MUSLIM COMMUNITIES OF SOUTH ASIA

Culture, Society and Power

Edited by

T.N. MADAN

Third Enlarged Edition

MANOHAR
2001

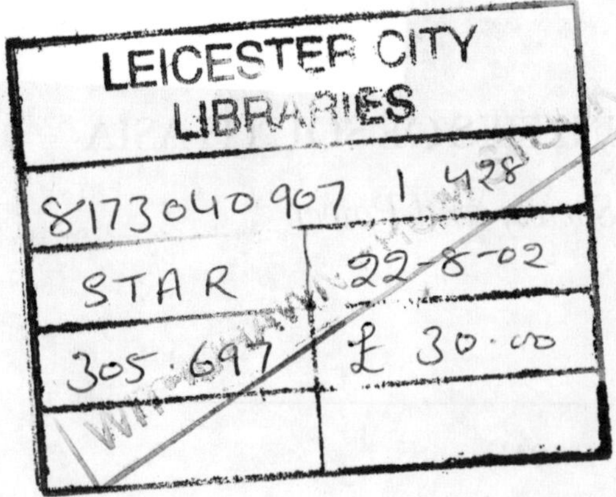

First published 1976
Revised and enlarged edition 1995
Third enlarged edition 2001

ISBN 81-7304-090-7

Published by
Ajay Kumar Jain for
Manohar Publishers & Distributors
4753/23 Ansari Road, Daryaganj
New Delhi 110002

Typeset by
A J Software Publishing Co. Pvt. Ltd.
305 Durga Chambers
1333 D.B. Gupta Road
Karol Bagh, New Delhi 110005

Printed at
Replika Press Pvt Ltd
Delhi 110 040

For
GHAUS ANSARI
author of
Muslim Caste in Uttar Pradesh (1960)
pioneer
in the study of social organization among the
Muslim Communities of South Asia

Contents

LIST OF MAPS

LIST OF FIGURES

LIST OF TABLES

Preface

The third edition of *Muslim Communities of South Asia* contains three new papers published earlier in *Contributions to Indian Sociology*. Two of these, by Rita Brara and Deepak Mehta respectively, are about India and illustrate how variously Muslim identity in South Asia has been defined diachronically or synchronically. The third new paper by Dennis McGilvray is about Sri Lanka, and this too pertains to the processes of identity formation. I am grateful to all three authors for their consent to include their essays in this volume. McGilvray was particularly helpful in responding to my request for shortening his paper. His contribution replaces Mohamed Mauroof's essay on aspects of religion, society and economy among the Muslims of Sri Lanka that appeared in the first two editions of this book.

I am gratified by the response of reviewers and readers to the second edition of this book. It is this response that has encouraged me and the publisher to bring out a third enlarged edition.

Delhi
16 September 1999

T.N. MADAN

Acknowledgements

I would like to thank warmly the following persons for their help in the preparation of this book:

All the authors whose work is presented here, for their ready and positive response to my request to allow me to include their essays in the volume. I am particularly grateful to Professor Hamza Alavi who rewrote and expanded his excellent paper mainly to clarify some significant theoretical issues. I am further indebted to the authors for their gracious consent to allow the Institute of Economic Growth to retain the royalties that may accrue from the sale of this book and use the same for strengthening the resources of *Contributions to Indian Sociology*.

Mr Ramesh Jain of Manohar Publishers & Distributors, New Delhi, for his proposal to bring out this book, and for his perseverance and persuasiveness, without which it would have never seen the light of day. I am now further obliged to him for bringing out the third enlarged edition of the book.

Mr Tejeshwar Singh of Sage Publications India Private Ltd., New Delhi, the present publisher of *Contributions*, for his understanding and unfailing courtesy.

The editors of *Contributions*, particularly Dr Patricia Uberoi, for their advice and support.

Further, it is noted here, in fulfilment of copyright formalities, that all the papers included in this book, except Hamza Alavi's, were originally published in *Contributions to Indian Sociology* (New Series) in volumes specified in the bibliography at the end of the Introduction.

T.N. MADAN

Introduction

T.N. MADAN

There are more Muslims in South Asia today, numbering almost 400 million, than in any other region of the world. Only Indonesia has a larger Muslim population than India, Bangladesh, or Pakistan. Divided into a number of subregional and national communities, the interaction of Islam and (to use Aziz Ahmad's phrase) 'the Indian environment' has played a crucial role in the making of their history and sociology. While historians have for long regarded South Asia as an area of immense if not unique interest from the Muslim point of view, and many approaches and schools of historiography flourish, high-quality sociological studies of these Muslim communities are rather rare. Some improvement in this regard has been, however, noticeable, in recent years.

The beginnings of the current surge of interest may be traced to discussions of the scope of the sociology of India in the early 1970s, following the publication of Louis Dumont's *Homo hierarchicus* in 1966 (English translation, 1970) and the inauguration of the second series of *Contributions to Indian Sociology* the following year (1967). These discussions drew attention to, among other issues, the constrictive identification of Hindu society with India, treating communities other than the Hindus as minorities of relatively less scholarly interest. Imtiaz Ahmad, an influential participant, wrote that, in the absence of enough studies of non-Hindu communities in their mutual relatedness, and in relation to the Hindus, 'we may have Hindu, Muslim, or Christian sociologies, but hardly a sociology of India' (1972: 177). He complained that leading figures in the field (notably M.N. Srinivas, Louis Dumont, and Milton Singer) had failed to remedy this deficiency, because of both the inadequacy of ethnographic studies of non-Hindu communities and the biases of these authors' theoretical frameworks. More recently some scholars have argued that the preoccupation with Hindu society has been carried over from Indology, which itself reflected the skewed perspectives of Orientalist scholarship of the late nineteenth century.

Sympathizing with the need for broadening the scope of the sociological studies of India in terms of both theoretical perspectives and empirical contents, I decided to devote a volume of *Contributions to Indian Sociology*, of which I was then the principal editor, to a discussion of the Muslim communities of South Asia. The contributors were invited to address the question of Muslim identity in the region in cultural and sociological rather than historical and religious (or theological) terms. The resultant volume was composed of two articles each on Bangladesh and India, and one each on Nepal, Pakistan, and Sri Lanka. Besides, Imtiaz Ahmad contributed a concluding note (from which I have quoted above) on the need for expanding the scope of the sociology of India. This volume of *Contributions* (no. 6), published in 1972, was well received by readers and reviewers. In view of the response, it was reissued in 1976 in a hardcover edition, under the title of *Muslim Communities of South Asia: Culture and Society*. The book sold out quickly, but could not be reprinted owing to a change in the publisher's priorities.

In the twenty-seven years since the publication of the special issue of *Contributions*, sociological and social anthropological studies of Muslim communities of South Asia have made considerable progress, although the volume and quality of published work devoted to India still falls short of what it should be. This is regrettable, particularly when one thinks of the impressive achievements of historians working on medieval and Mughal India. *Contributions* has tried to augment this rather meagre corpus, not only be publishing work of acceptable standard when offered to it, but also by inviting authors from India and abroad to write for it. By now more than two dozen articles (including the original set of eight) have been published (see Bibliography, pp. 23 ff.). To meet a persistent demand, sixteen of these essays have been collected in the present volume, which is offered to interested readers as a revised and enlarged edition of *Muslim Communities of South Asia*, with the subtitle expanded to include *Power* alongside of *Culture* and *Society*.

The present volume is a miscellany, a book of readings rather than one having a single, precisely defined theme. Broadly speaking, the essays comprising it contribute to our understanding of three key themes in the sociology of South Asian Muslim communities, namely: (1) attributes of cultural identity, (2) modes of social organization, and (3) dimensions of power. Some elaboration of the issues discussed by the authors may be helpful in introducing the contents of the book.

(1) *Attributes of Cultural Identity.* Two kinds of answers are possible to the question, 'What does it mean to be a Muslim in South Asia?' First, there is the textual or essentialist answer, according to which one is a Muslim in South Asia in the same way as one is so anywhere else, that is by affirmation of the fundamental tenets of faith (belief in Allah, the revealed book, angels, prophets and the day of judgement) and through adherence to the basic behavioural obligations (namely bearing verbal witness to the oneness of Allah and the finality of prophecy in the person of Muhammad, offering the appointed daily prayers, observing the yearly month of fasting, giving of charity, and performing the pilgrimage to Makkah). Ordering one's life in terms of the ideal expressed in the *shari' ah,* or holy law (as given in the Qur'ān, the conduct of the Prophet's own life, and his sayings), is included in the essentialist definition. In other words, one is a Muslim by virtue of one's membership of the *ummah,* or the universal community of Muslims. Such membership is ratified, as it were, by significant rituals and ceremonies, most notably circumcision, which transforms the individual body from mere organic substance into a socially recognized and spiritually refined person (see Mehta's essay in this volume). Hereafter, essays included in this volume are identified by the letters *tv* placed in parentheses; other sources are identified by the author's name and the year of publication.

Second, there is the sociologically informed answer that emphasizes the historical and local aspects of cultural identity, which is thus shown to be context sensitive. According to this view, a person is a Muslim not only by what he believes but also, and even more importantly, but what he does. This implicates others, including Hindus, Buddhists, and Sikhs, in South Asia in the everyday life of Muslims there. These others are 'outsiders' in terms of the Islamic ideology, but they often are significant role players alongside Muslims in the social, economic and political domains of society and, therefore, 'insiders'. In addition to predictability, contingency also enters into such social situations.

Those themes are discussed by Rita Brara, T.N. Madan and Dennis McGilvray in their contributions to this volume. Brara shows how, in the context of the retention of political power, the ruling house of the pre-1947 native state of Malerkotla, which was of Afghan descent, developed resemblances with non-Muslim (Hindu Rajput) ruling classes in the manner in which marriage ties, gift giving, etc., were employed for the said purpose. In contrast, McGilvray discusses a particularly delicate situation in contemporary Sri Lanka. Here the urban elite have fostered an Arab Muslim identity and distanced themselves from Hindu and Christian Tamils who are engaged in a separatist (in their own eyes independence) movement for the creation of an autonomous Tamil homeland and nation-state in the north-eastern regions of the country. In the process a potentially dangerous split has occurred between the given physical (geographical) location of these Muslims and an 'imagined' location that negates (transcends as it were) the 'given' reality. Madan also describes the loosening of traditional inter-community ties between Muslims and Hindus in the Kashmir Valley following the emergence of a modern political consciousness.

An emphasis on the specific should not, however, slip into a one-dimensional representation. To recall Ernest Gellner's image (from another context), the pendulum swings but does not rest in either of the two extreme positions, and it flies off only in extraordinary circumstances. In other words, the tension of the dialectic of the universal and the particular is the essence of the matter.

This dialectic in the context of South Asia was the subject of a lively debate in the pages of *Contributions*. Taking up issue with Imtiaz Ahmad's thesis that a synthesis has been worked out in South Asia, between the high Islamic and custom-centred traditions, so that they 'co-exist as complementary and integral parts of a common religious system', bestowing upon Indian Islam a distinctive character, Francis Robinson (a historian) observed:

> In Islamic history, in general, there has been a movement towards, or occasionally away from, the pattern of perfection. In South Asia, in particular, over the past two hundred years, learned and holy men have shown unusual activity and imagination in spreading knowledge of that pattern more widely. . . . It may be that (in the recent past) Bangladesh (than in India) . . . what there cannot be, as Ahmad suggests, is a state of equilibrium. (1983: 201)

It may be added here that Imtiaz Ahmad's thesis is the theoretical foundation of four volumes of essays by various authors, edited by him, dealing with 'caste and social stratification', 'family, kinship and marriage', 'ritual and religion', and 'modernisation and social change' among Muslims in India (published by Manohar, New Delhi).

While Robinson castigated what he considered a cavalier attitude towards the textual and historical perspectives, Lucy Carroll, commenting on the volume on the family, regretted that, with a solitary exception, the authors did not pay serious attention to classical Islamic law, as they should have done, for it is valid for Muslims everywhere: 'divergence between everyday customary practices and the provisions of the law does not mean that the law can be put aside and ignored' (1984: 219). Gail Minault (a historian) and Veena Das (a sociologist) joined issue with Robinson, and reiterated the importance of the empirical and the contingent—of the particular in relation to the universal. They both stressed the benefits of interdisciplinary research. Minault (1984) drew attention to the persistence of local customs in the face of Islamicization. Das recommended that 'the sociology of Islam . . . apply itself seriously to the investigation of folk theologies, on the one hand, and the meanings and use of scripture in the everyday life of the Muslim, on the other' (1984: 297-8). Later, Charles Lindholm contributed to this discussion (his essay is included in this volume), arguing that the study of subcultures is of crucial importance for not only our understanding of them, but also of Islamic culture as such. Resistance to assimilation illumines the whole scene, he suggested convincingly.

Further, it is obvious that, in dealing with the problem of cultural identity among the Muslim communities of South Asia, it is imperative to acknowledge the possibility of a multiplicity of theoretical perspectives. This is not all, however. We must also recognize that the social actors themselves may have multiple viewpoints which the student should seek to interpret. Not only may the different social positions of role players, such as people of noble lineages and commoners, produce a variety of internally generated images of social reality, the same set of persons may activate different identities in unlike contexts.

Thus, Victor de Munck (*tv*) points out that the Muslim villagers he studied in Sri Lanka see themselves as villagers, Sri Lankans, members of a Sufi brotherhood, Sunnis, or reformist Muslims, depending upon the context. Seemingly they experience no tensions in doing so. The case of the Muslim Tamils of Sri Lanka with their strategies of inclusion and exclusion (see McGilvray, *tv*) has already been mentioned earlier.

Similarly, Aparna Rao (*tv*) presents a fascinating analysis of how individual and ethnic identities among the pastoral Bakkarwal of the western Himalayas are comparable to the multipurpose boundaries between the different levels of local organization characteristic of their society. Elsewhere, Richard Kurin and Carrol Morrow write that, 'for Pakistanis, all Muslims are "religion" brothers, all Pakistanis "country" brothers, and all human beings "blood" brothers. Unities are taken to be generated by similitude, not diversity. The level of similitude may vary, from the very particular to the universal' (1985: 248). In short, cultural identities exhibit many complexities, whether viewed from the outside or the inside. They are also reflected in modes of social organization, but may not be presumed to determine the latter.

(2) *Modes of Social Organization.* It has often been stated that caste as a mode of social organization is so pervasive in South Asia that even Muslim communities give evidence of the operation of its principles in terms of marriage preferences, occupational specialization, social ranking, etc. Although there are differences among South Asia specialists whether to define caste culturally (in terms of values), as Louis Dumont does, or structurally (in terms of interests), in the manner of, say, Fredrik Barth, the relevance of a caste model of social organization has been asserted by many scholars. When the need for qualification has been felt, authors have written of 'caste analogues', 'caste substitutes', or caste as a 'residual category'.

One way of clarifying what otherwise appear as controversial social classifications is to clearly distinguish between 'self-ascription' and 'other-ascription'. This is particularly important in places where Muslims live alongside considerable numbers if not majorities of non-Muslims (Hindus, Buddhists, etc.), which is what we find in Bangladesh, India, Nepal, and Sri Lanka. In the Kashmir Valley (in India) what the Muslims themselves, who are the majority community, regard as specialist occupational groups, rendering economic services to the Hindus, the latter consider castes, providing ritual services with an economic content. Incidentally, rural social organization in Kashmir is one of the best examples known to us in ethnographic literature of the coexistence of two different cultural ideologies within one social framework (see Madan, *tv*). The participation of Muslim occupational groups in the caste system of the predominantly Hindu country of Nepal is more intimate than in Kashmir as it includes the affirmation of some key Hindu cultural values, such as the Brahmanical notion of ritual purity, by. Muslims (see Marc Gaborieau, *tv*). J.B.P. More (*tv*), however, considers caste unimportant in the self-perception of Sri Lankan Muslims. Objectively, caste is not a major feature of community rural organization in Bangladesh, it is not absent, but its place is being taken by, howsoever incipiently, class (see Bertocci, *tv*).

Some scholars have demonstrated the persistence of caste-linked principles of social organization even outside the original (South Asian) cultural setting. Pnina Werbner (*tv*) reports that caste survives among Pakistani migrants in England. New relations of power and economic domination are articulated in a caste idiom, she writes, and ratified through marriage. Migration does not dissolve the traditional social organization; it only redefines some elements within the whole. She analyses the mutually reinforcing relations between caste and kin groups, on the one hand, and caste and its apparent opposite, class on the other.

The usefulness of caste as an empirically existent group, or as an analytical category, has been questioned, however, in relation to contemporary Pakistani society by some scholars. While Saghir Ahmad (1970) expressed a general preference for class in place of the rather vague notion of socio-economic status, or the rigid concept of caste, as a tool of analysis, Hamza Alavi (*tv*) presents a wealth of carefully analysed ethnographic material to argue that, in contrast to the communities of the plains of north India, the basis of Muslim social organization in Punjab (Pakistan) is kinship and the modes of exchange and gift-giving associated with it. The importance of kinship and descent as the first principles of social organization is also attested to in the detailed analysis of local groupings among the pastoral Bakkarwal of the western Himalayas provided by Aparna Rao (*tv*).

A fairly wide range of forms is, thus, found to characterize social organization among the Muslim communities of South Asia. The characteristic groups include 'brotherhoods', lineages, clans, tribes, castes, or caste-analogues, and socio-economic classes. While religion (Islam) is the ideological bedrock upon which different types of social organization are constructed, they survive the disruptions caused by such overwhelming social processes as migration (see Katy Gardner, *tv*) and modernization. It may not be, however, the primary factor in all situations. Linguistic affinities or economic transactions are sometimes found to cut across religious (Muslim as well as non-Muslim) boundaries and create secular relationships of mutual support, distanciation or hostility (see McGilvray, *tv* and J.B.P. More, *tv*). Above all, 'power' in its religious and secular manifestations is a crucial theme of everyday life among South Asian Muslim communities.

(3) *Dimensions of Power.* Power is generally understood in political terms in sociological literature, but such a perspective is restrictive in

respect of Muslims anywhere, for the civil and political aspects of life are, in principle, not set apart from religion but encompassed by it. Traditionally, Islam was presented by its learned men as faith (religion), way of life (culture and society), and power (holy law and the State) in one seamless whole. It goes without saying, however, that strains between these different aspects are inevitable and always present empirically. This is insightfully brought out by Brara (*tv*), who shows how ties of marriage and kinship and the rules of inheritance and succession may be managed in ways that are oriented more to the retention of the power and status of ruling classes than to any orthodox Islamic ideals. Akbar Ahmed (*tv*) focuses on the conflation and confrontation of spiritual authority and temporal power in the persons of a traditional *mullah* with secular ambitions and a political agent representing the modern State, who is respectful of religious values. Besides power and authority, contestations of different types of legitimacy also are a component of such situations.

Varieties of power are reflected in the strategies employed in their pursuit. The complexities of such strategies are illustrated by the manner in which piety and power have been asserted to be interlinked by Muslim learned and holy men, and by Muslim politicians, in the nineteenth and twentieth centuries (see Usha Sanyal and Gopal Krishna, *tv*). It is obvious that the objective of piety may be secular power as well as the attainment of moral perfection. When moral virtue and grace (*barakat*) produce extraordinary powers, the blessed holy men (such as the *pir*) begin to perform miracles, heal the sick, and bestow material benefits on people. The inroads of secularization, which make the sick seek medical aid and goad the enterprising into entrepreneurship, lead to a decline in the scope of mystical powers and a redefinition of roles. This is more likely to happen in non-traditional settings such as the one in which Bangladeshi migrants find themselves in England (see Katy Gardner, *tv*).

At home, in the South Asian countries, too, such redefinitions occur. Besides, new power equations in the political arena are established or contested. Victor de Munck (*tv*) shows how national politics and pan-Islamic processes impinge upon the lives of Muslim villagers in Sri Lanka in a manner that creates new meanings for old practices (such as community festivals) which served as identity markers in the past, but do so now less significantly. McGilvray (*tv*) too elaborates in rich detail the interplay of ethnic identity and politics in contemporary strife-torn Sri Lanka. Similarly, Gopal

Krishna (*tv*) suggests that following the division of the Muslims of the subcontinent into three national communities—Indian, Bangladeshi, and Pakistani—living under differently conceived political regimes, the dialectic of religion and politics among them is bound to follow different trajectories. In short, culture, society, and power are linked in diverse, meaningful ways. The exploration of these relationships intellectually challenging and conducive to a better understanding of the social reality. This is, I believe, amply borne out by the essays comprising the present volume.

The objective of the foregoing observations is only to indicate the broad concerns of the contributing authors. I have made no effort to present a general statement on all the major issues raised—this would have been a formidable task—nor even to summarise the essays. An introductory essay serves its purpose if it gets the reader interested in the book, and I hope I have succeeded in doing this.

BIBLIOGRAPHY

The bibliography lists papers on the Muslim communities of South Asia published in *Contributions to Indian Sociology* between 1970 and 1999 (vols. 4 to 33). The papers that have been neither included in this book, nor cited in the Introduction, are marked by an asterisk.

Ahmad, Imtiaz. 1972. 'For a sociology of India', 6: 172-8.

Ahmad, Saghir. 1970. 'Social stratification in a Punjabi village', 4: 105-25.

Ahmed, Akbar S. 1983. 'Islam and the district paradigm: Emergent trends in contemporary Muslim society', 17: 155-83.

*Ahmed, Akbar S. 1983. 'Nomadism as ideological expression: The case of the Gomal Nomads', 17: 123-38.

Alavi, Hamza A. 1972. 'Kinship in West Punjab Villages', 6: 1-27.

Bertocci, Peter J. 1972. 'Community structure and social rank in two villages in Bangladesh', 6: 28-52.

Brara, Rita. 1994. 'Kinship and the political order: The Afghan Sherwani chiefs of Malerkotla (1454-1947)', 28: 203-42.

*Caroll, Lucy. 1978. 'The reception of the Muslim family laws ordinance 1961 in a Bangladeshi village: A critique of Jean Ellickson, "Islamic institutions: Perception and practice in a village in Bangladesh"', 12: 279-86.

Caroll, Lucy. 1983. 'The Muslim family laws ordinance, 1961: Provisions and procedures. A reference paper for current research', 13: 117-43.

Das, Veena. 1984. 'For a folk theology and theological anthropology of Islam', 18: 292-300.

de Munck, Victor C. 1994. 'Sufi, reformist and national models of identity: The history of a Muslim village festival in Sri Lanka', 28: 273-94.

*Ellickson, Jean. 1972. 'Islamic institutions: Perception and practice in a village in Bangladesh', 6: 53-65.

Gaborieau, Marc. 1972. 'Muslims in the Hindu kingdom of Nepal', 6: 84-105.

*Gaborieau, Marc. 1978. 'Aspects of the lineage among the Muslim bangle-makers of Nepal', 12: 155-71.

Gardner, Katy. 1993. 'Mullahs, migrants, miracles: travel and transformation in Sylhet', 27: 213-36.

Gopal Krishna. 1972. 'Piety and politics in Indian Islam', 6: 142-71.

Kurin, Richard and Carol Morrow. 1985. 'Patterns of solidarity in a Punjabi Muslim Village', 19: 235-49.

Lindholm, Charles. 1986. 'Caste in Islam and the problem of deviant systems: A critique of recent theory', 20: 61-73.

Madan, T.N. 1972. 'Religious ideology in a plural society: Muslims and Hindus of Kashmir', 6: 106-41. (Nb: This article appears under a changed title and with a postscript in the present volume.)

*Mauroof, Mohamed. 1972. 'Aspects of religion, economy and society among the Muslims of Ceylon', 6: 66-83.

*Mayaram, Shail. 1991. 'Criminality or community? Alternative construction of the Mev narrative of Darya Khan', 25: 57-84.

McGilvray, Dennis. 1998. 'Arabs, Moors, and Muslims: Sri Lankan Muslim identity in regional perspective', 32: 433-83.

Mehta, Deepak. 1992. 'The semiotics of weaving: A case study', 26: 77-113.

———. 1996. 'Circumcision, body and community', 30: 215-43.

Minault, Gail. 1984. 'Some reflections on Islamic revivalism vs. assimilation among Muslims in India', 18: 301-5.

More, J.B.P. 1993. 'Tamil Muslims and non-Brahmin atheists, 1925-1940', 27: 83-104.

Rao, Aparna. 1988. 'Levels and boundaries in native models: Social groupings among the Bakkarwal of the western Himalayas', 22: 195-227.

Robinson, Francis. 1983. 'Islam and Muslim society in South Asia: A reply to Das and Minault', 20: 97-104.

Sanyal, Usha. 1994. '*Pir, Shaikh* and Prophet: The personalization of religious authority in Ahmad Riza Khan's life', 28: 35-66.

Werbner, Pnina. 1989. 'The ranking of brotherhoods: The dialectics of Muslim caste among overseas Pakistanis', 23: 285-315.

The Two Biraderis: Kinship in Rural West Punjab[1]

HAMZA ALAVI
(1994)

I. TWO TYPES OF *BIRADERI*: LINEAGES AND CLANS

Kinship institutions are central to the ways in which political as well as social life in Pakistani rural society is organized. The central institution of kinship in rural West Punjab is the *biraderi* (spelled as *biradari* by some authors), which is usually a tightly knit corporate group and which, typically, is subject to the authority of a *biraderi panchayat* (i.e. council). The biraderi is a basic unit of social organization. In the political arena a candidate normally seeks to recruit whole biraderis rather than individual persons. At the provincial and national levels, biraderis of landlords function as powerful blocs. The phrase 'the biraderi system' has gained wide currency in Pakistan, although it is evident that those who bandy about that phrase are not always very clear about its precise meaning.

Two quite different types of structures of kinship are to be found in rural West Punjab and, accordingly, two different types of biraderis. These are described below.

(1) *Biraderi as lineage*: In one case kinship is based on what is known as the structure of patrilateral parallel cousin marriage or, in other words, marriage with father's brother's daughter (FBD). Although, ideally, men are expected to marry their father's brother's daughter, this is not always feasible, for such a cousin of an appropriate age may not always be available or desired. One may therefore marry a more distant paternal cousin. The operative rule, it may be said, is not quite literally one of marriage with a partilateral parallel cousin but that of lineage endogamy. In some conditions men may marry women of

*This is a revised and substantially enlarged version of a paper on 'Kinship in West Punjab Villages', published in *Contributions to Indian Sociology* (n.s.) 6, December 1972; reprinted in T.N. Madan, ed., *Muslim Communities of South Asia.* New Delhi: Vikas, 1976.

other biraderis, known as *rishtedar*, who have a special relationship with the biraderi. The pressure, in any case, is towards confining marriages within a group, whether the natal biraderi, or, less frequently, an extended group consisting of the natal biraderi and a rishtedar biraderi. I[1] will label this endogamous biraderi as 'Type A'.

This structure of kinship is more accurately described as one of 'lineage endogamy' rather than its more familiar description as that of patrilateral parallel cousin marriage. Bourdieu, however, takes a diametrically opposite view. He chides social anthropologists for using the concept of 'lineage endogamy' instead of 'patrilateral parallel cousin marriage' which, he suggests, is a more accurate description (1992: 30ff.). That, of course, is not literally true. Bourdieu has reasons for opting for the narrower definition which we will take up in the last section of this paper.

(2) *Biraderi as clan.* In the second, quite different, type of kinship system, the biraderi is made up of a number of exogamous patrilineal *gots* (or *gotras*). In contrast to the very small biraderis of type A of the endogamous system, biraderis in this second, exogamic, kinship system are very large. I will refer to this type of biraderi as 'type B'.

We need English equivalents for each kind of biraderi, to distinguish between them because of ambiguity that arises from the fact that in the indigenous language the word 'biraderi' is employed in two quite different senses; each representing a quite different structure of kinship. There is no difficulty about settling for an appropriate English word for the biraderi of 'type A', which is a lineage. But it is not quite so straightforward when it comes to finding an appropriate English word for the biraderi of type B. On reflection and after consulting some colleagues, I have settled for the word 'clan'. Judging from the opinions that I have received, this will be controversial. We shall revert to this question in Section III below.

Endogamy, exogamy and incest

Bourdieu, echoing the prejudices of Lévi-Strauss, dismisses patrilateral parallel cousin marriage as 'quasi-incest' (Bourdieu 1985: 30).[2] These ethnocentric judgements are surprising coming from social anthropologists. What is more to the point, they are ill-informed, not only about Islamic law and practice about incest, but also about the incest rules of European Christian churches. The major churches do not consider union between first cousins to be incestuous.[3] The Islamic law of incest, on the other hand, is more restrictive. For a Muslim the prohibited kin are *mahram*, which means not only 'prohibited' but also 'inviolable', 'sacred' or 'holy'.

A Muslim is not permitted to marry anyone who is mahram to him or her; that would be incest. For each individual his or her mahram are an ego-focused kindred that includes the person's (i) siblings (and step-siblings), (ii) a descendant or a descendant of siblings, (iii) an ascendant or sibling of an ascendant. It is further provided that (iv) a man may not marry his wife's mother at all; or his wife's sister, during the lifetime of his wife. There are some small variations between Muslim sects about the last prohibition. Mahram rules do not generate ancestor-focused descent groups. Rather, for each individual, they define a unique set of kin who are in a mahram relationship. Relationships between individuals who are mahram to each other are expected to be close and affectionate, notably those between a maternal uncle and his niece.

Biraderi and class

An additional complication derives from the effects of class differences on kinship practices and organization. The degree of cohesion among biraderis of different classes is not the same. Biraderis of (i) substantial landowners, (ii) biraderis of their dependent peasantry such as sharecroppers and landless labourers, and (iii) those of independent small peasant proprietors, all differ. Biraderis of small independent peasant proprietors are the paradigmatic case, the other cases being variants of it.

II. BIRADERI AS LINEAGE

Biraderi in the 'endogamous system', our biraderi of type A, is a patrilineage, a small tightly knit and involuted group in which affinal ties overlap agnatic ties and reinforce them. The word biraderi signifies both vertical ties of common descent as well as horizontal ties of brotherhood. Etymologically it refers to 'brotherhood', the word '*birader*' being cognate with 'brother'. The etymology emphasizes horizontal fraternal ties. Anthropologists might emphasize more the vertical lines of descent which is also implied in the concept of biraderi. Members of a biraderi are all descendants of a known male-ancestor. A woman who is not already a member of her husband's biraderi becomes one when she marries, and, at the same time, she ceases to be a member of the biraderi in which she was born. All kin in a single household are thus members of the same biraderi. In the Punjabi cultural system a biraderi is thought of as a collection of related households.

Semantic structure of the term 'biraderi'

The precise connotation of the term 'biraderi' alters with progressive contextual restriction of the concept, from the most general to the most specific. It may be looked upon as a term with a sliding semantic structure the vertical axis of which is the principle of descent and the horizontal axis the principle of fraternal solidarity. A movement along the scale of meanings from the most general to the most specific also represents a progressive axial movement from the vertical semantic component of the term, namely, the principle of descent, to the horizontal semantic component, namely the principle of fraternal solidarity. Corresponding with the shift in connotation, a progressively restricted group of kin are denoted by the term.

In its most general meaning as a descent groups biraderi includes, in principle, all those between whom actual links of common descent can be traced in the paternal line, regardless of the number of generations that have elapsed. In this sense, therefore, biraderi is indefinite in size. There are examples, although rare, that illustrate this general principle, for total strangers have been able to establish mutual links of common descent and have embraced each other as members of a single biraderi. It is crucially important, though, that in such cases the actual lines of common descent be demonstrated. It must be said that there are occasions when 'reliable evidence' is conveniently conjured up to serve the purposes of the powerful. In principle, however, just putative claims of common descent would not suffice. The actual line must be demonstrated, reliably, generation by generation.

A second, more restricted, connotation of biraderi derives from the practical consideration that written genealogies are not always available in an illiterate society, except among big land-owning families, for whom the ownership of such records is often a source of pride. Without written records, the boundary of the biraderi is determined by the possibilities and limits of recognition of kin ties.

Numbers as well as physical distance impose limits on the social interaction that keeps mutual recognition alive. Memory fails to trace relationships beyond a few generations; and practical considerations limit the scope of regular social interaction and participation in rituals through which the boundaries of the biraderi are reiterated and maintained. With succeeding generations, branches of distant kin tend to drift beyond the scope of regular contact and, indeed, the horizon of memory, into separate biraderis. The genealogical depth of biraderis, therefore, tends to be relatively shallow—about four or five generations, in contrast with the depth of 'lineages of recognition' among the Hindus of Malwa that extend to as many as ten generations (Mayer 1960: 169). I shall adapt Mayer's terminology and designate the biraderi at this level, of the knowledge and mutual perception of common descent, as the *biraderi of recognition.* Structurally, the concept of biraderi as such emphasizes descent, whether used generally or as biraderi of recognition. The boundary of the latter, however, is delimited by the fact of actual mutual knowledge of links of common descent and is empirically determinable, as against the mere potentiality of an extended boundary that exists in the former case.

A third, yet more restricted, meaning of the term biraderi, while still premised on common descent emphasizes the horizontal semantic component of the term, namely fraternal solidarity. It denotes those households of a 'biraderi of recognition' who actually participate in a ritual exchange of prestations called *vartan bhanji* on certain ceremonial occasions. Participation in such a relationship is no casual or dependent on the whim of individuals. It is unfailingly regular between the groups of participating households. Member households of this smaller, solidary, group affirm and reaffirm their fraternal ties on each occasion by virtue of their participation in vartan bhanji (as will be shown below). Further adapting Mayer's terminology, I shall label such a group of households as the *biraderi of participation.* In the event of fission in a biraderi of participation, the rules of vartan bhanji require that the break be ritually made and signified by exchange of appropriate final prestations that put a seal on the break and proclaim it publicly and unequivocally. Breakaway households constitute new biraderis of participation and affirm their new loyalties by resuming prestations of vartan bhanji within the new group. They make a clean break from households that remain with the old group, notwithstanding the existence of ties of affection between any households across the divide. When breaks occur, the cleavages do not divide households at random. Rather they tend to follow segmentary lines, along lines of descent. Households need to stay together with the closer relatives, regardless of sentiment. Otherwise they would be isolated and vulnerable, separated from near kin. Equally, when sections of a biraderi of recognition, that have split into separate biraderis of participation, are reconciled, they reunite by resuming vartan bhanji with each other.

A further restriction in denotation of the term 'biraderi' arises from a distinction between those households of 'biraderis of participation' the members of which reside in a single village and others that are dispersed elsewhere. The biraderi of participation that includes groups of households in several villages, is referred to, where the context demands it, as 'the entire biraderi', in contrast to 'biraderi of the village'. This last is the fourth level of the connotation of the term 'biraderi'. At this level interaction among the related households is the highest and ties (or pressures) of group solidarity are the strongest.

Segments of a biraderi within a village are known as *pattis.* The term 'patti' has a dual meaning: It refers not only to subdivisions of a local biraderi but also to corresponding subdivisions of its ancestral lands in the village. Refugees from India when asked about their pattis might sometimes reply that they had left their pattis behind in India. *Abadkars*, or colonists who were brought into the district during the last 100 years from various parts of the Punjab might sometimes give similar replies. Although the term 'patti' was thus, historically, applied to ancestral land, I never came across the term being used to refer to actual divisions of land in the district itself. It used to connote subdivisions of biraderis, the word patti refers to its segments that are descended from a named apical ancestor.

Marriages within a large biraderi type A

It will be useful at this point to tabulate and analyse marriages in a large biraderi type A, which is the most widespread form of kinship amongst Muslims of West Punjab. As will be seen from Table 1, marriages are in the main confined to the biraderi. The exceptions illustrate very well the underlying principles of endogamy that govern exchanges in marriage.

In Table 1, I have classified the actual distribution of marriages of men of a single biraderi of type A, a large lineage comprising 193 households of Duddhi Rajputs who live in a village called

TABLE 1. MARRIAGES OF MEN OF DUDDHI RAJPUT BIRADERI OF CHAK 237 HB

Name of Patti	Within own patti			With other pattis				Biraderi outside village	Biraderi Total	Other Dudhi	Other Zats	Grand Total
	FBD	Others	Total	FZD	MBD	Others	Total					
Jamali	23	35	58	1	-	3	4	10	72	3	6	81
Fattah	14	15	29	-	2	16	18	4	51	3	2	56
Nawab	6	4	10	2	-	8	10	-	20	1	6	27
Wazira	4	2	6	1	-	1	2	1	9	2	4	15
Rohilla	15	4	19	-	2	6	8	5	32	14	3	49
Bahadur	10	2	12	1	1	1	3	4	19	2	2	23
Nihal	10	14	24	-	-	6	6	1	31	-	5	36
Total	82	76	158	5	5	41	51	25	234	25	28	287

Chak 237 HB. The biraderi was divided into seven pattis (sub-lineages), each of which was named after the apical ancestor of the patti. The cultivators in the village, who were small peasant proprietors who cultivated their own land, were from the same biraderi. *Kammis*, or 'village servants', are not members of the biraderi and are not included in this survey.

In choosing a spouse, a man has priority of claim for the hand of is father's brother's daughter (FBD). Accidents of demography do not always make such a match convenient or possible. A woman who is in a structurally equivalent relationship, such as FFBSD or FFBD or, more generally, a member of the patti or finally the biraderi, is chosen. The value system requires that marriages be confined within the biraderi though a few marriages with members of other biraderis, known as rishtedars, may take place.

It will be seen from the table that the overwhelming majority of exchanges in marriage were confined to the biraderi, i.e. 234 (or 81.5 per cent) out of a total of 287. Of these, 209 marriages were between households of the biraderi in the same village; 158 or 55 per cent of the marriages were with women of the bridegroom's own patti. Of these only 82 or 28.5 per cent were with father's brother's daughter.

Zat

When asked, members of this biraderi described their '*zat*' as Duddhi Rajput. But the meaning of the word zat, as they understood it, was by no means clear. All that they could say was that Duddhi Rajput is 'just their name', i.e. like a surname. To them the word zat did not indicate a position within any ranked social order. They did not recognize any holistic hierarchical social order to which all zats could be said to belong and be classified accordingly. Nor were there any rules, rituals or ceremonies through which any status ranking with other zats could be manifested. The essential elements of 'caste' were missing.

The figures of marriages, in Table 1, demonstrate absence of any special significance of zat names, for having the same zat name did not result in any preferences in marriage. Of the 53 cases of marriages with other biraderis, marriages with women from biraderis bearing 'other zat names' (28) exceeded those with women from biraderis that shared the zat name of Duddhi Rajput (25). Members of all other biraderis are equally *nokh* (strangers) whether they call themselves Duddhi Rajputs or not. Nor did the well-known categories of Syed, Mughal and Pathan affect social interaction in any way. There are no collective ceremonies of any kind, or occasions through which zat ranking might be manifested.

Etiquette of status ranking

Some difference of status are reflected in the etiquette that persons from different backgrounds observe when villagers gather in the evenings to gossip after a day's work and smoke the hookah. A lower status is generally accorded to kammis but there was little evidence of status difference between the rest of the community.

In one village of small peasants that included biraderis of Dogars, Jats and Mughals, one found everyone in that village sitting around, sharing the communal hookah equally, with no sign of any precedence or differentiation. The Mughals denied any suggestion that they enjoyed any special status; others likewise denied that there was any kind of hierarchy of status.[4] it must be said, however, that one was a visitor to that village and, as far as one could see, there were no kammis around at the time.

The lower status of kammis was manifested more clearly in Chak Tekwala where villagers would gather around in the evenings at the landlord's *dera* (walled courtyard or 'men's house') where he held court. All cultivators, including sharecroppers, sat on chairs or *charpais* (the all-purpose string bed) and puffed at the hookah in turn as it was passed round. The landlord had his own hookah which he shared with visiting landlord friends. The rest of the gathering shared a common hookah. Kammis, 'village servants', would squat on the ground. They would not touch their lips to the nozzle of the common hookah, but would wrap their hands round it and take puffs of smoke through their fists. In that way they manifested a lower status. But the underlying logic of that was not embedded in the ascribed status of kammis, derived from birth as the following examples show.

The underlying principle that determined status was made clear by the treatment of a new *imam*, or preacher, who was brought to the village to lead prayers in the mosque. Earlier, the duties of the village imam were performed by a small farmer, who did not take any payment for his work. On special festive occasions he would accept a cash present as *salaami*, offered by a few better-off villagers. Following a factional split, the dominant landlord decided to bring a new imam to replace him. The young, new imam was the son of a smallholding cultivator from a village some distance away. He had studied at a religious school at the district town. He had no source of income of his own and became a full-time servant of the village. It was arranged that, like all kammis, he would be paid a share of the crop by all cultivators of the village, at harvest time. By accepting that mode of remuneration, notwithstanding the fact that he was the son of a landholding peasant, he was accorded the *de facto* status of a kammi. He had to sit on the ground, like any kammi at the landlord's dera, and smoke the communal hookah through his fist. Despite his role as the village imam, no more respect was given to him than to any (other) kammi. The villagers explained that like any kammi he was everybody's *seypi*.[5]

Contrary to the status loss of the well born imam, there are a number of cases of kammis gaining a higher status; their kammi birth being of little consequence. There was, for example the case of a *lohar* (blacksmith) who ceased to be a kammi (despite his origin) following a change in his economic role. Given rapid expansion of farm mechanization, there was an acute scarcity of skilled repairers of mechanical equipment. The lohar, who had gained some skills, went into business on his own account, repairing farm machinery for cash payment for each job. He took work from many villages around. He had changed his status. Although he was from a kammi background, he was no longer regarded a kammi. When he came to the village on business, he was received by the landlord of the village, if not with the cordiality reserved for another landowner, with a modicum of courtesy that he would not show to a mere kammi. The one-time lohar would sit on a chair (higher in status than the *charpai*, and obviously higher still than having to squat on the ground) at the dera in the evening, and he would smoke the hookah from its nozzle without the indignity of having to take puffs through his fist.

A third case of changed status of one-time kammis was that of a small biraderi of *nais* (barbers) who had come as refugees from India and settled in the village. Under the rules of allotment of land abandoned by Hindu and Sikh refugees in 1947, to incoming Muslim refugees from India, the nai biraderi were allotted land on the basis of one acre per person in every household. They now became cultivators. With the acquisition of land their status changed, regardless of their kammi origin. In keeping with their new status, they added a suffix to their name and called themselves 'Nai-Bhatti'.

They became a respected and influential group in the village and no one seemed to attach any significance to their nai origins.

These three examples show that status in Punjab is not fixed by birth; it can change with changes in occupation or, rather, with changes in modes of remuneration.

Inter-biraderi marriages

Marriages outside the biraderi are looked upon as hypergamous; but use of the term 'hypergamy' in this context places a special construction on the word. Ordinarily, hypergamy implies an already existing system of status ranking of the respective marriage groups. But, in the present case, there is no prior status ranking of biraderis. Allocation of relative status occurs as a *consequence* of an exchange in marriage between two biraderis. The bride-giving biraderi is then deemed to have placed itself in an inferior status. Keeping daughters within one's own biraderi is an index of social prestige. Wealthy peasants and landlords generally boast: 'We take girls (from other biraderis) but do not give ours.' It is often poorer peasants who are wife-givers.

In practice, such a change in relative status occurs only where an exchange in marriage between two biraderis is exceptional, a one-off affair. That does not happen in the case of regular inter-biraderi marriages which occur especially amongst small landholders and poor peasants. In the latter case, it is usually the first exchange that presents the biggest hurdle. In most cases such an exchange can be traced to quite exceptional circumstances—such as *watta*, when a brother and sister from one biraderi simultaneously marry a pair of siblings from another biraderi, so that neither biraderi is demeaned.

Once a relationship of exchanges in marriage between two biraderis is established, it is not uncommon for more marriages to follow, without the need for a further watta. When two biraderis give and take wives from each other the question of hypergamy or relative status between them does not arise. Affines who are not members of a person's biraderi are known as rishtedar and are distinguished from other biraderis with whom marriage relationships do not exist, who remain *nokh* or *ghair* (strangers). Thus, it will be seen that even in the case of departures from strict lineage endogamy, the tendency to confine exchanges in marriage within a group, in this case biraderis of rishtedars, persists.

Marriage and power

Control over marriages is a major factor in maintaining the cohesion of biraderis and in sustaining the authority of biraderi panchayats. The ultimate sanction that a biraderi panchayat may impose on a household is to 'expel' it from the biraderi. When that happens those who are expelled become 'non-persons' in the society. They become vulnerable and disgraced. The most distressing aspect of such punishment for the family is that it cannot expect to be able to get spouses for its sons and daughters. This is not a punishment that anyone want to invite. As a result the authority of the biraderi panchayat is very great. Its effective lever of power is control over the circulation of women in marriage—in other words, over reproduction. It is very rare indeed for its authority to be defied. Having looked closely at a number of villages over a period of fifteen months, I came across only one case of a man who had been expelled by his biraderi. His wife had then left him and returned to her father. The man was almost literally a broken man who had virtually lost his eyesight due, as he said, to years of weeping!

Some biraderis regulate marriages more strictly than others. The degree of cohesion of biraderis appears to depend directly on their strictness in enforcing biraderi endogamy and, furthermore, on the ability of the biraderi panchayat to regulate marriages within the biraderi itself, adjudicating disputes as they arise. Disputed rival claims in a patti are adjudicated in the first instance within the patti. Adjudication passes to the higher level of the biraderi panchayat where the parties to a dispute do not belong to the same patti or, even where they are both members of the same patti, if any of them defies the patti decision. The ultimate authority to excommunicate a household lies exclusively with the biraderi panchayat.

Rules of biraderi endogamy, structured around the ideal of patrilateral parallel cousin marriage, do offer considerable scope for manipulation. There is a recognized hierarchy of priority of claims among biraderi members to be given the hand of a fellow biraderi member's daughter in marriage to a youth. Such claims are graded according to the proximity of relationship, links through the paternal line having priority. An elder brother has the highest ranking claim for his younger brother's daughter's marriage to his own son.

Such a conception of a general order of priority of claims, however, is not applied mechanically, without regard to 'other factors', which the biraderi panchayat may choose to bring into play.

Such 'considerations' give the panchayat flexibility in adjudication of rival claims. It is this degree of freedom in using its own judgement in weighing up rival claims, that gives the biraderi panchayat its independent power in deciding in favour of one claim or another. It thereby gains the power that it exercises over the biraderi. In the event of a dispute, a plea would be accepted that the boy's father had shown no interest in the girl, until her father's intention to give her to someone else became known. His case would be further weakened if it could be shown (or accepted) that his behaviour towards the girl's household or members of her extended family, or generally towards members of her patti, had been uncooperative and not too friendly. Such considerations are by their nature often very vague and can be interpreted flexibly by the biraderi panchayat. It is in this freedom to interpret, or even override 'accepted rules' about priority of claims for the hand of a daughter in marriage that the authority and power of the biraderi panchayat resides.

Vartan bhanji: maintaining biraderi solidarity

The operative level of biraderi is the biraderi of participation, as indicated above. Membership of the biraderi of participation is defined and reiterated through a ritual of prestations and counter-prestations, called vartan bhanji. The term itself indicates the transactional essence of the ritual, for the word 'vartan' means 'dealings' or 'buying and selling'; and 'bhanji' means sister's daughter (an object of affection). Prestations given in vartan bhanji are called *neondra* or *nyota.* The ritual of vartan bhanji takes place, at specific times, on special ceremonial occasions such as marriages or circumcision ceremonies, when the prestations are given to the head of the household celebrating the occasion by representatives of all other households of the biraderi of participation.

An essential feature of vartan bhanji lies in an obligation on each household of the biraderi of participation to reciprocate the prestation, the neondra, at appropriate times in a customary manner. Because of that explicit obligation, it would be inappropriate to conceive of the prestations as 'gifts', i.e. as 'prestations which are in theory voluntary, disinterested and spontaneous, but are in fact obligatory and interested' (Mauss 1954: 1). They are obligatory even in theory. The reciprocation is not simultaneous. An initial prestation, for the moment, remains unreciprocated until an appropriate occasion when the receiver can proffer neondra in return. Until then, the initial prestation leaves behind a symbolic debt, which is 'owed' by the receiver of the neondra to the household from whom he receives it. That symbolic debt represents the tie that binds every two households of the biraderi and thereby all its households. When an appropriate occasion arrives the household that had received the initial prestation, gives neondra in return, giving an amount in excess of outstanding ritual debt so that the excess creates a fresh 'debt' in the reverse direction.

Thus prestations given in vartan bhanji generate a perpetual cycle of creation and reversal of mutual ritual debts that symbolize the ties and obligations of biraderi membership. Half of the amount given as neondra notionally 'repays' and extinguishes the outstanding debt and the other half of it creates a fresh obligation in the reverse direction. In this way, the roles of symbolic 'debtors' and 'creditors' are exchanged regularly between every two households of the biraderi and thereby between all households of the biraderi of participation. The permanent bond between them is symbolically expressed in the form of the regular exchange of ritual debts, which are constantly reversed, but which always remain, as tokens of their mutual bonds.

Vartan bhanji is central to the management and ritual cohesion of biraderis. Participation in it identifies members of the biraderi of participation. Prestations exchanged in vartan bhanji are not to be seen in the same way as ordinary gifts, which may be given on the ceremonial occasions when vartan bhanji takes place, but such (other) gifts are given quite separately from neondra, and at a different moment in the ceremonial proceedings, which leaves no room for confusion between the two. Gifts that are given separately from neondra are expressive of dyadic relationships between donors and recipients. Unlike neondra given in vartan bhanji they do not impose any ritual obligation on the recipient to reciprocate in like measure. On the other hand, the essential significance of neondra in vartan bhanji is a collective one, for it symbolizes biraderi ties. Neondra is given by a household as a ritual affirmation of its continued membership of the biraderi of participation. This is quite independent of good or bad feelings between any two households. Even where there is hostility between households, vartan bhanji must be continued between them, unless either of the households wishes to terminate its membership of the biraderi of participation, which would be an extreme step to take. Vartan bhanji thus not only defines membership of the biraderi of participation, as will be explained below, it also provides a ritual procedure for termination of that relationship in the event of fission of the biraderi.

Mechanics of vartan bhanji

When vartan bhanji takes place, the prestation, namely neondra or nyota, is given by all households of the biraderi of participation to the head of the receiving household. At an appropriate stage in the proceedings, of say a wedding, a *mirasi* ('bard') announces to the gathering that the time has come for those who are to give neondra to do so. He sits with the bridegroom and a senior member of his family (usually his father's eldest brother) and, if the latter is illiterate, as is often the case, also with a literate person, a *mullah* or the schoolmaster, who records the names of the donors and the amounts of neondra in a book called *behi* (account). The cash given as neondra is received and counted and the mirasi then announces in standard sing-song phraseology the name of the donor and his household and the amount given. It is then recorded in the behi. The record is preserved and is a valued family possession. It is the basis on which the recipient in turn reckons his own obligation to reciprocate on a subsequent occasion. I came across only one case in which no written record of neondra was kept; it was the case of a small biraderi of landless labourers where only a few households were invited to the wedding. On the other hand, I found written records kept even by kammi households as well as by cultivators and landowners big and small, regardless of the fact that most of them were illiterate.

The amounts which are given in vartan bhanji are generally fixed by the custom of particular biraderis, and are not varied to express differences or changes in sentiment between one household and another. Because vartan bhanji imposes an obligation on the recipient to reciprocate in like measure, he is not necessarily grateful for being given more than the conventionally established amount. Rather, it would be quite proper for a person who feels that he has been given an amount which would raise the stakes too high, to accept only a part of the amount offered and thus limit his own reciprocal obligation in subsequent cycles of vartan bhanji when he would be the giver. Return of the excess amount does not imply any offence to the donor. The excess may be returned at once or, in cases where a tacit understanding exists, privately later. This convention opens the possibility for poor relations of rich landowners to keep up appearances by giving a large amount as neondra publicly at ceremonial occasions, it being understood that a part of the amount would be returned later by the rich relative. In such cases only the actual amount that is retained is entered in the recipient's written records of amounts received in vartan bhanji, amounts which have to be later reciprocated. This allows rich households to be spared the embarrassment of a public demonstration of the poverty of their relatives and, contrariwise, poor households are spared the burden of having to sustain large payments to rich relatives which may force them to sever biraderi connections for financial reasons. This practice is usual where there are only a few poor relatives in a rich biraderi, especially if they all reside in the same village and must therefore all keep up membership of the biraderi of participation. But if the number in each of the respective groups of rich and poor relatives is large enough, they tend to drift off and form separate biraderis of participation.

The dynamic role of vartan bhanji is embedded in the principle that the return prestation does not simply cancel out the first prestation that was received. This may not at first sight be quite obvious to an outside observer, for he or she is likely to observe apparently equal amounts being exchanged between pairs of households on successive occasions. The people themselves do not see the reciprocal payments to be equal. In their eyes in every case there is a net excess of payment over the previous balance of account between the households, even though on the face of it the same amount is actually paid each time between the two parties. This is because each time there is a net amount that is 'owed' (ritually) by the household to whom a prestation is to be made. This is how it works.

A new household receives a certain amount as neondra on the first occasion, when it begins participation in vartan bhanji. It must, on subsequent occasions repay that amount and give as much again so that its own ritual debt is extinguished and a reverse symbolic debt in its favour is created at the same time. The previous 'creditor' now becomes the 'debtor'. On subsequent occasions our first household will find itself giving to and receiving from the other household identical amounts. Each payment will notionally consist of two parts:

one part of the amount paid extinguishes the pre-existing debt and the other part creates a fresh debt in the reverse direction. Some observers are puzzled by the perversity of the peasant mind, when they insist that payments that can be seen to be exactly equal every time they are made, are nevertheless 'unequal'. To restate it concretely, say ten rupees is the going rate of payment for every occasion. In the eyes of the participants not ten but five rupees are actually 'paid' (creating a 'debt' in its favour), for half of the amount went towards repayment of its pre-existing 'debt'. It is the excess of five rupees that creates the fresh 'debt' which will be entered in the recipient's behi, as the outstanding amount now owed by him. Although the amount 'owed', i.e. the 'previous reckoning', as entered in the recipient's behi, is only five rupees, ten rupees are actually paid each time, successively, from either side, leaving as a result an uncovered, ritual, debt on the receiver equal to half the amount that is actually paid. Thus, these apparently equal prestations given by one side or the other on every ceremonial occasion are, logically, 'unequal'. That, at least, is how it is seen.

The dynamic role of vartan bhanji cannot be understood if the prestations are looked upon merely as 'gifts', as for example Eglar (1960: *passim*) mistakenly sees them. Because of her failure to distinguish the formal and ritual payments made under vartan bhanji from (other) 'gifts' (that are in fact given quite separately), she fails to recognize the structural role of vartan bhanji in biraderi organization. Although she uses the term vartan bhanji, she includes under that rubric all kinds of gifts, quite indiscriminately. It is only if prestations under vartan bhanji are distinguished from other gifts, and neondra given in vartan bhanji seen in its role in a perpetual cycle of regular reversal of symbolic debts between participating households that signify bonds of the biraderi, that its true significance emerges.

Because of its importance, prestations given in vartan bhanji are carefully recorded in the behi, the relevant entries being made at the moment when the payments are made, during the course of the ceremony itself. Illiterate peasants get the help of a mullah or school teacher or a literate friend, for this. But the transactions are invariably recorded in writing in the behi. For every household the behi is a treasured possession and many of them were shown to me proudly. The behi has three columns. In the first column is shown the figure of the 'past reckoning', i.e. the amount of ritual debt outstanding.

The second column records the actual amount of neondra received. In the third column, the 'excess' of the neondra over the previous reckoning is entered, as the basis for future transactions. This notionally overbalanced reciprocation does not lead to an escalation of the amounts exchanged, as in the case of *potlatch*. Unlike ordinary gifts which are also given (such as *salaami*—see below), the amount of neondra in vartan bhanji is conventionally fixed in every biraderi at a low figure, so as not to overburden any member of the biraderi. These amounts cannot be varied at whim by households offering neondra. They must stick to the conventionally established figure.

The operation of vartan bhanji, as a mechanism that ratifies membership of the biraderi of participation, is best considered in association with a ritual of transmission and formalized acceptance (or rejection) of invitations to the ceremonial occasions on which vartan bhanji takes place. This plays a crucial part in the management of potential or actual conflicts that may arise within the biraderi. The invitations are symbolized by pieces of brightly coloured thread, called *mohli*, one of which is presented to the head of the invited household on behalf of the inviting household. The ritual mode of transmission and mode of acceptance of the mohli conveys certain messages between households, as will be explained below. The two rituals, namely the sending of mohli and vartan bhanji work inseparably; together, they constitute a very efficient mechanism by which tensions, between households of the biraderi of participation are managed and its membership held together.

Vartan bhanji as 'mutual aid'

A practical consequence of vartan bhanji is that it brings substantial financial aid to the recipient household, at a time when it is involved in considerable expenditure for ceremonial purposes, without, at the same time, imposing any significant burden on the households that give neondra, for each has a small amount to pay. These payments add up to a quite substantial sum for the host household, and is a most welcome help at a time of need. This utilitarian aspect of vartan bhanji is, sometimes, taken to be its *raison d'être*. That would be a misconception. To think of vartan bhanji in such a narrowly utilitarian way would obscure its latent function in affirming and regulating membership of the biraderi of participation. The latter is far more significant, though less easily perceived.

Pakki and katchi vartan: biraderi and non-biraderi

The structural significance of vartan bhanji in biraderi organization becomes clearer if we consider the distinction that is made by the people between *pakki* (cooked, ripe, firm or permanent) and *katchi* (raw, unripe, weak or temporary) vartan. The circle of households with whom these respective forms of vartan bhanji are transacted, and their modes of operation, are different. It is only in *pakki vartan* that we see the full operation of the institution and its complementary mechanism of ritualized responses. It takes place only between households between whom permanent bonds exist. These are, above all, members of the biraderi of participation. In cases where inter-biraderi marriages have taken place, pakki vartan also includes the *nanké* of the head of the household, i.e. the household of his mother's father, her siblings, and her father's brothers; and/or, as the case may be, the *sauré* of the head of the household (and or those of his sons), i.e. the households of his (their) wife's father or siblings and of her father's brothers.

Katchi vartan signifies a courtesy relationship, temporary by nature, rather than permanently embedded in kinship. It takes place principally with close friends and neighbours in the village. There is no permanent obligation on either side to continue the relationship, and there are no collective sanctions if it is discontinued. Vartan with such a household ceases, for example, when they leave the neighbourhood. In the case of katchi vartan no formal invitation is sent, by way of mohli, and there is no participation in the ceremonial feast. Instead, uncooked food is sent to their house in token quantity, i.e. just about enough for one person. Similarly, the amounts given as neondra in katchi vartan are smaller than those given in pakki vartan. The latter, by contrast, is unaffected by distance: members of the biraderi are invited and in fact come from long distances to participate in weddings and other *rites de passage*, such as circumcision ceremonies.

Puggi

It is rare for pakki vartan to take place with households outside the biraderi. But it may take place, exceptionally, between households of *puggis*. These are very close friends whose mutual bonds are sealed by a special ritual. When friends decide to become puggis, their close friendship is sanctified through an elaborate ceremony, during which they exchange their *pugs* (turbans). That solemnizes their new relationship and signifies their ties which are taken to be as close and as strong as those between brothers. It is a very precious relationship, not undertaken casually. Cases of such ritualized friendship are quite rare.

We can look at two examples. In one case the two puggis were a tractor driver in Chak Tekwala and his one-time comrade in arms who lived in a distant village. They had both served in the army during the Second World War and fought shoulder to shoulder in Burma. They had gone through the ceremony of exchanging their pugs and practised pakki vartan with each other. In explanation the tractor driver said, 'We stood together as true brothers when together we looked at the face of death; how can we now cease to be brothers in the face of life.'

A rather different case was that of two small landholding peasants, one of whom was a refugee from India and the other an original inhabitant of the area. During the upheavals accompanying the Partition, when large number of peasants, Indian and Pakistani, Hindus, Muslims and Sikhs, were driven across the new border in opposite directions, powerful landlords tried to grab as much of the land abandoned by the refugees as they could. The local peasant and his biraderi rallied to help the incoming refugee and his biraderi in their fight against a big local landowner who tried to grab the land that was allotted to the refugees. Out of that incident, a close friendship between the two men, each a leading figure in his own biraderi, grew. They went through the ritual of becoming puggis. But, in their case, despite their new ties as puggis, the two households practised only katchi vartan between them. Amongst small landholding peasants the integrity of their biraderis and the ritual of vartan bhanji are taken very seriously. They do not relax and extend boundaries of pakki vartan too readily.

Importance of funerals

Participation in funerals is of utmost importance and households are not easily forgiven if they fail to send a representative on such an occasion to commiserate with the bereaved and say prayers for the dead. Biraderi members as well as friends are all expected to attend funerals. In practice, virtually everyone from the village would attend the funeral of a fellow villager. Even when a biraderi is split, it is not unusual to find one-time fellow members of a split biraderi turning up for a funeral. On the other hand, some irreparable splits in biraderis had been caused by failures to attend funerals. The powerful sentiment that is associated with funerals is exploited by men with political ambitions, who make a point of attending every funeral in their constituency and thereby consolidating links with followers. People would say: 'We support him because he shares our joys and sorrows.' It is sharing of the sorrow that really counts.

After every funeral friends and relatives of the bereaved household go to their hut to say prayers for the dead (*fateha*). In the case of big landlords it is a very elaborate affair that lasts for forty days of collective recitation of the Quran, with meals provided. Bereaved poor labourers sit on a mat outside their huts for not much more than a few hours. Visitors come and go. Each visitor needs to stay no more than five minutes. On arrival he would ritually raise his hands in front of his face in silent prayer for a few seconds. Before leaving he would embrace the head of the bereaved household as an expression of sympathy. Then he would leave, for a poor man's visitor is probably equally hard pressed by the demands of work. It is all quickly over. But as tokens of sharing of sorrow such visits are of enormous significance in the local culture.

Vartan bhanji and class

The manner of observance of the ritual of vartan bhanji between unrelated landlord households is ambiguous and controversial. Some landlords use vartan bhanji and the notion of pakki vartan to seal political alliances with allies who are not members of their biraderi. They would describe their relationship with political allies as pakki vartan. Others, especially small landholding peasants, would scoff at such claims and insist that it was in fact only katchi vartan; pakki vartan was not possible with just friends. Small landholding peasants, for whom biraderi solidarity is of vital importance in standing up against the power of big landlords, are much concerned about emphasizing the importance of the biraderi and sanctity of its rituals. They would point out that pakki vartan could be practised with biraderi members alone. Even if one dislike a person, if he was a member of the biraderi one would have to engage in proper vartan with him. It was not a question of choice. They would say, landlord alliances are here today and gone tomorrow. They are not binding ties like those of the biraderi.

Landlords who are less dependent on biraderi solidarity and more so on political alliances, and who feel free to pick and choose their allies, from one election to another, initiate or terminate vartan bhanji with them as it suits them. For landlords, political allies are valued participants in their rituals which are not too rigidly restricted to the biraderi. Politics is a major preoccupation of most landlords, and some of them would not hesitate to exploit the ceremonial of vartan bhanji to consolidate friendships and proclaim political alliances. The landlords' view of the world may have influenced Eglar's (1960) reading of the situation, for she went with a landlord friend to his village, to stay with his family for her research.[6] I shall comment on some aspects of her work below. Her understanding of the Punjabi rural society, it is quite evident, was heavily influenced by her host's perceptions.

Terminating biraderi ties

When there is a break in a biraderi, termination of relationships between rival households cannot be completed unless the outstanding ritual debts, under vartan bhanji, are cleared up and the symbolic ties dissolved. Prestations of vartan bhanji do not therefore just cease when there is a fission in a biraderi. A final prestation must be made to extinguish the outstanding ritual debt, to free a household from the ties of biraderi.

The role of vartan bhanji in the organization of the biraderi is made quite manifest by the procedure that is followed in the event of a conflict which precipitates a rift in the biraderi. A household terminates its biraderi relationships by presenting to the household from whom it wishes to break relationship, an amount of neondra that is exactly equal to the net amount which is 'owed' by it on account of its ritual debt. The final payment extinguishes it. This final prestation does not include the normal additional amount in excess of the outstanding 'debt' that would have reversed it, and thereby continued the ongoing dynamic of vartan bhanji that symbolizes biraderi ties. The tie is terminated by ending ritual debts on both sides. This final prestation, in the event of conflict, makes it quite clear that neondra is not a gift, in the ordinary sense of the word, but is symbolic of reciprocal ties and obligations of biraderi. It is unthinkable for anyone not to remit the final prestation when he makes a break from the biraderi, for in that case he would not have extinguished the ritual debt and the relationship that it symbolizes. Nor would the receiving household refuse to accept it, for only by doing so they too end the relationship.

In such an event, the final prestation is not brought by a member of the household concerned, which does not participate in the relevant ceremonial event. The money is sent with a kammi, usually the nai. The amount given and the name of the sender of the neondra is loudly announced during the ceremonial proceedings both by the kammi who brings the money and the representative of the receiver. The kammi clearly announces the fact that the neondra being paid is exactly equal to the outstanding obligation, 'no more and no less', and that there is no more reckoning to be done between the two households. This formally seals the break.

Other gifts

There is a gift associated with vartan bhanji, which supplements neondra. Called *veyl,* it consists of cash gifts given by wedding guests to mirasis who sing and dance at the function. These amounts too are recorded and regarded as a 'debt' of the household celebrating the occasion. On a similar occasion that is celebrated by the donors, the 'debtors' must reciprocate this by making corresponding gifts to the donors' mirasis. The receiving households are anxious to keep such obligations within strict limits; when their set limit is reached they request the donors to stop. Nowadays professional groups of mirasis are engaged to sing and dance at weddings, and a minimum fee is guaranteed by the host household. When the total veyl reaches the set limit, the head of the household usually passes the word around for the veyl to cease.

The reciprocal obligation of the host's household is limited to customary and reasonable amounts given as veyl. If an exceptionally large amount were to be given he is not to feel obligated by it. A rather more interesting variant of this is that of a (friendly) status contest between two rival guests, which takes the form of each of them giving ever higher amounts of veyl, not in his own name but in the name of his rival, who, in turn is obliged to retaliate. This goes on until one of the two decides to stop or has no more money left in his pocket, which is the usual face saving excuse to stop. He thus acknowledges defeat. It is a status game indulged in only by rich landowners. Needless to say, in this case the host household is under no obligation to reciprocate later.

Other forms of gifts also are exchanged, which do not fall in the category of vartan bhanji. A wedding and circumcision ceremonies, biraderi and other guests may give additional amounts as gifts. These non-obligatory gifts are known as salaami. Salaami is given at a different moment in the ceremonial proceedings than neondra, so that the two cannot be confused. It is customarily given by close relatives or by rich patrons. Large amounts are sometimes given to show off the wealth and status of the giver. Not all households give salaami. Amounts given as salaami do not involve any obligation to reciprocate in like measure. Gifts are also made by heads of households to their married daughters (or sisters) on occasions when their households celebrate weddings or circumcisions.

A rather different category of gift is called *laag*, which is given by the host household celebrating an event, to its village servants. The word laag is taken to imply a 'right' or 'due'. There are specific laags which have to be paid to village servants who perform specific roles at the various ceremonies. Laag too does not constitute part of vartan bhanji.

Eglar on Punjab village life

It is necessary, in this context, to comment on the work of Zekiye Eglar (1960), who has written one of the very few book-length studies of a Pakistan village which is widely cited. Her account and interpretation not only differ from mine but raise large questions. She correctly emphasizes the basic characteristic of exchange of prestations in vartan bhanji when she states that 'While there should be reciprocity, there should never be an equilibrium. The things exchanged should not exactly balance, because this would bring her relationship to an end' (ibid.: 125). Despite that recognition, Eglar confuses prestations that are a part of vartan bhanji (and 'reciprocal') and other gifts and payments that are not. For example she includes under vartan bhanji: 'the daughter's right in her parent's home . . . (which) . . . is constantly validated through gifts she receives on her visits and on all major occasions in her own and her father's household' (ibid.: 106). Her confusion is evident for she soon tells us also that: 'Important as is the role of the daughter in the exchange of gifts, those gifts that are given to a true daughter are not vartan bhanji' (ibid.: 114). Nevertheless, rather extraordinarily she then concludes that: 'It is on this basis, namely the exchange of gifts, that a household can deal with people beyond its immediate circle of relatives and friends and can have vartan bhanji with the village as a whole' (ibid.: 107).

It is clear that Eglar has not grasped the ritual role of vartan bhanji in reiterating the ties of the biraderi of participation. She does not see the essential differences between ritual prestations exchanged in vartan bhanji and other 'gifts', namely salaami and laag which are not part of the ritual of vartan bhanji and the significance of which is not the same. Nor does Eglar appear to be aware of the distinction between katchi vartan and pakki vartan. She misses entirely the structural significance of vartan bhanji in biraderi organization. For her it is no more than gift exchange that 'establishes goodwill with kinsfolk and non-kin' (ibid.: 107, 176). Eglar's work, therefore, needs to be read with care (see endnote 6).

Invitations by mohli and signalling of conflicts

The structural role of vartan bhanji is best understood if we look at the associated mechanism of ritualized transmission of invitations for the ceremonial occasions on which vartan bhanji takes place. The invitations are sent with the nai and they elicit formally graduated responses from the household that receives the invitation. These are conveyed by the nai back to the inviting household, who thereby receive messages about the state of their mutual relationships. This signals potential conflicts in advance, so that there is an opportunity to resolve them before the ceremonial occasion in question or to precipitate an open break. The ritual transmission of invitations by sending *mohli* with the nai, and formalized responses to the invitations, are therefore a vital complementary mechanism that works, as part of vartan bhanji, to regulate relationships within the biraderi and in the management of tensions within it.

When the date of a wedding (or a circumcision ceremony) is set, the inviting household despatches the nai with mohli to all the households of the biraderi of participation who are all invited to participate. An invitation to a household usually implies an invitation to (any) one male adult of the household, except in the case of very close relatives. The mohli (or *ganth*) which the nai takes with him is a hank of threads of various bright colours. The nai approaches the head of the invitee household and informs him of the date of the wedding and gives him one strand of the thread, the mohli, which he pulls out from the hank. The mohli ritually conveys the invitation. When the invitation is accepted, the head of the household takes the mohli in his hand. He may tie it on the wrist of a child of his family, which would be a way of expressing affection and goodwill for the inviting household. He then gives a customary gift, in cash, to the barber. The amount is fixed by tradition in each biraderi, and is higher for near relatives and less for distant relatives. This customary amount is not varied by the invitee, except when he wishes to convey to the inviting household that he has a grievance against it. The head of the invitee household may demonstrate his pleasure and affection towards the inviting household by his cordiality towards the barber and offers of food, and hospitality for the night if appropriate. He may, if he pleases, also give him an additional rupee or two before he departs. Such additional payments are given later and quite separately from the fixed ritual payments which are made when the mohli is presented.

Where the household receiving mohli has some grievance against the inviting household, which it wishes to be resolved, one that is not serious enough to signal a threat of a break in relationship, the head of the household accepts the mohli, but gives the barber less than the customary amount or nothing at all. If reconciliation takes place later, this deficiency is then made good to the nai. Or, he may not treat the barber very lavishly (although, if the latter has come from afar, he will not ordinarily fail to give him some food). He may go further and show displeasure by his demeanour or he might make some pointed remarks. The responses are all finely graded and the nai is well experienced in judging their significance and the precise degree of displeasure. If the conflict is very serious, and the invitee wishes to break off the mutual relationship, he will refuse to accept the mohli, or he may take it and throw it on the floor. The worst insult conveyed through a poor suffering nai, that I have on record, is one where the barber was abused and beaten up and asked to hang his mohli on the (ubiquitous) thorny *kikar* tree in the invitee's compound. The nai was then sent back to report to his master what his relative thought of him and his invitation. The immediate issue arose because the invitee household had been led to expect that the present wedding would be solemnised with his own daughter. He felt jilted. The angry father would not have taken matters quite so far but for the fact that there were already signs of a growing rift within the biraderi. That would explain the change of mind on the part of the boy's father in the first place in not asking for the hand of his relative's daughter. Hence the dispute over the impending wedding only provided an occasion to precipitate the rift in the biraderi that was already expected because of a wider conflict that was brewing. Individual households, otherwise, do not push matters quite so far on their own.

The importance of ritually graded responses is that it gives some idea in advance to the inviting household of the strength of feeling on the other side, either of affection or resentment, and of prospects of reconciliation. Heads of households usually have a good idea already of any impending grievance, although in some cases a message would be sent with the nai just to make sure. If the inviting household desires reconciliation, it will take steps to repair the relationship. If the matter is not very serious, the head of the household may depute a son, a brother or a nephew—or go himself—to conciliate the aggrieved party. If the matter is serious, he may take with him a delegation of 'respected' elders, including persons who are likely to have influence with the other party, such as an influential landlord whose presence would pressurise the other party. Such a delegation of mediators is called a *meyla* or a *parain.* The term parain is used also for a mutually agreed 'arbitration tribunal' to adjudicate a dispute. Such a parain usually has, besides representatives of each contending side, some mutually agreed referees or independent members, who carry weight and can ensure compliance with the final agreed decision.

Fission and fusion of biraderis

In the event of conflict, biraderis break along segmentary lines rather than into random groups of households. Cleavages tend not to cut across descent lines. Individual households align themselves with members of their own patti regardless of their personal feelings towards households on either side. It is only rarely that a household finds itself compelled to align itself with more distant kinsmen and pitted against closer relatives. That is an unhappy situation because it would then be isolated and vulnerable in the midst of distant kin. It would not feel fully accepted by the other households with whom it has cast its lot. Occasionally, however, where two major branches of a biraderi break away from each other, it may so happen that a minor patti, instead of aligning itself as a whole with either one or the other of the two biraderi groups, is itself divided between them. That happens when the branch itself is small and weak, and its individual member households have strong ties with influential households of the section of the divided biraderi with whom they choose to cast their lot. Ties of neighbourhood and affinal ties or promises of marriage carry weight with such individual households when making up their minds. In such cases these households have a great incentive for making attempts to prevent a split. They try and promote reconciliation and reunification of the biraderi, sometimes by inviting influential outsiders to mediate.

Economic classes and biraderi organization

We have so far examined general features of the structure and organization of biraderis. On closer examination we shall find that there are very significant differences in the way in which biraderi rules and relationships operate amongst different classes of the population. There are aspects of the ethnographic data which would be difficult to interpret, and regularities that would be obscured, unless we were to look at them against the background of the class organization of the rural society. Rules and rituals of biraderi relationships do not function in identical ways, and with equal force, amongst the different rural classes.

We may divide the rural population into four categories, namely:

(i) *Landlords*, who own substantial amounts of land and employ sharecroppers and/or wage labourers;

(ii) *poor peasants*, who are either landless, or own too little land to secure an adequate livelihood, so that they have to seek employment as sharecroppers or wage labourers, and are economically dependent on their landlord patrons;

(iii) *independent small landholders*, who cultivate their own land; (ideally) they neither work for others nor do they exploit the labour of others as their employees;

(iv) *kammis* or 'village servants', such as the barber, blacksmith, carpenter, potter, etc. The essential criterion of being a kammi is that he is paid by cultivators in the form of a prescribed share of their crops. Persons of kammi origin may achieve a non-kammi status if that circumstance changes.

The above fourfold classification is a simplification in two ways. Firstly, there can be some overlapping between adjacent categories. For example, it is not possible to define with precision the line of demarcation between landlords who depend entirely on the labour of others for the cultivation of their land, and the better off 'small landholders' who rely mainly on their own family labour, but supplement it to a greater or lesser extent to tide over seasonal peak operations. Likewise, very poor small holders may rely heavily on sharecropping of landlords' land or on labouring for wages so that, effectively, they fall into the category of 'dependent peasantry', although they own some land.

Secondly, a complication can arise from the fact that there are some mixed biraderis which include households of landlords along with households of small peasant proprietors. In such biraderis the substantial capacity of landlords to offer patronage and protection to their poorer kinsmen tends to give them the upper hand.

We shall consider below differences between biraderis of the three different economic categories.

(i) Weak biraderis of the rural poor

Biraderi organization, the ideology of biraderi solidarity and the practice of biraderi endogamy are the weakest in the case of economically dependent sections of the rural population, namely sharecroppers and labourers. Not infrequently they do not have biraderi panchayats that enjoy the power and authority to adjudicate disputes amongst them, or take political decisions for the group as a whole. That is because authority and power over them are the prerogatives of their landlords to whom they are subject. The authority of the landlord overrides any authority that their own biraderi panchayat can exercise. The dependent peasantry often take even their own domestic disputes, such as that between a father and son, to their landlord for adjudication.

The landlord's power and authority are rooted in his ability to impose effective economic sanctions over his sharecroppers and labourers. The fact that he is in a position to adjudicate disputes itself contributes further towards enhancing his power and authority. Furthermore, he can get his henchmen to beat people. Besides, it is not uncommon for landlords (who exercise much control over the local police and the administration) to get defiant men jailed at will or, equally, to get men out of jails when it suits them. This power is used quite commonly by landlords to discipline the peasantry. Therefore, the dependent peasantry and even independent small peasants, who do not have a strong biraderi behind them, have to be subservient to landlords. There can be exceptions to this rule, though relatively rare. This happens particularly in cases of members of a large biraderi who work for several different landlords, so that no single landlord dominates them. But their autonomy is limited and precarious. They may have a slightly stronger hand if they also happen to own plots of land, so that they are not wholly dependent on the landlord for their subsistence. But in general, few among the dependent peasantry, dare defy their landlord. Their biraderi panchayats limit their jurisdiction on their internal, domestic, issues and leave larger political issues subject to the authority of the landlords. Not infrequently the landlord adjudicates also on their internal biraderi and family matters.

In the matter of marriages, biraderis of sharecroppers and labourers are not very strict about the practice of biraderi endogamy, although there is a general preference for it. They would marry a daughter outside the biraderi where there is some material advantage in doing so, for they have no status to lose. Nor are they reluctant to seek wives for their sons outside the biraderi if there can be some advantage in that. Biraderi as a social institution is visible amongst them mainly on ceremonial occasions such as weddings, when they get together for celebrations.

(ii) Flexible landlord biraderis

Biraderi organization tends to be weak also amongst big landlords. Households of their biraderis tend generally to be dispersed over several villages in contrast to biraderis of small peasants or labourers who are more concentrated. An indication of this is given by the size of the *mauza* which is a village plus the land attached to it. In Sahiwal district, for example, the gross farm area per *mauza* averages at about 1,000 acres. That cannot accommodate many households of landlords whose individual holding can be several hundred acres each. Households of a landlord biraderi are, typically, dispersed over many, though often nearby, villages. Within a single village it is possible to have a couple of medium sized landlords. In their own village, landlords rely on their own resources of power, which are ample; they do not have to rely on their biraderi at the village level. Their biraderi relationships are more likely to come into play in building coalitions in larger political arenas.

The rule of biraderi endogamy is observed fairly strictly by landlords when taking a first wife. They may, however, take a second, third or fourth wife from outside the biraderi without difficulty. Landlords generally boast that they 'take women (from other biraderis) but do not give them'. This boast is generally true. The prime consideration here is that of status. Marriages to men outside the biraderi would cause a loss of status for the biraderi that gives the bride. When taking a bride from outside the biraderi, it is generally insisted that a first wife be taken from within the biraderi before taking an 'outside' bride. In the case of landlords, this condition is not usually enforceable by sanctions. Nevertheless, a landlord would not like to antagonize fellow biraderi members over such a petty matter. Women are disposable chattels and the condition of prior marriage to a woman of the biraderi is not a serious problem for the man. Cases are known where a landlord wishing to marry a woman from outside the biraderi, either for 'love' or in pursuit of a political alliance, has been forced, nevertheless, to take a woman of his own biraderi as his first wife before he is allowed to marry the other woman. This can be quite tragic for the woman of the biraderi who is married for the sake of convention, her life already in ruins in front of her even as she steps into the bridal chamber.

Big landlord biraderis lack a tight formal organization or a panchayat capable of taking enforceable decisions. Instead of an authoritative biraderi panchayat the custom among landlords is to have informal gatherings, usually at the house of a respected elder member of the biraderi, where they discuss issues before them. They may either achieve a consensus or they may part without agreement. Unlike tightly organized and disciplined biraderis of small landholding peasants who have effective panchayats that exercise authority and impose discipline, big landlord biraderis are relatively undisciplined and more tolerant of dissident opinions and actions. This varies according to the nature of the issues before them. It would be a small matter for a landlord to acquiesce with the sentiment of fellow biraderi members in a relatively petty matter such as that of taking a first wife from the biraderi before he marries a woman from outside the biraderi. Political issues are more serious matters. Landlords may be in competition with fellow biraderi members in local political arenas for posts in local government bodies. Such local rivalry is usually good humoured, for they need to work with each other in larger political arenas, viz., the district, provincial and national levels of politics, where solidarity between them can be quite high. It is this phenomenon of powerful blocs of landlord biraderis that has come to be known in popular parlance, in Pakistan, as the 'biraderi system'. The advantages of having a fellow biraderi member in a position of political influence or power is no small consideration. In provincial and national elections the roles of solid blocs of big landlord biraderis is quite notorious.

In the case of mixed biraderis, where a big landlord has a large number of poor relatives living with him in the same village, there tends to be a greater emphasis, by the poor relations especially, on biraderi *solidarity*, as distinguished from biraderi *discipline* which a big landlord would not tolerate. The landlord relies on his economic power and patronage in asserting his authority in the village at large and pulling together followers of his faction. His fellow biraderi members can provide him with the core of his faction, by virtue of the ideological bond of biraderi solidarity. Because of his power and his capacity to bestow patronage, his poor relations are not averse to the idea of biraderi solidarity which they invoke to assert a prior claim to his favours. In such situations, the landlord does not allow properly constituted biraderi panchayats, vested with formal authority, to exist. If they did, that would conflict with his desire not to compromise his own authority. But, if his wealth and power are not enough to give him a commanding position, and if he happens to depend too heavily upon the support of his fellow biraderi members for his success in local political arenas, the balance can shift in favour of the majority of biraderi members, and some kind of biraderi panchayat can emerge. One finds gradations between these poles. Even a dominant landlord has to make a show (at least) of respect and consideration for his biraderi and, alternatively, even in 'democratically' constituted biraderi panchayats, wealthier members tend to pull greater weight than others.

(iii) Unified biraderis of small, independent peasant proprietors

The most cohesive and tightly knit biraderis are those of independent small landholders, the so-called 'middle peasants', who (ideally) work their own land with their family labour, being neither dependent on a landlord for employment as labourers nor themselves significant employers of labourers. In their case, biraderi solidarity, and the authority and discipline of biraderi panchayats, tend to be far tighter than among other rural classes. For the independent, small peasant proprietors, the unity and solidarity of their biraderi is of vital importance. As single households, they would be vulnerable against the power of big landlords. Collectively, they can hold their ground against the latter.

Their panchayats adjudicate disputes within the biraderi and regulate much of their social life. More significantly, the panchayats negotiate political deals on behalf of the biraderi, so that the biraderi acts as a single unit in factional and political affiliations. In large biraderis there may be patti panchayats that govern affairs that are internal to the patti. In each village or hamlet there is a panchayat for the local group. At a higher level, there is a panchayat for the entire biraderi of participation, which meets when it is called upon to adjudicate disputes. Very often these disputes are about the conflicting claims of biraderi members for the hand of a girl to be given in marriage to their sons in preference to other claimants.

The panchayats are neither formally elected nor do they hold office purely by ascription. Panchayat members *emerge*, in the course of their practical involvement with biraderi affairs, as persons effective in dealing with biraderi matters. There is a tacit acknowledgement of the ability, wisdom and fairness of biraderi members who are accorded the privilege and the right to sit as members of the panchayat. Although officials and academics often refer to them as the village 'elders', they are in fact not generally the older men of the village. Typically, they are men who are just in their thirties and forties, active as well as mature enough to function as effective members of the panchayat. There are cases in which there are in fact two, complementary, biraderi panchayats that operate in parallel, each within its own sphere. One, composed of relatively younger men, would deal with relations of the group with the outside world, i.e. matters that involve the administration, land revenue officials, the police or politics. The other panchayat, made up of older men, adjudicates on disputes about marriages and similar 'internal affairs' of the biraderi. Exchanges of women in marriage are controlled by the 'senior' biraderi, which is also invested with the power to impose the ultimate sanction of expelling offending households from the biraderi. Expulsion would leave the household isolated and vulnerable and would force it to seek a landlord patron to whom it would submit in return for protection. But that entails a high price. In the case of one fugitive household, the landlord who offered them protection extracted cheap labour from them.

An even greater penalty for the expelled household would be the problem of finding spouses for their sons and daughters; for no one from their own biraderi would (or even be able to) give (or take) a daughter in marriage. Marriage outside the biraderi is both dishonourable and difficult. In the light of the cultural norms, it would be less dishonourable for their son to take a wife from outside the biraderi. But who would give a daughter to such a household? Men will therefore often contain bitter hatred against fellow biraderi members, and continue vartan bhanji with them, as a price for remaining within the fold of their biraderi. Single households do not choose to break away from their biraderis. If they have to leave it, that would only be because they are expelled from it, which is done only in extreme circumstances. That is the ultimate sanction which a biraderi panchayat can impose. Outside the biraderi one becomes a non-person, shunned, humiliated and despised by all.

III. BIRADERI AS CLAN

My discussion of biraderi of type B, the biraderi as clan, will be more limited than the detailed account that I have given in section II of the endogamous biraderi of type A, the biraderi as lineage. My research was focused on the latter. There was, however, a large clan of Rangarh Rajputs with exogamous gots (or gotras), who lived in villages about twelve kilometres away from where I was based. That was not near enough to allow me to be a participant observer. What I have to offer is, hopefully, enough to provide at least a starting point for consideration of this alternative system, and to put the subject of kinship in Punjab into a wider perspective.

The clan

In the exogamous system, the biraderi is the endogamous group that envelops constituent exogamous gots. To avoid confusion, I have decided to use the word 'clan' to distinguish this type of biraderi from biraderi based on lineage. For the exogamous segments of clans there is no problem in employing the indigenous word got (or gotra), which is unambiguous and widely understood in South Asian anthropology.

The clan boundary defines the limits of exchanges in marriage between its constituent gots. Whereas the biraderi as lineage tends to be very small, so that there are usually several of them in a single village, biraderi as clan is very large so that one clan is spread over many villages. In Pakistani Punjab, the exogamous system is to be found among Rajputs, Jats, Meos, etc., who originated from East Punjab and Haryana (from Ambala to Gurgaon), regions now in India. These groups moved to the canal colonies of central and southern Punjab as colonists (*abadkar*) before the Partition or as refugees (*muhajirs*) after 1947.

All gots have distinctive names. The practice of got exogamy is understood as avoidance of marrying someone with the same got name. Thus a Chauhan may not marry a Chauhan but will marry a Powar, and so on. A woman of one's own got is regarded as a sister and union with her would be incestuous. In contrast to the involuted form of the small endogamous biraderis of type A, in which both affinal as well as agnatic ties are contained within the biraderi, in the case of biraderi of type B, affinal ties radiate out horizontally from the constituent exogamous gots, and unite them as segments of a single unified biraderi, the clan. These large biraderis, or clans, are also corporate groups, the affairs of which are subject to the authority of a biraderi panchayat at the highest level. Constituent gots and members of the clan in each village have their own panchayats which operate at the appropriate levels. The overall biraderi or clan panchayat is made up of representatives of constituent gots and meets when an occasion arises, to deal with matters that affect the entire clan.

Corporate character of biraderi of type B—the clan

The clan of Rangarh Rajputs that is settled in the Pakpattan-Okara area, consists mostly of small peasants. Some of them have served in the police or the army. They came as refugees from Indian Punjab. They practise got exogamy. Whereas in India, they said, they used also to observe village exogamy, now they are not very strict about that. Marriage entails a very large bride price. After marriage a woman's parents have nothing to do with her, or so they claimed. 'If my daughter leaves her husband and wants to come back to me, I will have no alternative but to kill her with my own hands, with this sword', said one of my informants, brandishing his well cared for sword. The daughter belonged to her in-laws and the father had no more claims on her.

Rangarh Rajputs of the area had an overarching panchayat for the entire clan. But day-to-day matters were dealt with by panchayats that functioned at local levels. The capacity of their village level panchayat in getting members to work together, was demonstrated by their ability to set up and run a very successful cooperative society in a large village, which had helped its members to install 42 tube-wells for irrigation. Tube-wells cost between Rs. 10,000 and Rs. 12,000 (in 1968), and this was a lot of money for small peasants.

A special event took place which demonstrated the corporate character of the clan as a whole. An occasion arose for the Rangarh Rajputs to convene the grand panchayat of the entire clan, their supreme council. The grand panchayat does not meet often, but only when major issues arise that affect the whole clan. I was not permitted to be present at its deliberations, nor would any of my informants divulge the issue that had caused it to be convened. But several of them, individually, were prepared to describe its procedure.

For the meeting of the grand panchayat, delegates from the constituent gots of the clan from miles around gathered at the village of a senior member of the clan. The delegates would begin to arrive by the afternoon. At sunset they would together say their evening prayers. That would be followed by a ceremonial meal. When everyone had finished eating, they would, one by one, ceremonially drink a glass of water, saying a prayer (*dua*) over the water before drinking it. Then they would all sit down to business. From the moment that the panchayat members sit down for their formal proceedings, following the ceremonial drink of water, it was said, no one is allowed either to eat or to drink, until the issue before the panchayat is resolved. 'It may take the whole night, it may even take the whole of next day. It may take days! But they are not allowed to get up for anything and they can neither eat nor drink', said one of my informants, dramatising it. One can see the symbolic importance of this elaborate ritual. In that summer heat, there is great pressure on thirsty and tired delegates to come to some compromise and agreement. That pressure would force compromises that would hold the clan together. The collective prayers, the ritual drinking of water, and all the ceremonial are obviously designed to heighten the sense of occasion, and to underline the weight of responsibility of panchayat members and the importance of the deliberations of the grand panchayat. Local village panchayats do not have such ceremonials; their proceedings are rather more mundane and routine. The grand panchayat of the biraderi bears the burden of holding the entire, widely dispersed, biraderi together. It deals with all matters that might potentially threaten its unity. The ultimate sanction of expulsion from the clan would, in principle, be imposed if anyone defied decisions of the clan. This decision was for the grand panchayat to take. But, said my informants, that had never actually happened.

Caste, subcaste, and kinship

Because of the two, quite different, meanings of the indigenous word biraderi we need English terms to distinguish them. There is no terminological problem regarding the biraderi of type A, which unambiguously is a lineage. We have difficulty in settling for an appropriate term for the biraderi of type B, the overall endogamous kin group that envelops constituent exogamous gotras. I have proposed the term 'clan' for this biraderi. But that is controversial and needs to be discussed.

The term currently used in Indian anthropology to designate groups analogous to our biraderi of type B, is 'subcaste'. A basic objection to this would be that we are moving unceremoniously into the vocabulary of caste simply because we have failed to address the problem of finding a suitable term within the vocabulary of kinship for this kin group. A shift from a discourse of kinship into the discourse of caste in this way is methodologically unsound. For us this procedure presents a special difficulty, for it is by no means settled that the Muslim society of Punjab that we are dealing with here is a caste society. One would argue the contrary. In any case, imposing the term 'subcaste' would prejudge an unsettled issue. My suggestion that the institution of caste does not exist among Muslims of the Indus plain is not based on an ideological position that caste cannot exist amongst Muslims because it is not sanctioned by their religion. Nor can we accept the opposite argument without examining the social structure of the Indus plain.

When we looked at the perception of zat by members of the Duddhi Rajput biraderi of the village 'Chak 237 HB', we found that the concept had little meaning for them. They did not see that the notion of zat meant that they occupied any status within a ranked caste order. We can now move beyond that particular case and try and look at the issue of 'caste' among Muslims of the Indus plain in a broader perspective. Scholars have made a case for the existence of Muslim castes in the Gangetic plain. But that cannot be extrapolated to Muslims of the Indus plain without the warrant of ethnography. There is some evidence to suggest that the social structure of the Indus plain is qualitatively different from that of the Gangetic plain.

Caste, clan, and tribe in the Indus plain

Ecological and historical reasons explains the contrasting social structures and cultures of the Indus plain and the Gangetic plain respectively. The arid plains of Punjab and Sindh—the Indus plain—were, until the development of canal colonies beginning from the late nineteenth century, peopled for centuries by semi-nomadic tribal people who inhabited the riverine areas, irrigated by annual flooding of the rivers. They kept herds of water buffalo and practised perfunctory agriculture when the summer floods receded, having irrigated the thirsty land. It was a precarious existence. For centuries, invaders from the West crossed this barren land without a second look, and headed for the wealth of the Gangetic plain. The agriculturally rich Gangetic plain sustained a much more elaborate (and stratified) social structure and culture.

The domain of religious belief dramatically underlines the contrast between the two regions with their very different social structures and cultures. It is surely sociologically most significant that the Indus plain generated successive religious beliefs that were antithetical to Brahminical orthodoxy of the Gangetic plain. Buddhism was the dominant faith in the Indus plain for many centuries before the advent of Islam. By contrast and remarkably, despite six centuries of Muslim imperial rule based on the Gangetic plain, conversions to Islam in the heartland of the empire (and of Brahminical orthodoxy) were minimal. It was on the periphery of Muslim imperial rule, in the Indus plain, where Delhi-based imperial control was tenuous and problematic, that conversions to Islam were maximal. It was on the soil of the Indus plain, too, that the Sikh faith, yet another religious heterodoxy vis-à-vis Brahminical orthodoxy, was born. This raises fascinating questions about the relationship between the respective social structures in the two regions and their ideological concomitants. For heuristic purposes, we could invert the familiar ideological argument that caste does not exist in the Indus plain because of Islam into a converse proposition, namely that this region was more susceptible to the appeal of Buddhism, Islam, and Sikhism because of its relatively simpler ('tribal') social structure.

Several anthropological studies point to the unique social structure of the Indus plain. A very interesting comparative study of caste ranking in different regions of India and Pakistan was undertaken by McKim Marriott who found that: 'Most people of the Middle Indus districts are contained within a large number of hereditary ethnic groups which may better be called '*tribes*' and '*line-ages*' [*sic*] *rather than castes* since they are not agreed to occupy distinct corporate ranks universally in relation to each other' (Marriott, 1965: 63; italics added). Marriott's study was limited to the Middle Indus region. But his findings can, arguably, apply to the whole of the Indus plain. Thus Ibbetson also noted that: 'Throughout the Western Plains and in a somewhat lower degree throughout the Cis-Indus Salt-Range Tract . . . we find the distribution of the landowning classes based upon tribe rather than upon caste' (Ibbetson 1916: 16).

The 'tribal' structure did not long survive changes that were set into motion by colonial rule. A key factor in that process of profound social change was the conversion of land into State enforced private property, instead of possession by tribal appropriation. A very limited number of big landholdings in some parts of the region, especially near major conurbations, did pre-date British rule. But after the colonial dispensation big landed magnates proliferated everywhere. They were invested with rights of ownership in large tracts of land. It seems anachronistic that the so-called 'feudalism' in Pakistan was directly a product of colonial rule.[7] In the light of these changes, tribal organization and solidarity lost their essential function, namely that of providing access to land, and atrophied. Tribes soon fragmented into small self-contained lineages, for the social glue that had held them together as clans and tribes had dissolved. But, despite the new economic stratification that emerged, the society of the Indus plain did not become a hierarchically stratified and ritualized social system in the sense of a hierarchy of caste. Its social hierarchy was to be an economic one.

Retrieving the term 'clan'

Given the above considerations, it seems quite doubtful, to say the least, that the concepts of caste and subcaste can legitimately be applied to the social system of the Indus Plain. We must look for our terminology within the vocabulary of kinship. The term that appears to be the most appropriate is 'clan'. But there is no unanimity about the meaning of the term 'clan' in South Asian social anthropology. Fox observes:

> yet strangely, in all the varied literature . . . no clear definition of 'clan' appears either in Indian native terms or in anthropological terminology. Instead, 'tribe', 'clan', 'family' and 'lineage' are confusingly used by different authors to refer to the same thing. . . . The confusing or contradictory terminology applied to these clans is not wholly a matter of ethnographic naivete. Rather the lack of precise definition mirrors the complex social situation in which groups were embedded, a complex born not of kinship structure but of the political and economic role they performed in the state.
>
> (Fox 1971: 19-21)

Terminology in this area of scholarship is clearly in considerable disarray, which places on the community of scholars the burden of examining and systematizing it and seeking a viable consensus.

Radcliffe-Brown (1950) deplored the use of the term clan which he complained was: 'without any clear definition' (ibid.: 40). Writing in the African context he chose 'tribe' to describe the overall endogamous group so that for him the word 'clan' was therefore available to refer to exogamous divisions of tribes (cf. ibid.: 41). But we cannot mechanically follow that route. If we were to insist on using the word clan to refer to 'exogamous divisions', namely gots or gotras, as is currently done, we may well ask, what are they the 'divisions' of ? We cannot shift gear into the terminology of caste and say that they are subdivisions of subcastes. That would methodologically be unacceptable. Nor can we say that the unit is a tribe, as Radcliffe-Brown can say in the African context. Tribe would not be an appropriate term for our purposes. What other term do we have that can be used for the purpose, if we insist on using up the term 'clan' to denote gotra? If we insist on that, we have no suitable term left within the available vocabulary of kinship. We can begin by giving up the use of the term subcaste.

The seminal work of Adrian Mayer (1960), on caste and kinship in central India, opened the way for an explicit separation of discourses of caste and kinship. Making a distinction between what he called 'external aspects of caste' and 'internal aspects of caste' he noted that: 'The difference between the roles of an individual as a caste and a subcaste member can thus be seen as one of belonging to a village and belonging to a spatially and genealogically extended kin-group' (ibid.: 6). He made the important point that the term 'subcaste' was really about kinship. He wrote: 'Subcastes are primarily endogamous bodies . . . marriage is a more important criterion of subcaste' (ibid.: 157-8). What was referred to in the literature as 'subcaste' was in fact the overall endogamous group within which exchanges in marriages between related gotras of Ramkheri were confined. Mayer continued: 'The subcaste itself is not a formal local unit, save where there is endogamy within a handful of villages. . . . The roles are instead made manifest in what I term the "*kindred of recognition* . . ."' (ibid.: 161). In Ramkheri this was a subjectively perceived boundary, within which exchanges in marriage took place, as 'recognized' by those concerned. The subcaste also had councils. But Mayer would hesitate to attribute to them a corporate quality (personal communication, H.A.).

Clan would appear to be the most appropriate term, from within the available vocabulary of kinship, for our biraderi of type B. The next higher-level term, tribe, as we have noted, would be inappropriate in our case, although it is quite appropriate in the African case that Radcliffe-Brown was concerned with in the passage quoted above. Our difficulty would be solved if we were able to retrieve the term 'clan' for this more useful and necessary purpose. This we can do, giving up its use to refer to gots or gotras for which we can happily use the indigenous word instead, for it does not stand in need of an English equivalent.

One option that we can take note of is that we can adopt the term 'sib' for gotra. Sib is not much favoured by the Anglo-Saxon tradition in social anthropology. But that is perhaps not a sufficient reason for our refusing to adopt the term if it were to be accepted that it suits our purpose and solves our problem. In the context of China, Feng,[8] amongst others, uses the term 'sib' for the exogamous group that is analogous to gotra (Feng 1937: 173). It is a term that Murdock (1965) also advocates.

There may be resistance to the idea of using the word sib for gotra. If so, our best alternative may be to opt for my earlier suggestion and use the indigenous terms 'got' or 'gotra', without searching for an English equivalent. There would be no problem in that case for the term gotra is unambiguous, unlike the word 'biraderi' which because of its two different meanings stands in need of English equivalents. Furthermore, we do stand in need of an alternative, within the vocabulary of kinship, for subcaste. If we retrieve the word 'clan' to mean biraderi of type B, a substitute for the misused term 'subcaste', our problem will have been solved. I hope that colleagues in South Asian social anthropology will accept the idea.

IV. THEORETICAL ISSUES

Structured kinship and commodification of women

Structured kinship, whether based on exogamy or endogamy, is based on control exercised by men over the circulation of women in marriage. Women are treated as commodities and chattels, exchanged or appropriated for the purpose of perpetuating male-controlled lineages and clans. In structures based upon patrilineal kinship, control over the procreative powers of women is essential for perpetuation of lineages and clans. Beyond that, control over the circulation of women also establishes social bases of power that is exercised over members of the kin groups by men who are in charge of panchayats. Kinship is, therefore, very much about power. Men who control kin groups have a large stake in the continued subordination of women, which is a means towards subordination of the entire group.

Other factors too enter into the equation. In the Indus plain it is only just over a century ago that the basis of rural social organization was tribal. That was essential for control of land by members of the tribe. That function of tribal organization, namely the appropriation of land, no longer exists. But new functions for kin organizations have taken its place. With the emergence of political systems based on universal adult franchise biraderis, of both types, tend to operate in the political arena as vote banks. That provides panchayat leaders with a considerable source of power. Tightly knit biraderi organizations serve the needs of small peasants too. At the village level, small peasant proprietors, who are individually weak and vulnerable, are nevertheless able, as powerfully unified kin groups, to confront landlord power. These factors work towards a perpetuation of the commodification of women, the basis on which the unity and power of kin groups rests. Kinship therefore is not a purely cultural phenomenon.

How stable are these structures of kinship? In the urban context we find that functions of kin groups begin to atrophy and rules of kinship tend to weaken. Structured kinship yields to more fluid, 'unstructured' patterns of marriages, so that conditions are created where the personal qualities of both men and women begin to enjoy a greater scope and freedom to develop. Communities and groups tend to drift away from the custom of arranging marriages according to the old codes. When this happens, conditions for women to be able to realize themselves as free and equal persons in society, improve. The possibility improves of their being able to pursue their lives, as individuals in their own right, in equality with men. This trend is accentuated with the growing importance of women's education and careers. Educated men want to marry educated women, the rich want to marry glamorous women, businessmen want to establish affinal ties with powerful bureaucrats, the not-so-well-off want a wife who can hold a good job and earn money to underpin the meagre family budget. There is a pronounced trend therefore in the urban milieu in Pakistan for the constraints of structured kinship to erode, although, given cultural inertia this is progressing more slowly than it might otherwise do. But, finally, in our patriarchal society, despite these changes, the initiative in the choice of a spouse still remains with men.

Exchange vs. appropriation of women

The structure of patrilateral parallel cousin marriages, or lineage endogamy as we may prefer to call it, is to be found exclusively in Muslim societies, from North Africa to Indonesia and beyond. It would, however, be inaccurate to call it the 'Muslim system of kinship', for not all Muslim societies have such a structure of kinship—as in the case of our biraderi as clan. Because it differs so much from other kinship systems, there is a great deal of ill-informed prejudice against it. This is to be found in the writings of Christian missionaries of the past and the derivative ideas of nineteenth century armchair social anthropologists, who speculated about the world comfortably ensconced in their university chairs.

In more recent times, similar prejudices have still been voiced. We may consider the ideas of Claude Lévi-Strauss. It is quite extraordinary that in his celebrated *tour de force* (Lévi-Strauss 1969), while analysing virtually all 'The Elementary Structures of Kinship' (as he calls them) that are known, Lévi-Strauss implicitly omits the structure of patrilateral parallel cousin marriage from the ambit of his analysis; it happens to be the one structure of kinship that does not fit in with his conclusions. After executing a brilliant exercise in the algebra of kinship based on exchange, he arrives at the not very surprising conclusion that all 'elementary structures of kinship' are indeed based on exchange!

At this point I must make a point about terminology. In opposition to 'elementary' structures of kinship, Lévi-Strauss posits the concept of 'complex' structures. The former is rule-governed kinship. By contrast 'complex structures' are not rule governed, for as Lévi-Strauss points out, the 'determination of the spouse (is left to) other mechanisms, economic or psychological' (ibid.: xxiii). It is easy to see that the concept of 'complex structures' is a contradiction in terms, for it refers to a fluid situation where marriages are not governed by rules that can generate kinship structures. The term 'complex structures' does not refer to structured kinship at all. I will therefore refrain from using the meaningless term 'complex structures', and therefore its counterpart, 'elementary structures of kinship'. I will substitute for them the pair of terms, 'structured' and 'unstructured' kinship, terms that are self-explanatory.

The omission of patrilateral parallel cousin marriage in Lévi-Strauss' monumental work can hardly be attributed to amnesia, for he does make a passing reference to it in his discussion of incest. The refusal to discuss it seriously, it seems, stems from a deep-seated prejudice so that he is unable to accept the fact that such a structure of kinship is at all a viable structure of kinship. This came out in the course of correspondence between us, which offers an insight into his thought on the subject. Proceeding deductively from abstract theoretical premises and transcendental concepts, in the hallowed French tradition that despises the empiricism of the English, Lévi-Strauss *logically* concluded that patrilateral parallel cousin marriage cannot sustain an 'elementary structure of kinship'. It mattered little if reality pointed the other way. To sustain this view, he went to extreme lengths to re-interpret facts to fit theory. This became clear from our correspondence of twenty-two years ago. As our exchange of letters proceeded, Lévi-Strauss, increasingly, veered towards the view that where endogamous structures appear to exist, that is an illusion, for behind such structures of kinship there lurks the principles of exchange. For 'evidence' of this he finally sheltered behind the work of Cuisenier (1962) who, by a magical twist in the presentation of his data, turned an endogamous system into an exogamous one! It is a pity that Lévi-Strauss himself did not enlarge on these themes in his *magnum opus* itself, which would have given the scholarly community a basis for discussion. In the circumstances we shall look at his views as they unfolded through our correspondence. They deserve to be made public. My only regret is my own failure in not being able to take this up two decades earlier.

The ball was set rolling by critical comments on the first draft of my paper on kinship in West Punjab, which were made by Maurice Freedman invoking Lévi-Strauss. The paper was later published without the section in which I proposed a distinction and opposition between two alternative structural principles underlying structures of kinship, namely the principle of 'exchange' (that figures as the exclusive principle in Lévi-Strauss's work) and an alternative principle of 'appropriation'. I suggested that it is the latter that underlies the structure of patrilateral parallel cousin marriage. I emphasized further that these two principles were mutually opposed and exclusive so that any dilution of the one by the other would cause erosion and breakdown of structured kinship. In the course of correspondence with Lévi-Strauss that ensued during April-May 1972,[9] I put these ideas to him. He did not accept them and put certain counter arguments that we shall look at.

Before taking up the interesting issues that arise from the correspondence, I should underline some of the propositions that we shall look at.

Before taking up the interesting issues that arise from the correspondence, I should underline some of the propositions that Lévi-Strauss makes in his book that have a bearing on our discussion. He wrote:

(i) 'The native mind sees matrimonial and economic exchanges as forming an integral part of a basic system of reciprocity'. (Lévi-Strauss, 1969: 33)

(ii) 'No matter what form it [marriage] takes it is exchange, always exchange, that emerges as the fundamental and common basis of all modalities of the institution of marriage.' (ibid.: 479)

(iii) 'Exogamy provides *the only means* of maintaining the groups as a group, of avoiding the indefinite fission and segmentation which the practice of consanguineous marriages would bring about. If these *consanguineous marriages* were resorted to persistently or even over-frequently they *would not take long to "fragment" the social group* into a multitude of families. . . . This is the danger which is avoided by the more complex forms of exogamy.' (ibid.: 479; italics added)

This last proposition about the consequences of *consanguineous marriages* is cru\cial for our present discussion. It probably explains Lévi-Strauss's fundamental belief that patrilateral parallel cousin marriage, which after all is based on consanguineous marriages, cannot be a basis of stable 'elementary structures of kinship'.

How can we reconcile such an *a priori* view with all the empirical evidence that we have from so many societies stretching from North Africa to Indonesia, that do have stable kinship structures based on patrilateral parallel cousin marriage? We have examined one such case of structured kinship in this paper, a structure that is based exclusively on consanguineous marriages. Does that mean that Lévi-Strauss's proposition as in (iii) above is not valid? My own view is that there Lévi-Strauss does put his finger upon an important truth. But he does so in a one-sided and distorted way because of his deep-seated prejudice against endogamous structures of kinship. If we broaden his theorem we can rescue its valuable insights, extending the framework of analysis to admit the principle of appropriation as well as the principle of exchange.

Consanguinity and stability of kin groups

Lévi-Strauss's insight in his proposition as per (iii) above is important. Consanguineous marriages would undermine an *exogamous* kinship system for, as he points out, by renouncing 'a limited or very restricted share in the women available . . . [the exogamous principle] gives everybody a claim to a number of women whose availability . . . theoretically is as large as possible and is the same for everyone' (1969: 42). Consanguineous marriages in an exogamous system would destroy the principle of reciprocity and reduce the availability of women to other groups if any group were to appropriate its own women at the same time. It must be said, however, that the converse applies when we are concerned with endogamous systems. In that case, surely, the Lévi-Strauss principle needs to be inverted for its insights to be applicable to the structure of patrilateral parallel cousin marriage. Here consanguineous marriages are not only not incompatible with that structure; they are its very basis. By inverting the Lévi-Strauss theorem we realize that in a system resting upon appropriation of women by the lineage, the system would tend to break down if, contrariwise, its women were at the same time given in 'exchange' to other groups. Considering that we are dealing with two different structures of kinship, based upon opposed principles, we need two alternative formulations of the Lévi-Strauss theorem, inverting his proposition to derive the second. The conclusion is obvious. The two principles, of exchange and appropriation, as alternative principles of structured kinship, are mutually exclusive.

Either of these alternative principles, namely that of exchange and that of appropriation, can generate stable kin groups—but each of a different kind. The truth that underlies Lévi-Strauss's theorem, in (iii) above, is that *in either case*, infringement of the basic structural principle, whether it is exchange or appropriation, would tend towards dissolution of structured kinship and therefore erode the stability of the kin groups. The ultimate principle is simple enough: 'You cannot eat your cake and have it too'! Under the rule of exogamy, by virtue of men of the group forgoing access to their own women, they make available to themselves, on a reciprocal basis, the choice of a much greater number of women of other groups within the system. Such a system would be undermined if men of a group tried to have it both ways and, while claiming access to women of other groups, appropriated their own women, marrying them themselves. Contrariwise, if within a system of consanguineous marriage, i.e. under patrilateral parallel cousin marriage, the women of the group were made available to other groups, that would undermine the availability of women for men of the first group and the stability of the system would be jeopardized. What Lévi-Strauss did not realize is that it works both ways. His formulation is flawed, but not without a large element of truth in it. It only appears to be false because its true insight is presented in a partial and one-sided form.

When I put to Lévi-Strauss my notion of a binary opposition between the two principles of 'exchange' and 'appropriation' as alternative constitutive principles of structured kinship, I did not entirely expect that he would instantly accept it. What was a surprise, however, was the basis of his 'defence' (letter dated 11 April 1972) for what he refused to accept was the very fact that structured kinship can exist at all on the basis of patrilateral parallel cousin marriage. His suggestion was that what I took to be an endogamous structure was, in reality, based on exchange after all! Since he has not written on the subject himself, he referred me instead to an article by Cuisenier (1962). That article is an extraordinary, intellectual conjuring trick. Both Lévi-Strauss and Cuisenier follow a strange logic.

Cuisenier studied marriages among Ouled Arfa, a fraction of the Drid tribe in southern Tunisia. In good Lévi-Straussian tradition he tries to show that the Ouled Arfa kinship, supposed to be based on the 'structure of patrilateral parallel cousin marriage', was in truth an exogamous system. He arrives at that conclusion by a strange distortion of his own data. To begin with, he tells us that only 21 per cent of the marriages were actually with FBD. Cuisenier takes too literally the notion of patrilateral parallel cousin marriage, as against lineage endogamy, as a basic structural principle and he finds it wanting. Proceeding on the basis of his narrowed definition he concludes that: 'this frequency [of 21 per cent of marriages with FBD] is too small for parallel cousin marriage to be accepted as the norm in the Arab system of kinship'.

Cuisenier wants to go much beyond the warrant of his ethnography and prove that the kinship system that he was examining was in fact based on exchange, as Lévi-Strauss too would have it. So we see some extraordinary jugglery in the presentation of his data. In an earlier part of the article Cuisenier tells us that Ouled Arfa marriages with FBD numbered 21 per cent of the total, 50 per cent of marriages were with patrilateral kin other than FBD, leaving 29 per cent of the marriages with 'outsiders'. Disregarding the fact that on the basis of his own figures, more than 71 per cent of the marriages were endogamous, rather strangely, in the final part of the article, there is a miraculous inflation of 'exogamy'. Referring to Murphy and Kasdan's (1959) suggestion that patrilateral parallel cousin marriage was 'not invariable', Cuisenier continues:

> It is necessary to carry this idea further: from the structuralist point of view the number of exogamic marriages is as important in the Arab kinship system as the number of endogamic marriages. Instead of concentrating on endogamy of the parental lineages equal attention should be devoted to the study of exogamous practices. (1962)

Then without any explanation Cuisenier tell us that two-thirds of the marriages were 'exogamous'. Such a statement could only be justified if we were to classify all marriages other than with FBD as exogamous! That would be contrary to what social anthropology understands by the concept. Both he and Lévi-Strauss rest their case on a rather dubious representation of the data.

Taking Cuisenier's demonstration as his basis, Lévi-Strauss re-iterated his views to me in a letter dated 28 April 1972, from which it would be useful to quote:

> As for parallel cousin marriage, I do not believe that it may exist alone, but as one aspect of a system which implies exogamic marriage as well. Of course, this 'exogamic' aspect need not belong to the field of elementary structures. Arab societies were obviously astride elementary structures and complex ones. Instead of exchanging women they were exchanging bonds of alliance.

On a statistical level, we should always find in these societies a balance between 'inside' marriages and 'outside' marriages, which may be expressed as a *combination* of '*endogamy*' and '*exogamy*' or, if you prefer calling it that way, of 'exchange' and 'appropriation' (or rather 'appropriation and exchange'). (Italics added.)

This new notion of a '*combination of endogamy and exogamy*' runs counter to Lévi-Strauss's own theorem as in (iii) above, that consanguineous marriages would undermine and disintegrate an 'elementary structure' of kinship (based on exchange) and indeed, it runs counter also to the broader formulation of the principle that I have advanced. We cannot have structured kinship that combines exchange and appropriation. It has to be the one or the other or, alternatively, a dissolution of the system into unstructured kinship. When suggesting, therefore, that these two opposed principles are combined as Lévi-Strauss proposes above, he is going against the grain of the one profound insight that he does put forward. It is regrettable that Lévi-Strauss is prepared to go to such extreme lengths in his last ditch attempt to reject the notion of the structure of parallel cousin marriage or, rather, the principle of endogamy, as a viable basis of structured kinship.

What would in fact happen if the two principles were to be 'combined'? We can consider an example. Kinship amongst the Muslims of Bangladesh permits patrilateral parallel cousin marriage and marriages can be made within the *gushti* or lineage. But it is not a rule for structured kinship. In practice, the principle of exchange has entered the picture, combined with the principle of appropriation. Marriages are freely made outside the gushti. As a result, 'structured kinship' has dissolved. Kinship among Bangladeshi Muslims is 'unstructured'. Marriages with FBD or a member of the gushti are no longer the rule. Marriages are determined by strategies rather than rules. In the language of Lévi-Strauss, the spouse 'is determined by other mechanisms, economic or psychological'. The current practice is to marry a person of equivalent social and economic status. A new kind of loose groupings has taken form, a loose network of intermarrying households of similar wealth and status. Households that belong to such a network are known as mutual *shambandis.* Shambandis are not a patrilineal kindred. Like rishtedars in Punjab, links between them are affinal. Structured kinship has dissolved. For Pakistan this may well be the face of the future, for it is already a growing tendency in urban Pakistan.

NOTES

1. I hope that the reader will bear with me when I eschew the conventional and scholastic first person plural pronoun 'we', in favour of the humble singular 'I'. I will use the plural 'we' when in a given context I associate the reader with myself.
2. Lévi-Strauss's phrase has been translated into English as 'fraternal incest', which is a peculiar expression (1969: 14). It is presumably intended to mean 'sibling incest'.
3. The Roman Catholic Matrimonial Tribunal prohibits marriage with a first cousin without dispensation. Infringement of that rule is not incest nor a sin. The Canon of the Anglican Church does not include first cousins in its list of prohibited kin with whom union would be incest.
4. The note in my diary records the reply: '*yé oonch neech ki kyą baāt kahen. Bas, Mian Saheb hi hain jo sab sé ooper hain*!' (laughter), i.e. 'What can we say about who is superior and who inferior. It is the Mian Saheb (a big landlord of the area) who is above everyone.
5. The word *seypi* denotes the role of a *kammi* as a receiver of payment in the form of a share of the crops, whereas the word *kammi* emphasizes the work he does—his functional role in the rural economy.
6. I was told this by Raja Mohammad Afzal Khan, whom Eglar had befriended. He had followed her work in the field. Raja was head of the Village-Aid Organization in Pakistan at the time.
7. For reasons of space I cannot embark here on a discussion of the thorny question of 'tribal' society of the Indus plain and the creation by the colonial regime of a new class of landed magnates, who are unscientifically labelled 'feudal'. For a theoretical discussion see Alavi 1980, 1981 and 1983. For an excellent historical account see Roseberry 1988.
8. Han-Yī Feng was a leading authority on Chinese kinship, whose work was used by Lévi-Strauss as an authoritative source on the subject.
9. I shared the correspondence, as it progressed, with Adrian Mayer and Alice and Daniel Thorner and with Maurice Freedman. I am deeply indebted to Alice Thorner for her great generosity in translating for me the article by Jean Cuisenier, which was central to Lévi-Strauss's defence.

REFERENCES

Alavi, H. 1980. 'India: Transition from feudalism to colonial capitalism'. *Journal of Contemporary Asia*, 10, 4.

———. 1981. 'Structure of colonial social formations'. *Economic and Political Weekly* XVI, 10/12 (Annual Number), 475-86; reprinted in Utsa Patnaik, ed., *Agrarian Relations and Accumulation*. Bombay: Oxford University Press.

———. 1983. 'India: The transition to colonial capitalism'. In Hamza Alavi, et al., *Capitalism and Colonial Production*, pp. 23-75. London: Croom Helm.

Bourdieu, P. 1992. *Outline of a Theory of Practice.* Cambridge: Cambridge University Press.

Cuisenier, J. 1962. 'Endogamie et exogamie dans le mariage Arabe'. *L'Homme* 2, 2 (mai-août).

Eglar, Z. 1960. *A Punjabi Village in Pakistan.* New York: Columbia University Press.

Feng, H. 1937. *The Chinese Kinship System.* Philadelphia.

Fox, R. 1971. *Kin, Clan, Raja and Rule: State-hinterland in pre-industrial India.* Berkeley: University of California Press.

Ibbetson, D. 1916. *Panjab Castes.* Lahore: Punjab Government Printing Press.

Lévi-Strauss, C. 1969. *The Elementary Structures of Kinship.* London: Eyre and Spottiswoode.

Marriott, M. 1965. *Caste Ranking and Community Structure in Five Regions of India and Pakistan.* Poona: Deccan College.

Mauss, M. 1954. *The Gift.* London: Cohen and West.

Mayer, A.C. 1960. *Caste and Kinship in Central India.* London: Routledge and Kegan Paul.

Murdock, G.P. 1949. *Social Structure.* New York: Macmillan.

Murphy, R.F. and L. Kasdan. 1959. 'The structure of parallel cousin marriage'. *American Anthropologist* 61, 1: 17-30

Radcliffe-Brown, A.R. and D. Forde. 1950. *African Systems of Kinship and Marriage.* London: Oxford University Press.

Roseberry, J.R. 1988. *Imperial Rule in Punjab : 1818-1881.* Lahore: Vanguard.

Islam and the District Paradigm: Emergent Trends in Contemporary Muslim Society

AKBAR S. AHMED
(1983)

Although Said's *Orientalism* (1978) captured and expressed what was a powerful trend among Third World scholars, it may be time for us to move ahead from that position—to turn inward and dispassionately examine our own societies. Self-knowledge may assist us in improving them. This article is, accordingly, an exercise in social anthropology: it is neither philosophic nor historical in content. I will discuss Muslim society as it is, not as it should be. I believe social anthropology has much to contribute both in academic thought and in practical affairs (see, for instance, Ahmed 1980b). My aim here is to identify what is stirring in the Muslim world, as also to investigate its causes by elucidating the principles of social process in contemporary Muslim society, with special reference to Pakistan.[1] I will also analyse the dialectics of forces creating tension between tradition and modernity in Muslim society in these last decades of the twentieth century. The unrest remains largely unstudied and, on the surface, inexplicable. Its complexity and the diversity of the contexts within it appears to defy easy analysis.

Perceptible beneath the ferment are shadowy figures, no more than simulacra, in the shape of religious leaders—*mullahs*, *maulvis*, *sheikhs*, or *ayatullahs*—who explicitly challenge the ideological tenets of the modern age. For instance, emphasis is placed on the central role of God and a reversion to fundamentalist ideology; revulsion is expressed against materialism as a philosophy and code of conduct; and the target is not the king or president as a symbol of the State, but the modern State apparatus itself. Further, contrary to accepted belief, these movements are a result of general economic betterment, not deprivation. They are revolutionary in form and content; death and destruction follow in their wake. Transformation of the social and political structure, not merely a change of government, is desired; it is not only the kings of Islam who sleep uneasily.

A traditional analysis of these movements casts them as revolts against legitimate authority—translated from notions of State and nationhood, order and rebellion, the major themes of modern political discussion. A corollary of this hypothesis is the simplistic placing of such endeavours within an anti-western framework. Muslim revolts, from Sudan to Swat, and their leaders have interested the West over the last few centuries and provided the stereotype of the 'mad *mullah*' (Talhami 1981; Voll 1981; Churchill 1972: 29). The implicitly hostile reaction of the West to contemporary movements of Islamic society and their anti-establishment religious leaders may be partly explained as a historically conditioned response to this stereotype.[2] During the colonial phase of modern Islamic history, the movements were explicitly anti-western and anti-colonial, but not today. In fact, the phenomenon is much more complex than it appears. These movements are aimed primarily *within* society and operate through local ethnic patterns. Opposition to established authority, whether Islamic or extra-religious, is a secondary feature.

In the last few years, movements have taken place in very different regions—from Kano in Nigeria to Wana in Pakistan. The attack on the mosque at Mecca—the very core of the Islamic world—illustrates the seriousness and significance of the contemporary Muslim mood. Recent events in Iran provide dramatic evidence of the revolutionary aspects of Islamic movements. Many other such upheavals, smaller and less dramatic, may have gone unreported, and more can be expected to take place. Understanding these movements and their long-term impact on social structure and organization is fundamental for Muslims and those dealing with Muslim societies. Anthropological methods may provide useful tools for this task through the analysis of small, traditional Muslim groups in situations of change and conflict. Certain methodological adjustments may, however, be required for such analysis.

They study of power, authority, and religious status (the central issues of Muslim society) by political scientists, sociologists and historians has rested largely on traditional methods and holistic analysis. These studies tend to concern themselves with the problems of rulers, dynasties, legitimacy, succession, and the control of armies and finances, on the one hand, and with issues of orthodoxy and legality, on the other. Conceptually, the canvas and the configuration are large; the area covered and the time spans are also extensive. It may be heuristically useful to look also beneath the surface of the large configurations of Muslim society and away from their main centres of power when examining social structure and process. Rather than the typical anthropological village, however, the focus of attention should be the critical intermediary level, the district or agency, the study of which remains neglected.[3]

Three broad but distinct spheres of leadership, interacting at various levels, may be identified at the district or agency level of society—traditional leaders (usually elders), official representatives of the established state authority, and religious functionaries. The last group is the least well defined, and hence ambiguity in its locus and elasticity in its role are apparent. Each group is symbolically defined in society by its base of operations—the house(s) of the chief or elders, district headquarters (flying the government flag), and the central mosque. Personnel from these three spheres of leadership vie for power, status, and legitimacy in society. The competition is exacerbated by the fact that all the major participants are Muslims; there are no simple Muslim *vs.* non-Muslim categories to fall back on as in the recent colonial past. Some form of alliance and collaboration between traditional leaders is characteristic of district history. It is the religious leaders who must confront the other two if he is to expand his role in society. This leads to an important question: Who speaks for society?

Having identified some of the core features at the district level, I will proceed to construct what may be termed the Islamic district (or agency) paradigm of the socio-cultural process—one that is conceptually precise, empirically based and placed within the regional political framework.[4] The Islamic district paradigm may assist us in discovering the meaning and structure beneath the diversity of contemporary Muslim society. The paradigm, it is suggested, is a predictive model. It will, therefore, help us both in examining Muslim society and in predicting developments in it. At the core of the Islamic district paradigm I shall place ethnographic analysis; not only is it the most relevant but may allow me, as a social anthropologist, to make some contribution. This article is thus constructed around an extended case study of traditional agnatic rivalry[5] in a tribal Agency in Pakistan, the central actor of which was the Mullah of Waziristan.[6] My own role as Political Agent from 1978 to 1980 allows me to comment on the narrative from within the structure.

The district paradigm, by definition, suggests the perpetuation of one aspect of the colonial encounter. The district structure and personnel, with its official head the District Commissioner (or, in the Agency, the Political Agent), were imposed by the British. Since colonial times, status and authority in the district have rested largely in district officials as representatives of an omnipotent central government. District officers were the *mai-baap* (mother-father) of the South Asian peasantry. The continuing importance of the district and its clear association with the colonial past, heightens tension in society. Although 'native', the administrative personnel reflect ambivalence in their dealings with other groups in society and may be viewed by them as distant and unsympathetic. The contemporary power and importance of district officials is further exaggerated by the suspension of normal political activities (a common phenomenon during periods of martial law). The district paradigm may be of direct use for the study of other tribal agencies in Pakistan and perhaps for other Pakistani districts as well. It may perhaps also be usefully applied, although with reservations regarding the contextual framework, in other countries with large Muslim populations where the British colonial administrative structure survives, such as Bangladesh and even Nigeria.

The case in hand is based in South Waziristan Agency, Pakistan. The Agency population, according to the last official census in 1972, was about 3,00,000, divided into two major Pukhtun tribes, the Mahsuds and the Wazirs. The tribes—segmentary, egalitarian, acephalous, and living in low-production zones—are somewhat similar to other Muslim tribes in North Africa and the Middle East (Ahmed and Hart 1982). There are about 2,50,000 Mahsuds and about 50,000 Wazirs. The Agency also has smaller nomadic groups (Ahmed 1983a). It is about 3,936 sq. miles in area and is the largest and southernmost of the North-West Frontier Province's seven Federally Administered Tribal Areas. A Political Agent heads the administration and represents the government. His powers are vast, and the tribes call him 'king of Waziristan' (*de Waziristan badshah*). South Waziristan shares a border with Afghanistan in the west and Baluchistan, across the Gomal river, in the south. It is distinguished for the most part by desolate valleys and barren mountains.

Recent colonial history is important to Waziristan.[7] Innumerable British soldiers have died here in savage encounters. In the 1930s there were more troops in Waziristan than in the rest of the Indian subcontinent. In 1937 an entire British brigade was wiped out in the Shahur Tangi. The ability of the tribes as fighters is well-recognized:

'the Wazirs and Mahsuds, operating in their own country, can be classed among the finest fighters in the world', wrote the British Indian Army General Staff (1921: 5). To John Masters, who fought in Waziristan, the tribes were 'physically the hardest people on earth (1965: 161). Some famous British Imperial names are associated with Waziristan, such as Curzon, Durand, Kitchener, and T.E. Lawrence (whose note to the South Waziristan Scouts is on display in the Scouts Mess at Wana). Tradition, in name and custom, is preserved. The main western gate of the army camp at Wana, the summer agency headquarters and main settlement, is still called the Durand Gate, and the main picket is Gibralter. Bugles still play at sunset as the Pakistani flag is lowered and the entire camp comes to a halt for those few minutes. Farewells to officers are conducted with traditional ritual in the Scouts Mess, with the band (in kilts and bagpipes) providing music. The romantic aspect of the colonial encounter which created a 'mystification' in British eyes is perhaps most evocative in Waziristan (Ahmed 1978). Their participation in the 'Great Game' between Imperial Russian and Imperial Britain further added to the importance of the Waziristan tribes (Ahmed 1979).

Beginning in the late 1960s, a mullah among the Wazirs mobilized Islam to forge a particular tribal ideology into a political movement against the Mahsuds, accusing the administration of supporting the latter. A migrant from neighbouring Bannu district, he built a beautiful mosque at Wana, unique in the Tribal Areas, and a complex of schools and dormitories around it. With his emergence in the politics of the Agency, the mosque came to symbolize the Mullah and his policies. The Wazir Mullah defined the boundaries within society. His objectives were explicit: transformation of the social structure and organization. His method was ambiguous, alternating between a secular political paradigm and a religious-charismatic one. This ambiguity gave him room to manoeuvre and partly explains his social and political success.

The story, however, begins with the migration of Maulvi Khan to the Agency. An appointment as mullah in their small *kacha* (mud) mosque was offered to Maulvi Khan, father of Noor Muhammad, by the Mughal *khel*, a cousin lineage to the Bizan khel. Wana was a small settlement at the time. 'There are only about 120 houses altogether of these tribes living in Wana, where they will be found chiefly at Mughal khel village just outside the camp' (Johnson 1934a: 8).

The maulvi soon established his reputation in Wana as a man of piety and devotion. He distributed *taweez* (a religious talisman) and acted as a *desi hakeem* (native medicine man). A son, his first, was born to him in 1931 in his Bizan khel village in Bannu district, and was named Noor Muhammad ('light of the Prophet Muhammad'). Shortly after maulvi moved his entire family to Wana.

Maulvi Khan sent his son, Noor Muhammad, to Multan in the Punjab for religious schooling at the Dar-ul-uloom as a *talib* (religious scholar, from Arabic). The school was organized and supervised by Maulana Mufti Mahmood.[8] After completing his education Noor returned to Wana. He inherited his father's position after his death.

The Mullah distributed taweez to cure the ill and provided counsel for the grieving. Men and women brought him their problems. He was soon reputed to possess healing powers. His taweez were symbols of this power. Payments were made to him in gratitude for such favours; dyadic links were cemented with prestations. Economic favours were exchanged for spiritual patronage. The Wazirs had found a spiritual leader they could trust. He was becoming the symbol of reviving Wazir pride and identity. For them he was building an emotionally contagious atmosphere suggesting spiritual powers around his person.

Apart from the religious functions he had assumed, the Mullah imposed a general Wazir peace in the area. Those quarrelling among themselves were fined and punished by the Mullah. His peace patched old cousin enmities, such as the one between Jalat and Bangul. He also began to arbitrate actively between groups in conflict. Clearly he was simultaneously appropriating the roles of the traditional elders in a *jirga* and the political administration in this regard. Various larger developments in Pakistan helped provide a suitable frame for the Mullah's emergence and I shall briefly refer to them later.

The late 1960s and early 1970s were characterized by new sources of wealth—internal (Ahmed 1977) and external, such as remittances from employment in the Arab States (Ahmed 1980a, 1981). For the first time, the tribesman with initiative could make considerable money. Some of the Wazirs' money was diverted to the Mullah: he seemed to be their champion, and he needed funds for his organization. The Mullah's religious organization supported complex economic networks. He invested some of the money in items that would confer prestige among Pukhtuns: Japanese cars, buses, guns, and lavish feasts for visiting politicians. Recent Waziristan history may be viewed as a function of the Mullah's emergence and politics.

Two important economic developments in the Agency coincided with the construction of the new mosque at Wana. First, a market (*adda*) sprang up between the mosque and the main road. In the late 1950s and early 1960s encroachments resulted in a cluster of small mud shops. The Scouts protested, as this violated rules prohibiting civilian construction near their posts and camps. Numerous letters were exchanged and meetings held between the Commandant of the Scouts, the Political Agent, and his superior the Commissioner, but the market continued to grow. Because it was on the property of the Mughal khel Wazirs, it came to be known as Adda Mughal khel. Eventually there were 400 shops, each not more than a small room or two. The market became a thriving centre of commerce for the Agency. The organization of the mosque and the market were interlinked by their guiding genius, the Mullah. The mosque was popularly called Adda Mughal Khel mosque, that is, the mosque of the Mughal khel market. Second, a major dam, the Gomal Zam Project, was started by the government in Wazir territory. The Wazirs provided labour and were given building contracts. Both developments generated local money.

A magnificent mosque costing between Rs. 7,00,000 and 8,00,000 (about U.S. $ 70,000-80,000) was soon completed. The minarets and dome were resplendent with tiles and glass of many hues. The interior reflected depth and space. A stream passed through the mosque, and coloured fish were kept in it. No monument so splendid had been seen in that—or any other—agency before. Elders from other agencies came to admire the mosque and compliment its builder. The Mullah basked in this acclaim and concentrated his energy on expanding an organization around the mosque. He built a *madrassah* (religious school) adjacent to the mosque and dormitories for visiting talibs (scholars), most of who were sons of Wazir elders. A set of rooms was built for the Mullah on the second floor of the mosque, overlooking its courtyard. As a mark of deference, people now referred to him as '*maulvi sahib*' rather than by his name.

In 1971, after the war with India (which resulted in the break-up of East Pakistan), Z.A. Bhutto emerged as the political leader of Pakistan, rallying a dispirited nation. In his political style Bhutto appeared to offer a viable model. The Mullah watched and learned.

Both were relatively young leaders with considerable political skill and organizational ability, who relied on their charisma and oratory to secure and stir their followers. Both spoke in the language of hyperbole and poetic populism. Their demeanour bordered on arrogance, and they brooked no opposition. Their critics accused them of opportunism. The politics of the 1970s in Pakistan were cast in the mould of. Bhutto, and these politics had their impact on Waziristan.

The Mullah, considering that the time was ripe for it, made a bid in the early 1970s for the control of the minds of the Wazirs. He was moving from a religious to a political role. For instance, he forbade the use of radios in the adda as un-Islamic. Having banned the radio, he listened to it avidly. Selecting information from the radio commentary or news, he would 'predict' national events at the Friday congregation in the mosque. His announcement of the National Pay Commission is one such example. The Mullah informed his following that he was praying for an increase in salary for the poorly paid Wazir *khassadars* (tribal levies) and Scouts (who received about Rs. 200 to 250 a month). An increase in the official salaries was being debated in the nation during 1972-3, and an announcement on the matter was imminent. The debate was reported in the mass media. Forbidden from listening to the radio and generally illiterate, the Wazirs were unaware of the national debate. When the government announced an increase in salaries, they took it as an example of the Mullah's powers to predict and influence events. The khassadars were particularly impressed and committed a monthly contribution of Rs 4 each to the mosque fund.

Shortly after, the Mullah imposed various taxes on almost every aspect of commercial activity at the adda, ostensibly to support the mosque. Each shop paid a monthly contribution of Rs. 10. Smaller charges were imposed on other items, for instance, Rs. 2 for a camel-load (usually of wood), Re. 0.25 per crate of apples, and Re. 0.50 per animal. The khassadars, to display their loyalty, further increased their monthly contribution to Rs. 5. Fines brought in.more money. A shop owner violating the radio ban could be fined Rs. 500 by the Mullah's armed supporters, the *chalweshti*, and also beaten up by them. Mir Askar, the Khojal khel elder who remained defiant, was regularly fined and manhandled by the chalweshti. Wazir *maliks* receiving a timber permit were expected to donate half its market price to the mullah. Estimates of the income from these sources vary from Rs. 20,000 to Rs. 30,000 daily. The Mullah kept half the amount and the other half was divided among the chalweshti (who organized its collection) and his followers. No audit of these sums was conducted nor were the figures made public.

The Mullah had been biding his time before challenging the traditional leaders of Wazir society, the maliks and the *pirs* (religious leaders). When he felt reasonably secure he openly scorned them. Traditional and somewhat ineffective leaders (like Malik Pasti, the Mughal khel elder), or established religious figures (such as the pir of Wana), were under considerable pressure from the tribe. They held their peace 'to save their self-respect'. An occasional bomb blast (like the one at Malik Pasti's home)[9] or ambush (such as of the Khojal khel elders) made sure the point of the Mullah's authority was not lost on recalcitrant elders.

Political administration read the Mullah's attack on their traditional allies, the maliks, as a prelude to his challenging established authority. . .

> His first target was the institution of Maliki. He started condemning the Maliks openly and at times he abused them on the pulpit. The idea was to weaken the institutional arrangements so that he could bulldoze his way by shattering all the norms and forms of administration. The Maliks started feeling uneasy but owing to his deepening influence on the tribe they found themselves absolutely helpless. They had no other option but to join his umbrella where they felt they could shelter themselves against the wrath of the *teeman* (populace—common people) who would go into a state of frenzy at the slightest provocation by Maulvi. (Political Agent's Office 1977: 4)

Dismissing traditional leaders as 'Government toadies' who only worked for their own selfish interests, he built up an alternative leadership. Around himself he gathered the *dolas kassi* (twelve men), mainly from Zilli khel, which assumed the status of his cabinet and conducted affairs on his behalf. The cabinet included emergent and eloquent *kashar* like Ba Khan (Zilli khel). The chalweshti was streamlined to ensure immediate implementation of his decisions. Those who opposed his wishes were incarcerated for short periods in a jail organized for this purpose. Many traditional Zilli khel elders, like Jalat, supported him whole-heartedly as they saw in him a viable form and focus of opposition to traditional opponents such as the Mahsud. The Mullah, in bypassing traditional leadership and exposing it as impotent and corrupt, had created a powerful base in the teeman. The teeman, which included women and children, showed their confidence in him through expressions of personal loyalty. Traditional leaders had been outflanked by the Mullah's approach to the Wazir. The Mullah had become the very embodiment of Wazir aspirations.

Three economic issues formed the main platform of the Mullah—first, he emphasized the Wazir nature of the market at Wana; second, he challenged Mahsud rights to the timber funds from Wazir forests that were distributed among the agency's tribes in the form of timber permits; third, he demanded an alternative route for the Wazirs, bypassing the Mahsud area, to the Settled Districts along the Gomal river. Each demand had clear social and political implications. The Mullah would not lead the Wazirs to the promised land but bring the promised land to the Wazirs.

At the same time, the Mullah imitated and developed some of the formalistic aspects of bureaucracy associated with the Political Agent. Armed guards escorted him wherever he went; *mulaqats* (meetings) with him were arranged by formal, often written, requests through his supporters. He issued chits to his followers ordering admission to official schools or medical dispensaries; he wrote asking officials to give interviews 'to the bearer of this note'. His requests were honoured and his whims humoured. These were visible symbols of his growing importance in and to society. By appropriating some of the form and content of the Political Agent's function, he was setting himself on a collision course with that office.

From being a traditional Mullah serving the tribe, he had now emerged as a leader representing, and speaking for, the tribe. The transformation from a sub- to a super-ordinate position in society was as visible as portentous; however, the passage from one category to the other was smooth and not marked by any dramatic event. The Mullah was impressed and somewhat awed by his own growing popularity: 'there was such a multitude of people which reminded people who had performed *haj* of Arafa [where the Holy Prophet preached]' (Noor Muhammad: 21-2). He perceived a sense of destiny pervading his actions. Addressing himself, he noted: 'God Almighty has given you status and influence matched by few men in history' (ibid.). He referred to himself in the third person, traditionally used by Muslim royalty. Indeed, the theme of royalty was not far from his mind: 'When they insisted you address the gathering they introduced you as *the uncrowned king* [*badshah*] of *Wana'* (ibid.). The title was underlined thrice by the Mullah. As we noted, there was another claimant to the title in the Agency and it is a notorious principle of history that no realm can support two kings.

The Mullah's campaign to discomfit the Political Agent and thereby ensure his transfer also continued unabated. A course of action was charted out by the Mullah which was repeated at Wazir jirgas:

> no one should see the Political Agent. However the Ahmedzai Wazir may keep their relations good with the APA Wana. If the Government is not going to transfer the present Political Agent, then the Ahmedzai have no objection to it but no Ahmedzai will see him. Defaulters will be liable to pay penalty of Rs 20,000. Maulvi urged for allowing vehicle traffic on Gomal Road. He added that the Political Agent is trying to make friction among the Ahmedzais but they should remain alert and may not disturb their unity. (Situation Intelligence Report of Wana Tehsil, 20 May 1973)

Acts symbolizing humiliation of the administration now became commonplace in Wana. A dog was placed on a cot which was carried by a large procession. The dog, representing the Political Agent, was then given a sound thrashing. This symbolic representation of relations between the administration and the Wazirs was to be repeated in the next months.

Those who still saw the Political Agent were punished: 'After the speech of Mullah Noor Muhammad, Khudaimir Matak Khel, (member of dolas kassi) announced that Malik Hakim is fined for seeing the Political Agent, South Waziristan, some days back. The amount of fine is not known and will be told to them after three days.' (Situation Intelligence Report of Wana Tehsil, 20 May 1973.)

The Political Agent, faced with the multi-dimensional aspects of the growing Wazir-Mahsud problem in early 1973, decided on firm action by taking two steps. First, he abolished the Timber Committee which dealt with disposal of the Agency timber and permits for timber. The timber permits were now sold from his office. In the context of the hysteria being built up in the Agency, the action did not please or suit either the Mahsuds or the Wazirs. Although the Wazirs continued to buy permits and resell them at an inflated price they resented the dissolution of the Committee. The Mahsuds insisted the permits be sold in the open market and not at fixed prices.

Second, he ordered the arrest of the Mullah's cabinet, the dolas kassi and chalweshti. The adda would be blown up if they refused to surrender. Blowing up the adda would cost the Wazirs a loss of millions of rupees. The shops did a thriving business with their money locked in them. The order was kept secret until it could be implemented the following day. As the Political Agent's relations with the Commandant of the Scouts were strained (a fact advertised and exploited by the Mullah), the action was ordered when the Commandant was away from the Agency. Unfortunately for the Political Agent, the Commandant arrived in Wana late at night and, it was widely rumoured, upon learning of the plans passed on the information to the Mullah (Noor Muhammad: 102). The Mullah immediately called an emergency meeting of his key men. He observed that in the past 'whenever the Scouts came to arrest our people they ran and hid in fields and mountains' (ibid.). Tomorrow, he commanded, 'no one will offer themselves for arrest and if necessary they will fight' (ibid.).

At the crack of dawn heavy guns were placed around the adda which was surrounded by the Scouts. The APA, Wana, leading the official party demanded that the dolas kassi and chalweshti come forth and hand themselves over to him. The Mullah's men were prepared. The chalweshti Commander, designated *jernail* (from general) by the Mullah, returned the message that 'he was not General Niazi [the commander of the Pakistan Army in East Pakistan who surrendered to the Indian in December 1971] and would not surrender alive' (Noor Muhammad: 103). The APA issued written order on the spot for the adda to be blown up. These orders were countermanded by the Commandant. Confusion and a sense of anti-climax prevailed in Wana. A stalemate had developed and by the end of the long, cold day it was apparent that the Mullah had won a major moral and political victory for the Wazirs: 'The 22nd of February, 1973', he observed in his notebook, 'has added a new chapter to the history of the Ahmedzai Wazirs' (ibid.: 102). He exulted that 'Two to three Wazirs faced each Scout's sepoy and all night the sepoys shivered in the rain and cold' (ibid.: 103). The Mullah had publicly defied and humiliated the political authorities and got away with it.

Shortly after, the Political Agent made another attempt to curb the Mullah's influence by arresting some of his Wazir supporters. The Mullah convened an emergency jirga at Wana. He ordered that 'all Wazir maliks and leaders present themselves at Adda Mughal Khel in three days and anybody absent will be severely dealt with' (Noor Muhammad: 106). The administration was warned to release his men before the jirga or face dire consequences (ibid.). On the third day the atmosphere in Wana was highly charged as some 2,000 armed Wazirs gathered to await the Mullah's orders when into this rally drove the Commandant. He had brought the Mullah's men with him. They had been unconditionally released by the Political Agent. 'I expect he will not go awry again and repent his wrong actions' (ibid.) commented the Mullah about the Political Agent.

Matters in the Agency deteriorated and the next two years saw scattered and persistent confrontation between the adversaries. The Political Agent saw the Mullah at the centre of the problems. The Mullah countered by adopting several lines of action. His most effective strategy was the articulation of his sermons in the mosque where he declared *jihad* against the Mahsuds. Having raised Wazir emotions to a high pitch he condemned the Mahsuds as *kafir.* The Mahsuds had dominated and exploited the Wazirs against the spirit of Islam, he argued. They were no better than the Hindus. The time had arrived to rid themselves of the Mahsuds. The imminent jihad would be between good and evil, between Muslim and Hindu. God was on the Wazir side. If, he declared in his fiery sermons, a Wazir killed a Mahsud it would be the equivalent of killing a Hindu kafir. If, on the other hand, a Wazir was killed by a Mahsud, he would become a *shaheed* and win paradise as he had been killed by a kafir. The Wazirs were inflamed by his rhetoric. By deploying religious arguments in a fundamentally tribal conflict the Mullah was bringing about an internal fusion in society between the spiritual and the social.

Simultaneously, the Mullah opened the issue of an alternative route for the Wazirs, hitherto closed, from Wana along the Gomal river to the Settled Districts. The Gomal road bypassed the Mahsud area unlike the main Agency road from Wana to Jandola. The problem of the Gomal route is a Pandora's box. The conception of a separate road is tied with that of a separate Agency. A separate Agency would deprive the Mahsuds of the entire timber funds. It would also reduce the importance and size of the Agency. Above all, for the Mahsuds, it would allow their agnatic rivals to escape from the Agency arena and establish their own identity.

The Mahsuds, unable to dismiss the Mullah as an 'unbeliever', stepped up their attack on his character (debauch, homosexual, practiser of black magic, etc.), which indirectly reflected on Wazir morality. The Mahsud impugned the Mullah's 'Pukhtunness' and accused the Wazir of being without shame of deviating from Pukhtunwali. Mystification of Pukhtunness was a strategy employed by the Mahsuds to counter the accusation of being kafir by the Mullah. An ethnic counter-attack was made for a religious attack. Feelings on both sides ran high. The battle hysteria divided the Wazirs and the Mahsuds sharply and the two camps began to prepare for armed confrontations.

The Mullah opened a new front in late 1975. He ordered the main Agency road to be blocked. In December, a Wazir war party (*lashkar*) gathered at Dargai in the Maddi Jan area for this purpose. Traffic was totally suspended, and the Agency was cut off from the outside world. The Prime Minister of Pakistan ordered that the road be reopened. The Political Agent, accompanied by a strong Scout force, moved from Jandola towards Wana to reopen the road, and simultaneously tanks were moved into the Agency from the Settled Districts. Any movement by the Wazirs, on foot or in vehicles, was banned. A fierce and bloody encounter took place at Maddi Jan in which five soldiers were killed and many more wounded. It was estimated that thirty Wazirs were killed or wounded. Others clashes causing loss of life also took place on the same day. The Wazirs remained defiant, and a few days later they blocked the Agency road again. It appeared that the sequence of events would be repeated. Orders were issued from Islamabad to reopen the road 'at all costs'. The Scouts moved in considerable strength from Jandola, but this time they faced no opposition; the Wazirs had melted into the night, and the road was deserted.

An abortive attempt to involve the Wazirs from outside the Agency was made. The involvement of Wazirs from the North Waziristan Agency or Afghanistan would have extended the theatre of conflict beyond the Agency borders and created serious complications for the government. Already Kabul was watching developments in Waziristan with interest; ideal material was at hand for its claim that Pukhtuns in the North-West Frontier Province wanted to secede.

The Mullah now ordered general civil disobedience. The Wazirs blocked the main roads, shot at the Scouts, and, at the climax of the movement, imposed a physical boycott on the Wana camp. Major clashes between the Wazirs, the Mahsuds, and the administration took place involving the death of many tribesmen and soldiers. The Agency was in flames; on the Durand Line such a situation has international ramifications. After obtaining clearance from the highest authority in the land, the administration acted in May 1976. Armed tanks were moved into the Agency, and the Air Force was alerted. The Scouts destroyed the Wana markets of the Wazirs and arrested the Mullah's 'cabinet' and, eventually, the Mullah himself. He and his key men were tried, found guilty and sent to jail in Hazara, across the Indus. The action, possibly the most serious of its kind in the history of the Tribal Areas, became the centre of controversy. The Wazirs were left in disarray, the Mahsuds jubilant, and the administration self-righteous. Afghan propaganda described the conflict as a simple Pukhtun struggle for autonomy against a Punjabi-dominated central government. Indeed, not since the merger of the Frontier States (Swat, Chitral, Dir and Amb) in 1969 had such a live issue presented itself to Kabul. Kabul's propaganda underlined the ethnic nature of the Mullah's struggle and pointed out that some of the key men in the drama (the Central Interior Minister, the Chief Secretary of the Province, and the Political Agent) were non-Pukhtuns and hence, they argued, unsympathetic to the Pukhtuns.

Why did the Wazirs respond to the Mullah? Was it clan or lineage pride—what may be termed 'primordial ethnicity'—based on the memory of humiliation at the hands of the Mahsuds? Was it promises of economic betterment? (Certainly some of the central issues were economic in nature.) Was it the hope of a separate Agency, with all its political and social implications? Or the Mullah's wealth, with which he could patronize the elders and the poor? Or the Papa Doc Duvalier syndrome—irrational fear of the evil eye and the immediate fear of thugs who could rough up doubters or close their shops? The Wazirs thought they were using the Mullah to say and do things that they could not do themselves. In the end, did the Wazirs use the Mullah, or did he use them? (The answer may be, both.) Considering the intensely democratic and egalitarian nature of ideal Pukhtun society, is the Mullah's emergence and success in peacetime an aberration? What are the social factors that caused it? All these questions are important for the study of leadership, social structure, and organization among Pukhtun tribesmen.

The breakdown of the ideal model implies the creation of tension in society on three levels: (a) social—women visiting the Mullah with various personal requests provided the enemies of the Wazirs grounds to talk about deviant Pukhtun behaviour and the hint of immorality; (b) political—the Mullah led a challenge to the established authority of the State which assumed the form of a rebellion; and (c) religious—

the Mahsuds were condemned as kafirs and a jihad declared against them. Since tension is implicit in the Mullah's work, to accept him posed as many dilemmas for the Wazirs as to reject him. This raises fundamental questions about human behaviour.

The study also raises important issues with wider theoretical ramifications such as the role of Islam in society, the emergence of religious leaders like the Mullah, the nature of the concept of jihad, and the necessity to construct an Islamic district paradigm. Islam is a religion preaching unity and equality among its followers, and the mullahs traditionally uphold Islamic ideology among the tribes. The Wazir Mullah both divided the Muslims and created a highly centralized organization around himself with a well-defined hierarchy.

The neglect of the role of the administrative structure in studies of tribal societies has recently been criticized (Asad 1973). I have illustrated how administrative interaction can affect tribal policy and strategy. Indeed, the administration may be viewed here as the third 'tribe' of the Agency, with its own boundaries, sets of symbols, and ritualized behaviour. Formal interaction with the other two tribes is characterized by ritual. The third has its own esoteric written and spoken language which is not understood by the other tribes—English. The Political Agent may be seen as the 'chief' of the tribe and the South Waziristan Scouts as its 'warriors'.

The 'personalities' of the main actors—the Mullah, the Political Agent and the Colonel—are important governing factors in the drama. Perhaps we need to re-examine the idea of personality in the social sciences. Why do we oppose 'personal' factors to 'structural' and 'categorical' ones? If persona are the loci through which opposed forces flow, then the person is also one of those forces.

To the Wazirs, the Mullah seemed a rational and sympathetic religious leader determined to secure their honour and rights. To his followers the blatant tilting of the administration towards the Mahsuds, the arrest of the Mullah, and the 'capture' of the mosque were tantamount to heresy. They argue that the house of God was desecrated and his faithful servant, the Mullah, arrested. Their continuing boycott of the mosque is explained as an Islamic response to a captured house of worship. Religion is not merely metaphysics. For all people the forms, vehicles, and objects of worship are suffused with an aura of deep moral seriousness. Religion carries with it a sense of intrinsic social obligation; it not only includes intellectual conformity, but demands emotional commitment. The Mullah's jihad had this effect, and the commitment is still explicitly expressed in the society.

The Mullah relied largely on his charisma—his powerful rhetoric, personality, and organizational skills—to win the hearts of his followers. Above all, he gave them group pride and identity. He was palpably neither *qazi*, saint or sufi with a reputation derived from lifelong abstinence, meditation or scholarship (Keddie 1972). None of this mattered to the Wazirs. A Pukhto proverb sums up the relationship of followers to their *pir* (saint): 'Though the pir himself does not fly, his disciples would have him fly' (Ahmed 1973: 19). The Wazirs saw their pir in miraculous flight. They entertained high hopes, partly because of their need for a saviour to deliver them from their enemies. The ground was thus fertile for the emergence of a leader who could organize cultural and religious forces on behalf of his followers. 'Now it is at such time—when a genuine sense of injustice, or danger, etc., reaches a certain points—that a closed complex opens up to the transcendent religions' (Rahman, personal communication).

In certain actions, however (for instance, in encouraging their children and women to pay the Mullah homage), the Wazirs violated a cardinal principle of Pukhtunwali and left themselves open to charges of shamelessness. It became fashionable to ask Wazirs, 'Are you first Muslims (implying the laws of Islam) or Wazirs (implying those of the Mullah)?' Either way, the answer posed dilemmas for the Wazirs. It also put their loyalty to the Mullah to a severe test. To answer 'Muslim' would negate Wazir 'primordial ethnicity' and its manifestations in society, the movement and the Mullah. Such jibes, common among the administration and the Mahsuds, further embittered the Wazirs and reinforced loyalty to their leader.

Islamic religious groups providing leadership in society may be broadly divided into three overlapping categories. The first two are defined by their functions, the third by genealogical links with holy ancestors. The first, the *ulema*,[10] defined by religious and legal learning, includes the *mufti*, *qazi*, *maulana*, and maulvi; the second, defined by esoteric, sometimes unorthodox practice, includes groups such as the sufis; and the third, defined by genealogy and thus claiming superior social status, consists of the *sharifs* or *sayyids* (descended from the Prophet) and the *mians* (descended from holy men). The ulema represent the orthodox, bureaucratic, formal and legalistic traditions in Islam. They interact with the State even at the highest level and advise the kings, captains, and commanders of Islam. In contrast, the mystical orders largely restrict themselves to the rural areas, shunning worldly pursuits and avoiding formal interaction with the administration. They command the hearts as well as the minds of their followers. The holy lineages and their members command a vague and generalized respect, especially if they live up to the behavioural ideal, which is pacific, dignified, and neutral with regard to warring groups. What is of interest here is the difficulty in placing the Mullah in any one category easily.

The difficulty is not simply taxonomic, but related to the ambiguity and elasticity of his social role. Not quite the learned mufti (sure of his orthodox Islamic knowledge) or the sufi (sure of his Islamic faith), the mullah is forced to define and create his own role. He may, indeed, borrow from all three categories, elevating himself to maulvi in one place (as in this case) and mian in others (Ahmed 1980a: 167). In general, the mullah occupies a junior position in the religious hierarchy and is defined as 'a lesser member of the religious classes' (Algar 1969: 264). Except in extraordinary circumstances the mullah restricts himself largely to the village level of social and political life. He appears to thrive in crises. Although the mullah's role is one of the most interesting and important in village and rural society, it is also one of the least studied. The serious writing of the ulema and the imaginative practices of the sufis appear to attract the most scholarship.

The Mullah of Waziristan was a Wazir, that is, a Pukhtun, from Bannu. He was not a sayyid or a mian. The distinction is important in the Pukhtun universe. The claims to superiority of the sayyid and the mian are backed by marriage rules and idealized behaviour patterns. Pukhtuns, notoriously endogamous and reluctant to give their women to non-Pukhtuns, are prepared to waive their prejudice for the sayyids (Ahmed 1980a; Barth 1972). They are settled between Pukhtun clans, a placement which is symbolic of their role as mediators between warring groups. The mullah is more often than not a poor Pukhtun of a junior or depressed lineage. The translation of the role from religious to political spokesman within society was thus inevitable once the Mullah had attracted a following. No lineage structure constrained him; as the son of a migrant member of a junior lineage, he remained outside the local lineage charter yet part of the larger Wazir tribe. From a mullah supervising religious functions he became a leader promising specific political goals.

The religious groups just described provide idealized models of moral behaviour. The story of the Mullah of Waziristan is not to be interpreted as an indictment of this class; it is, rather, the saga of one man and his struggle. His opponents perhaps exaggerated what they saw as his moral turpitude in order to contrast it with the behaviour expected of those belonging to religious groups. The question thus arises of relating the concept and role of mullah to a larger framework. Among Pukhtuns the mullah remains subordinate to the lineage elders and usually does not feature in the genealogical charter (Ahmed 1980a). As I have shown (ibid.), Pukhtun elders saw political activity as their preserve and restricted the role of the mian or mullah to religious functions. The important function of the mullah is to organize and supervise rites of passage based on Islamic tradition. Among Pukhtuns there is little evidence of the oscillation between two forms of society suggested in the 'pendulum-swing theory' (Gellner 1969b). Social leadership is firmly lodged in the lineage charter (Ahmed 1980a). In any case, the mullah in a Muslim society has no proselytising function. He must explore other areas if he is to enhance his role and authority in society.

A mullah may rise to power in extraordinary times, rallying Muslims against invading non-Muslims (Ahmed 1976). In the Tribal Areas, mullahs have led widespread revolts against the British with singular courage and conviction (for example, in 1897). Their bold stand provides a contrast to those quiescent elements in society that preferred to sit on the fence in the struggle against the British (traditional leaders and bureaucrats, in terms of the district paradigm). Men such as Adda Mullah, Manki Mullah, Palam Mullah, Mastan Mullah, and, in Waziristan, Mullah Powindah and the Fakir of Ipi seemed to appear from nowhere to mobilize society and lead the struggle. Some, like Mastan Mullah of Buner in Swat, known as *sartor baba,*[11] claimed, or were believed to possess, magical powers in their fight for Islam. The struggle, to the mullah, was a jihad, to be conducted irrespective of success.

The role of the mullah is negligible when the invading army is Muslim; a jihad cannot be invoked against Muslim brothers in the faith. When the Pukhtun tribes fought the Mughal armies, representing a Muslim dynasty, they were led by traditional tribal leaders. The Mullah of Waziristan provides an interesting example of a mullah who mobilized an entire tribe by creating a religious battle hysteria against kin groups belonging to the same sect and local administrative unit in peacetime. The Waziristan case may be interpreted as a mullah's rejection of his traditional role, a rejection that created problems for society at the same time as it afforded possibilities for the mullah.

This discussion of mullahs raises the related issue of the definition and role of saints and holy men in Islamic society. I have argued elsewhere (Ahmed 1976) that it is misleading to use the 'gloss saint' for mullah as some anthropologists have done (Bailey 1972; Barth 1972). Mullahs aspiring to spiritual status through mumbo-jumbo, such as the Wazir Mullah and Barth's Nalkot Pacha of Swat, usually employ transparent tricks and devices to convince people of their special powers. The sayyid or mian, assured of his position, does not need to do this. The Wazir Mullah installed a wide-angle viewer (sent by a follower from the Arab Gulf states) in his door. He could thus 'foresee' and predict who his visitor was, what he looked like, or what he was wearing. His capacity to see through doors was taken as further evidence of his powers. The Wazirs believed he possessed 'the magic eye' (*de jado starga*). Even educated people believed that the viewer was a magical device. Nalkot, whom I visited in 1976, described to me the devices he employed. His favourite was to stitch a thin piece of wire under the skin of his stomach and then, in front of a selected gathering, to 'eat' another bit of wire; as the audience watched in amazement, he would slowly pull out the first wire. 'Am I to blame', he asked, 'if people are so simple and believe everything?' Not only did people believe in is powers, but some elevated him to the role of 'saint', and in anthropological literature it is this characterization that prevails (for further discussion, see Ahmed 1983b). Similar stories are told about the Mullah Powindah, the earlier and better-known religious leader of Waziristan. This Mullah's grand-nephew Ahmedo Jan, one of the leading elders of the Agency, told of various devices his ancestor had employed to illustrate his powers. A favourite was to predict that the *niswar* (snuff) his followers were addicted to would turn to faeces if they did not give it up. At night his selected companions would place dog faeces in the niswar containers, and on rising in the morning his followers would marvel at the mullah's powers. Such tricks win some following that can be manipulated to consolidate the mullah's leadership.

Anthropology must be hermeneutic; it can only be so if the anthropologist manages to 'get inside' the local culture to some extent. On the basis of subjective criteria, we may understand what the Wazirs respond to the call for a jihad. For the orthodox Muslim, the crime of Akbar the Mughal, the most famous case of imperial heresy in South Asian Islam, lay in his attempt to redefine Islam; for the majority of Muslims in the Agency, the crime of the Mullah lay in his redefinition of the jihad.[12] Scholars of Islam have held different opinions on the exact nature of the jihad, a discussion that dates to the time of the Prophet. However, its importance for the believer is not in doubt. The Quran is explicit about the central role of the jihad.

> Fight in the way of Allah against those who fight against you, but begin not hostilities.
>
> Lo! Allah loveth not aggressors. (*Surah* II, *al-baqarah*, verse 190)

Verse 191 of the same surah actually employs the term kafir with reference to the preceding verse. Jihad is an all-encompassing struggle, a total commitment. Muslims are exhorted:

> Go forth and strive with your wealth and your lives in the way of Allah!
> (*Surah* IX, verse 47)

Sufis quote the Prophet as distinguishing two forms of jihad: the lesser jihad or holy war and the greater jihad, or the struggle against one's own passions. The importance of the moral life is thus emphasized (Hodgson 1974: 228). Modern sufi scholars, too, emphasize 'personal striving' in defining jihad (Algar 1969: 263), as do contemporary Islamic scholars: one must also admit that the means of jihad can vary—in fact, armed jihad is only one form' (Rahman 1980: 63). Jihad, then, is 'systematic endeavour' against *fitna* and *fasad* (oppression and injustice) (Maududi 1948) to 'establish the Islamic socio-moral order' (Rahman 1979: 37). Recent western scholarship discusses jihad mainly as an instrument against the European colonial venture (Dale 1981; Peters 1979).

For our purposes, jihad may be defined as 'a holy struggle in the way of Allah'. There is thus no theological support for a jihad against fellow Muslims. However, the jihad becomes operative when *takfir* (declaring someone an unbeliever or a non-Muslim) is involved. The Quran and the Prophet define a Muslim as a person reciting the *kalima* (the declaration of faith in the uniqueness of God and the prophethood of Muhammad). The Mahsuds fitted neither the unbeliever nor the heretic category. To condemn them as kafirs was, in itself, an act of considerable audacity. The mullah's jihad clearly rested on a weak theological but a strong sociological base.

Was the Wazir movement an outright rebellion, a struggle for political rights, or an attempt at transforming the social structure or defining ethnic boundaries? A common answer suggests itself for these questions—it was all of these things to different men at different times. The ambiguity of the answer and what it meant for the Wazirs reflects the range of interpretations open before us. The ambiguity is compounded by the ambiguity surrounding the Mullah himself.

If a certain ambiguity exists in the perception of the terms under discussion by insiders, a similar set of problems faces outsiders who comment on Muslim society. Herein, perhaps, lies the challenge of studying society. The richness and diversity of the subject are brought out clearly in the work of the two outstanding scholars of tribal Islam (Geertz 1968, 1973; Geertz, Geertz and Rosen 1979; Gellner 1969a, b; Gellner and Micaud 1973). Indeed, the opposed models they build to explain social structure and organization—the former emphasizing culture, the latter segmentary structure—point to the methodological fecundity of the discipline. Alternatively, Muslim anthropologists have suggested the need for an 'anthropology of Islam' (el-Zein 1977). Will this 'anthropology' be another name for 'the sociology of Islam', the social and sociological interpretation of basic religious themes by Muslim social scientists (Shariati 1979)? Is the endeavour to be defined by religious rather than academic schools? Surely, this would subtract from, rather than add to, the understanding of human groups.

A question that arises from the above discussion is: How Islamic are these tribes? In a sociological and cultural sense they may be defined as Islamic. A tribesman equates his Pukhtun lineage with Islam: to him the two are inextricably bound together. Concepts such as jihad are therefore potent and meaningful to him. Although he is aware of certain deviations from Islamic theological tradition, especially regarding women's rights, he is never in doubt about his Muslimness. I have criticized Barth (1972) for omitting the framework of Islam and its symbols from the analysis of Muslim tribal society (Ahmed 1976).[13] This tradition in anthropology derives in the main from the study of non-Islamic African tribes (Fortes and Evans-Pritchard 1970; Gluckman 1971; Middleton and Tait 1970). The question of relating religious to tribal identity has engaged anthropologists studying tribal groups, both Pukhtun (Anderson 1980;

Beattie 1980; Canfield 1980; Ghani 1978, forthcoming; Tavakolian 1980) and others (Geertz 1968; Geertz, Geertz and Rosen 1979; Gellner 1969a, b; Vatin 1980). The exercise in itself serves little purpose, and the debate generated may be misleading. We may more usefully pose the problem as the tribesman himself views it. To the tribesman Islam provides the political and socio-religious formations within which his Pukhtunness operates. The two are in harmony, and he sees them as a logical construct. They are closely interrelated; to suggest a dichotomy is false. Rather, the understanding of religion as being *outside* structure is to be viewed as a European one. The differentiation of religion and political systems into discrete categories is orthodox methodology in western thought.

A recognition of the overlapping of Islam and Pukhtunness partly explains the success of the Mullah. Once Islam was equated with kinship and the Islamic idiom employed, his success in leading and consolidating the Wazirs was ensured. The instruments for maintaining and reinforcing the Wazir ethnic boundary were drawn from an Islamic frame; the mosque was the base of the Mullah's operation and the key symbol of Wazir identity.

The dichotomy separating Islam and Pukhtunness is palpably sterile. Whether embarking on a religious war or stealing cattle, the Pukhtun invokes his God.[14] His objectives may be at fault, but not his sincerity and correctness in invoking assistance from heaven. Rephrasing from 'Islam versus Pukhtunness' to 'Islam and Pukhtunness', bringing Pukhtun custom and tradition in accordance with Islamic tradition, may be a more useful way of approaching the problem. The discussion could be still more fruitful if it analysed the use of Islam by religious leaders (such as the Mullah) to consolidate their position, especially in changing times. Thus the discussion shifts from the ideological base of the tribesman to questions of strategy and the choices open to him.

Anthropological studies of Muslim society may be broadly divided into village and tribal studies. The village, in the main, whether Turkish, Egyptian, or Pakistani, shares many of the characteristics of villages in other parts of the world; it is a peasant and rustic, largely self-sufficient universe somewhat isolated from larger developments and defined by village boundaries. It is in the study of Islamic tribal societies (a small percentage of the population in comparison with peasant groups) that anthropology has made important and original contributions. Here, too, however, there is a methodological bias in conceptualizing the universe in blocs sometimes so large as to cross national borders. While I am in partial agreement with the idea of conceptualizing the Sanusi, the Tijaniya, the Berbers and the Bedouin as wholes for purposes of analysis, I object to the application of this approach *in toto* when interpreting empirically observed reality, which may not conform to holistic theory. Although a Wazir conceptualizes himself as part of a large tribal configuration, a universe which includes his lineage kin in North Waziristan Agency and across the border in Afghanistan, his empirical restriction to the Agency is underlined in times of need. In spite of appeals for assistance, no kin arrived to participate in the struggle against the Mahsuds. The boundaries of the Wazir ethnic universe *in fact* tended to coincide with the administrative boundaries of the Agency.

On the surface and for purposes of general analysis, I have assumed a two-bloc Pukhtun political system corresponding to the Wazir and Mahsud tribes. Segmentary and political boundaries have been conceptualized as coinciding and thus upholding the segmentary principle of organization. In fact, there are smaller blocs within the major ones that may cross tribal boundaries to seek alliances. For instance, the second bloc among the Mahsuds, opposing the major one, supported the Wazirs in larger issues. Among the Wazirs the smaller clans opposed the major Zilli khel clan and were usually sympathetic to the administration.

When conceptualizing the tribe as a political unit in holistic arguments it will be well to keep in mind that the present administrative boundaries do not always correspond with tribal boundaries. Districts and agencies—indeed, along with the international Durand Line—were created at the turn of the century by the British, often without regard for tribal boundaries. Major tribes (such as the Mohmands or the Wazirs) were divided by the international border; others were untidily distributed between district and Agency (the Afridis, for example, are in Kohat district and Khyber Agency). The Ahmedzai Wazirs were separated from their Utmanzai Wazir cousins (who were confined to North Waziristan Agency), and placed with their traditional rivals, the Mahsuds, in South Waziristan Agency. Like other tribes in the region, the Ahmedzai Wazirs have confronted the fact of British-created borders for three generations. On either side of the Durand Line, differing political, educational and economic factors have widened the gap between Wazir and Wazir. New political realities have forced the creation of new social boundaries that take precedence over traditional alignments. We may thus conceptualize the Wazir tribe as a unit but must keep in mind administrative realities on the ground. An understanding of the Islamic district paradigm is important in illuminating some of the problems thus created.

The graphic depiction of the argument (Figures 1 and 2 and Map 1) allows it to be clearly visualized. Figure 1 depicts, in encapsulated form, the Wazir-Mahsud genealogy. Ideally, the segmentary theory suggests that the Ahmedzais would be assisted by their Wazir kin when in conflict with the Mahsuds. The Mahsud clans, in turn, would unite against the Ahmedzais (the unity of the Dre Mahsud, the three Mahsud clans, remained unshaken by internal politics and was a formidable factor in defeating the Wazirs).

Map 1 reminds us that while the Wazirs live in Afghanistan and North Waziristan Agency, the Mahsuds are confined to South Waziristan Agency. Not only are the Utmanzai Wazirs separated by administrative boundaries from their Ahmedzai cousins, but the Ahmedzai themselves are divided by the international boundary.

If Map 1 is superimposed on Figure 1, the importance of administrative boundaries in affecting tribal life will be made clear (see Figure 2).

The Wazirs find themselves restricted by the Agency borders. The inability of their kin to come to the assistance of the Ahmedzais of South Waziristan Agency in times of crisis was clearly brought out in the extended case-study discussed earlier. (The boundaries work both ways: Wazirs who wish to escape the Agency administration may cross the international border to their kin.) We may conclude that for historical and administrative reasons it would be more meaningful to analyse tribal groups within their contemporary political situations, or with specific reference to the Islamic district paradigm.

The notion of segmentation in tribal structure is one of the major contributions of anthropology to Islamic tribal studies. Can the data

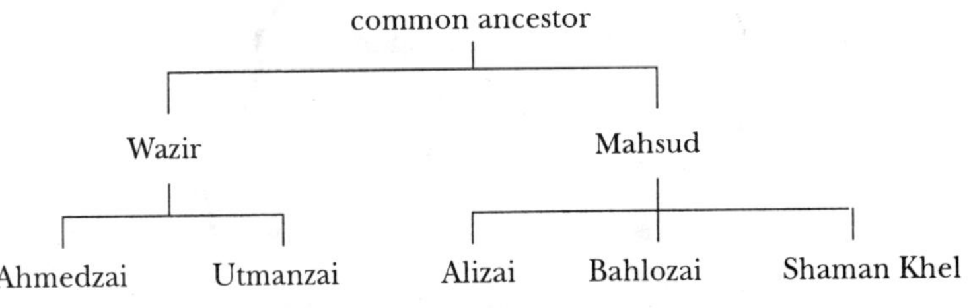

FIGURE 1. WAZIR-MAHSUD LINEAGE

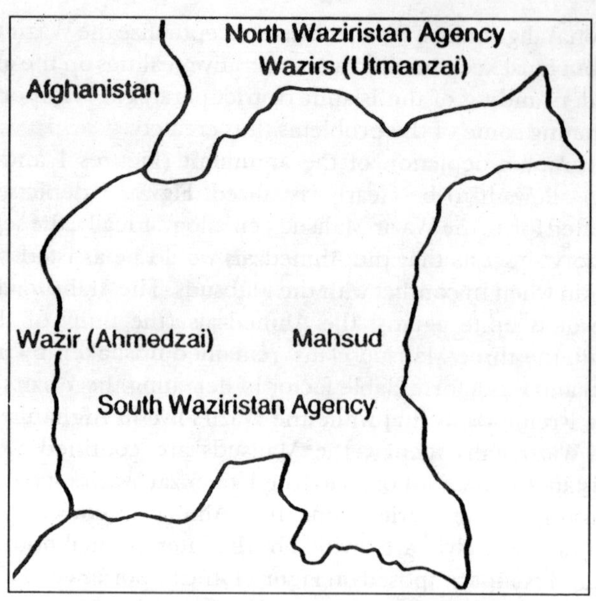

MAP 1: SOUTH WAZIRISTAN AGENCY (PAKISTAN)

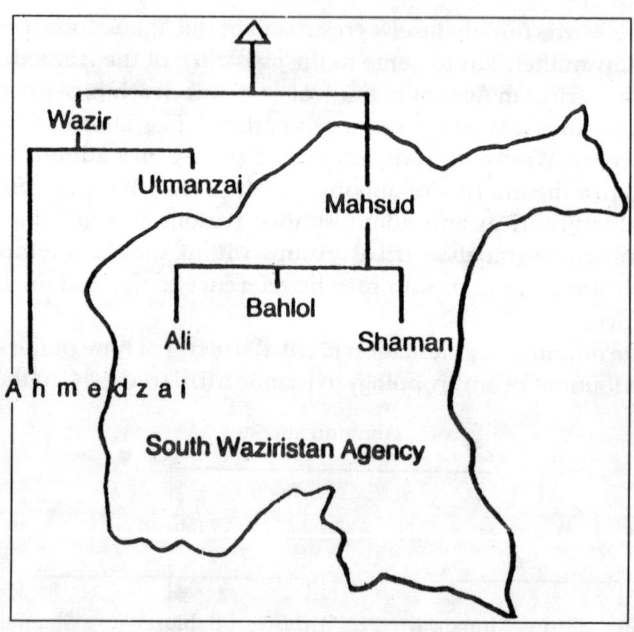

FIGURE 2: WAZIR-MAHSUD LINEAGE AND THE AGENCY

of the Waziristan case study be interpreted as traditional segmentary politics in the classic mould? The first important elaboration of the segmentation theory was Evans-Pritchard's Nuer study. The theory became, and remains, popular in examining Islamic tribal groups. Studies of the Berbers of the Atlas by Ernest Gellner and the Somali nomads by I.M. Lewis are highly regarded examples, and Evans-Pritchard himself applied the theory to the Cyrenaican Bedouin. In a sense, the segmentation theory has thus returned to its natural place of origin, in the segmentary genealogical charters of Islamic tribal groups, whence it originated a century earlier in the writings of Victorian scholar-travellers such as W. Robertson Smith. Recently there has been considerable and mounting criticism of the segmentation theory, particularly in America. The criticism is led by Clifford and Hildred Geertz and younger American anthropologists such as Dale Eickelman and Larry Rosen (is the lineup itself suggestive of tribal divisions between British and American 'cousins'?). The following, in capsule form, are some of the major criticisms: segments are neither balanced nor equal; on the contrary, there is disparity in political resources, and this is exacerbated with the emergence of lineages claiming seniority. Further, in times of political crisis, groups do not combine according to segmentary patterns. In spite of these criticisms satisfactory alternative explanations have not been put forward.

This study has illustrated the usefulness of the segmentation theory if the criticism is kept in mind. The degree of segmentation and segmentary consciousness are high in Waziristan society and *are so locally perceived.* Political action is articulated on the basis of the relationships defined in and by the genealogical charter. The agnatic rivalry between the Wazirs and the Mahsuds may be interpreted as a fundamental articulation of segmentary opposition. Mahsud inheritance of poorer lands, which presupposes junior lineages in the tribal charter, reinforced solidarity and sharpened strategy. Indeed, it may be stated that the genesis of the Waziristan problem is lodged in the genealogical charter; to understand the charter is to unravel the mysteries surrounding the problem. We may conclude that the segmentation theory retains its usefulness for examining Islamic tribal groups with the caveat that it must be conceptualized as a blueprint for social identity and not for political action.

I have touched upon the dangers of applying the segmentation theory too literally. Surely examples, such as the inability of Wazirs outside the Agency to assist Agency Wazirs against the Mahsuds, expose its weaknesses. Other variables (that may be termed 'cultural') are important in understanding Wazir social life. Culture is broadly defined here as customs consisting of the three interacting variables of word, deed, and concept. The response of the Wazirs to the Mullah was partly psychological and partly religious (what Parkin [1978] has termed 'the dynamics of cultural autonomy'). The local response among the Wazirs crystallized into what I have called primordial ethnicity. This was partly the creation of the Mullah. He was simultaneously cause and effect of the phenomenon. Traditional segmentary alignments were reordered by the Mullah's politics. The classic articulation and expression of segmentary lineage politics was thus altered. The usefulness of the segmentation theory is clearly reduced in situations of social and economic change. In such situations the Islamic district paradigm illuminates both the factors and the processes of change.

Can universal principles of behaviour, suggesting predictive models, be adduced from this case study? Is the Mullah's story of revolt against an established administrative apparatus a harbinger of things to come in the Islamic world? Can we relate the Mullah's movement to the current wave of fundamentalist revivalism surging in many Muslim countries? Is he to be seen as a modern revolutionary leader or a traditional product of Muslim structure and organization? Is he the model leader of the future? Are we witnessing a shift in style and loci of leadership away from urban, westernized elite? It is too early to provide clear answers, although tentative answers in the affirmative are suggested. There is almost no literature on such leaders and movements in the contemporary Muslim world. The Wana example shows what may be in store for Islamic governments and societies in the coming decades.

The example of the Mullah of Waziristan suggests the strength and universality of what I have referred to as the Islamic district paradigm of social and political life. Contradiction is implicit in the paradigm and suggests tension in the society; the Wana case testifies to the relevance of the paradigm and the need for fuller investigation.

NOTES

1. The themes of this article are explored at greater length in my book (Ahmed 1983b).
2. The apprehensions which have revived as a result of recent developments

are expressed by one of the leading Western authorities on Islam (Rodinson 1980: xi-xii):

The Iranian revolution and the (already disquieting) Muslim fundamentalist movements whose hopes it nurtured, changed all that, helped by the rising price of that petroleum with which Allah endowed his followers in such ample quantities. Once again the Muslim world became an entity jealously guarding its uniqueness, its own culture, comprising much more than just spirituality. And might not this entity again become a threat, as it had only three centuries ago when the Ottoman armies laid siege to Vienna? Might the way of life so valued by the West be in serious danger?

3. The district was the basic and key unit of administration in British India (Woodruff 1965). It was further divided into subdivisions and *thanas*. The district, in turn, was part of a division, which formed part of a province. In the Tribal Areas, the Agency corresponded to the district in the administrative Universe. Although I call this intermediary level 'district' to help conceptualize the unit of analysis, district (or Agency) boundaries do not always correspond with ethnic ones, a fact which continues to create political problems. In some cases new ethnicity has developed as a result of a new district—for example, Hazarawal in Hazara district (Ahmed 1984). Pakistan, like India, retains the administrative structure it inherited after independence in 1947. Most districts and agencies remain largely rural in character and somewhat isolated from national developments. There is a vast body of literature on district life, most of it written by British district officers themselves; for a recent contribution, see Hunt and Harrison (1980). Academic neglect of the topic may be partly due to methodological considerations, as the district does not correspond either to the larger subject-matter—State, nation, or region—traditionally studied by political scientists, sociologists, and historians, or to village society studied by anthropologists.
4. I shall refer to the paradigm as 'district' rather than 'agency' because the former is older and better known.
5. I shall use the term 'agnatic rivalry' for conflict between males descended in the patrilineage from a common ancestor.
6. 'Mullah' is a generic name for a religious functionary. *The Oxford English Dictionary* defines it as a 'Mohammedan learned in theology and sacred law'. I refer to the Waziristan *mullah* with a capital 'M' to distinguish him in the text. (In its usage of 'Mohammedan' here the *Oxford English Dictionary* continues to offend Muslims. 'Mohammedan' implies 'a flower of Mohammed', and Muslims hold that a Muslim is, as the word implies, a 'believer' in Allah and his follower only. 'Mohammedan' has been dropped from circulation even by Orientalists, who once used it [see, e.g., Gibb 1949].) 'Waziristan', when used generally, refers to the area of North and South Waziristan Agencies. The name derives from the Wazir tribe. Wazir in Arabic and Urdu means 'minister'.

7. See Bruce 1929; Curtis 1946; General Staff 1921, 1932, 1936; Howell 1925; Johnson 1934a, 1934b and Johnston 1903.
8. Maulana Mufti, based in Dera Ismail Khan, was to become an eminent leader in Pakistan politics. His simple habits, austere living standards and reputation for incorruptibility made him a respected and popular figure. He headed the Jamiat-i-Ulama-i-Islam (JUL), a party of religious scholars of Islam, as President and generally opposed the politics of the established governments, led by General Ayub Khan in the 1960s and Bhutto in the 1970s. Against the latter's Pakistan People's Party (PPP), he allied with the Pukhtun nationalists, the National Awami Party (NAP), and was Chief Minister, NWFP, from 1972-3. Until his death in 1980 he proved a strong and loyal patron to Mullah Noor Muhammad.
9. The Mullah's antipathy towards Haji Pasti can perhaps be explained by the memory of his father's employment as mullah with Pasti's father.
10. Singular *alim*, from *ilm*, meaning 'knowledge of the Quran, hadith, etc.'
11. *Sartor* is literally 'black head'; the name implies one whose head is uncovered as a result of poverty, grief, or some personal obsession (here an obsession with the cause of Islam). Baba is a term of respect for an elder.
12. Jihad has been used in the contemporary world in dramatically non-traditional ways. For instance, in April 1981 an Indonesian Muslim group called the Komando Jihad ('Holy War Command') hijacked a DC-9 belonging to Garuda Indonesian Airways. Indonesian commandos foiled their attempt at the Bangkok airport, killing all five hijackers. Although the idiom of jihad was employed, the case remains obscure. Jihad is also used for other daily, even secular, activity; there is at least one daily newspaper called Jihad in Pakistan.
13. Barth, perhaps acknowledging the criticism, has recently re-examined his earlier work in 'Swat Pathans Reconsidered' (Barth 1981). The study of Swat is not, however, over; see Meeker (1980).
14. An anecdote illustrating this point is recounted by Mahsud (1970: 92):

    Mr. Mattak Khan is an ideal man I can quote. In his youth he had been a famous dacoit having a gang of daring and skilful fighters and artful thieves. He has a notorious record in this regard. But he has all along been very religious minded. He prays regularly, observes fasts, pays *zakat* [compulsory alms]—even from his stolen things. He serves religious leaders with great zeal and honesty.

    One of his stories goes thus: He and his gang came out on an expedition of stealing cattle from a village in Jandola. He was telling me that they prayed their later afternoon [third] prayer at such and such place and started for the destination: prayed their evening prayer at such and such place and again moved ahead. At mid-night after the night prayer they reached the spot.

Like in the rest prayers of this day, they humbly prayed to Allah, besought great pirs and vowed to shrines to bless them with success. They held positions and started breaking through into the cattle band. After having successfully stolen the cattle, they made for their homes. Soon a group of armed villagers followed them. It was the morning prayer time; they prayed to Allah to save them and help them carry the cattle safely. They vowed that out of these cattle so many will be sacrificed and given in charity in the name of Allah and they called upon pirs; through their tactics they were successful in bringing the cattle to their homes. Honest to their promises, they slaughtered some sheep and goats at shrines, gave some of them to Maulvis in charity—Maulvis have established that they are the most rightful receivers of charity. They Maulvis well in the know about these cattle, accepted these under the pretence that these were *halal* [pure] for them as they did not steal these and were given to them in the name of Allah and holy persons.

REFERENCES

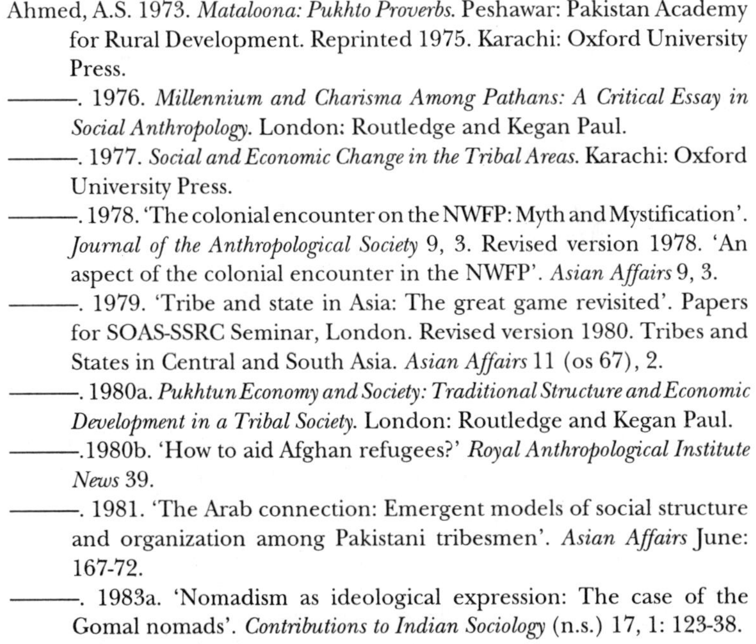

Ahmed, A.S. 1973. *Mataloona: Pukhto Proverbs.* Peshawar: Pakistan Academy for Rural Development. Reprinted 1975. Karachi: Oxford University Press.

———. 1976. *Millennium and Charisma Among Pathans: A Critical Essay in Social Anthropology.* London: Routledge and Kegan Paul.

———. 1977. *Social and Economic Change in the Tribal Areas.* Karachi: Oxford University Press.

———. 1978. 'The colonial encounter on the NWFP: Myth and Mystification'. *Journal of the Anthropological Society* 9, 3. Revised version 1978. 'An aspect of the colonial encounter in the NWFP'. *Asian Affairs* 9, 3.

———. 1979. 'Tribe and state in Asia: The great game revisited'. Papers for SOAS-SSRC Seminar, London. Revised version 1980. Tribes and States in Central and South Asia. *Asian Affairs* 11 (os 67), 2.

———. 1980a. *Pukhtun Economy and Society: Traditional Structure and Economic Development in a Tribal Society.* London: Routledge and Kegan Paul.

———.1980b. 'How to aid Afghan refugees?' *Royal Anthropological Institute News* 39.

———. 1981. 'The Arab connection: Emergent models of social structure and organization among Pakistani tribesmen'. *Asian Affairs* June: 167-72.

———. 1983a. 'Nomadism as ideological expression: The case of the Gomal nomads'. *Contributions to Indian Sociology* (n.s.) 17, 1: 123-38.

———. 1983b. *Religion and Politics in Muslim Society: Order and Conflict in Pakistan.* Cambridge: Cambridge University Press.

———. 1984. 'Hazarawal: Formation and structure of district ethnicity in Pakistan', plenary paper presented to the American Ethnological

Society. In David Maybury-Lewis, ed., *The Prospects for Plural Society*, pp. 104-20. American Ethnological Society.

———. The reconsideration of Swat Pathans: Methodological problems in studying the other (forthcoming).

Ahmed, A.S. and D.M. Hart, eds. 1982. *From the Atlas to the Indus: The Tribes of Islam.* London: Routledge and Kegan Paul.

Algar, H. 1969. *Religion and State in Iran*, 1785-1906. Berkeley: University of California Press.

Anderson, J.W. 1980. 'How Afghans define themselves in relation to Islam?' Paper presented to the A.A.A., Washington, D.C., December.

Asad, T., ed. 1973. *Anthropology and the Colonial Encounter.* London: Ithaca Press.

Bailey, F.G. 1972. 'Conceptual system in the study of politics'. In R. Antoun and I. Harik, eds., *Rural Politics and Social Change in the Middle East*, pp. 21-74, Bloomington: Indiana University Press.

Barth, F. 1972. *Political Leadership among the Swat Pathans.* London: Athlone Press.

———. 1981. *Selected Essays of Fredrik Barth: Features of Person and Society in Swat: Collected Essays on Pathans*, vol. 2. London: Routledge and Kegan Paul.

Beattie, H. 1980. 'Effects of the Saor Revolution in the Nahrin area of Northern Afghanistan'. Paper presented to the A.A.A., Washington, D.C., December.

Bruce, C.E. 1929. *The Tribes of Waziristan: Notes on Mahsuds, Wazirs, Daurs, etc.* His Majesty's Stationery Office for the India Office. Confidential.

Canfield, R.L. 1980. 'Religious networks and traditional culture in Afghanistan'. Paper presented to the A.A.A., Washington, D.C., December.

Churchill, W.S. 1972. *Frontiers and Wars.* Harmondsworth: Penguin Books.

Curtis, G.S.C. 1946. *Monograph on Mahsud Tribe.* Government of NWFP. Confidential.

Dale, S.F. 1981. *Islamic Society on the South Asian Frontier.* London: Oxford University Press.

el-Zein, A.H. 1977. 'Beyond ideology and theory: The search for the anthropology of Islam'. *Annual Reviews of Anthropology* 6: 227-54.

Fortes, M. and E.E. Evans-Pritchard, eds. 1970. *African Political Systems.* London: Oxford University Press.

Geertz, C. 1968, *Islam Observed.* New Haven: Yale University Press.

———. 1973. *The Interpretation of Culture.* New York: Basic Books.

Geertz, C., H. Geertz and L. Rosen. 1979. *Meaning and Order in Moroccan Society: Three Essays in Cultural Analysis.* Cambridge: Cambridge University Press.

Gellner, E. 1969a. *Saints of the Atlas.* London: Weidenfeld and Nicolson.

———. 1969b. 'A pendulum swing theory of Islam'. In R. Robertson, ed., *Sociology of Religion*, pp. 127-38. Harmondsworth: Penguin Books.

Gellner, E. and C. Micaud, eds. 1973. *Arabs and Berbers: From Tribe to Nation in North Africa*. London: Gerald Duckworth.

General Staff. 1921. *Operations in Waziristan, 1919-1920*. Compiled by the General Staff, Army Headquarters, India. Calcutta: Superintendent Government Printing Press. Confidential.

———. 1932. *Summary of Events in North-West Frontier Tribal Territory, 1st January 1931 to 31st December 1931*. Simla: Government of India Press, Confidential.

———. 1936. *Military Report on Waziristan, 1935*. Calcutta: Government of India Press. Confidential.

Ghani, A. 1978. 'Islam and state-building in a tribal society: Afghanistan 1880-1901'. *Modern Asia Studies* 12, 2: 269-84.

———. Sharia in the process of State building: Afghanistan 1880-1901 and dispute in a court of Sharia (forthcoming).

Gibb, H.A.R. 1949. *Mohammedanism: An Historical Survey*. London: Oxford University Press.

Gluckman, M. 1971. *Political, Law and Ritual in Tribal Society*. Oxford: Basil Blackwell.

Hodgson, M.G.S. 1974. *The Venture of Islam*, vols. 1, 2 and 3. Chicago: University of Chicago Press.

Howell, E.B. 1925. *Waziristan Border Administration Report for 1924-25*. Government of India. Confidential

Hunt, R. and J. Harrison. 1980. *The District Officer in India, 1930-1947*. London: Scholar Press.

Johnson, H.H. 1934a. *Notes on Wana*. Government of India. Confidential.

———. 1934b. *Mahsud Notes*. Government of India. Confidential.

Johnston, F.W. 1903. *Notes on Wana*. Government of India. Confidential.

Keddie, N.R., ed. 1972. *Scholars, Saints and Sufis: Muslim Religious Institutions Since 1500*. Los Angeles: Near Eastern Centre, University of California.

Mahsud, Minhaj-ud-Din. 1970. 'Impact of education on social change in South Waziristan Agency'. M.A. thesis. Punjab University.

Masters, J. 1965. *Bugles and a Tiger*. London: Four Square.

Maududi, Abdul-ala. 1948. *Al-jihad fil-Islam*. Lahore.

Meeker, M.E. 1980. 'The twilight of a South Asian heroic age: A rereading of Barth's study of Swat'. *Man* 15, 4: 682-701.

Middleton, J. and D. Tait, eds. 1970. *Tribes Without Rulers*. London: Routledge and Kegan Paul.

Noor Muhammad, Mullah. n.d. Personal diaries, in Urdu (unpublished).

Parkin, D.J. 1978. *The Cultural Definition of Political Response: Lineal Destiny Among the Luo*. London: Academic Press.

Peters, R. 1979. *Islam and Colonialism: The Doctrine of Jihad in Modern History.* The Hague: Mouton.

Political Agents Office. 1966-80. 'Official correspondence. Tank/Wana: PA's Office' (unpublished). Confidential.

Quran, the Holy. Trs. M. Pickthall. Karachi: Taj Co.

Rahman, F. 1979. *Islam.* Chicago: University of Chicago Press.

———. 1980. *Muhammad.* Trs. A. Carter. New York: Pantheon Books.

Said, E.W. 1978. *Orientalism.* London: Routledge and Kegan Paul.

Shariati, A. 1979. *On the Sociology of Islam.* Trs. H. Algar. Berkeley: Mizan Press.

Talhami, G. 1981. 'The Muslim-African experience'. Paper presented to the Islamic Alternative Conference. Arab Institute, June.

Tavakolian, B. 1980. 'Sheikhanzai nomads and the Afghan State'. Paper presented to the A.A.A., Washington, D.C., December.

Vatin, J.C. 1980. Introduction to *Islam, religion et politique. Revue de I'occident Musulman et la Mediterranee* 1.

Voll, J. 1981. 'Wahhabism and Mahdism'. Paper presented to the Islamic Alternative Conference. Arab Institute, June.

Woodruff, P. 1965. *The Men who Ruled India. The Founders,* vol. 1; *The Guardians,* vol. 2. London: Jonathan Cape.

The Ranking of Brotherhoods: The Dialectics of Muslim Caste among Overseas Pakistanis

PNINA WERBNER

(1989)

CASTE AND ISLAM

It is widely regarded as self-evident that overseas South Asian communities cannot develop a caste 'system' (Pocock 1957). While continuing to uphold endogamous practices, such communities lack both hereditary specialization and interdependence, and a hierarchical organization based on a ritual model of perfection (ibid.: 290). It is assumed, further, that although caste as ranked hierarchy may articulate or underpin urban as well as rural relationships, caste as system is restricted to pre-industrial cities. The present paper re-examines the validity of these hypotheses in the light of research among overseas Pakistanis in Britain. It asks in what senses can caste be said to persist as a 'system' among communities of overseas Pakistanis in British industrial cities. To answer this question the paper examines first the nature of Punjabi Muslim castes in general and the underlying dialectic informing Muslim caste as a conceptual system. What are the cultural and moral premises informing Muslim caste categories? The paper then examines how such premises explain patterns of mobility and shifts in dominance or hegemony within a particular local community of overseas migrants living in Manchester.

The ongoing debate on the nature of Islam in India is locked in controversies raised by two seminal essays by Barth (1959, 1960) and Dumont's response to them. In his essay Dumont (1972: 247-63) spells out the central dilemmas raised by the apparent persistence of caste among Muslims (and other minorities) in India. Despite the evident conflict between the egalitarian values of Islam and the fundamental inequalities between men implied by caste, Muslims in India continue to foster a caste-like system of ranked, named and endogamous social entities, a system which bears striking similarity to the Hindu caste system. This apparent persistence of caste among Muslims raises, he argues, problems both in relation to his definition of Hindu caste, and in the context of more general theoretical issues regarding modes of cultural-historical analysis. Islam in India, like Christianity, appears impotent in the face of the vitality of caste attitudes.

Dumont criticizes Barth's attempt to disassociate social organization from its cultural-historical determination. Barth, it will be recalled, while recognizing the Hindu origins of contemporary Swat social organization, bases his analysis of caste on its social structural features as a 'summation', a congruent cluster of statuses (occupational, kinship, political, etc.). This tendency towards congruence makes caste systems different, he argues, from other class and ranking systems which 'give simultaneous recognition to a multiplicity of conflicting hierarchical criteria' (1960: 113). However, to explain the stress on purity and pollution at the extremes of the Swat caste system Barth resorts to secondary explanations. The purity and ascendancy of the saintly Sayyids is determined by descent, whereas the lower castes' status is determined by their polluting occupations (for a more forceful exposition of this viewpoint, see Srinivas 1984).

For Dumont the most distinctive feature of the Hindu caste system is the disjunction (rather than congruence) between status and power, expressed in the priority of the sacred and the opposition between the pure and the impure. This sanctioning of hierarchy by religious belief is, he argues, even in the face of Barth's evidence, apparently absent among Muslims.[1] Dumont's conclusion implies a continuously unresolved dialectic between the opposed principles of hierarchy and inequality in the Muslim caste system. In Dumont's view, the association of Muslims and Hindus has created 'a Muslim society of a quite special type, a hybrid type which we are scarcely in a position to characterize, except by saying that, lying beneath the ultimate of Islamic values are other values presupposed by actual behaviour' (1972: 258).

An important theoretical advance in our understanding of Muslim caste systems may be found in Dumont's more recent work in which he revises his earlier assumption that universal religions cannot accommodate this disjunction between power and purity within a holistic order. In early Christianity, he argues, the disjunction between the sacred and secular orders persists as an expression of the tension between the inworldly social order with its inequalities of power and ranking and the outworldly relationship between man and God, based on a presumption of universal equality. Outworldly individualism encompasses inworldly inequalities of power (1983: 7). In such societies the ritually pure mediate between the inworldly and outworldly and are thus placed at the extreme top of the hierarchy. The outworldly Church encompasses the inworldly State within a holistic order. These moral philosophical premises informing early Christianity are applicable with a few modifications to popular Islam in South Asia where pure descendants of the Prophet mediate between God and individuals otherwise locked into a holistic inworldly order.

The ensuing tension or dialectic between conflicting premises of equality and inequality must be recognized if we are to bring together the sociological and cultural-historical within a single theoretical framework. Such a dialectical approach can help explain the persistence of caste as a system among overseas labour migrants in Britain. More broadly, it explains why worldwide ongoing processes of Islamicization (I. Ahmad 1976a; Robinson 1983) do not obviate Muslim caste systems but come to be constitutive of them. As part of this process of Islamicization, competing Islamic movements associated with different interpretations of the 'perfect' Islamic order (Das 1984) may be incorporated into localized Muslim caste hierarchies (although they do sometimes cut across them). Hence, a contextual analysis is undoubtedly essential (I. Ahmad 1976a; 1978b, 1981; Minault 1984); cultural-historical processes necessarily unfold differentially within localized contexts.

A second limiting feature of Barth's analysis is its restricted application to rural communities or pre-industrial cities. It is recognised that caste-like structures are consonant with a mercantile society, or societies based on hereditary trades requiring 'a minimum of organizational complexity' (Coon 1953: 153, 171, cited by Lindholm).[2] In Barth's view caste hierarchies are generated where 'individuals have intimate face-to-face relations with each other in many different spheres of activity. Differentiation in such societies can only be maintained if individuals in their different capacities are ranked consistently' (1960: 142).

In this sense caste as ranked hierarchy may articulate or underpin urban relationships only where these conditions hold. But what place can notions of caste possibly have in post-capitalist industrial cities? How is it that for Pakistanis in Manchester, caste, rather than disappearing permanently, has been resurrected and renegotiated as an ongoing system of categorical relations validating status and defining marriage options?

Such a process is quite inexplicable without a cultural-historical perspective. It remains essential to recognize the power of culture, regarded as a coherent set of ideas, images and norms, to determine action and generate structure. Given such a perspective, Barth's basic hypothesis remains brilliantly predictive: in communities of labour migrants status discrepancies are renegotiated in order to recreate the appearance of status congruence. The principle of congruence between ritual, kinship, economic and political domains, once re-established, is articulated in the idiom of caste.

The dialectic between the explicit egalitarian ethos of Islam and the unstated, implicit values of caste and hierarchy is arguably an inversion of a parallel dialectic within the Hindu caste system itself. Thus Parry (1979), in his study of Rajputs in north India's Kangra district, finds a 'structural contradiction' between values of hierarchy, on the one hand, and equality, on the other, revealed in periodic attempts to suppress hypergamous marriage in favour of marriage between equals. For Muslims the dialectic would seem to be given an alternative ideological expression, as the explicit ideology is continuously undermined by the implicit and yet quite pervasive counter-ideology of caste and inequality.

Caste for Pakistanis in Manchester is no longer underpinned by land-ownership or clear occupational specialization. During the early phases of migration Nai, Musali and Rajput worked side by side in the same factories. Nevertheless, I shall argue, emergent relations of power and economic dominance are articulated in the idiom of caste and ratified through marriage alliances. As the migrant community sinks roots locally, and establishes a local politico-economic order, a localized caste ranking re-emerges as significant. Migrants may attempt to change their caste affiliation or disguise their origins, but caste as an overarching principle is re-established. Whether this will remain the case for future generations is not yet clear, and is beyond the scope of this paper. It is conceivable that for youngsters growing up in Britain the confrontation will not be between Hinduism and Islam, but between patrimonialism and individual choice.

PUNJABI MUSLIM MIGRANTS IN MANCHESTER

Most Punjabi Muslims living in Manchester originate from small villages with one, or at most two, landowning castes. Manchester, very much like South Asian cities (cf. Pocock 1960), encompasses a large range of castes, from Sayyids to Musalis. Rather than disappearing, caste divisions in Manchester are thus probably more elaborate than in most migrants' home villages (Urban migrants, of course, are used to this complexity). And since migrants come from many different parts of the Punjab and beyond, the relative ranking of castes is ambiguous and subject to current negotiation.

Most Pakistanis in Manchester condemn the caste system while practising it, and assert the basic equality and brotherhood of all Muslims. This assertion is borne out by their behaviour in many different contexts, for no obvious distinctions are made between fellow Pakistanis in matters of hospitality, feasting and worship, as well as in matters of economic cooperation. Indeed, the absence of food prohibitions and other transactional diacritics between castes makes the continued value accorded to caste membership by local migrants somewhat problematic. On the face of it, it cannot be said, for example, that caste in Manchester constitutes the 'summation' or 'cluster' of statuses. Barth suggests it does in rural Pakistan. Caste membership would appear instead to be reduced to single, and apparently irrelevant, status attributes amongst many others.

Since most Pakistanis in Manchester do not follow their traditional caste occupations,[3] why, and in what sense, does caste continue to constitute a meaningful category of interaction for them? The history of migration to the city gives clues to the re-emergence of caste. Before discussing this history in detail, let me consider first some of the specific features of the Punjabi Muslim caste hierarchy. My data accords closely with that of I. Ahmad (1976b, 1978b) for Uttar Pradesh, but is perhaps worth reiterating, given the misunderstandings which have arisen about the Punjabi Muslim caste system.

At the heart of the uneasy compromise, Punjabis make between the Islamic ethos of equality and the inequality implied by caste, is a cultural serendipity: Islamic rules of exogamy are notoriously lax, permitting marriage with a wide range of close kinsmen and consanguines, and this is coupled with a prescriptive preference for patrilateral parallel cousin marriage. The familiar complexity of the

Hindu marriage system with its wide range of marriage prohibitions and elaborate rules of exogamy is entirely absent among Muslims, possibly with some notable exceptions (cf. Alavi 1972). As a result, the fiction of equality is sustained despite the very high level of endogamy practised by Punjabi Muslims; and, indeed, the same fiction disguises the *de facto* legitimation of inequality within stratified Muslim societies throughout the Middle East.

Punjabi Muslim castes have been studied from a Marxist perspective (Alavi 1971, 1972; Saghir Ahmad 1971, 1977) according to which caste is a mere epiphenomenon of relations of dependency or exploitation. Eglar (1960), although lacking any clear theoretical stance, also denies the significance of elaborate caste categories for Punjabi Muslim villagers. This consensus has, I would argue, stultified any meaningful discussion of Punjabi Muslim caste. The hiatus is all the more remarkable in the light of my own research, which reveals the persistent significance of caste among overseas Punjabi Muslims in Britain.

On the whole the Punjabi caste hierarchy fits well with the general pattern reported elsewhere (Barth 1960; I. Ahmad 1976a: 319-33, 1978b: 1-18). Punjabi Muslim *zats*, or castes, are social categories which resemble Hindu castes in being (i) hereditary; (ii) ideally endogamous; (iii) recruited both from occupational categories and ethnic groups; (iv) comprehensive and ranked hierarchically in a 'system', with persons of high ritual pedigree located at the top of the hierarchy (Sayyid), followed by 'conquerors' of Muslim and Hindu origin, followed by categories of agricultural cultivators and artisan castes, with service castes and those coming in contact with polluting substances located at the bottom of the scale (see Figure 1). Like Hindu castes, moreover, zat membership is based primarily, though not unambiguously, on patrilineal descent, so that endogamy, while preferred, is often breached, with children assuming the caste of their fathers (On similar notions among Hindus cf. Parry 1979). The caste status of the offspring of marriages between castes of radically different statuses is, however, highly ambiguous.

Punjabi Muslim castes differ from Hindu castes in that (1) the Muslim zat system is not based, except at its extremes, on notions of ritual purity and pollution. This implies, among other things, that commensality between members of all zats is permitted, if not always practised in domestic contexts. (2) Attendant to this, ritual services are not necessarily provided by the highest caste of descendants from

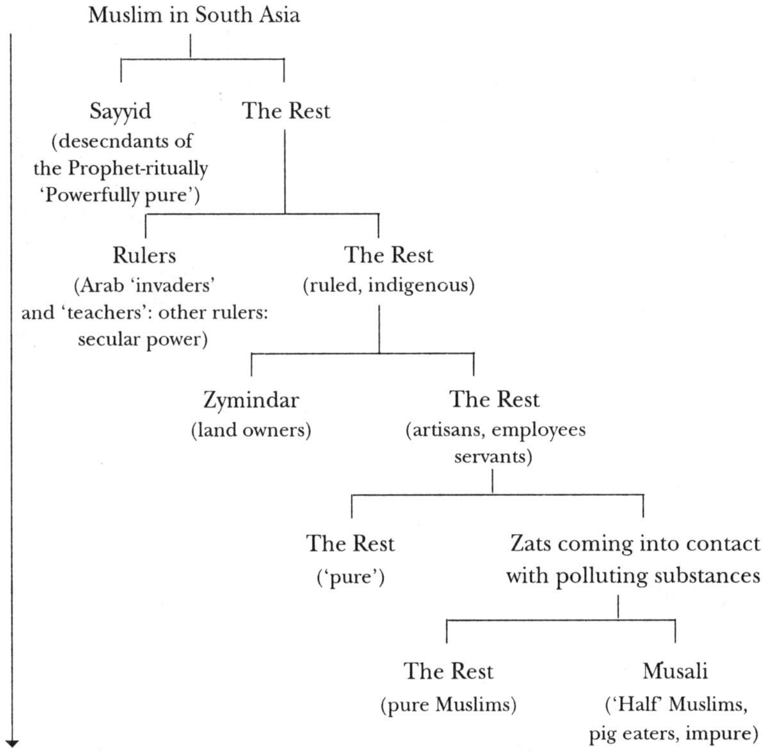

FIGURE 1. THE SYMBOLIC STRUCTURE OF THE MUSLIM *ZAT* SYSTEM

the Prophet, the Sayyids, but by lay specialists. Persons occupying mediatory roles as 'saints' (*pir*) or holy men do, however, usually claim to be Sayyids, while members of the Barber caste perform certain ritual services during rites of passage, much like their Hindu counterparts.[4] (3) Islam denies the validity of caste-like distinctions and all Muslims are equal in matters of law, worship and religious conduct.

The absence of notions of contagious pollution or commensal barriers and food prohibitions makes marriage the most highly significant symbolic ranking mechanism for Muslims. In Manchester, as elsewhere (Parry 1979), inter-caste marriages are the most problematic for migrants, since these contain implications regarding the relative ranking of the marriage partners. Marriage is notionally hypergamous, although this feature is underplayed in marriages between parallel cousins or in exchange marriages. The preference for marrying first cousins persists in Manchester as a means of bringing over to Britain close relatives from Pakistan. This preference is not, however, a sufficient explanation for the continued local significance of caste. This significance is to be understood in terms of the types of social networks maintained by migrants, and changes in the occupational structure of the community in Manchester.

Friendship among Pakistanis cuts across both caste and kinship boundaries. The local tendency towards the formation of regionally based networks contributes to the persistent significance of caste in Manchester, for it facilitates the flow of information between Manchester and Pakistan. Inter-caste marriages are quickly known in Pakistan and the prestige of migrants affected by them. Caste, therefore, cannot be ignored as long as migrants remain 'double rooted'. It is partly this embeddedness of migrants within networks spanning both Pakistan and Britain which makes caste a social category of continued significance. It is, moreover, within friendship circles that invidious comparisons regarding caste identity become important, in the context of *local* competition for status and prestige.

As children reach marriageable age, close friends may discover quite suddenly that a marriage bar divides them, and that upper-caste persons will not contemplate marriages between their children and those of the lower-caste friends. For despite the preference for endogamous marriages, marriages between castes of more or less equal status do occur, and this is reported in Pakistan as well (cf. Saghir Ahmad 1977: 73-5; Eglar 1960: 28-9; Alavi 1972: 7).

THE CASTE HIERARCHY IN MANCHESTER

At the top of the caste hierarchy of Punjabi Muslims, Sayyids tend to maintain strict endogamy while Pathan, Mughals, Qureshi, Siddiqui, and other 'ruler' castes marry hypergamously with castes of somewhat similar status such as Sheikh and Rajput. In general, however, the major marriage bar, outside the Sayyids, is between castes known collectively as 'landowners' (*zymindar*), and those known collectively as 'servants' (*kammi*). The landowners are those who, until the turn of the century, were the only castes entitled to own land, while the 'servants' include artisan and service castes (cf. Ullah 1958: 174).

The distinction is somewhat similar to that between twice-born and Shudra classes among Hindus, although the zymindar appear to be a somewhat broader category. Intermarriage among land-owning castes is, as mentioned, reported to be relatively common in Pakistan, and the same phenomenon of what might be called 'super-casteism' is also found in Manchester.

The caste hierarchy in Manchester appears to approximate to the list in Table 1. It must be stressed, however, that there is no complete agreement regarding caste ranking (Cf. Saghir Ahmad 1971, 1977: 79-83), and most caste members tend to place their own castes somewhat higher in the caste hierarchy than others place them. The notion of ranking is, however, inherent in the concept of zat, and it was assumed among all migrants that castes—even those within the zymindar class, were ranked, although there might not be complete agreement on exactly how they were ranked. This feature of caste is, of course, common among Hindus as well (for a comparative account cf. Parry 1979).[5] Table 1 shows the caste hierarchy in Manchester, based on informants' evaluations. Within each major class there are sub-classes, each divided into zats and zat 'sections'. The lower the level of division, the greater the equality implied between its constituent subsections. The list by no means exhausts all the castes represented in Manchester, but it includes those the members of which I encountered personally in the course of my research, and comprehends the more inclusive caste categories which are the significant units of endogamy. Of particular interest is the positioning of the Arain, Darzi and Rawal castes within the hierarchy, for it is these castes which have changed status in Manchester.

Among Pakistanis, as among Hindus, relations of inequality or hierarchy pervade the system at all levels, and shifts in status necessarily involve a transformation either in caste status or in caste identity. Generally speaking, there are two chief patterns of caste 'mobility': A local caste group may raise its status through economic success and religious purification. Alternatively, a group or section of a lower caste may break away from its caste of origin and change its caste affiliation. Caste categories are divided into smaller sections, usually regarded as descended patrilineally from a single putative ancestor (e.g., Gujar Khatana, Gujar Phaswal). The sections of various castes bear similar names and make affiliation of sections to higher castes possible. The rise in status of segments to higher order segments can

TABLE 1. THE PAKISTANI CASTE (*ZAT*) HIERARCHY IN MANCHESTER

Class and Sub-Class	Caste	Caste sections represented locally	Typical family surname used locally
Zymindar			
Ritually pure	Sayyid	Various (?)	Shah, Alawi, Awan
'Conquerors'	Pathan	Various sections	Khan
('Rulers')	Mughal	with zat suffix	Mughal
(Learned scholars)	Qureshi, Siddiqui		Qureshi, Siddiqui
Indigenous rulers	Rajput	Chohan, Koker, Pangwari, Gaher, Bhatti	Raja, Chohan, Koker
'Traders'	Sheikh		Sheikh
Cultivators	Jat (cultivators)	Kalo, Gelna, Bajewa	Choudhry (headman)
	Gujar (herders)	Ningrial, Kateck, Ningial, Waraich Khatana, Chohan, Chechi, Phaswal, Gorshi	
	Arain (vegetable-growers)	none	
(Indeterminate)	Kashmiri	Dar, Bhatti, Molek, Dar Bat	Dar
Kammi			
Skilled artisans	Darzi (tailor)	Caste	None
	Lohar (blacksmith)	Sections of castes	Lohar
	Tarkhan (carpenter)	in the Kammi	None
	Rawal (itinerant pedlars)	class with similar	
Service castes	Kisai (butcher)	names to	
	Kaspi (weaver)	those of	
	Mochi (shoemaker)	Zymindar	
	Tobi (washer)	caste	None
	Nai (barber)	sections	
	Mirasi (bard)		
	Musali (sweeper)		

take place at different levels of the caste hierarchy, as Parry has shown is the case for north Indian Hindus.

To fully understand processes of caste mobility we need first to examine the Punjabi Muslim notion of *biradari.* Castes, it must be remembered, are mere categories and do not form either corporate groups or actual units of endogamy. Members of castes bearing the same name are widely scattered and the effective unit of 'recognition' and 'participation' (cf. Mayer 1960), is the local group for marrying within the caste or, as it is known in Pakistan and north India, the biradari. The chief reason, in my view, why the significance of Punjabi Muslim caste has not been recognized stems from a misunderstanding of the cultural construction of biradari. For Punjabi Muslims the biradari encapsulates the contradictory ideas of equality and inequality. It disguises the immanence of caste behind a facade of fraternal kinship. It is thus necessary to elucidate the complex relationship between Muslim caste, regarded as a ranked set of categories, and biradari, regarded as a localized marriage circle, as these are played out in the context of migration.

THE RANKING OF BROTHERHOODS

While Barth and Ahmad, as we saw, stress the continued relevance of castes for South Asian Muslims, others regard caste categories as vestiges of a prior order. Alavi (1972) and Eglar (1960), for example both argue that all 'landowning' castes among Pakistanis are equal within a single 'caste' or 'class' category. The elaborate distinctions between castes or caste sections are, in their view, of no significance in the villages they studied, either in relation to marriage prescriptions or for the ranking of status. The unit of ranking, Alavi argues, is the far smaller unit of the village patrilineage—the biradari—which is named after an apical ancestor five generations from the living (and not by a caste and caste section name). This, according to Alavi, is also the main unit of endogamy. Saghir Ahmad (1977), while arguing that an analysis in terms of caste distinctions would provide little insight into the social structure of the village he studied, accepts the existence of a cultural 'system' of ranked zat categories even within the landowning class. His view is, however, that occupation and property ownership are more significant parameters for structural analysis.

I would argue, however, that the exclusive definition of the biradari as a lineage points to a fundamental analytic confusion: Biradaris for Punjabi Muslims, as for their Hindu counterparts, are units of endogamy *within* the caste, and they are also, as Parry shows, the primary vehicle of strategic marriage alliances and caste mobility. Alavi says of the notion of 'biradari' that it is a 'term with a sliding semantic structure' (1972: 2). In more common anthropological parlance, he is referring to the segmentary nature of the caste system. Thus Parry, following Beteille (1964, 1965) and Dumont (1972), argues:

> . . . that Kangra people conceptualize their society in terms of a segmentary model and that neither in language nor in behaviour do they signal any radical or absolute distinction between the nature of the groups of different orders of inclusiveness. The boundaries which mark divisions within the caste, divisions between castes, between 'clean' and 'untouchable' caste and even between men and gods are not of qualitatively different kinds, but are different only in the degree of emphasis and elaboration they receive. (1979: 3)

The biradari, Alavi recognizes, may include, depending on the context of action, a wider or more restricted group of people (cf. Eglar 1960: 76-7). Like Eglar and Saghir Ahmad, he emphasizes that the biradari is a *patrilineage,* although an extremely shallow one (ibid.: 3), defined by patrilineal descent from a single apical ancestor. Neither he nor the other two scholars give an example of such a patrilineage except as it exists in a single village. From their own accounts, however (cf. in particular Eglar 1960: 77), my own research, and the accounts of others in north India (especially I. Ahmad 1976a and 1978a), it is clear that the principle of patrilineal descent operates in defining the biradari *at the village level only.* Here the biradari is the 'maximal lineage' in Parry's terms. At the wider, inter-village level, the biradari is a recognized marriage circle composed of members of a single caste and named section who live in relatively large number of villages within a locality, and who traditionally inter-marry with one another. Only one informant among the many with whom I discussed this issue claimed that the notion referred to the village kin groups exclusively; all other informants stressed its wider application as a concept referring to all kinsmen, affines, and affines of affines. It would appear that only in the unlikely instance where the rate of marriage within the village is absolute can the village patrilineage and the biradari as a marriage circle be said to coincide. Thus, Alavi reports that in one village he studied, 73 per cent of all marriages were contracted within the village and only 27 per cent were contracted within the caste section outside the village (1972: 6-7).[6] None of the village genealogies I recorded showed this remarkable tendency towards village endogamy. In most of them under 40 per cent of the marriages were within the village, and there was a tendency to renew links between villages in consecutive generations

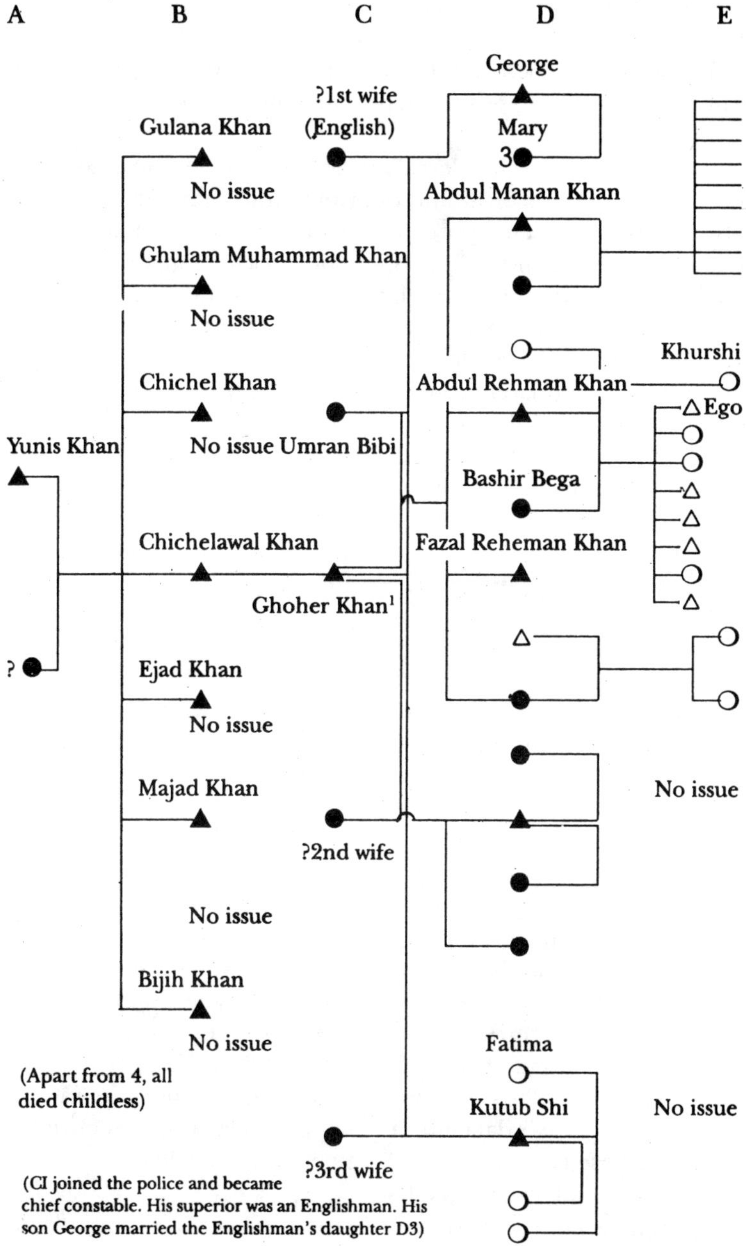

FIGURE 2. URBAN GENEALOGICAL MEMORY

through matrilateral marriages, a pattern commonly found among Hindus as well.[7]

The distinction between the biradari as a village kin group and as a marriage circle is important to bear in mind, for while at the village level the principle of patrilineal descent (*nasab* or *nasal*) may operate, at the inter-village level the principle of inclusion or exclusion in a biradari is based on affinity or prior affinity rather than descent. My informants in Manchester were adamant that the biradari was a bilateral kindred and included, in addition to cognatic kinsmen, affines, the consanguineous relatives of affines and even the affines of affines. Indeed, in tracing links between people in Manchester, no attempt was usually made to trace connections through descent beyond the grandparental generation, particularly if a more recent affinal link existed. Members of a biradari are descended from a single apical ancestor only to the extent that the caste is regarded among Muslims as, ultimately, a descent group, even though its members cannot trace actual links with one another. Seen in terms of marriage alliances, descent, while possible, is irrelevant.

Hence, while putative patrilineal descent of biradari members may well be assumed in Pakistan, it cannot be expressed by migrants in detailed genealogical information. Genealogical information known as '*shajra nasab*', (family tree) is often recorded in Pakistan by genealogists and is referred to by informants when information is sought. The main purpose of such 'family trees', however, is to prove a family's pedigree for marriage purposes, since marriages are supposedly contracted only between 'good' families. In so far as genealogical *memory* is concerned, beyond the village level social and group relations are not articulated in the idiom of unilineal descent, and there exists no explicit ramifying segmentary system expressing relations between village lineages in such an idiom of descent. A village lineage may be said to have been founded by an apical ancestor known to have come from a named village elsewhere in the Punjab, thus recognizing an agnatic link between the two villages, but no further segmentary levels can be specified. This genealogical pattern appears to be common throughout north India. In Kangra, for example, Parry's data indicate that while clans and subclans are putatively based on common descent, actual genealogical links are traced only at a localized level.

I obtained about twenty bilateral genealogies from migrants living in Manchester. The greatest genealogical depth appeared in the village genealogies I recorded, where there was a memory of an apical ancestor three generations from the living, and four generations from my informants. Most genealogies of migrants from urban backgrounds were much shallower and many did not even recall the name of their great-grandfather, although they did know some of the descendants of his siblings. An exceptional case was that of one informant who came from a landed family; he recalled the names of antecedents four generations from himself, but a closer inspection of the genealogy he gave (Figure 2), reveals that he could recall only the descendants of his grandfather in the present generation. The rest of those listed in prior generations were said to have died childless, or to have left Pakistan.

To understand fully the notion of biradari it must be related not to unilineal descent but to the wider category of the caste or zat, and its use resembles that among Hindus. It is, in Blunt's words, 'the *zat* in action' (1969: 10). At the village level, the biradari is a corporate descent group which often acts as a faction in local-level politics (cf. Alavi 1971; Saghir Ahmad 1977). At the inter-village level it is a circle of intermarrying affines. As such it is non-corporate and its boundaries undefined except when it refers to a number of village lineages who are known traditionally to intermarry. Otherwise it is family-focused, with each family and village lineage having a slightly different marriage 'circle' or chain of marriages; even this circle changes over time as new marriages are contracted and old affinal links left unrenewed. The circle might be quite large: I recorded one village genealogy of small landholders in the Jhelum district, in which the village lineage had ties of affinity with lineages in twenty-two other villages and towns in Pakistan within a radius of over 50 kilometres (cf. also Saghir Ahmad 1977: 47). On the other hand, the rate of *inter-caste* marriages in the genealogies I recorded was rather low—in most cases far less than 8 per cent (cf. Appendix).

It must be stressed, therefore, that biradari does not simply imply a kin relationship. Consanguineous kinsmen are known as *rishtedar* and this term is extended to include their spouses as well. Rishtedar are either *nazdik* (close) or *dur* (far), and a distinction is also made between *sakke* (real) and classificatory kin.

References to group categories vary contextually, as one notion is used in contrast to another. Hence, when biradari is used in contradistinction to rishtedar in Manchester, it is used to imply a more distant relationship than that of traceable kinship. When contrasted with zat, the latter term implies the absence of any relationship and is used about caste members with whom no links of consanguinity or affinity are thought to exist. At the widest and vaguest level biradari is interchangeable with zat and is applied to all caste members within a single locality, or even within a country. The reference of the term thus varies with the context of action or debate, and the significant unit often emerges in situational opposition to like units of a similar order. While the use of the notion of zat implies ranking as well as non-kinship, biradari, meaning 'brotherhood', implies equality as this is defined situationally. The very flexibility of the notion of 'biradari' makes its application in Manchester possible, and there too its significance is situational and contextual rather than constant.

As mentioned, there appear to be important differences in the genealogical memories of migrants originating from villages and towns; the latter do not attempt to encompass all members of the biradari living in town within a single unilineal descent group, unlike genealogies of village caste groups. Even in village genealogies, there is an area of ambiguity at the third ascending generation regarding the exact relations between ancestors. This is shown in the genealogies in Figures 3 and 4. In Figure 3 the relationship between two branches of a village biradari was presented as that between a man and his brother's son. In Figure 4, representing the genealogy presented three years later by the wife of the initial presenter, the two men were given as brothers. On both occasions, a whole branch of the village biradari was initially not unmentioned, and was only revealed to me after a great deal of probing. The members of this branch were said to be 'poor and uneducated' and to have 'less land than we have'. Their omission was all the more remarkable because the wife's mother's mother came from this branch, there had been a number of other marriages between the two family branches and once their existence was revealed, she could provide information regarding all living members of the family branch, their marriages, current residence and children. The other family branch, which had been mentioned on both occasions, was said to be composed of members who were 'rich and educated'; it included in its numbers an advocate of the Punjab High Court and a college principal. However, I was told that this branch was now 'separating' from 'us', because no recent marriages had taken place between the two branches. The emphasis, even with regard to village genealogies appears thus to be on the

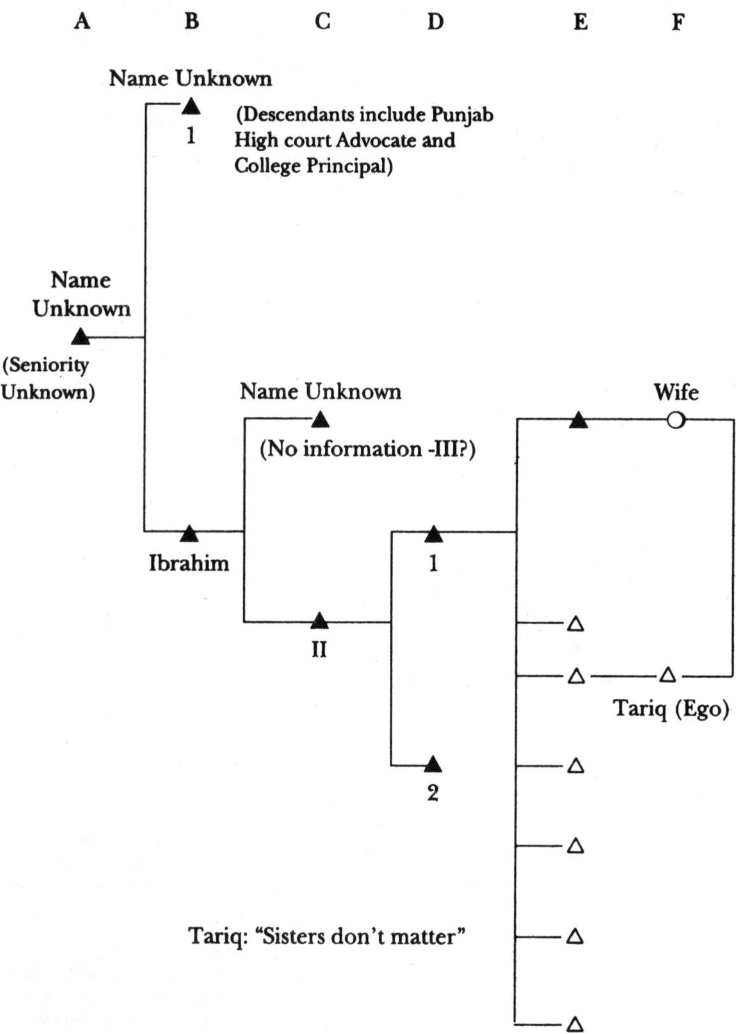

FIGURE 3. VILLAGE *NASAL* (1975) GIVEN BY TARIQ

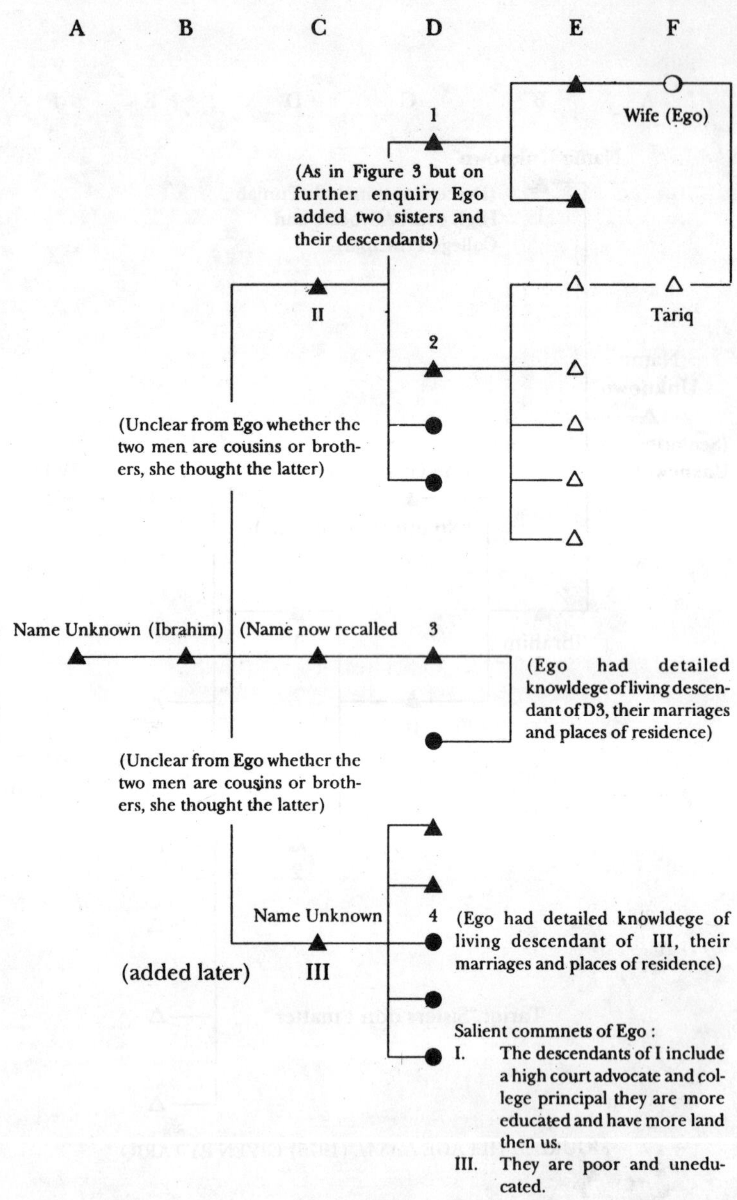
A
B
C
D
E
F
1
Wife (Ego)
(As in Figure 3 but on further enquiry Ego added two sisters and their descendants)
II
Tariq
2
(Unclear from Ego whether the two men are cousins or brothers, she thought the latter)
Name Unknown
(Ibrahim)
(Name now recalled
3
(Ego had detailed knowldege of living descendant of D3, their marriages and places of residence)
(Unclear from Ego whether the two men are cousins or brothers, she thought the latter)
Name Unknown
4
(Ego had detailed knowldege of living descendant of III, their marriages and places of residence)
(added later)
III
Salient commnets of Ego :
I. The descendants of I include a high court advocate and college principal they are more educated and have more land then us.
III. They are poor and uneducated.

FIGURE 4. VILLAGE *NASAL* (1978) GIVEN BY TARIQ'S WIFE

closest relatives with whom marriages are still being contracted.

Although biradaris, if regarded as marriage circles, are not as explicitly ranked as are marriage circles in Gujarat state in India (cf. van der Veen 1972; Lambat 1976), the fact remains that caste members marry within their class with those of equal wealth, power or education. This in turn means that marriage circles are usually homogeneous with regard to their class composition and social standing, and can, in this sense, be ranked. When some members of a single extended family rise on the social scale, as in the case of the advocate's family mentioned above, they may cease to intermarry with their less successful kinsmen; and over a generation or two the family will split into two separate biradaris.

The mutability of kin relations among Punjabi Muslims and their relativity to performance are mentioned both by Eglar (1960: 100) and by Alavi (1972: 9). In Manchester, too, migrants emphasize that kinship extends only where there are ceremonial exchanges, relations and mutual aid. Parallel and cross-cousin marriages can also be understood as arising out of this view regarding the ephemerality of kinship. A well-known Punjabi proverb quoted to me in Manchester cautions that 'When the fence gets old you must put new wood in it' (*purani bar-nu nawan chapa lagana zaruree ay*)—i.e., new marriages with relatives are necessary if the kinship relationship is not to crumble away and disappear. As families become scattered through labour migration, marriages between cousins, the children of widely dispersed siblings, become important for sustaining the kinship connection. Relations with more distant relatives of the old biradari, however, are often not considered worth renewing through new marriages.

LABOUR MIGRATION AND THE DEFINITION OF BIRADARI

The scattering of the family through labour migration was remarkable in all the genealogies I recorded. In some instances migrants came from refugee families, which may have precipitated their dispersal; but even among non-refugees, dispersal was very marked. Families were scattered both in different towns in Pakistan and all over the world. The major countries of immigration, apart from the United Kingdom, appeared to be Canada and the United States, Denmark, Germany, Libya, Saudi Arabia, and the other Gulf States. One woman from Karachi, for example, had close relatives in India, Australia, Britain, the Sudan, Saudi Arabia and the United States; her husband had relatives in Malaysia, Austria and Libya as well. Only in one case that I recorded, an informant appeared to have, outside Pakistan, relatives only in Britain.

In the circumstances, many home villages and towns of migrants have become temporary bases and centres of communication for widely dispersed kinsmen. Indeed, in one case that I know of, a large patrilineal homestead is maintained by a matrilateral relative as all the male joint owners are absent from their home town. Many migrants of village origin have changed residence in Pakistan itself, to a town near their village, after they immigrated to Britain. This form of double urbanisation is, at times, linked to their attempts to raise their status simultaneously both in Manchester and in Pakistan; or to family quarrels and divorces, precipitating a move from the village; or to the desire to invest in urban land or businesses.

Their geographical mobility has affected the marriage patterns of migrants. Most of the new marriages contracted in Manchester are contracted within the zat category. If this happens repeatedly, the caste category will be transformed over time into a recognized biradari. This is more likely if the local caste membership is large, with some already linked by prior kinship or affinal ties forged in Pakistan, and if a large proportion of caste members are successful economically.

A locally negotiated caste hierarchy re-emerges once migrants begin to sink roots locally and enter the local competition for status. As in South Asia, this case ranking has economic, political and religious dimensions, and is ratified symbolically through hypergamous inter-caste marriages. To appreciate this process, a brief review of the history of migration to the city is needed.

CASTE AND THE HISTORY OF MIGRATION TO MANCHESTER

Pakistani migration to Manchester may be regarded as composed of three parallel yet distinct migratory movements or flows. For a time, during the late 1950s and early 1960s, the three movements appeared as one. Yet in reality, the arriving migrants followed distinct migratory patterns. These streams may be classified as the 'trader' migrants, the students, and the worker migrants.

(i) *The 'trader' migrants.* A well-documented feature of Asian migration to Britain was the early pre-war arrival of migrants from the Punjab who became door-to-door pedlars. They settled in the larger cities: in London, Birmingham, Manchester, Leeds, Glasgow or Newcastle. They worked in factories for brief periods only, and entered almost immediately after their arrival into different sectors of the clothing and garment trade. In Manchester today they occupy a distinct vertically integrated economic enclave (Werbner 1987).

Within this general category of 'trader' migrants in Manchester, there appeared to be three major subgroups, each a biradari. One groups was that of East Punjabis, mainly from the Jullunder area, and mainly of the Arain zat. After the partition of India and Pakistan in 1947 this group moved as refugees into the Canal Colonies in the Punjab—to the Sahiwal, Multan and Bahavarpur areas, and to the large cities—Lahore, Rawalpindi, Faislabad and Karachi. At the same time that they were moving as refugees into the newly formed State of Pakistan, they began arriving in Manchester in quite large numbers, following a pattern of chain migration. Most became market traders, and later wholesalers, in the garment and clothing trades. Some of the largest wholesalers and manufacturers in the city today come from this group. Seen in aggregate, members of the group are extremely powerful economically, employing female machinists and young male workers from within the community, and providing custom and credit to a large number of manufacturers and retailers. Politically, the group has always been extremely influential, controlling the Central Mosque Management Committee (Werbner 1985) and other key voluntary associations. Members of the group meet regularly at large weddings and mortuary rituals (Werbner 1986, 1988). While split by factional infighting, they nevertheless tend to worship at the Central Jamia Mosque of Manchester and to follow Sunni 'Barelvi' traditions. These traditions stress the intercessionary role of saints or Sufi *pirs* in mediating between the individual and God.

A second biradari following a similar pattern was also originally from East Punjab. The family was already established in trading and the kin group extended into Singapore and Malaysia. After partition members of the kindred, of the Rawal biradari, settled in Wazirabad, Gujranwala, while some began migrating to Manchester. They too entered successfully into market trading and shopkeeping. One prominent branch of the family owns a successful small hotel, another is a large wholesaler. The group, while small, has prospered economically. Some (though not all) of its members are very religious, but unlike the Arain they prefer a more puritanical form of Reform Islam centred around another local mosque. The Sunni Islam they advocate stresses the direct access of individuals to God through prayer and religious learning. They thus deny the disjunction between the inworldly and outworldly characteristic of Barelvi traditions.

A third biradari, also with international trading links in the Far East, came somewhat later, in the 1950s. Many members of this kindred were tailors by occupation. They too originated from Gujranwala, but mainly from Gujranwala town itself and its surrounding villages. Several members of this family had served as tailors for the British army, or in other administrative capacities, and many were stationed in Cyprus. After the independence of Cyprus, they immigrated to Britain. Today many are successful manufacturers, a few are wholesalers as well. Key members of this group are known for their piety, education and religious knowledge. They too advocate a stream of Reform Islam. One of their members is a founder member and *maulvi* of the Reform Islam Mosque and one-time president of the UK Islamic Mission. He is very active in the religious circles and has led many parties on Haj to Mecca. His wife and sister often lead communal Quran readings, and the family is dedicated to religious service.

Members of all three groups and especially the two Gujranwala biradaris, are literate and relatively educated. A few prominent members of the Gujranwala biradari have university degrees. They are all Punjabis, and they have incorporated newcomers from their groups into trading and manufacturing after brief periods in factory wage employment.

(ii) *The students.* The second major migrant flow to Manchester was that of students. Like other major British cities, post-war Manchester attracted a large number of students to its educational institutions. Many of them stayed on in the city, either to practise (as accountants, doctors, etc.) or to go into business. They were mostly born in India, and their families had moved into cities of Pakistan after partition. Most of them were Punjabis, although there were some Urdu speakers from Delhi, Lucknow, and other parts of UP, and a few Gujarati speakers from Karachi. Virtually all belonged to higher castes, including Sayyid, Qureshi, Pathans, Mughal, Siddiqui or

Sheikh, and the main cultivating castes (Jat, Arain, Gujar). A few were Mhemanis from Karachi. Many had connections with the 'trader' East Punjabi migrants. In any case, the community in those days was very small, and concentrated residentially in certain areas of the city around the University (cf. Werbner 1979), all of which made for links between the two groups. Between them the students-turned-professionals and the large wholesalers in the garment trade controlled the Central Jamia Mosque, and most other communal institutions for many years. The ex-students, however, continued to marry within their respective biradaris, recruiting wives primarily from Pakistan.

(iii) *The worker migrants.* The third flow of migrants to the city occurred after the other two groups were well established. During the late 1950s and early 1960s the pattern of migration to the city changed. While the East Punjabis and students were bringing over wives and families, young bachelors from West Punjab—primarily from the Gujarat and Jhelum districts—began arriving in Manchester.[9] These men did not come from refugee families but from small landholding families and biradaris with deep, extensive roots in their village localities. The traditional supplementary occupations in these *barani* (rainfed) areas was of service in the army and the police. Although most of the men were moderately literate and educated, some to high school level, there was no tradition of trading in their families. They came to Manchester to work in local factories or in public transport services (the buses and railways), and they remained wage earners until the most recent economic recession and its associated factory closures and cut-backs of the mid or late 1970s. The migrants were not connected to the trading families, and only a small minority attempted to move into market trading, shopkeeping or manufacturing. Like the earlier pedlars, however, this enterprising minority was to lay the foundation for the group's entry into business in the 1980s. As in the other two migratory flows, caste membership was related to area of origin. Although migrants came from a variety of castes, including some service kammi castes, most notably from the Mirasi (Bard) and Nai (Barber) zats, the vast majority appear to have originated from the Gujar and Rajput landowning castes. They were not, however, from a single biradari, but from several discrete biradaris. It has thus taken them some time to acknowledge links across the different kindreds, even within the same zat.

Although the flow of migrant 'workers' has been the most recent, they appear to be the largest group numerically. (There are no statistics on this matter, and I base this statement on mobilization events.) Initially marginal to the community and its institutions, they have recently begun to reassert their political status, basing their power on their numerical strength rather than their economic superiority. In their political struggles, they stress their proud land-owning origins and influence in Pakistani politics. As their local commitment has grown they have also become more conscious of other caste members, beyond their current biradari. This is true, for example, of members of the Gujar caste who, though quite numerous in Manchester, have only begun to develop a 'consciousness' of their unity in the city. Although Rajputs claim to be placed above Arain in the caste hierarchy, and Gujars claim to be their equals, they acknowledge the Arain's superior local status and recognize the need to reassert their own local standing.

As migrants have come to be more settled in Britain, they have begun to use the notion of biradari not only in its most restricted sense (to refer to the current localized marriage circle within the caste), but with reference to a series of segmentary contexts—it is once again a term with a 'sliding semantic structure'. This was made clear in an interview with a local Pakistani community activist who had lived in the city with his wife since 1960, was a member of the Mosque Committee, had married children living locally and had sons working as market traders. He began our conversation by stressing the small number of kinsmen (rishtedar) he had living locally. Apart from a married sister and a brother, there were about five or six 'houses' (*ghar*—agnatically defined families) living in the city who were related to him. During the course of the interview we discussed another community leader and his stand on various political matters in the mosque, and I commented, since I knew this leader and his family very well, that he had a large biradari in Manchester. At this my informant remarked that his own biradari was just as large. Henceforth the discussion turned to the membership size of various castes in the city. Thus, for example, my informant—himself a Rajput—thought there were many people of the Gujar biradari living locally. He used the notion of 'family' in English and biradari in Punjabi interchangeably, but the discussion was about caste membership and the implication was that all migrants with the same caste identity were somehow related to one another. This, despite the clear distinction he had made earlier between caste members and consanguineous kin. As a politician, my informant had an interest in emphasizing the unity of caste members, and in the context of political confrontation biradari was defined by him as the local zat. My informant—Rajput—also claimed to know all members of his zat living in Manchester, although he knew some of my Rajput acquaintances by reputation only.

The political arena is not the only one in which the unity and kinship of local zat members may be claimed. As I mentioned earlier, economically well-established migrants of a single caste also regard themselves as belonging to one biradari. The most striking example of this in Manchester is the Arain caste. All the members of this caste I met in Manchester claimed to belong to a single biradari: Arain was, they said, a biradari. For them zat and biradari are locally synonymous. There is a saying among Arain: 'If you lift up a brick, you will find a relative', and indeed, many of the Arain in Manchester are able to trace distant kinship and affinal links with one another.

The ranking of the Arain caste appears to have undergone a shift in Manchester, and especially in the eyes of migrants from West Punjab. In the caste hierarchy, the Arain are ranked below the landowning class. Eglar reports that in Gujarat district Arain was not a landowning caste, although its members were entitled to own land (1960: 32). Ullah (1958: 172) ranks it near the bottom of the caste scale, among the kammi, in the village he studied. In Manchester, however, Arain are clearly accepted by all Pakistanis, including those from West Punjab, to be a landowning caste and many rank Arain as high as the Rajput caste. Such ranking has been validated by at least one inter-caste marriage. Members of the cultivating castes like Gujar and Jat usually rank the caste in the same order as themselves. One member of the Gujar caste said, 'Everyone in Manchester says they are Arain' and recounted a story about a low-caste acquaintance whom she had heard claiming to be an Arain. There is thus a recognition among other landowning castes in Manchester that to be an Arain is to have a slight edge in the local competition for status and prestige.

Similar changes in status have occurred for the Rawal and Darzi castes. Rawal, said originally to be an itinerant pedlar kammi caste, are now said by its members to have been the original rulers of the Rawalpindi area. Members of the Darzi caste claim that they are 'really' of Rajput origin, while acknowledging that they had been tailors by occupation. Some claim they were 'really' Nai before they became Darzi. The claims of both Darzi and Arain have been validated by inter-caste marriages with members of the Rajput (and in the case of Darzi also Arain) groups. However, in the case of a Darzi I know, the marriages have all been of daughters to male members of higher castes.

MIGRATION AND CASE MOBILITY

I have argued that as in rural Uttar Pradesh (I. Ahmad 1976b) so too in Manchester the achievement of caste mobility among Punjabi Muslims is clinched when marriages formerly not contemplated take place. Caste ranking is, in other words, tested and proved through inter-caste marriage. Here a further word of explanation may be necessary regarding the prevalent patterns of 'caste mobility' recognized in South Asia.

The literature records a number of forms of caste mobility.[10] Perhaps most widespread is the process of 'Sanskritisation' commonly occurring when members of an intermediate caste achieve enhanced (secular) status through an accumulation of power or wealth. Their enhanced status is accompanied by a collective decision to adopt brahaminical practices, to 'Sanskritise' the caste. Such changes in ritual and dietary observances may or may not be accompanied also by transformation of caste identity. A similar process has been called 'Ashrafisation' and 'Islamisation' among Muslims (cf. Vreede-De Stuers 1968; Ahmad 1978).[11] This trend towards increased religiosity is evident in both the Darzi and Rawal groups, of kammi origin. They adhere to a puritanical form of Islamic worship associated with the Deoband or the Wahabi Islamic schools, and stress religious scholarship and the ability of each individual to worship God independently and directly through learning and personal devotion.

Caste mobility—especially of the more inferior castes—may also occur, as I argued above, when a small segment of a larger caste unit breaks off from the caste, calls itself by a separate name and marries endogamously. This type of caste mobility is facilitated among Muslims by their ability to marry close kinsmen, for even a relatively small kindred group can arrange suitable marriages internally during the period of caste identity transformation, before they have established themselves as a caste section of a more elevated caste. There is no need for them to seek marriage partners far afield, as

Hindus are compelled to do, and this means that the mobile section may be a far smaller kinship unit than it must necessarily be among Hindus. An instance of this form of mobility in Manchester was that of a group from the Bard (Mirasi) caste. This group claimed to be Shi'ite and, as such, Qureshi or Qazi by origin, even though their caste status was well known locally. They worshipped in the Shi'a mosque, thus setting themselves apart in matters of worship. Several of the younger members of the group were, or were studying to be, professionals, but they did not assert their claims to high-caste status aggressively. Instead, members of this group preferred to marry internally, with very close relatives, primarily matrilateral first cousins, and not test their claims publicly. It is quite possible, however, that further claims to high-caste status could well be accepted a generation hence when the children of the professional generation' reach marriageable age. Here an element of *collusion* enters: once a group has established itself economically and politically, it is not necessarily in anyone's interest to invoke their caste origins.

Rather than intensified religiosity, mobile groups may of course choose to 'westernise'. On the whole however such a trend was evident in Manchester only among a small minority of elite caste members, mainly professionals and a few wealthy businessmen. Far more evident was the growing trend towards religiosity.

It is theoretically possible for a socially mobile individual to marry an impoverished woman of a higher caste and assume her caste name (Vreede-De Stuers 1968: 6). This type of individual mobility appears, however, to be rare in Manchester. Individuals usually achieve wealth only through cooperation with a wider group of kinsmen with whom they have continued relations of debt and trust, and whom they are unable to disown. It is whole kindred group which attempts to transform its caste identity, rather than a single individual within it.

The various forms of social mobility may be summarized in a general hypothesis. The hypothesis posits a contrast between *individual* social mobility and caste mobility, each form varying also according to the prior caste status of the group or the individual. Table 2 sums up this central hypothesis. Very generally, landowning castes validate their enhanced dominance through hypergamous marriages, while continuing to follow a mild form of popular Islam. Mobile individuals from within the landowning caste groups attempt to contract marriages with partners from an enhanced educational or wealthy background. Mobile kammi castes intensify their religiosity, choosing very often to stress religious learning and individual autonomy; they marry endogamously within a highly restricted kinship span and attempt to change this subgroup's caste affiliation.

As the number of mosques in the city has grown, it almost seems that they parallel the different biradaris and their particular strategies. There is a continuous drive towards status congruence: education, piety, wealth and political reputation are regarded together as people try to assess the local standing of different groups. But even more important, I think, is the fact that choices are determined by caste background and the values associated with the caste hierarchy: the move from employment (dependence) to self-employment (and control over others); the fierce battles for political office; the increasing religiosity, especially among those from lower castes; the renewed esteem and belief in saints and the local growth of Sufism. Purity, power, autonomy and control—the central ingredients of a caste hierarchy—determine choices and thus, ultimately, the collective history of the local community. Seen over time, the dialectic is evident: the move has been away from a caste society to a suppression of distinctions and then to their renewal; from an intensification of religiosity with its egalitarian practices to its refraction in groups defined by differentials of status and wealth. Equality continues to be the highest value, epitomized in the notion of the biradari as a brotherhood, but it is constantly being undermined by ideas about ranking and relativities of honour and status. The biradari is, after all, a ranked group.

The marriages contracted by Pakistanis in Manchester all seem to illustrate that caste mobility is not simply a matter of the 'manipulation of meaning', or the use of symbols and emblems for personal advancement. Caste membership is an important aspect of a Punjabi's identity, and it defines a field of relationships that can be appealed to in terms of values of equality and brotherhood. A change in caste identity is not, therefore, undertaken lightly, and it necessarily involves a period of relative social deprivation. It is unlikely to occur very often, and is a slow and painful process. So too the shift in caste ranking is gradual, and occurs only within the limits of the cultural logic of the caste ranking order. The types of legitimation used to explain this ranking order (descendants of the Prophet, rulers, etc.) change very slowly and set strict limits to the possible changes in the ranking order itself. Change occurs only within these limits.

TABLE 2. SOCIAL MOBILITY OF PAKISTANIS IN MANCHESTER

	Individual social mobility		'Caste' mobility		
	'High' castes	'Low' castes	'Landowning' castes	Artisan castes	Service castes
Situation	Personal social mobility—increased wealth/education	Personal social mobility—increased wealth/education	Large proportion of caste members socially mobile—wealth/education	Large proportion of caste members socially mobile—wealth/education	An extended kin group: social mobility—wealth/education
Marriage strategy	(Divorce) Remarriage with wife of urban/educated background	Marriage with woman of higher caste and poor family	Tested through inter-caste marriage—emphasis on biradari of caste members	Tested through inter-caste marriage if possible—emphasis on biradari of caste members	(1) High proportion of first cousin marriages (2) Testing through 'outside' marriage once new caste identity established
Caste	No change in caste—caste irrelevant	Take on in-laws' caste identity	Caste position in the caste hierarchy rises: no change of caste identity	Possible change of affiliation to wider caste category, but no attempt to hide caste identity	Break away of family circle from caste of origin: hiding of former caste identity and new affiliation to a higher caste

(contd)

(Table 2 contd)

	Individual social mobility		'Caste' mobility		
	'High' castes	'Low' castes	'Landowning' castes	Artisan castes	Service castes
Religion	Irrelevant		Public religiosity/ emphasis on western-type values	High degree of religiosity; denial of caste importance through an emphasis on Islam and Islamic ritual	Public religiosity but also an emphasis on western-type values
Case cited	Marriages beyond the biradari or between members of different landowning castes (several cases in in Manchester)	(Reported by Vreede-De Stuers. I did not encounter a case of this type in Manchester)	Arain	Darzi Rawal	Mirasi Nai

CONCLUSION

The analysis of the Muslim zat system raises general theoretical questions about the relation between legitimate and 'unofficial' ideologies. The contrast is not between 'real' and 'ideal', or 'emic' and 'etic'. Both Islam and zat ideologies are explicit and systematic. To argue that the egalitarian ethos of Islam is dominant is, moreover, also misleading since this ideology is continuously undermined by the underlying stress on rank and hierarchy.

The persistence of caste categorization and caste labelling among Pakistani migrants in Manchester stems, I have argued, from the semantic elasticity of the notions of 'zat' and 'biradari', as these are applied to critical levels of social action: familial, economic, political and religious. Caste is not simply a set of residual categories imported from Pakistan. Its viability and continuing relevance for migrants are attested to in their marriage strategies and religious behaviour. The concern of Pakistani migrants with hierarchy continues to be all-pervasive, and is underpinned by the rapid social mobility and wealth of the more fortunate members of the community. Like the vast majority of their British neighbours, they regard class, status and occupation as major concerns. But for British overseas Pakistanis the relation between these and the caste system has been crucially reinstated.

The notion of biradari, we saw, mediates between caste, kinship and locality. For more settled migrants in Manchester, its reference has expanded to include fellow caste members within the city. And because caste has remained a significant category of interaction, strategies of caste mobility have re-emerged locally. As in Pakistan, so too in Manchester: Pakistanis are caught in a dialectic of equality and inequality, of brotherhood and ranking. For a younger generation growing up in Britain, the contradiction between these ideologies or systems of belief is sharpened, highlighting the cultural and personal dilemmas implied by their uneasy coexistence.

APPENDIX: MARRIAGE

Tables A and B are based on fourteen genealogies collected from urban and rural migrants in Manchester. Although I have attempted to select the more reliable genealogies they are inevitably inaccurate. The difficulty of recording genealogies of absent persons is itself indicative of the selective memories of migrants. Although all the migrants interviewed were very cooperative, the exercise appeared to most of them to be futile. It was also remarkable that they rarely remembered the names of children or spouses of relatives born or married while they were in Manchester. Marriages contracted by members of collateral branches were often described simply as marriages within the 'biradari' or as marriages between unrelated persons. This contrasted with the description of marriages of siblings or of first cousins seen regularly, which highlighted the complexity of consanguineous and affinal relationships between the marriage partners, thus making it seem likely that the information provided about the marriages of distant or infrequently seen relatives might be partial or incomplete (see Table B).

In order to attempt to compute rates of endogamy I have selected four genealogies and examined the relationship in marriages of ego's own generation only.

Two of the genealogies are of urban migrants (Arain and Pathan); two are of rural genealogies (both Gujar, one from the Jhelum district, and one from Gujarat district).

These figures are comparable with the rates throughout the Middle East.

TABLE A. RATES OF ENDOGAMY

No. of marriages (Rural/Urban)		1st cousins/ mo's bro.	(1st pat. par. c.)	Exchange/ multiple affinity	Within biradari/ zat	Inter-caste
(R)	15	7	(6)	2	5	1
(U)	20	6	(3)	4	9	1
(R)	16	2	(1)	5 (2 2nd pat.)	9	
(U)	21	10	(1)	3	8	0
Total	72	25	(11)	14	31	2
Perc.	100 %	35 %	(15%)	19 %	43 %	3 %

TABLE B. MARRIAGE PATTERNS

No.	of marriages	1st pat. par.	1st mat. par.	Mos/bro falsis cross c.	Exchange/ multiple affinity	Classif. or 2nd cousins	Intersection/ caste	No. villages/ towns	No. foreign count.	No. divorces
1.	22				2		2	3	8	2
2.	19	1			4	1		7	3	
3.	12		1		2		2 (ca. sec.)	6	1	
4.	23	4		2		4	1	6	1	1
5.	47	5	3	3		1	1 (Irish)	11	5	1
6.	39	4		1	1	4	2 (ca. sec.)	16	5	
7.	22	1	3	1	6		3 (ca. sec.) 1 ca.	6	1	
8.	58	1			2	2	4 (all foreign)	3	7	
9.	30	3				2	5 (2 foreign)	4	5	
10.	25	1	2	2	3	2		5	4	
11.	40		3	2	3	2	4 (hyperg.)	6	4	1
12.	38	6	3	2	5	16	1	8	3	2
13.	21	1	1	1	1	5	1	2	2	
14.	22		2	2	1	4	1	8	5	

NOTES

1. Dumont's contention that there is no disjunction between power and purity among Swat stems from his confusion of the role of saints and Maulvis (1972: 374, fn. 104b). Saints who are powerfully pure descendants of the Prophet's daughter can act as intercessors with God. They are placed above the dominant ruler Khans in the caste hierarchy. Maulvis, who are mere lay religious officials with some Islamic learning, are placed below them.
2. Lindholm (1986) presents an illuminating cross-cultural comparison of caste-like structures in different Middle and Near Eastern societies. In accepting Dumont's interpretation of Barth, however, I feel he does not do full justice to the brilliance of the latter's highly integrated analysis.
3. The exception are a few goldsmiths, barbers and artisans.
4. On the role of the Barber in ritual cf. Leach (1958).
5. Alavi denies the internal ranking of zymindar castes (1972: 26). He argues that for Muslims below the level of *ashraf*, caste ranking is obscure in the literature as well as in fact. This obscurity should not be confused with the ambiguity of ranking in the middle range of Hindu castes. In the latter case the principle of ranking is not in question, and ambiguity in ranking is accompanied by the process of Sanskritisation, by which changes in caste are established and proclaimed. There is no analogous process among Muslims (1971: 115). My view, as demonstrated below, is that the *principle* of caste ranking does always exist, as does the equivalent process of ritual intensification.
6. A possible explanation of this high rate of endogamy might be that the village was composed of refugee families who were first establishing marriages with one another in the current generation before seeking them with other villages.
7. This goes against Alavi's view that small landholders marry mainly within the village (1972). The village did, however, have a high rate of labour migration.
8. Cf. also Inayat Ullah who reports that castes are divided between factions (*pati*) (Ullah 1958). This usage of pati was one I also encountered in Manchester in relation to one intrafamilial dispute.
9. There are some migrants in Manchester from peripheral areas: Mirpur, the North-West Frontier, Baluchistan and Karachi, as well as those originating from various other regions of India (Gujarat, Uttar Pradesh, etc). These migrants either form small encapsulated groups or attach themselves to one of the other major categories of migrants.
10. For Hindu caste mobility cf. Blunt 1969: 50-5; Bailey 1957; Srinivas 1968; Pocock 1972; van der Veen 1972; Parry 1979. For Muslims cf. Barth 1959: 13-31, 1960: 113-46; Vreede-De Stuers 1968: 4-7; I. Ahmad 1978b: 171-206.

11. Jeffery (1976) also emphasizes the assumption of class lifestyles and symbolic modes of behaviour, but this would seem to be only one aspect of a more general pattern of social mobility.

REFERENCES

Ahmad, Imtiaz. 1976a. 'Introduction'. In I. Ahmad, ed., *Family, Kinship and Marriage among Muslims in India*, pp. xvii-xxxiv. New Delhi: Manohar.

———. 1976b. 'Caste and kinship in a Muslim village in Uttar Pradesh'. In I. Ahmad, ed., *Family, Kinship and Marriage among Muslims in India*, pp. 319-45. New Delhi: Manohar.

———. 1978a. 'Introduction', In I. Ahmad, ed., *Caste and Social Stratification among Muslims in India*, pp. 1-18. New Delhi: Manohar.

———. 1978b. 'Endogamy and status mobility among the Siddiqui Sheikhs of Allahabad, Uttar Pradesh'. In I. Ahmad, ed., *Caste and Social Stratification among Muslims in India*, pp. 171-206. New Delhi: Manohar.

———. 1981. *Ritual and Religion among Muslims in India*. New Delhi: Manohar.

Ahmad, Saghir. 1971. 'Social stratification in a Punjabi village'. *Contributions to Indian Sociology* (n.s.) 4: 105-25.

———. 1977. *Class and Power in a Punjabi Village*. New York: Monthly Review Press.

Alavi, Hamza. 1971. 'The politics of dependence: A village in West Punjab'. *South Asian Review* 4: 111-28.

———. 1972. 'Kinship in West Punjab Villages'. *Contributions to Indian Sociology* (n.s.) 6: 1-27.

Barth, Fredrik. 1959. *Political Leadership among Swat Pathans*. LSE Monographs in Social Anthropology 19. London: Athelone Press.

———. 1960. 'The system of social stratification in Swat, north Pakistan'. In E.R. Leach, ed., *Aspects of Caste in South India, Ceylon and North-West Pakistan*, pp. 113-45. Cambridge Papers in *Social Anthropology* 2. Cambridge: Cambridge University Press.

Bailey, F.G. 1957. *Caste and the Economic Frontier: A village in Highland Orissa*. Manchester: Manchester University Press.

Beteille, A. 1964. 'A note on the referents of caste'. *European Journal of Sociology* V: 130-4.

———. 1965. *Caste, Class and Power*. Berkeley: University of California Press.

Blunt, E.H.A. 1969. *The Caste System of Northern India*. Delhi: S. Chand.

Coon, C. 1953. *Caravan: The story of the Middle East*. New York: Holt.

Das, Veena. 1984. 'For a folk theology and theoretical anthropology of Islam'. *Contributions to Indian Sociology* (n.s.) 18: 293-300.

Dumont, Louis. 1972 (1966). *Homo Hierarchicus*. London: Paladin.

———. 1983. 'A modified view of our origins: The Christian beginnings of modern individualism'. *Contributions to Indian Sociology* (n.s.) 17, 1: 1-26.

Eglar, Zekiye. 1960. *A Punjabi Village in Pakistan.* New York: Columbia University Press.

Jeffery, Patricia. 1976. *Migrants and Refugees: Muslim and Christian Pakistani Families in Bristol.* Cambridge: Cambridge University Press.

Lambat, Ismail A. 1976. 'Marriage among the Sunni Surati Vohras of south Gujarat.' In I. Ahmad, ed., *Family, Kinship and Marriage among the Muslims in India,* pp. 49-81. New Delhi: Manohar.

Leach, E.R. 1958. 'Magical hair'. *Journal of the Royal Anthropological Institute* 88: 146-64.

Lindholm, Charles. 1986. 'Caste in Islam and the problem of deviant systems: A critique of recent theory.' *Contribution to Indian Sociology* (n.s.) 20: 61-96.

Mayer, A.C. 1960. *Caste and Kinship in Central India.* London: Routledge and Kegan Paul.

Minault, Gail. 1984. 'Some reflections on Islamic revivalism vs. assimilation among Muslims in India'. *Contributions to Indian Sociology* (n.s.) 18: 301-6.

Parry, Jonathan P. 1979. *Caste and Kinship in Kangra.* London: Routledge and Kegan Paul.

Pocock, David F. 1957. '"Difference" in East Africa: a study of caste and religion in modern Indian society'. *Southwestern Journal of Anthropology* 13, 4: 289-300

———. 1960. 'Sociologies: Urban and rural'. *Contributions to Indian Sociology* 4: 63-81.

———. 1972. *Kanbi and Patidar.* Oxford: Clarendon Press.

Robinson, F. 1983. 'Islam and Muslim society in South Asia'. *Contributions to Indian Sociology* (n.s.) 17: 185-203.

Srinivas, M.N. 1968. 'Mobility in the caste system'. In M. Singer and B.S. Cohn, eds., *Structure and Change in Modern India,* pp. 189-200. Chicago: Aldine.

———. 1984. 'Some reflections on the nature of caste hierarchy'. *Contributions to Indian Sociology* (n.s.) 18, 2: 151-67.

Ullah, Inayat. 1958. 'Caste, patti and faction in the life of a Punjab village'. *Sociologus* 8: 36-46.

van der Veen, Klaas W. 1972. *I give thee my daughter.* Assen: Van Gorcum.

Vreede-De Stuers, Cora. 1968. *Parda: A Study of Muslim Women's Life in Northern India.* Assen: Van Gorcum.

Werbner, Pnina. 1979. 'Avoiding the ghetto: Pakistani migrants and settlement shifts in Manchester'. *New Community* 7: 376-89.

———. 1985. 'The organisation of giving and ethnic elites'. *Ethnic and Racial Studies* 8, 3: 368-88.

———. 1986. 'The virgin and the clown: Ritual elaboration in Pakistani Weddings'. *Man* (n.s.) 21: 227-50.

———. 1987. 'Enclave economics and family firms: Pakistani traders in a British city'. In Jeremy S. Eades, ed., *Migration, Labour and Social Order*, pp. 213-33. ASA Monograph 25. London: Tavistock.

———. 1988. 'Sealing the Koran: Symbolic orientations among Pakistani migrants'. *Cultural Dynamics* 1, 1.

Mullahs, Migrants, Miracles: Travel and Transformation in Sylhet

KATY GARDNER
(1993)

I. INTRODUCTION

Dominating the courtyard of the homestead of Abdul Hossain is a large and ostentatious shrine. Decorated with Arabic designs and words, and surrounded by flags, the shrine (*mazaar*) is similar to hundreds of similarly venerated graves scattered over the landscape of rural Sylhet, in north-east Bangladesh. It proclaims for all to see that the late Abdul Hossain is a *pir*. It is a social recognition of his spiritual power; by giving offerings and directing prayers towards it, believers can gain the help of an intermediary with privileged access to God. The presence of a pir in their lineage is thought to signify great religious purity amongst family members. As part of a pir's lineage, they are inherently more holy than others. Indeed men in subsequent generations will inherit their ancestor's holiness and, if they study and lead pure lives they may themselves become pirs, receiving the devotion, submission and offerings of disciples who come in search of guidance and help.

All this is familiar in South Asia, where pirs (often described as Sufi saints [Ewing 1980: 1]) are key figures in local Islam. Pirs, it is argued, enabled 'orthodox' Sunni faith to merge with indigenous culture when it was first introduced to the region, thus ensuring its acceptance amongst the masses (Cashin 1988; Haq 1975; Roy 1982; Saiyed 1989). Whilst the notion of 'syncretic' Islam is highly problematic,[1] it rightly indicates the embeddedness of the pir in South Asia: in Bengal, pirs and their shrines are as old as Islam.

Abdul Hossain's case is, however, distinctly contemporary. Unlike most pirs, he had no followers during his lifetime, and claims that he is a pir have only been made some years after his death. His cult is also exclusively confined to members of his immediate patrilineage. Indeed, their assertions that they are now part of a pir lineage, and as such are more inherently holy than the hoi-polloi, are generally scoffed at by more distant relatives and neighbours. The legitimacy of a pir is always of course a social construct (Ewing 1980). But of particular interest in the construction of Abdul Hossain's pir-hood, is its relationship to change in his family's economic status and their subsequent attempts to transform their own religious status. Like many other local shrines, the mazaar of Abdul Hossain is partly a result of overseas migration. More than the donations of devoted disciples, it was funded by remittances sent by family members in Britain.

*

The shrine is a useful entrance to the two main themes of this paper: the spiritual transformations and miracles of pirs; and the economic opportunities, and subsequent economic transformations of migration. Both types of transformation are interrelated; but rather than migration unilineally affecting religious beliefs and behaviour, the relationship is more circular.

Originally, I suggest, migrants were part of the culture of miracles. The economic transformations resulting from migration have however led to a gradual rejection of charismatic pirs. But rather than moving away from their cults to complete monotheism, change has come internally; the cults have themselves been transformed. The legitimacy of this new breed of pirs no longer rests upon charisma and miracles, but instead upon scripturalism and notions of 'orthodoxy'. Abdul Hossain's family, for example, asserts that his power is derived from his knowledge of Quranic texts and Islamic learning. Unlike the followers of most pirs, they do not claim him to be the agent of miracles and today, activities at his *urs* (death anniversary) are very different from those of most pir cults. There is no singing, ecstatic dancing or *dhikir* (repetition), but instead recitation of the Quran and *namaz* (formal prayer). Like so many of their neighbours, Abdul Hossain's family members are also migrants.

Tiny and kin-based as it is, the cult is thus part of far wider processes in Sylhet, and intimately tied to sweeping changes that have come to the region in recent decades. These have been largely engendered by the widespread migration of many Sylhetis abroad, primarily to Britain, but also to the Middle East, USA and Western Europe. This and the consequent enrichment and leaps in social status of migrant families, is closely associated with growing Islamic 'purism' in the area (and by this I mean the increasing influence of Quranic text reference of the *Shar'iat* and stress on *adab* or correct procedures). These practices, and the boundary between what is and is not acceptable are the subjects of continual negotiation between different groups.

Pirs, and the continually disputed criteria for their legitimacy, straddle this boundary. Although some of the most orthodox disclaim any allegiance to pirs, others have redefined their pirs as Sunni holy men of the highest scriptural tradition, separating themselves from the cults of charisma and miracles which are increasingly left to the poor and powerless. There is therefore a growing polarization between purist activities and belief and what is increasingly being interpreted by the economically and politically powerful as 'incorrect' religious behaviour.

II. A CULTURE OF MIRACLES: BENGALI PIRS

No comprehensive description of Bengali Islam is possible without reference to pirs (Roy 1982), although at times the category covers such a broad range of characters that there is danger of it becoming meaningless. In general it is associated with Sufism (Ewing 1980; Lewis 1985; Nanda and Talib 1989), but this too covers a whole spectrum of beliefs and categories (Baldick 1989; Cashin 1988; Wilson 1983). In Sylhet pirs are sometimes saints of the highest order such as Shah Jalal (who, it is generally agreed, introduced Islam to Sylhet), or the 360 disciples who came with him and who have acquired pir status (Roy 1982). The term may also be used for various figures shared with local Hindus such as Kwaz, the 'saint' of fishermen (Blanchet 1984; Saiyed 1989), or simply for ordinary *mullahs* (clergy) when the speaker wishes to denote particular respect.

In the cults of living pirs, devotees express extreme deference and subservience (Nanda and Talib 1989). The pir is believed to possess special spiritual power, which allows him to communicate with God, and to be a vehicle for miracles. Only through his guidance, it is believed, can God be found. Many followers of pir cults in rural Sylhet speak of their need for a guide to teach them holy ways and act as an intermediary with God. Others may visit the pir at times of particular need: sickness, economic crisis, marital problems, and so on, bringing material offerings (*shinni*) such as sacrificial meat. The pir usually responds to requests for help with *tapiz* (amulets), *foo* (blowing on supplicant), or in some cases the utterance of a *mantra* (blessing with holy power). How effective these are depends on how powerful the pir is thought to be, or how 'hot'. The hotter a pir, the more transformative power he is thought to have.[2]

In Talukpur, the migrant village where I worked, not everybody follows a living pir. Whilst all villagers told me the greatest pir is Shah Jalal, only a small proportion claimed to have a living pir. Most of those who did belonged to the poorest families, which have not enjoyed the benefits of migration. These families cited a holy man in Eeshabpur a nearby village as their pir. Generally they had been introduced through kin, or had inherited cult membership from their parents which they would pass on to their own children. Others cited different pirs, usually living locally. Whilst many did not visit their pir, regularly, all told me they would visit in times of need. The following are statements made by the villagers who today tend to be the poorest and most marginalized, about their pir.

> People carry him from here to there on their heads. They bring a throne and carry him on it. What this man says has effect. . . .
>
> The pir gives directions on how to lead my life. He shows me a straight path. I serve him and he tells me to fast pray and in what way to lead my life. If I do the things which my guru orders then I will go straight to Heaven. I sit by the pir and he tells me how to order my life. . . .

The power of a pir is thought to increase at death (Troll 1989). Their graves are venerated as shrines, whilst disciples or male next of kin usually inherit the saintly mantle. Like the caliph, the line of descent from the prophet the pir creates a holy line, in which descendants are closer than others to Allah. Many Sylheti cults are based around shrines of the dead. Soil and water from these are believed to contain *mortaba* (spiritual power) and effect cures in the sick. On the anniversary of the pir's death an urs is held. This usually involves singing into the night, drumming, and ecstatic dancing. Although I was never able to attend, the few villagers prepared to enlighten me whispered that ganja (marihuana) and prostitution were sometimes present at urs.

The legitimacy of pirs is generally based upon evidence that they are the vehicles of miracles seen as proof of their special relationship with God. These miracles invariably involve the transcendence of 'natural' law and reversal of apparent realities. These events were recounted by the followers of a local pir:

He didn't go [visiting] by boat, but wearing shoes, walking over the water. This is the proof of his saintliness; then people believed he was a saint, that he had strength, and they called him pir. . . .[3]

Some people were saying our pir was a cheat. One day they decided to prove whether he was pir or a fake. They hid some copper in the house where he was staying, then they closed the doors and set fire to it. Later, they found that those coins had melted but the pir had been not touched.

A child lay dead, her funeral shroud around her. The pir appeared and looked into her face and suddenly she was alive. Then he turned himself into a tiger, and ran off into the jungle.

Pirs, then, can transform their bodies and transcend elements which defeat normal men and women. They usually have healing powers and people who are not followers of a specific cult often visit when sick. If he is alive they will receive the pir's foo and amulets, if dead they will take soil from his mazaar. Because he has a special relationship with God he may also be able to influence events in a follower's life and for this reason pirs are often visited in times of crisis. An amulet or blessing may bring back an errant husband make a woman fertile or cure a man of sickness. Specialist pirs also exist who can find stolen property or detect thieves. Again, these pirs are often only visited in times of pressing need. Through devotion to a pir, then, followers are given a chance of escaping a state of affairs which seems inevitable.

This transformative ability extends to economic affairs. In the lines of a devotional song popular amongst labourers: 'My guru is a precious thing. He makes iron into pure gold.' Indeed whilst the pir's power is spiritual, and may be strengthened by his own asceticism, he may have the power to bring wealth to his followers. Poverty brings one closer to God, followers of pirs assert; but in turn, closeness to God can bring prosperity. Local myths often stress the economic transformations brought about by pirs. In one, the family of a labourer who stumbled upon the relics of a dead pir's grave was rewarded with great prosperity when they built a mazaar on the site and venerated it as a holy place. A similar link between holiness and wealth is echoed in many devotional Sufi songs:

Oh Great Guru, nobody returns from your court empty-handed: Allah gave his riches to Roussel; Allah disappeared;

Khaza received Allah's wealth and stayed in Ajmir; Khaza, everyone goes to your shrine:

If somebody wants something, he will give from his unlimited treasures.[4]

It is this which brings me to migration which, too, has led to economic transformation. I suggest later that overseas migration from Sylhet was originally informed by beliefs in the miraculous. But while the earliest migrants were initially part of the culture of the pirs and their miracles, many now follow a different religious path. Their transformation has been so radical that they now reject the charismatic pir, changing him into something more fitting to their new social and religious status.

III. MIRACULOUS TRANSFORMATION AND MIGRATION IN SYLHET

As Eickelman and Piscatori point out (1990: 259), the relationship between migration and religious change has been little examined by anthropologists. With a few exceptions, studies of labour migration are mainly located under the broad rubric of political economy concentrating upon economic and political change but neglecting the ideological concomitants of such change. Those studies which do exist tend to focus entirely upon how religious belief and behaviour are affected by migration rather than examining the interrelationship of economic change and ideology as a two-way process. In Sylhet, however, whilst labour migration is at one level controlled by external economic forces it is itself influenced by ideologies of transformation central to local Islamic belief. In turn, migration and economic prosperity have contributed to religious change and especially to a rejection of belief in miraculous transformation.

There are interesting similarities between the miracles of the pirs and migration. Both involve transformation on many levels. Just as the pir cited earlier can 'turn iron into pure gold', migration has enabled many families to reinvent themselves as high status landowners. Like the miracles of the pirs, travel involves a crossing, and redefinition of boundaries (Eickelman and Piscatori 1990: 5). More significantly, the spirit with which migration takes place often involves belief in the possibility of miracles, of being able to turn the world around and be transformed. As we shall see, in both instances, reality is not necessarily fixed; the given order of affairs can be changed.

Migration to Britain from Bangladesh is a peculiarly Sylheti phenomenon. Although South Asians have always migrated overseas (Clarke 1990), and migrants to the Middle East come from all over Bangladesh (Islam et al. 1987). Migration to the UK has been mainly monopolized by Sylhetis who, from the nineteenth century onwards were employed by British ship companies and travelled the world as crew (Adams 1987; Eade 1986). Their success is partly explained by the fortuitous success of a number of Sylheti *sarengs* (foremen, who controlled employment), who understandably favoured their kinsmen and fellow countrymen in recruitment. Although work on the ships was punishing, by village standards profits were considerable: a year's work in a ship's engine rooms might enable a man to buy land or build a new house. Anyway, many seamen did not confine themselves to the seas, jumping ship once they had docked, and seeking their fortune on dry land. Most of those who smuggled themselves ashore did so in London. A small but steadily increasing population of Sylhetis was established in Britain by the early 1950s (Adams 1987; Peach 1990).

Over the 1950s, the numbers increased dramatically. The post-war British economy needed cheap and plentiful labour, much of which was recruited from South Asia. It was a case *par excellence* of chain migration: just as ship workers helped their kin find work, so also British-based Sylhetis now helped each other to migrate. By the late 1960s, however, the situation had changed. British industry had declined, and immigrant labour was no longer in demand. New laws, radically curtailing entrance to Britain, were introduced. Alarmed by the increasing insecurity of their situations, most migrants responded by applying for British passports and sending for their wives and children (Ballard 1990: 219-47). At the same time, many Sylhetis switched from redundancy-prone factory work to the business of restaurants capitalising on a growing British appetite for curry. Since the early days when single men travelled to the West and returned every couple of years to their villages, things have greatly changed. Children are born and bred British, and the notion held by many migrants in the 1960s and 1970s that their stay in Britain was strictly temporary, and only to earn money, has increasingly faded (Carey and Shukur 1985; Eade 1990).

Meanwhile in Sylhet, a new form of labour migration had appeared by the 1970s, with the increasing importance to the Bangladesh economy of labour migration to the Middle East (Hossain 1985; Islam et al. 1987). Legally migrants can only enter these countries with official work contracts, which are sold by brokers for considerable sum. In Sylhet, many households without members in Britain have quickly taken advantage of this new opportunity, obtaining contracts for their young men and hoping for similar economic rewards. Other migrants enter illegally. These men face great insecurity. Working casually, often in the construction industry, or as street vendors, they have no legal rights and, if caught, face immediate deportation (Owens 1985). Although some have grown rich from Middle Eastern earnings, many do not recoup the initial capital expenditure. Others are cheated by brokers who take their money, but never deliver the promised contracts. In spite of such experiences, however, migration is perceived as the main economic opportunity available, and many households send their sons abroad more than once.

Just as the nature of migration has changed, so have the migrant villages (Gardner 1990, 1991). Those with high levels of overseas migration are startlingly distinct. Rather than the mud and thatch huts typical of Bangladesh, these villages are filled with stone houses; sometimes two or even three storeys high. The migrant villages seem prosperous, replete with material evidence of their overseas success and a far cry from the impoverishment of much of rural Bangladesh. Similar remittance-induced 'booms' have been noted elsewhere in Asia (Ballard 1983; Kessinger 1979; Watson 1975).

In Sylhet, most migrant families have indeed enjoyed a success story of sorts. The original migrants, whilst not usually destitute, were by no means the wealthiest of their villages. Some were even landless, helped in their migration by the patronage and loans of better-off kin or neighbours. Many were originally small landowners with just enough capital to pay for the initial costs of migration. These men returned home rich, investing their earnings in land, the vital commodity upon which the well-being and position of all households in rural Bangladesh depends. Most became moderate, or very large, landowners (Gardner 1990).

And so by the 1970s, when men who had been working in Britain had accumulated enough money to convert themselves from small owner-cultivators or sharecroppers to large landowners, people began to appreciate that fortunes could be made abroad. Given these leaps in fortune, foreign countries have increasingly been viewed as a source of great bounty, the means of economic transformation. In the eyes of those who have never been abroad, migration is something of a miracle:

> Now if I go to London I'll get big and strong.... Our poverty will be over. (A landless sharecropper.)

A poor man can get rich-but only by going abroad. (A sharecropper)

This economic miracle is very real. In Talukpur, landowning is strongly correlated with migration to Britain and the Middle East. Of the seventy households, only twenty-six are not involved in migration; over half have family members in Britain, and the rest are in the Middle East. Of the twenty-five landless households, only one has experienced migration to the West, whereas of the twenty-seven richest landowning households, i.e. those with over six acres, only one has no migrant members. These patterns have radically changed since the 1950s. Most households with British migrants were originally small to medium landowners, and some were landless. Within a few decades, their economic positions have been transformed.

Correspondingly, those without access to foreign wages have found it increasingly difficult to compete in the struggle for local resources. During the period of most intense migration in the 1960s. when migrants struggled to buy as many fields as possible, local prices shot up. To buy fields today foreign income is crucial. Other price rises—in labour, basic commodities and agricultural technology—have also contributed, making it increasingly hard for a small plot without capital behind it to be viable. The processes of land loss are as common in Sylhet as elsewhere in the country (Hartman and Boyce 1983; Jansen 1987). But in migrant areas, high prices offered to owners may have been a further incentive to sell, and once landless they had little chance of climbing back on to the landowning ladder. In sum, there has been increasing polarisation between the migrants and the non-migrants.

Migration overseas has thus become something which non-migrants dream of, and aspire to. Families without migrants constantly seek ways to gain access to the opportunities which they perceive migration to offer, however low their chances might seem to the dispassionate outsider. Many households sell their few fields to fund a trip to 'Saudi', and even if cheated once will take further loans to try again. In Talukpur several households have lost all their land through their desperate attempts to join the category of 'migrant': a common fate in Sylhet.

Whilst the economic transformation brought about by migration is of a different order to the miracles of pirs, I suggest that belief in the latter has influenced the spirit in which migration has been carried out. One example of this is the risk-taking involved in migration. As we have seen, potential migrants sometimes gamble away all their land on the chance of buying a work contract for the Middle East. When they are cheated, or the illegal migrant caught and deported before he can recoup his expenditures, their households tend to accept the disaster as part of the destiny which they tried to change through migration, but failed. In this view, life is something which can be radically changed, if God will it.

The lives of successful migrants are often filled with instances of risk-taking. Some, for example, have become involved in gambling, the illusory promise of instant fortune. The life histories of older British-Sylhetis often illustrate the connection between risk, gambling and migration. Problems with gambling were mentioned to me by several families with male members in Britain, and the earlier stages of migration: leaving for Calcutta, jumping ship, hiding out illegally, and going wherever there appeared to be economic opportunity, all involved risk. Contrary to Rodinson's conclusion that Islamic entrepreneurs tend to shy away from potential risks, preferring investments which bring certain gains (1974: 161), it seems that amongst Sylheti Muslims, at least, risk is an accepted element in the quest for economic transformation. Rather than a slow but steady process of accumulation, many prefer to gamble everything in the hope of a miracle.

In many cases, the gamble has paid off and the economic and social positions of the migrants have been transformed. Not only have they acquired land, but they have built new houses, educated their children, hired extra labour so that family members no longer need to work in the fields, and generally become high status landowners. This has not simply involved worldly change, but in many cases also a transformation of religious status which, in turn, has involved a rejection of the culture of miracles.

Migrants tend to present themselves as more pious than other villagers. By sending their sons to *madrasas,* contributing to funds for local mosques, and being freed from manual labour to spend more time studying the Quran, many migrant families have become highly religious. Many can now afford to perform *haj,* usually on their way back from Britain, or after working in the Middle East. This is of course the ultimate spiritual transformation: *hajjis* are deemed to have been purified of worldly sin and are treated with special respect and deference. As part of their reinvention some families have literally rewritten their histories, renaming their lineages with Islamic titles such as Khan and Sheikh. In Talukpur, various lineages have only been known by these prestigious titles for one or two generations. As others comment: 'They only started to write their name like that after he made money in London.' This use of prestigious Islamic titles by those whose economic status has improved has been described in many Muslim groups of South Asia (Vreede-De Stuers 1968: 3). In these cases, religious behaviour, and outward signs such as Islamic titles, are used to indicate a change in social position: relative religiousity becomes the explicit issue in implicit negotiations of status and power.

IV. MIGRATION AND THEOLOGIES OF THE SELF

Given these worldly changes, it is not surprising that many successful migrants now have very different ideas about destiny from poorer non-migrants. While the poor tend to declare that 'Allah gave us this position, so how can we change it?', the rich often assert that 'Allah helps those who help themselves'. Migrants and non-migrants also express remarkably different opinions about their relationship to God. Everyone agrees that 'Allah has no partners', but poorer, non-migrant villagers argue that only those with God-given mortaba can pray to Allah directly: ordinary mortals must use a pir as an intermediary in their relationship to God. In the theology of many of the richer men in Talukpur, however, Allah can be approached directly, and wealth is the reward He gives the pious. Thus, whilst the followers of living pirs are unable to face God directly, because in the words of one man: 'I am nothing', migrants tend to make statements similar to this one of a return migrant from Germany: 'If a man leads a pure life, prays, does Haj and attends religious events, then he can pray direct to God.'

Related to these differences, those who visit living pirs in Talukpur today are invariably poor men and women, who have little power to control their circumstances. It is these people who speak openly of the pir that their family follows, or who visit pirs in times of trouble. It is the poorest villagers, too, who most often state that they cannot approach God alone, and need an intermediary. For them, the pir is a middleman to an unapproachable God: at times he may be treated almost like a deity himself.[5] In Talukpur it is not true that only the poor have pirs; but the richer men, who have taken control of their own destinies, tend to have different beliefs about fate and their relationship with God. Rather than a simple dichotomy between migrants and non-migrants, then, there is a continuum: most of the younger, better educated men of migrant families tend not to believe in living pirs. Many richer men visit pirs in times of extreme crisis, but even then do not wear tapiz for, as one woman explained it: 'Men don't like to wear amulets because others would see them in the bazzar, and they'd be ashamed.' It is these men who are increasingly opposed to the miraculous cults.

In the second part of this paper I shall show how alongside, and partly because of the economic transformations of Sylheti migration, there has been a shift in attitudes towards God, and in religious behaviour. This involves a new emphasis on scripturalism; Islamic purity, and the international community of Islam. It has also entailed a rejection of what are now termed 'impurities', or activities which are closer to Hindu or tantric practices than those of Sunni orthodoxy. Alongside growing economic differentiation, then, has come religious differentiation in which the richer and educated members of the village continually seek to dismiss the religious activities of the poor as 'impure' or 'incorrect'. Pirs, however, are still important, for some families seeking to assert their new social status have reinvented their pirs or claimed that they themselves are descendants of a pir. The pirs of rich migrant families have thus themselves been transformed.

V. THE NEW PURITY, MIGRATION AND RELIGIOUS CHANGE

While reformism is nothing new in the history of religion (Caplan 1987a), it is true that the direction of change in many contemporary Islamic societies is towards a 'new traditionalism', an increasing puritanism which seeks to reject the old, localized ways (see, for example, Gilsenan 1982; Roy 1982). In Sylhet, modernity, if that is how we are to describe the increasing importance of international migration and foreign revenue in the area, has been met with increased religious fervour. Indeed, return migrants are often the keenest to assert a traditionalism (in this case in the form of religious orthodoxy) which, as many writers have shown, is invariably a social construct, the product of contemporary circumstances and continual reinterpretation of the slippery past (Bourdieu 1977; Cohen 1985; Hobsbawm and Ranger 1983). Clearly, modernity must not be confused with secularization (Caplan 1987a: 10).

I defined purism earlier as stress on adab: correct religious procedure as laid down by the Quran and other sources of Islamic law such as the Hadith and Shar'iat. It is concerned with the 'fundamentals' of the Islamic tradition, presented as enshrined in the holy text. Such concepts of 'orthodoxy' are however highly problematic (Baldick 1989: 7). Movements aiming to purify local Islam, or what we might term Islamic 'revivalism' are not new to South Asia, but have tended to erupt periodically, especially in the face of external threats such as British colonialism (Metcalf 1982; Roy 1982). The link of Islamic 'revivalism' to political resistance or its rise as a reaction to political inequality has been noted in many parts of the Muslim world (see, for example, Geertz 1968; Gellner 1981). In the Sudan, for example, where Sufi saints, or marabouts were politically and economically powerful, the puritanical Wahabi movement has challenged the hierarchy of the marabouts through their rejection of mysticism and insistence on Muslim equality (Amselle 1987). In a similar vein, as Asim Roy has argued, Islamic revivalism in Bengal at the end of the twentieth century was a reaction against colonial domination and heralded a rejection of traditional Bengali syncretism (Roy 1982). This argument provides a useful insight into the link between colonialism and religious reformism. It is especially pertinent for people who have a long history of contact with the West, and who today are continuing that relationship through migration.

Islamic purism in Sylhet is not simply the product of overseas migration, but it is linked with it. At the most practical level, this has to do with economic change. Within migrant villages it is predominantly the richest men (who usually have experience of migration, or whose close kin have migrated) who are most interested in enforcing what they define as 'orthodoxy'. This is the key to the acquisition of status, and it is the richer families who are most able to manipulate its definition. I suggest that this association with doctrinal purity and economic class has always existed, and that there has always been religious heterogeneity amongst local Muslims in Sylhet. Roy for example, mentions the presence of a small Ashraf elite in Bengal, descendants of the original Muslim invaders (1982). A minority of wealthy and educated people probably always leaned to the higher-status Sunni textual tradition. For the vast majority, however, this was out of reach since they could not read Arabic, or afford many of the religious activities which I describe below.

Migration has meant that in some parts of Sylhet, whole villages, or many households within them, have become relatively prosperous. Suddenly religious activities, which have always been revered, have become accessible. As we have already seen, families can now pay for sons to learn Arabic, can perform haj, and so on. It is not surprising that they should seek to differentiate their religious activities from those of the poorer, illiterate neighbours. At the same time, far wider processes have affected the way that Islam is viewed locally. Missionary movements such as Tablighi Jama'at[6] and the political parties such as Jama'at i' Islam have grown rapidly over recent decades. The growth of mass communications, which can reach remote villages such as Talukpur, has aided the spread of doctrinalism, and nationally the ideal of the community of Islam has in many ways taken the place of secular Bengali nationalism (Eade 1990). Similar processes have been at work all over South Asia.

There are other links between overseas migration and increased purism in Sylhet. Migrants to Britain and the Middle East have moved from an Islam based around localized cults and moulded to the culture and geography of the homelands, to an international Islam of Muslims from many different countries and cultures. This international Islam is one of universals: the holy texts are the only common language, and Mecca is the only universally perceived centre (Metcalf 1982: 12). This, of course, is not confined only to migrant communities, but involves a global spread of ideas, and perceived homogeneity (Gilsenan 1982: 18). In this perspective, the localized shrines of Sylheti pirs can only be perceived as peripheral.[7] In their new locations, Bengali Muslims had now, with other Muslim groups, to construct new communities based around the ideals of an international brotherhood of Islam and a central body of texts.

Travel and moving into a foreign culture may also prompt a heightened sense of 'being a Muslim' (Eickelman and Piscatori 1990: 16). The increasing importance of this identity, and its expression through revivalist movements is a common reaction both to imperialism (Metcalf 1982) and to being a beleaguered minority. As Caplan notes (1987a: 22), amongst all so-called 'fundamentalist' groups is a strong sense of 'otherness'. Thus, while not all migrants are interested in Islamic revivalism, many have been forced to define themselves first and foremost as Muslim, and in their religious institutions, their mosques, madrasas and festivals, increasingly join with other Muslims to create a universalist Islam (Eade 1990).

VI. RELIGIOUS PRACTICE IN TALUKPUR

It would be incorrect to present religion in Talukpur in terms of a straightforward dichotomy between 'purists' and non-purists. Amongst the majority Muslim population, there is much shared ground. All Muslims believe in certain basics (the five pillars of faith, the Day of Judgement, Heaven and Hell, and so on), and all attempt to follow basic Islamic laws.[8] Religious behaviour is thus a continuum, with the most puritanical situated at one end, and the least at the other. This continuum tends to reflect economic levels within the community. Those who are the most puritanical reject religious practices not derived directly from what they define as the Tradition. As the *imam* of one of the richest household's private mosque put it:

> Is not all milk white? Yet one drop of urine from a cow will ruin the whole bucket. Is it not so that one tiny prick will burst a balloon, one hole will sink a boat? In this way, one mistake will spoil someone's religiosity.

The purist end of the continuum is represented by the mosque and the village madrasa—the small Islamic college where students learn Islamic history and Quranic verse by heart. This madrasa and its students are part of the Tablighi Jama'at movement. Every year they organize a *wa'az* (preaching): an event for all local men, where renowned mullahs (those learned in the Quran and other holy texts) come to the village to preach and pray. The event lasts for twenty-four hours: the prayers and words of the mullah are broadcast across the fields all night. Men who attended told me that the sermons stressed the need for increased purity and rejection of 'incorrect' practices. The visitors had also urged them to keep their women in stricter purdah.

The behaviour of family women is an immediate indicator of piety, and extremely important for families anxious to assert their religious status. The less women are seen by outsiders, the more 'correct' the family is seen to be. This, like many other external signs of piety, is far easier for richer families to maintain. Seclusion costs money. The verandahs built around houses, the rickshaws and even *shrori* (covered sedan chairs) hired to carry women, the *burqas*, and, most importantly, the ability to keep women within the household and not send them out to earn wages, all demand a certain level of prosperity, which many non-migrant families do not have. Most landless women in the village are forced to seek work outside their own household. As they say, 'Who can bother with purdah when her belly is empty?'

Other external indicators of piety are also more available to the richer families. All of these are seen as increasing the virtue which an individual accumulates over his or her lifetime and which is reviewed on the Day of Judgement. Such activities include Haj, donations to the mosque or madrasa, and the *korbani* (offering of generous sacrifice) at religious festivals. Orthodox households may also hold *milads* (functions in which local mullahs and madrasa students visit for prayers and donations of shinni). These are held to mark the death anniversary of an ancestor, or on various dates in the religious calender,[9] and can generate religious merit for the entire household. Again, only the more prosperous households can afford to hold a milad.

Religious virtue can also be gained through knowledge of Islamic texts and of Arabic. For households which can pay the costs, this can be taught to children by a resident mullah. Those who have read the Quran are also accorded special religious status, as are those who can write Arabic. Hajjis too, as we have seen, have a special spiritual status. It is thus possible to invest financially in religious merit, which not only ensures a smooth transition to Heaven, but much worldly power too.

In many ways purism is defined not so much by what it represents, but more by what it opposes. The most puritanical of the village seek to banish a host of beliefs and customs which, as they are marginalized, are increasingly associated with the 'ignorance' of women and poor men. Examples of activities dismissed as 'ignorant' or 'incorrect' are devotion to Kwaz, the pir (or Hindu god) of water, or to Loki, a spirit of the house.[10] The poorest Muslim women pray and offer shinni (ritual offerings, usually food) to both Kwaz and Loki, but women from richer households deny belief in them. Other activities said to lead to punishment in this or the after-life include singing, use of drums, and dancing. In the company of the most pious, those who have performed haj, for example, such activities can barely be mentioned. All the songs which I recorded, many of which were devotional Sufi songs, were sung in secret by women or landless labourers, far from the ears of the household head.

It is this secrecy which most indicates the degree of division in Talukpur. Whilst economic and social power does not determine an individual's beliefs, the puritanical tend to be the most powerful men of the village. It is these men who are most keen to impose their new pieties on women and labourers who, in turn, are increasingly ashamed of their activities. 'We'll tell you when Abba goes to the bazaar!' the women of my household would declare, and it was only as his figure disappeared down the path that the stories of spirits and the songs would start. Likewise, when landless women showed me their traditional Bengali dances, the doors of their hut had first to be bolted. Reflecting the same division certain information is seen as directly oppositional to religiosity. Discussions about magic, the healing powers of medicine men, and spirits, invariably had to stop when Abba was saying his prayers, even though he was in another room.

Many of the activities which the puritanical condemn are central to the pir cults of the poor. Since urs involve singing, dancing and drumming, they are depicted by the religiosity respectable as shocking in the extreme. At an urs of Shah Jalal, held during my fieldwork, a return migrant attacked a group of excited worshippers for their dancing and drumming.[11] The assertion that Allah can only be approached through an intermediary is extremely suspect to purists, who argue that God can always be approached directly, so long as one is *pak* (pure). In their eyes, the devotion paid to a pir may come dangerously close to worship of him. Various other methods to gain closeness to Allah are also extremely dubious. Ecstatic trance, possibly reached through ganja, meditation and tantric practices are roundly condemned. As one madrasa student put it:

> Bad pirs are those who play music for prayer. For us this is bad: we call them pretender pirs. There's one like that I know of, who smokes ganja, drinks, and plays drums and sings as he prays. There are two types of pir, you see. One is good, and the other is *marifot* (tantric).

Significantly, purists tend to be against miracle-making, dismissing the miracles attributed to lesser-known pirs. As one man commented of a pir's shrine in a predominantly landless neighbouring village: 'No one in Talukpur believes in him. He's a poor man's pir.' A Talukpur sharecropper, however, told me the pir was extremely powerful and could walk on water. Such stories are said by the rich to be superstitious and their miracles, the tricks of fakes. Asked if they believe in local pirs and the stories told of them, return migrants, especially from Britain, referred to them disparagingly as evidence of the stupidity of the illiterate labourers who follow them. Since they have the power to control so much of their own lives, they appear to have no need of such miracle-making. It is interesting that purists also condemn gambling, the worldly path to transformation. I suggest that it is no coincidence that they are against both types of miracles—that of the pir and that of gambling. Theirs is now a world of certainties, in which virtue and wealth can be gained through steady investment, not risk and God-granted grace.

An example of the changing attitudes of richer villagers to the cults of living pirs is given by Heron Shah, a pir who has lost support in Talukpur. Originally, villagers told me, many people believed in him, and would flock to his homestead for his blessing. But in recent years, he has lost legitimacy, for the richer migrant families who once were his followers stopped believing in his miracles. As he became more desperate to prove his powers, he became more ridiculous. Eventually he claimed to predict his own death, but as one woman put it: 'We all went to see, on the day he said he would die, but nothing happened. That man didn't die. So how can we believe in him?' What is interesting is not that Heron Shah did not die—for what happened could have been interpreted in many ways by believers—but that his followers now refused to believe in his miracles.

VII. ECONOMIC CLASS AND RELIGIOUS REINVENTION

The creation of religious 'correctness' involves continual restyling of religious practice. In this, what is and is not 'proper' is defined by the most powerful. As they create religious status through 'orthodoxy', the criteria of which they also define, the religious activities of those without power are marginalized and presented as opposed to what is 'correct'. Meanwhile, people continually attempt to modify their behaviour in accordance with that of the most powerful. For example, some of the men who had been to the Middle East but were none the less landless were chary of admitting their devotion to local pirs. Religious practice not only marks out particular groups, it also reproduces them. The powerless are associated with unrespectable form of worship and are thus accorded even lower status, whilst the rich reiterate their power and status through their participation and knowledge of a system of beliefs which is of great prestige.

Lionel Caplan has suggested that to understand religious behaviour we must focus upon power relations between groups (Caplan 1987b). The hierarchy of religious discourses in Talukpur must indeed be interpreted politically. I suggest that whilst some degree of religious heterogeneity may have always existed amongst Muslims in Talukpur, as economic polarisation has increased, so too has religious differentiation. Rather than a united shift from the pluralism of traditional Bengal to the monotheism of modernity (Roy 1982), there is instead continual conflict and confusion within the village over religious activities, with the alternative views very much related to relative degrees of secular power.

Other writers have focused upon the link between ecstatic Sufi cults and social marginality. Michael Gilsenan, for example, has argued that Sufi mysticism in Egypt and the Middle East has an inherent appeal to the poor and marginal. There, scripturalism is monopolized by the wealthier and better educated, simply because it is not accessible to the poor, whose own charismatic cults the rich despise (1982: 86). This is a useful insight which to an extent can be applied to Sylhet. But we must also be cautious of creating false dichotomies between charismatic cults and textual 'orthodoxy'. By describing them in terms of an opposition between mysticism and purism, the flexibility of the cults is hidden, for cults initially associated with mysticism can change within themselves. In Sylhet, the cults of those whose economic positions have improved have been transformed into respectable 'orthodoxy'. The pir is not inherently oppositional to purism, for interpretations of his role are malleable. Indeed, rather than rejecting pirs, many rich families now seek to improve their status through close association with one. But instead of being lowly followers, subject to his holy authority, they now claim to be his official keepers, or of his lineage.

VIII. THE REINVENTION OF PIRS

Earlier, I quoted a madrasa student distinguishing between what he termed 'good' pir, and those who are marifot—or part of an ecstatic, tantric tradition. These he condemned as sinful. The student was part of the Tablighi movement, and told me that he did indeed have a pir, based in Sylhet town. This man, was also mentioned by other villagers as their pir. He is presented by them as a stern proponent of doctrinal Islam, and his followers in Sylhet publish a regular newsletter, urging people to take up more pure ways. When I asked what sort of person he was, the student replied: 'Human, like us. He has much knowledge of religion, and teaches us.'

The pir, it seems, is appearing in a different guise. Shah Jalal is a good example of the way that cults can be reinterpreted by groups competing for religious prestige. Although some of the most orthodox men in the village claimed that they did not have a living pir, all without exception told me they were followers of Shah Jalal. Today Shah Jalal is represented by many in wholly purist terms. Those threatening such an image are not likely to be tolerated (such as the revellers who were attacked by an orthodox Londoni at the urs). The *khadims* (official caretakers) of the shrine now stress the historical legitimacy of Shah Jalal as a Yemeni soldier who brought Islam to Bengal. They dismiss stories about his miracles, stressing that he was mortal, but now is close to God. Claims about the miracles of other pirs, they also told me, were 'superstitions, which you get in all religions'.

Similar reinterpretations have been made for smaller pirs. A shrine in the same village as Abdul Hossain marks the grave of a pir whose family lives locally. Again, this pir is not associated with miracles, and certainly not with marifoti practices. Again too, his family is rich and of high status, and would certainly not wish to be associated with the miraculous cults of the poor. As a relative and follower of the pir put it:

> It's not a singing and dancing urs. It's a time when my brothers invite many mullahs and madrasa students, and they pray for others, and read the Quran. Then they sacrifice cow and prepare a big meal which everyone eats. Then they pray again, and everyone goes their own way.

These cults are clearly very different from those of the landless speakers cited earlier, at least in the way they are presented to outsiders. All the marks of 'correct' praxis are there: the formal prayer, sacrifice, and the presence of mullahs. If they were once charismatic mystics no one admits it. They have been 'routinised' (Weber 1947: 334), stripped of their spiritual powers to become holy men who uphold the social order rather than threaten it through their miracles.

But this is not the only difference between the cults of the rich and those of the poor. Not only are the former's pirs now presented in different terms but, most interestingly many claim the pirs as their ancestors. Indeed, rather than pirs dying out in the face of puritanism, in recent decades there has been an outbreak of new shrines and revelations of pir-hood. Rather than the legitimacy of these ancestral pirs being demonstrated through miracles, it is often revealed through the dreams of mullahs. Such claims tend to be made by the richer, migrant families. In the case of Abdul Hossain, a mullah employed by the family as a teacher, is said to have received in a dream the revelation that the dead *dada* (paternal grandfather) was a pir. And the woman who described her pir continues as follows:

> My mother's lineage is a pir's lineage. Yasin Ali was the leader of the village—he was so rich and powerful that lights shone from his place just like a palace. And his family did so many good work that one of his line was made a pir by Allah. But during his life people didn't realise it. After he died, a mullah dreamt it and people then realised he was a pir, so my brother established that mazaar.

If the claims are accepted or at least tolerated by others, such families can identify themselves as of pir descent, the most prestigious title possible. Not only does this bring secular status, but also hereditary religious merit, passed down along the line. For in contrast to Islamic ideals of total equality, the notion of succession from the Prophet involves belief in a God-given hierarchy. As is often pointed out, Islam is used to legitimize widely different political arrangements (see, for example, Geertz 1968).

Another way of acquiring special spiritual blessing and status for the lineage is through revelation that a pir has been buried on homestead land. Since Sylhet is famous as the land of pirs and since not all of Shah Jalal's legendary disciples remains have been discovered, a great many claims are possible. Again, revelations are usually made in the dreams of people with Islamic learning, often madrasa students given board and lodging by a family. If a burial place is said to lie in the land of a family, and they build a shrine in that place and mark it with special respect, then great fortune, it is said, will fall to them. They will also become the caretakers of the shrine, itself a holy and prestigious function. Obviously only landowners can make such claims.

Sometimes the claim is simply that a pir rested at a particular spot or prayed there. This too leads to the place being marked as particularly holy and to the construction of a shrine. Both types of shrine are continually appearing in Sylhet. An educated informant told me that since the 1970s hundreds of new shrines dedicated to a disciple have appeared. The claims are invariably made by the rich or the mullahs whom they support.

CONCLUSION

Ernest Gellner has suggested that Islam is in a state of constant flux between monotheism and pluralism (1981). These modes of faith are associated with different political systems, which whilst apparently applying only to Middle Eastern tribal systems, Gellner assumes to be definitively 'Muslim'. On a similar tack, Leach (1983) has argued that religions involve radically different features over time. In 'icons of subversion', devotees are directly inspired, and God gives charisma independently of the existing political hierarchy. Over time, however, this changes into an 'icon of orthodoxy', where humans are important before deities. Only superior mediators, who usually have a high position on the social hierarchy, can act as intermediaries. Here, religion upholds established political hierarchies and God gives them legitimacy. In both arguments, religious behaviour is holistic; it is assumed that meanings are shared and when change occurs it is spread evenly throughout the religious community.

The evidence presented here admittedly covers only a very short time scale. But Abdul Hossain and the other pirs of rich migrants indicate that rather than one mode of faith merging gradually into another, change may also occur *within* cults. Indeed, not only can different modes of faith coexist, but they can also be represented by a single icon: pluralism, in the form of the pir, can express the ideal of monotheism. Thus, whilst outward features of faith need not necessarily change, they are instead transformed internally. They are also used and understood by different people in different ways, as the case of Shah Jalal, with his purist caretakers and intoxicated celebrants, illustrates.

The modes of faith are arranged hierarchically too, for the doctrine of the most powerful is by definition the most dominant (Caplan 1987b: 14). Combined with this, the meanings given to each general type shift according to context. Whilst the general message of international reformism is primarily one of the equality of Muslims united against the pagan, non-Muslim world, in the local context it is the language of hierarchical difference. And ironically, whilst the cult of the mystical pir stresses spiritual hierarchy, its accessibility to followers, and messages which link poverty with holiness, work against secular hierarchy.

Rather than being discrete and bounded, there are numerous cross-over points between the different modes of faith. Both are poles of a continuum towards which different social groups tend to gravitate. Indeed, elements at one end can be reinterpreted and used by those clustering towards the other. This is so for the pirs who, rather than being discarded by the rush towards reformism, have been reinvented. The pirs of the rich have shifted from being, in Leach's terms, agents of subversion to being those of orthodoxy. Meanwhile the poorer and less powerful villagers, while accepting the dominant discourse and struggling to follow it, also continue to place their faith in local charismatic intermediaries.

We have thus come full circle. Pirs have the power to transform, to perform miracles which can change everything. But so too does migration. The transformations of migration are, however, of a different order. With their newly found wealth and social status migrants and their families have been able to aim for the highest degree of religious piety as defined by themselves. Thus, while demonstrating their dynamism, the pir cults of the rich can also be manipulated by the powerful in the construction of status. No longer dependent upon the pir for his miraculous interventions (which they say they do not need), the prosperous families of migrants reinterpret the pirs, and use them to legitimate and build their religious prestige. Miracles, and the granting of holiness by God irrespective of secular hierarchy, become less important than the hereditary ability to be closer to God than others. The religious status of the families is transformed, but not through the miracles of the pir. Instead, their transformation results from the migration and the economic and political power which it has engendered. And in turn, the pirs of the self-defined purists are also transformed: no longer crossing the boundaries of nature, they are stripped of their charisma and become learned holy men. No longer agents of the supernatural, these pirs of the rich are instead agents of a new doctrinalism which, though it may unify Muslims internationally, is increasingly divisive within Talukpur.

NOTES

1. 'Syncretism' implies a creole religiosity born from the mixture of 'pure' or 'orthodox' Islam with indigenous culture. Since everywhere Islam is expressed and interpreted in different ways, and nowhere exists in a 'pure' form, the term must be treated with suspicion.
2. South Asian notions of and religious transformation are further discussed by Parry (1979: 327).

3. A similar story is told about Shah Jalal, the great Sylheti pir. According to this, when first journeying into the district, he crossed the rivers which lay across his path by spreading his turban cloth on the water, and using it as a raft. Once again, spiritual power overcame 'natural' elements.
4. Devotion to Chisti of Ajmer, sung by labourers in Talukpur.
5. For further discussion of intermediaries in monotheistic traditions see Gellner (1981) and Hume (1976).
6. This north Indian movement of spiritual renewal dates from the 1920s and exists throughout the world. Its main aim is spiritual guidance: spreading correct religious practice amongst Muslims.
7. There is an interesting parallel here with Turkish migrants in Germany whose concepts of core and periphery, in both religious and secular domains, have also shifted (Mandle 1990).
8. Shared 'basics' include the prohibition of alcohol and pork, daily prayer, fasting, the seclusion of women and, for men, weekly attendance at the small village mosque.
9. In much of the Muslim world milad is the commemoration of the Prophet's birthday. In Talukpur, however, the term is used more loosely.
10. Loki is almost certainly a version of the Hindu goddess Lakshmi. Mention of Kwaz is also made by Blanchet (1984) and Saiyed (1989).
11. Another event shunned by the purists is the annual festival of Muharram. This is of course a Shi'ite festival, marking the martyrdom of Mohammed's grandson Hussain. Despite the fact that Bangladeshi Muslims are predominantly Sunni, it is, however, celebrated by some groups, though only attended by the poorest men in the village. As a woman I was not able to go to the shrine where it was held, but the labourers and rickshaw drivers in the nearby bazaar downed their tools for the day for the celebration. There, I was told, they would perform dhikir (repetition of God's name), wail, and flagellate themselves. Respectable village elders conceded the holiness of the occasion, but said they would never attend.

REFERENCES

Adams, Caroline. 1987. *Across Seven Seas and Thirteen Rivers: Life Stories of Pioneer Sylhet Settlers in Britain.* London: Tower Hamlets Arts Project.

Amselle, Jean-Loup. 1987. 'A case of fundamentalism in West Africa: Wahabism in Bamako'. In L. Caplan, ed., *Studies in Religious Fundamentalism,* pp. 79-94. London: Macmillan Press.

Baldick, Julien. 1989. *Musical Islam.* I.B. Tauris.

Ballard, Roger. 1983. 'The context and consequences of migration: Jullunder and Mirpur compared'. *New Community* 11, 2: 117-36.

———. 1990. 'Migration and kinship: The differential effects of marriage rules on the processes of Punjabi migration to Britain'. In C. Clarke et al., eds., *South Asians Overseas*, pp. 219-49. Cambridge: Cambridge University Press.

Blanchet, Therese. 1984. *Women, Pollution and Marginalism: Meanings of Birth and Ritual in Rural Bangladesh.* Dhaka: Dhaka University Press.

Bourdieu, Pierre. 1977. *Outline of a Theory of Practice.* Cambridge: Cambridge University Press.

Caplan, Lionel. 1987a. *Studies in Religious Fundamentalism.* London: Macmillan Press.

———. 1978b. *Class and Culture in Urban India.* Oxford: Clarendon Press.

Carey, Sean and Abdus Shukur. 1985. 'A profile of the Bangladeshi community in London'. *New Community* 12, 3: 405-17.

Cashin, David. 1988. 'The influence of the esoteric cults upon the sufis of Bengal'. Unpublished paper for Bengali Seminar, Stockholm: Stockholm University.

Clarke, C. et al. eds. 1990. *South Asians Overseas.* Cambridge: Cambridge University Press.

Cohen, Anthony. 1985. *The Symbolic Construction of Community.* New York: Tavistock.

Eade, John. 1986. 'The politics of community. The Bangladeshi community in London'. Unpublished thesis. London: University of London.

———. 1990. 'Nationalism and the quest for authenticity: the Bangladeshis in Tower Hamlets'. *New Community.* 16, 4: 493-503.

Eickleman, Dale and James Piscatori, eds. 1990. *Muslim Travellers: Pilgrimage, Migration and Religious Imagination.* London: Routledge and Kegan Paul.

Ewing, Katherine. 1980. 'The pirs of sufi sants in Pakistani Islam'. Unpublished thesis. Illinois: University of Chicago.

Gardner, Katherine. 1990. 'Jumbo jets and paddy fields: Outmigration and village life in rural Sylhet'. Unpublished thesis. London: University of London.

Gardner, Katy. 1991. *Songs at the River's Edge: Stories from a Bangladesh Village.* London: Virago Press.

Geertz, Clifford. 1968. *Islam Observed: Religious Development in Morocco and Indonesia.* Chicago: University of Chicago Press.

Gellner, Ernest. 1981. *Muslim Society.* Cambridge: Cambridge University Press.

Gilsenan, Michael. 1982. *Recognising Islam: An Anthropologist's Introduction.* London: Croom Helm.

Haq, Muhhamud. 1975. *A History of Sufism in Bengal.* Dhaka: Asiatic Society of Bangladesh Publications, No. 30.

Hartman, Betsy and James Boyce. 1983. *A Quiet Violence: View from a Bangladesh Village.* London: Zed Publications.

Hobsbawm, Eric and Terence Ranger. 1983. *The Invention of Tradition.* Cambridge: Cambridge University Press.

Hossain, Anwar. 1985. *Remittances from International Labour Migration—A Case Study from Bangladesh.* Dhaka: Bangladesh Manpower Planning Centre.

Hume, David. 1976. *Natural History of Religion.* Oxford: Oxford University Press.

Islam, Muinal, et al. 1987. *Overseas Migration from Rural Bangladesh: A Micro-study.* Rural Economics Programme. Bangladesh: University of Chittagong.

Jansen, Eirik. 1987. *Rural Bangladesh: Competition for Scarce Resources.* Dhaka: University Press.

Kessinger, Tom G. 1979. *Vilaytpur: 1848-1968. Social and Economic Change in a North Indian Village.* New Delhi: Young Asia.

Leach, Edmund. 1983. 'Melchisdech and the emperor: Icons of subversion and orthodoxy'. In E. Leach and D. Aycock, *Structural Interpretations of Biblical Myth*, pp. 69-89. Cambridge: Cambridge University Press.

Lewis, Peter. 1985. *Pirs, Shrines, and Pakistani Islam.* Pakistan: Christian Study Centre. CSC Study Series 20.

Mandle, Ruth. 1990. 'Shifting centres and emergent identities: Turkey and Germany in the lives of Turkish Gastarbeiter'. In D. Eickelman and J. Piscatori, eds. *Muslim Travellers: Pilgrimage, Migration and Religious Imagination*, pp. 153-71. London: Routledge and Kegan Paul.

Metcalf, Barbara. 1982. *Islamic Revival in British India: Deoband 1860-1900.* Princeton: Princeton University Press.

Nanda, B. and L. Talib. 1989. 'Soul of the soulless: An analysis of the *pir-murid* relationship in Sufi discourse'. In C. Troll, ed., *Muslim Shrines in India*, pp. 125-44. Oxford: Oxford University Press.

Owens, Roger. 1985. *Migrant Workers in the Gulf.* London: Minority Rights Group Report 68.

Parry, Jonathan. 1979. *Caste and Kinship in Kangra.* London: Routledge and Kegan Paul.

Peach, Ceri, 1990. 'Estimating the growth of the Bangladeshi population of Great Britain'. *New Community* 16, 4: 481-91.

Rodinson, Maxine (trans.). 1974. *Islam and Capitalism.* New York: Pantheon Books.

Roy, Asim. 1982. 'The *pir* tradition: A case study in Islamic syncretism in traditional Bengal'. In F. Clothey, ed., *Images of Man: Religion and Historical Process in South Asia*, pp. 112-42. Madras: New Era Publications.

Saiyed, Anwar. 1989. 'Saints and dargahs in the Indian subcontinent: A review'. In C. Troll, ed., *Muslim Shrines in India,* pp. 240-56. Oxford: Oxford University Press.

Troll, C., ed., 1989. *Muslim Shrines in India: Their Character, History, and Significance.* Oxford: Oxford University Press.

Vreede-De Stuers, Cora. 1968. *Parda: A Study of Muslim Women's Life in Northern India.* Assen: Van Gorcum.

Watson, James, 1975. *Emigration and the Chinese Lineage: The Manns in Hong Kong and London.* California: University of California Press.

Weber, Max. 1947. *The History of Social and Economic Organisation* (ed. Talcott Parsons). New York: The Free Press.

Wilson, Stephen, ed., 1983. *Saints and their Cults.* Oxford: Oxford University Press.

Community Structure and Social Rank in Two Villages in Bangladesh

PETER J. BERTOCCI
(1972)

In this paper I discuss aspects of social stratification in two Bangladesh villages which I studied in 1966-7.* My purposes in this effort are threefold. Firstly, I wish to provide a modicum of ethnographic data from what is now South Asia's newest nation and has been one of its least studied regions, at least by anthropologists. Secondly, I hope to contribute to the study of South Asian social stratification systems by focusing on a region of this culture area where caste is not a major feature of rural community organization. Finally, I want to suggest some of the ways in which highly diffuse and indeterminate forms of community organization interplay with the rural class system to produce what passes for 'the village' and its extensions in the part of Bangladesh. In the latter connection, I note the previous work of Marriott (1965), whose perceptive observations in the face of little available data find substantial, if not total, confirmation in my own work.

The two villages which provide the data for this paper lie only a few kilometres from the *moffusil* town of Comilla, some 100 kilometres to the south-east of Dacca, in one of the most densely populated areas of Bangladesh. They are, in the Bengal context, referred to as 'local' or socially defined villages (*gram*), but their respective memberships cross cut the boundaries of four land revenue units (*mauzas*) which date from at least the turn of the century. Taken together, the two villages cover a total land are of just under a square kilometre. In a manner consistent with the overall reported population densities for this part of Bangladesh, the mauzas where the villages are found contained in 1967 the homesteads of some 700 people. One of them, here pseudonymously called Hajipur, contained 322 persons in mid-1967. The other, the boundaries of which overlapped three *para* or 'neighbourhoods' of three separately named mauzas, had 245 inhabitants at that time; I have called it Tinpara (*tin para*: 'three neighbourhoods'), in part to reflect its composition from parts of three different mauzas. The majority of the population of both villages was Muslim about 20 per cent were Hindus, members variously of the weaver (*jugi* or *debonath*), carpenter (*chutradar*), barber (*napit* or *sil*) and washerman (*dhopa*) castes. This paper will centre primarily on the Muslim majority, although the Hindu minority plays a significant role in many aspects of total community life.

I have elsewhere described the overall social organization of these villages in some detail (Bertocci 1970). For the aims of this paper, I outline the major features of social organization in this part of Bangladesh, with special reference to the problem of social stratification.

(1) Rural communities in this area are the product of an exceedingly dense population, adapted, under pre-industrial technological conditions, to a monsoon, deltaic environment.

(2) While their populations are inevitably crowded together, the pattern of rural settlement is dictated, in anticipation of heavy monsoon rains, by 'the lay of the land'—i.e. the location of relatively high ground which is the most desirable terrain for homestead construction. Hence, the pattern of settlement is scattered and, while the result of locational choices related to local topography, it is socially random and not the result of any pre-ordained preference for spatial arrangement.

(3) Given this ecological setting, the social basis of community organization, as it occurs above the level of the individual, homestead-based patrilineal kin group, is related to the relative proximity of dwellings the socially random settlement pattern has produced. The proximity of homesteads helps to influence the frequency and relative quality of interaction between members of their kin groupings, thereby contributing to the social solidarity of the population involved.

(4) The 'village', then, consists of what I call 'homestead clusters', the members of which interact more frequently with each other than they do with those of similar clusters lying further away. In each homestead cluster, the lineages, among members of which are included the most 'affluent' of the community, as a whole exercise the preponderance of social influence and political power. These lineages can for convenience be called *sardari* lineages in that those of their members who are the local community 'influentials' are known as *sardars* (also *matabbars*). It is sometimes the caste that within the 'village' there exist several subgroupings, the members of which

are variously loyal to one or the other of several sardars. These groupings are designated locally by the term *reyai*, a word apparently from Arabic, *rai'yah* meaning 'citizen', and derivations of which in standard Bengali (e.g. reyati) carry the connotation of 'protege'. Hajipur, for example, has three sardars and consequently three reyais. Where, as in the case of Tinpara, one sardar dominates local affairs, the term reyai corresponds in fact to organizationally formal and interactionally constant links to surrounding similar groupings.

(5) This direct linkage with other socially defined villages in contiguous or otherwise nearby mauzas is not merely a matter of formal organization. It is underlain by an extensive network of kinship relations, given territorial coherence by the scattered location of individual cultivators' land fragments, and buttressed sentimentally by the interaction which the spatial distribution of mosques and Id fields affords in uniting members of diverse villages in congregational worship.

(6) The political unity of several grams in this manner is given formal expression by the fact that the sardars from each of its constituent units constitute collectively a kind of 'Council of Elders' whose traditional duty it has long been to exercise judgement in disputes involving members of this larger multi-village community. The whole ensemble is, indeed, referred to as the '*samaj*'—the little 'society' for the villagers who constitute it. It should be stressed that any matter, particularly one of conflict and schism, though it may only involve two neighbours or two brothers in the same homestead, comes to the attention of, and is deemed relevant to, other people who may live well removed from the immediate 'turf' of those initially concerned. Any local public event is subject to the scrutiny of all and especially, where the peace is threatened as it so often is, of the traditionally powerful sardars.

(7) In a summary manner, one can characterize Comilla villages as, on the one hand, socially and territorially intensive, to the extent that the intimate ties of the gram serve to foster the cohesiveness of very small social groupings. But, quite crucially, the social organization of these villages is also extensive in character, in that dyadic and group ties, which bring individuals and groups together over a geographic area far broader than that of the single small 'village', all directly affect the daily lives of those who inhabit the latter. In this wider context, the 'village' as an organizational unit is an ephemeral and elusive entity, the social cohesiveness of which is tenuous. In the

context of particular events, the 'village' emerges as a structural unit of larger social groupings, of which the samaj is one of the most important.[1]

CASTE AND CASTE IDEOLOGY

Rural Comilla *thana*[2] is notable for the very paucity of the caste groupings, Hindu or Muslim, one finds in its villages. Few Muslims in the thana, including those in the villages under discussion, perform those traditional service occupations which are associated with varying degrees of low status and ritual pollution. Most males above the age of 15 in these villages report farming as a major occupation, although half of these are engaged in other tasks for supplementary income, as workers in newly developed town factories, as (usually menial) service holders, in petty trade or as manual labourers of some sort. Three are school teachers, four are *imams* and, among the Hindus, most practise their traditional occupation to some extent. Thus, in neither village are there any Muslims engaged in those occupations historically associated with middle and low ranked serving castes; indeed, members of these Hindu castes still remain relatively numerous in the area and their services are widely utilized by Muslim cultivators who often travel some distance to avail themselves of such services. The skills and defiling occupations which are still the relative monopoly of these Hindu castes appear to remain in low supply relative to the need for them, as indicated by the distance cultivators are willing to travel to obtain them. None the less, as yet few Muslims have taken them up as source of livelihood.

It should be noted, however, that there do exist some Muslims in Comilla thana who perform these tasks and whose services are used by people in villages like Hajipur and Tinpara. In the interviews I conducted on this subject, I was able to elicit consistent reference to certain Muslim groupings outside of the villages which were associated with occupations traditionally conceived of as defiling, and having thereby low rank. Among such Muslim 'functional groups' were those whose members were washermen and sweepers. More interestingly, certain groups that perform specifically Muslims services were mentioned in this category. Among these are butchers (*khasai*), some of whom would appear regularly in the local market with fresh meat, although their place of residence is near the town. The *hajjams*, whose task is to perform the ritual circumcision of Muslim boys, regularly tour the thana in the winter, although they are not widely distributed residentially in it. Such groups are referred to by Muslim cultivators in Hajipur and Tinpara as distinct from themselves and of lower status. 'They are a caste, a separate community (*jat*)', declared one of my informants about the hajjams, 'No one will arrange a marriage with them.'

The important point here is that although there exist caste groupings among these Bengali Muslims, they are not widely distributed in Comilla thana as corporate groups and concrete structural units of local villages. Thus, one of the key logical conditions for elaborate caste ranking, as Marriott (1965: 6ff) has suggested, is not fulfilled in this part of East Bengal. With caste groupings few and far between, no such ranking system can exist—and, indeed, here it does not exist. When interaction takes place between the members of endogamous, low-ranked groups and cultivators in village like Hajipur and Tinpara, it is no doubt stratified in that members of subordinate groups are, after all, interacting with 'their betters'. But such interaction is dyadic and functionally specific. Since the low-ranked groups in question rarely reside in cultivator-dominated villages, their relationships with cultivators lack the functionally diffuse and sentimentally complex quality one finds in communities composed of many residential, interdigitated caste groupings. Thus, elaborate social ranking in this part of East Bengal is limited not merely by the paucity of the relevant caste groups, but also by the fact that these, although they exist, rarely interact as concrete structural units of residential social systems. Caste, as an organizing principle of rural society, is not significant, even though one might say, given the persistence of certain low-ranked, endogamous Muslim occupational groups, that '*jati* thinking'—as Gould (1969) has put it—certainly forms part and parcel of the ideology of social relations held by most cultivators.

It is of course true that the traditionally reported orders of South Asian Muslim society—the *Ashraf-Ajlaf* ranking categories—have played a role in the ideology of status in East Bengal. It is, for example, a commonplace finding of the censuses and other ethnographic commentary of the colonial period that 'most' or 'nearly all' the Bengali Muslims considered themselves to be *Shekhs*. Mention is also made in these sources of the existence of a large number of Muslim castes or caste-like groups, ranked well below

Shekh and other Ashraf statuses. My own efforts at historical research on the matter confirm these truisms superficially in the first instance. Indeed, by the turn of the present century, well over 95 per cent of the Muslims of East Bengal were reporting themselves as Shekhs in the censuses. Moreover, the rapid increase, after 1872, of this nearly universal self-definition was accompanied in fact by an absolute decline in the number of Muslim 'caste' or 'caste-like' groups—e.g. *jola, kulu, nikari,* etc.—despite the absolute increase in the overall population of the region (see Bertocci 1970: 73-104). Indeed, the evidence suggests an overall increase in 'horizontal solidarity' and the 'freeing of (Muslim) caste from its traditional, local and vertical matrix', to borrow Srinivas' useful terminology, and, in effect, the emergence of a broadly homogeneous Muslim peasant class (1968: 114).

Nicholas (1969), in commenting on the 'ethnic homogeneity' of the whole of the Bengal Delta (East and West), notes in this reference and elsewhere (1963) the widespread existence in the most populous areas of the delta of villages characterized by relatively meagre caste stratification. In Hindu-majority West Bengal, peasant cultivating castes such as the *Mahisyas* are dominant in villages with scarcely half a dozen resident caste groupings. Similarly, he argues, one might see the Shekhs of East Bengal as a dominant Muslim 'caste' in the region. The data on caste and caste ideology I have here reported for Hajipur and Tinpara support this notion. That is, to the extent that they preponderate numerically, and reside in villages with few, *if any,* other Muslim castes, and refuse to marry into Muslim occupational communities they consider lower than themselves in rank, the 'Shekhs' of Comilla thana clearly constitute a kind of 'dominant caste' for the area as a whole.

But, as Imtiaz Ahmad (1967) has pointed out, the traditional Ashraf-Ajlaf categories usually bear only the most tangential relationship to the system of social rank in local Muslim communities of a given region or subregion. Indeed, it is hard, except by the most direct questioning, to elicit spontaneous self-reference as Shekh from informants in Hajipur and Tinpara. Indeed, local categories of social rank, which are the focus of the remainder of this essay, are couched amid a different set of referents. 'Shekhs' though they may have once been and may still be, the Muslims of Hajipur and Tinpara respond to another system of internal ranking and status. To this I now turn.

THE ECONOMIC BASES OF SOCIAL CLASS

It is useful, following Marx and Weber, to think initially of class in economic terms. The relationship of different groups to the means of production, as well as their differential access to goods and services, provides the link between economy and society. At the same time, it is necessary to distinguish both conceptually and empirically between the economic bases of social structure and another of its crucial dimensions, that of status, defined by Weber as 'every typical component in the life fate of men that is determined by a specific, positive or negative, social estimation of *honor*' (Gerth and Mills 1958: 186-7). As Weber has put it, however:

> class distinctions are linked in the most varied ways with status distinctions. Property as such is not always recognised as a status qualification, but in the long run it is, and with extraordinary regularity. (ibid.: 187).

It is possible to identify both economic class and social status groups in Hajipur and Tinpara and to establish a certain correlation between the two. Table 1 gives us the means to begin this analysis by showing farm size in the villages (combined).

TABLE 1. FARM SIZE IN HAJIPUR AND TINPARA

Acres	Number of farms*	Percentage
0.00	10	9.80
0.01-0.49	17	16.67
0.50-0.99	18	17.65
1.00-1.49	15	14.71
1.50-1.99	13	12.75
2.00-2.49	8	7.84
2.50-2.99	6	5.88
3.00-3.49	6	5.88
3.50-3.99	-	-
4.00-4.49	2	1.96
4.50-4.99	4	3.92
5.00-8.00+	3	2.94
Total	102	100.00

Hajipur: 100.68 acres; 54 farms
Tinpara: 58.68 acres; 48 farms
1.5 acres per farm: median land ownership per farm, both villages = 1.15

*There are actually 104 *chulas* or economic household units, but three of these in Hajipur are combined in a lineal collateral joint ownership arrangement despite separate chulas. Hence, the actual number of farms = 102.

In a peasant society, land-ownership and land relations provide the key link between economy and social structure. In addition to the fact that land types influence importantly the pattern of rural settlement, these, plus the degree of plot fragmentation, along with the norms of possession, help to locate the foci of rural people's activities and thus the territorial as well as social organization of their communities. Finally, relative differences in land-ownership and control are crucial, if not the sole, determinants of the distribution of status, power and influence.

In the latter connection, it is possible to distinguish broad categories of cultivators ranked with respect to land-ownership and economic activities, as I attempt to do in Table 2. This is a procedure used by Marxist students of peasantry who *begin* discussions of social stratification with categories based primarily on economic rank (see e.g. Mao Tse-tung 1965a, 1965b; Alavi 1965; Hinton 1966, Chapter 2 and Appendix C; Gough 1968-9). This procedure serves

TABLE 2. LAND-OWNERSHIP BY CATEGORY—MUSLIMS ONLY

Category	Number	Per cent	Type of peasantry
Landless:			
Own 0.00 acre	9	10	Poor and landless peasant 50%
Land poor:			
Own .1-1.22 acre			
Median .50 acre	39	40	
Marginal:			
Own1.23-2.40 acres	25	26	Marginal subsistence peasants 39%
Median 1.80 acre			
Subsistence:			
Own 2.41-3.50 acres	12	13	
Median 2.80 acres			
Surplus:			Surplus farmers 11%
Own 3.51+acres	10	11	
Median 4.80 acres			
Totals	95	100	100%

Statistical note: Mean land-ownership is 1.60 acres; median ownership is 1.22 acres; range of ownership, all farms, is 0.00 to 10.40 acres. The median has been taken as the better index of central tendency in this instance. In each category, the range exhibits a similar spread and hence median ownership in each is given to indicate general levels of ownership within each class.

as a means whereby the link between economy and social structure can be perceived. The next step in the analysis is to study the correlations between economic and political power, either synchronically or diachronically, and, where exact correlations between the two cannot be established, to explain the manifestation of power under the given conditions. Finally, a holistic study of social stratification seeks further to understand the relationship—or its lack—between these variables and those of status and general lifestyle.

Table 2 represents the beginnings of such analysis for the Muslims of Hajipur and Tinpara. The categories in this table are not wholly arbitrary, for in choosing them I have attempted to follow the natural groupings of ordinally ranked data as they have emerged in analysis. Moreover, while the categories are mutually exclusive and collectively exhaustive, the reader will rightly assume progressive shadings in land-ownership at either end of each category in the arranged continuum. About two-thirds of the farms are less than two acres in size, the latter acreage commonly taken by students of Bangladesh agriculture to be the minimal amount of land needed to maintain subsistence level of income over time.[3] In a *good* harvest year, the cultivator with two acres or a little more can manage to feed his family, repay debts and save a little of his production to pay for future capital expenses; in a word, he can barely subsist. In a *bad* harvest year, however, the same 'two acre farmer' will face difficulties in meeting these needs. Thus, the subsistence farmer stands not far from marginality, as I have tried to indicate in Table 2. Indeed, half of the subsistence farmers in Table 2 are deeply in debt, which suggests that they face downward economic mobility in a peasant society where land is the sine qua non of well-being. By contrast, the surplus farmer, who is likely to own upwards of four acres, is well able to withstand the vicissitudes of most years and can in fact count regularly on a small crop surplus which he can put to various economic uses, not the least frequent of which is the lending of money or rice to his less fortunate neighbours. Thus, a surplus farmholding allows its owner typically to augment his income by lending activities, taking the land of his debtors in mortgage (which is by custom usufructuary). In the literature on Bangladesh agriculture and rural society the term *mahajan* (moneylender) refers more often than not to the surplus farmers. It is, therefore, on this basis that I have attempted to construct a broad preliminary typology of peasantry in Table 2, with land-ownership as the major criterion. If land-ownership is taken as a major indicator of relative status and power, it will be apparent from the data presented in Tables 1 and 2 that social relations among most heads of households in these villages are relatively egalitarian. Indeed, it is probably true that rural society in Bangladesh is more egalitarian than the kinds of social relations found commonly in other areas of South Asia. But, as Table 2 suggests, one can find distinctions in social rank in villages like Hajipur and Tinpara.

Absolute smallness in farm size should not obscure the importance of small differences in land-ownership and associated economic activities associated with them as these reflect clear variation in class, status, lifestyle and power.

INDICATORS OF STATUS

With respect to the symbolic indicators of relative status, it is to be noted that in these villages and in Comilla thana generally, lineages and homesteads bearing specific titles or names are commonly found. The origins of these are quite diverse, as I shall demonstrate, and there are differences in the significance of one title or name as opposed to another. Lineage titles denoting high status often function as patronymics whereas other titles do not. In this sense they contradict the more usual situation, which corresponds to the *hadith* often cited in support of Islamic egalitarianism: 'There are no genealogies in Islam' (see the discussion in Levy 1965: 53-73). That is, a man born into a family with the titles of *Majumdar* will retain that title as a patronymic, whereas a man born into an untitled family will be known simply as, for example, Abdur Rahman, son of Jainal Abedin, Village X, Thana, etc.

There are four kinds of names or titles commonly associated with lineages and homesteads in Hajipur and Tinpara. Among these, two kinds are what may be called 'traditionally high status' titles or names associated with (a) landed aristocracy, positions in the revenue collection system of pre-independence times or in government administration and (b) religion. Among these are to be found lineage titles which function as patronymics, although not all have this characteristic. Of the two remaining kinds of titles—or, better put, names or common appellations—some are associated with (c) occupation, in a service or artisan capacity, others with (d) personal characteristics of a given member or members of the family remembered of some reason. The latter are not patronymics, but merely localisms by which neighbouring families in the villages have come to call a given homestead. In Comilla thana the following examples of these names and titles were found:

(A) Traditional high status, secular

Majumdar: according to Sinha (1962: 39), majumdars were the keepers of the records of land transfers in the revenue system; the title was apparently also often conferred by the Mughal aristocracy on local holders of revenue collection rights, be they Hindus or Muslims; thus historically associated with ownership and control of land (*jum*, Persian; *jomi*, Bengali; land), a patronymic.

Choudhuri: according to Webster (1910: 82ff) a title (of Persian derivation) conferred by Mughal rulers on the managers of estates, either Hindu or Muslim; also historically associated with ownership or control of land; a patronymic.

Bhuiya: apparently derived from Sanskrit *bhumi*, meaning 'earth, ground' (*bhui*, *bhui* in Bengal); also associated historically with the famous '*baro bhuiya*' or '12 Bhuiya families' of pre-Mughal and early Mughal times in Bengal (see Wise 1874); a patronymic.

Mahisan: from the Bengali *mahis*, meaning specially 'water buffalo', not historically a title granted in association with land-ownership or revenue so far as I know; but associated with the ownership of a lot of land in that its bearers claim historically to have been cattle traders, a profession which requires large amounts of grazing land, as well as trading capital; a patronymic.

Kaji: from the Arabic, *qadi*, the title of an ecclesiastical judge, among whose important functions were and still are the registration of marriages and divorce; a patronymic, usually preceding its bearer's given name; most commonly pronounced *kazi*.

Munshi, Kerani, Muhuri: all terms for 'clerk' or, especially the latter, 'deed-writer'; these positions were historically associated with the administration of revenue collection; they may be, but are not always, patronymics.

(B) Traditional high status, religious

Khondakar: from the Persian *Khawandgar*, 'Circumcisor of Muslim boys'; according to Wise (1903: 28-9) a priestly class which functioned importantly in the spreading of Islam in Bengal; the title is for this reason, apparently, high status, despite the Persian meaning of its origin which, as I have noted earlier, refers to an occupation which is considered 'defiling' (that of the hajjams); present-day bearers of this title may or may not be religious leaders; a patronymic.

Haji: a title borne by one who has performed the religious duty of pilgrimage of *Hajj*; not a patronymic.

Maulana: a religious leader of usually greater training than that of a more common imam, who is allowed to lead mosque prayers; a certain degree of scholarship is attributed to *maulanas*, who are recognized as authorities on religious and certain legal matters; tends to be religiously prestigious.

Pharaji: commonly spelled *Faraizi* or *Faraidi*, especially with reference to the important Islamic revivalistic and social movement of the nineteenth century in Bengal; the term appears to be derived from the Arabic *fard*, which refers to a category of 'moral acts' which are encumbent upon and essential duties for Muslims; perhaps because it reflects special piety and orthodoxy, it appears to connote a high degree of respectability for its bearers; it is not a personal name, but usually attached to a homestead (e.g., *Faraizi Bari*).

(C) Occupational titles, secular and religious, but not of especially high status: some examples

Imam, Molla, Moulvi: local circles, religious congregational leaders, with sufficient training to be accepted by the Faithful as leaders in limited capacities; conveys honourable, but not especially high, status.

Kobiraj: 'native doctor'; either of persons or animals.

Kathmistri: wood worker, carpenter (as distinct from the Hindu caste carpenter).

(D) Names of homesteads denoting personal characteristics: examples

Mal: Bengali meaning 'strength, force, high value'. One homestead in Hajipur is sometimes called *Mal Bari* because of the forceful character of the (now deceased) head of its resident lineage.

Pagali: from the Bengali *pagal* or 'mad'. This name attaches to a particular homestead in village Reshompur near my study area, where there formerly lived a widow who is reputed to have vigorously resisted all attempts to deprive her of her land by inheritance. The constant battles and litigations in which she is said to have been engaged earned for her the title of 'pagali' or 'madwomen' (itself a commentary on the status of women in rural Bengali Muslim society). The homestead in which her descendants live became known thus as *Pagali Bari*, or 'Home of the Mad Woman', a source of amused embarrassment to its current inhabitants.

Ordinary villagers in Hajipur and Tinpara, when asked to identify with respect to status either their own or other families with which they may be associated in marriage, will refer to these kinds of appellations if they are relevant. This is the phenomenon I encountered when making a census and recording genealogies, which surprised me because I had expected that when so queried people would respond with the term Shekh or other such Ashraf (or Ajlaf) titles. Not all lineages or homesteads have names or titles, however, and when asked to identify these in any way which denotes status, usually informants said that the people in question were simply '*grihasthi*', a term the local dialectal pronunciation of which given here is probably related to the Sanskrit *grihastha,* which refers to the 'householder' stage of the traditional Hindu four 'stages of life'. By this it appeared to mean that the person or family in question was merely a 'common villager', someone 'just like anyone else', but none the less 'respectable'.

My concern with names and titles is not merely ethnographic, for an awareness of the differences in status they connote, facilitates an understanding of social stratification in Hajipur and Tinpara, where status, in the Weberian sense, is often empirically distinct from class as an economic grouping. Villagers themselves discriminate between *ucho-bangsho* (high status lineage), *madhya-bangsho* (middle status lineage) and *nichu-bangsho* (low status lineage) families and appear to do so on the basis of a title, or its lack, as much as anything else. This appears to be common in other parts of Bangladesh as well, as Glasse (1966) shows for the Matlab Bazar area, where villagers also are disposed to rank titles in this manner.

Not all those in Hajipur and Tinpara with traditionally high status titles, either secular or religious, are particularly wealthy. This is the case partly because of the considerable differences in landholding which obtain within the same homestead. The homestead is the residential locus of a patrilineally extended family, with which may also be living matrilateral kinsmen and even families of non-kinsmen or affines. The homestead is further broken down into individual economic segments or families which may be either sub-nuclear, nuclear or joint; these are known as chula (hearth, oven) or, less commonly, *khana* (eating groups) and represent either sub-lineal segments of the patrilineage or matrilateral and unrelated co-residents. Ownership of land is not based on a corporate lineage principle and each sub-unit represents an economically separate group. These chulas or households have been represented in Tables 1 and 2 as 'farm', indicating their separateness as individual producing units.

In Tables 3, 4 and 5, individual Muslim-owned farms are compared on the basis of land-ownership and relative rank as indicated by the possession of traditionally high status title or its lack. Table 3 begins this analysis with a presentation of rank according to the land-ownership type developed in Table 2. As indicated in Table 3, 39 of the Muslim family farms in Hajipur and Tinpara belong to persons whose homesteads are given a traditionally high status title. When these 39 are compared on a percentage basis by land-ownership, as in Table 3, association with high status titles is relatively evenly distributed across the range of land-ownership categories. By contrast, the vast majority (77 per cent) of the 56 farms belonging to Muslims of 'low status', i.e. possessing no title, are associated with marginal and land poor ownership. Table 4 indicates that while some 77 per cent of farm families associated with high status titles are landless/ land poor or marginal subsistence in general peasant type, 23 per cent of them are surplus-producing farms, and that 90 per cent of all surplus farmers are high status in rank. Conversely, Table 5 shows that 98 per cent of the families with no title (or low status) are landless/land poor or marginal subsistence in peasant type, while

TABLE 3. LAND-OWNERSHIP AND STATUS—MUSLIMS ONLY

Land-ownership category	Low status		High status	
	N	%	N	%
Landless	6	11	3	8
Land poor	27	48	11	28
Marginal	16	29	10	26
Subsistence	6	11	6	15
Surplus	1	1	9	23
Total	56	100	39	100

TABLE 4. TYPES OF PEASANTRY IN RELATION TO HIGH STATUS TITLE

Peasant type	N	%	Title	N	Total	% per class*
Landless/ Land poor	14	36	Majumdar	8	14	31
			Mahisan	1		
			Munshi	-		
			Haji	-		
			Faraizi	3		
			Khondakar	2		
Marginal/ Subsistence	16	41	Majumdar	1	16	41
			Mahisan	6		
			Munshi	3		
			Haj	1		
			Faraizi	2		
			Khondakar	3		
Surplus farmer	9	23	Majumdar	3	9	90
			Mahisan	4		
			Munshi	1		
			Haji	-		
			Faraizi	1		
			Khondakar	-		
Total	39	100			39	40

*40 per cent of all farms owned by titled persons or families. The percentages in this column reflect the N of all peasant types with high status titles.

TABLE 5. TYPES OF PEASANTRY IN RELATION TO LOW STATUS TITLE

Peasant type	N	%	% per class*
Landless/Land poor	33	59	69
Marginal/Subsistence	22	39	59
Surplus farmer	1	2	10
Total	56	100	60

*60 per cent of all farms owned by untitled persons or families. The percentages in this column reflect the N of all peasant types with low status titles.

only 2 per cent of these are surplus farm families. These data show two general things. On the one hand, possession of the trappings of rank (a high status title) is in absolute terms the sole possession of no one peasant type in these villages. To this extent they reflect the comparatively remarkable social and economic egalitarianism of Bangladesh peasantry. On the other hand, the data tend also to confirm an overall association of land-ownership with relative social rank and thus to bear out Weber's dictum to the effect that while property and status do not always coincide, in the long run they tend to do so 'with extraordinary regularity'.[4]

ECONOMIC ACTIVITIES AND LIFE-STYLES

Classes in any society evince differential patterns of behaviour, are charaterized by unequally distributed access to goods and services and, as exemplified by marriage patterns, may be seen to unite families along horizontally stratified lines. With respect to all of these characteristics, some differences can be perceived in Hajipur and Tinpara between the peasant types I have attempted to delineate.

Table 3 indicates differences in the distribution of control over productive resources, which is taken as the basis for the peasant class typology I have tried to construct. In general, land poor peasants have reached their situation as a result of loss of property through chronic indebtedness, particularly via the mortgage of land as security against small loans. Marginal and subsistence farmers confront a similar potential, but their economic situation often presents a mixed bag of activities in each specific case. While many of these farmers are heavily in debt, as a rule they own and cultivate their own land; paradoxically, however, a good number of petty moneylending transactions can be found among their activities as well. Indeed, the lending of money is so constant and ubiquitous a feature of social and economic activity in these villages, it is difficult to say that the 'exploitation' implied in them is the unique province of any one peasant class. Moreover, available land tenure data for Bangladesh as a whole indicate that while for the country as a whole outright tenancy is not great, nearly 40 per cent of the nation's farms are of the owner-cum-tenant variety. This fact suggests a high degree of mutual dependence on land lease and sharecropping arrangements by marginal, subsistence and even surplus farmers to supplement their holdings in any given season. But, in the end, as with status, the ability to engage in moneylending or the renting out of land is clear related to the possession of at least the median amount of land,[5] a fac which takes on significance in the context of social mobility, discussed below.

With respect to non-economic differences among the groups, relatively high status and the ability to maintain it also is differentiated along class lines. Larger homesteads and houses (*ghar*) of better construction are more common among surplus farm families than others. A common indicator of relative wealth could be seen in the fact that the more fortunate cultivators had sufficient land to have a pond within the homestead where members of the homestead could bathe in private. Rich peasants often entertain visitors in a separate building, known as *kachari ghar*, maintained by the lineage for the reception of guest. These symbols of relative affluence are especially important in the maintenance of what Weber calls 'status honour'. Indeed, the Muslim term and concept of *izzat*—personal or group prestige or honour—is a manifestation of Weber's notion *par excellence*. In no way is the izzat of a family better evidenced than in its ability to maintain the 'privacy' of its women and to entertain guests in a manner consistent with both the norms of purdah as well as of genteel hospitality. The poorer families, who women must bathe in the ponds of others near the cultivation fields, unhidden from public view, and must hide behind screens in houses when guests are entertained for lack of a kachari ghar, must constantly be reminded thereby of their relatively low status. It was, by contrast, my own properly Quranic experience 'never to look upon' the wives and mature daughters of my more wealthy village acquaintance; although over time, I came to know the men well. But in the homes of the poorer villagers less precaution was taken to ensure that my presence would not 'embarrass' the ladies of the house and in several cases I was able to banter with women while they worked in their compounds; even in these houses, such occasions were rare. Thus, in Hajipur and Tinpara, general differences in wealth and status overlap with distinctions in behaviour and access to goods and services which facilitate the maintenance of 'status honour'.

Status distinctions may also be seen in the pattern of marriage alliances. From the earliest point in my research I was interested in the degree to which class or 'caste' lines, once defined would correspond to marriage patterns. At a number of points I discussed the matter with villagers and was most often told, with varying tones of insistence, that economic considerations were of the greatest import in the selection of spouses. As one informant put it: 'Nowadays if one's economic position is good, one's lineage status is also good.'

This statement seems to ring true in no small measure. The most important consideration in the selection of husbands for one's daughters seems to lie in the economic well-being and social status of the potential husband's family. It was often touchingly put to me that a father wanted above all his daughter to be married into a homestead where she would 'be happy'. This meant that her marriage should be into a homestead the members of which were economically secure enough that a young wife would not have to perform more than the normal domestic duties. In some of the more wealthy families, for example, domestic servants are often employed. Conversely, the wives of the poorer homesteads' members must not only contend with the tasks of their own husbands' homesteads, but are also often sent to work as domestic help or 'hired labour' during the harvest seasons in the homesteads of the more wealthy villagers. It is a matter of izzat (status honour), as I have pointed out, for those who can afford it to provide adequately for the observance of purdah. Thus, in the selection of a prospective husband, it is a matter of some concern that there be minimal risk that the bride's *lajja* ('modesty', 'natural shyness', or 'sense of shame') will be offended. Finally, concern for the girl's relations with the women in her 'father-in-law's house' is a further element in attempting to assure for her a 'happy' married life. For, as is common elsewhere in South Asia, a young bride's relations with her husband's elder brother's wives, and, above all, her mother-in-law, may be tense. For this reason, a perceptive informant once told me, families in which many divorces are known to have taken place are often avoided as sources of marriage partners; frequency of divorce is taken as a sign of a family where the men are inordinately demanding and mean or with whose women it is difficult to get along.

The families of girls being considered as brides are also investigated to ascertain locally their economic situation and status. In this connection local sardars are often consulted as independent checks, if a bride is sought far from home. In addition to the economic well-being and status of the family, some personal considerations are operative. It seems to be a matter of some concern that the girl in question be properly 'religious', that is, that she can and does 'read' the Quran during the appropriate prayer periods (in most cases this amounts to her reciting what she can remember of the appropriate prayers). For this reason, I add parenthetically, it is common to find proportionally more girls present in *madrasas* (Islamic schools) than in public schools, since from the point of view of the family who must find her the best possible match, it is more important that a girl be familiar with the formal niceties of religious observance than with simple arithmetic or the Bengali alphabet (although in families where the sons have attained a significantly higher average of education, it is common to seek a bride who is at least to some extent literate). Finally as village men, at least, will regularly attest, it is desirable that a girl will be reasonably good-looking—or, as regards local standards, 'fair-skinned', a physical characteristic which, I suspect, is valued for prestige reasons as much as for ideal notions of physical beauty.

In Hajipur and Tinpara the choices of marital alliance tend to exhibit a certain coalescence along the lines of the status groups I have delimited above. Genealogical data from 31 patrilineages, including several from villages lying near the two I focus on here, reflect this fact. Of the 31, some 14 bore traditionally high status titles and 17 did not. A count of all marriages recorded in those genealogies for which data on lineage status were obtained shows that the titled lineages married into others of like status at an average rate of 42.3 per cent of their total marriages recorded. By contrast, non-titled grihasti lineages show evidence of marriage into titled lineages at an average rate of 13.4 per cent of their total recorded marriages. Thus, the tendency for titled lineages to intermarry was over three times the rate of grihasti lineages to marry into them.[6]

These data point to a certain independence of status from class taken as a purely economic category. Status would appear to be as much a consideration in marriage choice as is economic well-being, even where the two do not coincide. Thus, a titled family can obtain desirable marriage partners for its sons and daughters even if its economic situation (*abastha*) is comparatively modest. This is particularly the case if the basis for its status is religious. For example, the family of Hajis in Hajipur has a marriage rate of 44.4 per cent with other families bearing both secular and religious titles, despite the fact that the Haji family possesses only the subsistence amount of land. It should be further pointed out that within a given lineage the individual households (chula) may vary greatly with respect to economic well-being. In a titled lineage with one or more rich cultivator or surplus farmer families, the latter have predominance within the lineage and are largely responsible for the maintenance of the status honour of the whole kin group. As Table 4 indicates, 90 per cent of the surplus farmers in Hajipur and Tinpara are members of titled lineages or homesteads. A subsistence, marginal or poor peasant household in the patrilineal kin group of the homestead or lineage in question has the advantage of status which, one might say, is 'paid for' in the long run by the fortunes of the lineage as a whole, in particular its more wealthy segments, either in the past or at the present point in time. The statements of the villagers to the effect that economic well-being is the major consideration in marriage choice may be seen in this context. The extent to which status alone is a consideration finds demonstration also in the analysis of actual marriages over time, as is possible with genealogical data. Thus, only indirectly can it be maintained that those 'whose economic situation is good' also have high lineage status.

MOBILITY IN THE SYSTEM

The data presented above reflect a good deal of openness in social stratification, as far as status is concerned, in that even among titled lineages the absolute majority of marriages are with non-titled lineages. In short, mobility between high status and non-high status groups is clearly evident.

A high degree of mobility of individual families between economic classes and status groups is an important feature of social stratification in Hajipur and Tinpara and probably has been so far a long time. Given that the economy of these villages is one of general scarcity, with the population size and the vicissitudes of agriculture in a monsoon climate, it is unlikely that a family can maintain superior wealth for long without some difficulty. This is partly because ownership of property is individual, not corporate or communal. Inheritance is partible and stresses equal division among males. A certain proportion of the patrimony is also legally designated for females in shares which, while in total disproportionate to that given to males, are also equally divided among those women who inherit. Thus, over time, unless land is consistently accumulated, a given lineage taken collectively becomes vulnerable to the inexorable problems of agriculture in a monsoon environment, as its property is progressively segmented into uneconomic units. At the same time, other families with subsistence holdings or a little more may be rising, especially if they are able to engage successfully in lending activities, in particular the taking of land in mortgage, over a given period of time. Thus, there appears to occur a regular rise and fall of families, with decline of wealth (and hence a key basis for power) for some and increase of these for others, in a process which probably evinces a three to four generation periodicity.

The assignment of status seems to follow the rise and fall of various families in this respect. Villagers in Hajipur and Tinpara are quick to distinguish between long-standing and recently acquired titles. For example, they will readily inform one of which local families among, say, the Majumdar homesteads, are the 'real' or 'original' (*ashol*) Majumdars, who are perceived to have gained the title 'legitimately' in the past for performance of the requisite services, and which of them are merely 'so-called' (*dak*) Majumdars, in those cases where the title has been merely been recently adopted by rural upstart *parvenus*. Similarly, members of poor peasant families will sometimes claim to have enjoyed the status of a secular title in past generations, but will end their tale of woe by stating that they can no longer claim it. One is reminded, in short, of the proverb common to Muslims everywhere on the subcontinent which states: 'Last year I was a *jolaha* (weaver), this year I have become a Shekh, and if next year's crops are good, I shall be a *Syed'*. As I have suggested here, and elsewhere attempted to show with concrete case study examples (Bertocci 1970: 98 ff), the process this proverb reflects has a double cutting edge as it works itself out, in both upward and downward directions.

CLASS AND POWER

There remains for discussion the way in which this embryonic and as yet highly flexible class system is linked to local and also wider expressions of social and political power. As I have noted earlier, the homestead clusters, which are the basis of village organization in part, are internally solidified by the formal allegiance the constituent homesteads members render to the dominant sardari lineages. In village Hajipur, in 1967 there were three such lineages and three sardars. Of the ten homesteads which comprised this socially defined village, these three lineages taken collectively claimed ownership of well over half the cultivation land of the village. Within each sardari lineage, one found wide variation of ownership among the individual households (chulas); any of them and the individual sardars themselves, while by no means 'poor peasants', were not in every case the most wealthy members of their respective lineages. In Tinpara there were two sardari lineages, but in contrast to the situation in Hajipur here only one sardar could be said to be truly 'dominant'; this man personally owned around 12 per cent of all the cultivation land claimed by Tinpara villagers collectively and in nearly all respects he could be said to be the real arbiter of Tinpara affairs. In both villages the sardars' homesteads were the most common focus for recreational activities, the members of their lineages played key roles in organizing religious and ceremonial activities for each village as a unit, and at that time, the sardari lineages in both villages were prominent in the organization of cooperative societies under the aegis of the well-known Comilla cooperative experiment. In effect, little of importance in the collective lives of people in Hajipur and Tinpara took place without the active participation and leadership of the sardari lineages.

Moreover, the relations between the sardars and their role in the samaj, the multi-village political unit I have described above, contribute, importantly to the formation of a wider, territorially extensive community organization which, I would argue, is the hallmark of rural society in this part of Bangladesh. As I have noted, a manifest function of the samaj as a political grouping is the resolution of conflict within its territory. But a latent function of this multi-village grouping must also be seen—that of the regulation of relations among the sardars themselves as representatives in most cases of the dominant lineages in their respective bailiwicks. When a man becomes a sardar, for example, his accession to this position is ritually sanctioned in a feast (*davat*) to which he invites the other sardars in the samaj. In this manner the newcomer to the sardari ranks, even when he has inherited the position, must legitimize his political status, for the sardars are jealous of their prestige and insist on some method of formally sanctioning admission to their number. A man of new found wealth and prestige who wishes to become a sardar must give such a feast, and refusal of the other sardars to attend amounts to a denial of acknowledgment to the seeker of sardari status.

The ceremonial and political functions of the samaj and its constituent sardars finds reflection in the marriage alliance of the latter. Of the five sardars in Hajipur and Tinpara, four are bearers of high status titles and their lineages contain surplus-farmer households within them. Because of the wide dispersal of marriage ties throughout the thana (see Bertocci 1970: 122-6) I was unable to identify the extent to which people in Hajipur and Tinpara have married into sardari lineages outside their own samaj area. But analysis of marriages within the samaj area has been possible. On the basis of genealogical data I calculate that the five sardari lineages of Hajipur and Tinpara show an overall rate of intermarriage with other sardari lineages of the same smaj of 11.4 per cent of all marriages. The sixteen non-sardari lineages which are found among the Muslims in these two villages married into the sardari lineages of local smaj at a rate of 8.7 per cent of all recorded marriages over several generations. While the difference between the rates of sardari lineage marriage arrangements between the two groups is not statistically significant (using Fisher's Exact Test p=.1135), the direction of the difference is toward a clearly higher rate of intermarriage between sardari lineages than that between sardari and non-sardari families. Thus, while the sardars do not form an exclusively intermarrying group, they tend to choose each other's lineages as sources of mates more often than they allow such alliances to take place with *non-sardari* lineages. At the same time, the fact that non-sardari lineages can have access to mates from sardari families is an important one. For, from the perspective of intermarriage, the samaj as a grouping is unified in two ways. On the one hand, intermarriage between the dominant sardari families from each sub-unit of the samaj helps to solidify ties at the upper levels of power and influence within the smaj itself. On the other hand, the fact that non-sardari lineages can gain access to sardari families via marriage adds to the multiplicity of ties between the more and the less powerful within the samaj as a whole, thereby increasing its cohesion as a group. It might be added, however, that this kind of intermarriage across economic, political and status lines also increases the potential for conflict. For disputes over inheritance of land are typically common sources of schism in these villages, while ironically the aim of intermarriage—so often at the heart of such conflict—is continuity, its opposite.

Finally, the samaj and the sardari system of political leadership may be seen to play crucial roles in linking rural communities to official organs of government and national political parties. Under Ayub Khan's Basic Democracies System the Union Council, an amalgam of villages and mauzas electoral wards of which cross-cut the 'natural' community groupings I have outlines here, reflected these traditional rural leadership patterns and their class base. In 1967, of the fourteen Basic Democrats (Union Councillors) in the Union where Hajipur and Tinpara lie, twelve were Muslims and of these, none were either sardars or from sardari lineages. The extent to which this particular Union Council appeared to reflect the economic and social bases of power and influence common in Bangladesh villages is consistent with the findings of Rehman Sobhan (1968: 88-9), as well as others, for the former province of East Pakistan as a whole.

Over and above this mode of linkage of the rural areas' traditional political system to national institutions of power, it is likely that the dominant rural class groupings have served, and may continue to serve, national elite which come to power in the new State of Bangladesh. Ayoob (1971), among others, has suggested that the wealthier peasants of rural East Bengal were crucial in mobilizing the large electoral majority obtained by the Awami League in December 1970. This class, he argues (and my limited village research tends to confirm his notion), had direct linkages to urban areas by virtue of the fact that many of its members had become part of the newly urbanized 'white collar' intellgentsia, small business and student elements which provided the political base of Bengali nationalism and the Awami League. As Ayoob puts it, these elements, the origins of whose urbanization were quite recent, retained 'intimate contacts and strong family ties with the Bengali countryside'. As a result, 'they were able to draw the more politicized sections of the rural population . . . into their struggle for a place in the sun' (Ayoob 1971: 48). Although this statement must await confirmation from detailed study of the Awami League's power base, I believe that it is a good hypothesis. Moreover, if true, it fits well with the general agreement on the middle class constituency of the Awami League by pinpointing the crucial connections of the party to the dominant surplus farmer or, in Ayoob's terms, middle peasant class in the countryside. It would also suggest a fair amount about the kinds of constraints under which it will be possible to implement the agricultural and rural administrative policies of the present ruling party in Bangladesh.

In general, then, the data and analysis presented here hopefully suggest, at least, something of the way in which East Bengali peasant communities have in the recent past been connected with the larger

State system of which they are a part. While it is true that, as a group, the peasants of Bangladesh form a remarkably homogeneous mass, I have tried to show that there exist among them important distinctions of wealth, status and power. These internal economic and related social status differences are intimately tied to the actual workings of rural communities. Moreover, the differentiation I have tried to show tends to produce an embryonic, often insecure, surplus farmer or 'middle peasant' class, based on a system of land control and moneylending which, in various forms, has a long history in Bengal. As before, the temporary 'winners' in that system fill the intercalary roles which link peasant communities individually and collectively to the State—and now to the new nation itself.

NOTES

* *Acknowledgements*: Fieldwork on which this article is based was made possibly by an NDEA/Fullbright-Hayes Fellowship. I wish to thank Professors Philip Calkins and Ronald Inden of the University of Chicago, for their helpful comments on an earlier version of this paper. Similarly, I appreciate the criticisms offered by my colleagues in the National Seminar on Pakistan and Bangladesh, Columbia University, to whom these ideas were first presented in a formal manner. Professor Hamza A. Alavi, of the University of Leeds, and my own departmental colleagues, Professors Carleton W. Smith and James Dow, have at various points been helpful in the methodological analysis presented here. Needless to say, none of these colleagues are responsible for any errors of fact, interpretation or analysis which may remain. Finally, this paper is written in the 'ethnographic present'.

1. One ought not to speak of the samaj as 'the' definitive territorial or structural unit if, indeed, we must have one at all. Samaj groupings in turn interlink over market areas. If indeed, social interaction has any focal coalescence which could be qualitatively and quantitatively determined in any geographically bounded way, then perhaps the local market (*hat*), with its hinterland, might be said to serve as that focal point. I owe, however, to Professor Ronald Inden the suggestion that samaj and the reyai groupings, cultural entities form the substance of 'community' in symbolic sense. For rather than as being purely territorial entities, they also imply concrete social and political bonds which link individuals both interactionally and ritually in association quite apart from local kin groups. To the extent that members of reyais and samaj units on ritual occasions (e.g. marriages, religious celebrations, etc.) share food (a cultural substance, following Lévi-Strauss) and follow a commonly

enjoined code for conduct which buttresses enduring, diffuse solidarities, these groupings constitute the cultural essence of community. Indeed, one might say that the institutions, reyai and samaj, combining patron-client vertical ties with territorially extensive horizontal ones, constitute the East Bengali local expression of the *umma muslima* itself. This is, however, the subject of another essay.

2. The thana—literally 'police station'—is a unit of political administration roughly equivalent to the *tehsil* in other parts of South Asia and, in Western terms, has been likened to an American county. Comilla thana was 275 sq. kilometres in area in 1966-7, with a population of about 2,18,000.
3. I have elsewhere attempted to derive a concrete empirical referent for the designation of two acres as the 'subsistence level' of farm size (Bertocci 1970: 60-1). Here I can only draw the reader's attention to the fact that a farmer with one acre is likely to produce little more than 900 kilograms of paddy per year, assuming that he cultivates during the summer and autumn seasons, the dry winter being a loss without mechanised irrigation. In the process of husking the farmer is left with around 725 kilograms of rice. Estimates in the 1960s have tended to show that the average East Bengali rural family of 5.5 consumes about 800 kilograms of this staple food per year. Certainly, then, most families in villages like Hajipur and Tinpara live from year to year on the barest margins of subsistence (see figures on average and median, as well as range, of farm size in text). One can thus calculate roughly that around two acres are needed to yield a subsistence crop consistently, particularly given the problems of traditional agriculture on the Bengal delta. Those with substantially more than two acres are on the edge of surplus and peasants with four acres and above are, in this overall minifundist context, surplus farmers.
4. I tested a null hypothesis to the effect that the untitled and titled groups were random samples of the same population, i.e. that there was no statistically significant association between land-ownership and social rank as indicated by high status title. The mean land-ownership (2.36 acres) proved to be in fact significantly greater than that of the untitled group (1.14 acres), at the .01 level using the 't test' of the difference between two means (calculated t = 3.4685, df = 93).
5. The relationship of land-ownership and creditor activities—lending money and renting out land—was tested with Fisher's Exact Test. Creditor activities were associated with landholdings above the median amount at a statistically significant level (p = .0033).
6. On the basis of genealogical analysis, I hypothesized that there would be a systematic tendency for titled lineages to intermarry at a higher rate than that at which they would allow non-titled lineages to marry into them. This hypothesis was confirmed, the correaltions proving significant at the p = .0079 level using Fisher's Exact Test.

REFERENCES

Ahmad, Imtiaz. 1967. 'The Ashraf-Ajlaf categories in Indo-Muslim society', *Economic and Political Weekly* 11: 887-90.

Alavi, Hamza. 1965. 'Peasants and revolution'. *Socialist Register* 11: 241-77.

Ayoob, Mohammed. 1971. 'From martial law to Bangladesh'. In Pran Chopra, ed., *The Challenge of Bangladesh*, pp. 40-59. Bombay: Popular.

Gerth, Hans and C. Wright Mills, eds., 1958. *From Max Weber: Essays in Sociology*. Oxford University Press (Galaxy edition).

Glasse, Robert. 1966. 'La societe musulmane dans le Pakistan rural de l' est'. *Etudes Rurales* 22-24: 188-205.

Gough, Kathleen. 1968-9. 'Peasant resistance and revolt in South India'. *Pacific Affairs* XLI: 526-44.

Gould, Harold A. 1969. 'Toward a "Jati" model for Indian politics'. *Economic and Political Weekly* IV: 291-7.

Hinton, William. 1966. *Fanshen: A Documentary of Revolution in a Chinese Village*. New York: Knopf.

Levy, Reuben. 1965. *The Social Structure of Islam*. Cambridge: Cambridge University Press.

Mao Tse-tung. 1965a. 'Analysis of the class in Chinese society'. *Selected Works of Mao Tse-tung*, pp. 13-21. Peking: Foreign Languages Press.

———. 1965b. How to differentiate the classes in the rural areas'. *Selected Works of Mao Tse-tung*, 137-9. Peking: Foreign Language Press.

Marriott, McKim. 1965. *Caste Ranking and Community Structure in Five Regions of India and Pakistan*. Poona: Deccan College Research Institute.

Nicholas, Ralph W. 1963. 'Ecology and village structure in deltaic West Bengal'. *Economic Weekly* 15: 1185-96.

———. 1969. 'Islam and Vaisnavism in Rural Bengal'. In David Kopf, ed., *Bengal Regional Identity*, pp. 33-47. East Lansing: Michigan State University Asian Studies Centre, South Asia Series, Occasional Paper No. 9.

Sobhan, Rehman. 1968. *Basic Democracies, Works Programme and Rural Development in East Pakistan*. Dacca: University of Dacca, Bureau of Economic Research.

Srinivas, M.N. 1968. *Social Change in Modern India*. Berkeley: University of California Press.

Webster, J.E. 1910. *Tippera. Bengal District Gazetteers*.

Wise, James. 1874. 'On the Barah Bhuiyas of Eastern Bengal'. *Journal of the Asiatic Society of Bengal* XLIII, Part 1, No. 111: 197-214.

———. 1903. 'The Muhammedans of Eastern Bengal'. *Journal of the Asiatic Society of Bengal* LXIII, LXV and LXVII, Part III, No. 1: 463-76.

Muslims in the Hindu Kingdom of Nepal

MARC GABORIEAU

(1972)

What does it mean to be a Muslim in a non-Muslim environment? Nepal, where a Muslim minority lives scattered among Hindus, provides an illustration of this kind of problem. It is a Hindu kingdom—the last one—where Hinduism is the State religion and where, until quite recently, Hindu law founded on the *dharma-shastra* applied to all subjects, including Muslims. It offers, therefore, a pure case of Hindu environment and institutions.

According to the census of 1961, among the nine and a half million inhabitants of Nepal, there were 2,80,597 Muslims, i.e. 2.97 per cent of the total population. They are divided into three groups of unequal size: most of them are settled in the southern plain, the Tarai; 1,127 Indian Muslims live in the Kathmandu Valley; finally 6,656 Muslim bangle-makers, called Churaute, are scattered in 45 villages all over the hills of central and the western Nepal. In this paper we shall consider only the last group, which has been associated for more than two centuries with the numerically, socially and politically dominant Nepali-speaking Hindu population who have created the institutions of the present kingdom of Nepal.

We shall further narrow the scope of the discussion by limiting ourselves to socio-religious aspects, posing the following questions: How do the Muslims identify themselves in relation to the Hindu majority? What is the status ascribed to Muslims in the caste society? In other words, we shall see how religious beliefs and the acceptance of social order founded on ritual purity determine in part the status of Muslims in a Hindu environment. These ideological factors, of course, are not the only ones; but we shall concentrate on them because they are the most important in a Hindu society.[1]

In January 1964, I was walking through the district of Gorkha some 40 miles from Kathmandu. At midday I entered a hamlet and asked for food; a woman answered: 'we cannot prepare any food during day time, because we are now in the month of *Ramazan*'. That is how I became aware of the presence of Muslims in the hills of Nepal. The people of this hamlet looked like the Hindus of the surrounding villages: same dress, same type of houses, same way of living: nevertheless, they were set apart as Muslims (*Musalman*) opposed to their Hindu neighbours. It will be of interest to analyse the various meanings both Hindus and Muslims give to this opposition.

Let us begin with an examination of the Nepalese law: Hinduism being the State religion, what is the legal status of Muslims? We read in the First Legal Code of 1853:[2]

> All people of a caste (*jat*)[3] wearing the sacred thread (*Upadhyaya* Brahmans, *Rajput, Jaisi* [Brahmans], *Kshatri*...), all people of a caste who drink alcohol and cannot be reduced into slavery, people of European caste, of Muslim caste, people of a caste whose touch does not require purification by aspergation of water [but] from whose hand water is not accepted, all people of a caste whose touch requires purification by aspergation of water, in the whole territory ruled by the Gorkha (dynasty), are allowed, barring the slaughtering of cows, to perform all acts considered as duty (*dharma*) in their own religion (*majhab*) according to the traditions of their family (*kul*). Nobody should get angry (with anybody) in this matter. If, in case of a quarrel in such a matter, anybody comes to complain in a court, the man who has done something which may prevent another man from practising his religion, should be punished by a fine of a hundred rupees; if he does not pay the fine, he should be imprisoned according to the law. In case anybody lost his life in course of the quarrel, if the murderer is of a caste who may be put to death, his life should be taken in exchange of the life [of the victim]; if he is of a caste who cannot be put to death, all his property should be confiscated according to the law and he should be imprisoned for life. (Code 1952: vol. v, no. 1, 1 and Code 1963: no. 10, 224)

Leaving aside for the time being the long list of castes which raise the problem of the status of Muslims in the caste society, let us study the rights of the Muslims insofar as they belong to a religion different from the official one. I use here the word religion to translate the legal concept of majhap or majhab (in Arabic mazhab) which is general and neutral, and applies to any of the great religions. Dharma here means duty, but in later legal documents it is used to designate all religions classified as Hindu and is opposed to *mat*: creed, which applied to non-Hindu religions.

What is meant by Hindu? The legal codes of 1853 and 1963 are silent on the subject but the Code of 1952 goes into some details: strictly speaking, Hindu means the traditional Shaiva and Vaishnava sects (*Shiva Vaishnava adi sanatan dharma*); but Buddhism (*bauddha mat*) traditionally enjoys the same rights (Code 1952: no. 29, 16). Other sects, either ancient or modern, are also accepted and the following list is given: *arya samaji, brahmasamaji, radhakrishna, vallabhi, jhannashanna, jain, nastik ramkabir* (Code 1952: no. 29, 15). The codes are silent about tribal religions, like those of the Rais or the Limbus, but legal practice shows that they enjoy the same status as Hinduism. Thus, from the point of view of the law, all those religions or sects are classified as Hindu.

They are opposed to Islam and Christianity (as well as, curiously enough, *kabir panthi*), which are characterized as foreign and irreligious creeds (*videshi vidharmi mat*), destroying the traditional religion and caste order.

What are the rights given to the followers of those non-Hindu religions and especially Muslims? To quote again the code: 'they are allowed to perform all acts considered as duty in their own religion, according to the tradition of their family'. And in fact no restrictions are placed on religious practices. Muslims can freely perform all private and public ceremonies: they take out noisy *tazia* processions during the month of *Muharram* and have their mosques and cemeteries; they are allowed to establish religious trusts (*guthi*), in order to maintain the latter and to finance ceremonies. In the field of personal law, some usages, either Islamic or customary, are recognized by the code. For instance, a Hindu is not allowed to marry a member of his paternal lineage within a certain number of generations (varying according to caste) but an exception is made in favour of Muslims, so that they can, if they want, marry the paternal parallel cousin (Code 1853: 551-2, 536-7).[4] Similarly special clauses were made to codify the customs of the various Muslim groups in the matter of adultery and remarriage (Code 1853: nos. 5, 6, 8, 677; Code 1952: nos. 21, 22, 110).

But these clauses concern only minor points: on other matters—especially inheritance—they have to follow Hindu law and all cases-even those where only Muslims are involved—are tried by State courts presided over by Hindu judges. Some clauses of the law weigh heavily on them. To quote the 1935 Code, they are allowed to practise their own religion 'except for doing acts prohibited in the code, including the slaughtering of cows' (Code 1952: vol. v, no. 1, 1). The last prohibition is of importance for Muslims who outside Nepal are traditionally beef-eaters. Even on the occasion of *baqra'id*, i.e. festival of the cow, they can sacrifice only buffaloes. I will here mention only one more prohibition. While Hinduism has been constantly gaining ground among the tribal people for the past two centuries, partly through the Hindu monarchy and partly through imitation of higher castes, non-Hindus are prevented from making converts from among Hindus, even if they be foreigners. Only people who were already Muslims (or Christians) when they entered Nepal, or were born there from Muslim (or Christian) parents, enjoy the freedom of practising those religions. This rule has been constantly followed by the present dynasty. As soon as King Prithivi Narayan entered Kathmandu Valley in 1768-9, he expelled the Catholic missionaries and their local converts. Francis Hamilton notes a similar restriction regarding the spreading of Islam as early as 1802-3: 'While at Kathmandu, several Hindus, of high caste, among our followers, chose to embrace the Musalman faith, and thereby subjected themselves to severe restrictions and disgrace' (Hamilton 1819: 37-8). the first official document on the subject which has come to my notice is an article of the Code of 1952:

> Spreading kabirpanthi, Christian, Islamic and other irreligious and foreign creeds; delivering, for the purpose of spreading them, speeches which may corrupt the religion of the people, converting any member of the brahman caste or any of the castes from whose hand water is accepted, is prohibited. If anybody does so or attempts to do so, this person, as well as the person who has abandoned his traditional religion to adopt one of the above-mentioned creeds, are deemed to have committed an offence. If the courts, the police or the local authorities do not lodge a complaint against them, the government must lodge a complaint and inquire into the case. (Code 1952: vol. v, no. 29, 15)

A similar clause occurs in the 1963 Legal Code:

> Inside Nepal, nobody is allowed to preach creeds like Islam and Christianity which destroy the dharma practised by the Hindu people; or to convert to those creeds people practising the Hindu dharma. If anybody attempts to convert people, he should be imprisoned for three years; if he has actually [converted people] he should be imprisoned for six years; and then, if he is a foreigner, he should be expelled from the country. If anybody practising the Hindu dharma becomes converted to any of the above-mentioned creeds, he should be imprisoned for one year, and then if he is a foreigner, he should be expelled from the country. If he has only attempted to become converted, he should be punished by a fine of a hundred rupees. When somebody has become converted, the conversion is nullified, and he remains in the Hindu dharma. (Code 1963: no. 1, 223)

And finally, until the promulgation of the new code of 1963, non-Hindus were impure in the eye of the law. The earliest and best illustration of this attitude is given by Hamilton who wrote, referring to his stay at Kathmandu in 1802-3:

> When any woman has been discovered with a Musalman, the whole kingdom is thrown into confusion. Even if she has been of the lowest caste, she may have given water to some person of the caste immediately above her own. He may again have given it to a higher caste and thus the whole inhabitants may have been involved in sin and disgrace. This can only be expatiated by a ceremony called prayascitta, in which the Prince washes in the river with great ceremony, and bestows large sums on the Brahmans, who read expiatory prayers proper on the occasion. The expense of an expiation of this kind, which was performed during our stay in this country, was, by my Brahman, estimated at two thousand rupees; but the natives alleged it amounted to ten times this sum. (Hamilton 1819: 20-1)

The codes also declare non-Hindus impure: we shall deal later on with this fact and see its bearing on the problem of the rank of Muslims in the caste hierarchy. Let us here only point out an article of the 1853 code which has been hitherto little noticed: in the chapter on exchange of food and drink, Christians and Muslims are listed with untouchable castes from whose hands only raw and dry eatables can be accepted (Code 1853: no. 2, 369).

Thus, in the eye of the law, all religions (majhab) are not equal: Hinduism is the dharma, the religion *par excellence*, and enjoys complete freedom and protection. Islam, which represents a challenge to the belief and social order of the Hindus, is tolerated with restrictions.

How far does the law reflect the attitude of the Hindus toward the few Muslims who live among them? Although they are not interested in the details of Islamic observances, they are struck by some features which seem strange to them, or, one may say, they choose to notice only such features. Thus, Muslims do not perform their ablutions in the same way as Hindus do; the former bury their dead, the latter cremate them; for the latter, the sacred direction is east, while the former turn toward Mecca, which happens to be situated west of Nepal and India. Adding up a few similar facts, Hindus generalize and come to the conclusion that Islam is *ulto dharma*, reversed religion; that Muslims consciously do just the opposite of what Hindus consider to be normal behaviour. They even go a step further and make up stories. They for instance tell of a Muslim who was sitting among Hindu friends chewing a piece of arecanut which, while he was talking, fell on the ground. He felt embarrassed, asked the Hindus: 'What do you do in such a circumstance?' They answered: 'For us, whatever thing has been in contact with the mouth, even one's own mouth, is polluted (*jutho*): it cannot be eaten.' The Muslim quietly picked up the arecanut and chewed it again, choosing deliberately the reverse of the Hindu way.

All Hindus, of all castes, consider Muslims as impure. Hamilton, while writing about untouchables, remarked: 'These castes can scarcely venture to draw near any other Hindu, but would consider themselves as much degraded by eating, drinking or cohabiting with a Musalman or a Christian' (1819: 37).The same feeling is expressed in a ballad I recorded from a minstrel belonging to the *Gaine* caste, one of the lowest among the untouchables. A rat has fallen on the plate of the King Bijaya Bhar and he refuses to eat from it, saying:

> We eat game, deer killed by dogs; all the people eat curd defiled by the mouth of cats. But the rat (*musa*) is called Muslim (Musalman); we Hindus, we do not eat food touched by Muslims.[5]

Finally—if not openly, at least indirectly in legends—Muslims play the part of the enemy. People who rank as *Kshatriya* (*Thakuri* and Kshatri castes) pose as Rajputs and in their written or oral genealogies they tell how their ancestors had to leave Rajasthan to escape the persecution of Muslims. An even more widespread story is that of the Emperor Aurangzeb who confiscated the sacred threads of so many Brahmans that he could fill 74 carts with them—more precise versions say 74 and a half! Many Hindus believe that they came to the hills at that time. Neither tale seems to be grounded in history; they merely express an inner feeling of hostility between Hindus and Muslims.

Thus common people express the same attitude toward Muslims as the law does, though in another language. Islam is opposed to the dharma, and Muslims endanger Hindus by their impurity and hostility. How to explain this attitude? A clue was given long ago by Hodgson:

> The penal code of Nepal, a Hindu state, is necessarily founded on the *Shastras*, . . . the law expressly confounds Mohammadans with the outcastes of its own community. . . . If the followers of Islam are not expressly ranged with ordinary outcastes by the Hindu law Shastras, it is merely because the antiquity of the books transcends the appearance of the Moslems in India;

since, by the whole spirit and tenor of those books, 'all who are not Greeks are barbarians'—all strangers to Hinduism, *Mlecchas.* (1880: 236-7)

The Sanskrit word mleccha is a blanket term applying to all people who do not share in the Hindu culture; it is also used by the Nepalese legal codes in association with the words musalman and seems usually to designate Europeans (Code 1853: no. 38, 390; Code 1952: vol. v, 106; also see Macdonald 1970: 145). The Nepalese when dealing with Muslims and Christians, follow an old Hindu tradition. A few references to the dharma-shastra will be enough to substantiate this statement: mlecchas are characterized as those who do not follow the usages of the Hindus and their institutions of *varna* and *ashrama*; who eat cow flesh (see, e.g. Kane 1930-62: IV, 117). They are considered impure (ibid.: II, i, 384 and III, 882-3); rules were made to prevent caste people from being polluted by them and to purify those who had been forcibly defiled (ibid.: II, i, 575 and IV, 117). But, on the other hand, just as the king had to protect heretics, so 'he had to take into consideration the duties and usages of the four varnas and 18 low castes. The 18 low castes said to be outside the pale of the varna and ashrama are enumerated by Pitamaha, viz., washerman, shoe-maker, *nata*, bamboo-maker, fisherman, mleccha, *Bhilla, abhira, matanga* and 9 others' (ibid.: III, 284-5). No doubt, the Nepalese attitude toward the Muslims (acceptance and protection accompanied by severe restrictions) continues the tradition of the dharma-shastra. But some features seem to come from another source: the neutral and general term majhab does not correspond to any Sanskrit concept; Muslim thinkers do sometimes use mazhab with that meaning; but most probably the Nepalese legislator has in mind the western concept of religion. This double reference to Islam and Christianity brings us back to the end of the eighteenth century, when the new Kingdom of Nepal was created. It was a time of Hindu renaissance when the Marathas and later the Sikhs (and the Nepalese had contacts with both) were fighting Muslims and the British: 'when the banner of Hinduism dropped from the hands of the Mahrattas in 1817, they solemnly conjured the Nepalese to take it up, and wave it proudly, till it could be again unfurled in the plains by the expulsion of the vile *Feringis,* and the subjection of the insolent followers of Islam' (Hodgson 1880: 240). This may explain why the present dynasty has insisted, more than the preceding ones, on banning cow slaughter and proselytism. It sought to protect the tradition from foreign influence and penetration.

Turning now to the viewpoint of Muslims, let us try to see what it means to them to be followers of Islam. We could directly ask them the question but this kind of approach soon proves disappointing: in their answer they give an image of what they should be, not of what they are in fact. In Islam beliefs, rituals, injunctions and prohibitions are so well codified that even an ignorant villager of the Nepal hills knows more or less how he should behave to be a good Muslim and pretends that he is such. I prefer to turn to quite a different approach, asking: What is the minimum of beliefs and practices a Muslim should stick to on pain of losing his own identity? We can observe Islam reduced to such a minimum in a few villages of the Karnali Basin in western Nepal, where reformist and revivalist propaganda from the plains has not yet reached: to be a Muslim there means adherence to the following.

First, professing that there is only one God. This belief is outwardly marked in their way of greeting people. As an old man of Dullu put it: 'A Muslim should never bend his head in front of anybody except God.' Therefore, while lower caste people prostrate themselves in front of Brahmans, or sons in front of fathers, a Muslim, when greeting superior people will never bow: he will stand upright, raise his hand to his forehead, and say *salam.*

Secondly, they are submitted to a law (*shariat*) revealed by God, which provides the norm for conduct in all aspects of life. The fact that there is such a law is never questioned, but it is not integrally obeyed; and it is interesting to note the rules which are considered important and cannot be dispensed with. The hill Muslims adhere to their own rules of ritual purity—which are different from those of the Hindus—and have preserved in their own dialect the Arabic words *ghusl* and *wuzu* for major and minor ablutions; they abstain from all food and contacts considered as polluting, especially pork and (at least in public) alcohol. Ceremonies of the life-cycle are unequally preserved: birth rites have been borrowed from Hindu neighbours; but circumcision is considered necessary and they have periodically to call for that purpose, a barber from the plains. The Islamic exchange of consent (*nikah*) cannot be dispensed with in the course of the marriage ceremonies; and they bury their dead according to the codified ritual. Other practices, which are enjoined as obligatory by the religious law, are unequally followed: alms to the poor (*zakat*) are collected on the day of the breaking of the fast (*id-ul-fitr*); but daily prayers and the fast of ramazan are most often light-heartedly dispensed with. For many people the only prayers performed during the year are those of the two great festivals: Id-ul-fitr and Baqr-id. By sticking to this minimum Muslims, in their beliefs and rites, set themselves apart from the Hindus.

But, curiously enough, the main emphasis is on festivals which are not canonical: those in honour of saints. Everywhere, the cult of Shah Madar of Makanpur has been introduced by *madari faqir,* who are settled in most of the villages. In addition, in the central hills, the martyrs Hasan and Husain are venerated during the first ten days of the lunar month of Muharram; further west the fair of Ghazi Miyan is held in the beginning of the solar month of *Jesth.* Those festivals are celebrated with much more solemnity, and with a more active participation of the people than the canonical ones. We will understand why this is so when we realize what they mean for the local Muslims. In actual history, Hasan and Husain were killed by Muslims, Ghazi Miyan by Hindus; but in the mind of the hill Muslims, the two legends blend curiously, and the story of the former is shaped on the same patterns as that of the latter: it runs briefly as follows.

The heroes are Muslims: their marriage is going to take place and the rejoicing has begun to the sound of auspicious music. Suddenly there is news that the enemies, who are Hindus, are coming to attack; the auspicious music is changed into martial music and the heroes, mounting their horses, rush to fight the enemies. They are finally killed and the story ends in lamentation and funeral music.

While in the celebration of the canonical festivals, Muslims can hardly find any outlet for their emotions, during Muharram and Ghazi Miyan fair they can express successively joy in evoking the marriage, aggression when they commemorate the battle in a sham fight, and finally grief when they sing lamentations, for this legend tells of the greatest sorrow: death on the day of marriage. And one should emphasize that the main theme of those festivities, where Muslims express themselves without restraint, is an irreducible enmity between Hindus and Muslims.

To sum up this rapid review, Muslims identify themselves in opposition to Hindus by sticking to the main tenets of Islam and by expressing, through festivals and legends connected with them, their hostility.

So whatever viewpoint one adopts—that of the legislator, that of the Hindu folk, or of the Muslim folk—one comes always to an irreducible opposition between Hindus and Muslims. What is a most sacred duty for one is considered as just the reverse by the others, to the Hindus who follow their dharma Islam is *vi-dharmi*, ulto dharma; conversely for Muslims who practice submission (islam) to the only God and His revealed law, who follow the true religion (*din*), Hinduism is infidelity and idolatry. We cannot help recalling what Al-Baruni wrote nine centuries ago: 'They (Hindus) differ from us [Muslims] in religion as we believe in nothing in which they believe, and vice versa' (Sachau 1964: 1, 19). For Hindus of all castes Muslims are impure; and the latter have to agree to be treated as such. Finally, in the background, each community is convinced that the other is the enemy. In normal circumstances, this feeling remains hidden and is expressed only indirectly through legends but in periods of crisis, it can come to the foreground. I was able to witness such an explosion in a village of central Nepal in October 1965. It was the time of the *dasai* festival and Hindus and Muslims were playing together at the *rohote ping*, a kind of vertical merry-go-round. For several hours the atmosphere was very cordial, Hindus and Muslims addressing each other as *mama*, maternal uncle, a term denoting a warm relationship. Then, one of the pillars supporting the merry-go-round broke down; to replace it, a Muslim set about cutting a tree belonging to a Hindu; the latter got angry and a quarrel arose. For the affectionate term of address 'maternal uncle', the crude words Hindu and Musalman, accompanied by filthy abuses were substituted. Incidentally, this was the time soon after the Indo-Pakistani war and news about it had come through the radio. In spite of the neutral policy of the Nepalese government, Hindus, in their discussions, unanimously sided with India and Muslims, more or less, identified with Pakistanis. Some Muslims had witnessed Hindu-Muslim riots in India and were afraid; in fact, during my stay in the village, tension went on rising.

I began by analysing the opposition between Hindus and Muslims in order to emphasize it for, since it usually remains in the background, it could easily pass unnoticed. Now, keeping it in mind, let us see how the Muslim minority fits in the environing society. The latter being a caste society, the question arises: is a rank ascribed to the Muslims in the caste hierarchy? In anthropological literature, there are two ways of dealing with this problem: one is simply to avoid it, arguing that, because of the difference in religion, Muslims stand completely outside the caste society (see Srinivas 1955: 22). But such an attitude disregards the fact that traditionally Hindu governments and authorities, far from considering Muslims a complete outsiders, codified their relations with Hindus—just like the dharma-shastra made rules for dealing with the mleccha. For instance, the *shastri* of Poona wrote of Muslim status as if it was equivalent to that of unclean castes above untouchables (see Steele 1868, quoted in Orenstein 1965: 139). Hodgson pointed out long ago that Nepalese law did deal with the question of the status of Muslims: 'This law expressly confounds Mohammadans with the outcaste of its own community' (1880: 236). He went on to explain what he meant by: 'He who may give water to a pure Hindu to drink, is within the pale of Hinduism; he whose water may not be drunk by a pure Hindu, is an outcaste, an utterly vile creature, whose intimate contact with one within the pale is foul contamination, communicable to the pure by the slightest and most necessary intercourse held with them, and through them to all others' (ibid.: 244).

Since traditional Hindu authorities did assign a rank to Muslims, we are justified in following the second approach, like that of Orenstein or Mayer. In what sense and by which criteria can Muslims be considered to have a rank in the hierarchy of castes?

For Nepalese Muslims, we have to start from the observations of Hodgson: these call for two remarks. First, having probably in mind the traditional distinction between *sa-varna* and *a-varna*, 'those within the pale' and 'outcaste', he calls the latter 'non-Hindus'. Now, in the eyes of the law as well as of the people, low caste people 'whose water may not be drunk' are considered to be Hindus; the line separating Hindus from non-Hindus is not an horizontal one, but a vertical one drawn—we shall see on which criteria—between low castes and Muslims. Secondly, in his list of 'outcastes', Muslims are enumerated in the last position: does it mean that they rank lowest? Hodgson enumerated the castes at random ignoring the actual hierarchy existing among them. We must then first study this hierarchy to see where Muslims stand.

The whole society, as Hodgson rightly pointed out, is first divided according to the criterion of acceptance of water: all the upper castes are pure (*chokho*) and freely accept water from each other. They are called *pani chalne*, i.e. those from whose hand water is accepted and make up approximately 85 per cent of the population. They stand together in refusing water from the hands of the rest of the castes, who are called *pani nachalne*, i.e. those from whose hand water is not accepted. We shall simply call them impure. They make up about 15 per cent of the population.

Pure castes are further divided according to the criterion of initiation. The twice-born, who are allowed to wear the sacred thread are called *tagadhari* and make up about 65 per cent of the total population. They are divided into the following castes: Brahmans, Thakuri (the royal caste called Rajput in the legal code) and Kshatri. Below them are placed those who cannot perform the initiation ceremony. Since in Nepal they are allowed to drink alcohol—while twice-born are not—they are called *matwali.* The comprise the uninitiated *khas* of western Nepal and the Tibeto-Burmese speaking tribes who—it should be emphasized—are all considered pure. They make up about 20 per cent of the whole population. We need not, for the problems discussed in this paper, go into the details of the complicated hierarchy existing among pure castes and sub-castes.

More important are the subdivisions among the impure ones. The criterion of touch is applied: the lowest castes are considered so defiling that, if anybody belonging to a pure caste comes into physical contact with such a low caste man, he must purify himself. This is done simply by taking a little water in one's hand and sprinkling it on one's body. The castes are therefore called *chchoi chchito halnu parne,* i.e. those whose touch requires [purification by] aspergation of water. We shall call them untouchable. In contradistinction, the impure castes whose touch is not defiling are called *chchoi chchito halnu na parne,* i.e. those whose touch does not require purification by aspergation of water.

Now what is the rank assigned to Muslims in this hierarchy? One should notice that, in the article of the code we translated at the beginning of this paper, Christians and Muslims come, in the enumeration of castes and groups of castes, in-between the pure and the impure categories. Since the enumeration is a hierarchical one, they are not placed there by chance; if we look at the chapter devoted to impure castes, we see all Muslims and mleccha listed among impure but non-untouchable castes (Code 1853: 680-1; Code 1952: 106; see Macdonald 1970: 145).

The status thus assigned by the law corresponds to the rank given by village Hindus to the Muslims. And the Muslims themselves acknowledge their low position. Thus, a woman once refused water to my porter belonging to the Tamang tribe on the ground that he could not accept it from a polluted caste. When he asked her which caste she belonged to, she answered 'Musalman caste'. This happened in a hamlet in the district of Gorkha. But the touch of a Muslim is not considered polluting. In some remote areas a few very orthodox Brahmans may purify themselves after touching a Muslim, but this is not considered obligatory. People who live in the neighbourhood of Muslims, and know exactly who they are, touch them freely and never purify themselves; but they will not fail to sprinkle themselves with water if they happen to touch any member of the artisan castes classified as untouchable.

Thus it is not enough to say, as Hodgson did, that Muslims are considered as outcastes; they are assigned—at least from the viewpoint of the pure castes—a definite rank in the last but one level of the social hierarchy, above the untouchables. This situation does not seem to be peculiar to Nepal. Thus, Orenstein writes:

> The main Muslim bhauki (lineage) had the traditional occupation of butcher, thus its members were associated with death. Furthermore, Muslim tradition permitted eating of beef. By 'ritual' criteria Muslims ought to have been ranked among Harijans. Yet the political rulers in this region, as in much of India, had at one time been Muslims, and the local Muslims were identified with them; hence they ranked as touchable, albeit a low caste. (1965: 144-5)

Orenstein starts with the presupposition that Muslims should rank as untouchable, and uses two arguments in support of it. First, in the particular case cited by him, they are butchers. This argument does not hold good, however, because all over India butchers are considered impure but they rank higher than untouchables. Muslims get here exactly the rank which would be expected if we should consider only their occupation. The second argument is that Muslims are beef-eaters: it is a more serious one and, if valid, we should expect Muslims to be generally classified as untouchables. But does this reasoning *in abstracto* correspond to anything in the traditional Hindu society? Since his observations do not correspond to his theoretical expectation, Orenstein has to build up a historical explanation: Muslims should have ranked lower, but they were upgraded because they, at one time, had political power in the area.[6] Against his argument, we should point out that since the seventeenth century, Maharashtra has witnessed an interesting movement of Hindu renaissance; Hindu law founded on the dharma-shastra was rigorously enforced (see, e.g. Gune 1953) and we should not expect that any concession would be made to Muslims from the point of view of ritual status. Nepal offers contrary evidence. It has been governed for centuries by Hindu kings and Muslims were always a small minority without any political power; nevertheless, they were never considered untouchables.

I then propose a simpler hypothesis: the rank of impure but not untouchable assigned to Muslims in Nepal by the local Hindus as well as by the written law should be considered as the traditional and normal rank of Muslims and generally of the mleccha in a Hindu society.[7] In fact, whenever we get a precise description for any part of India, we see Muslims ranked in the aforesaid manner.[8] This should be considered as rule: and we should conceive as exceptions calling for an explanation only the cases where they rank either lower or higher. They are lower when they belong to untouchable castes converted to Islam: they retain their previous defiled status even in the eyes of other Muslims. They may be higher only in areas where the Muslim community is numerous and politically dominant, as for instance in the Delhi area or in Kashmir, where water is accepted from their hands. (See Dumont 1970: 58; also see Madan 1972.)

Pursuing our enquiry on the status of Muslims in Nepal from the point of view of the pure castes, let us see what are the rules governing sexual relations between the latter and the impure but not untouchable castes and whether they apply also to Muslims.

In Nepal hypergamy is widely practised. For a man of pure caste, women are like water: he is allowed to have relations with women of all the castes from whose hand he can accept water. But sexual relations with a woman of an impure though not untouchable caste are not permitted: up to 1963, they constituted a state of offence (*rajkhat*) punishable by the tribunals. If the guilty man had taken neither food nor water from the hands of the woman, he had only to pay a fine (*dand*) and to undergo a penance (*prayascitta*); but if he had taken food or water from her, he was degraded and integrated into her caste. As for the woman, if she had given neither food nor water to the man, she was not considered guilty; if she had, she was severely punished (Code 1853: no. 1, 670; no. 6, 671; no. 9, 672; no. 14, 673; no. 1, 676). Conversely, woman of pure castes were allowed to have sexual relations only with men of an equal or superior status: if they had relations with impure but not untouchable Hindus, they were degraded to the status of the man and integrated into his caste (Code 1853: nos. 1, 4, 668; no. 4, 671).

The same rules do not apply when the impure person involved is a Muslim. The punishment is more severe for a Muslim woman:

> In case a woman of Musalman caste had sexual relations with a man of a superior Hindu caste from whose hand water is accepted, including tagadhari, if through the man she has polluted the food or water [of other pure people], she should be imprisoned for two years; if she has not polluted food or water, she should be imprisoned for one year.

Secondly, the rules of degradation differ; the 1952 code is quite clear on the subject:

> If a person belonging to the Hindu dharma and a person professing a foreign and irreligious creed, have had sexual relations or exchanged water and food, and [the former] has lost his caste according to the code and must be integrated into a lower caste, one should not integrate a man belonging to the Hindu dharma into a caste professing a creed opposed to the Hindu dharma. If a person, either pure or impure, professing a creed classified as opposed to the Hindu dharma and a person of Hindu dharma belonging to any caste from the brahmans to those whose touch requires purification by aspergation of water, have sexual relations, then, after inflicting the punishment prescribed by the code, the man and the woman should be separated. If, after having been separated, they again have sexual relations, the woman should be imprisoned for six months, the man for one year; man and woman should be separated and, if they are foreigners, they should be expelled from the country. (Code 1952: no. 29k, 16)

The Code thus makes a distinction between loss of status and integration into a lower caste. But where can the degraded person go?

In fact, casual sexual relations, especially at the time, of festivals, are ignored. The question of their being allowed or not arises only when a child is born of such a union or when there is a more permanent union. I had the opportunity to know about several cases of the latter kind. In a village of central Nepal, two men of pure caste fell in love with Muslim girls. One was a Kshatri boy, whose parents tried their best to separate him from the girl: they sent him to study first in Kathmandu and then in India. But hc always came back to the girl. They finally had to give way and allow him to live with her. As he could no longer stay in the Kshatri hamlet, he shifted to the Muslim hamlet and himself became a Muslim. The other man was a Gurung who married a Muslim girl in the same manner. In the same village there were three Hindu women (a *Thakurani,* a *Samnyasini* and a *Gurungseni*) from pure castes who lived with Muslim men. These men and women, as well as the children born of such unions, were considered as full members of the Muslim community. Thus the distinction maintained in law between loss of status and integration into the non-Hindu community does not operate.

How to explain this discrepancy? According to the Code, the guilty partners should be separated and the Hindu should be integrated into a caste where he can fit; but practically where could he fit? All Hindus will reject him and consider him impure because of his connections with the Muslims, who in turn feel flattered to accept in their community a person of higher status. Thus, in practice, if not in legal theory, Muslims in relation to pure castes are treated exactly like any impure but not untouchable caste in terms of the rules applicable to acceptance of water, contact and sexual intercourse.

Now where do they stand in relation to the castes classified at their level? In the Code, we find the following list: Castes from whose hand water is not accepted [but] whose touch does not require purification by aspergation of water:

Musalman
Madhesh ka teli (oil-pressers of the plains)
Kasai (Newar butchers and milkmen)
Kusle (Newar tailors and musicians)
Dhobi (Washerman)
Kulu (Newar drum makers)
Mleccha
Chaudara (*Churaute*: Muslim bangle-makers of the hills).

Mleccha and hill Muslims come at the end of the list while other Muslims come in the beginning. Does the foregoing reflect a hierarchical order? In the accompanying text, criteria to ascertain the relative rank of those castes are discussed in detail, and the following hierarchy is presented:

Kasai
Kusle
Hindu dhobi
Kulu (Code 1952: vol. v, nos. 7-10, 106-7; also see Code 1853: nos. 8-11, 679-81 and Macdonald 1970: 144-7).

Teli are left out probably because they live in the plains; and the text not only fails to ascribe a definite rank to the Muslims and mleccha in relation to the other Hindu castes, but even ignores the problem. A clue however is given in another chapter:

> In case a Muslim had sexual relations with a woman of the Hindu Kasai, Kulu, Dhobi'. . . castes from whose hand water is not accepted, if he gave her cooked food or water, he should be punished by a fine of a hundred rupees; if he gave her neither cooked food nor water, he should be punished by a fine of seventy rupees. (Code 1853: no. 4, 637)

It is thus clear that neither food nor water can be exchanged between those Hindu castes and Muslims, and that sexual relations are prohibited. These rules can lead to two divergent interpretations: either Muslims stand lowest in a linear hierarchy, or they are apart. The first one cannot hold good for two reasons: low castes do not provide their services to the castes they consider inferior to themselves and this is a recognized criterion in Nepalese law:

> The caste of the Hindu Dhobi who does not eat from the hand of those seven castes and who does not wash the clothes of those [seven] castes from whose hand water is not accepted and whose touch requires purification by aspergation of water . . . is superior to those seven castes. (Code 1952: no. 8, 106)

Now the Dhobi washes the clothes of Muslims, who cannot therefore be considered inferior to him. Secondly, Hindus cannot be integrated into the Muslim community, while they can be degraded from one to the other of the above mentioned castes (Code 1853: no. 7, 677). We have therefore to choose the second interpretation: according to the law, impure but not untouchable Hindus stand on one side in a linear hierarchy, while Muslims stand apart on the other side.

In the actual behaviour of the people the same opposition holds good: Hindu castes refuse cooked food and water from the Muslims; the latter, while they accept food or water from the pure castes situated above them, refuse to take anything from the impure castes at their level. But what would happen in case of avowed sexual relations? I did not hear of any actual instance, but one would expect the Hindu partner to be rejected by his own caste and to have no other choice but to come into the Muslim community; if this hypothesis proved true, people, here again, would act against the written law.

In brief, at the level of impure but not untouchable castes, Muslims cannot fit into a linear hierarchy, and the opposition between Hindus and Muslims hold good. If we were to compare the foregoing analysis with the treatment of the same problem by anthropologists for other parts of India, we would contrast with Orenstein who inserts

Muslims in a linear hierarchy. We reach a conclusion similar to that arrived at by Mayer, who places them at the level of status but apart from Hindus (see Orenstein 1965: 138-9 and Mayer 1960: 40).

Let us finally analyse the relations of Muslims with the untouchable castes, who are listed below in hierarchical order:

Kami (blacksmiths, goldsmiths, wood-turners) / *Sarki* (leather workers)
Damai (tailors and musicians)
Gaine (begging minstrels)
Badi/ Bhand (begging musicians and dancing girls/jesters)
Pode (Newar executioners and fishermen)
Chyamakhalak (Newar sweepers) (Code 1853: 681, Code 1952: vol. v, 106).

Muslims on their part refuse to accept not only food, but water from these castes: for instance, in a village of central Nepal, a Muslim woman had just brought a pot of water from the fountain and put it under the verandah when a Kami came to sit nearby. I heard the husband telling his wife hurriedly to put the pot inside the house for fear that the Kami would touch it and thereby pollute it. Similarly, a Muslim had performed his ablutions and was sitting under the verandah waiting for the prayer time. He told a Damai who was sitting nearby not to touch them lest he should become defiled and have to wash again before saying his prayers. Muslims thus consider the touch of untouchables as polluting. They also say that they would not allow avowed sexual relations with untouchables. I failed to discover any instance of them in the villages where I enquired though this may be so because they were no recent cases or because they were concealed from me. It is difficult to decide but even the hiding of facts would be an indication of their pretension to rank above untouchables. This claim is well illustrated by the following anecdote. A Kami had stayed for seven years in Dacca and had become converted to Islam. When he came back to his village, he renewed some contacts with his family, but was no longer considered as a full member of his caste. Every Friday he would come to the Muslim hamlet to join in the prayers. Local Muslims were impressed by his good religious education and by his remarkable ability at chanting the Quran; but they would not accept him as a member of their community. Like any other untouchable, he was prevented from entering their houses.

How do untouchables react? They serve Muslims as patrons through permanent relations of the *jajmani* type: this kind of subordination is not as such a criterion of rank but in some instances—as we have seen above in the case of the Dhobi—it can be relevant. Damai play auspicious music for the ceremonies of the castes they consider superior to themselves and for those only; they do not provide their services to castes like Gaine and Badi, who rank lower and have to make their own music. But they do play music for the marriages of the Muslims and they thereby acknowledge that they stand lower than the latter in the social hierarchy. Moreover, when untouchables greet Muslims, they use the same kind of salutation as toward and saying *jaya deu.* So, on this plane where exchange of services comes into consideration, untouchables acknowledge their inferiority.

But, on the other hand, they try to nullify this subordination by claiming they have a higher status of ritual purity than Muslims. They will refuse to accept food or water from their hands. The *mijhar* (a kind of caste headmen appointed by the government for the untouchables) used to insist on the observance of these rules and to enforce penance for any breach. For instance in a *patta* (letter of appointment) issued by the main Damai mijhar to his delegate in the Lamjung district for 1963, it is stated that penances should be enforced for acceptance of water and food and for sexual relations with 'outcasted Damai, Teli, Dhobi, Badi, Gaine, Musalman, Pode, Chyamakhalak, Kulu, Kishthanai (Christians)'.[9] And while impure but not untouchable Hindus—like the pure-can be degraded and integrated into an untouchable caste, an exception is made for Muslims who are not accepted in any Hindu caste, even among the lowest.

If any man or woman of a caste whose water is not accepted but whose touch does not require purification by aspergation of water, Muslims excepted, has sexual relations with a person of a caste whose touch requires purification by aspergation of water, [then] if [the person of non-untouchable caste] is a married woman, her husband may [punish the lover] according to the law; but if the husband does not punish [the lover] or if the woman is unmarried or a widow, or if the person [of non-touchable caste] is a man, since such an act is an offence against the state (raj-khat) the guilty person, in case he (she), after the sexual relations, has given cooked food or water to those who interdine with him (her), should be marked on his (her) left cheek with one letter of [the name of] the caste of the person with whom he (she) has been convicted of having had sexual relations and should be sold as a slave. But if he (she) has not given cooked food nor water to his (her) commensal relations, one should mark his (her) cheek with one letter, integrate him (her) into that (untouchable) caste and let him (her) free; he (she) should not be sold as a slave. (Code 1853: no. 12, 672)

To conclude, when one tries to ascertain the rank of Muslims in the caste hierarchy, one cannot come to any unequivocal conclusion. Their position varies according to the criteria used, and the point of view one chooses. We took into consideration the following criteria: acceptance of food and water, pollution by touch, sexual relations and loss of caste status, exchange of services. When we analysed the point of view of the pure castes and that of Muslims themselves, in their actual behaviour, the Muslims appeared, according to all criteria as if they were a caste just like any Hindu caste, with a definite degree of impurity that of the impure but not the untouchable. But a complication arises from the point of view of the law which—in contradiction to the solution chosen by the people—prohibits integration of fallen people into the Muslim community, thereby trying artificially to keep a separation between Hindus and Muslims. If we take the point of view of the Hindus of impure castes, we see that on the one hand they have to serve Muslims and accept to be treated as impure by them. But on the other hand they compensate by treating Muslims as impure and by refusing to accept any of them in their own castes—thereby, curiously enough, acting in full accordance with the law.

We can now explain the divergent attitude of anthropologists when they have to deal with the problem of the rank of Muslims in a caste society. If they focus on facts like the difference of religion, or the hidden hostility we analysed in the beginning of this paper, they may emphasize the opposition between Hindus and Muslims and consider the latter as remaining outside the caste society. And the Nepalese law, for reasons both religious and historical, tends to emphasize such separation. But this ignores the other aspects of the problem: Muslims do themselves follow, in their dealings with Hindu castes, the rules of purity prevalent in the environing society. Therefore, a rank must be assigned to them. While their status in relation to the pure castes is clear, problems arise as to where they stand in relation to the impure castes. Here again divergent interpretations are possible according to the criteria one chooses to emphasize. By criteria of contact (touch) and exchange of services they are impure but not untouchable; by the criterion of exchange of food and water, and of sexual relations they should rank lower than untouchables. If one realizes, that, in the last analysis, nobody accepts anything from them and that, while Hindus rejected by their own caste can become Muslims, no Muslim will even be admitted in any Hindu caste, one may consider that they stand completely apart from the hierarchy of impure castes. But the last two interpretations are not acceptable: they ignore the fact that similar problems arise when one tries to ascertain the rank of some Hindu impure castes. The clearest example is that of the Dhobi, about whom contradictory statements are made: his touch is not polluting and he refuses to serve untouchables and ranks higher than them in general estimate. On the other hand, the latter refuse to accept food or water from him (as clearly stated, for instance, in the patta of Damai we quoted above): that is why he is considered, by some observers, as ranking among the lowest castes. Similar problems arise in Nepal in the case of Kulu (see patta of Damai quoted earlier) and *Sarki*. The ambiguous position of the Muslims is thus shared by some Hindu castes. Since for the latter the criteria used by higher castes, and by the interested castes themselves, are given prominence to establish their rank in the hierarchy, we have to do the same for Muslims and consider that they are impure but not untouchable in the same sense as the Dhobi is.

I have tried in this paper to analyse the principles which the Hindu social order is founded, and to demonstrate how they have worked to determine the status of Muslims. The core of the discussion centred on the problem of status: insofar as Muslims are followers of a non-Hindu religion, a specific degree of impurity is ascribed to them, which in turn determines their rank in the social hierarchy, and this modern attitude appears clearly as a continuation of the tradition of the dharma-shastra. The position of Muslims in the Hindu society of Nepal is thus quite intelligible. The anthropologist may also draw a lesson from the foregoing analysis. Europeans being also considered as mleccha, Hindus give them the same status as they do to Muslims; they are bound to observe the rules and restrictions linked with this status and to remain in this low and ambiguous position.

NOTES

1. The reader interested in a discussion of other aspects (historical, economic) and in the other Muslim groups of Nepal may consult the following publications: Bista (1967: 129-34), Gaborieau (1966a: 121-32) and Gaborieau (1966b: 81-91).

2. In this paper I use three different versions of the legal code, corresponding to three phases of the legislation:
   (1) Code of 1853, quoted from *Shri Surendra Vikram Shaha Deva Ka Shasan Kal Ma Baneko Muluki Ain*, Kathmandu, V.S. 2022.
   (2) Code of 1952: revised version of the 1935 code, quoted from a reprint of 1955, *Muluki Ain*, vol. V, Kathmandu, V.S. 2012.
   (3) Code of 1963, quoted from the first edition, *Muluki Ain*, Kathmandu, V.S. 2017.
3. In the legal code, as well as in common speech the word *jat* conveys the two following meanings: (1) status of ritual purity; and (2) class of people having the same status. The status may be determined either by being a member of a Hindu caste *stricto sensu*, by being a member of a tribe, or by being the follower of a non-Hindu religion. For reasons of convenience we shall always translate jat by the English word 'caste'. For ethnographical data and bibliography concerning all the castes mentioned in the code and in this paper, the reader may consult Macdonald (1970: 139-52).
4. But the clauses in favour of Muslims are not found in the codes of 1952 and 1963.
5. Ballad of *Sarumai Rani*, recorded from Gokul Gaine, Jumla, November 1967.
6. One can read the same argument in Dumont (1970: 206):

   'For their part the Hindus had to adjust themselves for long periods and over large regions to political masters who did not recognize Brahmanic values, and they did not treat even the most humble Muslim villagers as untouchables. In fact the Muslims occupied a superior position in society than that which would have resulted from the application of Hindu values alone.'
7. At least in the medieval and modern period: in the dharma-sastra, mleccha are considered as untouchable (see Kane 1930-62: II, 169, 173 and 384).

   'But so far as mleccha are concerned these restrictions of untouchability have been given up long ago at least in pubic. Similarly the washerman, the worker in bamboo, the fisherman, the *nata*, among the seven well known *antyaja* are no longer untouchable in several provinces (though not in all) and were not so even in the time of Medhathiti and Kulluka' (173).

   Since the status of several Hindu castes, who were ranked as untouchable in the dharma-shastra and never had any political power, was raised progressively, there is nothing to warrant the hypothesis according to which the status of Muslims (mleccha) was raised because of their political power.

8. The best description, with an analysis of the various criteria involved, is found in: Mayer (1960: 34 and 40). See also Orenstein (1965: 138 and 144-5).
9. Quoted from a copy in my possession.

REFERENCES

Bista, D.B. 1967. *People of Napal.* Kathmandu.

Dumont, L. 1970. *Homo Hierarchicus: The Caste System and its Implications.* London: Weidenfeld and Nicholson.

Gaborieau, M. 1966a. 'Les Musalmans du Nepal'. *Objects et Mondes* 6, 2: 121-32.

———. 1966b. 'Les Curute du Moyen Nepal. Place d'un groupe de Musulmans dans une Societe des castes'. *L'Homme* 6, 3: 81-91.

Gune. 1953. *Judicial System of the Marathas.* Poona.

Hamilton, F. 1819. *An Account of the Kingdom of Nepal.* Edinburgh.

Hodgson, B.H. 1880. 'Some account of the system of law and police as recognised in the State of Nepal'. *Miscellaneous Essays Relating to Indian Subjects*, vol. II, London.

Kane, P.V. 1930-62. *History of Dharmashastra.* Poona: Bhandarkar Oriental Research Institute.

Macdonald, A.W. 1970. 'La Hierarchie des jat inferieurs dans le *Muluki ain*', *Exchange et Communications, Melanges offerts a Claude Levi-Strauss.* Paris.

Madan, T.N. 1972. 'Religious ideology in a plural society: The Muslims and Hindus of Kashmir'. *Contributions to Indian Sociology* 4: 106-41.

Mayer, A.C. 1960. *Caste and Kinship in Central India.* London: Routledge and Kegan Paul.

Orenstein, H. 1965. *Gaon: Conflict and Cohesion in an Indian Village.* New Jersey: Princeton University Press.

Sachau (trans). 1964. *Alberuni's India.* Delhi: National Book Trust.

Srinivas, M.N. 1955. 'The social structure of a Mysore village'. In McKim Marriott, ed., *Village India*, pp. 1-35. Chicago: Chicago University Press.

Steele, A. 1868. *The Law and Customs of the Hindu Castes within the Dekhun Provinces.* London.

The Social Construction of Cultural Identities in Rural Kashmir

T.N. MADAN
(1972)

I borrow myself from others; I create others from my own thought. This is no failure to see others; it is the perception of others.

Maurice Merleau-Ponty

In this essay I am concerned with defining the socio-cultural identities of the Muslims and Hindus of rural Kashmir. Such an exercise will have first to take note of the attributes that the two categories of people themselves judge to be of critical importance. I shall thus examine the images that Muslims and Hindus have of themselves and of each other. Once the attributes have been defined, discussion will be focused on real life interaction observed in the course of field-work. To give historical depth to the material obtained through interviews and observation, limited use will be made of selected published works. I will not burden the discussion with ethnographic and historical details, but concentrate on exploring the general principles that may be shown to underlie what people believe in and what they do. In other words, the aim will be to combine the views from *within* and *without*. Needless to emphasize, doing so is not an exercise in simple accumulation of points of view—the attempt is to examine not the two views *per se* but the relation between them.

Situated in the Himalayas at an average altitude of 6,000 feet above sea level, Kashmir proper—not to be confused with the state of Jammu and Kashmir of which it is a part—is a basin 135 kilometres long and 40 kilometres broad. It is located approximately between 33-35° N and 74-76° E, and has an area of 15,879 square kilometres. The people of Kashmir partake of the common cultural heritage of the subcontinent of India, Bangladesh and Pakistan. At the same time, they have their own distinctive cultural traits, social structure, and historical experience. In this respect, the Kashmiris are like any other regional community such as the Bengalis, Maharashtrians or

Tamils; but the insights which our study of them is likely to offer would seem to be rare if not unique.

As a culture area, the Kashmir Valley is of crucial importance for our understanding of, for example, the synthesis of Muslim and Hindu world-views and such fundamental principles of social organization as caste. It has not, however, received from anthropologists and sociologists the kind of close attention that it richly deserves.[1]

Kashmir has a population of 24,35,701 of whom 8,32,280 live in the southern district of Anantnag. It is primarily from a village of this district that the ethnographic content of this paper is drawn. I have also visited a few other villages in this district and in the central district of Srinagar (population 8,27,697). The rural areas of these two districts are generally believed by Kashmiris to be culturally similar. The northern district of Baramulla (population 7,75,724) is, however, said to be culturally somewhat distinct in several respects. The present essay may therefore, be said to be generally descriptive of the rural areas of the two districts of Anantnag and Srinagar. The rural population of Anantnag is 7,58,046, or 91 per cent of the total. The corresponding figure for Srinagar is 4,04,444, or 48 per cent (India 1972a, 1972b).

Muslims occupy a position of overwhelming importance in the population of Kashmir. They call themselves Musalman which is the Persian form of the word Muslim (see Hughes 1935). They form 94 per cent of the total population in the three districts taken together—95 per cent in Anantnag and 91 per cent in Srinagar. If we consider only the rural population of Anantnag, Muslims again account for over 95 per cent of it. The rest of the population consists almost exclusively of Hindus, though Sikhs also are present in a few villages. It must be noted here that there are no Hindus at all in about 56 per cent of the villages of the Anantnag and Srinagar districts (India 1943). Village boundaries are not, however, impassable barriers, and exclusively Muslim settlements would often seem to have various kinds of relationships with Hindus in adjoining villages.

The native Hindus of Kashmir all belong to the Brahman *varna* and are divided into two endogamous subcastes. The Kashmiri Brahmans call themselves Bhatta and are generally known in India as Kashmiri Pandits. 'Bhatta' is the Prakrit form of the Sanskrit *bhartri* which means 'scholar', 'doctor', or the same as the Sanskrit *Pandit.* Since I have elsewhere used the term Kashmiri Pandit (see, for example, Madan 1965). I will continue to do so here. How Kashmir came to have a single Hindu caste will be described later. I shall first take up the problem of Muslim identity.

MUSLIM IDENTITY: MUSLIM REPRESENTATION

The problem of mutual identification among the Muslims of rural Kashmir does not arise very often. Within a village all adults know each other. The average population of a village in the district of Anantnag is 511 (India 1966: 5). When a person goes to another village, he stays with his relatives; the purpose of the visit most often is to renew contact with them. A Muslim tenant on a visit to his landowner in another village will stay with him and, if the latter also is a Muslim, eat with him. A Pandit landowner will supply uncooked victuals to the tenant, who will cook his own meal in the compound. Utensils for the purpose will be borrowed for him by the landowner's household from one of their Muslim neighbours. Mutual recognition in such situations is not problematic; but it is important, for Hindus and Muslims observe different degrees of mutual avoidance.

Even when one encounters total strangers, there are several visible signs which identify them as one's co-religionists or otherwise. Thus, Muslims and Pandits do not dress identically: the differences may not appear striking to an outsider but a Kashmiri would never make a mistake in this regard. Besides difference of male and female dress (of headgear, gown, trousers, and sometimes even footwear), many Pandits wear *tyok* on their foreheads: it is a mark of saffron or some other coloured paste, elongated among men and round among women. Muslims grow a beard more often than Pandits, and of a distinctive cut. There are differences of speech, mainly lexical (see Kachru 1969: 21-7). Though native Kashmiris look very much alike (see Raychaudhuri 1961 and also Bhattacharjee 1966), two recent Muslim immigrant groups have distinctive features and speak a non-Kashmiri dialect called *Paryum* (literally, foreign, alien).

Identification of people in terms of the Muslim-Pandit dichotomy is thus not difficult in the rural areas, except perhaps when the stranger is from a town or is an urbanized villager, and thus likely to be without any of the above visible signs. Purposive interaction with a stranger is dependent upon the initiation of a specific process of identity establishment. This process usually follows a predictable pattern.

The most crucial cue lies in the family name. Muslim personal names in rural Kashmir are identical with similar names anywhere in the world. Family names often refer to the fact of descent: the Baig, Mausodi, and Sayyid are descended from early immigrant families, and the Shaikh, who constitute the overwhelming majority of Muslims, from converts.[2] The immigrant families fall into three categories: Arabs, Mughals, and Pathans. There is a fourth category of immigrant Muslims who entered the valley late in the nineteenth century. They are called Gujar (cowherd) or Bakkarwal (goatherd), and constitute two somewhat distinctive groups. They are the Muslims who, as mentioned above, speak a non-Kashmiri dialect among themselves.

Not many Shaikhs use that appellation along with their names. It is more common to use other types of family name. One of the most widely prevalent of such names among Kashmiri Muslims is Bhat, which is, of course, the same as Bhatta, and obviously bears testimony to the fact of conversion. There are other examples of this kind of surname such as Pandit, Koul (Sanskrit *kaula,* originally the name of a Brahman sect), Naik and Ryosh (Sanskrit *rishi* or saintly, learned man). There is still another category of common family names which refer either directly to one's hereditary family occupation or indirectly through association. Thus, an Ali Khar is a blacksmith (*khār*) and a Rasul Navid is a barber (*nāvid*). A Samad Vagay will readily be recognized as a milkman, and even referred to as Samad Gur, for the Vagays are milkmen (*gūr*).

All types of surname are called *zāt,* and enquiries about them are made in the effort to obtain identity specification. The important question is what does zāt denote? Apparently it points to birth, as does the well-known word *jāti* used elsewhere among Hindus. The Kashmiris, however, use the word zat in a broader sense to connote essence or inherent nature. *Bad-zāt* is a term of abuse and is used to condemn an evil-natured or mean person rather than to rēfer to lowly birth, which would seem to be the primary meaning of the term in the original Arabic-Persian (see Steingass 1957). Similarly, Kashmiri Muslims refer to God as *Zāt-i-pak,* the one whose nature is pure. Zāt is also used in classifying breeds of cattle or varieties of inanimate objects such as paddy or timber.[3]

When used as part of a person's name zāt has the narrower meaning of either birth (e.g. Sayyid, Shaikh) or hereditary occupation (e.g. Khar, Navid, Gur). It does not, however, necessarily indicate a person's actual source of livelihood: a family of any occupational category may have enough land not to want to exercise their traditional calling: or a particular individual may choose to enter a new occupation. These facts are ascertained by inquiring about *kār*, a general term for work or occupation, or about *kasb*, skills.[4] It may be noted, however, that people rarely move from one skilled or specialist occupation to another, though agriculture is deemed to be open to all. Agriculturists are called *zamīndār* and non-agricultural artisan groups are designated *nāngār*, literally 'those in search of bread'.

At this stage it will be helpful to introduce some ethnographic details from a village.[5] Utrassu-Umanagri is situated 19 kilometres east if the town of Anantnag. It is a rather large bi-nucleated—hence the hyphenated name—village of about 1,542 acres, inhabited by 2,644 persons (see Madan 1965). Of these, 2,122 persons (80 per cent of the total population) are Muslims and the remaining 522 are Pandits. The Muslims are divided into two cultural subgroups; 1,352, or 64 per cent are natives and 770, relatively recent immigrants.

The natives engage in a variety of economic pursuits. Over half of them, totalling 121 households (728 persons), are agriculturists—peasant proprietors or proprietors-cum-tenants. Another 111 households (624 persons) fall in the traditional category of Nangar, though after the abolition of big landed estates in the state in 1950 (see Bamzai 1962: 716-18), there are no completely landless Muslim households in the village. Enquiries made by me in other villages indicate that the Nangar generally account for about one-third to one-half of all Muslim households. They never seem to outnumber the Zamindar. As will be pointed out below, several of the households of Utrassu-Umanagri that I have classified as Nangar in arriving at the above proportions are doubtful cases. But I will first give the distribution of the Muslim households in terms of occupation (see Table 1).

Besides the occupational categories listed in Table 1, I came across the following in the other villages or in the town of Anantnag: (i) Aram (vegetable gardener); (ii) Band (minstrel); (iii) Barbuz (grain parcher); (iv) Gada Hainz (fisherman); (v) Hainz (boatman); (vi) Kawuj (attendant at Hindu cremation sites); (vii) Sangtarash (stone-cutter); (viii) Torkachhan (wood carver): (ix) Vonya (grocer).[6]

The Muslim Zamindar households of Utrassu-Umanagri may be deemed to be those who have no source of income other than cultivation of land, whether self-owned or leased in, or of both types.[7]

TABLE 1. NATIVE MUSLIM HOUSEHOLDS BY TRADITIONAL OCCUPATION

Occupational category		Number of households
1. Zamindar (landowner-cultivator, tenant)		121
2. Nangar		
(i)	Dob (washerman)	2
(ii)	Dosil-Chhan (builder-carpenter)	8
(iii)	Domb (messengers of revenue officials)	2
(iv)	Dun (cotton carder)	6
(v)	Gur (milkman, cowherd)	5
(vi)	Hakim (physician)	2
(vii)	Jalakhodoz (rug-maker)	1
(viii)	Kandur (baker)	2
(ix)	Kanyul-Shakhsaar (basket-maker)	10
(x)	Khar (blacksmith)	6
(xi)	Kral (potter)	4
(xii)	Navid (barber)	6
(xiii)	Puj (butcher)	3
(xiv)	Sech (tailor)	6
(xv)	Sonur (silversmith)	1
(xvi)	Tabardar, Arikash (wood-cutter, sawer)	10
(xvii)	Tilawoni (oilseed-presser)	3
(xviii)	Thonthur (coppersmith)	2
(xix)	Vatul (cobbler)	3
(xx)	Wovur (weaver)	19
(xxi)	Mallah (religious functionary)	10
	Total	232

there are no landless labourers in the village though many agriculturists work on daily wages for other landowners during busy seasons. Muslim Zamindars are small landowners. The average size of the holding is just under an acre and three quarters, but this figure is somewhat misleading in respect of the Muslims since it is based on all holdings, including those of Pandits. There are 636 land-ownership registration among the native Muslims of the village, the basis of registration being the individual and not the household. Recalling that there are 1,352 native Muslims, it will be noticed that the registrations are indicative of the already mentioned fact of widespread ownership of land. Of these registrations, 139 are in respect of holdings of 1 to 3 acres, 27 in respect of holdings above 3 but below 6 acres and only 2 in respect of holdings above 6 acres. All the rest are below 1 acre. The ceiling on agricultural land was fixed at 20 acres through legislation in 1950. No Muslim household lost any land at that time. Only one Muslim landowner had more than twelve acres and was thus affected by the tenancy reforms which fixed the share of the tenants, at three-quarters of the produce in respect of such holdings. A large number of tenants mostly Muslims, received small shares from about 170 acres of land that were compulsorily acquired from Pandit landowners and redistributed among the tillers by the Government.

Turning our attention to the Nangar, it may be noted that:

(i) The names of all such groups, except the Domb, are directly descriptive of skilled work of some kind, or of non-skilled but specialized services. The Domb have a traditional calling but their names does not originate in it. They seem to be descendants of a low caste (see Lawrence 1967: 311), may be of the Domba mentioned in early historical accounts of Kashmir (see Pandit 1968).[8]

(ii) Whereas most of the Nangar in the village are stable groups following their respective hereditary occupations, some of them represent the arrival of relatively recent skills in the village, or seem to be more open to recruitment than others. The Bakers, Rug-makers and Tailors of the village, though natives, have had no predecessors there. Butchers and Weavers seem to be relatively open categories. Only one of the four Butcher households have a tradition of being meat sellers. Similarly, the Weavers seem to be an assorted category, only some of whom are Weavers by birth. Incidentally, most of the Weaver households have a secondary occupation—the breeding of silkworms. Sericulture and silk-weaving have been carried on in Kashmir for several hundred years (see Bamzai 1962: 451).[9]

(iii) Some of the households following the above occupations own shops. The Butchers are a good example and so are the Tailors; but the former also sell meat at their homes and the latter divide work between home and shop. Shopkeeping is not treated as an occupation by any group in the village, but grocers in the nearby town of Anantnag have a long tradition of it. Generally speaking, shopkeeping in the rural areas is merely indicative of the mode of augmenting income by a group or household.

Finally, a few words about the Gujar and Bakkarwal. As already stated, they number 770, and constitute 98 households. They live on the upper boundaries of Utrassu-Umanagri, along and deep inside the forests. Some of the Gujar—the group which came earlier than the Bakkarwal—have taken to agriculture and sedentary life, and a few have even intermarried with native Muslims. There are 71 registrations of land-ownership in the names of the Gujar. However, most of them continue their traditional occupation, as do the Bakkarwal: they graze sheep and cattle, their own and those of other people in exchange for grain, and sell dairy products. Most of them leave the village during the winter months in search of warmth and pastures for their flocks. The Gujar and Bakkarwal are an important element in the life of the village but they are not of it. They look different from native Muslims, speak their own dialect, live in distinctive huts, follow their own traditional pursuits and customs, and have a system of social control centred round the *jirga* or tribal council.

Occupations such as the above are widespread and stable categories in rural Kashmir and are, therefore, employed by the people themselves as indicators of socio-cultural identity. In any particular village one encounters them as groups of households, usually but not necessarily related by ties of kinship and/or marriage. The Zamindar category is the melting pot, as it were, inasmuch as anybody might become a cultivator, even if he has no land of his own. The various Nangar groups are, however, characterized by a low degree of occupational mobility and a high incidence of endogamous marriages. Only 9 per cent of the adult Muslims of the village are in skilled or specialist occupations other than those indicated by their zāt. A count of marriages among the Nangar, spread over two generations, revealed a little under two-thirds of them to be endogamous. (Here it may be noted that marriage between both parallel and cross cousins takes place among Kashmiri Muslims, but is not prescriptive.)

When asked to explain these cultural regularities, my Muslim informants generally stressed three considerations. (i) The most specific of these is what be called practical considerations. Since every Nangar is assured of a clientele for his goods or services, it is only reasonable that he should pursue his traditional occupation. His relations with his clients are generally on a hereditary and family-to-family basis; land-owning households pay for goods and services in kind according to predetermined scales, while the other pay in cash. Barter is rarely practised nowadays. The most practical as well as efficient way of learning a craft is to start when quite young, by helping the older members of one's household in their chores.

One's son is one's natural apprentice as well as one's successor. (ii) Endogamous marriages are desirable for reasons of compatibility. There are often differences in the lifestyles of different groups. Boatmen and Mallah are good examples. Moreover, women often help men in their chores; a Carpenter's daughter would obviously be of no help to a Potter, or a Barber's daughter to a Boatman. (iii) Both pursuit of hereditary occupation and endogamy are commendable as being *inherently* right. The word zāt (in its adjectival form of *zāti*) is employed in this context also.

It follows from the foregoing that we ask: how does one acquire one's essential nature, one's true identity, or zāt, in terms of which certain actions become inherently right or natural? This was not a question which my informants generally welcomed as they felt that they were being pushed against the wall. Several of them, however, interpreted the word zāti as meaning 'at the root or base', which was further paraphrased as 'at or by birth'. One might translate this statement to mean that one's essential nature is endowed upon one by the circumstances of birth. The notion of zāt is genealogical, but stands for more than the fact of birth.

If the foregoing is a culturally valid position to adopt in respect of the self-ascription of Kashmiri Muslims, the most crucial question that arises is, who is a Muslim?

There seems to be general agreement among the Muslims of rural Kashmir that anyone who avows to be a Muslims is to be regarded as such. They maintain that this is what the Quran teaches. They further assert that a pious Muslim (i) believes in the oneness of God and in Muhammad as His prophet; (ii) offers prayers (*namāz*) at the appointed times; (iii) gives alms (*zakāt*); (iv) keeps the prescribed hours of fasting and eating (*roza*) during Ramazan; and (v) performs the pilgrimage to Mecca (*hajj*) when he has enough savings for the purpose. My informants pointed out that lack of means, poor health, and preoccupation with household responsibilities often prevent a person from offering prayers, giving alms, observing roza or performing hajj. Such unwilling transgressions of the desired conduct are to be forgiven a person if he reaffirms the most important tenet of Islam by solemnly reciting the *Kalimah* on being challenged: *Lāillāh illallah Muhammadur Rasūl Allah*—there is but one God and Muhammad is His prophet.[10]

To deny such a person the status of a Muslim is to turn against the will and voice of God and the Prophet. The *accident* of birth is irrelevant in this regard. One of my educated urban informants, a Shaikh, stressed this point by asserting that he who embraces Islam out of conviction is a better Muslim than he who follows it as the religion of his parents. 'Such a man is deservedly called *shaikh,* the leader who points the path to others.'

In the course of my fieldwork I heard of about a dozen cases of recent conversion of Pandits to Islam. I was able to interview one of these converts and to discuss his case with a number of my informants, Pandits as well as Muslims. Since this case throws considerable light on the notion of zāt in relation to religious identity. I will briefly discuss it here.

He told me that his name was Ghulam but that, before conversion to Islam, which took place about twenty years ago, he was known as Darshan Krad, and belonged to a Pandit family of Utrassu-Umanagri. His *gotra* name was Shandalya. He had been much persecuted by his cousins, particularly because he was a bachelor.[11] He had several Muslim friends in the village and they showed him greater sympathy and understanding than his own kin, who robbed him of his property and would have willingly starved him to death. His Muslim friends fed him and gave him shelter in their homes. Ultimately, he became a Muslim. He was, however, very badly treated by Muslims once he changed his religion, he said. Though he is living with a Muslim household of the village, he is doubtful whether they will give him a decent burial. It is for this reason that he begs and not merely to keep himself alive. He is obviously saving for the rainy day and hopes to have enough money for a shroud for his dead body and for its burial. He lamented his moral and physical condition and called his act of conversion 'a stupid act' (*budhi-vināsh*) by which he became a 'breaker of *karma*' (*karma-khandit*). As he sees himself, he is a totally lost man.

The Pandits, to whose homes he comes to beg, generally pity him, but treat him as a fallen man who is of course no longer a Brahman, even though he had been born one. Urchins ask him to sing Brahman devotional songs (*līlā*) and promise him handfuls of rice. He often obliges them. My Pandit informants said that he had given me a fairly accurate account of what had happened, but that he had omitted to tell me that he had been promised a Muslim girl in marriage to make him give up his religion. This might in fact be true as Ghulam told me that Muslims often tempt Hindus by 'showing them birds' and by making false promises. He did not say, however, that this had been his own undoing too. The Pandits look at such cases as a kind of wicked game which some Muslims play at the former's cost. It was alleged that such Muslims derive mean satisfaction from a Pandit's fall.

When I discussed this pitiable man's case with some Muslim informants, they made two points. First, they maintained, it was imperative that one should distinguish between a person who becomes a Muslim out of conviction and one who embraces Islam in the hope of material gain. To them Darshan's conversion was not a true conversion: he had not been impelled by the best of motives. Nevertheless, a Muslim household has given him shelter, though nobody gave him shelter, though nobody gave him a wife. What more could he expect?

Secondly, my informants said, Ghulam is a bad Muslim. He does not observe the essential rules of behaviour. For example, he begs and eats at Pandit homes. No good Muslim eats food cooked by Pandits. 'The plain truth', as one informant put it, was that Darshan was born a Pandit and could not possibly be as good a Muslim as he himself, i.e. the informant, who was a zāti Muslim.

The conclusion that seems permissible on the basis of the foregoing discussion is that, the alleged teachings of the Quran notwithstanding, in actual practice the Muslims of rural Kashmir attach crucial importance to the fact of birth in the determination of a person's nature and his legitimate socio-cultural identity. Whether this is an Islamic notion or not, it certainly accords well with Hindu belief.[12]

HINDU IDENTITY: HINDU REPRESENTATION

One of the most striking characteristics of the social organization of the native Hindus of Kashmir is that they consist mainly of two Saraswat Brahman subcastes. There is also one Vaishya caste, but it is very small in numbers and is found only in some towns. To the best of my knowledge, this is a social situation unparalleled in any other cultural region of the subcontinent. It is almost like a deliberately set up laboratory situation, and its study should yield insights into the Hindu caste system unobtainable elsewhere. The first question that must be answered is, how has this peculiar situation arise?

Fortunately we have a precious historical document to fall back upon: the twelfth-century Sanskrit chronicle *Rājataranginī* by Kalhana.[13] A perusal of this work yields two relevant conclusions regarding the social structure of Kashmir before the arrival of Islam early in the fourteenth century. First, it is obvious that there were many castes among the Hindus. All the four *varṇa*—Brahman, Kshatriya, Vaishya, Shudra—are mentioned and, besides, we read of castes, sects and classes such as the Chandala, Damara, Domba, Kayastha, Kirata, Nishada and Tantrin. It is not always clear, however, which is which. Thus, the Damara and Kayastha, it seems were classes of landowners and civil servants respectively, rather than castes. Tribal groups of various kinds are also mentioned. Of these, the Ekanga and Lavanya seem to have been professional soldiers.

The second relevant conclusion is that the caste system in Kashmir between the seventh and fourteenth centuries does not seem to have been characterized by stringent exclusiveness in the relations between social groups. We read in the *Rājatarangiṇī* of low caste Domba queens of Kshatriya kings. Kalhana particularly mentions a low-caste *āramika* (vegetable grower) who had successfully entered the ranks of the Kayastha. A probable reason for the relatively flexible social organization may well have been the influence of Buddhism which was introduced in Kashmir during Ashoka's reign in the first quarter of the third century BC and dominated the cultural life of the Kashmiris for almost a millennium.

By the beginning of the eighth century, Hinduism had reasserted itself in Kashmir—the Brahmans, who led the resistance to Buddhism seem also to have spearheaded this revival. They continued to play a prominent role in the political and cultural life of the Kashmiris until the arrival of Islam in Kashmir. The presence of Muslim (Turkish) mercenaries during the eleventh century is noted by Kalhana. It was only a couple of hundred years later, however, that the Islamization of the valley began, first through the persuasion of missionaries and then through the persecution by some of the early Muslim kings. The most prominent of the early missionaries was Sayyid Bilal Shah of Turkistan, who was associated with the Suhrawardi school of Sufis (see Hughes 1935).[14]

The Hindu dynasties had an inglorious end. External invasion, court intrigues and internal disorder resulted in the emergence of the first Muslim king of Kashmir, Rinchana (1320-3). He was a Buddhist prince, a refugee from Tibet at the court of the Hindu king. This combination of circumstances and Rinchana's personal valour led to his seizure of the kingdom. He beseeched the Brahmans to allow him to become a Hindu but they refused. He then turned to

Bilal Shah who readily accepted him within the Muslim fold. Thereafter, the Sayyid's mission as a proselytiser seems to have met with success after success. Of later missionaries who carried Islam into the length and breadth of Kashmir mention may be made of the saintly Sufi scholar, Sayyid Ali of Hamadan, who paid several visits to the valley beginning in 1327. Many Sayyids came to settle down in these parts around that time.

The scholarship, saintliness and peaceful intentions of some of the Sayyids found their counterpoint in the bigotry and fanaticism of some of the early Muslim kings. The most notorious of these was Sultan Sikandar (1389-1413), to whom historians have given the name of *butshikan* (iconoclast). Not only did he destroy virtually all the Hindu temples of Kashmir (see Kak 1936, text and plates), he also compelled his Hindu subjects to choose between Islam, exile or death. Whereas some chose one of the latter two alternatives, the majority of those who had resisted the missionaries now accepted defeat. It was thus that the Hindus of Kashmir, along with whatever Buddhists had remained, were converted *en masse* and Islam was established in Kashmir during the fourteenth century.[15] It seems that only a handful of Brahmans survived in Kashmir at the time of Sikandar's death in 1414; tradition puts the number at eleven. It is from them that the Pandits of today are said to be descended.

The most celebrated of the Muslim kings of Kashmir is Zain-ul-Abidin, remembered to this day as the *bud shah* (great king). His reign, spanning half a century (1420-70), reversed the policies of the preceding hundred years of Muslim rule by making it possible for Hindus and Buddhists to live in safety and with honour in their homeland. He abolished the *jizya*, a tax imposed on non-Muslims by his predecessors, called a halt to the destruction of non-Muslim places of worship, showed keen interest in Buddhist and Hindu philosophy and scholarship, and appointed the followers of these religions to high positions in his administration. In his magnanimous treatment of his non-Muslim subjects, he was the true precursor of Akbar, the Great Mughal, who followed a hundred years later.

Encouraged by the king, many Brahmans returned to Kashmir. The descendants of those who stayed behind during the darkest days, and of those who went into exile to return later, maintain a distinction amongst themselves to this day: the former are called *malamāsi* and the latter *bhānamāsi*.[16] More significantly, the Brahman families, presumably acting together,[17] seem to have taken the major decision to study Persian and thus laid the foundation of a changed social organization.

It is clear from Kalhana's account that the Kayastha category had traditionally been recruited mainly from among the Brahmans. They had for long been accustomed to playing an important role in religious, civic and administrative affairs. Zain-ul-Abidin, who had inherited an administration which was in a shambles, held forth to them the renewed possibility of a similar role. The language of the court and administration had meanwhile been changed from Sanskrit to Persian. The Brahman's decision to acquire proficiency in the latter language indicated their earnestness to seize the newly offered opportunities and become *kārkun* (the Persian word for civil servants, revenue collectors, etc.).

The Brahmans' decision raised a problem: what was to become of their traditional scholarship and philosophical heritage, and who was to ensure the proper performance of rituals so crucial to a Brahman's life? During the days of Hindu rule they had not faced such a problem, obviously because the Brahman and the king belonged to one and the same socio-religious system and used the same language—Sanskrit—in the performance of their respective roles. The problem that resulted from the separation of the socio-religious and politico-administrative spheres was resolved through a curious stratagem: a daughter's son would study *bhāshā* ('the language'), i.e. Sanskrit, and administer to the spiritual and ritual needs of his mother's natal family (see Kilam 1955: 53).[18] Designated Bhasha Bhatta, they were regarded as the privileged category compared to the Karkun; they were the Brahmans *par excellence*, indeed as in name. What began as an arrangement of convenience has since frozen into a rigid division into two endogamous sub-castes. What is more, the Karkun have arrogated to themselves the higher status. The Bhasha Bhatta are now called Gor (derived from the Sanskrit *guru*, 'preceptor', 'teacher'), which term today is unmistakably one of social contempt.

Both the Karkun and the Gor are divided into exogamous gotra categories. According to Lawrence (1967: 304) there are 103 Karkun and 18 'Levite' gotras among the Pandits. Koul (1924) mentions 199 gotras and names 189.[19] Within each gotra there are families which are identified by surnames called zāt or, relatively rarely, *kram*, meaning 'hereditary descent', and possibly indicative of social ranking. The zāt among Pandits are sectarian or family nicknames, the latter oftener than the former. These nicknames have their exact parallels among the Browns, Blacks, Longmans, Pidgeons, Swindlers and other such Anglo-Saxon surnames.[20] The Gor also have zāt but they rarely use the surname. It is instead customary to use the suffix *boi* (brother) with the personal name of each male priest. I have already pointed out that zāt has to do with the establishment of identity by birth among Kashmiri Muslims; the same applies to Pandits.

In none of the villages in the district of Anantnag which I visited did I encounter any other kind of Bhatta except the Gor and Karkun. All the 87 Pandit households of Utrassu-Umanagri are Karkun. The adjacent village of Kreri has seven Karkun and five Gor households. Pandit informants drew my attention to the presence of a doubtful and small category of Bhatta, the Buher, who are to be found only in urban areas. (There is a ward in the city of Srinagar named after them.) The Buher (also called Bohra) are Khattris, probably of Punjabi origin (see Lawrence 1967: 302; 1909: 40). Hutton (1951: 282) describes the Khattri as a trading caste of the Punjab and north-west India. The Buher are an endogamous caste of grocers and *halwai* (makers of confectionery, cheese, yoghurt and savouries of various kinds). In fact, the word *buhur* (singular of *buher*) is used in Kashmir in the sense of a grocer. The Pandits do not interdine with the Buher, nor allow them entry into their temples. The Gor do, however, perform priestly functions for them. The Buher have built a Vishnu temple of their own in Srinagar. On their part, they have adopted the lifestyle of the Pandits and would obviously like to be called Buher Bhatta. Already there are signs that, barring inter-marriage, the Karkun and the Buher are coming closer to each other in urban areas. The problems does not exist in rural Kashmir.[21]

In Utrassu-Umanagri and surrounding villages the Karkun are served by a large number of occupational groups. The first of these are, of course, the Gor. Each Gor household has a clientele, fixed on a hereditary basis, of both Karkun and Gor households. The latter are referred to as *yazaman* (derived from the Sanskrit *yajamāna*). When a Gor household dies out, its clientele is usually inherited by the nearest agnatic kin. A Karkun household may employ the services of the most readily available priest for minor purposes—such as consecrating routine food offerings, or determining auspicious dates for doing or buying something—but on all important occasions only the *kola-gor* (family priest) will do. If he is ill, in a state of pollution, or otherwise unavailable, it is his duty to provide a substitute.

Formerly the Gor were also teachers, not only of priestly lore but also of astrology, Sanskrit and *shāstra* (religious literature) in general. Nowadays, the only pupils they have are their own sons, though not even all of them are willing to follow their traditional calling. The performance of all but the most essential rituals is coming to be viewed as dispensable. The Karkun feel that they do not have the time or the resources for them. The Gor lament the decline of faith and they complain that even the essential rituals are sought to be abridged. Whatever the reasons, the Gor are beginning to turn away from priesthood. One of the young Gor of Kreri is a school teacher; another has joined the state militia. I was informed that the process of occupational change among the Gor is more visible in urban areas than in the villages.

The Karkun are, of course, dependent on the Gor for the performance of rituals. There can be no Pandits without the Gor. The latter's dependence on the Karkun is merely economic. It is not inconceivable that a small community of Gor could exist without the Karkun and draw their sustenance from land or service. The Karkun on their part look down upon the Gor and even consider them inauspicious. Several times during my fieldwork I noticed how a Karkun would return home if he met a priest just after he had started on an errand. There is general denigration of the Gor on account of their style of life and their alleged greed and lack of learning. Their worst fault would seem to be that they accept food and other gifts offered in the names of the dead.[22]

The Karkun-Gor relationship has always been hierarchical, being ordered in terms of religious values and moral judgements. The two groups seem to have changed places, however, since the emergence of the division between them about 500 years ago. Even so, as a category, the Gor are essentially pure, irrespective of how particular Gor may be regarded by their Karkun patrons. In principle the Karkun and the Gor are one: they are Brahmans—they are the Pandits.

For all other services the Pandits are dependent upon Muslims. An examination of these services is of great importance from the point of view of this discussion as it will enable us to grasp the definition of Muslim identity by the Pandits.

MUSLIM IDENTITY: HINDU REPRESENTATION

As stated earlier, Utrassu-Umanagri is a bi-nucleated village. The settlement of Utrassu is older than anybody can remember. Umanagri is, however, quite recent: it was founded about 200 years ago. I have given the details elsewhere (see Madan 1965: 38-40), and will here confine myself to pointing out that originally there were no Muslims in Umanagri. The Pandits found it impossible to carry on without the services of Muslim cultivators, artisans, village servants, and other specialist groups, and therefore invited them to come from other villages and settle down in Umanagri. This historical fact only serves to underline what my fieldwork has revealed.

Being Brahmans, the Pandits are traditionally debarred from a large number of occupational activities. Thus, they cannot engage in polluting activities such as barbering, washing clothes, obtaining oil from oilseeds, removing and skinning dead animals, making shoes, winnowing pans and drums, slaughtering goats and sheep,[23] and so on. There are so many other types of activities which are not polluting, but which no Pandit would engage in because they involve manual labour, no matter how light. Some of the poorer Pandits in Utrassu-Umanagri do engage in cultivation or cooking—the former only in their own village and the latter only outside it—but at the cost of being treated as socially inferior by the others.[24] Ownership of land, service (public or private) and shopkeeping are the only sources of household income among the Pandits of Utrassu-Umanagri (see Madan 1965: 149-50).[25] In such a situation it is not at all surprising that the Pandits should regard Muslims as an essential component of their social system. In this connection it is worth mentioning that the 1941 census shows only two villages in the Srinagar-Anantnag district inhabited by Pandits alone though, as stated earlier, 56 per cent of the villages are exclusively Muslim.

In the Pandits' conception of them, Kashmiri villagers are characterized by the simple but sharp distinction between themselves and the Muslims. The latter are regarded in principle as being ritually impure. They are referred to as *mleccha* (of lowly birth, outsiders); theirs is the world of *tamas* (darkness, ignorance). Muslims are outside the pale of values by which a Pandit is expected, as a Brahman, to order his life. In practice, however, the Pandits consider some Muslims less polluting than others.

In Utrassu-Umanagri no Pandit eats food cooked or even touched by a Muslim. There are no exceptions to this rule except the acceptance of clarified butter from Milkmen, Gujars and Bakkarwals. (Some Pandits also accept yoghurt and fresh cheese from these three groups but others disapprove of the practice, which seems to be recent.) If transgressions occur they are so secretive that no Pandit claimed having actually seen another Pandit eating with a Muslim. There seems to have been some kind of sumptuary ban on the consumption of such forbidden food until about 1925, when Maharaja Pratap Singh, a very orthodox Hindu ruler, died.

Pandits accept uncooked food from all but the lowliest of Muslims (namely, Domb and Vatal). Grains, vegetables and fruits are included in this category. Uncooked meat also is generally accepted but may be refused for fear of its being beef. (Killing beef cattle is a penal offence in the state, but it would seem the Muslims do sometimes slaughter such animals.) Unboiled milk is freely accepted from Milkmen, Gujars, Bakkarwals, and Zamindars but usually not from any other group. The Pandits are much more hesitant to accept water from Muslims. Some well-to-do households employ water carriers but invariably choose a Milkman or a Zamindar for the chore and provide him with a pitcher. A Pandit is not expected to drink even milk from a container belonging to a Muslim.

There is no sharing of the hookah between Pandits and Muslims. A Pandit does not touch any part of a Muslim's hookah—its vase of water, pipe or the *chillum* (tobacco-cum-fire bowl). A Muslim is allowed to smoke the chillum of a Pandit's hookah by holding it between his palms but is never permitted to use the pipe.

The Utrassu-Umanagri Pandits avoid any physical contact with the cobblers and winnowing-pan makers (Vatal), who skin dead animals and have traditionally been suspected by everybody of being carrion eaters. (I was informed that in urban areas, where there are two types of Vatal, namely, leather-workers and scavengers, the latter are treated with less repugnance than the former.) The Pandits do, however, buy the articles these craftsmen make. The Domb are also regarded as being very polluting and physical contact with them is strenuously avoided. In relation to other Muslims in the village, the Pandits are less anxious to avoid total physical contact. The more fastidious among them will wash their hands after touching a Muslim. I once saw a Muslim servant (a Zamindar) press the feet and legs of his Pandit master but the latter did not wash afterwards. (Only half a dozen or so Pandit households in Utrassu-Umanagri employ Muslim servants, all of whom are Zamindars.) Muslim-Pandit marriages are, of course, ruled out. Illicit sexual intercourse does seem to occur once in a while. This is a subject on which one has no evidence more reliable than village gossip. Among all Muslims, it is the Barber (Navid) and the midwife with whom Pandit men and women, respectively, come in most intimate physical contact. The Barber's services are particularly noteworthy and may be elaborated upon.

The Navid renders routine and occasional services to his Pandit patrons. The routine services consist of shaving the face and the head or cutting the hair. Shaving is regarded as *varzit* (derived from the Sanskrit *varjit*, forbidden) on certain days of the week and on most occasions when one has to perform a ritual. The act of having one's beard or hair shaved on such days is inauspicious in itself, and does not seem to have anything to do with the desire to avoid contact with a Muslim. That this is so is indicated by the fact that the Barber is called in to render his services on four highly important occasions of ritual performance. Sanskritic rites are interrupted to have a boy's *zarakāsai* (*zara* = baby hair, *kasai* = shaving, cutting) done; to have a neophyte's head shaved during *mekhlā* (the investiture ceremony also called *yagnopavit* or *upanayana*); and to shave the beard and hair of a mourner at the end of the period of pollution. These rituals would remain incomplete without the Barber's services. The Barber's touch is polluting, however, and the person who has been served by him on the special ritual occasions mentioned above must have a bath. On other occasions too having a bath is desirable, but washing of the face and head is all that may be done. The Barber also shaves and gives a haircut to a bridegroom before the latter leaves for the bride's home for the marriage ceremony. During the *lagan* (marriage ritual), one of the rites involves letting the bride and the bridegroom see each other's faces in a mirror. This mirror is customarily provided by the Barber of the bride's natal household.

For his routine services the Barber receives a number of measures of paddy from his patron at harvest time. Several Pandit households of Utrassu-Umanagri buy grain so as to meet the requirements of such payments to the Barber and other specialists. Many families pay for them in cash. On all special occasions the Barber receives the clothes, at least some of them, which the individual recipient of the services has on him at that time. The Barber also receives other gifts. He is treated as a well-wisher by his patrons, with whom he has hereditary relations.

I have described the Barber's services at some length because of their value as a paradigm of the relations between the Pandits and Muslim occupational groups. The essential elements of the paradigm may be recapitulated:

1. The services are of routine and special kinds.
2. They have a ritual significance for the Pandit and this is known to the Muslim specialist.
3. The specialist himself views them in economic terms, but recognises their traditional character.
4. The threat to his state of ritual purity arising from contact with a Muslim is tolerated by the Pandit because he is otherwise even more seriously in danger of being unable to enter or re-enter such a state.
5. The relations between the patrons and the specialists are on a hereditary basis and are paid for in kind, if possible.

I will take another crucial example: that of the relations between the Muslim Potter (Kral) and his Pandit patrons. The Potter supplies pots and pans of various kinds which he makes both for everyday use and for special occasions. Storage jars for grains, pickles and water; utensils for cooking, storing and serving food; smoking bowls; toys; and many other types of pottery are supplied by him. He provides a wide range of utensils in large quantities at weddings. It is on the occasion of Herath (a feast in honour of Shiva), however, that he makes for his Pandit customers the most unusual of all pieces of baked clay.

As I have described elsewhere (see Madan 1961: 129-39), Herath is celebrated over fifteen days during the dark fortnight of the month of *Phagun* (February-March). Each day has its appointed task; on the eleventh day the Potter carries a basket-load of pottery to each patron household for use in the kitchen and in the climactic rites during the last four days. The number of each type of the various pieces of pottery has to be just right. Shortages are regarded as bad omens and the Potter is rebuked for such lapses. Among the many objects he makes is the rather inconspicuous looking *sanipotul* (*sani* = worship, *potul* = idol), which is the *lingam*, to be installed as Shiva during the rites. It is obviously phallic in shape.

Though the Potters whom I questioned at Utrassu-Umanagri do not exactly know what kind of an idol the sanipotul is, they are all aware that it is the object of worship for the Pandits. As Muslims they have no use for such idols, and abhor idol worship, but as Potters they readily make the objects for their patrons. They look upon the work they do in economic terms; but not so the Pandits, who view the Potter's services in relation to such basic activities as the preparation of food and the performance of one of the most important domestic rituals of the year.

More examples of such relationships between Muslims and Pandits could be given, including that of the familiar Washerman and the unfamiliar (among Brahman communities) Butcher. The latter supplies the meat which the Pandit offers to some of his gods and goddesses. In fact, it is the Muslim Butcher who slaughters the sacrificial ram after the Brahman Gor has ritually rendered it sacred. Further, it is worth mentioning that, since the Pandits are major consumers of meat in Utrassu-Umanagri, the Muslim Butchers keep track of the capricious Hindu lunar calendar and avoid slaughtering too many animals on days on which Pandits abstain from eating meat.

Limitations of space prevent me from going into the details of more cases.[26] Suffice it to add that most of the services that Muslim specialist groups render their Pandit clientele are ritual liturgies when viewed from the receiver's end; but they appear as economic transactions, sanctioned by village tradition, when judged from the perspective of the giver. What are legitimately seen as occupational groups from the Muslim angle are castes, 'caste analogues' or 'caste substitutes' when viewed in terms of the Hindu caste system which they, in fact, help to constitute in Kashmir.

We will be justified in speaking of the social organization of mixed Kashmiri villages as a regional variant of the caste system if the cardinal principle of hierarchy is found applicable. It is obvious from the foregoing discussion that this certainly is so in the Pandits' ideological reconstruction of empirical reality. Moreover, the Pandits do not normally render any services to the Muslims, nor do they provide them with any goods. The only exceptions to this rule in Utrassu-Umanagri are a Pandit *hakim* (practitioner of Graeco-Arab medicine), and some moneylenders, and (if we may include them) shopkeepers. I encountered several instances of a Pandit astrologer being consulted by Muslims. It is clear that all these roles are prestigious. The Pandits' representation of village society is shown in Figure 1.

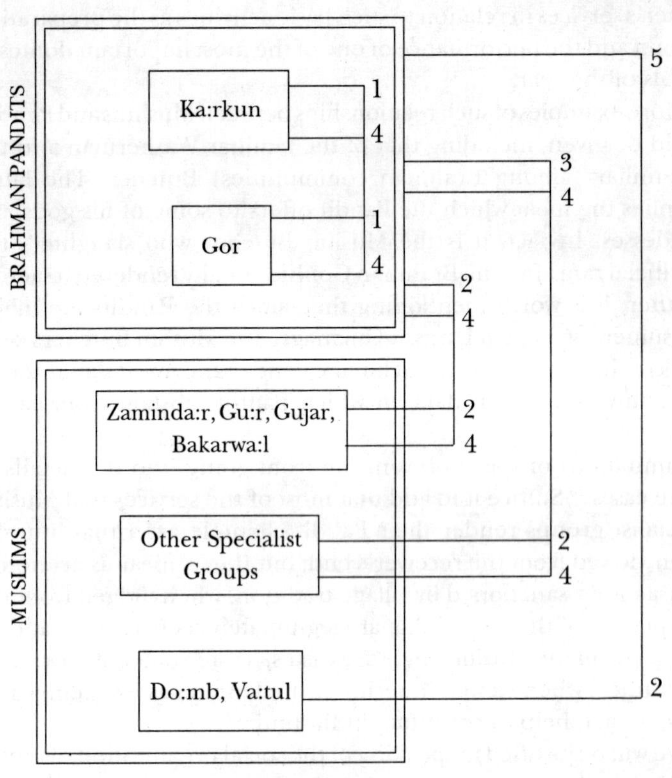

1 Acceptance of cooked and uncooked food.
2 Acceptance of uncooked foods, milk, and water.
3 Acceptance of uncooked food only.
4 Flow of goods and/or services without avoidance of physical contact.
5 Flow of goods and/or services with strict avoidance of physical contact.

FIGURE 1. PANDIT REPRESENTATION OF VILLAGE SOCIETY

It will be agreed that (i) the inferior status of Gor *vis-à-vis* Karkun, (ii) the inferior position of the Muslims *vis-à-vis* the Brahmans, and (iii) the division of Muslims into three ranked categories are all ultimately based on the same governing principle of superior dignity arising out of moral, i.e. religious considerations. As we move downwards from the Gor through the three rungs of Muslim occupational groups, the element of ritual impurity becomes increasingly salient.

The admission of Muslims into a common social fold is surreptitious, by the backdoor as it were: it cannot occur in terms of ideology but, paradoxically, is defended on the ground that without them the Pandit would lose caste or ritual purity. In other words, the empirical situation in which the Pandit finds himself compels him to establish relations of various kinds with Muslim occupational groups; he orders them in terms of hierarchy. Ideally he should have no relations with the Muslims: they are mleccha, and this word means both 'an outsider' and 'a person of lowly birth'. Common stereotypes about Muslims which I found prevalent among Pandits included, besides mleccha, 'dirty', 'polluted', 'unprincipled,' 'omnivorous', and 'lustful'. Individual Muslims are respected for personal qualities; the two Lambardars (minor revenue officials) of Utrassu-Umanagri are Muslims, and I saw Pandits treat them with the courtesy due to their official position. Muslim households with wealth may even be accepted as patrons: one Pandit household of the village cultivates a portion of the biggest Muslim Zamindar's land, though I was told that such a relationship is rare and amounts to a reversal of familiar roles.

As a category, however, Muslims are polluting and contact with them should be restricted as far as possible if it cannot be avoided. It is obvious that Pandits have accepted compromise to avoid being defeated. They are faced with a moral dilemma: to preserve their status as Brahmans they need goods and services which only the Muslims provide, but the latter are themselves a source of pollution. Since the danger emanating from Muslims can be controlled and rectified, the Pandit's choice has its merits. A Pandit saying is apposite in this context: *Yath na pūsh tath na dūsh* (whereof one is helpless, thereof one attracts no blame). This may be regarded as evidence of Pandit pragmatism; in Dumont's phrase, a concession to coexistence (see Dumont 1970: 206).

That this has not been an easy choice is illustrated by the manner in which Pandits switch codes when talking to Muslims. Though they all speak the same language, Koshur or Kashmiri, there are striking differences of lexical elements so that linguists have classified it into Sanskritized Kashmir (SK) and Persianized Kashmiri (PK) (see Kachru 1969: 21-7). The speakers of PK are Muslims. I found in Utrassu-Umanagri that their use of PK words is consistent: they employ them with whomsoever they are speaking. The Pandits switch from SK to PK when certain crucial words have to be used in conversation with Muslims. A Pandit will generally stick to such SK words as *ponya* (water; PK equivalent, *āb*), *khovur* (left; PK, *khofur*), and *shokrawār* (Friday; PK, *jummah*). He wavers when it comes to such words as God (SK, *Bhagvan*; PK, *Khodā*) and religion (SK, *dharma*; PK, *mazhab*), but generally uses the PK words when talking with a Muslim. I never found a Pandit use the SK greeting of *namaskar* when addressing a Muslim: there is no ambiguity at all on this point. A Muslim greets all, whether Muslim or Hindu, with *salām*; but a Pandit always says salām to a Muslim and namaskār to another Pandit. Namaskār is thus a marked term: when one hears it said, the only conclusion that may be drawn is that one Pandit has greeted another.

On being questioned, even the most intelligent of my Pandit informants would tell me no more by way of explanation than that it would be improper to say namaskār to a Muslim. 'Is that not obvious?' they asked me. It is apparent that saying namaskār, 'I bow to thee', to a Muslim is improper, for he is mleccha, an outsider. He cannot be fully admitted into the Pandits' company. There must be no blurring of zāti or natural distinctions, that is, of socio-cultural identities. Words like Bhagvān, dharma and, above all namaskār, are signposts which the Pandits have set up as a boundary maintenance device. Those within are Brahmans; those outside, mleccha. It is a kind of last ditch defence.

HINDU IDENTITY: MUSLIM REPRESENTATION

A question that arises from the foregoing discussion is, do Kashmiri Muslims also feel threatened by the Pandits? The answer, it seems to me, has to be in the negative, although Muslims regard Pandits being outsiders, non-Muslims. To understand this situation we shall now examine the Muslim representation of Pandit identity in relation to their own.

The Muslim's view of Pandits as non-Muslims has to be disentangled from his image of them as clients or patrons. Just as Pandits *qua* Hindus see themselves in opposition to the mleccha, Kashmiri Muslims *qua* Muslims identify themselves with the *umma*, the universal Muslim brotherhood, and regard Pandits as *kāfir* ('misbelievers'), destined to go to hell. Internal divisions among the Pandits do not interest the Muslims in the least.

The relationship is hierarchical, based on Islamic values. The exclusion of Pandits stems from moral abhorrence but has nothing to do with ritual pollution. Earlier I mentioned Pandit stereotypes of Muslims; these may now be matched by Muslim stereotypes of Pandits, equally derogatory and expressive of the wish to exclude the other. 'Faithless', 'unfaithful', 'double-dealer', 'mean', 'cowardly', 'corrupt' and 'dirty' are some of the epithets I heard Muslim informants use for Pandits.[27]

Kashmiri Muslims countenance marriage with Pandits no more than the latter do so with the former. They have no objection, however, to physical contact with the Pandits. The latter have free access to all parts of a Muslim house though they themselves do not allow Muslims into their kitchens and into any room where a ritual is in progress or where rituals usually take place (see Madan 1965: 46-50). The Barber and the Butcher, whose roles in Pandit religious ceremonies was discussed earlier, perform their assigned tasks just outside the ritually demarcated area. Similarly, the water carrier pours water into a vessel in the kitchen without stepping inside. Pandits are, however, debarred from entering mosques. Moreover, the Muslims of Utrassu-Umanagri do observe strict avoidance in respect of food cooked by the Pandits. 'It is *harām* (forbidden)'—the Quran prohibits it—is the most general explanation given. When pressed to elaborate this cryptic remark, some informants used the word *napak* (impure) to describe Pandit food. (Several other less significant explanations were given, including the belief that Pandit food is injurious to health because the curries contain asafoetida, and is tasteless as it lacks onions and garlic). A few Zamindars who have intimate relations with Pandit landowners were reported as given to eating food from their patrons' kitchens, but the number of such cases is negligible. Those who transgress this restriction are believed to be guilty of a moral lapse and therefore liable to suffer supernatural punishment. One of the villagers drew attention to his own brother, a sickly and poor Milkman, saying that the latter was an eater of Pandit food.[28]

There is one more category of people whose cooking the Muslims of the village do not accept because it is considered impure. The people concerned are the Domb and the Vatal. Whenever these families arrange a feast, they engage professional Muslim cooks who bring their own cooking and serving utensils. Other Muslims then readily join such feasts in the houses of these lowly groups, but do not otherwise eat with them. In turn they get invited to the homes of other Muslims but they are excluded in a subtle manner. On such occasions four persons eat from a single plate. Domb and Vatal guests will not be asked to share a plate with one another, or with any other Muslim, even if there are less than four of each of these groups present. Needless to add, the Domb and the Vatal are the two most strictly endogamous Muslim groups in the village.

Kashmiri Muslims clearly distinguish between dirty (*mokur*) and impure (nāpāk). The two conditions may exist together as in the case of the legendary pig—the animal is non-existent in Kashmir—the very sight of which is forbidden to the Muslim. The best example of the distinction between dirt and impurity was given to me by one of my informants when he explained why Muslims are expected to dry the penis with clay after urination. 'I may have put on new or washed trousers, but if even a drop of urine falls on them, I cannot enter the mosque for prayers.' Muslim ablutions prior to the saying of prayers (namāz) are quite an elaborate affair. However, their notion of pollution is in principle different from the Hindu notion inasmuch as they do not consider it permanent in any circumstances whatsoever. I was told that if the Domb or the Vatal should give up their present occupations, they too would be accepted as equals by other Muslims. This is of course difficult to confirm, and though there has long been evidence of upward mobility among Muslim occupational groups, I doubt if these two groups could easily live down the stigma of their names, which proclaim their zāt.[29] The Muslims point out that even a Pandit—any non-Muslim for that matter—can acquire true faith and become a believer (*mūmin*). This is of course the ideological position, but we have already noted the case of the convert Ghulam alias Darshan and have discussed the significance of the circumstances of birth in the determination of zāt.

Before we complete this discussion of the Muslim representation of Pandit identity, I would like to make a final comment on the notion of zāt among Muslims. The status of Sayyids is the key to this problem. I have already pointed out that Kashmiri Muslims are not an undifferentiated category, and that they themselves acknowledge this fact. My informants in Utrassu-Umanagri spoke to me of the division between the Sunni and Shia (see Levy 1962: *passim*), though there are no Shia in the village.[30] They also mentioned Sayyids, Mughals and Pathans with a certain degree of deference. Muslims falling into these categories are to be found in the town of Anantnag.[31] The position of the Gujar and the Bakkarwal has already been mentioned. I have also described how the native Muslims are composed of many occupational groups including the Domb and the Vatal.

The Sayyids are the descendants of Ali and his wife Fatima, daughter of the Prophet Muhammad. They are, therefore, entitled to respect. The Mughal and Pathan families are entitled to respect, but why? The Muslims of the village are dimly aware that these people were once the rulers of Kashmir. An equally important reason would seem to be that these groups have been Muslims longer than the others. The principle of proximity to the founder of Islam, which is apparent in view of the genealogical connection in the case of the Sayyids, and acknowledged by the Muslims, is also applicable to the Mughals and the Pathans. In terms of this logic Gujars and Bakkarwals should also be accorded deference but they are not, though they themselves look down upon the natives. The empirical situation is, therefore, somewhat ambiguous, but the cardinal principle of genealogical relationship emerges clearly in the exalted position of the Sayyids. It is misleading to regard them as the Muslim equivalent or Brahmans, as some writers have done, because the criterion of ritual purity—or perhaps even of moral superiority—is not applicable.

All the above internal divisions among Muslims are ignored when Muslims are juxtaposed with Pandits. The situation then is dramatized by being reduced to stark opposition between the believer and the 'misbeliever', the Muslim and the non-Muslim. The Pandit lies completely outside the fold of Islam. His present status is inconsequential to the Muslim; his potential status as a convert, though significant in ideological terms, does not really excite the Muslim, given the latter's notion of zāt. In an case, the convert is not a threat to the community of believers, which is open and to which he is in principle welcome. The contrast with the completely closed community of Pandits is too obvious to need further comment.

The answer to the question posed at the beginning of this section—namely why Muslims do not feel their identity threatened by interaction with Pandits—may now be given. As already explained, Kashmiri Muslims enter into relations with Pandits which they view as traditional economic transactions. The relationship is between a supplier of goods and services and his patron; religious differences are held in abeyance. It is a relationship of mutual dependence, but also asymmetrical. Whereas the Pandit cannot find substitutes or surrogates for Muslim occupational groups in his own community, Muslim specialists are free, at least in principle, to make their living by attending to the needs of their co-religionists alone. This is what happens in fact in many villages where there are no Pandits within the settlement or nearby. It is true that in mixed villages Pandit households have generally enjoyed enough economic power to make it worthwhile for the Muslims to serve them. The Pandits were favoured by and identified with the ruling class during the hundred years of Hindu rule between 1846 and 1947 (see Bamzai 1962: 553 ff.).[32] Economic need or advantage and political subordination of the Muslims do not, however, create among them a dependence on the Pandits in principle, which alone would be immutable; the existing dependence is purely circumstantial.

Dependence in deference to a principle characterizes the relationship of the Pandits with the Muslims. A Pandit cannot retain his ritual status without the crucial services of at least some of the Muslim occupational groups. The dependence is absolute, in principle as well as in practice. To put it differently: the Pandit keeps Muslims out of the *sanctum sanctorum* of his cultural universe, but has to let them into his social world; hence the strain and anxiety that he experiences. A Muslim, on the other hand, considers Pandits as outsiders, both ideologically and empirically. He does not feel threatened on either plane. This sense of security has been considerably heightened since 1947 by the policies followed by a succession of democratically chosen governments of the state which have been dominated by Muslims. The most noteworthy of the decisions taken have been in respect of land and tenancy reforms (the most radical in India), abolition or reduction of the debt burden of the peasantry, and provision of extensive education, health and transportation facilities in rural areas. Educationally, and perhaps economically, the Muslims of Utrassu-Umanagri are not yet the equals of their Pandit co-villagers, but politically they are on the right side of the fence. This would seem to be generally true of rural Kashmir (see Madan 1966).

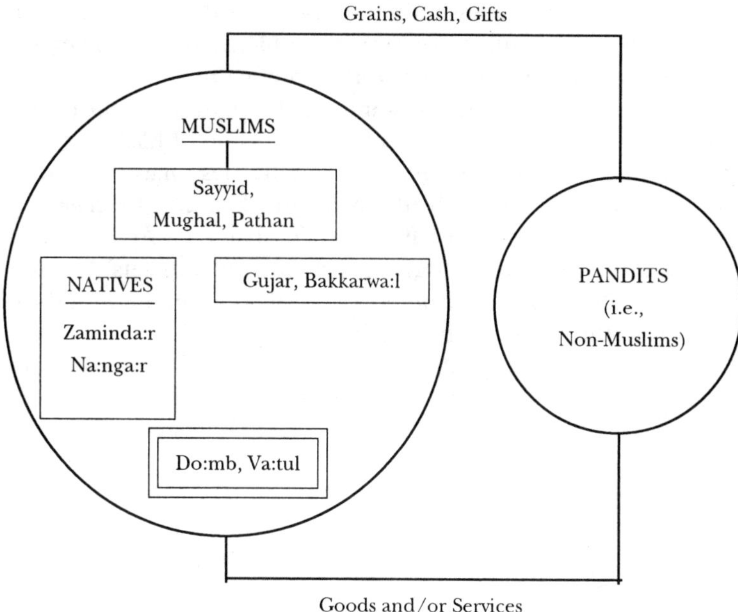

FIGURE 2. MUSLIM REPRESENTATION OF VILLAGE SOCIETY

The Muslim representation of village society is shown in Figure 2. If we compare it with the Hindu representation of the same society presented in Figure 1, it becomes clear that we are faced with a situation of dual identities and of dual social orders. The only respect in which the two social orders appear identical is the position accorded to the Domb and the Vatal. In this parallelism between the two representations may be seen the exemplification of the Hindu ethic of ritual purity. What explains it? This is a difficult question to answer. With Dumont,, we might attribute it to the permanence of 'psychological dispositions' (see Dumont 1970: 211). What I would like to stress, however, is the marginal nature of these two groups in both the versions of Kashmiri rural society.

CONCLUSION

It will be recalled that this examination of data, drawn primarily from a Kashmiri village, was undertaken with a twofold purpose. It was hoped that it would, first, enable us to define the respective places of

Muslims and Hindus in Kashmiri rural society and, secondly, provide some fresh insights into more general problems, such as the nature of Hindu-Muslim cultural 'synthesis' and of caste society.

We have seen that the Muslims and the Hindus differ in the images that they have of themselves, of each other, and of Kashmiri rural society. This is a familiar situation in societies characterized by cultural pluralism, with each ethnic category being 'self-ascribed' as well as 'other-ascribed' (see Barth 1970). The data from Utrassu-Umanagri reveal that each group has, in fact, two sets of representation, one stemming from ideological considerations and the other from the compulsions of living.

At the ideological level there is complete mutual exclusion. That this fundamental opposition between Hindus and Muslims exists throughout South Asia, is well known.[33] What is missed, however, is the very important though apparently paradoxical fact that both ideologies command identical behaviour towards non-believers—total exclusion—and are in that sense mutually reciprocal and reinforcing. In other words, Kashmiri rural society, when subjectively defined, comprises two social orders, not one.

At the empirical level we encounter another set of relations, those between the Muslim occupational groups and their Pandit clients or patrons. As we have already seen, the Muslims view these relations in economic terms, while the Pandits regard them as ritual liturgies with an economic content. This content is not to be equated with the value of goods or services transacted, for the Pandits' stakes are higher than can be measured by the economic yardstick. Thus, though the Muslims and the Pandits are mutually dependent, there is no reciprocity of perspective, if we take the surface level view of the situation. At the deeper level, however, there is agreement. The duality of the social orders is thus overcome. In the words of Lévi-Strauss (used, of course, in another context), 'it is not the resemblances, but the differences, which resemble each other' (1962: 77).

The relationship of the ideological and empirical situations may thus be seen as one of complementary opposition. The emic definition of the relationship would, however, seem to be as that of independence. Viewed in its own terms the empirical situation is a harmonious whole; in ideological terms it is a compromise, a concession to the exigencies of coexistence (see Dumont 1970: 206). Compromise and concession spell ideological defeat; and it is as much in terms of it as of economic interdependence that, viewed from the outside, a synthesis may be seen to have been worked out by the peoples of Kashmir.

Turning to the problem of caste, we have seen that both Muslims and Pandits recognize the notion of zāt as the crucial factor in identity specification and in determining an individual's natural or moral conduct. Further, Muslim specialist-Pandit patron relations were seen to be a close approximation to the familiar *jajmānī* pattern. It was, in fact, argued that from the Pandit's point of view a caste system does exist in Kashmir. The significance of this situation lies in that it demonstrates more clearly than any other regional social framework that the castes of a 'Hindu' society, other than Brahmans, are not necessarily 'Hindu' by religion. The Kashmir data reveal how the Brahman will conjure up a system of caste substitutes even out of a non-Hindu environment. His capacity to do so is, of course, dependent upon both ideological compromise and politico-economic power. In the recent past—between 1846 and 1947—the Pandits had the monopoly of both political and economic power in rural Kashmir. In 1947 they lost the former. Though economically they are yet no worse off than they were earlier, their economic monopoly has certainly been broken and their association with land-ownership has been abolished. The future may yet hold an unprecedented challenge to the Pandits in the form of the withdrawal of cooperation by Muslim specialists. There have been a few straws in the wind to indicate that such an eventuality cannot be ruled out.[34] It remains to be seen what solution the proverbial Pandit ingenuity will find for such social and ritual lacunae.

The above considerations should not mislead us to conclude that the Kashmiri Muslim social order itself is a modified system of castes, as might be suggested by the manner in which some scholars have dealt with so-called Muslim castes (see, for example, Dumont 1970: 210; Ansari 1960; and Hutton 1951: 2). The temptation to do so is particularly strong in Kashmir where the bulk of the Muslim population is of Hindu ancestry (see Lawrence 1967: 286 but also 306). It is an easy way out but fails to attach sufficient importance to the Muslims' self-ascription today. I do not mean to suggest that the anthropologist should not venture beyond native models of social reality; he must not, however, ignore them.

Another pitfall would the temptation to discuss Kashmiri rural society solely in terms of a system of economic classes based on occupation, on the ground that the caste model is totally inapplicable to Muslims in view of their ideology (see, for example, Saghir Ahmad 1970). I trust this discussion has convincingly show that our understanding of the peculiarities of rural social organization in Kashmir is dependent upon a prior knowledge of the Hindu caste system, which is not the same thing as saying that Muslim groups are modified castes.[35] The class model is an independent construct.

The inescapable conclusion—it seems so to me at least—is that, instead of trying to completely assimilate the Muslim and Pandit representations of Kashmiri rural society, we should acknowledge the existence of dual social orders, which are, however, accommodated within one overarching framework. The latter is defined partly in cultural terms (language, customs, etc.) and partly in terms of the politico-administrative set-up. Its members are not, as such, the Muslims and the Pandits, but rather people, *Kashir* (that is, Kashmiris), who either have the Muslim identity or the Pandit identity. Within this overall framework, the Pandits need the alternate Kashmiri identity to function, whilst the Muslims do not, but only use it conveniently because that is the framework within which they can, given the Pandit requirement, deal with their Hindu co-villagers. This is precisely what I mean when I claim that, while Pandit identity is intrinsically a caste structured one, Muslim identity is not so, and, again, the Kashmiri one is. Moreover, such a view of the relation between religious ideology and ethnic identity may turn out to be of value beyond Kashmir in helping us comprehend the situation not only of Muslims but also of other non-Hindu groups in South Asia and, *mutatis mutandis*, even of Hindus in such places as Sind in Pakistan or in Afghanistan.

POSTSCRIPT

The social organisation of rural Kashmir, evolved over more than six centuries, came under severe pressure in the mid-1980s with the emergence of Muslim fundamentalist and secessionist (pro-independence) forces. In early 1990 the Kashmir Valley was literally taken over by armed Muslim militants, who resorted to terror tactics, including abduction, arson and murder. Many groups called upon the Pandits to agree to live under Islamic laws (*Nizam-i-Mustafa*) or go away. One of the Pandits of Utrassu-Umanagri was killed, a couple of others barely escaped the same fate. This resulted in unprecedented panic, and well over 90 per cent of the 2,00,000 or so Pandits of the valley abandoned their hearths and homes and migrated to safer places or refugee camps outside Kashmir. The situation remains the same until today (January 1994). Recently some militant groups have called for the return of the Pandits; it remains to be seen what comes out of it.

These developments have delivered a death blow to the composite culture and harmonious social relations described in this essay. A return to the traditional ways of life in rural Kashmir appears very remote.

NOTES

1. Literature of general interest on Kashmir, including travellers' accounts, is considerable; sociological studies of Kashmiris are few. Lawrence's book (1895; rpt. 1967) and *Gazetteer* (1909) are invaluable sources of information. He toured the valley during the 1890s in his capacity as settlement commissioner. The only published, major social anthropological study is Madan 1965. For a general introductory account and bibliographies, see Crane 1956. Suggestions regarding future research are given in Madan 1969.
2. Shaikh, an Arabic word (pl. *shuyukh*), literally means an old man or man of authority. The term seems to be widely used in South Asia to designate Muslims descended from Hindu converts (see Gait 1911; see also *Chamber's Twentieth Century Dictionary*). In Kashmir: 'The census of 1891 does not show the division into which the Muslamans of the valley fall, but it may be stated that the great mass of the village people come under the head Shaikh, and are descendants of the original Hindus...' (Lawrence 1967: 306). It is likely that some Shaikhs, particularly in urban areas, are descended from immigrants.
3. Gould mentions a similar use of the term jāti among villagers in eastern Uttar Pradesh:

   > One also speaks of *jātis* of... animals... of botanical objects... (and even of) woven fabrics.... What we see operating here is *ethno-conceptualisation.* In this instance Indians are manifesting a long established, culturally patterned tendency to regard endogamous, ritually and functionally differentiated social units as if they were natural species. (1969: 23)

   Marriott and Inden have been engaged in working out a general thesis regarding jātis as natural genera (see Marriott and Inden 1974).

   Eglar reports from the Punjab in Pakistan: 'When a mature person is asked about his *zat,* which means caste and also identity, he is most likely to answer: "What identity can a human being have? The only one who has an identity is the Almighty. I am a carpenter (or *zamindar*, or barber or this, that) by occupation"' (1960: 29).

An interesting use of the word zāt appears to have been made in Mughal administration. A *mansabdār*, or noble, was accorded a double rank. His so-called zāt rank apparently gave recognition to his social status, and his salary was determined in terms of it; his *sawār* rank stipulated the number of troopers he was expected to maintain (see Gascoigne 1971: 105).

4. Barth (1960: 118) has recorded in identical use of these two terms among the Swat Pathans who, however, use *quom* for caste status.
5. My first period of fieldwork in Kashmir, the longest so far, was in 1957-8 when I was a scholar at the Australian National University. Since then I have returned to the area of original fieldwork for several short spells. I was there last in 1986. The tense employed in this essay is of the ethnographic present.
6. The various census reports on Kashmir seem to have failed to distinguish between the traditional role and hereditary occupational groups. Thus, the 1931 report lists groups like *Derwish* (Muslim mendicant) and *jogi* (ascetic) which are not such groups. Many other functional roles could be mentioned: e.g., *dāndur* (greengrocer), *galadār* (grain dealer), *ghāsi* (grass cutter), *hamāmi* (attendant at public baths), *varinya* (midwife) and *vāza* (cook). A hereditary group which I heard mentioned was that of the Galawan who reared and stole horses (see Lawrence 1967: 311). The 1941 census report lists Potters, Blacksmiths, Carpenters and Oil-pressers, and groups all the rest together as Shaikh unless they happen to be Sayyid, Mughal, Paṭhan or Rajput (see India 1943).
7. There were only a handful of literate Muslims in Utrassu-Umanagri in 1958; the oldest of them was about 18. This fact ruled out government service as a major source of livelihood for them. The two *lambardār* (revenue collectors) of the village were, however, Muslims. A few more were employed as forest guards.
8. 'Dom: A widespread caste of scavengers, musicians, and sometimes weavers, traders or even money-lenders; possibly representing an aboriginal tribe of some influence and power (Domra, Dombu)' (Hutton 1951: 279).
9. See note 6.
10. Whenever Kashmiri Muslim villagers have to cite the authority of religion, they invariably invoke the Quran. Being generally illiterate they are unable to cite a specific chapter or verse. Far from being a disadvantage, their illiteracy and ignorance have emerged as a source of strength inasmuch as doubt has been banished from their lives. Whatever the source of their beliefs, they attribute them to the unimpeachable authority of the holy book. Distinctions between the

sunnah, hadīth, and *īmān* (see Hughes 1935) are not generally made by common people; only the literate are aware of them.

11. On the sad lot of a bachelor among Kashmiri Pandits, see Madan 1965: 101-2.
12. Though all believers are called brothers in the Quran (49, 10) and a hadīth (saying attributed to the Prophet Muhammad) contends that genealogies count for nothing among Muslims (see Levy 1962: 56-7) it is well known that Islam was never able to eradicate earlier social inequalities among the Arabs (see Smith 1903: 42-55 and Levy ibid.: 53-90). Besides, 'Birth as a principle of status honour was considerably important in the early Muslim society in India' (Ahmad, I. 1966: 279; see also Ashraf 1959: 61-3).
13. Kalhana composed the *Rājatarangini,* 'River of Kings', in eight cantos of Sanskrit verse in the middle of the twelfth century. Though he draws upon both legendary and historical material, his work has been acclaimed as a historical text in the true sense of the term (see Pandit 1968: xiii ff.).
14. The following account of the political history of Kashmir is based on Kak 1936.
15. The similarity between the Kashmir and Bangladesh situations is striking:

    'Here [in Bengal], in the course of the thirteenth and fourteenth centuries, a whole countryside turned to Islam. It is thought that the decaying Buddhism of the Pala dynasty in Bengal had been superimposed upon their rustic animism, that the substitution of the Brahminical Sena Kings for Palas had meant a lowering of status and caste restriction, and that the Muslim conquests of Bengal with its casteless religion offered a welcome avenue of social escape.' (Spear 1967: 34)

16. I have been unable to establish the exact meanings of the two terms. The common suffix *māsi* (probably derived from *mās,* month) suggests a calendrical connotation; the two groups do, in fact, observe the same important ritual occasions on different dates during the Hindus' leap year.
17. There is evidence in the *Rājatarangini* that Brahmans often acted as a corporate group, for instance, to effectively intervene in affairs of State.
18. The choice of a daughter's or sister's son would seem to have been made in view of the fact that, since agnates suffer pollution together, such a kinsman would be unable to help in the performance of purificatory rituals of his yajamān; non-agnatic kinsmen would not be similarly handicapped except by rare coincidence. The practice seems to have been prevalent in the Punjab also and Hutton curiously consider it as evidence for the fusion of the matrilineal and patrilineal cultures (see Hutton 1951: 156-7).

19. For a discussion of the nature of gotra among the Pandits, see Madan 1962.
20. For an account (partly fanciful perhaps) or Pandit family names, see Fauq (n.d.).
21. There are a few Kashmiri speaking Hindu families in Srinagar called the Purib or Purbi. They are probably descended from an immigrant Brahman group. Some informants told me that the Purbi came to Kashmir from the Chambha Valley.
22. I was told in Srinagar that there is a special category of Gor called *Achor*, who alone accept such offerings. They collect the goods under cover of darkness, either from the home of the gift-givers or from the nearest bathing ghat. See Dumont 1970: 58 on the 'Mahabrahman'.
23. Kashmiri Pandits eat mutton, wild fowl and fish, but not domestic fowl or their eggs (see Madan 1975).
24. Things have begun to change since 1947 following the many drastic political and economic changes that have taken place in the state. During 1957-8, nine Pandits of Utrassu-Umanagri were working as labourers in an Indian Army ammunition depot 6 kilometres from the village (see Madan 1965: 146-8).
25. The 1931 Census report lists government service as the traditional occupation of the Pandits (see India 1933).
26. The case of the Muslim Kawuj—attendants at Pandit cremation sites in Srinagar, and probably in other towns—requires close study; particularly their relations with other Muslims should be of interest. Kashmiri Muslims regard everything dead (except fish) as polluting.
27. Probably the stereotype of Pandits most widely used by Kashmiri Muslims is *dāli-Bhatta*, 'the *dāl* or lentil curry Pandit'. Dāl is considered the very opposite of mutton curries; dāl eaters are represented as cowardly and meat eaters as brave and courageous. Vegetarianism is actually no more than an occasional dietary restriction among the Pandits. Exceptions apart, I have encountered no vegetarian Pandit households in many years of contact with rural Kashmir, though there are vegetarian individuals. The Muslims also eat dāl but never on festive occasions (see Madan 1975b). A well-known Kashmiri saying is: *Bhattas phaka, Musalmanas shraka, Shias baka*, the Pandits fast on important occasions, the Muslims wield the sword (to slaughter sheep and goats), and the Shias weep.
28. I discussed the Muslim attitude to Pandit food with a *mufti* (a person 'learned in the Quran and Hadith in the Muslim works of law'—Hughes 1935) who is also a college professor. He disapproved of the villagers' attitude and maintained that they were acting out of ignorance and under the influence of long established habits. In this connection it is worth noting here that a Muslim Washerman of Utrassu-Umanagri once told me of how he had fallen ill after he had eaten 'unusual meat'

with some acquaintances in a neighbouring village. On my asking for clarification, he said he suspected that he had been served beef. I doubt if many Kashmiri Muslims would feel likewise about eating beef; what is remarkable is that even a few of them should. The influence of Pandit neighbours is an obvious but unsatisfactory explanation. I guess one has to fall back upon Dumont's other suggestion, 'psychological dispositions' (see Dumont 1970: 211), preferably qualified as *residual*.

29. Lawrence calls the 'social system in Kashmir. . . delightfully plastic':

> '. . . there is nothing to prevent Abdulla the Dum (Domb), calling himself Abdulla Pandit if he chooses. At first the people would laugh, but after a time, if Abdulla Pandit prospered, his descendants would exhibit a lengthy pedigree table tracing their family back to one of the petty Rajas, lord of three villages and possessor of a fort, the ruins of which still stand in Abdulla Pandit's village'. . . . (1967: 307)

Unless things have changed beyond recognition over the last 75 years, which I doubt, Lawrence's account seems rather exaggerated. I found no forts in ruins in the Kashmir countryside and the people, Muslims and Pandits, alike, take little interest in genealogies beyond half a dozen generations at best.

30. 'At the census of 1890 no distinction was made between the Musalmans of the Sunni and Shiah persuasions, but it may be roughly said that the Shiahs form only about 5 per cent of the total Musalman. The Shiahs chiefly reside in Zadi Bal ward of Srinagar and in the Kamraj (Baramulla) district, though they are found in other parts of the valley'. (Lawrence 1967: 284)
31. According to the 1941 census Sayyids formed 7 per cent of the Muslim population of Anantnag district, Pathans 3 per cent, Rajputs 2 per cent and Mughals 1 per cent.
32. Lawrence notes that the Dogra rulers have vested revenue administration in the hands of the Pandits, who manned it from the lowest to the highest levels (see Lawrence 1967: 400-1).
33. There is widespread agreement on this point. See, for example (i) Aziz Ahmad (1964: 73): 'As a religio-cultural force, Islam is in most respects the "very antithesis of Hinduism"'; (ii) Dumont (1970: 211): '. . . Hindus and Muslims form two distinct societies from the point of view of ultimate values'; (iii) A.K. Saran (gist of a statement made by him in the course of a conversation with me in 1970): 'When the Muslims came to India, the Hindus had only two valid courses of action open to them: a fight to the finish or conversion to Islam. Instead they made a soft choice: they swallowed the poison and pretended they had not died. But only the gods can perform such feats.'
34. Since 1947 some Muslim specialists of Utrassu-Umanagri have on two occasions threatened to deny their services to the Pandits: the Potters

in around 1948 and the Barbers in 1967. See also Madan 1966.

35. Imtiaz Ahmad has, for several years now, been pleading for the study of the nature of interaction between Hindus and Muslims (see, for example, Imtiaz Ahmad 1965, 1966). He believes that the Muslim occupational groups of Uttar Pradesh, whom he has studied, are appropriately described as 'caste analogues' but does not clarify from whose point of view—the anthropologists', the Hindus', or the Muslims'.

REFERENCES

Ahmad, Aziz. 1964. *Studies in Islamic Culture in the Indian Environment.* London: Oxford University Press.

Ahmad, Imtiaz. 1965. 'Social stratification among Muslims'. *The Economic Weekly* 10: 1093-6.

———. 1966. 'The Ashraf-Ajlaf dichotomy in Muslim social structure in India'. *The Indian Economic and Social History Review* 3, 3: 268-78.

Ahmad, Saghir. 1970. 'Social stratification in a Punjabi village'. *Contributions to Indian Sociology* (n.s.) 4: 105-25.

Ansari, Ghaus. 1960. *Muslim Caste in Uttar Pradesh.* Lucknow: The Ethnographic and Folk Culture Society.

Ashraf, K.M. 1959. *Life and Conditions of People of Hindustan.* Delhi: Jivan Prakashan.

Bamzai, P.N.K. 1962. *A History of Kashmir.* Delhi: Metropolitan.

Barth, Fredrik. 1960. 'The system of social stratification in Swat, North Pakistan'. In E.R. Leach, ed., *Aspects of Caste in South India, Ceylon and West Pakistan.* London: Cambridge University Press, pp. 113-45.

Barth, Fredrik, ed. 1970. *Ethnic Groups and Boundaries.* Boston: Little, Brown.

Bhattacharjee, P.N. 1966. 'Distribution of the blood groups . . . and the secretor factor among the Muslims and the Pandits of Kashmir'. *Z. Morph. Anthrop.* 58, 1: 86-94.

Chamber's Twentieth Century Dictionary. 1959. London: W. & R. Chambers.

Crane, Robert I., ed. 1956. *Area Handbook on Jammu and Kashmir State.* Chicago: Chicago University Press for Human Relations Area Files Inc.

Dumont, Louis. 1970. *Homo Hierarchicus: The caste system and its implications.* London: Weidenfeld and Nicholson.

Eglar, Zekiye. 1960. *A Punjabi Village in Pakistan.* New York: Columbia University Press.

Fauq, M.M. n.d. *Tarikh-i-Aquam-i-Kashmir* (in Urdu), 3 vols. Lahore: Zafar Brothers.

Gait, E.A. 1911. 'Caste'. In J. Hastings and J.A. Selbie, eds. *Encyclopaedia of Religion and Ethics.* New York.

Gascoigne, Bamber. 1971. *The Great Moghuls.* New York: Harper and Row.

Gould, H.A. 1962. (Review of) *Caste Ranking and Community Structure in Five Regions of India and Pakistan by McKim Marriott. The Eastern Anthropologist* 15, 1: 73-103.

———. 1969. 'Toward a "Jati Model" for Indian politics'. *Economic and Political Weekly* 4, 5: 297-300.

Hughes, T.P. 1935. *A Dictionary of Islam.* London: Allen.

Hutton, J.H. 1951. *Caste in India.* Bombay: Oxford University Press.

Census of India. 1931. Vol. XXIV. *Jammu and Kashmir,* Part II. *Imperial and State Tables,* 1933, Jammu: The Ranbir Govt. Press.

———. 1941. *Jammu and Kashmir State.* Vol. XXII, Part III: *Village Tables and Housing Statistics,* 1843. Jammu: The Ranbir Govt. Press.

———. 1961. *Jammu and Kashmir, District Census Handbook, I: Anantnag District,* by M.H. Kamili, 1966. Srinagar: Vishinath Printing Press.

———. 1971. *Series I, Paper I: India, Final Population,* 1972. Faridabad: Govt. of India Press.

———. 1971. *Series I, Paper II: India, Religion,* 1972. Faridabad: Govt. of India Press.

Kachru, Braj B. 1969. *A Reference Grammar of Kashmiri.* Urban: Department of Linguistics, University of Illinois (mimeo).

Kak, R.C. 1936. *Ancient Monuments of Kashmir.* London: Royal Asiatic Society.

Kilam, Jia Lal. 1955. *A History of Kashmiri Pandits.* Srinagar: G.M. College.

Koul, Anand. 1924. *The Kashmiri Pandit.* Calcutta: Thacker, Spink.

Lawrence, Walter. 1967 (1895) *The Valley of Kashmir.* Srinagar: Kesar Publishers.

———. 1909. *Imperial Gazetteer of India: Jammu and Kashmir.* Calcutta: Superintendent Government Printing.

Lévi-Strauss, Claude. 1962. *Totemism.* London: Merlin Press

Levy, Reuben. 1962. *The Social Structure of Islam.* London: Cambridge University Press.

Madan, T.N. 1961. 'Herath: A religious ritual and its secular aspect'. In L.P. Vidyarthi, ed., *Aspects of Religion in Indian Society,* pp. 129-39. Meerut: Kedar Nath.

———. 1962. 'Is the brahmanic gotra a grouping of kin?' *Southwestern Journal of Anthropology* 18, 1: 59-77.

———. 1965. *Family and Kinship: A study of the Pandits of rural Kashmir.* Bombay: Asia.

———. 1966. 'Politico-economic change and organizational adjustment in a Kashmir village'. *Journal of Karnataka University: Social Sciences,* 2: 20-34.

———. 1969. 'Urgent research in social anthropology in Kashmir'. In B.L. Abbi and S. Saberwal, eds., *Urgent Research in Social Anthropology,* pp. 101-5. Simla: Indian Institute of Advanced Study.

———. 1975. 'On living intimately with strangers'. In Andre Beteille and

T.N. Madan, eds., *Encounter and Experience: Personal Accounts of Fieldwork.* New Delhi: Vikas/Honolulu: University of Hawaii Press.

———. 1976. 'The gift of food'. In B.N. Nair, ed., *Festschrift for A. Aiyappan.*

Marriott, McKim and Ronald B. Inden. 1974. 'Caste systems'. *Encyclopaedia Britannica.*

Pandit, R.S. 1968. *Kalhana's Rajatarangini: The saga of the kings of Kashmir.* New Delhi: Sahitya Akademi.

Raychaudhuri, T.C. 1961. 'The Pandit and Mohammedan of Kashmir: An anthropometric study'. *Eastern Anthropologist* 14, 1: 84-93.

Smith, W. Robertson. 1903. *Kinship and Marriage in early Arabia.* London: Black.

Spear, Percival. 1967. 'The position of the Muslims, before and after partition'. In Philip Mason, ed., *India and Ceylon: Unity and diversity,* London: Oxford University Press, pp. 30-50.

Steingass, F. (compiler). 1957. *Persian-English Dictionary.* London, Routledge and Kegan Paul.

Levels and Boundaries in Native Models: Social Groupings among the Bakkarwal of the Western Himalayas

APARNA RAO

(1988)

Most anthropologists have been confronted by problems of translating and interpreting local terminology and concepts into western terms commonly used in the analysis of contemporary social phenomena. While native terms may often appear translatable, the accompanying denotations and connotations may not always be so. Without a full grasp of the latter no interpretation of native models of social organization can, however, be meaningful. This is not to say that it is not possible, and even indispensable, to explain local terms: indeed, without this, no cross-cultural comparison would be possible. Nevertheless, Malinowski's warning (1922: 176) that 'nothing is so misleading in ethnographic accounts as the description of facts of native civilization in terms of our own' is still relevant.

In this paper, I explore the problems of comprehension and translation implicit in the analysis of concepts crucial to the understanding of one universal and major aspect of culture, namely, the organization of the community and the domestic group. 'Finally', 'household', 'community' and 'group' are terms which may reasonably gloss native terms; but they are also organizing concepts with different, complex denotations and connotations in different cultural contexts. When there is change within these contexts, these concepts also undergo a certain modification. But change in social organization does not always imply lexical change. What does change is the value and the connotation of existing terms. The semantic choices on which these changes are based often reflect broader processes of socio-economic transformation.

The paradigmatic framework selected here is that of the pastoral Bakkarwal[1] of Jammu and Kashmir. Some of the terms they use could, at first glance, be translated as 'family', 'household', 'camp' or 'community', but such straight translations would ultimately hinder comprehension rather than facilitate it. The use of these terms among the Bakkarwal differs situationally, and their use has also changed over time. A very large number of anthropologists have observed that in many nomadic pastoral societies the '. . . sense of the boundaries . . . is frequently relatively vague' (Khazanov 1983: 119). My experience among the Bakkarwal suggests that although there is a certain permeability of boundaries within this society, there is no vagueness. There is, on the other hand, a multiplicity in the meaning of boundaries and the use of classificatory taxons is entirely context-specific. The multiplicity in the functioning of each of these boundaries can be synchronic or diachronic; as in the case of individual identity, each Bakkarwal has in every new context a 'pool of signs . . . as it were, from which to choose' (Madan 1972: 84). It will be shown that among the Bakkarwal a limited number of terms (signifiers) represent a multiplicity of concepts (signifieds). There are numerous economic and social reasons for this. It is postulated that their nomadic pastoral lifestyle and the seasonal change implicit in such a lifestyle represent the first knot of reasons. Above all, however, and this is the second postulate, the fairly recent ethnogenesis and the immigration of the various component parts of this community into their present areas and the resultant demographic flux explain the lack of correspondence between the number of terms and the number of connotations. It is this process of ethnogenesis, and this relatively recent immigration, which represent the forces binding Bakkarwal society in all its aspects. Without a precise and contextual understanding of their terminology at various levels of organization, no clear understanding of concepts and of factual behaviour of the Bakkarwal is possible.

THE CONTEXT OF ENQUIRY

The people who form the subject of this study are Islamic (Sunni), nomadic goat and sheep breeders. The earliest documentary reference found so far to nomadic goat and sheep breeders in Kashmir dates back to the last quarter of the nineteenth century, and the first explicit mention of the term Bakkarwal was made in 1899 (McDonell 1899: 15); later references found date from the early years of this century (Census of India 1911: 181; Bryant 1913: 3; C.S. 1914). In fact, this community first emerged as a corporate group

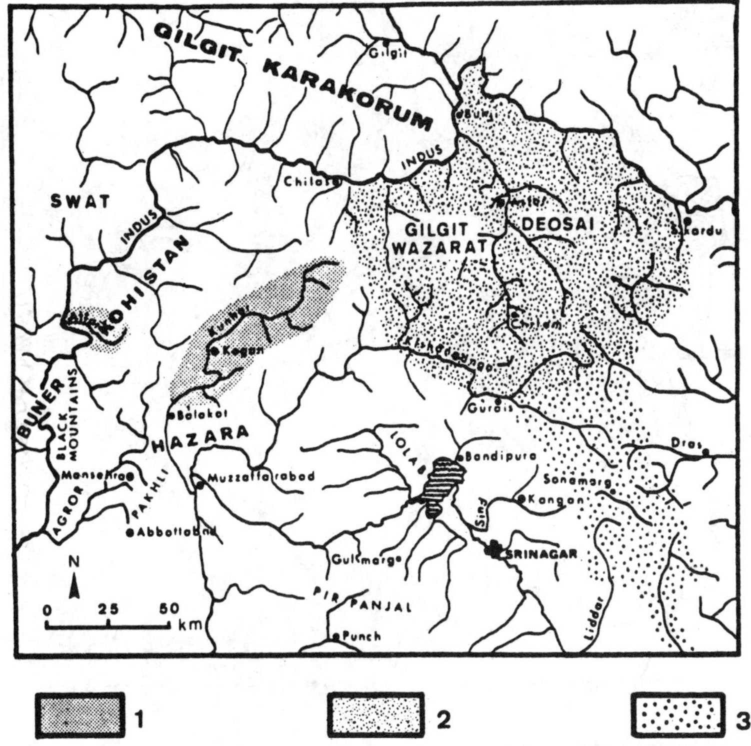

1 = areas of origin of Bakkarwal forefathers; 2 = summer pastures of the Bakkarwal and their forefathers till 1947; 3 = princial summer pastures of Bakkarwal since 1947.

FIGURE 1: BAKKARWAL PASTURES AND AREAS OF ORIGIN

only in the early years of this century (Rao 1988; 1990). It is a conglomeration of families, whose ancestors belonged to different ethnic groups, spread over large parts of South Asia. The numerically most important among them was represented by the Gujar, who live as peasants and/or pastoralists in large parts of Pakistan and north and western India, and in pockets in Afghanistan. However, families from other Islamic ethnic groups of the area, such as the Awan and Pashtun of several clans, were also drawn in to form the Bakkarwal community. In Jammu and Kashmir, all Gujar are Sunni Muslims and their traditional activities range from sedentary agriculture

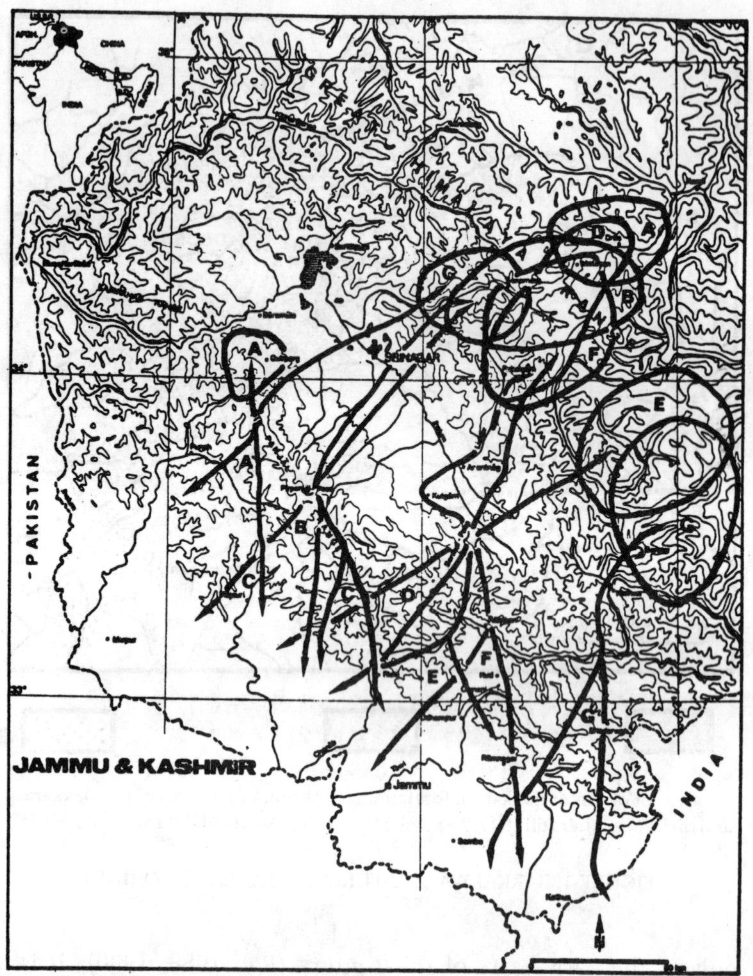

FIGURE 2: OVERVIEW OF SUMMER AND WINTER AREAS OF THE WAKKARWAL TODAY AND THEIR PRINCIPAL MIGRATION ROUTES

accompanied by a limited amount of multistock transhumance to nomadic uni-stock animal husbandry, together with little or no agriculture. Between these two extremes one finds several types, depending on the precise area and the specific sub-group of Gujar (Rao and Casimir 1985, 1987).

As stated earlier, the notion of time is of crucial importance in this study. Following Fry (1980), time was differentiated during the collection and analysis of data into historical time ('real' events which affected the lives of the people), life time (chronological measurement corresponding to a series of changes in individual life-cycles) and social time (graded roles and statuses at different period in the life-cycle). All Bakkarwal stated that their forefathers had entered Jammu and Kashmir some generations ago from the valleys of Allai and Kunhar (Figure 1), and this is corroborated by archival materials.

Till 1947 a very large number of the summer pastures of the Bakkarwal lay north of the Indo-Pakistan cease-fire line. With the partition of the subcontinent in 1947, their access to these pastures was cut off, and this has had many implications for Bakkarwal society. Their present summer pastures lie in semi-alpine and alpine zones, north and north-east of the Kashmir Basin at altitudes ranging between *c.* 2,500 m and *c.* 4,200 m (cf. Casimir and Rao 1985; Rao and Casimir 1987). Their winter area lies in the colline belt, between Punch and Kathua, at altitudes of *c.* 500 m-900 m (Figure 2). As already stated, and as their name implies, the Bakkarwal (<*bakri* = goat) are still predominantly goat breeders and their goats, which are known locally as 'kāgāni', are reported to have originated in the Kagan Valley, in Hazara (see Fig. 1). It appears that Bakkarwal economy has always depended principally on the sale of animals on the hoof; in addition, sheep wool and goat-hair were also always important sources of income in cash and kind. Even today, according to the official report of the Jammu and Kashmir Government's Planning and Development Department, the sale of herd animals and of animal products accounts for 54.15 per cent and 28.60 per cent, respectively, of the income of Bakkarwal families surveyed (PDD n.d.: Table 27). Milk was never sold, and still is not. In summer, if a family has enough animals and milk is plentiful, it is turned into butter, buttermilk, clarified butter and cheese. These are primarily for household consumption, but when there are surpluses, clarified butter is exchanged with farmers for maize, which is the staple of Bakkarwal diet. (For a detailed study of Bakkarwal diet and nutrition, see Casimir 1991.) Although the majority of Bakkarwal are subsistent on their herds, many have to draw on supplementary sources of income by hiring themselves out as shepherds for a few seasons, or as seasonal or daily contract labourers. Prosperous Bakkarwal with many horses and mules also hire out these pack animals, along with their sons or employees, for the trek to Amarnath, a place of annual pilgrimage for Hindus from all over India.

COMMUNITY, SUBDIVISIONS AND THE EMIC PERSPECTIVE

Classification is a condition for cognition and not cognition itself; cognition in turn dispels classification—Horkheimer and Adorno 1969: 196).

Some thirty years ago, Murphy and Kasdan (1959: 18-19) had pointed out the difficulties 'reflected in the variable application of European terms for kin groups, which sees a unit of essentially the same scope called by different writers a tribe, a confederation, a lineage, or a clan'. In Jammu and Kashmir, this problem reappears in the use of the term *kaum*, which has been variously translated in neighbouring cultural contexts (cf. Orywal 1986) as 'tribe', 'family' (Raverty 1860), 'local community' (Uberoi 1971: 405), 'caste', 'ethnic group' (Barth 1971: 115; 1959), 'kin group', 'sect' (Canfield 1973), 'patrilineal descent group' (Anderson 1975; Glatzer 1977: 119), 'nation', 'effective endogamous unit' (Ahmad 1978: 305), 'the entire Muslim community' (Ali 1978: 24), or 'clan' (Rao 1982: 198). Among the Hazara of Afghanistan, wrote Bacon (1958: 41), the term *qaum* is 'applied to groups at all levels . . . and there is no terminological means of distinguishing a group at one level from that at another'. In a north Indian town Berreman (1975: 93) found that this term could 'refer to religion, region or language, as well as to caste'. In Nuristan the range of connotations of the term are even greater, and Katz (1982: 170-1) writes: 'The precise category that *qaum* refers to is difficult to determine without reference to the context where it is used.'

The Bakkarwal speak of the *kashmiri kaum* and the *pandit kaum* in the Kashmir Valley and of the several dēsi kaum in their winter areas. Kaum is thus used here in the sense of an ethnic and regional category (kashmiri kaum, *dēsi kaum*) as well as in that of a religion or caste (pandit kaum). They also consider that the term Bakkarwal refers to both kaum and a *peshā* (an occupation, or trade). Literate informants, who were aware of politics at the provincial and national levels, sated that the only differences between them and the Gujar in Jammu and Kashmir—and for that matter throughout South Asia—lay in the fact that the Bakkarwal were small-stock breeders, whereas the 'other Gujar' generally owned large stock. Less wealthy Bakkarwal and those who were less aware of politics at regional and state levels, however, considered themselves akin to the Gujar, but distinct from all other communities. They cite various non-economic factors for these differences—differences in dress, appearance, language,[2] marriage customs, etc. Although certain prosperous, land-owning Bakkarwal do try and find Gujar brides and grooms for their offspring, especially in the Kashmir Valley, the Bakkarwal as a whole are endogamous. In a sample of 184 marriages analysed so far, only 5 (2.17 per cent) were found to be with non-Bakkarwal; of these, three were between Bakkarwal men and Gujar women, one between a Bakkarwal man and a Gujar-Bakkarwal (see below) woman, and one between a Bakkarwal woman and a Kashmiri villager. The marriages analysed were performed between *c.* 1900 and 1985. However, with the increasing tendency among the Bakkarwal to acquire land, build houses and thereby, as they explain, obtain the comforts and conveniences of a settled home for longer parts of the year, it is likely that the number of such community-exogamous marriages, especially with land-owning Gujar will increase, since a Bakkarwal with land prefers to give his child in marriage to someone who also has land.

But even such exogamous marriages may not necessarily lead to the Bakkarwal as a whole becoming predominantly exogamous. It is probable that it will lead rather to such families and their members becoming identified, and identifying themselves, with another local subgroup of the vast Gujar community, namely those who refer to themselves as the Gujar-Bakkarwal.[3] This distinct subgroup also tends to be endogamous, but when exogamous, its members marry prosperous and influential Gujar or Bakkarwal and draw not only the relevant partner, but also his/her family into the Gujar-Bakkarwal fold, instead of, for example, letting the exogamous individual or family integrate among the Bakkarwal.

The term 'Bakkarwal' is, however, used to identify oneself only towards persons who are not from, or familiar with the region; members of the local rural population can almost invariably recognize their interlocutor's ethnic identity on sight. Within the Bakkarwal community other categories and terms are used for identification, as we shall soon see.

The Bakkarwal are divided into the Allaiwāl (or Ilahiwāl) and Kun(h)āri. These divisions are the result of groupings of individuals and families who immigrated from the valleys of Allai and Kunhar. Khatana (1976a: 87) writes that these divisions do 'not have any direct functional relevance today', but this is true only to the extent that there is no abstract categorization, no taxon in Bakkarwali language for these two divisions. They are, however, considered as

TABLE 1. EXTENT OF ENDOGAMY WITHIN THE DIVISIONS KUNHĀRI AND ALLAIWĀL

Kunhāri-Kunhāri		Kunhāri Allaiwāl		Allaiwāl-Kunhāri		Allaiwāl-Allaiwāl	
N	%	N	%	N	%	N	%
80	96.4	2	1.1*	8	4.3**	82	87.2

*= 2.4 per cent of all Kunhāri marriages.
**= 8.5 per cent of all Allaiwāl marriages.

The division of the male partner is indicated first. N marriages analysed = 184. Percentages are calculated on all marriages analysed.

distinct units of neighbours (*hamsāyā*), and my field data clearly show that there are important differences between these divisions, and that the Bakkarwal and even many of the transhumant Gujar of the area are well aware of these differences. Dress and certain aspects of language help differentiate these divisions outwardly. An important difference in production activities is that while Kunhāri do not generally milk their sheep, the Allaiwāl do; other differences include names of certain smaller units of social organization within each of these two divisions. To a certain extent, even the taxon for these smaller units is different; while among the Kunhāri these units are known as *zāt*, among the Allaiwāl, both *zāt* and *khel* (a taxon more common in areas of Pushtun influence) are used. One of the major differences in social organization is that while Kunhāri fathers give their daughters dowry (*dāj*, or *samā*), Allaiwāl marriage negotiations are sealed by the bride price (*duniyā*).[4] Both in terms of norms and of factual behaviour, intermarriage (*nātedāri*) among the Kunhāri and Allaiwāl divisions is limited (cf. Table 1). The incidence of endogamy at this level has also not changed substantially over the past 60 to 70 years.

For the seven age groups (under 20 to above 70), endogamy among the Kunhāri ranged between 90.9 per cent and 100.0 per cent. In both cases the minimum applied to the age group 31-40 years, that is for partners born and brought up shortly before, during and after the partition of 1947, which caused considerable population dislocation in Jammu and Kashmir (see endnote 10). A few instances were noted of Kunhāri men 'becoming' Allaiwāl and vice versa; such cases are referred to by the Bakkarwal as those in which a man 'changes his *birādari*' and not his 'neighbourhood'. Only in such instances is the taxon birādari applied to the divisions Kunhāri and

Allaiwāl; why this is so will become clear in the course of this paper. In such cases of exogamy, say a Kunhāri man marries an Allaiwāl woman and lives with her kin, provided that they give him pasture[5] for his flock. This in turn, often depends on whether the woman has brothers or not. In my sample of 184 ever married men only 6 (3.2 per cent) were originally Kunhāri and had 'become' Allaiwāl, whereas one had switched from Allaiwāl to Kunhāri.

The two terms Kunhāri and Allaiwāl, which originally had only historical and geographical implications, took on new connotations in the early phase of the formation of the Bakkarwal community in Jammu and Kashmir (*c.* 1830-1910):

1. The ethnic composition of the valleys of Kunhar and Allai, whereby the Allaiwāl were known to contain major Pashtun elements, and
2. New geographical connotations in terms of distinct summer/winter pasture areas in the new area of colonization.

Today, both these connotations are relevant to a certain extent; additionally, however, there is by and large the connotation of two sets of affiliations, with regional and national political parties leading to what could almost be considered two factions. This new aspect has resulted partly from the political nature of the Bakkarwal institution of birādari.

THE DYNAMICS OF GENEALOGY, ECONOMY AND POLITICS

The term birādari, derived from the Persian *berādar* (brother), is used extensively in northern India and Pakistan to denote, strictly speaking, the patrilineage. By extension, however, it is often used to refer to a kind of sodality, i.e. to various formal and informal associations, even those beyond kin connections, all of which nevertheless have in common the concept of 'belonging together', of mutual cooperation in various degrees and in various spheres. The Bakkarwal speak of 'doing birādari' when a matter is to be solved amicably, in cases where mutual trust between the parties involved is of crucial importance. Not to help fellow birādari members amounts to being impious, irreligious and faithless—*bedīni.* When their ancestors first came to Jammu and Kashmir they were few in number; they intermarried and with these first steps towards creating a kinship network in their new land, they created the various birādari with their elementary, genealogical connotations: 'natedāri'[6] created the birādari, say the Bakkarwal. At this level the term birādari denotes a patrilineage to which one belongs by birth; hence, say the Bakkarwal, whatever one's crime one can never be expelled from the birādari. Furthermore, since the alliances the ancestors entered into were limited in number, they say, 'there are no new birādari, although there are now many more Bakkarwal'.

The ancestors immigrated in small groups and each of these was composed of one or more zāt and khēl, probably one dominant and a couple of others numerically weaker. Although taxonomically different, zāt and khel among the Bakkarwal are organically and functionally indifferentiable. Two such khēl and thirty-seven such zāt have been identified, and since the majority of these zāt names are also caste names among several Hindu and Muslim communities of the subcontinent, it is pertinent to briefly try and answer the question, 'Are Bakkarwal zāt "castes"?' Although probably dèrived from the same Indo-Iranian root as the term *jāti*, the term zāt (cf. Ansari 1960; Ali 1978: 24; Steingass 1973: 605) as used by the Bakkarwal cannot, I suggest, be glossed by the term 'caste', as it does not share any cultural or structural features with elements of the *varna-jati* system, and does not fulfil any of the commonly agreed upon basic requirements which are essential for a unit of social organization to be termed a 'caste'. There is no hierarchical ordering of Bakkarwal zāt; members of all zāt share the same occupation and there is no further specialization within the community. There is also no ideology restricting social intercourse among members of the various zāt, and although preferentially *zāt*-endogamous, the actual extent of *zāt*-endogamy is only 54.0 per cent (101 cases out of 187 first marriages among 29 *zāt*). In these *zāt*-endogamous marriages the incidence of marriage between persons who considered themselves related in some manner even before marriage has been fairly constant over the last six decades, but has changed in the past few years (Table 2).

Of the 118 marriages examined 61 (51.6 per cent) took place between persons who thought of themselves as related before marriage and 57 (48.3 per cent) between persons who considered themselves unrelated. Among these 61 again, there were 12 marriages each (19.6 per cent) among patrilateral parallel cousins and patrilateral classificatory parallel cousins (up to six generations), making these

TABLE 2. BREAK UP OF 118 BAKKARWAL MARRIAGES ACCORDING TO TIME OF MARRIAGE AND RELATIONS REPORTED BETWEEN MARRIAGE PARTNERS PRIOR TO MARRIAGE

Time of marriage	N	No. of marriages between relatives	%
between 1981-5	16	14	87.5
between 1971-80	30	14	46.6
between 1961-70	12	6	50.0
between 1951-60	10	7	70.0
between 1941-50	7	4	57.1
between 1931-40	3	1	33.3
between 1915-30	40	15	37.5
	118	61	51.6

the commonest marriages for all age groups. These were followed by marriages between patrilateral classificatory cross cousins [also up to six generations] with 13.1 per cent, the children of a brother and a sister (9.8 per cent), and exchange marriage with 8.1 per cent. If, however, all marriages between real and classificatory patrilateral parallel cousins are grouped together, this is found to constitute the largest single group of marriages for all age groups (39.3 per cent), followed by all marriages between real and classificatory patrilateral cross cousins (22.9 per cent). Contrary to the pattern in, for example. West Punjab (cf. Eglar 1960; Pfeffer 1983: 473), the incidence of matrilateral parallel cousin marriage was found to be fairly low for all age groups (6.5 per cent for real cousins and 6.6 per cent for classificatory cousins). Two main reasons were cited by Bakkarwal informants for allegedly preferring to marry within their respective zāt; namely, the solidarity of the birādari, especially at the economic level, whereby both zāt and birādari are conceived of as a patrilineage. Second, the emotional and moral security within the zāt, expressed by, for example, 'we know what we get' and 'it is safer to give and get within the same *rang*'. Rang literally means 'colour', but is used here to denote 'blood'. Marriage within the zāt thus implies purity of blood, a concept which is widespread among both Hindus (cf. Parry 1979: 85-6) and Muslims (cf. Ahmad 1978: 5) in India. Madan (1973: 109) reported a somewhat similar use of the term zāt among Kashmiri Muslims, to 'connote essence or inherent nature' and Goodfriend (1983: 121) found that among Muslims in Old Delhi 'purity of blood and bone are said to be the basis of *beradari*'. That the term *qawm,* in the sense of 'religious group' or 'sect' can also denote 'blood' is attested by Canfield's study (1973: 69) in central Afghanistan.

As Ahmed (1976: 50-1) has pointed out for Swat, Wakil (1972) for the western Punjab, and Honigmann (1960) for Sind, even a higher rate of zāt-endogamy would not necessarily point to zāt among the Bakkarwal being a caste-like element. A historical zāt-caste link cannot, however, be dismissed entirely, when one considers that (a) a majority of Bakkarwal *zāt* names are names of Hindu castes in neighbouring areas, and (b) among a neighbouring Islamic Gujar subgroup, namely the buffalo-breeding, nomadic Banihara, social units with similar names and classified under the taxon zāt or *gōt* are strictly exogamous (Hasan 1981: 50; 1986 for Uttar Pradesh and my own information for Jammu and Kashmir). On the other hand, Bakkarwal zāt are also comparable to clans, insofar as each of them constitutes, what Murdock (1949: 66-8) termed a 'compromise kin group': each Bakkarwal zāt consists of a group of persons who claim common ancestry, but are not able to trace it, and each zāt is also a part of a larger ethnic group. It is clear then, that the Bakkarwal taxon zāt subsumes a number of connotations; it is a folk concept of 'race', 'breed', 'clan', 'lineage' and 'solidarity group' (for examples of similar folk concepts beyond South Asia see Banton 1983: 32-59). In fact the Bakkarwal explicitly compare zāt, race and breed when they say: 'Just as we have different zāt, so do our goats—they too have different zāt, different *nasl* (literally pedigree, genealogy).' Implicit in such a statement is a qualitative difference, but this difference is not ranked for either goats or men. 'There are goats who give a lot of milk, others who give a lot of hair and still others who breed well. Similarly there are big zāt and small zāt; different zāt have different traditions.'

A zāt is generally classified as either Kunhāri, or Allaiwāl,[8] i.e. its ancestors came originally from either of the two areas Kunhar or Allai. But there are instances in which a zāt, or a part of it, can be classified as both Kunhāri and Allaiwāl; this is where we reach the nexus between the concepts of birādari, zāt and the pertinence of the Kunhāri and Allaiwāl divisions. the immigrants had established themselves in specific pastures in such a manner that 'each birādari used to have contiguous grazing areas',[9] a pattern which is still partly true. Furthermore, in the very early years of immigration most male members of a birādari belonged to one zāt, although dependent members of other zāt who had immigrated along with them were also considered fellow-birādari members. Soon, however, daughters and sisters were also given in marriage in limited numbers to men of other zāt, who then also became fellow-birādari members. One could now 'change' one's birādari and be recruited into one. The original and single patrilineage connotation of the birādari was thus affected and an additional connotation of this taxon now emerged. It now also meant the application of the term at the level of economy and alliance. After a while birādari-dynamics took on still other aspects: with population flux (cf. Table 3, although the actual figures are perhaps not entirely realistic), intermarriage, and geographical dispersal, the Bakkarwal formed new cooperative associations, each time with new goals, to deal with new, more local problems. Hence they developed new facets of 'fraternal' solidarity, one of which was political. The taxon 'birādari' grew in connotations accordingly. The Bakkarwal explain that even today 'a birādari can grow bigger or smaller-bigger through marriages and more children, and smaller if there is a big fight and a group separates and forms its own birādari.' Today, new birādari can thus be formed through a kind of segmentation, but in other senses and with other connotations than those referred to earlier in the patrilineage-context statement 'there are no new birādari'. In 1947, when the Bakkarwal community was split and dispersed by the partition[10] of the subcontinent and vast

TABLE 3. POPULATION FLUX AMONG THE BAKKARWAL BETWEEN 1901 AND 1981

Year	Population	Source
1901	466	Census of India 1901 XXIII A (II): XXII
1911	583	Census of India 1911 XX(I) Report: 220
1921	—	No data available
1931	5349	Census of India 1931 Part II. XXIV: 218
1941	15299	Cènsus of India 1941 Part III. XXII (II): 359
1951	—	No data available
1961	5941	Census of India 1961 VI(IIC): 220
1971	8755	Census of India 1971
1981	12000*	Census of India (unpublished estimate)

The figures from 1961 to 1981 indicate the number of persons who mentioned Bakkarwali as their mother tounge.

* Officials in charge of the Census of India (Jammu and Kashmir) 1981 estimated the number of respondents giving 'Bakkarwal' as their mother tongue at *c.* 12,000. This figure can be considered as minimum, since many Bakkarwalīspeaking respondents mentioned 'Gujari' or even 'Pahari'.

amounts of pasture land cut across by the cease-fire line between India and Pakistan, the Bakkarwal birādari shrank somewhat in number and size; but, above all, pasture land at the disposal of the existing birādari was greatly reduced. This, besides the population growth within the community since then, has led to increasing pressure on pastures and a concomitant sense of increased and acute economic competition within the community. This, in turn, has affected birādari organization and added new dimensions to this concept.

The implications of the single term birādari at the different levels of functioning among the Bakkarwal may perhaps best be explained by quoting various Bakkarwal informants and giving specific examples. The 'sliding semantic structure' (Alavi 1972: 2) of this term and its 'slippery' nature (cf. Marriott in Honigmann 1960: 836) will then appear most clearly:

1. The genealogical level of the patrilineage at which neither fission nor fusion takes place: 'brothers, cousins and their descendants'. At this level the birādari as a solidarity group is opposed today in Bakkarwal conversation to the egocentric individual symbolised by the expression '*nafase nafasai*' (lit. *nafsa-nafsi* = each one for himself).
2. The levels of production and consumption at which fission can take place: 'Formerly', say the Bakkarwal, 'the birādari helped replace dead or lost herd animals and damaged household goods and helped build burnt down dwelling.' Surplus stock is still often used by wealthy and pious men to bind social relationships of subservience within a birādari, a common feature in many pastoral societies (cf. Baxter 1975: 224; Pastner 1971; Swidler 1973). *Sakāwat,* (Rao 1995), compared by many Bakkarwal with the Islamic *zakāt,* is paid even today to a certain extent by prosperous Bakkarwal in a hereditary fashion to specific families within a birādari. Also, if for example a man grazes his flock in pastures which are recognized as traditionally belonging to another man of the same birādari, the former may not be required to pay the latter for grazing rights. Among the Bakkarwal there is, however, nothing comparable to the intricate gift exchange system which regulates birādari relations, say, in West Punjab (Eglar 1960; Wakil 1970; Rahat 1981; Pfeffer 1983). Migration units never cut across birādari lines.
3. The reproductive level, at which fission too can take place: 'before

deciding on a groom for my daughter I must ask the birādari.' It was also widely stated and observed on a few occasions that the birādari is involved in the choice of marriage partners, in marriage negotiations, and in solving marriage problems. There are also certain occasions when a birādari instigates separation and divorce, although these are rare (divorce rate: 1.0 per cent out of 277 marriages recorded).

4. The political level, which is also fissive and at which Bakkarwal representatives (*lambardār* and *mukaddam*) and politically active individuals (*kharpeñch*) function. This is the highest level and the largest possible native unit within which mediation is attempted in cases of dispute and conflict.
5. A fifth and entirely new implication of the term birādari can occasionally be observed among certain literate Bakkarwal, Gujar and Gujar-Bakkarwal. When talking to non-Bakkarwal and non-Gujar these men often refer to one another as belonging to 'our Gujar birādari'; this is to be understood in the context of growing mobilization of ethnic feelings on broader platforms (cf. Rao 1988). Here the taxons birādari and kaum are interchangeable, and the phenomenon is comparable to what Weiner (1978: 557) called 'the discovery of varna identities' among Hindus. In its exclusion of non-Gujar—and especially of Kashmiris—the usage of the term birādari here is also similar to the expression '*Hindu birādari*' (as opposed to Muslims) in pre-partition Punjab (Tandon 1961: 82). But this new connotation of the term birādari is not yet common currency, and all traditional Bakkarwal I spoke to felt that no Gujar could be a functioning member of any of the existing Bakkarwal birādari, at any level, nor vice versa. This minimal inter-ethic 'brotherliness' in contemporary Bakkarwal society may be partially explained by the fact that the ethnogenesis of this group is fairly recent. Additionally, Bakkarwal and Gujar compete to a certain extent for the same pastoral resources and that too in an area in which ecological risks are low: hence, unlike pastoral populations in arid areas among whom inter-ethnic friendship networks with peasants (e.g. Glatzer 1977; Torry 1979) or other pastoralists (e.g. Spencer 1973; Schlee 1984) often act as a kind of risk-insurance, here such networks are fairly redundant.

Like the term *mahal* in sedentary rural north India (Neale 1969: 13), 'birādari' here thus represents a knot of individual interests at various levels of social, economic and political interaction. All these levels are interdependent. An example of interaction between the first and the fourth levels can be found in the observation 'who will listen to one who is alone—an only son can never be powerful? Two complementary attitudes inform all these levels of the birādari; the first is formulated in the expression '*birādari karnā*' (lit., to do birādari), that is to trust completely, just as a man would trust his own brother. The second is symbolized by the proverb *jo bāi e wo e dushman*' (your brother is your enemy).[11] This is explained by the Bakkarwal thus: 'Your FBS, MBS and so on are your brothers, but they are also your worst enemies. A man in real trouble, has to call for help from others.' These 'others' are, also fellow-birādari members, but not in the genealogical sense of this term. As a woman, however, one can and does appeal in times of need to one's 'brothers' but here again, not only to those of the patrilineage, but also to matrilineal ones.

As already stated, since Bakkarwal birādari were originally only patrilineages, and hence composed, at least predominantly of only one zāt each, the terms birādari and zāt are still often used synonymously. This also explains why Bakkarwal zāt are generally concentrated area-wise.

MIGRATION, KIN GROUP AND FAMILY

As Shah (1974: 107-15) pointed out, the sociological discussion of family types and structures in India has long been hampered by lack of terminological clarity. A comprehension of Bakkarwal family types and of the structure of their domestic groups also requires terminological sorting out. Let us then first take a closer look at the terms *ṭolā* and *kumbā* as used among the community.

A ṭolā among the Bakkarwal is a migrating unit, and cannot be translated by 'household' as it can, for example in Kangra (Parry 1979: 157). The term is sometimes also used synonymously with zāt, since it is usually dominated by one zāt. As stated earlier, migrating units do not cut across birādari lines, and only occasionally hired shepherds (*ājri*)[12] and their families may belong to other birādari. There is, on the other hand, a great seasonal flux in the number of individuals in such a migration unit. Table 4 illustrates this flux on two migrations observed in 1983 and 1984. All members of any migration unit at its maximum do not move together, but they converge at short intervals towards specific locations and keep contact with one another throughout the migration periods, which

TABLE 4. SEASONAL FLUX IN TWO BAKKARWAL MIGRATION UNITS

Season	Beginning			Middle			End		
	Adults	Children[13]	N	Adults	Children	N	Adults	Children	N
Spring 1983	60	70	130	182	208	390	13	18	31
Autumn 1984	22	1	38	136	152	288	4	2	6

can last from two-and-a-half to five months, depending on the distance between summer and winter pastures. (For details on Bakkarwal migration see Khatana 1976b, 1986; FAIR 1980; and Kango and Dhar 1981.)

Except when used synonymously with zāt, the term ṭolā at its maximum is usually directly linked with a living adult male. But not every Bakkarwal man has a ṭolā linked to him; ṭolā are linked to specific men, whose economic and social status are high and whose consanguineal kin groups are very large. These men can be mukaddam, or kharpeñch, and in this respect a ṭolā is comparable to one aspect of the birādari as well. A ṭolā at its maximum generally consists of several kumbā, whereby each kumbā usually constitutes the units of humans and herd animals (*māl*) which actually move and camp together, or very close together during migration. Like a ṭolā at its maximum, a kumbā too is always linked to, though not necessarily named after, a specific man of some substance both economically and biologically. The Bakkarwal use the term kumbā to designate part of a zāt, or alternatively, a collection of nuclear or extended families descended from one living man—it is a specific type of descent group. When the Bakkarwal speak of A's kumbā, they imply that:

(i) A is alive; (ii) A has a large number of married sons and daughters who are also alive; and finally, (iii) A's male siblings recognize his authority over themselves, either because he is much older or richer than them. If this last requirement is not met, they speak of A's *ḍērā,* rather than of his kumbā.

The principle of the Bakkarwal kumbā is one of segmentation. Hence, say the Bakkarwal, 'there are no new birādari (here, patrilineages), but one kumbā (of old) has now become twenty kumbā. Additionally, the term kumbā also has the connotation of clique, or faction, as for example when the Bakkarwal say, 'When one of us becomes a doctor he works very well—but only for his own kumbā, and he takes no money from them.'

THE DEVELOPMENTAL CYCLE ḌĒRĀ DYNAMICS

For a study of Bakkarwal social organization, either in its synchronic or diachronic aspects, one must first examine their concept of ḍērā, a term derived from the Arabic and known in large parts of South Asia, but varying locally in connotation. For example, in rural, sedentary West Punjab the 'common sitting room of a village' or of a part of a village is called a ḍērā, or *dara* (Inayatullah 1958: 171), but among peripatetic Qalandar and Kanjar in Pakistan dērā denotes a camp (cf. Berland 1982: 85, 1987: 261-2).

The term ḍērā is connected in Bakkarwali usage to aspects of residence and location of individuals and their possessions, whether in one place or on the move. One meaning of the term is reflected in sentences in which the words ḍērā and māl are used to distinguish, within one and the same economic unit, between human beings and their herd animals. Somewhat like the term *halk* used by Brahui nomads (Swidler 1972: 71-2), ḍērā also denotes nuclear or extended family and kin group and can, depending on the context of reference, even extend to cover all material belongings, including herd animals, especially milch animals. It is this aspect of ḍērā that is taken into account when, for example, government ration cards are applied for ḍērā-wise, with the eldest male member of the ḍērā, or the head of the kumbā entered as 'head of the family'. Then there is the aspect of dērā expressed in a sentence such as, 'there are three ḍērā in this hut', i.e. there are units of individuals who cook and eat separately, although data reveal that they are usually closely related and may even constitute one loose unit for production purposes.

Most Bakkarwal spend the summer months in tents and the winter either in these tents or in thatched huts made of branches and reeds or grass. Some have built themselves log huts in their summer pastures and mud and wood huts in their winter grazing areas. During the spring and autumn migrations only tents are used. Whatever the type of habitat, 'when a Bakkarwal invites one to visit, he/she speaks of the ḍērā—of 'home'. Bakkarwal settlements, or local exploitation groups, also referred to as ḍērā, are at all times of the year small. In summer, camp sizes vary from one to nine tents (N = 42, x = 3.4 ± 2.3) and in winter between one and seven huts (N = 23, $\bar{x}$ = 3.5 ± 1.6). Settlement members are usually quite closely related and also share economic interests, such as herding activities, or in some instances joint landed property. An investigation of forty-six settlements (23 in winter and 23 in summer) revealed that none consisted of more than three generations.

When two Bakkarwal adults who do not know each other meet, they usually ask each other one of two questions: 'Where is your ḍērā (*dērō kit jēy e*)?' or, alternatively, 'With whom is your ḍērā (*ḍērā kiske nāl e*)? Each question implies a specific manner of perceiving the other's identity in terms of economy, kin group, or both. The first question implies that the respondent has an independent unit of his own; the second implies that the respondent's identity—and thus perhaps even his physical habitat—is linked to someone else's. The answer to the first question is straightforward: a camping area is named and with it generally, both the zāt and the birādari at various levels of connotation (levels 1 to 4) become fairly clear to the enquirer. The answer to the second question depends partly on the respondent's sex, but predominantly on his/her economic status and social position within the kin group. In Bakkarwali terms it depends upon the respondent's position within, and association with, the organization of ṭolā and kumbā. If in answer to the question 'With whom is your ḍērā?' a man replies, 'With X', he may mean that he is part of X's migrating unit at any point of time. Alternatively, he could mean that he camps with X. This is comparable to the use of the term ḍērā among the Hindu Pandits in Kashmir, who use it above all in the context of rural-urban migration to denote a temporary/ fixed abode away from home and under the tutelage of some important person or a broker who helps in finding work (T.N. Madan, personal communication).

Ḍērā is thus a Bakkarwal taxon with various meanings; in some contexts it signifies specific family types. However, when a young man speaks specifically of his own wife, his own small children and their personal clothes, bedding and utensils, he uses the term *ṭabbar*, rather than ḍērā. As opposed to ṭabbar as used, say in Kangra (Parry 1979: 157), or among Jat villagers in Punjab (Kessinger 1979: 43-4), among the Bakkarwal this term could, without great difficulty, be translated as a (an almost always incomplete) 'nuclear family'[14] (cf. also Eglar 1960: 75; Jettmar 1961-84). According to T.N. Madan (personal communication), Kashmiri Pandits achieve a greater degree of specification by using this term to refer to a man's wife and children. Among the Bakkarwal, the term tabbar is used by males only, and this too in a certain span of their life-cycle (Figure 3). Ṭabbar, ḍērā, and eventually kumbā are types of family which come

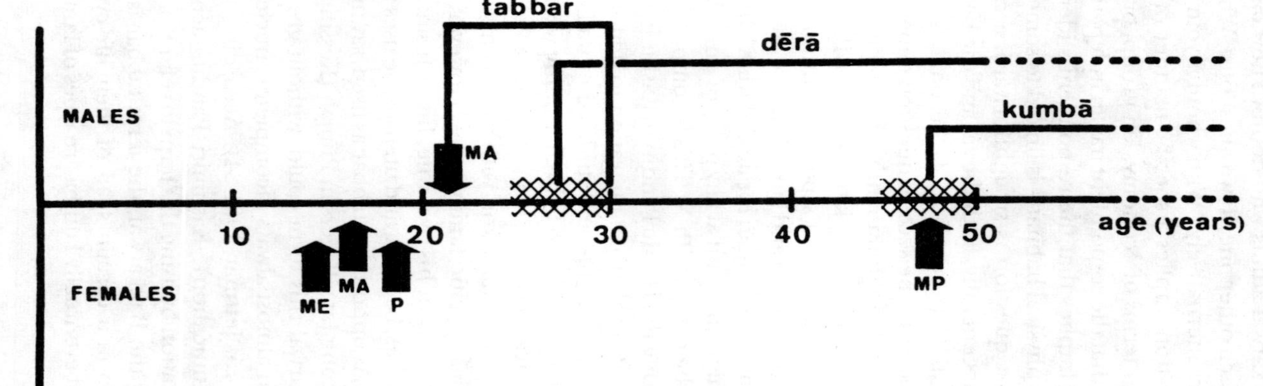

M = menarche ($\bar{x}$ = 14.3 ± 2.9, N = 74); MA = first marriage (females: $\bar{x}$ = 16.3 ± 3.5, N = 117; males: $\bar{x}$ = 21.3 ± 6.0, N = 97; P = first pregnancy ($\bar{x}$ = 18.0 ± 3.3. N = 96); MP = Menopause. The hatching indicates the time-span between the earliest and the latest occurences.)

FIGURE 3. DEVELOPMENT CYCLE OF BAKKARWAL DOMESTIC GROUPS AND INDIVIDUALS ACCORDING TO SEX AND AGE.

into being at different stages of a Bakkarwal's life, and correspond, among others, to different types and degrees of what Pasternak et al. (1976) termed 'incompatible activity requirements'.

Generally, residence among the Bakkarwal is patrilineal and virilocal, provided that the groom's father is alive and has enough animals and pasture, so that they do not have to work as hired shepherds. Living together may not always involve sharing the same tent, although if the dwelling is a hut it is always shared, for at least part of the day. But it does mean cooking together over the same fire and budgeting together in all respects. One speaks in such instances of the father's ḍērā, not the son's, whereby the ḍērā is viewed as a single unit in all socio-economic transactions with non-members. Only two cases were recorded (out of 908) in which, instead of a son, a son-in-law (DH) lived with his wife's parents, as part of their ḍērā; in these cases too, the ḍērā was viewed as a single unit and even religious tribute was paid only by the ḍērā head. When members of such a ḍērā simultaneously use two or more pastures in summer or in winter, ḍērā members are parted temporarily; while the milch animals remain with most of the family at the ḍērā in the lower pasture, the dry animals are taken by some of the younger men to graze at pastures, sometimes almost a week's journey away from the ḍērā. A seasonal split also occurs during migration, when different ḍērā join different migration units. Ḍērā also split into commensal and sleeping units, the former being larger than the latter.

Sons are generally married in the order of their birth. Unlike partition among Hindu agriculturists, among these Muslim mobile pastoralists, if all goes well, a man and his wife separate (*kanni*) from his parents in the lifetime of the latter, and form their own ḍērā, when the young couple have children and at least one of the man's male siblings is married and in his turn has young children. Thus, at the end, one is left with a unigenitural form of residence, usually one of male ultimogeniture. The timing of the separation depends on a number of factors. One factor—cited mainly be elderly Bakkarwal fathers—is the basic desire of the son to assert himself by breaking away from his father. It is claimed, however, that daughters-in-law, mothers-in-law, and women in general are instrumental in putting this desire into effect. This desire is also the factor most referred to in studies of other pastoral societies; among the Bakkarwal, however, the extended domestic unit with many married sons, their wives and children is not an ideal. Another factor cited by both men and women informants as determining the timing of the split are the relations between mother-in-law and daughter-in-law. Bakkarwal women hold that his relationship is likely to be smooth if the daughter-in-law's mother does not interfere; it is reported to be most probably an easy relationship if the girl is her own, or her husband's brother's or sister's daughter. But it appeared from numerous conversations with Bakkarwal women of various ages, and at different stages in the life-cycle, that the partition is principally triggered by the ratio between the number of persons to be cared for (especially young children and the aged) and the number of women and older girls who regularly participate in the daily productive (and to some extent reproductive) activities. When the workload of each adult woman in a household rises above a certain level, tension increases to such an extent that the decision to split is taken. Although it has been recognized in other pastoral setting that 'each tent should be fairly self-sufficient insofar as female labour is concerned' (Black-Michaud 1986: 170), it is rare that women's viewpoints and considerations based on women's labour in the household and pastoral spheres have been related to the developmental cycle of pastoral families elsewhere. In fact, in his definition of the viability of a pastoral domestic unit, Stenning (1958: 92) takes account exclusively of the labour such a unit can provide 'for the exploitation of its means of subsistence. . .'. Here I am arguing against such exclusive considerations, and pleading for a broader definition, which would include labour availability in all spheres of production and reproduction.

My observations suggest that among the Bakkarwal, when the ratio between 'eaters' (*khāṇālā*) and 'workers' (*kām karanālā*) reaches a certain level, it is considered desirable for a married son and his nuclear family to move out and form a separate ḍērā (Figure 4). Conscious steps towards restricting family size have, however, always been negligible. The decision to form their own household is made by the young Bakkarwal couple and agreed to, if not openly encouraged by the man's parents. If open conflict is not frequent, however, the man's parents want the new household to remain close by, rather than move away to another camp.

As among most pastoral populations studied recently (Irons 1972; Bates 1973: 169; Beck 1980: 337; Glatzer and Casimir 1983; Oboler 1985), among the Bakkarwal also herd size and well-being are intimately connected to labour availability and input. Unlike some

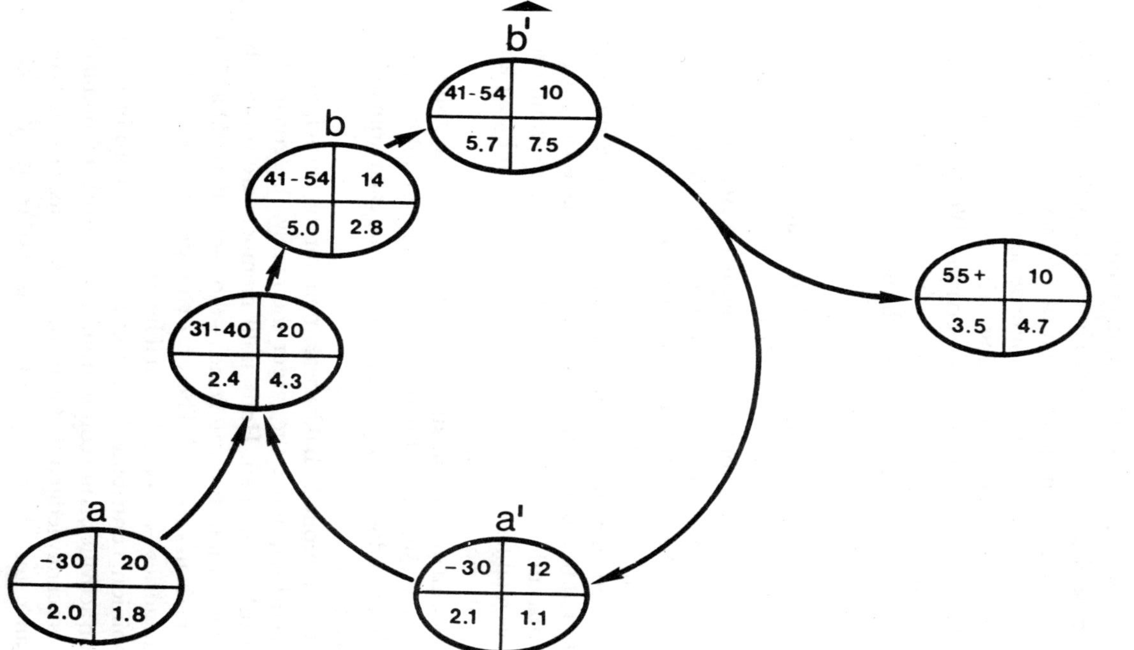

Each ellipse represents a phase in this cycle. Within each ellipse are given clockwise from the upper left section the age group, sample size, average number of 'eaters' and number of 'workers'.

FIGURE 4. DEVELOPMENTAL CYCLE OF BAKKARWAL DOMESTIC GROUPS

other pastoral groups, such as the Rendille of East Africa among whom married persons do not take an active part in herding activities (Sato 1984: 53), the Bakkarwal expect all males to herd livestock; older girls are expected to help in herding during the day. There is no upper age limit, or status limit for men, but wealthy men usually employ shepherds and every old and infirm men usually hand over herding responsibilities to their sons. There is no prescribed lower age limit either, and the male children of 7 or 8 years have been observed to help, especially in the lambing period. Generally, a boy of about 15 years is expected to start taking on herding responsibilities under his father's or elder brother's supervision. Whereas men can employ shepherds to help them with herding, most women have little access to domestic help from outside the household. Shepherds' wives are not normally expected to provide more than occasional help. Apart from an occasional, unmarried, young shepherd who may help out in his spare time by fetching water or chopping vegetables for the evening meal, adult men do not by and large participate in domestic chores. Throughout the year Bakkarwal women have to fetch water and firewood, cook, wash, clean and raise their children. In the winter[15] they must additionally fetch fodder, process wool, spin and weave; often they also take cooked food out to the men when they are out herding all day, and in the peak lambing and kidding season they must also help take care of the newborn lambs and kids. In summer, much time is spent gathering edible wild vegetables and, depending on herd size, milking and churning are laborious and time-consuming. Most women I spoke to felt that in a kanni ḍērā a woman has plenty of work to do if she has no children old enough to help; in an extended household all tasks are shared, but this does not necessarily mean that each woman has less work to do.

As already mentioned, Bakkarwal men rarely participate in household activities; hence the larger the family, the greater the burden of work on women. Household members are divided by Bakkarwal women into two categories—those of eaters (khāṇālā) and of workers (kām karanālā). These are considered to be mutually exclusive categories—an 'eater', even if he/she does, in the anthropologist's opinion, contribute directly or indirectly to production/reproduction activities, is not counted among the 'workers'. Similarly although it is acknowledged that a 'worker' also eats, he/she is not counted as an 'eater'. 'Eaters' are individuals who are either roughly under 12 years of age, or are too old and infirm to actively participate in household or pastoral work. Generally, in calculations of household effectives the number of 'eaters' includes the number of 'workers'. Table 5 compares the results of two sets of eater/worker ratios. One set of results may be described as the outcome of the etic approach, which assumes that 'workers' also eat; the other set of results represents the emic attitude of Bakkarwal women.

A sample of 20 Bakkarwal nuclear families in which the parents were between *c.* 30 and 40 years old shows that for an average of 2.4 workers there are 4.3 persons to be cared for. In such a family it is clear that the workload of the woman is extremely high, but then the possibility of splitting the household is also nil, since the 'eaters' are too young to form separate households. Such a nuclear family (N = 20 and 12) starts off on its own with, on an average, 2.0 and 2.1 adults and 1.8 and 1.1 children, respectively. Data on 10 extended families just before a married son left to form his own household show that here the proportion of working adults to non-working adults and children is on an average 5.7/7.5. As Table 5 shows, the eater/worker etic effectives vary minimally for these families throughout the development cycle. If, however, we take the emic viewpoint of Bakkarwal women into account, we find that the ratio of 1.3 in an extended family capable of splitting could perhaps, be considered an approximate threshold value. The ratio of 0.5 found in a sample of 14 other extended families which could have split, but chose not to, appears to strengthen this suggestion. The ratio of 1.3

TABLE 5. EMIC AND ETIC 'EATER' TO 'WORKER' RATIOS AMONG 86 BAKKARWAL HOUSEHOLDS IN DIFFERENT PHASES OF THE DEVELOPMENTAL CYCLE

		Average			Ratio	
Parents' age-group	Households (N)	No. of eaters	No. of workers	No. of eaters+ workers	Eaters/ (Eaters+ Workers)*	Eaters/ Workers**
-30(a)	20	1.8	2.0	3.8	0.4	0.9
-30 (a')	12	1.1	2.1	3.2	0.3	0.5
31-40	20	4.3	2.4	6.7	0.6	1.7
41-54 (b)	14	2.8	5.0	7.8	0.3	0.5
41-54 (b')	10	7.5	5.7	13.2	0.5	1.3
55+	10	4.7	3.5	8.2	0.5	1.2

*represents the results of the etic approach and **those of the emic approach.

for families with parents above 55 years is as high as for those who split, but here again, as in the case of the households with parents between *c.* 30-40 years, there is no member who could possibly leave and form his/her separate household. The PDD (n.d.: Table 5, page 293 figures of 4.1 adults to 1.6 children yield an eater/worker ratio of 0.3, but since the ages are not specified it is difficult to compare this meaningfully with data presented here.[16]

In the early stages of its development a kanni ḍērā is not necessarily economically independent; although it constitutes an independent cooking and sleeping unit it may well be that it has no herd animals of its own. The animals which it herds, together with other units, may be considered joint property. Alternatively—and this is more frequent—a man may receive as anticipatory inheritance a portion of his father's animals, but choose not to herd them separately. The money obtained by selling these animals is then also joint, forest grazing taxes are paid jointly, and milking is also done together. Milk products are however, made, consumed and eventually sold separately. When a woman gets herd animals as part of her dowry (among the Kunhāri), these, their offspring and the proceeds from their sale are hers, and when her husband's kanni ḍērā comes into being she takes them with her. But this livestock is also grazed jointly. The process of becoming economically independent is normally gradual. In a later phase of its life course a kanni ḍērā has its own herd and thus becomes an entirely independent economic unit. The herds are now formally separated. Within a given pasture territory the herds of each fully independent kanni ḍērā graze separately in sub-territories, but as long as they all belong to the same kumbā no territorial markings are used to demarcate grazing sub-areas.

I shall now briefly examine some aspects of Bakkarwal domestic groups, irrespective of the phase in the development cycle. In the ethnographic present of 1984-5, an examination of 202 such groups (78 of them [39.1 per cent] with a Kunhāri head, 113 [56.7 per cent] with an Allaiwāl head, 8 who had become either Kunhāri or Allaiwāl and 3 unknown) shows that 191 of them had married males as their heads, while only 11 had women as heads (five of these were Allaiwāl and six were Kunhāri). The percentage of domestic groups headed by women here (5.4 per cent) is lower than that for rural areas in Jammu and Kashmir (7.6 per cent; Census of India 1961) and much lower than the figure estimated for India as a whole (18.7 per cent); however, my data corroborate the suggestion that in India female-

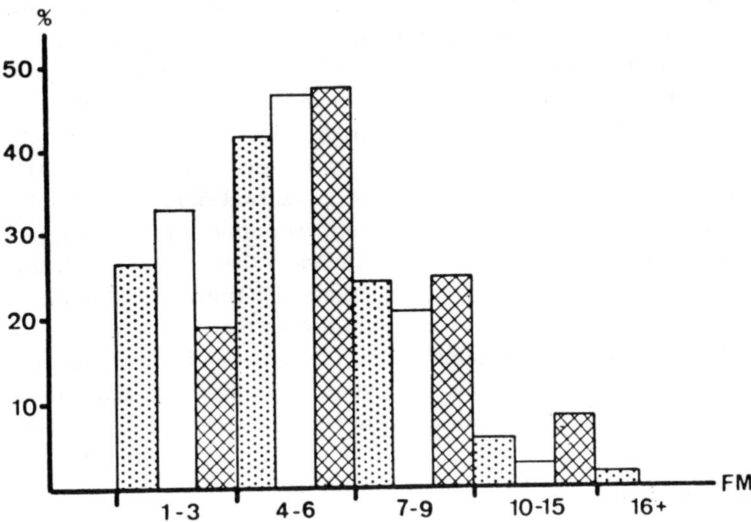

Open columns = SW (1969): Table 1, N = 185); hatched columns = Khatana (1976a: Table 3, N = 36); dotted columns = my data (N = 204)

FIGURE 5. BAKKARWAL HOUSEHOLD SIZE (FM) COMPILED FROM THREE BODIES OF DATA

headed domestic groups are poorer than those headed by men (cf. Agarwal 1985). The size and sexual composition of all the 202 Bakkarwal domestic groups examined varies minimally according to the Kunhāri and Allaiwāl divisions, but again there is a marked difference between domestic groups headed by men and those headed by women. The average size of all these domestic groups taken as a whole (N = 191) is 5.6 ± 2.9; Figure 5 shows that 40-50 per cent of Bakkarwal domestic groups have four to six members. The average size of domestic groups with male heads (N = 180) is 5.6 ± 2.8 among the Kunhāri and 5.9 ± 3.0 among the Allaiwāl; but the average size of domestic groups with female heads (N = 11) was found to be 3.5 ± 1.9; this appears to be in keeping with the general Indian pattern (Visaria and Visaria 1985). Similarly, data on domestic groups of both divisions, but with males as heads reveal that the average number of males per domestic group is 2.8 ± 1.7 (N = 189) and average 2.8 ± 1.7 (N = 185); these figures are lower than those advanced in PDD (n.d.: Table 2 page 279). However in domestic groups with female heads (N = 11: all except one widowed and between *c.* 50 and 70 years old) the average number of males and females is 1.5 ± 1.3 and 2.0 ± 1.9 respectively; one household has no males at all. Among the Bakkarwal the incidence of sex-selective out-migration is seasonal, very short term and on the whole negligible. Thus it can be asserted that unlike many other rural Indian women, a Bakkarwal woman can be head of a domestic group only when she does not have a living spouse. The Bakkarwal ḍērā in one of its aspects is a patrilineal unit of social and economic organization, and when a woman becomes its head it indicates that her kin group and that of her ex-husband are either very small in number and poor, or worse still, do not bother about her. In short, a woman as ḍērā head symbolises poverty and helplessness. The ḍērā head, the husband—*kārāḷo,* for which there is no female equivalent in Bakkarwali language—is both the worker and the one who gets work done; without a kārāḷo a ḍērā shrinks symbolically to a unit without work—or workers—simply to a unit of eaters.

CONCLUSION

In all societies there are different levels at which the forms and functioning of native models of social organization can be defined and comprehended, but as Walters (1982: 848) has argued, a clear and comprehensive picture '. . . will not be forthcoming until the interdependence of levels of explanation is understood'. In this paper I have attempted to identify and briefly discuss each of these levels among the Bakkarwal. At each of these levels decisions are taken which affect one or more individuals in different ways. Social and economic practice among the Bakkarwal affects social and economic structure and through the interrelationships of the different levels of organization this practice is to be comprehended as a continuous dialectic in the process of history. Figure 6 illustrates these levels and the boundaries between the various units of social organization. It also indicates the various levels at which interaction takes place between the Bakkarwal and the official organs of the State and government.

'Only things without a history are definable', was indeed a rather categorical statement that Nietzsche made, but few will contest that definitions are not always timeless; their validity is often contextual in both time and space. I have argued here that it would be rather meaningless to define certain Bakkarwal terms of social organization

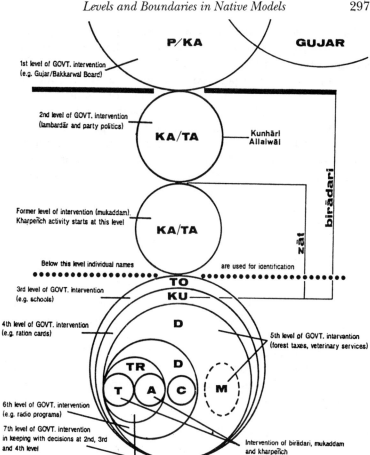

P = *peshā*; KA=*kaum*; TA=*taifa*; TO=*ṭolā*; KU=*kumbā*; D=*ḍērā*; TR=*ṭabbar*; T=*tabri* (wife); A=*ayāl* (children); C=*chullā* (hearth), M=*māl* (herd animals); Govt.=Government. For further information see text.

FIGURE 6. LEVELS AND BOUNDARIES OF BAKKARWAL SOCIAL GROUPINGS

with the finality that is often expected in ethnographic literature. I have shown how certain Bakkarwal boundary-maintenance terms take on different meanings at different levels and in different contexts. Since the different levels of social organization have an inherent dynamics, I have considered Bakkarwal domestic groups as '. . . whole processes through time [as well as] . . . samples of decisions' (Hammel 1984: 34).

The pre-colonial concepts and precise spatial relationships among ethnic groups in the area between eastern Afghanistan, Punjab and Kashmir remain fairly ambiguous. It is, however, certain that social and spatial boundaries between many of these communities were in frequent flux, and it is this permeability of boundaries which enabled several ethnic groups to get together and form a new corporate group—that of the Bakkarwal. The proverb quoted by Ibbetson (1916: 222) exemplifies the general situation in the area: 'Last year I was a *Julaha*; this year I am *Shekh*; next year if prices rise I shall be a *Saiyed*.' In fact, anthropologists are increasingly realizing that nomadic groups of herders in many parts of Africa and Asia are colonial constructs and that such discrete, homogeneous entities existed only in Census Handbooks and District Gazetteers. 'Colonial names for groups', writes Larick (1986: 166) of East Africa, 'gave permanent definition to continually changing ethnic allegiances'. The Bakkarwal are also a colonial phenomenon, insofar as their ethnogenesis took place during the colonial period and was largely influenced by colonial policies and administration. They exist today as an entity, whose boundaries delineated themselves gradually over a period of about 80 years; they are the result of a process of mutual accommodation of several, older boundaries (Rao 1988).

All of this could, perhaps, also explain why Spooner's observation (1973: 41), that in nomadic societies 'instability at the level of local groupings is balanced by conceptual stability at the level of larger social groupings' does not entirely fit the Bakkarwal case (see also Tapper 1979: 6). No doubt Bakkarwal social life is subject to frequent change through seasonal flux, determined by the nomadic way of life and the constraints of pastoral production. No doubt also that the cognition of this dynamics is reflected in their language at the most localized levels of social organization. 'Conceptual stability at the level of larger social groupings'—at the level of say, birādari—is, however, also absent. In fact it is less present here than it is at the more localized levels of ḍērā. Less instability at the ḍērā level among the Bakkarwal could be correlated to relatively recent immigration, low population density and individual territoriality of pasture resources (Rao 1992). The ancestors of the Bakkarwal came into their present areas as small groups of individual herders who did not all know one another. Their primary adaptive strategies consisted of flexibility, high competitiveness but basic equality in a society characterized by mechanical solidarity. Under such conditions it could well be that population density at the local level had to be kept within certain limits (cf. Forge 1972). This demographic factor, in combination with the 'conquest' of new areas and the highly predictable abundance of pasture land (cf. Dyson-Hudson and Dyson-Hudson 1980: 29-30) at least in summer, probably made for individual territories. This, in its turn made herding associations, for example of the Middle Eastern type, redundant and even impossible. Herding associations among the Bakkarwal are restricted to father-son associations (and occasionally include married brothers), whose well-being is ensured only by harmony and stability within a kumbā or ḍērā.

But lack of conceptual stability does not mean cognitive vagueness. Somewhat like individual and ethnic identity, both of which are in most cases of a multiple nature (for examples from contemporary north India see Berreman 1975; Kaur 1986), boundaries between various levels of Bakkarwal social organization are multipurpose and are the result of both short-term (seasonal) and long-term (life-cycle and ethnogenesis) change.

NOTES

* Dedicated to Professor Dr. Ulla Johansen on the occasion of her 60th birthday.

1. Data presented here were gathered between 1980 and 1985, over a total period of about 20 months in Jammu and Kashmir (Rao and Casimir 1982). Research was sponsored by the Institut für Volkerkunde, University of Cologne, the Department of Anthropology, Delhi University, and the Nehru Memorial Museum, Delhi; it was funded by the German Research Council (DFG). I would like to thank all these organizations. I would like to express my gratitude to several Bakkarwal individuals for their hospitality and for hours of patient conversation; Hajji Gul Bijar, Hajji Zimdi Bokra, Bedan Chauhani, Janti Jangal, Baso Kalo Khel and Sain Khatana deserve special mention. Ms. Andrea Mick helped me in sorting out and computing the quantitative data; Dr. M.J. Casimir, Dr. H. Lang and Professor T.N. Madan read previous drafts and made several important suggestions.

   Except for the term 'Bakkarwal', which has been transliterated, and for the names of persons and places, all local terms have been transcribed following the local pronunciation. Thus 'k' rather than 'q' has been used to spell 'kaum' and 'kh' rather than '*kh*' or 'x' to spell 'khel'. Incidentally, the double consonant in the term 'Bakkarwal' is never pronounced; the term is pronounced rather 'Bakarwal, or as 'Bakaral'.

2. Officials in charge of the Census of India (Jammu and Kashmir) 1981 estimated the number of respondents giving 'Bakkarwali' as their mother tongue at *c.* 12,000. This figure can be considered as a minimum, since many Bakkarwali-speaking respondents mentioned 'Gujari', or even 'Pahari'.
3. This community is not to be confused with what Khatana (1976a; 1992) refers to as Gujjar-Bakarwal: he terms all Bakkarwal thus.
4. It is likely that this bride price payment is a feature of earlier Pashtun influence. Incidentally, 'duniya' (literally = the world) is also used to refer to bride price among certain Pashtun nomads in East Afghanistan (Ferdinand 1982: 76).
5. Among the Bakkarwal grazing rights are entirely individualised, a fact which is of some relevance to my arguments towards the end of this paper. Pastures in Jammu and Kashmir are state property but the individual rights of herders are recognized by all. Forests where Bakkarwal herds browse in winter are also state-owned: while individual rights are recognized here, in certain forest circles browsing permits are allotted to them afresh each year (Rao 1992).
6. Cf. Punjabi: *nattā* = a relationship created by giving a sister, a daughter or other female kin in marriage.
7. The term khēl is transcribed in neighbouring contexts as khēl, or *xēl* and denotes various units of social organization (e.g. Barth 1959: 24; Glatzer 1977: 119; Anderson 1982: 7; Rao 1982: 119; Orywal 1986).
8. Occasionally, nowadays, zāt names are used as patronymes; the same applies to the term Allaiwāl or Ilahiawāl.
9. That a zāt can be composed of two or more regional sections (again without taxons) is exemplified by the Bokra (or Bokun) zāt, which is divided into the Gadvēl and Dacchinpar sections. It is said that the ancestors of these two sections immigrated at different times and hence occupied different pasture areas. Each of these two sections is now preferentially endogamous.
10. Several informants describe the social relations among the various Bakkarwal families, and the situation of the group as a whole at the time as confused and chaotic ('*this mis*': cf. Punjabi '*miss tiss*' = mixed grain, Bhai Maya Singh 1972: 754). The conflict between India and Pakistan in 1965 also divided many Bakkarwal families.
11. This is a somewhat watered-down form of the system of complementary opposition, widely reported in ethnographic literature.
12. An ājri is a Bakkarwal who does not have enough herds/pasture to subsist on and is thus obliged to work as a shepherd for another, better off Bakkarwal. In Swat '*ajār*' or '*ajāri*' is used to qualify all nomadic sheep or goat breeders (Van Banning 1985: 34).
13. Boys and girls below *c.* 16 years of age migrate together with younger siblings, women and the elderly, while boys above *c.* 16 tend to go with

their fathers, elder brothers or hired shepherds along with the herd animals.

14. Polygyny among the Bakkarwal is not uncommon (10.2 per cent, N = 274).
15. In their winter areas on the southern flanks of the Pir Panjal, Bakkarwal women were observed to spend about two hours each day collecting some 12-15 kg of fuel wood on an average of two such 2-3 km collecting-trips per day.
16. In a neighbouring agricultural context, Berreman (1978: 342) reports a maximum eater/worker ratio of 2.6, all of whom could live off an average of 4.5 acres of land. A discussion of the eventual differences in demographic and residential behaviour between mobile and sedentist populations or between agriculturists and pastoralists in the Himalayas would, however, be beyond the scope of this paper.

REFERENCES

Agarwal, B. 1985. 'Work Participation of rural women in the third world'. *Economic and Political Weekly* XX (51-2): A155-A163.

Ahmad, I., ed. 1978. *Caste and Social Stratification among Muslims in India.* New Delhi: Manohar.

Ahmed, A.S. 1976. *Millennium and Charisma among Pathans.* London: Routledge & Kegan Paul.

Alavi, H.A. 1972. 'Kinship in West Punjab Villages'. *Contributions to Indian Sociology* (n.s.) 6: 1-27.

Ali, H. 1978. 'Elements of caste among the Muslims in a district in southern Bihar'. In I. Ahmad, ed., *Caste and Social Stratification among Muslims in India,* pp. 19-39. New Delhi: Manohar.

Anderson, J.W. 1975. Tribe and community among Ghilzai Pashtuns. *Anthropos* 70: 575-601.

———. 1982. 'Cousin marriage in context: Constructing social relations in Afghanisthan'. *Folk* 24: 7-28.

Ansari, G. 1960. *Muslim Caste in Uttar Pradesh.* Lucknow: Ethnographic and Folk Culture Society.

Bacon, E. 1958. *Obok. A Study of Social Structure in Eurasia.* New York: Wenner-Gren Foundation.

Banton, M. 1983. *Racial and Ethnic Competition.* Cambridge: Cambridge University Press.

Barth, F. 1959. *Political Leadership among Swat Pathans.* London: London School of Economics. Monographs on Social Anthropology, 19.

———. 1971. 'The system of social stratification in Swat, north Pakistan'. In E.R. Leach, ed., *Aspects of Caste in South India, Ceylon and North-west Pakistan,* pp. 113-46. Cambridge: Cambridge University Press.

Bates, D.G. 1973. *Nomads and Farmers. A Study of the Yoruk of South-eastern Turkey*. Ann Arbor: University of Michigan, Anthropological Papers 52.

Baxter, P.T. 1975. 'Some consequences for social relationships of sendentarization'. In T. Monod, ed., *Pastoralism in Tropical Africa*, pp. 206-28. London: Oxford University Press.

Beck, L. 1980. 'Herd owners and hired shepherds: The Qasqa i of Iran' *Ethnology* 19: 327-51.

Berland, J.C. 1982. *No Five Fingers are Alike: Cognitive Amplifiers in Social Context*, Cambridge (Mass): Harvard University Press.

———. 1987. 'Kanjar social organization'. In A. Rao, ed., *The Other Nomads. Peripatetic Minorities in Cross-cultural Perspective*, pp. 247-65. Cologne: Böhlau Verlag.

Berreman, G.D. 1975. 'Bazar behavior: Social identity and social interaction in urban India'. In G. Devos and L. Romanucci-Ross, eds., *Ethnic Identity: Cultural Continuities and Change*, pp. 71-105. Palo Alto: Mayfield.

———. 1978. 'Ecology, demography and domestic strategies in the western Himalayas'. *Journal of Anthropological Research* 34: 326-68.

Bhai Maya Singh. 1972. *Punjabi-English Dictionary*. Patiala: Language Department, Punjab University (1st edn. 1895).

Black-Michaud, J. 1986. *Sheep and Land. The Economics of Power in a Tribal Society*. Cambridge: Cambridge University Press.

Bryant, F.B. 1913. *Note on a Tour of Inspection of Some of the Forests of the Kashmir State, dated 23.11.1912.* Indian National Archives: Foreign Dept. Procgs. Int. B. May 1913, nos. 121/2.

C.S. 1914. *Extracts from the Hon'ble the Resident's Gilgit Tour Diary During August and September 1913.* Jammu Archives: C.S. Old Records File No. 221/A-9 of 1914.

Canfield, R.L. 1973. *Faction and Conversion in a Plural Society: Religious Alignments in the Hindu Kush.* Ann Arbor: University of Michigan, Anthropological Papers 50.

Casimir, M.J. 1991. *Flocks and Food, A Biocultural Approach to the Study of Pastoral Foodways.* Cologne: Böhlau Verlag.

Casimir, M.J. and A. Rao 1985. 'Vertical control in the western Himalayas: Some notes on the pastoral ecology of the nomadic Bakkarwal of Jammu and Kashmir'. *Mountain Research and Development* 5.3: 221-32.

Census of India. 1901. *Vol. XXIII. A: Kashmir Part II. Tables.* 1902.

———. 1911. *Vol. XX. Kashmir Part I. Report,* 1912.

———. 1931. *Vol. XXIV. Jammu and Kashmir Part II. Imperial and State Tables,* 1933.

———. 1941. *Vol. XXII. Kashmir Part II. Important Elements,* 1942.

———. 1961. *Vol. VI. Jammu and Kashmir Part II. Cultural and Migration Tables.* 1962.

Dyson-Hudson, R. and N. Dyson-Hudson. 1980. 'Nomadic pastoralism'. *Annual Review of Anthropology* 9: 15-61.

Eglar, Z. 1960. *A Punjabi Village in Pakistan.* New York: Columbia University Press.

FAIR. 1980, *A Study of Migratory Shepherds.* Delhi: Ministry of Commerce (Foundation to Aid Industrial Recovery).

Ferdinand, K. 1982. 'Marriage among Pakhtun nomads of eastern Afghanistan'. *Folk* 24: 65-87.

Forge, A. 1972. 'Normative factors in the settlement size of neolithic cultivators (New Guinea)'. In P. Ucko, R. Tringham and G. Dimbleby, eds., *Man, Settlement and Urbanism,* pp. 363-76. London: Duckworth.

Fry, C.L. 1980. *Aging in Culture and Society: Comparative Viewpoints and Strategies.* New York: Praeger.

Glatzer, B. 1977. *Nomaden von Gharjistan.* Wiesbaden: F. Steiner Verlag.

Glatzer, B. and M.J. Casimir. 1983. Herds and households among Pashtun pastoral nomads. Limits of growth. *Ethnology* 22, 4: 307-25.

Goodfriend, D.E. 1983. 'Changing concepts of caste and status among old Delhi Muslims'. In I. Ahmad, ed., *Modernization and Social Change among Muslims in India,* pp. 119-52. New Delhi: Manohar.

Hammel, E.A. 1984. 'On the *** of studying household form and function'. In R. McC. Netting, R.R. Wilk and E.J. Arnould, eds., *Households, Comparative and Historical Studies of the Domestic Group,* pp. 29-43. Berkeley: University of California Press.

Hasan, A. 1981. 'The Jammu Gujars of Uttar Pradesh'. Unpublished manuscript.

———. 1986. 'Elements of caste among the Indian converts to Islam: A case study of Muslim Gujars of Uttar Pradesh'. *Eastern Anthropologist* 39, 2: 159-64.

Honigmann, J.H. 1960. 'Education and career specialization in a West Pakistan village of renown'. *Anthropos* 55: 825-40.

Horkheimer, M. and T.W. Adorno. 1969. *Dialektik der Aufklarung.* Frankfurt: Fisher Verlag.

Ibbetson, D. 1916. *Punjab Castes.* Delhi: B.R. Publishing Corporation (rpt. 1974).

Inayatullah, I. 1958. 'Caste, patti and faction in the life of a Punjab village'. *Sociologus* 8, 2: 36-46.

Irons, W. 1972. 'Variation in economic organization: A comparison of the pastoral Yomut and the Basseri'. *Journal of Asian and African Studies* 7: 88-104.

Jettmar, K.1961. 'Ethnological research in Dardistan 1958. Preliminary report'. *Proceedings of the American Philosophical Society* 105, 1: 79-97.

Kango, G.H. and B. Dhar, 1981. *Nomadic Routes in Jammu and Kashmir* (Part I). Srinagar: Directorate of Soil Conservation.

Katz, D.J. 1982. 'Kafir to Afghan. Religious Conversion, Political Incorporation and Ethnicity in the Vaygal Valley, Nuristan'. Ph.D. thesis, University of Wisconsin, Madison.

Kaur, R. 1986. 'Jat Sikhs: A question of identity'. *Contributions to Indian Sociology* (n.s.) 20, 2: 221-39.

Kessinger, T.G. 1979. Vilayatpur: 1848-1968. Delhi: Young Asia.

Khatana, R.P. 1976a. 'Marriage and kinship among the Gujar Bakarwals of Jammu and Kashmir'. In I. Ahmad, ed., *Family, Kinship and Marriage Among Muslims in India*, pp. 83-126. New Delhi: Manohar.

———. 1976b. 'Some Aspect of Transhumance in Mountainous Tracts—A Case Study of the Gujar Bakarwals of Jammu and Kashmir', M.Phil dissertation, New Delhi: Jawaharlal Nehru University.

———. 1986. 'Gujar-Bakarwal transhumance in Jammu and Kashmir Himalayas—responses of spring migrations'. In M. Husain, compiler, *Geography of Jammu and Kashmir*, pp. 86-116. Srinagar: University of Kashmir.

———. 1992. *Tribal Migration in Himalayan Frontiers*. Gurgaon: Vintage Books.

Khazanov, A.M. 1983. *Nomads and the Outside World*. Cambridge: Cambridge University Press.

Larick, R. 1986. 'Iron smelting and interethnic conflict among pre-colonial Maa-speaking pastoralists of north-central Kenya'. *The African Archaeological Review* 4: 65-176.

Madan, T.N. 1972. 'Two faces of Bengali ethnicity: Muslim Bengali or Bengali Muslim'. *The Developing Economies* 10, 1: 74-85.

———. 1973. 'Religious ideology in a plural society: The Muslims and Hindus of Kashmir'. *Contributions to Indian Sociology* (n.s.) 6: 106-41.

Malinowski, B. 1922. *Argonauts of Western Pacific*. London: Routledge and Kegan Paul.

McDonell, J.C. 1899. *Annual Report of the Forest Department, Jammu and Kashmir State for the Year Samwat 1955 (AD 1898-9)*, Lahore.

Murdock, G.P. 1949. *Social Structure*. New York: Macmillan.

Murphy, R. and F.L. Kasdan. 1959. 'The structure of parallel cousin marriage. *American Anthropologist* 61, 1: 17-29.

Neale, W.C. 1969. 'Land is to rule'. In R.E. Frykenberg, ed., *Land Control and Social Structure in Indian History*, pp. 3-15. Madison: University of Wisconsin Press.

Oboler, R.S. 1985. *Women, Power and Economic Change. The Nandi of Kenya*. Stanford: Stanford University Press.

Orywal, E., ed. 1986. *Die ethnischen Gruppen Afghanistans. Fallstudien zu Gruppenidentität and Intergruppenbeziehungen*. Wiesbaden: L. Reichert Verlag.

Parry. J.P. 1979. *Caste and Kinship in Kangra*. Delhi: Vikas.

Pasternak, B., C.R. Ember and M. Ember. 1976. 'On the conditions favoring extended family households'. *Journal of Anthropological Research* 32, 2: 109-23.

Pastner, S. 1971. 'Camel, sheep and nomad social organization: A comment on Ruble's model'. *Man* 6: 285-8.

PDD. n.d. *Report of the Gujjars and Bakarwal Survey, Poonch, Rajouri, Srinagar.* Srinagar: Directorate of Evaluation and Statistics, Planning and Development Department.

Pfeffer, G. 1983. 'Präskription und Geschichte: Grenzen in pakistanischen Terminologien'. In P. Snoy, ed., *Ethnologie und Geschichte: Festschrift fur Karl Jettmar,* pp. 471-86. Wiesbaden: F. Steiner Verlag.

Rahat, N. 1981. 'The role of women in reciprocal relationships in a Punjab village'. In T.A. Epstein and R.A. Watts, eds., *The Endless Day. Some Case Material on Asian Rural Women,* pp. 47-81. New York: Pergamon Press.

Rao, A. 1982. *Les Ġorbat d' Afghanistan. Aspects economiques d'un groupe itinerant 'Jat'.* Paris: Editions ADPF, Institut français d'iranologie de Téhéran.

———. 1988. *Entstehung and Entwicklung éthnischer Identitat bei einer islamischen Minderheit in Südasien. Bemerkungen zur Geschichte der Bakkarwal in westlichen Himalaya.* Berlin: Freie Universitat Berlin. Occasional papers Ethnizität und Gesellschaft.

———. 1990. 'Reflections on self and person in a pastoral community in Kashmir'. *Social Analysis. Journal of Social and Cultural Practice* 28: 11-25.

———. 1992. 'The Constraints of Nature or of Culture? Pastoral Resources and Territorial Behaviour in the western Himalayas'. In M.J. Casimir and A. Rao, eds., *Mobility and Territoriality,* pp. 91-134. Oxford: Berg.

———. 1994. 'Le berger dans une société islamique de 1 Asie du sud.' In D. Balland and J-R Pitte, eds., *Mélanges offerts au Professeur X. de Planhol.* Paris.

Rao, A. and M.J. Casimir. 1982. 'Mobile pastoralists of Jammu and Kashmir: A preliminary report'. *Nomadic Peoples* 10: 40-50.

———. 1985. 'Pastoral niches in the western Himalayas' (Jammu and Kashmir). *Himalayan Research Bulletin,* 5.1: 28-42.

———. 1987. 'Explorations in man-environment interaction in the western Himalayas: Notes on the pastoral Bakkarwal'. In V.S. Datye, J. Diddee, S.R. Jog and C. Patil, eds., *Explorations in the Tropics. Festschrift for K.R. Dikshit,* pp. 231-47. Pune: University of Pune.

Raverty, H.G. 1860. *Dictionary of the Pukh'to, Pushto or Language of the Afghans; with Remarks of the Originality of the Language.* London: Longmans.

Sato, S. 1984. 'The Rendille subsistence groups based on age-system'. *African Study Monographs,* Supplementary Issue 3: 45-57.

Schlee, G. 1984. 'Intra-und interethnische Beziehungsnetze nord-kenianischer Wanderhirten'. *Paideuma* 30: 69-80.

Shah, A.M. 1974. *The Household Dimension of the Family in India.* Berkeley: University of California Press.

Spencer, P. 1973. *Nomads in Alliance.* London: Oxford University Press.

Spooner, B. 1973. *The Cultural Ecology of Pastoral Nomads.* Reading. Mass.: Addison-Wesley.

Steingass, F. 1973. *A Comprehensive Persian-English Dictionary.* Delhi: Munshiram Manoharlal (rpt.).

Stenning, D.L. 1958. 'Household viability among the pastoral Fulani'. In J. Goody ed., *The Development Cycle in Domestic Groups,* pp. 92-119. Cambridge: Cambridge University Press.

SW. 1969. *Report of Socio-economic Survey of Gujjars and Bakerwals in Jammu and Kashmir State.* Delhi: Government of India, Department of Social Welfare.

Swidler, W.W. 1972. 'Some demographic factors regulating the formation of flocks and camps among the Brahui of Baluchistan'. In W. Irons and N. Dyson-Hudson, eds., *Perspectives on Nomadism,* pp. 69-75. Leiden: E.J. Brill.

———. 1973. 'Adaptive processes regulating nomad-sedentary interaction in the Middle East'. In C. Nelson, ed., *The Desert and the Sown,* pp. 23-41. Berkeley: University of California Press.

Tandon, P. 1961. *Punjabi Century 1857-1947.* Delhi: Orient.

Tapper, R. 1979. *Pasture and Politics, Economics, Conflict and Ritual Among Shahsevan Nomads of Northwestern Iran.* London: Academic Press.

Torry, W. 1979. 'Anthropological studies in hazardous environments: Past trends and new horizons'. *Current Anthropology,* 20, 3: 517-40.

Uberoi, J.P.S. 1971. 'Men, women and property in northern Afghanistan'. In S.T. Lokhandwalla, ed., *India and Contemporary Islam,* pp. 398-416. Simla: Transactions of the Indian Institute of Advanced Study 6.

Van Banning, H. 1985. 'Gujars in Swat-Kohistan (Noord Pakistan) Transhumante boeren en nomadische herders in the Kalam tehsil'. Ph.D. thesis, Amsterdam: University of Amsterdam, Antropologisch Sociologisch Centrum.

Visaria, P. and L. Visaria. 1985. 'India households with female heads: Their incidence, characteristics and levels of living. In D. Jain and N. Banerjee, eds., *Tyranny of the Household,* pp. 50-83. Delhi: Shakti.

Wakil, P.A. 1970. 'Explorations into the kin-networks of the Punjabi society: A preliminary statement'. *Journal of Marriage and the Family* 32, 4: 700-7.

———. 1972. 'Zat and *qoum* in Punjabi society: A contribution to the problem of caste'. *Sociologus* (n.s.) 22, 1/2: 38-48.

Walters, L.H. 1982. 'Are families different from other groups?' *Journal of Marriage and the Family* 44, 4: 841-50.

Weiner, M. 1978, *Sons of the Soil. Migration and Ethnic Conflict in India.* Princeton, NJ: Princeton University Press.

Tamil Muslims and Non-Brahmin Atheists, 1925-1940

J.B.P. MORE
(1993)

The relationship between the Hindus and Muslims of British India at the political and social level during the nineteenth and twentieth centuries is a subject of deep scholarly interest. Many studies have been done on this relationship but most of them concentrate on the northern provinces. Very few studies have been done regarding the southern province of Madras. It is difficult to point out even a single important study devoted exclusively to the Hindu-Muslim relationship in this province.

The study by R. Suntharalingam (1974) on nationalism in the Madras province of the Madras Presidency during the second half of the nineteenth century contains a section on the Muslims who, since the foundation of the Indian National Congress in 1885, were divided between pro-Congressists and anti-Congressists (Suntharalingam 1974: 352-3). Most of the other general studies of a socio-political nature, for instance, by David Arnold (1977), Christopher Baker (1976), David Washbrook (1976), and Eugene Irschick (1969), concentrate mainly on Brahmin and non-Brahmin roles in contemporary south Indian society and pay only peripheral attention (or no attention at all) to the Muslims or to the Hindu-Muslim relationship.

Susan Bayly of the University of Cambridge, in her recent work (1989) on south Indian society from 1700 to 1900, puts forward the thesis that there was no hardened frontier between the three religious communities of the south—Hindus, Muslims and Christians—because they shared many common customs, values and practices. She also asserts that there was no real gulf dividing Urdu-speaking Muslims and Tamil-speaking Muslims of south India during the same period (ibid.: 101). Bayly maintains that Islam (like Christianity) grew because Muslims identified themselves with the various aspects of Hinduism, especially 'low' Hinduism, and not because of the egalitarian or monotheistic message of Islam (ibid.: 1, 13, 458).

Further, she holds that the manifestations of Islam and Christianity which took root in south India should now be seen as fully 'Indian' religious systems (ibid.: 454). According to her, conversions took place because the converts wanted to elevate their standing within a locally recognized scheme of ceremonial rank and precedence (ibid.: 458). Her views and conclusions on south Indian Muslims very much resemble the views expressed earlier by scholars like Imtiaz Ahmad, who actually claims that 'the Islamic traditions and the indigenous custom-oriented traditions have blended to such an extent that they have become complementary integral parts of a single, common religious system' (Ahmad 1981: 15).

Kenneth McPherson, in his study of trends in the political evolution of the Muslims of the Madras Presidency from 1901 to 1937, distinguishes Urdu-speaking Muslims from Tamil-speaking Muslims (McPherson 1969: 381-402). But he fails to consider seriously the non-Brahmin Dravidian factor, which to my mind is crucial to the understanding of the evolution of the Tamil Muslims in their relationship with Urdu-speaking Muslims and the factor or factors that divide them.

The non-Brahmin movement, or the Dravidian movement as it is popularly known, comprised two trends: political and apolitical. In this paper, we will mainly concentrate on the apolitical trend, as represented by the Self-respect Movement founded in 1925, and its impact on the Tamil Muslims. This will throw light not only on the views and assertions of Susan Bayly, but also on some important aspects of south Indian society, for instance, the phenomenon of conversions to Islam, the plight of the low caste Hindus, the affirmation of Tamil Muslim identity, the division between Tamil and Urdu-speaking Muslims and the striking characteristics of Islam among the Tamil Muslims.

I. HISTORICAL BACKGROUND

The Madras Presidency came into existence due to the administrative and political needs of the British, who, by the end of the eighteenth century, had to a great extent consolidated their grip on south India. The supremacy of the British in this part of India became unquestionable by the next century, when the political influence of the Mysore Sultans was eliminated and the power of the Urdu-speaking Muslim Nawab of Carnatic (a region comprising large parts of the

Madras Presidency) was considerably reduced and the Nawabship itself abolished in 1855.

The Presidency as it existed during the nineteenth and twentieth centuries, comprised the predominantly Telugu-speaking Andhra region of the north, the predominantly Tamil-speaking country of the south, and the Malabar and South Canara districts of the west. The Tamil country alone, now equivalent to the state of Tamil Nadu, was made up of a great quadrant, a little over 1,28,000 sq. kilometres, lying between the sea and the Deccan plateau (Spate et al. 1960: 739). The Presidency itself, especially its Tamil component, was far removed from the Gangetic plain, the heart of political India and the north-western passes through which, for centuries, foreign people had made their way into northern India and beyond.

Urdu and Tamil-speaking Muslims

With the irruption of the newly Islamized Arabs into north-west India in the eighth century and the implantation of the Turkish Sultanate at Delhi a few centuries later, the course of India's history entered a new phase. Although the Musalman power was firmly established in northern India, no attempt was made by the Muslim monarchs to extend their sway over the Deccan and the extreme south of the peninsula until the closing years of the thirteenth century (Venkataramannaya 1942: 13). After this, it was only in the second half of the seventeenth century that the political influence of the Mughal emperors, who succeeded the Delhi Sultans, penetrated deep into the south. Emperor Aurangzeb conquered the Deccan and appointed a Nizam (governor) to rule from Hyderabad. Under the Nizam, with Arcot as the capital, the Carnatic Nawabs ruled large tracts of south-east India, until they were incorporated into the Madras Presidency by the British.

Before and during the rule of the Nawabs of Carnatic, a large number of soldiers, poets and administrators came and settled in south India from the Deccan and north India (Kokan 1974: 1-10). These settlers and their descendants made south India their home. But they did not severe their historical, cultural and ethnic ties with their northern Muslim brethren. They were mainly Urdu speakers. Being just a southern extension of north Indian and Deccani Muslim culture, they were never able to identify themselves fully with the predominantly non-Urdu-speaking local populations.

Long before the incursion of Muslims into northern India and their eventual establishment as a political power, however, there were Muslim colonies in southern India which had long-standing trading relations with the ancient Romans, Greeks and Arabs. In Tamil literature there are references to Muslims from the eighth century onwards. Islam in southern India actually owes its origin primarily to its direct contact with the Arab traders, who contracted marriage alliances with indigenous coastal women. The children born of these unions and their descendants were Muslims and their mother tongue was always Tamil or its derivative Malayalam. Since missionary activities seem to have taken place to convert the local people to Islam, local converts were also added to them from time to time.

The Tamil Muslims can be divided into three groups: the Marakkayars, the Lebbais and the Rawthers. In a recent article, entitled 'The Marakkayar Muslims of Karikal, south India' (1991a), I have shown that the Tamil Muslims, though they follow many non-Islamic customs and habits in their lives, still adhere strictly to the core Islamic principles like belief in One God, equality before God and brotherhood, Last Judgement and Resurrection. On the whole, the way of life and customs of these Muslims are centrally Islamic. In the non-central areas of living, they have been able to accommodate many non-Islamic customs which do not really contradict the central Islamic norms (More 1991a: 25-44).

The Marakkayars were Sunnites of the Shafi school, while the Lebbais and Rawthers were Sunnites of the Hanafi school. It seems that the Tamil Muslim subdivisions were not hierarchically ranked, but are of approximately equal status (Mines 1978: 162). Though it contradicts the claims of Susan Bayly, this view seems to confer the Tamil Muslims with a distinct identity in the Indian religious landscape and is generally held to distinguish them from the other Muslims, including the Madras Urdu-speaking Muslims.

One other historical factor that divides the Tamil Muslims from the Urdu-speaking Muslims is that the latter once belonged to the ruling class. Dispossessed of political power by the British, they flocked to Madras city, the capital of the Madras Presidency, in search of new avenues in employment and business (Dupuis 1960: 405). On the contrary, the Tamil Muslims were in all respects an independent Muslim group. Their social relationship with the Urdu-speaking Muslims was limited, though they shared the same religion,

Islam, with them. They seem to have taken little interest in who governed the country. The traditional and principal interests of many of them lay in trade and commerce, and they were especially proud of keeping up with the tradition of trade bequeathed to them by the Arabs.

Muslims and Hindus

Already in the 1830s, the abolition of Persian as the official language and its replacement by English and the vernacular languages, and the introduction of modern education in English had dealt a severe blow to the prestige and the influence of the Muslims throughout India. Both the Tamil and Urdu-speaking Muslims shunned modern western education and concentrated more on traditional methods of education. As time passed, the Tamil Brahmins, of all communities of the Presidency, had forged ahead in the field of education. By virtue of this, they had come to dominate also the public services and the political movements of the Presidency, for instances, the Madras branch of the Indian National Congress. By the turn of the century, the cleavage between Brahmins and non-Brahmin Hindu interests in the field of education, employment and politics became more and more glaring.

In 1906, the All India Muslim League was founded in Dacca to protect Muslim interests in India. Its Madras branch was founded in 1908. The very next year, separate electorates were accorded to the Muslims. Until about 1930, Muslim politics in the Presidency was dominated by the Urdu-speaking aristocratic merchant elite, centred in Madras city. The situation of the Tamil Muslims, who had their own powerful merchant elite and who until the launching of the Non-Cooperation and Khilafat Movements in the 1920s were impervious to national and pan-Islamic sentiments and usually kept a low political profile, underwent a sea-change. In fact, the Khilafat Movement drew the Tamil Muslims into national and international issues and made them join hands with the Urdu-speaking Muslims. They thus became conscious of their Islamic identity and there was certainly an awakening of their political consciousness, too.

The failure of the Khilafat Movement left them, like all other Muslims, disenchanted with the unreliable attitude of the Congress party. But being inexperienced in politics, especially national politics, they preferred to stay in the background, in spite of their considerable economic clout, while the Urdu-speaking Muslims occupied the front rank in both national and provincial politics. Besides, language was certainly a barrier for the Tamil Muslims in communicating with the mainly Urdu-speaking north Indian Muslims. This was another strong reason for them accepting Urdu leadership in politics until about 1930.

While the Congress and the All India Muslim League were evolving as nation-wide organizations, there came into existence in 1916 in the Madras Presidency the South Indian Liberal Federation or the Justice party. This party was founded by non-Brahmin stalwarts, exclusively for non-Brahmins. The Muslims and the Indian Christians were considered as non-Brahmins by the Justice party, the foundation of which was a reaction to Brahmin domination in public life. It is a peculiar domination because Brahmins, who constituted just about 3 per cent of the total population of the Presidency, had gained ascendancy over the remaining 97 per cent in the political, employment and educational fields.

This quickly led to a resentment of the traditional ritual and cultural domination of the Brahmins also. Many non-Brahmins claimed themselves to be Dravidians, the descendants of the original inhabitants of the soil, while the Brahmins were considered to be Aryan intruders into India. The caste system, which had privileged the Brahmins, was subjected to heavy criticism and the importance and development of Tamil were stressed.

Even within the ranks of the Congress, the non-Brahmins began to organize themselves against Brahmin domination. At the twenty-sixth provincial session of the Congress held at Tinnevely in 1920, a separate session of the non-Brahmins was held under the presidency of E.V. Ramasamy Naicker, member of a wealthy business family of Erode. Resolutions were passed demanding communal representation (Veeramani 1981: 32), and it was also decided at this conference that Tamil should be given equal status with Sanskrit.

Eventually, the disenchantment of Ramasamy with the Congress and its policies, dominated by Tamil Brahmin professionals in the south, led him to quit the Congress and start the Self-respect Movement in 1925. He and his followers trained their guns against the Brahmins, the caste system and the various Hindu religious mythologies. Their aim was to reform the Tamil or Dravidian society so that it became truly rational. Unlike the Justice party, which had a political and provincial character and which showed more interest in participating in the electoral and legislative process instituted by the British government rather than propagating or promulgating far-reaching social reforms in the Hindu society, the Self-respect Movement was purely a Tamil reform movement, with no political ambitions whatsoever.

It was during this period that the Tamil Muslims, too, became conscious of their Tamil identity. Tamil Muslim journals like *Dar-ul-Islam* were committed to the promotion of Tamil. The editor *of Dar-ul-Islam*, P. Dawood Sha, was a B.A. of the Madras University and a gold medalist of the Madurai Tamil Sangam. He was particularly interested in the promotion of chaste Tamil. In his journal, the Tamil *moulvis* and *alims* were heavily criticized for their inadequate knowledge of Tamil, both spoken and written (*Dar-ul-Islam*, 1 January 1923).[1] There were other Tamil Muslim journals like *Hifazatul Islam* and *Al Kalam* which defended the alims and moulvis.[2]

The Majlis-ul-ulema, founded in Tiruchirapalli in 1917 was an organization essentially funded by Tamil Muslim money (*Dar-ul-Islam*, 1 January 1923). The rich Tamil Muslim merchant, Jamal Mohammad, was the chief sponsor of this organization. During the fourth conference of the Majlis-ul-ulema in 1927, P. Khalifullah, a notable Tamil Muslim leader and lawyer from Tiruchirappalli, declared the need to start a Tamil Muslim daily for the benefit of the Tamil Muslims (*Al-Islam*, September 1927). Thus, while the non-Brahmin Hindus were promoting a Dravidian or Tamil identity, there was a certain awakening of linguistic consciousness among the Tamil Muslims too.

The Justice party, which captured power in the Presidency under the Montagu-Chelmsford Reforms of 1919, very soon discredited itself in the eyes of Muslims, by failing to satisfy the demands of its Muslim supporters. They were accused of catering to the needs of only high caste Hindus. In any case, the popular Muslim support for the party was never important at any point of time. Thus, the Muslims of Madras, especially during the later half of the 1920s were in a position where they could neither rely on the Congress nor the Justice party for their welfare. They generally kept aloof from the Civil Disobedience Movement launched by the Congress in 1929, and almost ignored the Justice party which was increasingly under the control of big landlords (More 1991b: 70). Moreover, during this period the prominent Muslim leaders of Madras, who were essentially Urdu speakers, were scattered in various organizations and factions, often quarrelling with one another (ibid.: 91-4). It was under these circumstances that the apolitical Self-respect Movement, fully committed to social reforms, came to play a crucial role in the Tamil country. This had far-reaching implications for Tamils in general and the Tamil Muslims in particular. In this paper, we are concerned only with its implications for the Tamil Muslims and their religion, Islam.

II. SELF-RESPECTERS AND MUSLIMS

Mainly for historical reasons, the Madras Presidency, especially its Tamil districts, has always been considered as the bastion of Hinduism. The emergence of the atheist Self-respect Movement in such an environment introduced an important ideological contradiction in Tamil society, which was essentially hierarchical in nature. The movement itself grew in a hostile atmosphere, though the Justice party leaders patronized it (Baker 1976: 83). By organizing public meetings and through the press, the Self-respect Movement led its virulent campaign against the Brahmins, the Congress and the Hindu religion in its popular forms. This very soon caught the attention and imagination of the Tamil people, including the Muslims.

But propaganda alone was not enough to assure its survival in the long run. So its strategy was to identify itself more and more with the causes and grievances of the various non-Brahmin Hindu castes who were considered to be socially depressed and backward. The Muslims, though a distinct group, were nevertheless considered to be socially backward in several ways. Through their propaganda machinery, the Self-respecters championed the Muslims' causes too, and highlighted their grievances. Thus there developed a relationship which inevitably was to have a lasting impact on the Tamil segment of the Muslims.

E.V. Ramasamy not only participated in the conferences held by the non-Brahmin castes, but also actively encouraged such conferences (*Revolt*, 8 May 1929).[3] Similarly, he also participated in many Muslim conferences organized in the Tamil areas. He was not only invited to speak at these conferences, but was also asked to preside over some conferences. He cleverly used such conferences to air his religious and political views, taking care not to offend the Muslims.

At the Prophet's birthday meeting at Satyamangalam on 8 August 1930, Ramasamy declared:

. . . I [say] to both Hindu and Muslim communities. It is not an exaggeration to [talk] about it. The philosophy of Islam most probably suits all people of the world. Because it is a religion that came into existence recently, it should be [said] that it is a reformed religion. . . . More than Muslims, Hindus are a greater obstacle to unity. The Hindu policy is full of superstitiousness, where there is no place for love and unity. . . . (*Kudiarasu,* 24 Aug. 1930)

At the Coimbatore district Muslim conference, he came out strongly in favour of separate electorates for Muslims because the majority of the Muslims wanted Muslim representatives to be elected by Muslim votes (ibid., 21 June 1931).

Moreover, *Kudiarasu,* the principal Tamil press organ of the movement, in its zeal to undo the Hindu caste structure more than in its love for Islam, encouraged the outcaste Untouchables to take refuge in Islam if they really wanted equality. According to *Kudiarasu* (19 April, 31 May, 25 Oct. 1931) Christianity could not give freedom because of its caste structure, and in Hinduism there was no freedom at all.

Ramasamy himself, during his speech at the Erode Municipal Elementary School to celebrate the Prophet's birthday, asked the Muslims to bring into their religion those who suffered and who were looked down upon, and make the happiness of equality and brotherhood that they (Muslims) enjoyed available to the depressed people (ibid., 24 Aug. 1930).

It should be noted that the Self-respect Movement did not stop with criticizing Hindu religious dogmas and practices, but also directed its criticisms against the un-Islamic customs of the Muslims as well as their religious teachers, the *mullahs.* It condemned outright customs like worshipping at *dargahs* (ibid., 3 March 1929) and the extravagant participation of both Hindus and Muslims in *allasamy pandigai* (Moharram) (ibid., 14 June 1931).

In its attack on the mullahs, the Self-respect Movement characterized them as Muslim *purohits* (priests) or Muslim Brahmins, whose dominance was still alive while the Hindu purohits' dominance was being destroyed. It further insisted that, while the Hindu non-Brahmins had awakened, the Muslim non-Brahmins had not, and attributed the Muslim bondage to the Islamic Brahmin to lack of education (ibid., 3 March 1929).

Ramasamy himself strongly criticized Muslim superstitious habits, though he conceded that Muslims gave more respect to reason than did the Hindus. He cautioned the Muslims against pulling *thers* or chariots on the occasion of festivals, in imitation of the Hindus (ibid., 9 Aug. 1931). He further said that:

> it will be a matter of laughter to others if Muslims, after having criticised the Hindus for going to Kasi [Benares] and Rameswaram [and] spending money in order to wash away their sins, go to Nagore, Muthupettai[4] and Mecca to do the same thing. (ibid., 9 Aug. 1931)

However, Ramasamy did not fail to point to the principle of brotherhood in Islam, and asked Muslims to make persons with other religious principles their brothers too. It was due to the brotherly spirit in Islam, he said, that he was incited to Muslim religious festivals, while it was a matter of shame that the Hindus did not invite him to their religious festivals (ibid.).

At Coimbatore on the occasion of a meeting held to celebrate the birthday of the Prophet, he further said:

> If Islam has spread in India, the reason is (the Muslims') feeling of brotherhood and equality. . . . If Islam is a superior religion, it should take over the whole Indian people, it should destroy all obstacles to achieve it.... It should be free to do anything which is reasonable. (ibid., 23 Aug. 1931)

Such daring pronouncements by a non-Muslim in Muslim meetings, especially on the occasion of the prophet's birthday, are certainly unique not only in the history of the Indian Muslims, but also in world Muslim history. They show the extraordinary degree of tolerance that prevailed among the Tamil Muslims during this period, permitting them to listen to criticisms directed against their way of life by people like Ramasamy, who never fully disowned their Hinduness. That the rationalist approach to religion found a considerable audience among the Tamil Muslims' is a historical fact that was bound to shape and define the trends of Tamil Muslims' behaviour in various fields in the years to come.

While the Self-respect Movement and its leader were thus contributing to reforming the customs and practices of the Muslims, the Muslims themselves were in their own way trying to reform Islam in Tamil Nadu by founding associations and using the medium of their journals and magazines in the most effective way. The foremost association was certainly the *Majlis-ul-ulema.* There were many other associations founded in various Muslim localities—the Muslim Sangam of Natchiyarkoil, the Samuga Seerthirutha Sabhai of Koothanallur (*Dar-ul-Islam,* July-Aug. 1923), the Muslim Vidya Sangam of Karikal (*Al-Islam,* Nov. 1927), to name a few.

The Tamil Muslim journals were particularly interested in defending Islam against all forms of attack and corruption,[5] and especially against un-Islamic customs. The custom of taking out *Kanturi* or *santhanakoodu* processions and the other un-Islamic customs associated with it (*Al Kalam*, May 1925, *Dar-ul-Islam*, 1 Jan. 1923), the custom of piercing large holes in the woman's or girl's ear in the name of beauty (*Dar-ul-Islam*, Jan., July-Aug. 1923), and all such customs resembling traditional Hindu practices were severely criticized.

Hifazatul Islam (Feb. 1930) even claimed that due to the opposition of its supporters, the santhanakoodu procession at Koothanalur was cancelled. Even the alims and moulvis were criticized heavily by some journals like *Dar-ul-Islam* (1 Jan. 1923) for their inadequate and corrupted knowledge of the Islamic religion. Moreover, various *maktabs* (Koranic schools) and *madrasas* were opened during this crucial period to impart Islamic education to young Muslims (More 1991b: 112-26). For the Muslims who were thus plunged into reforming their community, the reform propaganda of the Self-respect Movement in their favour was a welcome morale booster.

Thanks to the propaganda of the Self-respect Movement, the Tamil Muslims had developed a certain sympathy and goodwill for the movement and its leader E.V. Ramasamy. Specifically, the Tamil Muslims found in him a well-wisher of their community. Further, the Self-respecters' propaganda contributed to the increasing assertiveness of the low-caste Hindus. Some actually converted to Islam to shake off social discrimination on the basis of caste. In fact, in the twentieth century, the first major wave of conversions seems to have taken place in the Tamil districts between 1925 and 1935 (More 1991b: 198-202).

It appears that conversions to Islam were largely a rural phenomenon. The conversions took place mainly in the villages of Seliyampatti, Gokilapuram, and Narayandevanpatti of Madura district, in the village around the town of Kilakarai in Ramnad district and in the villages near Tenkasi in Tinnevely district (*Madras Mail*, 24 May 1932; Rifaye 1987: 66; interview with Rifaye at Madras). Between 1930 and 1935, at Tippanampatti in Tinnevely district, several Untouchables adopted Islam. This event was celebrated with pomp in the village itself (interview with A.K. Rifaye at Madras; Rifaye 1987: 66).

In the district of Madura, the Muslim proselytizing association, the

Isha-at-ul-Islam, which functioned from 21 December 1929, appears to have contributed to the conversion of at least 1,100 persons in the town of Cumbum and its neighbourhood, and 400 other persons from different regions of Tamil Nadu and Travancore (*Hifazatul Islam*, May 1934). In 1933, the first conference of the Isha-at-ul-Islam was held at Cumbum, under the presidency of the rich Lebbai merchant, Nawab C. Abdul Hakim. He declared during the conference that thousands of people waited to join the ranks of Islam and that rich Muslims should help with money to welcome these converts into the Islamic fold (ibid.; *Madras Mail*, 24 May 1932).

The age-old subordination, exclusion and even repression of a great number of low-caste Hindus by the high castes is a historical fact. The subordination and exclusion was particularly acute in Travancore and the southern districts of Tamil Nadu like Tinnevely and Ramnad. In these places, low-caste Hindus such as the Nadars, Ezhavas and Untouchables were customarily kept away from the Hindu temples. In fact, the conversions that took place during this period, in a way forced the Madras Legislative Assembly to adopt the Temple Entry Bill, which threw open Hindu temples to the Untouchables. Actually, during a speech in the Assembly over the Temple Entry Bill, the Congress leader T.S.S. Rajan, a Brahmin by birth, expressed his fear of the phenomenon of conversion to Islam, declaring that the Bill was necessary to prevent the Hindus from diminishing in numbers and weakening (Ramasamy 1947: 31-2).

The years between 1925 and 1935 were a period when the Self-respect Movement, founded in 1925, was indulging in a virulent campaign. Its constant exhortations to join Islam and its perennial criticism of the various aspects of Hinduism would have led many low-caste Hindus suffering discrimination to rethink their continuance as Hindus. The increasing activity and mobilisation of the Isha-at-ul-Islam might also have been promoted largely by the campaign of the Self-respect Movement.

The press organs of the Self-respect Movement, for instance *Kudiarasu* and *Viduthalai*, occasionally published articles urging the Untouchables to join Islam (*Viduthalai*, 24 Feb. 1935; More 1991b: Ch. 1). The leaders of the movement spoke at public meetings not only against the Brahmins, the Hindu gods and the caste system, but also about the grandeur of Islam and the necessity for the Untouchables to convert to Islam to obtain equality and liberty.

Among the factors that contributed to conversions, the foremost certainly was the oppression and discrimination of low-caste Hindus, especially Untouchables, in the Hindu social system. The conversion was to Islam, because of the professedly egalitarian and monotheistic nature of Islam and the propaganda done in its favour, especially by the Self-respecters. The low-caste Hindus embraced Islam not only to escape from social tyranny but also to find refuge in a social and religious structure where all are considered equal and where all, without restriction or discrimination, can worship the same God from the same place of worship. Status elevation was just one of the benefits accompanying conversion. In the light of the above, it is difficult to concede Susan Bayly's contention, at least as far as conversions during the twentieth century are concerned, that low-caste Hindus converted just to elevate their status in society, and not because of the egalitarian and simple monotheistic message of Islam.

As noted earlier, the Muslims of the Madras Presidency were disenchanted with the policies of both the Congress and the Justice parties, and were split between various Muslim organizations. The Tamil Muslims, who were not directly involved in national politics, found a valuable ally in the Self-respect Movement. Ramasamy in his turn, found a convenient platform in the conferences organized by the Tamil Muslims, from which he could air not only his political views, but also his opinions on religion. Though he continued to maintain that religious principles were an obstacle to Hindu-Muslim unity (*Kudiarasu*, 21 June 1931), he did not fail to stress the need for protection for the Muslims whom he considered to be more progressive and rational than the Hindus.

The development and influence of the Self-respect Movement, which dreamt of purifying the Dravidian or Tamil culture on a rationalist basis, sowed the seeds of a distinct Tamil or Dravidian consciousness among all Tamils, including the Tamil Muslims. Even those Tamil Muslims who were not overt sympathisers of the movement would not have been totally impervious to its propaganda. Consciously or not, the Tamil Muslims had to cater to the Dravidian factor in determining their future political and other activities, mainly because they were part of it linguistically, culturally and ethnically, though in religious terms they belonged to the wider-Indian Muslim and Islamic worlds.

Very soon, in 1937 itself, an occasion presented itself which was going to be a standing proof of Tamil Muslims' intimate involvement with the atheist, non-Brahmin Self-respect Movement. This involvement will constitute the next section of this paper. It will throw further light on the extraordinary relationship between the Tamil Muslims and the Self-respect Movement, the mass character of this relationship and the clear-cut affirmation of a Tamil Muslim identity.

III. ANTI-HINDUSTANI AGITATION

By the end of 1937, the ties between the Self-respecters and the Tamil Muslims had developed manifold. In fact, the Muslim Leaguer, P. Khalifullah, presided over the second North Arcot District Self-respecters' Conference, in which he pleaded for unity between Muslims and Self-respecters, but advised the latter to eschew atheist propaganda and to seek remedies through political and social agitation (*Madras Mail*, 30 Nov. 1937; *Swadesamitran*, 29 Nov. 1937). He and his supporters even trained their guns against the Brahmins, following the lead of the Self-respecters.

E.V. Ramasamy in his turn assured Muslims that atheism was not part of the official programme of the Self-respect Movement (ibid.). Thus, he was willing to dilute his strident anti-God propaganda for the sake of close relationship with the Tamil Muslims. This was a necessity at that moment, absolutely essential to his movement at this juncture when Hindustani was sought to be imposed in the Presidency and the Justice party was declining rapidly.

The Tamil Muslims did not object to the Self-respecters directing their criticism against their non-Islamic customs. In fact, this only contributed to reforming the lives of the Muslims on strictly Islamic lines. They actually welcomed such moves and were even extremely pleased when the Self-respecters extolled the lofty principles of equality and brotherhood in Islam. But what they could not tolerate was the Self-respecters' penchant for attacking God. I have earlier noted that the God is a core principle in the lives of the Tamil Muslims. By attacking God, the Self-respecters were creating a situation whereby it was becoming impossible for the Tamil Muslims to continue their relationship with the Self-respecters without compromising on their central belief in one God. No wonder Tamil Muslim leaders like Khalifullah, though they favoured the promotion of unity between the Tamil Muslims and the Self-respecters, cautioned the latter to avoid atheist propaganda.

Clearly, the Tamil Muslims did not want to compromise their centrally Islamic religious identity, in spite of the various unIslamic customs that they followed (More 1991a: 25-44). As a result, it is difficult to maintain that there was no hardened frontier between the Tamil Muslims and the Hindus, especially when the former clearly did not want to compromise on their core religious principles in their relationship with the Self-respecters, who after all never relinquished their Hinduness.

But in subscribing to the Aryan-Dravidian theory and in campaigning against the Brahmins (supposed to be Aryans) and the Brahmin domination in the Congress, the views of the Tamil Muslims and the Self-respecters converged. For example, at the Tanjore District Muslim Conference, Khalifullah made a scathing attack on the Brahmins by declaring that before the Muslims came to India there was no India, and that the Brahmins had no right to ask the Muslims to leave India, for they themselves had come from outside in search of livelihood (*Kudiarasu,* 16 June 1940). Through such attacks on the Brahmins, the Tamil Muslims re-emphasized their Tamilness or Dravidiannes and drew closer to the Self-respecters, their steadfast allies.

On his part, E.V. Ramasamy continued to address many Muslim meetings, in which he carried on his usual propaganda and asked the Muslims, the Justice party and the Self-respect Movement to work unitedly (ibid., 5 Dec. 1937; 9 Jan. 1938). At the same time, a sustained propaganda was carried on as usual, exhorting the Untouchables to convert to Islam, for that was supposed to be the only way to their salvation (ibid., 6 Feb. 1938). This brought the Tamil Muslims closer to the Self-respecters. As we shall see, the latter were to put to good use this support during the first anti-Hindustani agitation in the Presidency.

In fact, when the Congress party assumed office in 1937 in the Madras Presidency, with the Tamil Brahmin, C. Rajagopalachari as Prime Minister, a new phase of non-Brahmin and Tamil Muslim assertiveness had begun. Rajagopalachari had earlier coöperated with the Muslims during the Khilafat Movement, and was hailed as an able administrator. He introduced several measures during his tenure as Prime Minister of which his programme for introducing Hindustani as a compulsory subject in 125 secondary schools was the most shocking to his fellow countrymen. Contrary to all expectations, this single move of introducing Hindustani, turned a sizeable section of the Muslim and non-Brahmin communities, especially of the Tamil districts, against the Congress government. The element of compulsion in the study of Hindustani was not envisaged even by Gandhi or the Congress High Command.

The Hindustani controversy had arisen even before the installation of the Congress government. The Hindi versus Urdu controversy of the United Provinces was well known. Naturally, the Muslims of Madras feared that they were being obliged to learn a Sanskritized Hindi in the name of Hindustani. Rajagopalachari stressed that there was no difference between Hindi and Urdu except in script, and that Mahatma Gandhi referred to both Hindi and Urdu as Hindustani (*Swadesamitran,* 6 May 1937). He further said:

> Government employment is limited. All cannot get it, therefore one has to search for other jobs. For that and for business, knowledge of Hindi is necessary. Only if we learn Hindi, can the south Indian gain respect among others. (ibid.)

While Rajagopalachari was thus trying to assure south Indian participation in national affairs through the learning of Hindustani, he was blatantly accused by the Self-respecters of catering to the Brahmins' needs, because it was feared that it would be the Brahmins who would once again benefit first by learning Hindustani, as they had benefited earlier by taking to English education before the others. On the Tamil Muslim side, Khalifullah led the attack on Rajagopalachari's programme. He accused the Congress of seeking to revive Sanskrit, a dead language (*Madras Mail,* 21 May 1937).

The Hindustani move came as an opportunity to the Self-respecters to strengthen their already existing ties with the Tamil Muslims. Muslim Leaguers joined the Self-respecters to oppose the introduction of Hindustani. At several Muslim League meetings, resolutions were passed protesting against the compulsory study of Hindi or Hindustani in schools (T.N. Archives 1938a, 1937).

In the Madras Legislative Assembly, there was no unanimity of opinion against Hindustani among the Muslim League members. Actually, it was on this question of Hindustani that the real cleavage between the Tamil Muslims and the Urdu-speaking Muslims became apparent. Khalifullah, who was closely cooperating with the Self-respect Movement and was hailed by it as the real leader of the Muslim League (*Kudiarasu,* 26 June 1938), led a most uncompromising attack against Hindustani in the Assembly, regardless of the views of the Urdu-speaking Muslim League Assembly members and prominent leaders like Abdul Hameed Khan and Basheer Ahmad Sayeed. He was articulating his views not only as a Muslim Leaguer, but also as a Tamil and a sympathizer of the Self-respect Movement.

But Basheer Ahmad Sayeed strongly defended the government's programme in the Assembly, declaring:

> There is no controversy over this. the language (Hindustani) is one, the scripts are two.... This government wants to propagate this spoken language (Hindustani) which is a Muslim language. It is up to the Musalmans to say 'we welcome this movement'. We shall get the facilities for the speedy learning of this language by 11 or 12 lakhs of Moplahs in Malabar and 11 or 12 lakhs of (Tamil) Musalmans in Tamilnadu and an equal number in (the) Andhra and Kanarese areas.... It will be to our detriment, to the progress of the Muslim language and the Muslim community in this province, if we should participate in anti-Hindi agitation.... The Muslims should take up agitation for Hindustani. That Tamil will be seriously affected by the propagation of Urdu or the Hindustani language is certainly groundless and merely a cloak of agitation. (T.N. Archives 1938c: 309)

Likewise Abdul Hameed Khan wanted the Tamil Muslims and the Moplahs to study Urdu. According to him, Urdu was the language of the Muslims of India (ibid, 1939: 142).

The support that Urdu-speaking Muslims extended to Hindustani is understandable. Though Urdu was the cultural language of the vast majority of Muslims in India, it was not the cultural language of the non-Urdu-speaking Muslim majority of the Madras Presidency. The maintenance and the propagation of Urdu as the cultural language of all the Muslims of the Presidency was absolutely essential for the survival of the Urdu Muslims as a political force in the Presidency, for without the predominance of Urdu, the Urdu-speaking Muslims knew that it would be more and more difficult for them to stake their claim for the leadership of the Madras Muslims or to play an important role in Madras Muslim Politics. Many Urdu-speaking Muslims saw in the proposal to introduce Hindustani a golden opportunity to propagate their language among the other Muslims and thus maintain their influence.

Unfortunately for the Urdu-speaking Muslim leaders, the Brahmin/non-Brahmin controversy had instilled a new sense of cultural and linguistic assertiveness and pride among the Tamils, including the Tamil Muslims. Reflecting this new found assertiveness of the Tamil Muslims, Khalifullah defiantly declared in the Legislative Assembly:

> ... I may at once say that I am a Rowther myself; my mother tongue is Tamil and not Urdu. I am not ashamed of it; I am proud of it.... There is not one

village which has not passed its resolution against the compulsory introduction of the foreign language (Hindustani). (ibid., 1938c: 317, 483)

Moreover, the Tamil Muslims, perhaps conscious of their superior number, did not see any advantage for themselves in learning Hindustani. For them Urdu/Hindustani was the symbol of the linguistic and cultural dominance of the Urdu Muslims. Learning it would only prolong their cultural subordination to Urdu-speaking Muslims, in spite of the latter being a minority among Muslims in the Tamil country. Therefore, the anti-Hindustani agitation started by the Self-respect Movement appeared to provide many Tamil Muslims with a wonderful opportunity to shake off the dominance of Urdu-speakers once and for all. Naturally, they seized this opportunity, even if it meant strained relations with the Urdu-speakers, who were after all their co-religionists.

Khalifullah, the foremost of the many Tamil Muslims to oppose Hindustani, actually participated in the agitations launched by the Self-respecters and their leader, Ramasamy. The agitations were almost purely a Tamil phenomenon, affecting the Tamil district alone. They were particularly active in the districts of Tinnevely, Salem, Tanjore, Ramnad and North Arcot, all containing large concentrations of Muslims, where Muslim Leaguers joined with the Self-respecters to oppose Hindustani (T.N. Archives 1938b).

From Tiruchirapalli, Khalifullah and Ramasamy flagged off a march of 100 anti-Hindi volunteers to Madras city (Mangaiyarkarasi 1982: 135). A Tamil Muslim, Tiruppur Mohideen, was among the front rank leaders of the march. On 11 September 1938, the band of volunteers reached Madras, where they were welcomed by more than 1,00,000 Tamils, including a large number of Tamil Muslims, after covering a distance of 920 kilometres on foot in forty-two days (ibid.: 136).[6] The agitators used Congress techniques like picketing, black flag demonstrations and fasting to register their protest against Hindustani. Rajagopalachari used the Criminal Law Amendment Act and arrested many picketers. E.V. Ramasamy himself was arrested and convicted. In all, 1,198 arrests were made and 1,179 were convicted (Governor's papers 1938).

Tamil Muslims participated extensively in the agitations. In Madras, Khalifullah presided over an anti-Hindi rally (*Sunday Observer*, 3 July 1938).[7] At Dindigul, in the interior of Tamil Nadu, Janab Tanga Meeran led an army of people shouting slogans like 'down with Hindi' and 'Long live Tamil' (*Swadesamitran*, 12 Oct. 1938). At the meeting that followed, the secretary of the Madurai Town Muslim League, Janab B. Abdul Latif and other local Muslim leaders accused the Congress of introducing Hindi to destroy Tamil (ibid.). The Madurai District Muslim League organized a grand anti-Hindi march (*Sunday Observer*, 6 Nov. 1938). In Vellore in North Arcot district, a Tamil Protectors' march was planned (ibid., 28 Aug. 1938). Many more protest meetings and marches were organized by the Muslims in various parts of the Tamil districts, with the cooperation of the Self-respecters.

In all these meetings and marches the main theme of course was the protection of the Tamil language. But it was also a question of race. It was claimed openly that the Tamil Muslims belonged to the Dravidian stock and therefore they had the right to participate in the anti-Hindi war (*Viduthalai*, 14 June 1939).

That the anti-Hindustani agitation was a popular protest movement is also confirmed by the correspondence of the Governor of Madras' with the Viceroy. He wrote:

> . . . Compulsory Hindi has been the cause of great trouble in this province and it is certainly contrary to the wishes of the bulk of population. (Erskine papers 1939)

Certainly the anti-Hindustani agitators and sympathizers were gaining in strength, but Rajagopalachari, though aware of it, was unwilling to scrap his project. Fortunately, for him the resignation of the Congress ministries in November 1939, decided by the Congress High Command, put an end to his involvement in this most unpopular move.

On 8 January 1940, Ramasamy, who had earlier accepted the leadership of the Justice party, met Jinnah, the undisputed leader of the Muslim League, at his residence in Bombay. After the meeting Ramasamy declared:

> . . . Both Jinnah and Ambedkar supported my views on compulsory Hindi. . . . As Jinnah has recognised my policy concerning Hindi, the agitation (anti-Hindi) that I am going to start again, I hope, will be supported by all Muslims. (*Kudiarasu*, 21 and 28 Jan. 1940)

Realizing that things might get out of hand on this language issue, the government hurriedly chose to defuse the situation by deciding to abolish the compulsory study of Hindustani in schools and to provide for its study as an optional subject in the higher and lower forms. Jinnah was quick to send a congratulatory telegram to

Ramasamy at Erode for the scrapping of the compulsory aspect of the programme (ibid., 3 March 1940).

On the whole, the abolition of compulsion brought a lot of relief and rejoicing in the ranks of the Self-respecters and also of the Tamil Muslims. The rejoicing of the latter can be summed up in the words of Moulana Moulvi Sherfuddin Sahib of Vellore:

> . . . Our agitation of the past two years has ended triumphantly. Everyone knows about the major role that the Muslims played against compulsory Hindi. . . . Therefore the Muslims of Tamil Nadu are happy at the cancellation of compulsory Hindi. I also participate in this joy. I congratulate the Tamilians who were victorious. I congratulate Periyar E.V. Ramasamy for his victory (ibid.).

Thus the anti-Hindustani agitation came to an end. Non-Brahmin Hindu Tamils and Tamil Muslims were the main participants in it. They joined hands to defy the Congress government and Rajagopalachari, mainly in order to protect the Tamil language and the Dravidian stock from what they perceived as Aryan Brahmin intrusions. Rajagopalachari directly contributed to this movement, which was no doubt a powerful expression of non-Brahmin mass feelings of the previous twenty years and more, given that mass participation in politics was never envisaged either by the Montague-Chelmsford reforms of 1919 or the Government of India Act of 1935.

Mass mobilization for a major agitation like the anti-Hindustani agitation is not possible without the ground being prepared for it beforehand. As a matter of fact, the ground was prepared by the Self-respect Movement from 1925, in conjunction with the Tamil Muslims and other backward castes.

Throughout the anti-Hindustani agitation, the official Madras Presidency Muslim League, under the presidentship of the rich Tamil Muslim merchant, Jamal Mohammad, kept a low profile (More 1991b: 316). What Jamal Mohammad lost by not openly participating in the agitation, Khalifullah stood to gain. He was acclaimed as the prime Muslim hero and leader of the agitation among the Tamil Muslims. By joining hands with the Self-respecters, he and his Tamil Muslim followers asserted unequivocally their Tamil identity. The Tamil linguistic trend chalked out among the Tamil Muslims during this period was naturally bound to play a determining role in their future, especially in the field of politics. P. Khalifullah may be deemed the father figure of this trend.

IV. CONCLUSIONS

From 1925 the propaganda of the Self-respect Movement against Hinduism and the Brahmins, its zeal to reform Islam, its contribution to the conversion to Islam of low-caste Hindus, its championing of the causes and grievances of the Muslims and its vision of a rational Dravidian society, had won the admiration and sympathy of a sizeable section of the Tamil Muslims and instilled a certain pride and confidence in them as Tamils. It was the language agitation, however, which finally led the Tamil Muslims to affirm their distinct Tamil identity. This coincided with their growing interest, during this period, in reforming themselves on Islamic lines and in promoting their mother tongue, Tamil.

In the evolution of south Indian society, language has been both a divisive as well as an integrative force. The same language, Tamil, which played an integrative role in uniting a sizeable section of non-Brahmin Hindus and Tamil Muslims at one level, played a divisive role at another level by pitting a sizeable section of the non-Brahmin Hindus and Tamil Muslims against the sanskritised Brahmins and to great extent dividing the Urdu Muslims from the Tamil Muslims.

It is highly improbable that the Tamil Muslims would have, on their own, affirmed their Tamil identity without the influence of the radical, apolitical and mass-based Self-respect Movement. A common religion was not enough to create a monolithic Muslim identity to make them accept permanently the domination of the Urdu Muslims. In fact, the anti-Hindustani agitation provided them a golden opportunity to shake off this domination and assert their Tamil and Dravidian identity. Here is a case where language and supposed racial affinity cut across religion and mobilized the Tamil Muslims as a distinct group, having shared interests with the radical non-Brahmins. From the time of the anti-Hindustani agitation, this distinctiveness became an enduring feature of the Tamil Muslims, which was bound to have far-reaching implications for them, especially after independence in 1947.

During this period, language and ethnicity had proved to be greater force for group identity than religion. Religion could have been or can be a unifying factor under different circumstances and situations, but during this particular period the dynamics of language and ethnicity had the upper hand in shaping the destiny of various sections of south Indian society. During the Khilafat Movement in the early 1920s and later during the partition of the Indian subcontinent in the 1940s the Tamil Muslims identified themselves with the Urdu speakers and the north Indian Muslims on the basis of religion. But during the anti-Hindustani agitation, the same Tamil Muslims, as we have seen, joined hands with non-Brahmin Tamils in affirming their Tamil identity.

In the course of this paper, we have also shown that low caste Hindus converted to Islam because the latter provided them with an egalitarian social and religious order, unheard of in Hinduism. No wonder many seized the opportunity of conversion, especially under the influence of the non-Brahmin Self-respecters who ceaselessly extolled the egalitarian and fraternal values of Islam and vehemently criticized the Hindu caste system, traditions and values. This conversion from a state of discrimination to one of non-discrimination may involve an elevation in status as well. But claiming that conversions took place just because the low castes desired to elevate their status ignores both the existence of the age-old historical fact of social oppression and discrimination in south Indian society and the simultaneous existence of Islam, with its egalitarian ideology, in the same society.

Living in a predominantly Hindu milieu, the Tamil Muslims have been successful in maintaining their Islamic identity despite following many un-Islamic customs, mainly because of their attachment to such core Islamic values as monotheism and equality before God. They were not willing to compromise these central values, especially monotheism, for the sake of maintaining or strengthening their relationship with the atheistic Self-respect Movement, though they were quite willing to accept the criticisms directed against their un-Islamic customs by the non-Brahmin Hindu 'atheists. Their relationship with the non-Brahmin atheists, which in itself is unique in the history of Islam in the Indian subcontinent, actually emphasizes and brings out this most striking characteristic of Islam among the Tamil-speaking Muslims of south India.

NOTES

1. See *Al Kalam*, June 1924; *Hifazatul Islam*, February-November 1930.
2. Native newspaper reports, May-June 1929 (T.N. Archives); History of Freedom Movement B22, Non-Brahmin Movement, 1921-36 (T.N. Archives); Barnett (1976: 41).

3. *Revolt* was an English newspaper of the Dravidian movement.
4. Muslim holy places.
5. See, for example, *Al Kalam*, April-May 1925; *Taj-al-Islam*, October 1923; *Dar-ul-Islam*, September 1923; *Hifazatul Islam*, Jan.-Feb. 1934.
6. Interview with K.M. Sheriff, Tamil poet and nationalist, and K. Veeramani, leader of Dravida Kazhagam: Mangaiyarkarasi (1982: 136).
7. *Sunday Observer* was a Dravidian English paper.

REFERENCES

Ahmad, Imtiaz, ed. 1981. *Ritual and Religion among Muslims in India*. New Delhi: Manohar.

Arnold, David. 1977. *The Congress in Tamilnad: Nationalist Politics in South India, 1919-1937*. London: Curzon Press.

Baker, Christopher. 1976. *The Politics of South India, 1920-37*. Cambridge: Cambridge University Press.

Bayly, Susan. 1989. *Saints, Goddesses and Kings: Muslims and Christians in South Indian Society, 1700-1900*. Cambridge: Cambridge University Press.

Barnett, M.R. 1976. *The Politics of Cultural Nationalism in South India*. New Jersey: Princeton University Press.

Dupuis, Jacques. 1960. *Madras le nord du Coromandel*. Paris: Maissoneuve.

Erskine Papers, 1939. Tel R., Governor to Viceroy, No. 159c of November 1939 (immediate). London: India Office Library.

Governor's Papers. 1938. Madras Governor's Reports: Work of Congress Ministries in Provinces. From Governor Hope to Viceroy Linlithgow. London: India Office Library.

Irschik, Eugene. 1969. *Politics and Social Conflicts in South India: The non-Brahman Movement and Tamil Separatism, 1916-1929*. Berkeley: University of California Press.

Kokan, M.Y. 1974. *Arabic and Persian in Carnatic, 1710-1960*. Madras: Hafiza Press.

Mangaiyarkarasi. 1982. *Varalaru kanda vaikom veerar* (Tamil) (2nd edn.). Madras: Muruthamalaiyan Pathipagam.

McPherson, K. 1969. 'The social background and politics of the Muslims of Tamilnad, 1901-1937'. *Indian Economic and Social History Review* 6, 4: 381-402.

Mines, Mattison. 1978. 'Social stratification among Muslim Tamils in Tamilnadu'. In Imtiaz Ahmad, ed., *Caste and Social Stratification among Muslims in India*, pp. 159-69. New Delhi: Manohar.

More, J.B.P. 1991a. 'The Marakkayar Muslims of Karikal, south India'. *Journal of Islamic Studies* (Oxford) 2, 1: 25-44.

———.1991b. 'Evolution socio-politique des Musulmans du pays tamoul, 1930-47'. Doctoral dissertation, Paris: École des Hautes Études en Sciences Sociales.

Ramasamy, E.V. Periyar. 1947. *Ina izhivu ozhiya Islamay nanmarunthu* (Tamil). Erode.

Rifaye, A.K. 1987. *Samuthaya neerotathil sangamam* (Tamil). Tinnevely: Rifaye (Kottaram).

Spate, O.H.K., A.T.A. Learmouth and B.H. Farmer. 1960. *India, Pakistan and Ceylon—The Regions*. London: Methuen.

Suntharalingam, R. 1974. *Politics and Nationalist Awakening in South India, 1852-91*. Arizona: University of Arizona Press.

T.N. Archives (Tamil Nadu Archives). 1937. Fortnightly Reports, second half of December 1937.

———. 1938a. Fortnightly Reports, first half of January 1938.

———. 1938b. Fortnightly Reports, January 1938, February 1938, June 1938.

———. 1938c. *Madras Legislative Assembly Debates*, vol. VII.

———. 1939. *Madras Legislative Assembly Debates*, vol. XI.

Veeramani, K. 1981. *The History of the Struggle for Social and Communal Justice in Tamilnadu*. Madras: Dravidian Press.

Venkataramannaya, N. 1942. *Early Muslim Expansion in South India*. Madras: University of Madras.

Washbrook, David. 1976. *The Emergence of Provincial Politics: The Madras Presidency, 1870-1920*. Cambridge: Cambridge University Press.

Piety and Politics in Indian Islam

GOPAL KRISHNA
(1972)

'Islam, not only chronologically, is in its fourteenth century. . .' (Bernard Lewis 1972: 40). It is a feature of the still medieval character of contemporary Islam that in theory even low Muslims are not prepared to make any distinction between different spheres of human activity, above all between the spheres of religion and of politics. Nor would the believers concede that human pursuits have human ends in view. The medieval Islamic postulate that the true purpose of life was to serve God in this world and to prepare for the world to come still dominates the Muslim religious outlook. 'No sphere', says Grunebaum (1953: 108), 'Is left in which our doings are inconsequential for our fate in the hereafter.' An acute awareness of the ever-present and overwhelming supreme power of God permeates Muslim religious thought, and is the foundation of Muslim piety. It is He who guides or denies guidance to men in all they do. All ends are determined by Him and therefore all activity is, or should be in principle religious.

Muslim religiosity has manifested itself in two forms: mystical and orthodox. Both derive their inspiration from the Quran and the life of the Prophet. There are in the Quran impressive verses which speak of the majesty of God, urge man to devote himself to God, and point out the transient character of this world and the enduring rewards of the world to come (VI: 32, XXIX: 64, XL: 42, XLVII: 38).[1] For all Muslims the Prophet is a model of piety, and his life and the traditions associated with him are studied with great reverence.[2] From these proceeds the development of mystical piety, with its later expression by the Sufis, who emphasized love rather than fear of God. This form of piety was ecstatic, personal and other-worldly (Arberry 1950: 33-4). The sufistic religiosity, with its elevation of self-chosen poverty, was popular with the masses, but not only with them. Its indifference to observance enabled it to accommodate pre-Islamic animism, saint worship and cults of various kinds within the spiritual life of Islam (Gibb 1962: 176-218; Goldziher 1971: 255-344).

Since they were a later and unorthodox growth, the Sufi orders were for long outside the power structure of Islam, and often found themselves in conflict with the rulers and the *ulama*. Hence, apart from its ecstatic expression, this detachment from political power distinguished sufistic piety from its orthodox counterpart.

The texture of orthodox piety is different. It lays stress on the observance of the five obligatory religious duties and on good works, charity, the feeling of presence of God, obedience to the *Sharia*, and devotion to the community and to Islam. It is puritanical and intolerant of dissent. The ulama, who constitute the unique religious institution of Islam (no religious functions are assigned to them, yet they constitute the authoritative custodians of Islam, mainly on account of their role as teachers, and interpreters and administrators of the Sharia),[3] embody the true orthodox piety. In contrast with sufistic other-worldliness, this does not deny the worth of this world, but advises moderation in its enjoyment.[4]

The pious orthodox are deeply concerned with power and politics. For them the worldly power of Islam constitutes the visible proof of its status as the perfect religion. They keenly appreciate the need for community solidarity, and are well aware of the relevance of the political dominance of Islam for its spread among non-Muslims. Their interest in politics has never led them either to seek power for themselves or to make power serve the larger interests of society and be accountable to it. Power for the orthodox has only two purposes: to subdue non-Islam and maintain general peace. Medieval Muslim scholars placed the greatest emphasis on order, and obedience to rulers (who must be Muslims) is enjoined upon the believers in all circumstances except conditions of threat to Islam itself (Rosenthal 1958: 42; Grunebaum 1961: 127-40). The Islamic political tradition places a high value on leadership, and the *Khalifa*, the upholder of the Sharia, is also the *Amir-ul-Muminin*, the commander of the faithful. He is above all a military leader.

An integral part of the medieval Muslim belief system which continues to receive fervent adherence in our own time is that the Muslims, as recipients of God's guidance through the Prophet, constitute a chosen community charged with the task of living according to divine injunctions and spreading the message of God among non-Muslim humanity, who have forgotten, misread or distorted it. The Muslims, according to their self view, constitute a charismatic community (Watt 1961: 204) since their religion is perfect (V: 6), they have been declared 'the best community' (III: 106), and their prophet is the last Messenger of God (XXXIII: 40).

Islam was born and survived its initial phase of development in an environment of determined opposition from non-Muslims. This early experience made Muslims look upon non-Muslims, except for the 'people of the Book', with extreme hostility. The Quran is permeated with bitter sentiments against the non-believers, and threats of condign punishment in the hereafter are held out against them. This context of conflict generated a sentiment of abiding unity among the believers, which was strengthened by several Quranic injunctions. No student of Islam can but be struck by the violent contrast the Quran presents between the believers and their opponents. The Quranic world is divided between the two antagonistic blocs of the Muslims and the unbelievers, with the 'people of the Book' occupying an intermediate position.[5] Between Muslims and unbelievers there is no common ground. The word *Kufr*, applied to non-Muslims other than the 'people of the Book', carries a particularly odious meaning in the Quran (Izutsu 1959: 113-44). Perhaps in no other religious system has the power of antagonism towards adversaries been so successfully harnessed in the cause of community solidarity as in Islam.

Given this conflict between Muslims and non-Muslims at the inception of Islam, it is not surprising that the Quran placed a high value on *Jihad*, which in the words of D.B. McDonald 'narrowly escaped being a sixth *rukn* (fundamental duty)' (Gibb and Krammers 1961: 89). Although the true meaning of the term has been variously interpreted—as 'holy war against unbelievers' or as 'striving hard with yourself in the quest for submission to God'[6]—it undeniably expresses the militant element in the Islamic ethos. Muslim religious tradition accords great merit to the conquest of unbelievers.[7] The early Islamic conquests turned the Muslim state into a military establishment and, in the eyes of Muslim, confirmed the character of Islam as a conquering faith (Gibb 1953: 3). The extraordinary achievements of Muslims arms constituted for the faithful incontrovertible proof that Muslims were the chosen instrument of God, who caused them to prevail over the unbelievers—as was indeed promised in the Quran (XXXIV: 54-5, XLVII: 37). Awareness of being distinct and superior to others became an integral part of Muslim self-identification (Kruse 1971: 181).

Militant hostility towards adherents of other religions was part of the medieval religious ethos and was not confined to Muslims. But for Islam the task of subduing non-Islam has been a prolonged and far from successful struggle, and this has engendered certain attitudes towards non-Muslims, for which the Quran also provided ample authority (IV: 101, 140, IX: 56). It urged them to fight in the way of God (IV: 76, 93, 97, IX: 112, 125), and assured them of God's protection (II: 143) and of ultimate victory (XLVII: 37). The political creed of Islam as it emerged through its medieval history could be summed up as solidarity among the faithful and jihad against the unbelievers (Watt: 1986, 19). The key Islamic term *din* carries the double meaning of 'to subdue, oppress, govern by power', and 'to submit, yield to be obedient and submissive' (Izutsu 1964: 222). It is din to subdue, oppress and govern by power the infidels; it is also din to submit, yield and be obedient to the will of God. These are the two essential aspects of being religious in the Islamic way.

Throughout its long history in India,[8] Islam has had to contend with the presence of a large non-Muslim majority. Despite its political and military ascendancy in the greater part of the subcontinent for several centuries, Islam secured the adherence of no more than a small fraction of the population (Titus 1930/1959: 7-8). This failure may have been due to the lack of interest shown by most rulers, for obvious political considerations, in a policy of active Islamization, and to the resistance to conversion manifested by the local population. Whatever the reasons, the Muslim conquest of India in the end produced only a religious stalemate. The situation of Islam in India has remained for all these centuries curiously like its situation in the early phase of its growth in Arabia—that of a body of believers surrounded by a vast mass of unbelievers—and Arabian parallels must often have occurred to those with active religious sentiments.

The imperatives before those concerned with the expansion of Islam since its entry into India have been: (1) to keep Hinduism at bay; (2) to extend the following of Islam; (3) to make the new converts to Islam into proper Muslims.

The historical circumstances of Islam's association with India made Muslims deeply conscious of the critical importance of state power being subject to Muslim control. Islam could flourish only in *dar-ul-Islam.* Though the Hanafi doctors had allowed Hindus to be viewed as *dhimmis*—'people of the Book' entitled to follow their own religion and enjoy the protection of Islam on payment of *jizya* (which was imposed intermittently, depending upon the zeal of the ruler)—the Muslims, imbued with orthodox piety, always looked upon

Hindus with hostility. Given the relatively small proportion Muslims must have constituted in the total Indian population,[9] and the fact that Islam sat rather lightly on a majority of them, the orthodox ulama's concern to safeguard Islam from the insidious encroachment of the local religion becomes understandable. The limited success of this mission and the constant sense of threat account for their endeavour to sharpen the conflict between Islam and kufr, to purify Indian Islam of its local borrowing and to distinguish Muslims from non-Muslims on all possible counts[10] (Qureshi 1962: 86-103). The attempt to exclude Hindus from power, in cases where it was made, could never be carried very far because they were needed to administer the empire and they controlled the economy. Shaikh Ahmad Sirhindi and his followers could pour out the most fanatical hatred of the infidels, and yet the Mughal emperors, even the pious ones among them, could not act upon their advice and also govern the empire. Symbolic acts of militancy generated ill-will without furthering the cause of Islam. There was, in Indian conditions, an unresolvable contradiction between militant piety and the exercise of state power by the Muslims.

Sufi Islam, which by now had been incorporated into the main orthodox tradition, made its compromise with the local culture through the shared medium of ecstatic piety and by accommodations with local superstition.[11] This extended the following of Islam, but the task of Islamization remained. This became the prime concern of reformist movements associated with the Nakshbandia, the Wahabi movement of Sayyid Ahmad Shaheed, and the Tabilighi Jamaat in our own time.

Since the end of Islam's political supremacy in India in the eighteenth century, Muslim society has been passing through a crisis. Islam is ill-equipped to cope with political and military failure. Because power has been central to the Islamic mission it was only to be expected that the pious should endeavour to rebuild dar-ul-Islam. The Wahabi movement of Sayyid Ahmed Shaheed of Bareilly was the most sustained and wholly unrealistic, attempt to re-establish the Muslim state and to reform Muslim society by purging it of Hindu influences (Ahmad 1966). The failure of this movement, and of the 1857 mutiny, ended all hopes of restoring Muslim power. The struggle Indian Islam has put up since, without success, to retrieve its lost position has had far-reaching consequences for the situation of the Indian Muslims.

It is a traumatic experience for any people to suffer loss of power, and the more so far as self-conscious a people as the Muslims of India, whose situation had made power an indispensable element in their sense of well-being. Among obvious consequences were the decline of the Muslim nobility and contraction in the employment opportunities provided by the state.[12] But of greater consequence was the damage done to Muslim self-esteem, further aggravated by the spectacle of the Hindus making progress under the new dispensation.[13] The standard explanation for the state of decay which overtook Indian Islam was that Muslims had become corrupt and less religious.[14] The golden age of Islam was now placed in the beginning of Islamic history, the greatest period being that of the Prophet's lifetime and, following on this, that of the 'rightly guided' Caliphs; since then there had been nothing but decline. This pessimistic outlook on historical development is in sharp contradiction with the belief in the ultimate victory of Islam and in history as proof of Islam's invincibility—but myths about history are born from the historical circumstance.

The deep-seated change that Muslim society underwent in the aftermath of the loss of power has yet to receive the attention it deserves from students of Indian Islam. The contours of change, however, are clear. The erstwhile nobility became landowners, whose rights and privileges were guaranteed by the British authority, of which they became loyal supporters. The new western education created a modern middle class, which, over the decades, emerged as the leading class in Muslim society, replacing the nobility and the ulama as the chief protagonist of Muslim interests in politics.

The response of the Muslim elite to the crisis in politics was determined by the ideas then prevalent among Muslims about themselves and about others, along with a shrewd understanding of their own interests. Their advice to their community against participation in the national movement was born out of these considerations. Muslim political tradition did not provide for Muslims working with non-Muslims for a common political end, since no such end could exist. Secondly, Muslims had lost to the British, not to the Hindus, and insofar as they had to come to terms with the new political reality they had to make their peace with the British. This they did under the able leadership of Sir Sayyid Ahmad Khan (1817-19).

The leaders of the new middle class together with the landed interests developed a strategy of collaboration with the British, in opposition to the emerging Indian national movement, to further Muslim interests. This strategy made good sense on the assumption, widely held by the Muslim elite then and since, of a fundamental cleavage between Muslims and Hindus. The restraints and compensations of power which had hitherto governed the relations between the two communities were now removed, and the hostilities which had been held in check by considerations of prudence erupted into increasingly virulent opposition, frequently leading to communal violence (Mathur 1972: 1-52; Lambert 1951).

The fundamental political postulate maintained by the Muslim elite was that India could not be considered a nation, neither could it become one, because of the diversity in religion and culture of its inhabitants. For the same reason it could not operate a democratic system, since this rested on shared values and on a consensus regarding the goals of society and procedures for achieving them. No such consensus obtained in Indian society. Power had therefore to be distributed on the basis of equality of communities rather than of citizenship.

The loss of power resulted in an increased emphasis on power as a necessary element in the Islamic way of life, and on Muslim solidarity as a condition of survival as well as of successful confrontation with non-Islam. The state of decay of Islam produced a flood of apologetics which is still continuing.[15] Sir Muhammad Iqbal (1873-1938), who articulated Muslim sentiments very forcefully, wrote: '. . . religion without power is only philosophy' (Schimmel 1963: 42); 'Vision without power does bring moral elevation but cannot give a lasting culture' (Iqbal 1934/1958: 92); 'Christianity describes God as love, Islam as power . . . God reveals himself in history more as power than love' (Schimmel: 101); 'Power is more divine than truth. God is power . . .' (ibid.: 127); 'The most visible thing in our religion is struggle and power' (ibid.: 266). In Muslim architecture Iqbal is said to have 'admired most those buildings which seemed to express the vigorous character of the young and powerful Islam. . . . The beautiful form as such did not appeal to him' (ibid.: 145).

The medieval principle of social integration was religion; the modern principle is the nation. For Iqbal there was only one nation, consisting of all Muslims, and there was 'only one *millat* confronting the Muslim community, that of non-Muslims taken collectively' (ibid.: 198). Patriotism to him was a 'subtle form of idolatry'; 'the fact that the Prophet prospered and died in a place not his birthplace is perhaps a mystic hint to the same effect' (ibid.: 162). Iqbal was inspired, in the words of R.A. Nicholson, cited by Professor Schimmel, 'by the vision of a new Mecca, a world-wide, theocratic, utopian state in which all Muslims... shall be one' (ibid.: 197). Later, when nationalism had triumphed among the Muslims of West Asia (much to the distress of Indian Muslims), he modified his vision and hoped for a commonwealth of Muslim states. He also put forward the idea of a separate Muslim state to be carved out of the north-western areas of India, which later materialized in the form of Pakistan.

The ulama, whose attitudes were deeply coloured by the historical and contemporary conflict between Islam and the West—a major theme in Islamic history-did not concur with the political strategy of collaboration with the British.[16] Paradoxical as it seemed, the custodians of Islam preferred to make common cause with Indian nationalism in its struggle for independence (Faruqi 1963; Haq 1970; Hardy 1971). The ulama were pan-Islamists, and believed, with Jamal ad-Din al-Afghani,[17] that the freedom of the Muslim people required British rule in India to be ended. Subsequently they developed a tortuously argued case, with appropriate theological reasoning, for Indian independence as such (Haq 1970: 105-33; Hardy 35-40).

The remarkable decision of the ulama of Deoband to support the Indian National Congress and the sanction they accorded to co-operation with the Hindus (Faruqi, 43-5) constituted, coming as they did from the successors of Shah Waliullah and Shah Abdul Aziz, a radical departure from the traditional posture of the orthodox establishment. Since they were not interested in power for themselves the ulama were able to be patriotic. Nor did they see any clash between Indian independence and the interests of Islam, either in general or in India in particular. On the contrary, they declared the struggle for national independence to be a religious duty for the Muslims. In reconciling nationalism with Islam the ulama took the first step towards creating a basis for understanding between Muslims and non-Muslims.

The ulama's commitment to nationalism was limited to the expulsion of the British power from India: it did not comprehend the Congress ideal of creating an Indian nation transcending the divisions of religion. They believed in maintaining communal identities and indeed planned for a state structure designed to erect and preserve permanent barriers between Muslims and others (Hardy: 32-4).[18] But this should not lead one to overlook the significance of the ulama's active involvement with the national movement. Despite increasing opposition from the Muslim elite and the masses, and a split in their own ranks, the main body of the ulama persisted with their policy of support to the Congress. By doing so they introduced a radically dissenting note into India's Muslim political tradition. Against the totalitarianism of the modernists, who wanted the Muslims to constitute a single monolithic political entity against the non-Muslims, the ulama asserted their own right to independent judgement. It is an irony of the situation that by adhering to their controversial position the traditionalist ulama introduced a modern value—the legitimacy of plurality of opinion—into Muslim politics on the entrenched Muslim value of community solidarity against non-Islam.

The pan-Islamic sentiment of the ulama led them into the morass of the Khilafat movement (Niemeijer: 1972). Its failure demonstrated the insubstantial character of the pan-Islamic cause. The enthusiasm shown for it by all classes, of Indian Muslims, but particularly by the merchants and the urban lower classes, showed, on the other hand, the strength of their religious sentiment. The educated Indian Muslims' concern for the Turkish Khilafat was due to their need to reassure themselves of the power of Islam as a factor in their own situation in India, while the ulama's concern was for a venerated but decrepit institution of Islam which symbolized the religious unity of the Muslims world. The abolition of the caliphate completed the process of the political fragmentation of Islam[19] and finally established the ascendancy of nationalism among Muslim peoples.

In the subsequent evolution of Muslim politics, in the face of the growing separatist Muslim nationalism pioneered by the Aligarh modernists and nurtured on Muslim apologetics, the ulama did not waver in their adherence to a composite Indian nationalism. Their point of view, considerably diluted in effort to retain some following, did not command much support among the Muslims. In the frenzy of the partition movement the nationalist Muslim, who represented the creative response of Indian Islam to the situation of a dispersed minority community required to come to terms with nationalism, became a figure of derision in the community.

The defeat of the nationalist Muslim by Muslim nationalism has not invalidated the rationale of the Deoband ulama's position.

Experience is a better guide for judging the soundness of their view than the doubtful *hadith*, 'My community will not agree to error.' The decision made by Indian Muslims in 1946-7 in favour of sovereignty for a part of the community at the expense of the unity of the whole marked in reality the triumph of the modern idea of territorial nationalism over the medieval idea of the unity of the Muslim people. The implications of this development for Indian Islam are far-reaching.[20]

It would be a mistake to think that the success of Muslim nationalism, because it was led by nominal modernists, also represents the success of Muslim modernism. Modernism, 'primarily a function of Western liberalism' (Gibb 1947: 59), which emphasized humanitarian ideas and values, never found adequate expression in Indian Islam,[21] except in the thought of Maulana Abul Kalam Azad (1888-1958), the tragic and lonely figure of the twentieth century Indian Muslim and national politics. Though Sir Sayyid Ahmad Khan initiated the modernist movement, it soon disappeared into the quicksand of power politics and religious apologetics.

The 'essential principle of modernism', says Professor Gibb (1947: 57-8), 'is the Protestant principle of the right of free examination of the sources and the application of modern thought to their interpretation, irrespective of the constructions of the early doctors and legists . . .'. This is precisely what Maulana Azad did in his justly famous, but unfortunately incomplete, commentary on the Quran (1962: I; 1967: II). Rejecting the medieval authorities, he proceeded to interpret the Quran in the light of the historical and social context in which it was revealed, its language and the linguistic usages then current, and above all its general spirit.

The Quran, Maulana Azad argued, instils a spirit of humanism and tolerance. Every people have received their prophets, salvation is open to all, and there is no place for compulsion in religious matters. The Quran recognizes, in fact asserts, that the spirit animating all religions is essentially the same; differences are confined to observances, and these the Quran tolerates because observances will naturally vary according to place and time. Similarly systems of law will differ because they are designed to meet the requirements of particular circumstances. The true values are devotion to God and righteous living; good works are of more importance than religious labels. To establish unity among people is the primary purpose of religion, and instead of making invidious distinctions on the basis of religious adherence, the Quran urges all people to become true followers of their own religion, by whatever name they call it (I: 152-82).[22]

Unfortunately this liberal and humane interpretation of the Quran, with its advocacy of a generous attitude towards others, did not gain acceptance among Indian Muslims.

Historians have explored the growth of the new Muslim elite (or rather the old elite which mastered the new arts of politics) and its political activities; religious life under the new conditions, with the strains arising from loss of the assurance provided by dar-ul-Islam, has not been examined at all. Muslims themselves have emphasized the political aspect of their situation, and since political processes have had such far-reaching consequences it is natural that their study has received the most attention. But the religious life of Muslims under stress deserves careful scrutiny.

Dr. Titus mentions 14 Sufi orders operating in India at the time of Akbar (1959: 117), four of which (Firdawsiya, Suhrawardiya, Chistiya and Zaydia) seem to have survived into the twentieth century. Louis Massignon in his survey of the *Tarika* (Gibb and Krammers 1961: 575-8) mentions ten orders active in India, five of which were of Indian origin: the Chistiya, the Madariya, the Rasulshahiya, the Shattariya and the Warith Alishahiya. The Sufi orders began to decline in the nineteenth century under the attack of the modernists, based on rationalism and the new ideas of morality, which reinforced the opposition of the orthodox ulama who had never approved of the orders because of their deviation from 'pure' Islam. According to Massignon the 'acrobatics and juggling practised by certain adepts of the lower classes, and the moral corruption of too many of their leaders' had aroused the hostility and contempt of the Muslim elite against most of the orders, which have now practically disappeared.[23] The decline of the Tarikas should not of course be taken to mean a decline in popular forms of piety. Visits to the tombs of local saints, and above all to the *dargahs* at Nizamuddin (Delhi) and Ajmer, remain popular; belief in the capacity of saints to intercede with God for the petitioner is far from extinct.[24]

The orthodox tradition of piety had not contemplated subsisting without a Muslim state. In the changed political circumstances, the ulama constituted a force for stability and continuity in Muslim society. In the aftermath of the mutiny they turned to the task of establishing centres of Islamic learning, using for the purpose that powerful instrument of Muslim education and socialization fashioned by medieval Islam, the *madrasa*, which would train young men for the religious and social service of the community, direct Muslim religious life by issuing authoritative *fatawa* on day-to-day problems, and publish literature defending Islam against attacks from Christian missionaries, Hindu Arya Samajists and Muslim modernists.

The two great seminaries of Indian Islam, the Darul Uloom at Deoband and the Darul Uloom Nadwatul Ulama at Lucknow, were founded in 1865 and 1898 respectively. At both these centres, and at several less celebrated ones, traditional religious education is imparted, with special emphasis on the study of the Quran, the Hadith, the *Fiqh*, Islamic history, and Arabic language and literature (Faruqi 1963: 27-42; Haq 1972). Since the madrasas are maintained from public contributions, their success, in terms of the number of students they attract and the resources they mobilise,[25] testifies to the important place they occupy in the Muslim community's religious life. The madrasas are also an instrument of the 'Urduization' of Muslims from the non-Urdu-speaking areas of India,[26] because instruction in all madrasas is imparted in Urdu, the chosen language of Indian Islam. Professor Maqbul Ahmad of the Muslim University, Aligarh, has estimated that there must be 'about a thousand' madrasas in India (1971: 31).[27] These institutions of Islamic learning and training have produced a large number of ulama, variously qualified in religious studies, whose main work has been to serve Islam and the Muslim community in all possible ways, but above all imparting religious instruction to the young. Every major mosque has a school (*maktab*) attached to it where the *Maulevi*, trained at Deoband or at Nadwat or at one of the other centres of theological studies, teaches Muslim children the Quran, the life of the Prophet, rudiments of Islamic history and other useful sciences.

The religious and social life of the great majority of Muslims is guided in many of its details by the fatawa, or authoritative religious pronouncements, of the ulama of the various law schools. These pronouncements are made in response to specific enquiries and on matters of importance to the community. On issues arising under Muslim personal law these pronouncements carry considerable weight, while on other issues they express the opinion of the learned and influence the community's thinking. The fatwa device has been used for controversial purposes, the most celebrated case being the fatwa issued by the ulama of Mecca against Sir Sayyid Ahmad Khan

(Graham 1909: 139-40). Since every *alim* is entitled to give a fatwa, there could be contradictory pronouncements by different alim, as indeed did happen during the Khilafat agitation over the question of loyalty to the British Indian government.

Despite such abuses, the fatwa is still a powerful instrument for influencing Muslim opinion; on religious and personal law questions the fatwa enjoys the status of law with believing Muslims. The well-known centres of Muslim learning like the Darul Uloom, Deoband, and the Darul Uloom Nadwatul Ulama have special departments which issue fatawa in response to enquiries from Muslims all over India. The subjects covered by these pronouncements are very varied. For example, the Darul Uloom, Deoband, has issued fatawa on, among other things, religious duties (prayer, fasting, alms-giving, pilgrimage), marriage divorce, apostasy, the payment of taxes, social relations with Hindus and with lower castes, the status of women, taking interest on bank deposits, wills, claims to property, the use of a translation of the Quran in prayer, the use of loudspeakers in mosque prayers, the permissibility of the tooth-brush, and the right length of the beard for an *imam* (Darul Uloom, Deoband: Fatawa).

In recent history, Muslim religious life has expressed itself in the formation of dissenting sects and of religious and social organizations. There has also been an upsurge of interest in religious education and propaganda directed especially at the young. Common to all these phenomena is either the total absence or low infusion of politics in their orientation and activities. None of the bodies concerned engages in direct political activity, and such marginal semi-political activity as some have undertaken is inspired by concern for the preservation of Muslim culture and the distinct identity of the community. Their general purpose is to deepen religious feeling and strengthen community solidarity. Among themselves the sects and the organizations represent manifestations of religious dissent and of both moderate and militant orthodoxy.

The major dissenting sect in modern Indian Islam is the Ahamadiya, and the most pietistic the Ahl-i-Hadith. Both these developed in the Punjab in the last quarter of the nineteenth century, and could be seen as responses to the new situation of Islam following the loss of state power.

The deviation of the Ahmadiya from orthodox Islamic tenets—in holding the Quran to be created and prophesy not to have concluded with Muhammad—is so radical that they are looked upon by the orthodox as outside the pale of Islam (Nadwi: 1967), and indeed as a shade worse than unbelievers. The bizarre claims of the founder, Mirza Ghulam Ahmad (1838-1908), to be the Mahdi of the Muslims, the Messiah of the Christians, and the tenth avatar of the Hindus, earned him the hostility of all three communities. The Mirza's most interesting doctrinal modification, which is of considerable social significance, was the repeal of jihad. He held that God had gradually reduced the rigour of jihad until it was repealed by the promised Messiah, that is, by himself. The Ahmadiya, now split into two groups, regard themselves as Muslims, and are a prosperous and active community.[28]

The Ahl-i-Hadith emphasize the life of faith, piety and good works. Sensitive to suffering in this world and cultivating a penitential spirit, they are chiefly concerned with the Day of Judgment and the life hereafter. The Ahl-i-Hadith do not accept the doctrine of *ijma* (the consensus of the Muslim doctors, or, in its more recent usage, of the community),[29] nor do they recognize the four law schools. They insist upon the right of every believer to interpret the Quran for himself. In their emphasis on good works they come close to the Kharidjites,[30] and to medieval Sufis in their aversion to any association with rulers. Though their following is small, the Ahl-i-Hadith represent a unique tendency in modern Indian Islam.

There are three religious-cum-social organizations engaged in the work of Islamization—the instruction of Muslims ill-informed about Islamic doctrine and ritual, and the propagation of Muslim culture—and in the protection and promotion of Muslim interests: the Tablighi Jamaat, the Jamiat-ul-Ulama-e-Hind and the Jamaat-e-Islami Hind.

The Tablighi Jamaat is a purely religious movement, which sends out parties of preachers to different parts of India, and also to foreign countries. It enjoys a great deal of support among traders and the lower classes, who are generally characterized by greater religious enthusiasm. The founder of the movement, Maulana Muhammad Ilyas (1885-1944), emphasized the personal nature of true piety, and attached greater merit to devotion than to jihad. The movement is thoroughly orthodox in its opposition to secular education and insistence on conformity to the Sharia, seclusion of women and preservation of all outward forms of a Muslim culture. Ilyas rejected pursuit of power for religiously-motivated Muslims because he believed 'the aims of modern political authority and Islam do not coincide', and 'if Islam were to make any progress it must be divorced from politics' (Haq 1972: 170). An interesting aspect of the Tablighi movement was the use it made of rural preachers to bring the message of Islam to city-dwelling Muslims who had become careless of religious observances.

The Jamiat-ul-Ulama-e-Hind, a product of the Khilafat movement, has, ever since its formation in 1919, represented the nationalist ulama, nationalist in politics, orthodox in religion and conservative in social outlook (Faruqi, 67-91). In the 1920s the Jamiat organized the *Tanzim* (organization) and *Tabligh* (religious propaganda) movements to counter Hindu efforts to reclaim the converts to Islam. It opposed the Muslim League's demand for partition on the ground that it would not be in the best interests of Muslims. The Jamiat is active in spreading religious education, assisting Muslims affected in communal disturbances, helping widows and orphans, and settling purely religious issues such as the proper procedure for determining the visibility of the moon in the month of Ramazan. It promotes the study of Urdu, and campaigns against any change in Muslim personal law. It organizes religious courts for deciding matrimonial disputes. It is also active on behalf of the Arab cause against Israel.

In politics the Jamiat has always advised Muslims against forming a party of their own and in favour of working with a party that represents different social groups and fosters a sense of national unity, since this is in their general interest.

The Jamaat-e-Islam Hind, the successor organization to the original body founded by Maulana Abul Ala Maududi in 1941, is a fundamentalist militant movement which aspires to establish the 'rule of religion'. The Jamaat takes its starting point from Islam as the perfect religion and is uncompromisingly opposed to all modernist attempts to reinterpret it to make it conform to criteria of rationality or liberal humanitarianism. It holds that the guidance available to man in Islam is both clear and comprehensive and that what is needed is to make man act on it.

The Jamaat opposes nationalism, secularism and national integration. It believes in the coexistence of different communities with each retaining its own culture and identity. Its efforts are designed to establish as far as possible an autonomous existence for Muslims. It seeks to eliminate non-Islamic accretions and to keep

Muslims rooted in traditional Islamic culture, including the veiling of Muslim women. The Jamaat has a large and active propaganda apparatus. It publishes seven newspapers, of different periodicity, and Islamic literature in most of the Indian languages.

The growing concern felt by all Muslim organizations for the religious education of the young resulted in the establishment of the Deeni Talimi Council (Religious Education Council) in 1959. The Council has been active in establishing maktabs, and there are now said to be 12,000 of them in Uttar Pradesh alone (Shakir 1972: 118). They provide free primary education to Muslim children through the Urdu medium. Some Muslims believe that the maktab movement, born out of religious fervour, is likely to play a major role in the future of Islam, and that through these schools Arabic 'may well became once again the *lingua franca* of the Muslim world' (Kazmi 1971: 59).

In their contemporary predicament, the Muslim religious organizations have chosen to pursue the path of consolidation of the Muslim community though Islamization and through propagation of traditional Muslim culture. Professor S.C. Misra, in his pioneering study on *Muslim Communities in Gujarat* (1964), notes, 'People may not become better "Muslims" or better men in religious or moral terms but the quantum of practices which are, or are felt to be, Islamic goes up in daily life' (159). Islamization as a process of integrating the Muslim community is very old and has been operating in India for several centuries. It brings about social reform among the more backward sections of the community, but its major thrust is against modernization. It seems to hold special appeal to the middle and lower-middle classes, on whom the pressures of the contemporary world impinge most critically and in whom education has generated communal self-awareness.

The contemporary crisis in Islam has been characterized as a crisis of history by Professor W.C. Smith and as one of belief by Professor Geertz. Professor Smith tells us that 'the fundamental crisis in Islam in the twentieth century stems from an awareness that something is awry between the religion which God has appointed and the historical development of the world which He controls' (1957: 41). Professor Geertz analyses the corrosion of belief. He makes an important distinction between 'religiousness' and 'religious-mindedness', that is, 'between being held by religious convictions and holding them'. A decline in religious spirit is often accompanied by more strident religious-mindedness 'celebrating belief rather than what belief asserts' (1968: 61).

The recent history of Indian Islam confirms both these propositions. With their attachment to the 'beaten path' (Watt 1961: 156) sanctified by tradition and temporal success, Muslims have accorded special importance to history as a guide to conduct and as a source of collective pride. This has sustained them in adversity. To their way of thinking Muslim successes are the successes of Islam, while the failures are their own. The battle of Badr and the battle of Uhad demonstrate to the faithful the two ways in which God helps them, in failure as well as in success. It is therefore common for the pious to argue that political and military failures are ultimately due to the decline of religious spirit and if they only became 'better Muslims' they would be rewarded with the success they deserved. While it is conceded that the present does not seem in accord with the believed divine design, it is argued that since history is still evolving there is no reason to attach undue importance to the present. It is again Iqbal who formulates the Muslim attitude. He rejected 'the finality of the present', reminding Muslims that 'God will not change the condition of men, till they change what is in themselves' (*Quran* 13: 12); however, the promise of change (meaning the restoration of the old order) always remained. But it is likely that this type of reasoning now no longer carries conviction; in the face of prolonged adversity it neither reassures nor sustains hope. Indeed, such spurious argument, which is the stock-in-trade of Muslim apologetics, eventually undermines faith. The lack of evidence of concrete divine favour in the present produces doubt, leading by stages to scepticism and withdrawal. How far this process has gone in India it is difficult to say, but judging by the agitated calls of the 'religious-minded' for more active adherence to Islam, apathy, if not doubt, would appear to be widespread.

In politics the dilemma of Indian Muslims has become increasingly acute. Muslim nationalism provided no answers to their problems, as has become evident over the last twenty-five years. The major consequences for them of partition were to reduce considerably their proportion in the population, to remove from India all Muslim majority areas except Kashmir, and to discredit Muslim nationalism as a cause worthy of their support. Partition also deprived them of the remedy offered by the nationalist ulama—a contractual alliance with Indian nationalism—since it had been rejected by the majority

Muslim opinion. As a consequence Indian Islam is today without a relevant political heritage. For the greater part of the twentieth century prior to partition, politics had been used as any instrument of Muslim consolidation, based on the claim to the existence of a distinct Muslim nation and operating through the institution of the separate electorate. With the removal of both these supports the process of communal consolidation through politics has come to an end. In a political system based on the representation of citizens distributed over territorial constituencies and not on the representation of communities, the Muslims, as a geographically dispersed minority, have either to join with others in building a secular political society or to remain outside the political process.

There have been serious differences within the Muslim elite on the course Muslims should adopt in this radically altered political context. Prescriptions have varied from the political fragmentation of the community to a return to communal consolidation under a single Muslim political party. Several Muslim groups have attempted to organize Muslims on mild to extreme communalist platforms—for example, the Muslim League in Kerala, Tamil Nadu and West Bengal, the Ittehad-ul-Muslimin and Tamir-e-Millat in Andhra Pradesh, and the Muslim Majlis in Uttar Pradesh. But by and large Muslims have supported the Congress party, which, as a ruling party committed to secularism and the protection of minority interests, seems to offer them the best terms.

Resistance persists to the idea of Muslims dispersing their support among different political parties. The view that Muslims *qua* Muslims have common interests different from those of others and must operate in political as a single collective entity still holds much appeal for large sections of Muslim opinion. But the reality is different. The Muslim community in India is far from homogeneous. Because of its large size and dispersion over all the states, differences of language, economic conditions, sect, culture and traditions, are as much to be found within it as in the rest of Indian society. In the absence of an effective movement of communal consolidation these differences are asserting themselves, and the political pluralization of the Muslim electorate is continuing despite the impulses to the contrary.

The main challenges to Islam, as perceived by the orthodox, are presented by secularism and nationalism. The former, by making religion a private concern of the individual, threatens to reduce the sphere of life subject to religious direction and with it the cohesion of the Muslim community. Secularization in the realm of ideas makes religion peripheral, and with it ideas of the after-life, divine design in history and the uniqueness of any particular religious group. Religion is viewed as an aspect of social culture. Muslim orthodoxy has interpreted secularism in the Indian context to mean that there is no state religion, and that all communities are free to pursue their own religious life in freedom and without state interference; intellectual secularism is of course incompatible with adherence to Islam. Nationalism is rejected because of its tendency to seek in pre-Islamic culture the sources of national identity, and because of the links it establishes between Muslims and non-Muslims on the basis of a shared non-Muslims past as well as the shared aspects of contemporary culture. The preservation of the Islamic identity is seen to require rejection of the pre-Islamic past as a state of *jahiliya* (ignorance) and the accentuation of distinctions between the Muslims and others.

Because of the threat to Islam which it sees as inherent in the present Indian context, Muslim orthodoxy opposes any changes whatever in Muslim social practices. This, however, is a battle already lost, because the processes of change are inevitable and the instruments of control are not in the hands of the orthodox. The self-sufficiency of Muslim civilization has been irretrievably undermined.

This critical situation has generated considerable self-analysis, and, along with renewed assertions of unreconstructed orthodoxy, several new positions are emerging on what is relevant for Islam in contemporary India.

The orthodox, having sensed that pursuit of power is fruitless and seeing the corrosive effects of political activity on community solidarity, are beginning to advise Muslims to withdraw from politics, at least for the time being. An attempt is being made to dissociate religion from worldly success, with the argument that for Muslims the real reward lies in the world to come. A.A.K. Soze writing on 'Causes and Cure of our Backwardness' (*Radiance*, November 1972), says: '. . . religion has absolutely nothing to do with material progress of a nation. The laws of the rise and fall of nations operate in their natural course, irrespective of the theology of the nation concerned. Religion does not aim at guiding men on the path of material and worldly progress. Its aim is to enable man to win immortality and immortal bliss. This has nothing to do with material progress.'

He continues, 'Muslim kings of India turned Islam into a political rather than a religious force. Instead of appealing to the hearts of the people, since heart is the natural abode of all religious faith, they took recourse to war and political subjugation, and sealed the fate of Islam—at least for the time being—in this land.'

'The greatest service that the present day Muslim community can do to itself and to the cause of Islam is to preach the Divine message to the non-Muslims. Being politically and militarily weak, they can never appeal to arms. Hence they must appeal to hearts.' (The 'hence' is revealing.)

The most eminent representative of unreconstructed orthodox is Maulana Abul Hasan Ali Nadwi, Rector of the Darul Uloom, Nadwatul Ulama, Lucknow. Maulana Nadwi is a prolific writer and an active protagonist in the cause of Islam. His writings are devoted to asserting the excellence of Islam and to denouncing materialism, nationalism, western civilization and such other evil forces as have corrupted the Muslim elite and brought defeat to Islam. His heroes among Indian Muslims are Shaikh Ahmad Sirhindi, Shah Waliullah, Sayyid Ahmad Shaheed, Emperor Alamgir, Tipu Sultan, and Sir Muhammad Iqbal—all ardent defenders of orthodox Islam. Maulana Nadwi apprehends a great threat to Islam from the growth of informal apostasy among the Muslim elite. In despair he writes, 'A fast spreading Apostatic wave is sweeping over the Muslim society and yet no one cares. Even the Ulema and the religious leaders feel no anxiety about it' (1968: 7). 'Today the leading sections of the Muslim society almost everywhere are on the verge of the dissolution of faith. . . . There are many among them—to avoid saying a majority of them who do not believe in Islam as a creed and as an ideology. . . . If the present situation continues as it is the Apostasy will infiltrate into the masses as well and destroy the faith of the simple-minded Muslim peasants and artisans. It has been so in the West and it is going to happen here also in the East if the events are allowed to take their course and the All-powerful Will of the Providence does not intervene' (1968: 24-5).

Maulana Nadwi's primary concerns are the solidarity of the community at home and the success of Muslim powers abroad, which he associates with the success of Islam. In India, he maintains, Muslims are representatives of the 'Muhammadi-Ibrahimi' civilization, and the purpose of their stay here must be its defence, in which also lies their own safety. Muslims must not allow the line of demarcation between themselves and others to be blurred (1972b).

Maulana Nadwi's apologetics are saturated with hatred of non-Islam. He writes: 'A man should have not only emotional attachment to Islam: he should also hate all un-Islamic philosophies, thoughts and ideals' (1972a: 10). He wants Muslims so Islamized that their hearts are filled with 'love of Islam and abhorrence of un-Islam' (ibid.: 21).

There is nothing creative, challenging or generous about Maulana Nadwi's advocacy of a renewal of faith; nor is there even evidence of genuine learning. His 'unreflected conviction' (Grunebaum 1962: 188-9) does not enlighten, but reduces itself to mere reiteration of the uniqueness of Islam.

At the opposite extreme from the fundamentalists are the secularists, as yet few in number, whose most outspoken representative is Hamid Dalwai, a young social worker from Maharashtra. A thoroughgoing modernist, Dalwai does not accept any of the tenets of Islam, but regards himself nevertheless as a Muslim by virtue of being a product of Indo-Muslim culture. He finds much that is unacceptable in Muslim tradition, social practices and political outlook. He is relentless in his attacks on Muslim separatist sentiment and on the absence of humanism in traditional Islam, particularly in its dealing with non-Muslims. He exhorts Muslims to review critically their past, their laws and customs, and the ethos of their society. Such a self-scrutiny would reveal the need for a movement for reform in all respects (1968; 1971).

Dalwai is active in the cause of social reform, especially in the sphere of women's rights, and has launched a reform movement in his state under the auspices of the Muslim Satyashodhak Mandal and the Indian Secular Society. His radicalism is perhaps not unrelated to his non-Ashraf social background and to the fact that he comes from an area uninfluenced by Urdu culture.

The nationalist ulama continue to uphold the position that nationalities are, and must be, based on countries, not on religion, and therefore Islam cannot be a basis of nationality. Maulana Abdul Wahab, President of the Jamiat Ulama-e-Hind, recently reaffirmed this view in his presidential address to the Jamiat's session in May 1972. He stated further that while Muslims have genuine grievances, these often arise from problems that are common to all, though they are felt more acutely by Muslims. The Indian constitution is among the best, 'but the people have not moulded themselves according to it', although secularism, as viewed in India, is not opposed to religion, but gives freedom to every community to pursue its own religious life.

Among the intellectuals who adhere to Islam, Professor A.A.A. Fayzee, an eminent scholar of Muslim law, and Professor M. Mujeeb, Vice-Chancellor of Jamia Millia Islamia, New Delhi, have yet raised major issues on the interpretation of Islamic injunctions and the duties of Muslims.

Professor Fayzee has declared himself in favour of a sufistic position. 'Religion is the relationship between the human self and some unseen non-human entity' (1963: 33). Islam in his view has ceased to be dynamic and religious practices have become 'soulless rituals'; also 'the beneficial laws of early Islam have in many instances fallen behind the times . . .' (108). The traditional position that in Islam law and religion are coterminous can, in Fayzee's view, no longer be maintained, because law is a product of social evolution and must change with time and circumstances, while religion, in his sense of the term, is eternal. He states as his personal conviction that 'gradually all individual and personal laws, based upon ancient principles governing the social life of the community, will either be abolished or so modified as to bring them within a general scheme of laws applicable to all persons, regardless of religious differences' (82), and he maintains that such a development will not destroy 'the essential truth of the faith of Islam' (idem).

Professor Mujeeb advocates a wide-ranging reappraisal of Islamic tenets and outlook. In a controversial paper entitled 'The Status of Individual Conscience in Islam' (1970), he argued that the relevant question for Muslims was not 'how a Muslim can be a good Muslim', but 'where he should act according to his conscience as a Muslim' which is something required of him by the Quran. Sincerity, constancy of faith and the performance of good acts, and not formal allegiance to Islam, are the test of a believer. The demand for conformity with the alleged consensus of the community deprived the Muslims of his responsibility to act according to the dictates of his conscience. This has had damaging consequences for Muslim society in the past and has accounted for many of the failures of Muslims to act rightly in the light of the teachings of Islam.

Since Islam is a universal religion and its message is addressed to all humanity, it must follow that 'all problems should be considered not in the light of Islamic history alone, but in the context of world history.' He advocates the study of the history of all religions, 'not to see how far they have deviated, for of that God alone is the judge, but how close they are in essence to the fundamental human faith'. Studies of other societies should be undertaken 'to discover when and how the Islamic values we believe in have been realized in practice', and Muslims must recognize that 'the principles of Islam can be realized in practice by non-Muslims'.

The relationship between the individual and the community is conceived by Professor Mujeeb in a radically different way from the established pattern. 'Islam', he writes, is in 'essence an individualistic religion. . . . The true Islamic spirit seems to be that the individual should uphold the community as an act of his own will, and not that the community should absorb the individual will into its own.'

Proceeding from theoretical propositions to practical issues, Professor Mujeeb calls for a re-examination of Muslim beliefs regarding relationships with non-Muslims, and in matters relating to reform of the law, he advises Muslims to concern themselves with the content of the legislation and not with who has the authority to legislate.

Such advocacy of a radical recasting of the Muslims outlook, emphasizing the principles of freedom, responsibility, broadmindedness and humanity, is rare in the annals of Indian Islam. The sufistic spirit provides the religious basis for it from within the Islamic tradition. Professor Mujeeb maintains that the over-ridingly personal religion of the Sufis, 'with its inevitable emphasis on sincerity, has been the link between all religions, which differ widely in externals but are one in essence' (1972: 65). It also tends to dissociate religion and politics by making religion a personal rather than a collective preoccupation.

In politics, Professor Mujeeb argues, Muslims (as others) will have to view the state as a moral entity with a claim to their loyalty as citizens. Muslim tradition does not encompass such a view of the state, and in India the relationship between the state and the citizen has been viewed by Muslims as contractual. Muslims have yet to understand the spirit of political democracy, which requires responsible participation in public affairs with a view to achieving common goals. 'Understanding of this system of government would bring (the Muslim) closer to his fellow-citizens, with whom he has many common interests and these common interests would then acquire a moral quality' (1972: 71).

The developing secular polity in India will require Muslims to be participant citizens and not passive dhimmis, a concept alien to democratic thought. The integration of a plural society into a political system is the essence of political modernization, and is a process from which Muslims cannot be exempt.

A quarter of a century ago Professor Gibb had noted that 'the student who passes from the Near East to India cannot but be conscious of a more marked political content in its religious movements. . . . In contrast with the Arab lands, Islam in India can never free itself from its setting over against the vast Hindu majority; and this, of necessity, forces social and political issues into the context of religious life' (1947: 57). The crisis in Indian Islam may be susceptible to resolution on the basis of an emphasis on personal religious commitment rather than the pursuit of communal politics and a reinterpretation of the unity of the community in religious, and not in social, legal or political terms.

In the critical circumstances of today, issues concerning the place of the Muslim community in the emerging modern society, the true meaning of religious spirit, the relationship between the individual and the religious group and the attitudes which religious communities should have towards each other can no longer be avoided. This is what makes the current debate of such great interest to the development of Indian Islam and of Indian society. Fundamentalist reiteration of old formulae no longer suffices. In the thought of Professor Mujeeb there are the beginnings of a reformation.

The contemporary context for Islam in India is very different from anything that Muslims have known in the past. The intellectual categories of traditional Islam, defining social reality and the Muslims' place in it, have become irrelevant. The fundamentalists aspire to re-establish dar-ul-Islam, which is an impossible goal, even if it were considered meaningful and worthwhile. The ulama have no new ideas to offer beyond a composite nationalism and the preservation of the communal society. The modernist elite which in the past conceived and nurtured Muslim nationalism has retreated from public life, having seen the disastrous results of separatist politics for Indian Muslims. The more well-meaning modernists discuss whether Hindus should be declared the 'people of the Book', and if this would make for happier inter-community relations, not realizing that the whole Muslim conceptual schema—dar-ul-Islam and *dar-ul-*

Harb, dhimmi, the 'people of the Book', and so on—has no application in the Indian situation.

There is a growing drift away from religion, particularly among the elite. The sufistic religious spirit is to be found rarely. In its version, as presented by Professor Mujeeb, it is unlikely to be anything but an uncommon phenomenon. The mass of Muslims are making their adjustments as best as they can without any satisfactory guidance from a community leadership, traditional or modernist. The Muslim society is becoming differentiated, particularly its elite, and it no longer has the homogeneity which earlier had given it a relatively monolithic character. How Muslim religious life and Muslim politics will relate themselves to the Indian nation is again an open question.

POSTSCRIPT, 1994

Over the two decades since the above paper was written Islam has forcefully challenged the two forces that Muslims regarded as inimical to their civilization, viz., nationalism, which disrupts the unity of the Muslim Umma, and modernism, which places individual reason above the claims of the collectivity.

In the Islamic world nationalism has suffered an eclipse because of its failure to protect the autonomy of Muslim people, and modernism has lost some of its attraction because of its alienating consequences. To escape alienating and subordination Muslims have turned back to Islam, whose claim to supply answers to all types of problems Muslims find persuasive. But it is undoubtedly the case that accumulated resentment at the treatment accorded to Islam by the West in the post-war years has given rise to aggressive Islamic fundamentalism throughout the Muslim world. Islamic fundamentalism in West Asia arose in the aftermath of the failure of modernist nationalism and owed its appeal to the Muslim populations primarily as a more effective force against subordination to the West. It has been given powerful support by the clerical revolutionary regime in Iran and less spectacularly by the oil rich Arab countries of the Middle East.

In India the Islamic development has inevitably focused on local issues. Here the Muslim concerns have been the same that they were in the first quarter century after independence, namely, how do Muslim relate to India, and how do they ensure that the Muslim identity is preserved and Muslim rights are protected. Here, rather more acutely than elsewhere in the Islamic world, for Muslims religion and politics are closely intertwined, and the emphasis is more often on politics than on piety. Since the dominant Islamic tradition does not make a distinction between the two, the Indian context (of Muslims as a minority engaged in a continuous struggle to protect its interests and expand its zone of autonomy) ensures that being Muslim entails active engagement with the political process.

Among Indian Muslims the dominant opinion was always ambiguous towards nationalism because nationalism, nurtured on an ethnic past and culture and language, compromised the Islamic identity of Muslims by linking them with their pre-Islamic past, and in some measure distanced them from the Muslim Umma by establishing closer bonds with the non-Muslims of the nation. The pressure towards national integration was perceived by Muslims as an ever present threat to Muslim identity, and consequently much of Muslims politics has been focused on Muslim communal demands. The democratic politics of India has enabled Muslim leaders to mobilize Muslim opinion effectively on issues bearing upon Muslim personal law and on religious concerns focusing on the status of the Babri mosque in Ayodhya, as well as Salman Rushdie's novel, *The Satanic Verses* (1988). In the process of these agitations the agenda for 'national integration' has been defeated and Muslims have redefined 'secularism' to mean protection of minority rights and the strengthening of the plural character of Indian society. Nationalism has lost much of its earlier appeal and the pressure for 'integration' has subsided.

Muslim modernism, which once seemed so dominant, has also suffered an eclipse. The Islamic revolution in Iran has given fillip to Islamic fundamentalism throughout the Muslim world, and India has not been immune to it. Here the focus of Muslim opposition has been the state. The state, avowedly secular and solicitous of minority interests, made a very hesitant attempt to introduce reform of Muslim Personal Law in the area of maintenance provision for divorced Muslim women in the form of a new provision in the Code of Criminal Procedure (Section 125). Under this provision a maintenance award granted by the Madhya Pradesh High Court to a Muslim lady by the name of Shahbanu against her ex-husband

Mohammad Ahmed Khan became a cause *cèlébre,* leading to much litigation and a judgment by the Supreme Court upholding the award, holding the legal provision to be in accord with the precepts of Islam. This intervention by the Supreme Court in the realm of Muslim Personal Law occasioned one of the most massive Muslim agitations, organized by the Muslim Personal Law Board, a body consisting of some leading Ulama and politicians. The Muslim Personal Law Board claimed that the particular provision of the Criminal Procedure Code amounted to an interference with the Muslim Personal Law and thus violated the religious rights of Muslims. The agitation compelled the government to enact a new law, 'The Muslim Women (Protection of Rights on Divorce) Act, 1986', which conformed to the provisions of the Sharia in this matter. This episode demonstrated the limits to which the state could go in the area of legal reform.

The controversy over Rushdie's *Satanic Verses* and its early proscription by the Government of India, showed how effective Muslim opinion has become in matters Muslim consider important either from religious and/or from political point of view. Non-conformist Muslim intellectuals have suffered humiliation at the hands of Muslim fundamentalists and received little support within the community.

The agitation over the Babri mosque at Ayodhya since 1986 has further mobilized Muslims on behalf of a religious cause. This has had important political consequences, the chief among which must be reckoned to be the re-emergence of Muslims as a factor of great importance in north Indian politics.

For moderate and modernist Muslims these developments have posed a serious challenge: how to be good Muslims and yet promote reform within Islam so as to allow liberal and modernist tendencies to flourish to the benefit of Muslims. The dominant tendency of the Islamic tradition has been to sustain the fundamentalists, who claim, on good authority, that Islam is a perfect code and all talk of reform is illegitimate; they also assert the need for solidarity—another Islamic virtue—in the context of conflict with non-Islam. The liberal modernist is at a disadvantage when he claims to be a good Muslim and yet urges reform, thus betraying inadequate adherence to Islam. In the current climate in the Islamic world as well as in India the liberal tendency is on the retreat.

NOTES

1. All references are to A.J. Arberry's lucid translation, *The Koran Interpreted*, vol. I (i-xx) and vol. II (xxi-cxiv).
2. An empirical study of the conditions and problems of Muslims in India, recently carried out by the Centre for the Study of Developing Societies, Delhi, found that the Quran and one or other *Sirat* of the Prophet were most frequently mentioned as the two books which have influenced Muslims most.
3. An Egyptian author, Abdal-Rahman al-Jabarti, writing in 1820, testified to the high place the ulama occupied in Muslim society: '. . . God created mankind in five categories of descending importance. In the first category were the Prophets . . .' In the second category the Ulama who are the heirs and the successors of the Prophets, 'the depositors of truth and the elite of mankind'. Below them in rank were the kings and other rulers, and below them ranked the rest of mankind in two last categories. (Marsot, in Keddie 1972: 149).
4. There is an engaging picture of the pious orthodox scholar drawn by J. Barque: 'The scholar walks along the street, his eyes lowered, his prayer rug under his arm. Unctuous, his step expresses disdain for the sights of the world about him. Rather it seeks and obtains the veneration of the masses. . . . Only rarely has he given himself over the brutal asceticism or ill-bred pedantry. The master of religious science is at the same time the master of the right tone.' (Cited by K. Brown, in Keddie 1972: 127.)
5. To the 'people of the Book' Islam conceded the right to follow their own religions, while imposing on them inferior political status. The rest, classified as *kafirs,* had to choose between Islam and the sword. See Tritton (1970).
6. There is a tradition which makes the Prophet rank the 'greater warfare' (*al-jihad al-akhar*) above the 'lesser warfare' (*al-jihad al-asghar,* i.e. war against infidelity), and explain the 'greater warfare' as meaning 'earnest striving within the carnal soul'. See Arberry (1950: 75). the prophetic traditions are unreliable, and even the selections held to be authentic by Muslim doctors, i.e. those of Bukhari and Muslim, are not free from doubts. The classic study of the Hadith literature is by Goldziher (1971); for the latest statement on the state of Hadith scholarship, see F. Rahman (1966: Ch. 3). A contemporary justification for jihad has been offered by Professor Sayyed Hussain Nasr of the University of Tehran. He writes: 'War, in a limited sense at least, is actually in the nature of things and Islam, rather than leaving it aside as if it did not exist, limited by accepting it and providing religious legislation for it. One can at least say that the terrible wars of this century have not come out of the Muslim world . . .' (1966: 31).

7. Max Weber writes: 'This conception (of jihad) assumed the exclusiveness of a universal God and the moral depravity of unbelievers who are his adversaries and whose untroubled existence arouses his righteous indignation.' He adds that Islam was the first religion to produce 'a direct connection between religious promises and war against religious infidelity' (1965: 86).
8. Islam in India constitutes a very differentiated socio-religious system. There are many local variations and several sects within it. Differences of doctrine and ritual, and ethnic, social and cultural heterogeneity abound. The centre of Islam in India, however, has been in the north, and though there have been regional styles in Muslim culture, the dominant note of Indo-Muslim culture has been provided by the Muslims of North India. They also constitued, until recently, the most active segment of the Muslim population and have been the pace-setters in social, and political movements. Even now (1971) they account for 46.60 per cent of India's Muslim population. In other parts of India Muslim life has been strongly influenced by local cultures and manifests a rather different ethos. I confine myself in this paper to consideration of the religio-political movements in north Indian Islam. Within north Indian Islam differences of sect have been ignored, though they are not unimportant. The vast majority of Muslims are Sunni (Titus 1959: 86) and it is their ethos, beliefs and activities that are of primary relevance to our enquiry.
9. There are no estimates as yet of the religious composition of the Indian population during the centuries of Muslim rule. My surmise that the Muslim proportion in the Indian population must have been small rests on the fact that in 1881 Muslims constituted twenty per cent of the population, and had exhibited a tendency to have a relatively high rate of growth (Davis 1951: 179). If a backward projection were to be made, taking into account the possible additions through conversion, the share of the Muslims in the total population during the heyday of Muslim power would turn out to have been quite small. There must of course have been much larger concentrations of Muslims in some regions than in others, as in our own time.
10. The religious history of Islam in India remains to be written. The two general accounts available are provided by Dr. Titus (1959) and Professor Mujeeb (1967). The religious policy of the Mughals has been studied by Professor Sri Ram Sharma (1972). A detailed study of the Muslim revivalist movements in the sixteen and seventeenth centuries is to be found in the work of Professor S.A.A. Rizvi (1965). For an account of the more recent developments see Professor W.C. Smith (1946).
11. William Crook's revised edition of Herklots' *Islam in India* (1921/72) gives an idea of the enormous amount of superstition that had entered

into the lives of Muslims in Southern India. This work has served as the source for all subsequent writing on this subjects, for no other similar work has been done since Herklots publishing the English translation of the *Qanun-I-Islam* by Zafer Sharif in 1832. Sufi mysticism, says Professor Aziz Ahmad (1964: 119-39), owed little to Hindu influences and did not promote interaction between Hindus and Muslims. Professor Zaehner (1960) holds Hindu influences on Suffism as of prime importance.

12. W.W. Hunter (1817/1945) propagated the myth that Indian Muslims as a community had suffered greatly under early British rule; from then on by endless repetition the myth acquired the status of incontrovertible fact. It is only now that scholarly investigation is revealing the very differentiated consequences of and Muslim responses to British rule in different parts of India. In fact, Muslims as a community did not fare badly in nearly all areas, except Bengal. See Brass (1970), Seal (1968: 298-340).
13. Professor Theodore Wright has discussed this aspect, especially considering the impact of a reverse social status situation for hitherto dominant minority, in his paper on 'Identity Problem of Former Elite Minorities' (1972).
14. The best and often-cited work reflecting this line of thought is Hali's *Musaddus-i-Madd-u Zazr-i-Islam.* See Aziz Ahmad and G.E. von Grunebaum (1970: 95).
15. Professor Mujeeb has summoned up the features of this genre of writing and its impact on Muslims:

    'The modern Muslim's listlessness, his lethargy, his disregard for his own welfare, his betrayal of a great religious and cultural heritage was contrasted in eloquent terms with the faith, the energy, the splendour of earlier times. The Muslim was so carried away by the eloquence of the apologists that the achievements and the glories of the past came to life again, and the experience was so vivid and intense that the present was merged in the past, and the most spineless subject of the British Raj transformed himself in imagination into a conquering world force. Apologetics also generated a pride which made the Muslim look down on others, and if forced to face reality, he excused and even justified his own degradation by arguing that others were worse.' (1970: 130-1).
16. Opposition to British rule was not universal among the ulama. Dr. Hafeez Malik, referring to Bengal, mentions that the 'Local ulama, collaborating with the British, issued decrees approving of English education . . .' (1963: 149).
17. In the most comprehensive biography of Sayyid Jamaluddin al-Afghani yet published, Professor Keddie (1972: 191-9) draws attention to the radical rationalist ideas of al-Afghani. Fortunately for his popularity with them the pan-Islamist enthusiasts in India were unaware of these

ideas. They subscribed to his anti-imperialism and his support for a common national front in India against the British rule. For this very reason Sir Sayyid did not approve of him.

18. The criticism of the ulama that they were not whole-hearted nationalists (Dalwai 1968: 66-72; Karandikar 1968: 234-44), or that their concern to seek religious authority for political choices was ultimately counterproductive (Haq 1970: 146-7), seem to me to be irrelevant. The implicit idea that if secular nationalism had been presented to the Muslims without invoking religious authority it would have gained more support has only to be made explicit for its absurdity to be demonstrated. The ulama were bound to be limited nationalists and had to have religious sanction for their recommendations. Their great contribution was to put forward a meaningful alternative to Muslim separatism, and thus to keep open the possibility of Muslims living as citizens in a non-Muslim state. In this they were more realistic and better defenders of the interests of Indian Muslims than the Muslim nationalists. Their failure to carry with them the Muslim masses, and even a large section of the ulama, only testifies to the strength of separatist sentiment among Indian Muslims.
19. The juridical fragmentation of the Muslim umma into nationalities had taken place with the Ottoman Law of Nationality of 19 January 1869, which marked the end of dar-ul-Islam as well as of *dhimma* in the Turkish empire. (See Kruse 1965).
20. What for example, is now the status of Muslims nationalism? Does Pakistan symbolize it? Does it also do for Indian Muslims? These are explosive questions, not only for Indian Muslims but also for Pakistan. Pakistani historians have presented the emergence of Pakistan as a logical development of Indian Islam (Qureshi 1962; Malik 1963; Ahmad 1964, 1967; Aziz 1967; Sayeed 1968). The Indian Muslims are bound to reject such a view, and to repudiate any suggestion that Pakistan represents the sentiment of Muslim nationalism for the whole of the subcontinent.

    For Pakistan too the interpretation of its past, and the determination of its present and future role, pose many problems, especially after the emergence of Bangladesh. Does Pakistan represent the nationalism of the people of Pakistan or does it represent Muslim nationalism? It is clear now that there was no such thing as Pakistani nationalism, nor did Pakistan represent Muslim nationalism—perhaps there was no such thing either. Some Pakistanis once claimed, possibly some still do, that their nationalism is territorial—of the people of West Pakistan—and that they are the heirs to the Indus Valley Civilization. (Sir Mortimer Wheeler even published a book with the preposterous title, *Five Thousand Years of Pakistan*, London: Christopher Johnson (Publishers) Ltd., 1950.) If this were to become the dominant view in Pakistan it would give final quietus to the phantom of Muslim nationalism, and with it to the idea of religion-based nationality, which has already been repudiated in Bangladesh.

With the division of the Muslims of the subcontinent into three units, it is not possible for Indian Muslims to claim to be a political nationality on the basis of religion. The choice before them is between repudiating the principle of nationality itself, and adopting the principle of a single Indian nationality, not only as a legal but also as a political concept. The Muslim fundamentalists, represented by the Jamaat-e-Islami, predictably reject the concept of political nationality in its application to India. But on the whole the tendency among Indian Muslims is to avoid discussion on this subject, which is too sensitive in its implications.

21. An otherwise sympathetic student of Indian and Pakistani Islam, Professor W.C. Smith, notes the failure of moral sensitivity in Pakistan in face of the appalling violence in the partition riots (1957: 268). The reactions among Muslims in India and Pakistan to the oppression in East Bengal in 1971 were also lacking in sensitivity to human suffering. See, for example, Maulana Abul Hasan Ali Nadwi's disingenuous lament for the misfortunes of Islam because 'in a country with Muslim majority' 'the idol of language prevailed . . . national and racial zealotry smashed the brotherhood of Islam . . .' etc.; 'its most shameful aspect has been to arm the enemies of Islam with one more weapon against it' (1972a: 4-5, 7). There is not a word of sympathy for the victims of oppression. It is a remarkable feat to give a whole lecture without once mentioning the countries involved. The subcontinent is mentioned once.
22. The Quranic suras cited in support of these views are:

    II: 4, 5, 59, 106, 113, 114, 129, 139, 148, 177, 213, 285; III: 2, 18, 64, 74, 75, 78; IV: 161, 162, 163; V: 51, 68, 69; VI: 60, 108, 160; X: 19, 48, 99; XIII: 9; XVI: 38; XVII: 16; XIX: 36; XXI: 23, 24; XXII: 66, XXII: 23, 32, 51, 52, 53; XXXV: 23; XLII: 13; XLIII: 5; XLVI: 4.
23. The survey referred to in n. 2, shows that most of the respondents did not belong to any of the Sufi orders.
24. Even the very orthodox ulama of Deoband have allowed visits to the graves of pious men, holding them to be profitable for the visitors (*Fatawa*, Q. 503/5, vols. I-II, p. 335). They of course disapprove of acts of worship at the graves and all types of *piri-muridi.*
25. Darul Uloom, Deoband, had 974 pupils in 1970, and an income of Rs. 1,126,447; the Darul Uloom Nadwatul Ulama, Lucknow, had 288 students, and an income of Rs. 3,35,280 (Haq: 1972). No comprehensive data are available on the student population and the resource available to the madrasas in India, but on the whole they seem to have more students and more resources now than at any time since independence.

26. The process of Urduization is as it were the cultural extension of Islamization. The distinction between Urdu-speaking and local-language-speaking Muslims is of great social and political significance. The north Indian Muslims have tended to identify true Islamic culture with their own. It is striking that almost all over India, until recently, this claim was conceded by the non-Urdu-speaking Muslims. Urduization represents the north Indian Muslims' drive to bring about the cultural unification of Indian Muslims.
27. Dr. Mushir Ul Haq's study on *Islam in Secular India* (1972) provides detailed information on the madrasas in Uttar Pradesh and Bihar. He reports that 'at least 356 madrasas were functioning in 1969' in these two states, but thinks this is an underestimate.
28. See Titus (256-69), Ahmad and Grunebaum (77-84), Farquhar (1919: 137-48). The question of who is a Muslim, which first arose in the controversy between the Kharidjites and Muridjites, was raised in connection with the Ahmadiya, and as might be expected, remains unresolved. It was exhaustively debated by the Commission, presided over by Justice Munir, in its report (see The Munir Report, 1954) on the anti-Qadiani disturbances in West Punjab in 1953.
29. Dr. Hardy accurately characterizes it as 'the description of a principle rather than of an activity' (11). Ijma has always been utilized to legitimize the given state of affairs. It is a conservative rather than a democratic principle.
30. See Wensinck (1932/65) for the doctrinal controversy between the Kharidjites, who held good works necessary for a believer to be considered a Muslim, and the Muridjites, who believed faith (*iman*) to be sufficient. This latter view has prevailed.

    The material available on the Ahl-i-Hadith is very scanty. See Titus (195-7), Ahmad (1967: 113-22); Ahmad and Grunebaum (85-8).

REFERENCES

Ahmad, Aziz. 1964. *Studies of Islamic Culture in the Indian Environment.* Oxford: Clarendon Press.

———. 1967. *Islamic Modernism in India and Pakistan 1857-1964.* London: Oxford University Press.

Ahmad, Aziz and G.E. Von Grunebaum. 1970. *Muslim Self-Statement in India and Pakistan 1857-1968.* Wiesbaden: Otto Harrossowitz.

Ahmad, S. Maqbul. 1971. 'Madrasa system of education and Indian Muslim society'. In S.T. Lokhandwalla, ed., *India and contemporary Islam,* pp. 25-36. Simla: IIAS.

Ahmad, Q. 1966. *Wahabi Movement.* Calcutta: Firma K.L. Mukhopadhyay.

Arberry, A.J. 1950. *Sufism.* London: George Allen & Unwin.

———. 1955. *The Koran Interpreted*, vol. I (i-xx) and vol. II (xxi-cxiv). London: George Allen & Unwin.

Azad, Abul Kalam. 1962, 1967. *The Tarjuman al-Quran*, vols. I & II. Bombay: Asia Publishing House.

Aziz, K.K. 1967. *The making of Pakistan.* London: Chatto & Windus.

Brass, P. 1970. 'Muslim separatism in the United Provinces'. *Economic and Political Weekly*, Annual No. 5, 3-5: 167-86.

Brown, Kenneth. 1972. 'Profile of a nineteenth century Moroccan scholar'. In N.R. Keddie, ed., *Scholars, Saints and Sufis*, pp. 127-48. Berkeley & Los Angeles: University of California Press.

Crooke, William/G.A. Herklots, 1921. *Islam in India.* London: Oxford University Press. New Delhi: Oriental Books Reprint Corporation (1972).

Dalwai, Hamid. 1968. *Muslim politics in India.* Bombay: Nachiketa Publications.

———. 1971. 'Presidential address to the conference of forward-looking Muslims'. *The Secularist* (Bombay) 11-12 December.

Darul Ulom, Deoband. n.d. *Fatawa*, vols. I-VIII. Deoband: Kutubkhana Imdadia.

Davis, Kingslay. 1951. *The Population of India and Pakistan.* Princeton: Princeton University Press.

Farquhar, J.N. 1919. *Modern Religious Movements in India.* New York: The Macmillan Company.

Faruqi, Zia-ul-Hasan. 1963. *The Deoband Movement and the Demand for Pakistan.* Bombay: Asia Publishing House.

Fayzee, A.A.A. 1963. *A Modern Approach to Islam.* Bombay: Asia Publishing House.

Geertz, Clifford 1968. *Islam Observed.* New Haven and London: Yale University Press.

Gibb, H.A.R. 1947. *Modern Trends in Islam.* Chicago: Chicago University Press.

———. 1953. *Mohammedanism* (2nd edn.). London: Oxford University Press.

———. 1962. *Studies on the Civilisation of Islam.* London: Routledge & Kegan Paul.

Gibb, H.A.R. and J.H. Krammers, eds. 1961. *Shorter Encyclopaedia of Islam.* Leiden: E.J. Brill.

Goldziher, I. 1971. *Muslim studies*, vol. II (edited by S.M. Stern). London: George Allen & Unwin.

Graham, G.F.I. 1909. *The life and work of Sir Syed Ahmad Khan.* London: Hodder and Stoughton.

Grunebaum, G.E. Von. 1953. *Medieval Islam* (2nd edn.). Chicago: Chicago University Press.

———. 1961. *Islam, Essays in the Nature and Growth of Cultural Tradition* (2nd edn.). London: Routledge & Kegan Paul.

———. 1962. *Modern Islam: The Search for Cultural Identity*. Berkeley & Los Angeles: University of California Press.

Haq, M. Anwarul. 1972. *The Faith Movement of Moulana Muhammad Ilays*. London: George Allen & Unwin.

Haq, Mushir Ul. 1970. *Muslim Politics in Modern India*. Meerut: Meenakshi Prakashan.

———. 1972. *Islam in Secular India*. Simla: IIAS.

Hardy, Peter. 1971. *Partners in Freedom—and True Muslims*. Copenhagen: Student Literature.

Hunter, W.W. 1945. *The Indian Musalmans*. Calcutta: The Comrade Publishers.

Iqbal, Sir Mohammad. 1958. *The Reconstruction of Religious Thought in Islam*. Lahore: Shaikh Muhammad Ashraf.

Izutsu T. 1959. *The Structure of the Ethical Terms in the Koran*. Tokyo: Keio University.

———. 1964. *God and Man in the Koran*. Tokyo: Keio University.

Karandikar, M.A. 1968. *Islam in India's Transition to Modernity*. Bombay: Orient Longmans.

Kazmi, A. 1971. '*Maktab* Education in India'. *Islam and the Modern Age*. II, May 2. (New Delhi).

Keddie, Nikki R. 1972. *Sayyid Jamal ad-Din 'al-Afghani'—A Political Biography*. Berkeley & Los Angeles: University of California Press.

Kruse, H. 1965. 'The development of the concept of nationality in Islam'. *Studies in Islam* II. 1 January.

———. 1971. 'Traditional Islam and political development'. In S.T. Lokhandwalla, ed., *India and Contemporary Islam*, pp. 175-93. Simla: IIAS.

Lambert, Richard D. 1951. Hindu-Muslim riots. Unpublished Ph.D. thesis, Philadelphia: University of Pennsylvania.

Lewis, Bernard. 1972. 'The study of Islam'. *Encounter* 38, 1 January (London).

Malik, Hafeez. 1963. *Moslem Nationalism in India and Pakistan*. Washington: Public Affairs Press.

Marsot, Alaf Lutfi al-Sayyid. 1972. 'The Ulama of Cairo in the eighteenth and nineteenth centuries'. In N.R. Keddie, ed., *Scholars, Saints and Sufis*, pp. 149-65. Berkeley & Los Angeles: University of California Press.

Mathur, Y.B. 1972. *Muslims and Changing India*. New Delhi: Trimurti Publications.

Misra, S.C. 1964. *Muslim Communities in Gujarat*. Bombay: Asia Publishing House.

Mujeeb, M. 1967. *The Indian Muslims*. London: George Allen & Unwin.

———. 1970. 'The status of individual conscience in Islam'. *Studies in Islam*, VII, 3 July (New Delhi).

———. 1972. *Islamic Influence on Indian Society*. Meerut: Meenakshi Prakashan.

Nadwi, S. Abdul Hasan Ali. 1967. *Qadianism—A Critical Study*. Lucknow: Academy of Islamic Research & Publications.

———. 1968. *The New Menac and its Answer* (3rd edn.). Lucknow: Academy of Islamic Research & Publications.

———. 1972a. *Calamity of Linguistic and Cultural Chauvinism.* Lucknow: Academy of Islamic Research & Publications.

———. 1972b. *Islam—Mukammal Din Mustaki Tahzib.* Lucknow: Academy of Islamic Research & Publications.

Nasr, S.H. 1966. *Ideals and Realities of Islam.* London: George Allen & Unwin.

Niemeijer, A.C. 1972. *The Khilafat Movement in India 1919-1924.* S. Gravenhage: N.V. De Netherlanddsche Bock-En Steendrukkerij V/H H.L. Smitz.

Qureshi, I.H. 1962. *The Muslim Community of the Indo-Pakistan Subcontinent.* S. Gravenhage: Mouton & Co.

Rahman, F. 1966. *Islam.* London: Weidenfeld & Nicolson.

Rizvi, S.A.A. 1965. *Muslim Revivalist Movements in Northern India in the Sixteenth & Seventeenth Centuries.* Agra: Agra University.

Rosenthal, E.I.J. 1958. *Political Thought in Medieval Islam.* Cambridge: Cambridge University Press.

Sayeed, Khalid B. 1968. *Pakistan—The Formative Phase* (2nd edn.). London: Oxford University Press.

Schimmel, A. 1963. *Gabriel's Wing—A Study into the Religious Ideas of Sir Muhammad Iqbal.* Leiden: E.J. Brill.

Seal, A. 1968. *The Emergence of Indian Nationalism.* Cambridge: Cambridge University Press.

Shakir, Moin. 1972. *Muslims in Free India.* New Delhi: Kalamker Prakashan.

Sharma, Sri Ram. 1972. *The Religious Policy of the Mughal Emperors* (3rd edn.). Bombay: Asia Publishing House.

Smith, W.C. 1946. *Modern Islam in India* (revd. edn.). London: Victor Gollanez.

———. 1957. *Islam in Modern History.* Princeton: Princeton University Press.

The Munir Report. 1954. *Report of the Court of Inquiry Constituted under Punjab Act II of 1954 to Enquire into the Punjab Disturbances of 1953.* The Munir Report. Lahore: Superintendent Government Printing.

Titus, Murray T. 1959. *Islam in India and Pakistan* (revd. edn.). Calcutta: Y.M.C.A. Publishing House.

Trimingham, J. Spencer. 1971. *The Sufi Orders in Islam.* Oxford: Clarendon Press.

Tritton, A.A. 1970. *The Caliphs and their Non Muslim Subjects.* London: Frank Cass & Co.

Wahab, Abdul. 1972. *Khutba-e-Sadarat.* New Delhi: Jamiat Ulama-e-Hind.

Watt, W. Montgomery. 1961. *Islam and the Integration of Society.* London: Routledge & Kegan Paul.

———. 1968. *Islamic Political Thought.* Edinburgh: University Press.

Weber, Max. 1965. *The Sociology of Religion.* London: Methuen.

Wensinck, A.J. 1965. *The Muslim Creed.* London: Frank Cass & Co.

Wright, Theodore, P., Jr. 1972. 'Identity problem of former elite minorities'. *Secular Democracy* V, 1.

Zaehner, R.C. 1960. *Hindu & Muslim Mysticism.* London: The Athlone Press.

Pīr, *Shaikh* and Prophet: The Personalization of Religious Authority in Ahmad Riza Khan's Life

USHA SANYAL

(1994)

Ahmad Riza Khan Barelwi (1856-1921), a Sunni Muslim jurisconsult (*mufti*) and writer of voluminous legal rulings (*fatāwā*) over the course of approximately forty years from the 1880s to his death in 1921, was also a Sufi preceptor (*pīr*) to his followers. During his lifetime, and subsequently, he has been revered by is followers as the pre-eminent leader of a movement known as the 'Ahl-e Sunnat wa Jamā'at' (People of the [Prophetic] Way and the Majority Community). Detractors, of which there were many in the Indo-Muslim world (chiefly, though not exclusively, persons associated with the Dar ul-'ulum at Deoband), who have since the late nineteenth century disputed the implicit claim to universality that this term makes. Instead, they have labelled Ahmad Riza's followers 'Barelwi', after Ahmad Riza's patronymic which derives from his lifetime residence in Bareilly, now in west Uttar-Pradesh (earlier known as Rohilkhand).

Taking seriously the claim of the movement to be engaged in religious reform (*tajdīd*) on the prophetic model, I refer to it by its own term. Tajdīd however, held very different meanings for Ahmad Riza and his followers than it did for the Deobandis. In this paper I explore the Sufi dimensions of the movement, focusing in particular on the nature of religious authority in Ahmad Riza's life from three perspectives: Ahmad Riza's devotion to his pīr, and his view generally on the nature of a pīr's relationship with, and authority over, his disciples; his devotion to Shaikh 'Abd ul-Qadir Jilani, the founder of the Qadiri order of Sufis, with which he identified more closely than with other orders, though he was also affiliated with the Chishti, Naqshbandi and Suhrawardi orders; and finally, the place of the Prophet as a pivotal figure in his life.

Devotion to the three figures of pīr, *shaikh*[1] and Prophet was central to Ahmad Riza as a believer and to his perception of what it meant to be a 'good Muslim'. Nor were they unrelated to each other in his life: his writings make clear that each is a pathway, and a guide, to the next. The culmination of religious authority, in the world of men, is the Prophet.

One of the chief sources I will be drawing upon in this paper is Ahmad Riza's *Malfūzāt,* the collection of orally delivered homilies and responses to questions posed by followers, that was compiled by his son, Mustafa Riza Khan (d. 1981). Important, too, in this context is Ahmad Riza's *dīwān,* or anthology of poetry, entitled *Hadā'iq-e Bakhshish.* The poems, which deal for the most part with qualities of the Prophet, often have a simplicity and directness that give us additional insight into Ahmad Riza as believer. There is also an extensive collection of fatāwā by him on these themes. Indeed, this genre constituted Ahmad Riza's hallmark. In this paper, some of the relevant fatāwā will be drawn upon where necessary.

I. THE ROLE OF THE PĪR IN AHMAD RIZA'S LIFE

Ahmad Riza received *bai'a,* or initiation into discipleship, from Shah Al-e-Rasul of Marahra in 1877, two years before the latter's death. Ahmad Riza's own personal recollections and record of his pīr are rather limited in content which is understandable in the circumstances. Ahmad Riza was then about 21; Shah Al-e Rasul in his 80s. Nor does Ahmad Riza appear to have spent any length of time studying under his direction; indeed, it is related in the *Sirat-e A'la Hazrat* that he was ready for discipleship immediately he met Shah Al-e Rasul, and did not need the forty-day period of instruction which was customary prior to an initiation.[2] The lack of a close personal relationship is also indicated, I believe, by the fact that there is no mention, in Ahmad Riza's Malfūzāt or in the biographies of him, of dreams in which his pīr appeared to him, although he reported having seen a wide variety of people in his dreams, including his father, his grandfather, and the Prophet (Mustafa Riza Khan n.d.: vol. 1, 83; vol. 3, 68-9). As an adult, Ahmad Riza was to receive instruction from, and seek the advice of, Nuri Miyan, Shah Al-e Rasul's *sajjāda-nishīn* (successor) and grandson, who was about fifteen years his senior. Ahmad Riza respected Nuri Miyan as his pīr's sajjāda-nishīn and reportedly had a close personal relationship with him.

Despite the fact that Ahmad Riza did not have such a relationship with Shah Al-e Rasul, the latter held a special place of honour and regard in his life. This is clear from the fact that, from about 1905 or 1906 until his death in 1921, Ahmad Riza annually commemorated Shah Al-e Rasul's *'urs* (death anniversary) at his own home in Bareilly. For three days each year, from the sixteenth to the eighteenth Zu'l Hijja, the occasion was observed, in a spirit of both solemnity and devotion, with complete readings (*khatma*) of the Qur'an recitation of *na't* poetry honouring the Prophet, and sermons by the *'ulamā*. The highlight of the proceedings was the sermon (*wa'z, bayān*) delivered by Ahmad Riza, in which he spoke feelingly and eloquently (so the reports tell us) on a particular *ayat* (verse) of the Qur'an, Shaikh 'Abd ul-Qadir Jilani, and the Prophet (see, for example, *Dabdaba-e Sikandari*, 45: 50 (10 January 1910), 9; 46: 50 (26 December 1910), 12-13; 47: 51 (18 December 1911). Evidently, Ahmad Riza was an effective and powerful speaker, for the reports never fail to mention the religious transport and ecstasy of his listeners. One writer reported:

> Everyone was completely captivated (by his *wa'z*). Sometimes he makes you laugh, sometimes he makes you cry, sometimes he makes you feel agitated.

He continued:

> If you want to hear the true praises of the Prophet, you must hear them from the lips of A'la Hazrat (Ahmad Riza). The qualities with which he has been blessed by God make it clear that he is the *mujaddid* of the present century. . . . And at a time when such turbid fissures are opening up (among Sunnis), A'la Hazrat is a shield and a chisel.[3]

Others have reported, as well, on the eloquence of Ahmad Riza's sermons, and the huge crowds he drew (Bihari 1938: vol. 1, 97-8, 114).

It is noteworthy, in view of the fact that Shah Al-e Rasul died soon after Ahmad Riza became his disciple, that Ahmad Riza did not consider his relationship with his pīr, or with the Barkatiyya family, to have ended with this event. His relationship of discipleship appeared instead to embrace the Barkatiyya ancestors of Shah Al-e Rasul, and Nuri Miyan his sajjāda-nishīn, and to continue in time beyond his death. In a sense Ahmad Riza's relation with Shah Al-e Rasul transcended Shah Al-e Rasul, himself, reaching beyond him to the chain of spiritual (and actual) ancestors who were the source of his spiritual authority. The source of their authority, in turn, was in the final analysis their descent from the Prophet. The *shajara* or family tree, in which one's ancestors were listed by name down to oneself, was an important testimonial of authority linking its bearer to the Prophet. Ahmad Riza has a poem in his dīwān in which he traces his spiritual descent from the Prophet, through such eminent figures as 'Ali, Husain, 'Abd ul-Qadir Jilani, and his pīr Shah Al-e Rasul.[4]

In his Malfūzāt, Ahmad Riza illustrated the point that a person's relationship with his (or her) pīr reaches back to the pīr's own pīr, and so on, with a story about a poor man (*faqīr*) who asked a shopkeeper for alms. When the shopkeeper refused, the faqīr began to shout at him, and threatened to turn his shop upside down. This caused a crowd to gather around them. In the crowd was a man of vision who pleaded with the shopkeeper to accede to the faqīr's demands. He told the crowd that he had looked into the faqīr's heart,

> to find out whether there was anything there. I found it empty. Then I looked into his *pīr's* heart, and found that empty as well. I looked at his *pīr's pīr.* I found him to be a man of Allah. And I saw that he was standing by and waiting, wondering when the *faqīr* would finally carry out his threat. What had happened was that the *faqīr* was holding on tightly to his *pīr's* garment (*dāman*).[5]

The story conjures up an eloquent picture of a continuous chain of Sufi pīrs watching over the affairs of their disciples' disciples, many generations removed from them. Clearly, Ahmad Riza did not believe that the relationship of a *murīd* to his pīr ended at the latter's death.[6]

On one occasion, Ahmad Riza (1901: 9) was asked for a fatwa in answer to the question, why should a Muslim who had grown up in a Sunni home, and had the Qur'an and the *hadīs* to guide him in his daily affairs, seek a pīr? This was an important question, for it raised doubts about a human being's very need for discipleship. Ahmad Riza responded by saying that the Qur'an and hadīs contain everything: *sharī'at* (the law), *tarīqat* (the sufi path), and *haqīqat* (truth), the greatest of these being the sharī'at. Knowledge of the sharī'at however, has been handed down from one generation of scholars (*mujtahids,* those qualified to interpret the sharī'at, and 'ulamā) to another; had this not been so, ordinary people would have had no way of knowing right from wrong action. This being the case with matters related to the sharī'at, it is even more vital that there be a similar chain (*silsila*) for the transmission of gnostic knowledge (*ma'rifat*), for this cannot be extracted from the Qur'an and hadīs without a teacher (*murshid*). To try to do so is to embark on a dark road, and be misled along the way of Satan.[7]

Even if one is not seeking gnostic knowledge for its own sake, Ahmad Riza continued, one needs a pīr for a different, and more fundamental reason: Without a pīr one cannot reach Allah. The Qur'an commands one to seek a means (*wasīla*) to reach Him. This means is the Prophet. And the means to reach the Prophet are the *mashā'ikh* (pl. of shaikh). It is absurd to imagine that one can have access to Allah without an intermediary; as for the Prophet, access to him is difficult (*dushwār*, though presumably not impossible) without one. Ahmad Riza added that hadīs prove that there is a chain of intercession to God that starts with the Prophet interceding with Allah Himself. At the next level, the mashā'ikh intercede with the Prophet on behalf on their followers; they do this in all situations and circumstances, including the grave (*qabar*). It would be foolish in the extreme, therefore, for one not to bind oneself to a pīr and thus ensure help in times of need (Ahmad Riza Khan 1901: 12).

Finally, Ahmad Riza argued that union with the Prophet (through the succession of pīrs to whom one is related by means of one's own pīr is a matter of grace (*baraka*), in itself no small thing. If one's chain of transmission is through pīrs and mashā'ikh of eminence, this is all to the good in terms of the baraka that accrues to oneself. In this regard allegiance to Shaikh 'Abd ul-Qadir Jilani (founder of the Qadiri order of Sufis) is better than allegiance to other Sufi founders, for he is said to protect the Welfare of his murīds in all situations.

Ahmad Riza's Malfūzāt also contain references to the relationship that should obtain between a pīr and his murīd, and the conditions which should guide a person in choosing a pīr. He emphasized the importance of having the right intention or inner desire (*irāda*), or without this the relationship would be sterile, and 'nothing would happen'. The pīr's ability to guide his disciple was thus in part dependent on the disciple's purity of intention and his faith in him. The tie between them was indissoluble, and irreplaceable (Mustafa Riza Khan n.d.: vol. 3, 59-60). As Ahmad Riza put it memorably on one occasion, 'The fact is that the Ka'ba is the *qibla* of the body, and the pīr is the qibla of the soul'.[8]

A disciple attains supreme closeness to his pīr in the condition of *fanā fi'l-shaikh,* or total absorption in one's pīr. Once a disciple has attained this, Ahmad Riza explained, he will never be separated from his pīr, regardless of the circumstances. The pīr is there to guide and admonish him at all times. Ahmad Riza related the story of one such case to his followers:

Hafiz ul-Hadīs Sayyid Ahmad Sujalmasi was going somewhere. Suddenly his eyes lifted from the ground, and he saw a beautiful woman. The glance had been inadvertent (and so no blame attached to him). But then he looked up again. This time he saw his *pīr* and *murshid,* Sayyid Ghaus ul-Waqt 'Abd ul-'Aziz Dābagh. (ibid.: vol. 2, 45)

Given the importance of one's pīr, Ahmad Riza advised his followers to choose carefully. A pīr should fulfil four exacting standards. He must be a Sunni of good faith (*sahīh* '*aqidat*); he must be an '*alim* or scholar, one who has sufficient knowledge of the Law to solve his own problems and answer his own questions without having to ask someone else to interpret the *sharī'a* for him; the chain of transmission (silsila) should reach back from him, without a single break, to the Prophet; and finally, he should lead an exemplary life, and not be disobedient or wicked in his personal habits (ibid.: vol. 2, 41).

One sees here, as in other writings by Ahmad Riza, the emphasis on following the sharī'a which was also characteristic of pīrs of Marahra. In his Malfūzāt, he related several stories pointing out that ignorant Sufis, who have no knowledge of *fiqh* (jurisprudence), mistake Satan for God without knowing that they do so:

There was a *wali* (Sufi 'friend of God') who made large claims for himself. An ascetic heard about him. He called the *wali* and asked him what he could do. The *wali* said he saw Khuda (God) every single day. Every day Khuda's canopy ('*arsh*) spread itself on the ocean and Khuda appeared on it. Now, if he had knowledge, he would have known that it is impossible (*muhāl*) in this world to see Khuda, that this was something given only to the Prophet. At any rate, the ascetic called someone and asked him to read the *hadīs* in which the Prophet said that Iblis spreads his throne (*takht*) over the ocean. (When this had been done, the so-called *wali*) understood that all this time he had mistaken Satan for God, had been prostrating himself before Satan had been worshipping him. He rent his clothes and vanished into a forest. (ibid.: vol. 3, 22-3)

II. AHMAD RIZA AS PERSONAL PĪR

Ahmad Riza himself, while primarily an 'alim, specifically a mufti whose opinion was frequently sought on a wide range of issues, was pīr to a small number of disciples.[9] He founded the silsila Rizwiyya,[10] and in November 1915 ensured its continuity by appointing his elder son, Hamid Riza Khan, as his sajjāda-nishīn. The ceremony took place on the last day of the annual 'urs celebration that year for Shah Al-e Rasul (*Dabdaba-e Sikandari,* 51: 51 [8 November 1915], 3). Ahmad Riza placed his *khirqa* (robe) received from Shah Al-e Rasul, on Hamid Riza's shoulders, and his own *imāma* (turban) on his head, before reading the *sanad* (authority) of the sajjāda-nishīn in Arabic and Urdu. After his death in 1921, his disciples and followers affirmed their allegiance to Hamid Riza as his sajjāda-nishīn.[11]

In addition to his small circle of murīds, Ahmad Riza had a much larger circle of *khalīfas.* Some of these, such as Na'im ud-Din Muradabadi and Didar 'Ali Alwari, were prominent leaders of the Ahl-e Sunnat wa Jamā'at movement in the 1920s.[12] Many came to him from different parts of north India (central India, in the case of Burhan ul-Haqq Jabbalpuri, who, however, was a murīd) toward the end of their course of studies, attracted to him by his growing reputation for scholarship and for the particular point of view he espoused. The term '*khilāfat*' as it applied to these and other men did not necessarily denote a relationship of discipleship to Ahmad Riza. It was a loosely applied term, usually, it would appear, as an honorific that Ahmad Riza bestowed on those he wished to honour in this way. Granting khilāfat was an individual and public act, undertaken from time to time. Thus the *Dabdaba-e Sikandari* reported in January 1910 that on the third and last day of the 'urs for Shah Al-e Rasul at Ahmad Riza's house that year, Ahmad Riza bestowed the title of khalīfa on Maulana Zafar ud-Din Bihari by tying a turban (the *dastār-e Khilāfat*) on his head. Zafar ud-Din fell at his feet, and Ahmad Riza responded by giving him some 'necessary counsel' (*nasīhat*) (*Dabdaba-e Sikandari,* 45: 50 [10 January 1910], 9).

Ahmad Riza explained the difference between a khalīfa and a murīd by saying that there are two kinds of khilāfat, the ordinary ('*amm*) and the special (*khāss*) (Ahmad Riza Khan 1901: 14). The first kind obtains when a murshid (teacher) chooses to make someone he considers worthy (*lā'iq*), whether a student of his or a follower, his khalīfa and deputy (*nā'ib*). The teacher guides his khalīfa in matters related to Sufism (*azkār, ashghāl, aurād, a'māl*). The 'position' (*masnad*) is of religious (*dīnī*) significance alone, and there is no limit to the number of khalīfas that he may choose to have. This relationship ceases upon the death of the teacher. By contrast, in the second kind of khilāfat, the khāss or special one, the khalīfa continues in this role even after his murshid's death. The relationship is special because the khalīfa in this case is his murshid's sajjāda-nishīn, a position to which only one person may be appointed. In contrast, again, with the first kind, here the role carries worldly responsibilities for the maintenance of properties. Ahmad Riza went on to say that this position usually devolves upon the murshid's eldest son, though various shar'i conditions may obtain to alter the situation (ibid.: 15-21).

However, this twofold distinction between the sajjāda-nishīn on the one hand, and a large number of khalīfas on the other, does not convey the diversity of possible relationships between a murshid and his murīds or khalīfas. On examination, it appears that the relationship between a murshid and his murīd was not always as close or as intense as has been described above. In Ahmad Riza's own case, shortly before his death a large number of men and women came forward to take bai'a at his hands; so many that he had to deputise his two sons, Hamid Riza and Mustafa Riza, to officiate on his behalf (Hasnain Riza Khan 1986: 124). Obviously, those who became his murīds at this time did not enjoy a special relationship with him; nor, probably, had they made the careful and thoughtful choice that he had advised. These murīds do not fit the picture of one who was giving of himself or herself to the pīr in the total sense that is described in the literature, including Ahmad Riza's Malfūzāt. What had probably attracted them to him was the baraka that he, as a learned, upright and renowned pīr (and 'ālim), was believed to possess. Nevertheless, the term used in this case is also 'bai'a'.

Conversely, Ahmad Riza's relations with his khalīfas were not as distant as may appear from his twofold categorization into ordinary and special. His relations with them appear to have been rather loosely structured, individual and diverse. He was their murshid in the informal sense that they respected him greatly, and sought to promote the same ends as he in their own lives; but they did not necessarily live in Bareilly or take instruction from him. Na'im ud-Din Muradabadi (1882-1948), one of Ahmad Riza's khalīfas, was a forceful personality. He had already built up a reputation for disputation against 'Wahhabis'[13] and Arya Samajis in Muradabad before he came to Ahmad Riza's attention on account of an article he had written in a local newspaper (Na'imi 1959: 6-7). He neither studied under Ahmad Riza's direction, nor took bai'a from him, though Ahmad Riza's writings and point of view had influenced his thinking before they met. Once the two men got to know each other, Na'im ud-Din was a frequent visitor at Bareilly, and Ahmad Riza would summon him from time to time to represent the Ahl-e Sunnat wa Jama'at at debates in different parts of the country. For the rest, he was busy writing and debating, and in 1919-20 he set up a *madrasā* (seminary) in Muradabad (ibid.: 7-10, 20). The relationship between Ahmad Riza and Na'im ud-Din, then, was to a large degree that of intellectual companions, Na'im ud-Din respecting Ahmad Riza as the older and more widely read 'ālim.

On a day-to-day basis, Ahmad Riza interacted with a diffuse set of people who sought his advice on all kinds of matters, great and small. Some hours in the late afternoon were set aside for this purpose. As with Nuri Miyan, an important function Ahmad Riza performed *vis-à-vis* this wide circle of followers was that of curing or healing. A man who came to him asking for a prayer (*du'ā*) because he was beset with problems, was told:

> A *sahābi* [companion] went to the Prophet and said, the world has turned its back on me. He said, Don't you remember that *tasbīh* [prayer of praise] praising the angels, by the *baraka* of which we receive our daily food? Good fortune will come to you after your distress. At the time of the *fajr* prayer of sunrise, repeat this prayer ('*Subhan Allah bi-hamdihi subhan allah al-azim wa bi-hamdihi astaghfir Allah*'). Seven days after the Prophet had given the *sahābi* this advice, the *sahābi* returned. His fortune had changed so much, he said, that he didn't know how to describe it. You too [Ahmad Riza addressed the man] should repeat this prayer. If you miss the time of sunrise, say it in the morning after joining the congregation at the *fajr* prayer. And if some day you miss saying it even then, say it before sunrise [of the following day]. (Mustafa Riza Khan n.d.: vol. 1, 62)

The solution to a problem was not always so simple, however. When a man came to him saying that after many years of childlessness, he had six children only to lose five of them, and that he now had only a three-year old daughter left, Ahmad Riza gave the following detailed advice:

> Next time you are expecting a baby, come here and tell me within two months of conception. Also tell me your wife's and her mother's names.

Thereafter, *insha'llah*, arrangements will be made. Make sure everyone in your household is punctilious in offering *namāz*, and after every *namāz*, the Ayat al-Kursi should be repeated thrice a day—before sunrise, before sundown, and at bedtime. Even women who don't have permission to say the *namāz* [i.e. are menstruating] should repeat this *āyat*. But on such days they should say it with the intention not of repeating an *āyat* of the Qur'an but of praising of Allah. And on the days that they are permitted to read the *namāz*, they should also read the *qul* three times thrice a day (before sunrise, before sunset, and before sleeping). [*Detailed instructions on the position of the hands follow.*] There is an elderly man here who makes large lamps (*chirāgh*). Get him to make you one, and light it from the time conception takes place right until the time of birth. As for the daughter you already have, if she gets ill, light a lamp for her as well. That lamp will guard against sorcery (*sihr*), misfortune (*āseb*) and disease. And as soon as a new child is born the *azān* (call to prayer) should be repeated in its ear seven times, four times in the right ear and three times in the left. There should be absolutely no delay in doing this. If you delay, Satan enters [the child's body]. For forty days after birth, the child should be weighed against grain, and [the equivalent weight of grain] given in alms. After that, this should be done once a month until it's a year old; once every two months until it is two years old, and once every three months until it is three. In its fourth year, this should be done once every four months, and so too in its fifth year. In its sixth year, it should be done every six months. And from its seventh year on, once a year. Do this for your daughter as well. Since she is in her fourth year, weigh her every four months. Repeat the *azān* out loud in her ear for seven days at *maghrib*, seven times on each occasion. And for three evenings, the *Sūrat al-Baqara* should be read by a qualified reader (*khwān*) in a loud voice that will reach every corner of the house. At night the door of the house should be shut while saying '*Bism'illah*' and the same when opening the door in the morning. When going to the bathroom (*pā-khāna*), one should say the *Bism'illah* outside the door and enter with one's left foot first. And when leaving, one should extend one's right foot first. When taking off one's clothes or bathing, one should say the *Bism'illah* first. And when approaching one another, both husband and wife should remember to say this first. If you observe all this advice, *insha'llah*, no harm will befall you. (ibid.: vol. 3, 9-11)

Ahmad Riza's lengthy response shows the seriousness with which he viewed the man's problem. The ingredients of the cure were, essentially, simple ones: punctiliousness in observing the *namāz*, repetition of certain verses of the Qur'an (repetition of the Ayat al-Kursi being widespread as a cure), awareness of the details of every personal deed and of the correct way of performing it, and finally, the giving of alms on a large scale. A distinctive feature of his response, which recalls Denny's comment that reciting the Qur'an is in a sense a magical act (1985: 76), was that reciting a verse of the Qur'an repeatedly would ward off the problem at hand.

This was very clear when, on another occasion, Ahmad Riza was asked whether one can receive grace (baraka) only after one dies, or whether one may begin to do so during one's lifetime. In the course of his reply that grace may accrue to one both before and after death. Ahmad Riza alluded to Chapter 67 of the Qur'an, Sura al-Mulk,[14] which, he explained, intercedes for the person who prays to it. The *sūra* was portrayed anthropomorphically in the female gender:

> Nothing exceeds this *sūra's* ability to save [the dead] from the punishment of the grave and to convey peace and tranquility. If the punishing angels wish to come to the reader of this *sūra*, she [the *sūra*] stops them from doing so. If they try to come from another direction, she hinders them from there. 'He is reading me', she says. The angels say, 'We have come at His command, whose *kalām* [speech] you are.' Then the *sūra* says, 'Wait then, don't come near him until I return.' And the *sūra* puts up such a fight on behalf of the reader at Allah's court, pleading for his pardon. . . . If there is a delay in the pardon being granted, she argues, 'He used to read me, and You haven't forgiven him. If I am not your *kalām*, tear me out of Your Book.' The Lord replies, 'Go. I have forgiven him'. The *sūra* immediately goes to heaven. She collects silk cloths, pillows, flowers and perfumes from there, and brings them to the grave. 'I got held up coming here', she explains. 'You didn't get worried, I hope?' And she spreads out the cloths and the pillows, while the angels, commanded by God, go away (ibid.: vol. 1, 70-1).

While he attached considerable importance to the 'magical' as a cure to problems, Ahmad Riza also emphasized on numerous occasions, the role of individual effort, and of internal 'purity of heart' and purpose in achieving the desired result.[15] Just as a pīr could not by himself ensure the progress of the disciple unless the latter had the right 'intention', so also with the removal of obstacles. If the seeker was pure of heart, Allah never failed him. Ahmad Riza cited a *hadīs qudsi* (Divine Saying) in which Allah is reported to have said, '. . . And if he draws nearer to Me by a hands-breadth, I drew nearer to him by an arms length; and if he draws nearer to Me by an armslength, I draw nearer to him by a fathom; and if he comes to Me walking, I come to him running.[16] Clearly, though, the onus was on the individual to make the first move toward Allah before he could be helped.

In the same vein, Ahmad Riza cautioned his listeners not to

undertake the fast or the *hajj*, or go into seclusion toward the end of Ramazan (*e'tikāf*), for the wrong reasons: they must perform these deeds for Allah, not for themselves, although good would come to them as a result of having done them (ibid.: vol. 1, 29-30). And when judging the actions of others, they must be careful not to entertain doubts about others' sincerity as long as a possibility existed that they were well-intentioned (ibid.: vol. 2, 91, 93). One had constantly to be watchful over one's heart, which was ever given to disobedience (*ma'āsi*) and *bid'at* (reprehensible innovation). A time could come when a person became completely blind to the truth (ibid.: vol. 3, 63).

The Malfūzāt reveal the wide range of questions that Ahmad Riza dealt with in these daily conversations. Some related to personal appearance, such as the permissibility or otherwise of dyeing one's hair black, wearing one's hair long if one were a man, or wearing rings of various metals (ibid.: vol. 2, 102; vol. 3, 2). Others related to ritual practice, such as the correct manner of performing *wuzu'* (ablution) before prayer, the performance of the prayer itself, or the *adab* (etiquette) to be observed in mosque (ibid.: vol. 2, 88-9, 108-12). Sometimes conversation turned to marital relations, or to relations with non-Muslims (ibid.: vol. 2, 86, 97; vol. 3, 44). Beliefs about the dead, their intercession with the Prophet on behalf of the living, the Prophet's knowledge of the unseen: All these and other matters were discussed repeatedly. These daily conversations with people in the neighbourhood, town, and region in an around Bareilly must have been an important factor in Ahmad Riza's growth of influence and stature over the years. Although we have no way of knowing, his audience probably included some who were illiterate, on whom Ahmad Riza's advice and display of learning may have had a particularly powerful impact.[17]

In this examination of the nature of religious authority in Ahmad Riza's life, particularly in reference to the role of the pīr that we have looked at so far, it is clear that Ahmad Riza himself exercised considerable personal religious authority over his followers, as his pīr and other scholarly and pious men did over him. What were the likely sources of this authority?

Simon Digby has addressed this question in relation to the Chishti shaikhs in the Sultanate period (twelfth and thirteenth centuries) (1986: 57-8). Digby looks at a range of personal attributes which, as sources of prestige, enhanced the reputation and standing of a pīr at that time. These could include: 'learning and orthodoxy in conjunction with descent from the Prophet and . . . rank as a Sufi Shaikh', 'poetic sensibility', and 'the ability to construct, extend and organize a *Khanqah* (Sufi hospice); to feed, accommodate and attend to the material and spiritual needs of disciples and often numerous dependents; and to accommodate travellers according to Muslim precept and the expectations of hospitality' (ibid.: 61, 67). Most of these personal attributes (and Digby mentions others), with the exception of Sayyid ancestry, accurately described Ahmad Riza as pīr. Zafar ud-Din Bihari, Ahmad Riza's biographer, enumerates his qualities in a series of subheads throughout the *Hayat-e-A'la Hazrat,* including, among others: Islamic equality, kindness toward the poor, generosity towards others, depth of learning, and vigilance in the observance of *din* (Bihari 1938: 40, 46, 50, 131, 181).

It should be pointed out, however, that these values applied in the particular context of Ahmad Riza's vision of right belief and conduct. Zafar ud-Din sees no contradiction between 'Islamic equality', by which he means that Ahmad Riza treated people of low social status at par with those of high social standing, and Ahmad Riza's proverbial respect for Sayyids, whom he treated with a deference accorded to no one else on account of their descent from the Prophet (Bihari 1938: 203-8). A small example of this was that Sayyids were given twice as much food at a milād celebration (in honour of the Prophet's birth anniversary) as other guests at Ahmad Riza's household. Likewise, Ahmad Riza's refusal to have anything to do with Shi'is is interpreted as a sign of his uncompromising attitude in matters related to '*mazhab*',[18] Zafar ud-Din comments that people ignorant of dīn and *shar'* mistook Ahmad Riza's *mazhabi* firmness for rudeness or harshness (ibid.: 189-92). 'Wahhabis' of various descriptions, whose views Ahmad Riza devoted a lifetime to rebutting, were also understood to be outside the circle of people to whom he extended a courteous welcome. In all that Ahmad Riza said and did, he drew a clear line of difference between right and wrong belief and action. This unambiguity, backed by his unquestioned erudition, was perhaps his greatest source of prestige and authority in his follower's eyes.[19]

III. SIGNIFICANCE OF SHAIKH 'ABD UL-QADIR JILANI

The Qadiri order (tarīqat) named after Shaikh 'Abd ul-Qadir Jilani Baghdadi (d. 1166) is more popular in the South Asian subcontinent than in any other part of the Muslim world apart from Iraq, its place of origin. Ewing writes that 'Abdul Qadir Gilani . . . is regarded as the patron of all the Sufi orders in South Asia' (1980: 142). Among pilgrims to his tomb in Baghdad, South Asians outnumber those from other parts of the world (Schimmel 1975: 247). In the late twentieth century, Pakistanis (and Iraqis) are the chief source of the authority of the keeper of 'Abd ul-Qadir's tomb at Baghdad. The Pakistanis 'periodically send gifts which form the main source of the revenues of his establishment; the members of this family find it worthwhile to learn Urdu.[20]

'Abd ul-Qadir Jilani, who was born at Jilan in Iran, migrated to Baghdad as a young man. After spending several years in solitude as an ascetic, in the latter half of his life he decided to become a preacher. As a follower of the Hanbali school, he taught and preached at a madrasa of Hanbali Law, and also at a *ribāt* or monastery. Both institutions were famous in twelfth-century Baghdad, and 'Abd ul-Qadir was by all accounts very popular. His efforts as a preacher gained him the title 'Muhyi ud-Din' or 'reviver of the faith' which, allegedly, had grown weak at the time.[21]

To the Qadiris in the subcontinent, the founder of their order is known among other things (he has over ninety-nine names) as the 'Ghaus-e A'zam', or 'Greatest Helper'.[22] As the epithet 'Helper' or 'Succorer' suggests, he is viewed primarily as an intercessor with Allah. Padwick explains that 'While the *Shafa'a* [intercession] of the Prophet is his people's great hope for the life of the world to come, ['Abd ul-Qadir Jilani is an intercessor] concerning the life that now is' (1961: 240). He occupies a pre-eminent position in the hierarchy of saints, as we shall soon see; in some of the prayer manuals that Padwick studied, in fact, it is claimed that Allah gave him a seat 'with the spirits of the prophets . . . between this world and the next, between the Creator and the created . . .', which claim, Padwick comments, 'is remarkable, because entrance to that rank [that is, of the prophets] had been regarded as closed since the coming of Muhammad' (ibid.).[23]

In this respect, Ahmad Riza's views on 'Abd ul-Qadir's status *vis-à-vis* the Prophet and the other saints of the Sufi hierarchy were very clear. He definitely ranked him below the Prophet, but exalted him above all other saints. In one of his poems, he addressed 'Abd ul-Qadir with these words:

Except for divinity and prophethood
you encompass all perfections. O Ghaus

(*ulūhiyyat nubūwwat ke siwā tū*
tamām afzal kā qābil hai yā ghaus)
(Ahmad Riza Khan 1976: 252).[24]

Elsewhere he described how spiritual authority flows from Allah to the Shaikh:

From Ahad to Ahmad, from Ahmad to you
in this order the divine command 'Be' or 'Don't Be' is followed, O Ghaus
(*ahad se ahmad aur ahmad se tujh ko*
kun aur sab kun makun hāsil hai yā ghaus) (ibid.: 249).[25]

As this verse suggests, 'Abd ul-Qadir is seen to occupy the apex of spiritual authority below that of prophethood. Echoing the Shaikh's famous saying that 'My foot is on the neck of every saint', Ahmad Riza writes:

Who is to know what your head looks like
as the eye level of other saints corresponds to the sole of your foot
(*sar bhala kyā ko'i jāne ki hai kaisā terā*
auliya milte hain ānkhen wo hai talwā terā) (ibid.: 233).[26]

For Qadiris he is the Ghaus, or the *Qutb* (Axis or Pole), 'on [whom] the government of the world is believed to depend' (Subhan 1970: 104). Ahmad Riza explained the invisible hierarchy of saints as follows:

Every *ghaus* has two ministers. The ghaus is known as 'Abd Ullah. The minister on the right is called 'Abd ur-Rab, and the one on the left is called 'Abd ul-Malik. In this [spiritual] world, the minister on the left is superior to the one on the right, unlike the worldly *sultanat.* The reason is that this is the *sultanat* of the heart and the heart is on the left side. Every *ghaus*... [has a special relationship with] the Prophet. (Mustafa Riza Khan, n.d.: vol. 1, 102)[27]

Ahmad Riza went on to name the succession of *ghaus* and their ministers from the time of the Prophet down to Shaikh 'Abd ul-Qadir Jilani. the first ghaus in this list was the Prophet, followed by the four *khulafa-e rāshidūn* (Abu Bakr, 'Umar, 'Usmān and 'Ali), each of whom was in turn first the minister of the left hand to the current ghaus, and at the latter's death, replaced him in that position. They were followed by Hasan and Husain, down to Shaikh 'Abd ul-Qadir Jilani. The latter was the last occupant of the '*Ghausiyat-e Kubrā* (the Great Succourer [ship]); those who have followed have been, and will continue to be, deputies (nā'ib). Ultimately the Imam Mahdi will receive the Ghausiyat-e Kubra (ibid.).

It is to be noted that in this scheme of things, the Prophet and the first four khalīfas stand at the head of the spiritual hierarchy which ends in Shaikh 'Abd ul-Qadir Jilani. In this way the lines of succession by which spiritual, gnostic knowledge is handed down coincide with the ultimate sources of authority for knowledge of sharī'a which, of course, also culminate in the Prophet.[28] Ahmad Riza explicitly made this connection in one of his poems addressing the Shaikh:

> You are *mufti* of the shar', *qāzi* of the community
> and expert in the secrets of knowledge, 'Abd ul-Qadir
> (*mufti-e shar' bhi hai qāzi-e millat bhi hai*
> *'ilm-e asrār se māhir bhi hai 'abd ul-qādir*) (ibid.: Part 1, 27)

'Abd ul-Qadir Jilani's relationship with the Prophet was not merely one of spiritual lineage, however. It was also one of genealogical descent, for the Shaikh's mother was a descendant of Husain, and his father of Hasan. This double genealogical link with the Prophet earned the Shaikh one of his many names, that of 'Hasan al-Husain' (Subhan 1970: 176). For Qadiri followers this genealogy was of great importance for, as S.A.A. Rizvi notes, 'as a direct descendant of the Prophet Muhammad (through his daughter, Fatima), Shaikh 'Abdu'l Qadir was believed to have inherited every one of his ancestor's spiritual achievements' (1983: vol. 2, 54).

Ahmad Riza's poetry is again helpful in understanding the importance of this factor to him personally. In the following verses, Ahmad Riza uses metaphors from nature to describe the Shaikh. It should be understood that the words 'pure', 'beautiful', and 'lovely', stand for Fatima, Hasan, and Husain, respectively:

> Prophetic shower, 'Alawi[29] season, pure garden
> Beautiful flower, your fragrance is lovely
> Prophetic shade, 'Alawi constellation, pure station
> Beautiful moon, your radiance is lovely
> Prophetic sun, 'Alawi mountain, pure quarry
> Beautiful ruby, your brilliance is lovely
> (*nabawī menh, 'alawi fasl, batūli gulshan*
> *hasani phūl husaini hai mahakna terā*

nabawi zil, 'alawi burj, batūli manzil
hasani chānd husaini hai ujāla tera
nabawi khur, 'alawi koh, batūli ma'adun
hasani la'l husaini hai tajallā tera (1976 edn.: 234)

These verses indicate that Ahmad Riza saw Shaikh 'Abd ul-Qadir as the repository of the virtues of each one of his illustrious ancestors, not only that of the Prophet. This is the clearest indication we have had so far of his belief that religious authority flows both spiritually and genealogically. Ahmad Riza's choice of Sayyid as his own pīr had already indicated the importance he attached to genealogical descent from the Prophet. Further evidence that spiritual authority is handed down genealogically was seen in his nomination of his own eldest son for the sajjāda-nishīni.

As with other holders of religious authority, 'Abd ul-Qadir Jilani was a very real presence in Ahmad Riza's personal life as lived from day to day. He told his followers of a time when the Shaikh had answered his appeal for help during a visit he had made to Nizam ud-Din Auliya's tomb in Delhi. The tomb was surrounded by musicians and singers, making what seemed to him 'a great commotion' and causing him much distress. Invoking Shaikh 'Abd ul-Qadir's help with the words 'Ya Ghaus', he also addressed Nizam ud-Din, saying, 'I have come to your court. Release me from this noise.' As he entered the tomb, silence suddenly reigned. He thought the musicians had gone away, but as soon as he left the tomb, the noise returned in full swing. Then he knew that the Shaikh had answered his prayer.[30]

'Abd ul-Qadir was also a constant presence in his life in terms of ritual practice. This included saying the Fatiha in the Shaikh's name when a wish was granted, and celebration of the Shaikh's birthday on the eleventh of every month, a ceremony known as *gyārahwīn.* Zafar ud-Din Bihari records an occasion when someone asked Ahmad Riza to read the Fatiha (the opening sūra of the Qur'an) over some food, offered in the Shaikh's name in thanksgiving:

(Ahmad Riza) first had everyone do *wuzu'* (ritual ablution). The food was placed in a room and everyone gathered together in it. They faced the direction of Baghdad which is eighteen degrees north of the *qibla* (Mecca). Ahmad Riza directed everyone to say *Bism'illah,* and to follow this up with the *durūd Ghausia* (prayer calling down God's blessing on shaikh 'Abd ul-Qadir), seven times. Then they were to read a formula (in praise of the

Prophet) once, the *al-hamd sharīf* (giving thanks to God) once, the Ayat ul-Kursi once, and repeat 'Qul huwa Allahu Sharif (Allah is one) seven times. After reading the *durūd Ghausia* thrice, they should offer nazar (the food) to the Sarkar-e Baghdad ('Abd ul-Qadir Jilani). [After completing the reading] everyone said *Bism'illah* (once more), and sat down to eat. When they had finished, Ahmad Riza told them not to wash their hands immediately, but to turn in the direction of Iraq and raise their hands to do *du'ā* (prayer of supplication for 'Abd ul-Qadir). He said, the *Sadat* (pl. of Sayyid) are in the front row, in front of everyone else. After they had said the *du'ā*, everyone washed their hands carefully, as he instructed, and he moved the used water to a safe place, commanding each one to drink a little of it rather than rinse it out. (Bihari 1938: 202-3)

It only remains to be highlighted once again the significance of the Qadiri order and its founder, Shaikh 'Abd ul-Qadir Jilani, to Ahmad Riza in terms of religious authority. Most importantly, the Shaikh was a means (*wasīla*) of intercession with the Prophet and thence with Allah, and he was seen, consequently, as a kindly, caring saint who has his petitioners' interests at heart. His Sayyid ancestry, moreover, made him a perfect intercessionary agent, as religious authority was seen to flow through both spiritual and genealogical lines.

Indeed, it appears to me that we are now in a position to better understand the significance of Ahmad Riza to Sayyid ancestry. As many Muslims see it (and here I speak more generally), Sayyids are imbued with baraka or grace by virtue of their descent from the Prophet, and this quality may be passed on to others through contact with relics associated with them. When one considers that baraka is itself a source of expression of religious authority, it becomes apparent that Sayyids 'automatically' embody religious authority, though personal spiritual worth is of course also of great importance in determining how a man, or a pīr or shaikh, is evaluated. Zafar ud-Din Bihari wrote in his biography that Ahmad Riza always looked upon Sayyids primarily as a 'part of the Prophet', and only secondarily saw their personal qualities. Consequently, it was inconceivable to him that a Sayyid could be placed in the socially inferior role of servitor: Sayyids were to be served, regardless of material or social standing.[31]

A second, and rather different, point that emerges from this examination of the place Shaikh 'Abd ul-Qadir Jilani occupied in Ahmad Riza's thought, it seems to me, is that Ahmad Riza saw the Shaikh as uniting within himself both sharī'at and tarīqat, both the

Law and the Path. Although this point does not emerge as clearly from the literature—which, by its very nature, stresses the tarīqat aspect of belief and practice over sharī'at, and a more complete documentation of which would require us to examine 'Abd ul-Qadir's teachings as they emerge from his own writings—nevertheless, the history of the Qadir order in the subcontinent indicates that 'reformist' or sharī'a-minded Sufis have been an important element in the order. Belief in the miraculous, or in the inborn superiority of noble (Sayyid) descent, in no way contradicts emphasis on a 'sober' Sufism.[32] The evidence from Ahmad Riza's own life, his sayings as recorded in his Malfūzāt, and his writings, together with what we know of the nature of the ritual activities he participated in, all indicate (as noted previously) that esoteric beliefs and practices had to be within the bounds of the sharī'a, or, as Muslims would say, *ba-shar'* (with *sharīa'a*).

IV. AHMAD RIZA AS A 'LOVER OF THE PROPHET'

In the foregoing we have seen how the Prophet was the focal point and apex of religious and spiritual authority for Ahmad Riza, the goal to which devotion to pīr and Shaikh lead. For him all such forms of devotion are undertaken ultimately in order to reach Allah. His writings on the Prophet are extensive: Numerous fatāwā deal with the Prophet's attributes, as do his dīwān of na't poetry and his Malfūzāt. In the discussion that follows, I intend to highlight the main themes addressed by Ahmad Riza's poetry and Malfūzāt inso-far as they concern the Prophet.

Veneration of the Prophet has a long history in Sufi and popular devotionalism. It goes back to al-Hallaj (d. 922), Sana'i (d. 1131), Ibn al-'Arabi (d. 1240), and Rumi (d. 1273) among others.[33] Ahmad Riza's Malfūzāt indicate his familiarity with the lives and writings of a range of Sufis, such as Junaid Baghdadi (d. 910) the Persian poet Rumi, the Egyptian poet al-Busiri (d. 1298) who wrote the *Burda* in praise of the Prophet, and the Egyptian 'Abd al-Wahhab Sha'rani (d. 1565), for example (Mustafa Riza Khan, n.d.: vol. 1, 43, 92-3; vol. 2, 59-60; vol. 3, 29). Given his vast erudition, it is likely that his vision of the Prophet and of the latter's place in the life of the believer was shaped by this rich Sufi tradition of veneration of the Prophet. Schimmel points as well to the popularity of na't poetry in the subcontinent since the Mughal period, written first in Persian and later in Urdu and in regional languages such as Sindhi (1987: 207-13). Some of this poetry would have been familiar to Ahmad Riza.

The resemblance in the themes touched upon in the devotional poetry of the Muslim world generally, and those that Ahmad Riza writes about, indicates that he was, indeed, writing within the context of this larger tradition. Schimmel describes the poets' concerns as follows:

From earliest times, Muhammad, the messenger of God, had been the ideal for the faithful Muslim. His behaviour, his acts, and his words served as models for the pious, who tried to imitate him as closely as possible even in the smallest details of outward life . . . all the noble qualities of his body and his soul were described in terms of marked admiration. (1975: 213-14)

Schimmel places the beginning of a 'genuine Muhammad mysticism' in the early eighth century with the first formulation of the 'Nur-e Muhammadi' concept that Muhammad was created from God's light and preceded the creation of the world and of Adam. In the tenth century Hallaj took the idea a step further, writing that the Prophet is both the 'cause and goal of creation'. Proof of this belief was cited from the hadīs qudsi, 'If thou hadst not been, I would not have created the heavens.'[34] In subsequent centuries the concept of the 'Muhammadan light' was further developed until the theory of *fanā fi'l-rasul*, 'annihilation in the Prophet', emerged in later Sufism. The Prophet had by now definitely become an intermediary between man and God (Schimmel 1975: 215-16).

Ahmad Riza's writings, whether in his capacity as a mufti writing fatāwā, as a Sufi preceptor giving guidance to his followers in his Malfūzāt, or as a poet expressing his personal longings and passions, all indicate that he held views such as those described by Schimmel. One of his ideas about the Prophet, which is worth exploring here, is that of the relationship between Allah and the Prophet, for clarification on this point will help us understand one of the major areas of difference between Ahmad Riza and his followers on the one side, and other South Asian Muslims such as the Deobandis on the other. Ahmad Riza's own relationship of 'love' for the Prophet should consequently also become clearer.

In his Malfūzāt, Ahmad Riza responded to a query about the Prophet's intercession with Allah as follows:

Only the Prophet can reach God without intermediaries. This is why, on the Day of the Resurrection, all the prophets, *auliyyā* and '*ulamā* will gather in the prophet's presence and beg him to intercede for them with God.... The Prophet cannot have an intermediary because he is perfect (*kāmil*). Perfection is concomitant on (*Mutafara'*) existence (*Wujūd*); and the existence of the world is dependent upon the existence of the Prophet (which in turn is dependent on the existence of God). Inn short, faith in the pre-eminence of the Prophet leads one to believe that only Allah has existence, everything else in his shadow. (Mustafa Riza Khan, n.d.: vol. 2, 58)

The hierarchy, then is clear: Allah, the Prophet, the other prophets, the saints, and so on. Within this framework of the Prophet's essentially dependent relationship to Allah, however, there are no limits to the qualities that may be ascribed to him. Ahmad Riza quotes 'Abd ul-Haqq Muhaddis Dehlawi, and the Egyptian poet al-Busiri, in support of his view that,

setting aside the claim that Christians make (about Jesus being divine), you can say whatever you wish in praise of the Prophet for there was no limit to the Prophet's qualities. (ibid.: 58-9)

This belief in the practically limitless virtues and abilities of the Prophet, given him by God of His own will, is the basis for Ahmad Riza's assertion that the Prophet had knowledge of the unseen (*'ilm-e ghaib*), a claim denied by the Deobandis. This Knowledge was said by Ahmad Riza to include (though by no means to be limited to) the five things specifically said in the Qur'an to be known to God.[35]

In certain respects, the Allah/Prophet relationship is not as clear as the foregoing quotations would suggest, however. In the following passage from the Malfūzāt, Ahmad Riza made the point that the Prophet is not 'other than God' (*ghair-e khuda*):

(The Prophet had to teach his followers how to recite the Qur'an in the early days of Islam). After listening to the recitation of a *sahābi*, Abu Musa Ash'ari, at night (from his own house), he praised his reading the next morning. The *sahābi* said, O Prophet, had I known that you were listening, I would have read with even greater fervour (*aur zyāda banā kar parhtā*) . . . (Ahmad Ṛiza comments) The *sahābi* himself said he would have recited more forcefully for the Prophet, and the Prophet did not object. This proves that reading for the Prophet was not comparable to reading for one other than God (*ghair-e Khuda*). The Prophet's business (*mu'āmala*) is Allah's business. (ibid.: 44-5)

Ahmad Riza also gave other examples of the identification of the Prophet and Allah, such as A'isha's (d. 678) statement that she was repenting to Allah and the Prophet.

On another occasion, Ahmad Riza was asked whether it was

permissible to use lanterns and carpets (and similar expensive decorative items) at a milād function. He responded that it was permissible as long as the purpose of the decoration was to honour the Prophet, rather than some selfish or worldly motive, and reported this story:

> Imam Ghazali wrote in his *Ihya 'al-'Ulūm*, on the basis of a writing by Sayyid Abu 'Ali Rudhbari, that a believer had organized a *zikr* meeting (remembrance of the Prophet's name). He had installed a thousand lights in the meeting hall. A guest arrived, and seeing the lights, began to leave (in disapproval of the host's extravagance). The organizer of the function held him back, took him inside, and said, Any light that has been lit for one other than God should be put out. The man tried to do so, but none of the lights could be extinguished. (ibid.: vol. 1, 99)[36]

These quotations are rather startling at first in their apparent equation of the Prophet with God. We know, however, from numerous clearly stated passages in Ahmad Riza's works that he did not equate the Prophet with God. What we have here, I think, is evidence of Ahmad Riza's unusually strong sense of Muhammad's prophecy itself, in terms of the uniquely close relationship of God that this implied. I am helped in my attempt to understand this by William Graham, who, in his study of the hadīs qudsi or Divine Saying writes:

> In the Divine Saying one sees perhaps most clearly that aspect of Muhammad's mission that is most often ignored: his genuinely *prophetic* function as the ordinary man who is transformed by his 'calling' to 'rise and warn'—not only through his 'Book', but in all his words and acts. . . . Outside the scriptural Revelation, God's revealing goes on, and most vividly so in the action and speech of His messenger. In terms of religious authority, especially within the realm of personal faith and personal piety, the Qur'an and the varied materials in the Hadith form not two separate homogeneous bodies of material, but one continuum of religious truth that encompasses a heterogeneous array of materials. (1977: 110)[37]

Ahmad Riza, like the early Muslim community that Graham describes in his study, appears not to have made any distinction between Muhammad the Prophet, recipient and messenger of God's immutable word, and Muhammad the guide or leader, an ordinary mortal like those around him. For him, the Prophet was 'in all his words and acts' prophetic, and thus extra-human. While all believing Muslims see Muhammad as unique among humans in perhaps indefinable ways, by virtue of his calling, Ahmad Riza seems to have had a heightened awareness of Muhammad's 'genuinely prophetic function', causing him to place the Prophet at the centre of his own life as a believer.

As may be expected, these ideas are expressed particularly forcefully in his poetry. In the following verses, the subject is Muhammad's close relationship with Allah:

> The two worlds seek to please Allah
> God seeks to please Muhammad.
> (*Khuda Ki rizā chahte hain do 'ālam*
> *Khuda chāhta hai rizā-e muhammad*)
>
> Muhammad is the threshold to Allah
> Allah is the threshold to Muhammad.
> (*muhammad bara-e janāb-e ilāhi*
> *janāb-e ilāhi bara-e muhammad*)
>
> A vow was made for all time
> to unite Khuda's happiness with Muhammad's.
> (*baham 'ahd bandhe hain wasl-e abad ka*
> *rizā-e khuda aur rizā-e muhammad*)
>
> (Ahmad Riza Khan, 1976 edn.: 47)

In the following verse Muhammad is seen as Allah's beloved, completely united with Him:

> I will call you only 'Lord', you who are the beloved of the Lord there is no 'yours' and 'mine' between the beloved and the lover.
> (*main to mālik hi kahunga kih ho mālik ke habīb*
> *yāni mahbūb o muhibb men nahin merā tera*) (ibid.: 9)

On the Prophet's night ascension (*mi'rāj*), he became God's bridegroom:

> You went as a bridegroom of light
> on your head a chaplet of light,
> wedding clothes of light on your body.
> (*kya banā nām-e khuda asra kā dulhā nūr kā*
> *sar pe sihrāh nūr kā, bar men shahanā nūr kā*) (ibid.: 13)

As for his own relationship to the Prophet, Ahmad Riza made it a conscious object of his life to immerse himself in serving the Prophet in whatever capacity he could. Small details about him say this most eloquently: He used to sign himself as 'Abd ul- Mustafa ('Servant of Mustafa', this meaning 'the Chosen' or 'the Elect', being one of

Muhammad's names) on all correspondence, fatāwā, and other writings. When asked about this at one of his daily meetings, he replied that the name was the sign of good judgment (*husn-e zann*) in a Muslim, and cited a hadīs in which 'Umar was reported to have said that he considered himself to be the Prophet's follower (*bandā*) and servant (*khadīm*) (Mustafa Riza Khan, n.d.: vol. 1, 43). On another occasion, he told those gathered about him that if his heart were to be broken into two pieces, it would be found that on one part would be inscribed the first part of the *kalimā*, 'There is no God but Allah', and on the other would be written the second half, 'And Muhammad is His Prophet' (ibid.: vol. 3, 67).[38]

As was the case with Shaikh 'Abd ul-Qadir Jilani whom Ahmad Riza perceived as actively intervening on his behalf from time to time, so too did he experience the Prophet's presence in a very personal way in his life. When he was learning the art of divination (*'ilm-e jafr*), the Prophet appeared to him in a dream giving him permission (*izn*) to proceed with his study.[39] On his second hajj in 1905-6, he spent a month at Medina the Prophet's birthplace, being present there during the Prophet's birth anniversary celebrations on 12 Rabi'ul-Awwal. He spent this entire period, he said, at the Prophet's tomb, taking time off only once to visit the shrine of one Maulana Daghastani, and another time to go to (*ziyārat*) the tomb of Hamza, the Prophet's uncle. When he met the 'ulamā of Medina to engage in learned discussions, it was in the precincts of the Prophet's tomb (Mustafa Riza Khan, n.d.: vol. 2, 34-5). This was, for Ahmad Riza, the holiest place on earth; he was willing to go so far, indeed, as to say that Medina was better than Mecca, as in this verse:

O pilgrims! come to the tomb of the king of kings
you have seen the Ka'ba, now see the Ka'ba of the Ka'ba.
(*hājiyo! ā'o shahinshāh kā rauzā dekhō*
ka'ba dekh chuke ka'be ka ka'ba dekhō)[40]

In his belief, the Prophet is very much alive in his tomb, leading 'a life of sense and feeling', as do the other prophets. From his grave he helps his 'guests', those who visit his tomb, in whatever way he sees fit (ibid.: vol. 3, 28-30).

It was particularly in the hope of being honoured with a vision of the Prophet at his tomb in Medina, Zafar ud-Din Bihari writes, that Ahmad Riza had undertaken this second hajj. While waiting for him to appear, Ahmad Riza spent the first night composing a *ghazal*; the next night he presented the ghazal to the Prophet, and it was after this that 'his *qismat* [fortune] awoke. His watchful, vigilant eyes were blessed with the presence of the Prophet' (Bihari 1938: 43-4). Unfortunately, Ahmad Riza himself does not appear to have written about this experience.[41]

Ahmad Riza's personal devotion to the Prophet shines through in his poetry. Some poems have become popular nationwide in Pakistan and are recited particularly on the Prophet's birth anniversary. The simplicity, humility in the presence of the awesomeness of the Prophet, and grateful confidence in his forgiveness with which Ahmad Riza addresses the Prophet, are apparent over and over again, as in these verses from the extremely popular poem *Karoron dūrūd*:

> I am tired, you are my sanctuary
> I am bound, you are my refuge
> My future is in your hands.
> Upon you be thousands of blessings.
> (*khastāh hūn aur tum ma'az, bastā hūn aur tum malāz*
> *āge jo shai ki rizā, tum pe karoron dūrūd*)
>
> My sins are limitless,
> but you are forgiving and merciful
> Forgive me my faults and offences.
> Upon you be thousands of blessings.
> (*garche hain behad qasūr, tum ho 'afū-e ghafūr*
> *bakhsh do jurm o khatā tum pe karoron dūrūd*)
>
> (Ahmad Riza Khan, 1976 edn.: 195)[42]

It was entirely consistent with Ahmad Riza's personal piety and devotion to the Prophet that the latter's birth anniversary on 12 Rabi' ul-Awwal, known as *milād ul-nabi* (or *maulid*, both forms being derivatives of the Arabic root *walada*, to give birth), was celebrated on a grand scale. It was a time of rejoicing, eagerly anticipated by Ahmad Riza and his followers. The *Dabdaba-e Sikandari* reported in January 1916, for example, that on the Prophet's birthday 'the Muslims of Bareilly, Rampur, Pilibhit, Shahjahanpur and other towns performed the pilgrimage to A'la Hazrat [Ahmad Riza]', for this was one of the three annual occasions on which he consented to give a sermon (*Dabdaba-e Sikandari*, 52: 11 [24 January 1916], 3). In fact, it appears from Zafar ud-Din Bihari's account that he gave two sermons that day, one at 8 a.m. after the first (fajr) prayer, and the second in the evening after the last (*'isha'*) prayer. The sermons were delivered at his ancestral house (referred to as 'Purani Haweli', or 'Old Family Home'), in which his younger brother Hasan Riza lived. In addition to the 'ulamā who came from outside Bareilly, the elite of the city were also invited to attend. People considered it so important to listen to Ahmad Riza on this day, Zafar ud-Din writes, that no one of eminence in the town organized a similar gathering of their own at the same time.[43]

Preparations for the events began around dawn. The townspeople—Ahmad Riza's murīds, followers and admirers—bathed, donned their new clothes, and hurried to the mosque to greet him there at the time of the fajr prayer. After the obligatory prayers (*farīza*) had been offered, people lined up waiting for him to finish saying his prayers and hoped to get close enough to him to kiss his hand (*dast-bosi*).

Shortly thereafter, and again at night at the 'Purani Haweli',[44] began the recitation of na't poetry by a trained reciter (*na't khwan*), recalling the Prophet's qualities. Ahmad Riza ascended the minbar (pulpit) exactly at the moment of *qiyām* (literally, 'to say, to stand') when everyone in the meeting (*majlis*) stood up at the remembrance of the Prophet's birth (*zikr e wilādat*). Ahmad Riza stood in silence for several minutes, for his entrance had caused a tumult among the crowd, which was swelling in numbers and finding it hard to fit into the meeting hall. When the shoving and pushing had quietened down, he rinsed his mouth with water using a spittoon placed next to him, and began his sermon with the words '*Bism'illah ar-rahmān ar-rāhīm*'.

In his sermon Ahmad Riza said that Allah, who is intrinsic (*zāt*), chose the Prophet as His means of bringing the extrinsic (*ghair*) world to Him. Everything comes from Allah, and Muhammad distributes what He gives. What is in the one is in the other. The other prophets are a reflection or shadow of Muhammad, like stars reflected on water.

Allah made Muhammad from His light before he made anything else. Everything begins with the Prophet, even existence (*wujūd*). He was the first Prophet, as Allah made him before He made anything else; and he was the last as well, being the final Prophet. Being the first light, the sun and all light originates from the Prophet. All the atoms, stones, trees and birds recognized Muhammad as Prophet, as did Gabriel, and the other Prophets.

The majlis-e milād is held in order to recall God's blessings (*ne'mat*), and to bring Muslims together so as to remember the presence (*tashrīf-āwari*) and excellent qualities of the Prophet. The collective partaking of food (which follows at the end of a milād meeting), Ahmad Riza said, is not central to the milād's purpose; nor, however, is there any harm in it, for it is an invitation of people 'for a good purpose' (*dā'wat ala'l-khair*), and is therefore necessarily good.[45] Allah has said, '. . . . the bounty of thy Lord rehearse and proclaim!' (93: 11) Yusuf Ali 1983: 1753).

Ahmad Riza reminded his audience that Allah had brought all the prophets together and told them about the future porphethood of Muhammad. All, on Allah's command, bound themselves to believe in his prophecy, and were witness to the fact that the others did so. Thus Allah was the first to speak of the Prophet, and the first majlis to mention the Prophet was this meeting of the prophets. In keeping with this covenant, all the prophets from Adam to Jesus have remembered the Prophet's coming and his birth. Speaking about the circumstances of the birth itself,[46] he recalled its joyous celebration by the angels and the fear with which the event was viewed by the devils (*shayātīn*). The meeting ended with a na't calling down Allah's blessings (dūrūd) on the Prophet.

The practice of holding milād meetings, like that of celebrating the 'urs of a Sufi shaikh or pīr, reading the Fatiha in thanksgiving over an offering of food, or holding gyārahwīn functions in honour of 'Abd ul-Qadir Jilani, were matters of intense debate and argument among the 'ulamā at the turn of the nineteenth century. The Deobandi 'ulamā sought 'to avoid fixed holidays like the *maulūd* of the Prophet, the 'urs of the saints' (Metcalf 1982: 151) and other feasts; the Ahl-e Hadis, taking an even more disapproving attitude,

> prohibited 'urs and *qawwālli,* particularly opposing the *giyārhwīn* of Shaikh 'Abdu'l-Qadir Gilani. . . . They prohibited all pilgrimage, even that to the grave of the Prophet at Medina. . . . In their emphasis on sweeping reform, they understood Sufism itself, not just its excesses, to be a danger to true religion. (ibid.: 273-4)

Like the Deobandis, they too opposed the practice of milād.

In the 1980s, Imdad Ullah Muhajir Makki (1817-99) had addressed the controversy on this matter in his pamphlet *Faisla-e haft Mas'ala.* In his view, whether a milād was permissible (*ja'iz*) or not depended on the intention of the participants. If a person equated the details of the milād (such as holding it on a particular date and not other, distributing sweets, lighting incense sticks, or laying carpets) with ibadat or worship, at par with namāz and the Ramazan fast (*rozā*), then it was reprehensible. It was bid'at (reprehensible innovation) if a person considered it a religious obligation (*dīni farz*), a duty enjoined by the sharī'a. But as long as it was viewed as one among several means of honouring and remembering the Prophet, it was permissible.[47]

Apart from the controversy over the permissibility of holding a milād, however, debate also centred over a particular aspect of the milād function itself, namely the practice of standing up (*qiyām*) during a sermon when the Prophet's birth was recalled, and blessings were called down on him (*salāt o salām*). Ahmad Riza, answering a query about the permissibility of qiyām in an 1881-2 fatwa entitled *Iqāmat ul-Qiyāma*, responded by saying that the practice was viewed as commendable (*mustahsan*) by a majority of 'ulamā throughout the Islamic world—particularly mentioning leading 'ulamā in Mecca and Medina—for two reasons. The first was that it had been practised for hundreds of years, though admittedly not in the first three generations of Islam.[48] Ahmad Riza considered this a valid argument on the basis of the hadīs that what Muslims consider to be good is good in Allah's sight too, and that a practice which hundreds of 'ulamā have considered to be good over hundreds of years cannot be bad (Ahmad Riza Khan 1986: 25-6, 28-9). Second, standing up when the Prophet's birth is recalled, Ahmad Riza argued, was an expression of respect and honour (*tā'zīm*) for him (ibid.: 36).[49] Standing up as a mark of respect for the Prophet, was, for these reasons, a meritorious act that would earn great reward (*sawab*) (ibid.: 15-22). Ahmad Riza did not assert, as Metcalf writes, that the Prophet was actually present (though invisible to the audience) the time of qiyām,[50] though he cited with obvious approval and concurrence a statement by a Hanbali mufti that the Prophet's spirit is present at this time (ibid.: 23).

V. THE IMPORTANCE OF INTERCESSION IN THE EXERCISE OF SPIRITUAL AUTHORITY

This paper has highlighted the importance for Ahmad Riza of intercession on behalf of the believer with God, a role fulfilled most especially by the pīr, the shaikh, and the Prophet, though not limited to them. As Metcalf points out, the power of mediation is accessible to many: 'Not only the dead but the living could be intermediaries', including children (1982: 303). The intervention or mediation of certain categories of persons is, however, more powerful than that of others. That of the Prophet is best of all.

Ahmad Riza believed that such mediatory power (or grace, baraka) inheres most especially in lineal descendants of the Prophet; hence his marked respect for all Sayyids, regardless of social standing. This was probably a significant factor, as well, in his (and his father's) choice of Shah Al-e Rasul of Marahra, who was a Sayyid, as his pīr. It also accounts in part for his devotion to Shaikh 'Abd ul-Qadir Jilani.

As Ahmad Riza's care in observing birth or death anniversaries such as 'urs, gyārhawīn and milād indicates, he believed strongly that the dead continued 'to live' in a spiritual sense, and that they retained a specially close relationship with places they had been associated with during their lives. Moreover, their spirits were specially alert and their grace heightened on certain days (their birth or death anniversaries). For these reasons, supplicants were well-advised to observe such anniversaries, and exhibit the greatest respect for tombs. Such behaviour, pleasing to the shaikh or pīr whose intercession was sought, would find favour with him, and therefore be a source of benefit (sawāb) to the believer.

While having a pīr, or visiting the tombs of Sufi holy men and 'ulamā in far-flung places were not at par with the performance of obligatory ritual acts such as prayer or fasting, or substitutes for them, in Ahmad Riza's eyes they could only be a source of good and an aid for the believer. As he said in his fatwa in answer to the question as to why one needed a pīr, it was absurd to imagine that one could reach Allah without an intermediary. One senses in all his writings and in his Malfūzāt the humility of one who believed he needed help in getting access to Allah, and in working out his own salvation. He saw the position taken by the Ahl-e Hadīs, or 'Wahhabis', as he called them, rejecting the need for intermediaries, as a sign of their arrogance.

As for the Prophet, his status was so elevated, and his closeness to Allah so great, that for Ahmad Riza the Prophet had in a sense displaced Allah as the centre of his devotions. While Ahmad Riza's writings make clear that the Prophet's qualities and abilities were God-given, and thus contingent, while only God is intrinsic, the fact of prophecy itself had such a compelling force in Ahmad Riza's judgement that he viewed love of the Prophet as the best way of showing love of Allah. In all he did or wrote, love of the Prophet was a motivating factor.

In fact, it was a standard Ahmad Riza consistently applied in drawing boundaries between 'right' and 'wrong' action, and in distinguishing between Muslims who were on the right or wrong track. In my view it would be erroneous to conclude that because Ahmad Riza supported a mediatory, custom-laden 'Islam', he 'made less of a demand for individual responsibility' on himself or his followers than did the Deobandis or others (Metcalf 1982: 397). On the contrary, his whole life was spent defining how a Muslim should conduct himself or herself in his or her time and day, and in punctiliously following these standards of conduct and belief in his own life, while at the same time distancing himself from those Muslims of whose beliefs or practices he disapproved. I have also tried to show that he attached great importance to the intention with which an action was undertaken. What emerges, I think, is the distinctiveness of his 'style', compared with that of other Indian Muslims in the nineteenth and twentieth centuries, caused by the determining role in his life of the Prophet and of his defence of the Prophet against perceived disrespect or slight.

NOTES

1. I am deliberately using the term 'shaikh' here to denote the founder of one of the major Sufi orders, as distinct from a personal pīr, although the two terms are generally used interchangeably. This appears to be the only way of making the distinction between two entirely different levels of belief and ritual practice.
2. Hasnain Riza Khan (1986: 55). While the hagiographical literature sees this lack of a period of instruction as a sign of Ahmad Riza's high attainments, and gives him centre stage as it were in this event, the decision to seek bai'a from Shah Al-e Rasul was probably made by Naqi'Ali, Ahmad Riza's father, on Maulana 'Abd ul-Qadir Badayuni's advice. Naqi'Ali and Ahmad Riza did not know Shah Al-e Rasul personally. Why did 'Abd ul-Qadir, who was also a pīr, not make father and son his own disciples? I think it probable that they had expressed a wish to become disciples of a Sayyid, which he, as descendant of an 'Usmani family, was not.
3. *Dabdaba-e Sikandari*, 46: 29 (1 August 1910), 6. The occasion for this wa'z was an '*urs-e Nuri* at Marahra. A mujaddid is a renewer of the religious law, who seeks to ensure that the sharia is implemented and followed in people's lives. The effort of renewal is tajdīd.

4. Ahmad Riza Khan (n.d.: Part 1, 66-8). I am grateful to Mr. Nigar Erfaney of Karachi for his translation of this shajara.
5. Mustafa Riza Khan (n.d.: vol. 3, 29-30). The Urdu original reads 'shaikh' rather than 'pīr' as in my translation.
6. Indeed, it appears that the impending death of a pīr causes large numbers of people to seek bai'a from him before it is too late. See later.
7. Ahmad Riza Khan (1901: 9-11). This is based on a hadīs that says: 'When someone has no *shaikh*, Satan becomes his *shaikh*'. Cf. Schimmel (1975: 103).
8. Mustafa Riza Khan (n.d.: vol. 2, 65). The Ka'ba is the cube-shaped building in Mecca's Grand Mosque in the direction of which Muslims face to pray, while the qibla is the direction of prayer (i.e. facing the Ka'ba).
9. It is virtually impossible to estimate who these were, and how many. In addition to his two sons, Hamid Riza Khan and Mustafa Riza Khan, the names of a few others are known, such as Haji Kifayat Ullah, and Hafiz Yaqin ud-Din Qadiri. The difficulty with identifying Ahmad Riza's disciples is that the names cited in the literature are often of khalīfas rather than murīds. The difference between the two will be discussed later. See Bihari (1938: 139-40), Hasnain Riza Khan (1986: 124, 132).
10. By 'silsila' is here meant a chain of discipleship that culminates in particular pīr, not a Sufi order. The name Rizwi or Rizwiyya is derived from the 'Riza' in Ahmad Riza's name. A person who wrote 'Rizwi' after his name (probably as part of a string of epithets, written in descending order of importance, such as 'Sunni Hanafi Qadiri Rizwi Barelwi') would be signalling the pīr to whom he bore allegiance.
11. This occurred in the course of ceremonies marking the fortieth day of Ahmad Riza's death, on 8 December 1921. While I have not seen an account of the event, an announcement that this was intended was made by Hamid Riza in *Dabdaba-e Sikandari* 58: 13 (28 November 1922), 5.
12. See Mas'ud Ahmad (1987: 11) for a partial listing of Ahmad Riza's khalīfas.
13. A term used by the Ahl-e Sunnat in a loosely defined sense to include the 'ulamā of the Tariqa-e Muhammadiyya, Deoband, and Ahl-e Hadis, as well as modernist Muslim intellectuals such as Sir Sayyid Ahmad Khan.
14. Referred to in the text as 'Sura Tabaraka', after the first word in the sūra. I am grateful to Christian W. Troll for identifying the sūra for me, in a personal communication.
15. The individual, he explained on another occasion, is composed of *nafs* (the base instincts), *qalb* ('heart' in a metaphoric sense), and *rūh* (spirit) (Mustafa Riza Khan, n.d.: vol. 3, 63). For discussion of the background of this tripartite division in Sufi thought, see Schimmel

(1975: 191-2). For the importance of 'intention' in Sufism, see Padwick (1961: 52-4).

16. Mustafa Riza Khan (n.d.: vol. 4, 33). the translation is by Graham (1977: 127-30).
17. In this context see Robinson (1983: 194-5), wherein he refers to the 'special chemistry of personal contact' as a factor 'spreading Islamic knowledge and bringing about a wider observance of Islamic law'.
18. Zafar ud-Dın Bihari's use of the word 'mazhab' (Ar., *madhhab*) in this context is not strictly correct, for mazhab refers properly to the four main Sunni law schools of Hanafi, Shafi'i, Hanbali, and Maliki. Shi'ism is not, therefore, a mazhab. The word as used here is interchangeable with din, the faith.
19. See, in this context, Ewing (1988: 1-22).
20. Margoliouth, 'Kadiriyya', in *E12*: 382. The article has presumably been updated since Margoliouth's death, though the editor's name is not indicated.
21. Margoliouth: 380-3. Also, Jilani (1967: 1-14), for a biographical note on 'Abd ul-Qadir Jilani.
22. For a history of the Qadiri order in the subcontinent from the fifteenth century, when it was first introduced in that region, until the late nineteenth century, see Rizvi (1983: vol. 2, Ch. 2).
23. In this context, see also Rizvi's comment that, 'To all intents and purposes, the Qadiriyyas advocated the deification of their founder and all his descendants' (1983: vol. 2, 54).
24. The reference here is to a different edition from the one cited in note 4 of this paper. Hereafter, n.d. or '1976 edn.' will indicate which edition is being cited.
25. *Ahad* = The One, i.e., Allah; *Ahmad*-Muhammad.
26. This saying is extremely popular and widely known among Qadiris. For comments see, for example, Schimmel (1975: 247-8).
27. Subhan (1970: 104-6) gives the details of this hierarchy, which is considerably more complex than this brief summary indicates. Schimmel suggests that the concept of the qutb (or ghaus, for the two terms are interchangeable) as 'the highest spiritual guide of the faithful' bears a structural resemblance to the Shi'i concept of the hidden imām. See Schimmel (1975: 200).
28. Apparently, Ahmad Riza was here following a scheme outlined by 'Ali al-Hujwiri, the eleventh century saint popularly known in the subcontinent as Data Ganj Bakhsh. See his *Kashf al-Mahjūb.*
29. 'Alawi: 'of, belonging to,, 'Ali'.
30. Mustafa Riza Khan (n.d.: 3, 59). Although Ahmad Riza had invoked the help of both Shaikh 'Abd ul-Qadir and Nizam ud-Din Auliya, he interpreted this event as miracle (*karāmat*) by Shaikh 'Abd ul-Qadir

alone. The latter's miracles are numerous. Many are recorded in the secondary literature in English.

31. Bihari (1938: 201). Zafar ud-Din recounts an incident in Ahmad Riza's household when it was discovered that one of the household servants was a Sayyid. Ahmad Riza immediately ordered everyone in the house to serve him instead, to consider the salary he had been receiving as *nazar* (a gift), and to ensure that he was fed and cared for. After a while the man left of his own accord, made uncomfortable, undoubtedly, by the reversal of roles.
32. Evidence for the 'reformist' or shari'a-minded orientation of the Qadiris in the subcontinent may be found, for example, in Eaton (1978: 284-6). Rizvi (1983: vol. 2, 91-4) also indicates that some famous Qadiri Sufis such as Shaikh 'Abd ul-Haqq Dehlawi (d. 1642) were devoted to uniting sharī'at and tarīqat.
33. Schimmel (1975: 213-27) discusses the history of the veneration of the Prophet in the Muslim world specially as manifested in poetry. The subject receives fuller treatment in Schimmel (1987).
34. On the Divine Saying, see Graham (1977).
35. The kernel of Ahmad Riza's argument with the Deobandis on the 'ilm-e ghaib issue was that 'known to God' did not mean only known to Him, and not known to the Prophet. Ahmad Riza believed that Allah gifted such knowledge to the Prophet from time to time, including knowledge of the five things specifically mentioned in the Qur'an (31: 34). These were: knowledge of the Hour (of Resurrection), of when it would rain, of the sex of a child in the womb, of what a person would earn on the morrow, and of where one would die.
36. Rudhbari (d. 934) was a contemporary of Junaid Baghdadi. See Schimmel (1975: 54).
37. Graham argues that the very existence of the hadīs qudsi, which is record of a Divine Saying in the Prophet's words, and which thus straddles the boundaries of Qur'an and hadīs, should alert us against making a rigid distinction between the Prophet in his prophetic role and in his personal role. Graham finds evidence to believe that the earliest Muslims did not do so.
38. A lengthy poem on the *mi'rāj* adjudged (in a personal communication) to be Ahmad Riza's masterpiece by Professor Muhammad Mas'ud Ahmad, a scholar on Ahmad Riza and his work, again pictures the Prophet's ascension as a wedding. See *Hadā'iq-e Bakhshish* (n.d.): Part 1, 106-15 (see Khan 1976). The imagery of a wedding is also central to the notion of 'urs, for the word 'urs literally means 'marriage'.
39. However, he gave up it up of his own accord after some time. Mustafa Riza Khan (n.d.: vol. 1, 82-3).
40. Ahmad Riza Khan (1976 edn.: 96). See also Mustafa Riza Khan (n.d.: vol. 2, 47-8).

41. His lengthy ghazal is in *Hadā'iq-e Bakhshish* (n.d.), Part 1: 92-105. I have been unable to find any reference in it to his vision of the Prophet, though this is not surprising given Zafar ud-Din Bihari's information that it was written before he had this experience.
42. Although Ahmad Riza did not approve of music and would not have put his verses to music, this poem, as many others he wrote, has a lilt and rhythm that makes it easy to remember and recite.
43. Bihari (1938: 96-7). Zafar ud-Din does not tell us to which year his account refers, though I assume the proceedings were more or less standard from year to year.
44. The text of the Hayat-e A'la Hazrat is confusing here. Zafar ud-Din clearly refers to the fajr prayer and the dast-bosi (kissing of the hand) taking place in a mosque, and is also unambiguous in reporting that the sermons were delivered at the Purani Haweli. However, he then goes on to talk of the na't reciter, and Ahmad Riza, getting up on the *minbar* (pulpit) to speak, which suggests that the meetings followed directly after the prayers (fajr and 'isha') at the mosque itself, and that there was no change of venue. He also refers to the people crowding together at the mosque to do the dast-bosi and then getting as close to the minbar as possible. This does not sound like a 'by invitation only' affair. See Bihari (1938: 96-8) for the entire text concerning the milād meeting (majlis-e milād).
45. Bihari (1938: 108). Here he was defending his position on the legitimacy of holding milād functions against critics such as the Deobandis. See Metcalf (1982: 300-1).
46. Bihari (1938: 112). Gabriel calmed the fears of Amina, Muhammad's mother, and assumed the shape of a white hen when urging the Prophet to manifest himself. Again the image of a marriage comes up when Gabriel tells Muhammad (not yet born) that the procession (*barāt*) of the bridegroom of both worlds is fully adorned and ready (to start for the bride's house. the Prophet, as bridegroom, is awaited before it can set out.) It would appear that in this case the bride is the world rather than Allah.
47. Barkati (1986: 50-76). In the above I have attempted to sum up his position rather than lay it out in all its details.
48. This was an important admission, in terms of the argument, for it meant that the practice was an 'innovation' or bid'at. However, as Ahmad Riza argued at some length in this fatwa, it was a *bid'at-e hasana* or 'good innovation'. The argument was taken even further, and the tables turned on the opponents of the practice, when Ahmad Riza quoted an 'ālim from the Haramain (Mecca and Medina) as saying that because Muslims saw this as a good deed, those who opposed it were *bid'atis*! Ahmad Riza Khan (1986: 28-9).
49. Ahmad Riza offered detailed proof on both counts, arguing his point

of view in about thirty-odd pages. The second half of the fatāwā was specifically in rebuttal of Maulana Nazir Husain Dehlawi (d. 1902), the Ahl-e Hadis leader.

50. See Metcalf (1982: 301). Ahmad Riza did assert in another context, however, that the Prophet had the ability to be bodily present should he so desire.

REFERENCES

Barkati, Mufti Muhammad Khalil Khan, ed. 1986. *Faisala-e haft Mas'ala.* Lahore: Rumi Publications.

Bihari, Zafar Ud-Din, 1938. *Hayāt-e A'la Hazrat,* vol. 1. Karachi: Maktaba Rizwiyya.

Dabdaba-e Sikandari. 1910-22. Rampur State.

Denny, Frederick M. 1985. 'Islamic ritual: Perspectives and theories'. In Richard C. Martin, ed., *Approaches to Islam in Religious Studies,* pp. 63-7. Tuscon: University of Arizona Press.

Digby, Simon. 1986. 'The Sufi shaikh as a source of authority in medieval India'. In Marc Gaborieau, ed., *Islam and Society in South Asia,* pp. 57-77. Paris: Ecole des Hautes en Sciences Sociales, Collection 'Purusartha', vol. 9.

Eaton, Richard M. 1978. *Sufis in Bijapur 1300-1700: Social Roles of Sufis in Medieval India.* Princeton: Princeton University Press.

Encyclopeadia of Islam (2nd edn.). 1954. Leiden: E.J. Brill.

Ewing, Katherine P. 1980. 'The *pīr* or *sufi* saint in Pakistani Islam'. Unpublished Ph.D. dissertation, University of Chicago.

———. 1988. 'Ambiguity and sharī'at—A perspective on the problem of moral principles in tension'. In K.P. Ewing, ed., *Sharī'at and Ambiguity in South Asian Islam,* pp. 1-22. Berkeley: University of California Press.

Graham, William A. 1977. *Divine Word and Prophetic Word in Early Islam: A Reconsideration of the Sources, with Special Reference to the Divine Saying* or hadith qudsi. The Hague: Mouton.

Jilani, Abd Al-Qadir. 1967 (trans. Aftab ud-Din Ahmad). *Futuh al-ghaib* ('The revelations of the unseen'). Lahore: Sh. Muhammad Ashraf.

Khan, Ahmad Riza. 1976. *Hadā'iq-e Bakhshish.* Karachi: Medina Publishing Company.

———. 1986. *Iqamat ul-Qiyama: Yani, Khare ho kar salt o salam parhna.* Karachi: Barkati Publishers (rpt., originally published in 1881-2).

———. n.d. *Naqa 'al salafa fi ahkām al-bai'a wa'l khilāfa.* Sialkot: Maktaba Mihiriyya Rizwiyya, rpt. (originally published in 1901).

Khan, Hasnain Riza. 1986. *Sirat-e a'la Hazrat.* Karachi: Maktaba Qasimiyya Barkatiyya.

Khan, Mustafa Riza, ed. n.d. *Mulfūzāt-e a'la Hazrat*, 4 vols. Gujarat (Pakistan): Fazl-e Nur Academy.

Mas'ud Ahmad, Muhammad. 1987. *Neglected Genius of the East: An Introduction to the Life and Works of Mawlana Ahmad Riza Khan of Bareilly (India) 1272/1856-1340/1921.* Lahore: Riza Academy.

Metcalf, Barbara D. 1982. *Islamic Revival in British India: Deoband, 1860-1900.* Princeton: Princeton University Press.

Na'imi, Mu'in ud-Din. 1959. 'Tazkira al-ma'ruf hayāt-e sadr al-afāzil'. In *Sawād-e A'zam.* Lahore: Na'īmi Dawākhāna.

Padwick, Constance E. 1961. *Muslim Devotions: A Study of Prayer-Manuals in Common Use.* London: S.P.C.K.

Rizvi, S.A.A. 1983. *A History of Sufism in India*, vol. 2. Delhi: Munshiram Manoharlal.

Robinson, Francis. 1983. 'Islam and Muslim society in South Asia, *Contributions to Indian Sociology* (n.s.) 17, 2: 185-203.

Schimmel, Annemarie. 1975. *Mystical Dimensions of Islam.* Chapel Hill:: University of North Carolina Press.

———. 1987. *And Muhammad is His messenger: The veneration of the Prophet in Islamic piety.* Lahore: Vanguard.

Subhan, John. 1970. *Sufism, Its Saint and Shrines.* New York: Samuel Weiser.

Yusuf Ali, A. 1983. *The Holy Qur'an: Text, Translation and Commentary.* Brentwood, Maryland: Amana Corporation.

Kinship and the Political Order: The Afghan Sherwani Chiefs of Malerkotla (1454-1947)

RITA BRARA

(1994)

The relation of the kinship pattern to the polity has perhaps always posed questions to anthropological writing. From its early beginnings with Morgan, it has been sustained as a problem worthy of attention in tribal societies. Approaches to kinship that have emerged from the exploration of a tribal context continue to animate discussion on the role of kinship in relation to the polity in the civilizations of the non-European world.

The correspondence of the lineage and the political organization in what were termed 'acephalous' societies in Africa gave rise to the concept of a lineage-based and segmentary state (Fortes and Evans-Pritchard 1941). The idea of the segmentary state, especially as developed by Southall (1956, 1965) in the course of his study of Alur society, has been employed for apprehending the character of pre-colonial polities in India (Fox 1971; Stein 1977; 1980).

In pioneering attempts to understand the nature of the pre-colonial state in India, it was apparent that the conception of a centralized state floundered in the face of the autonomy exercised at regional and local levels (Cohn 1962; Frykenberg 1963; Shah 1964). However, the organization of the polity in pre-colonial north India does not coincide with the idea of a segmentary state that may apply to a lineage-based tribal society. The constituent units of the Indian polity were not identifiable as lineage segments that would combine or break up along genealogical divides. Apart from the lineage, religious (Hindu-Muslim) and cultural affiliations (caste or *kaum/jaat*), often cross-cutting each other, entered the very formation of political entities. These multiple identities facilitated a gigantic nexus of alliance and exchange relations across regions, provinces and even empires that is overlooked by the segmentary polity theorists.

From the standpoint of a second tradition in the social sciences, the debate concerning the nature of the pre-colonial state in India has centred on whether or not it can be characterized by feudalism or the feudal mode of production, the Asiatic mode having been rejected in view of inadequate evidence. Insofar as the debate relates to kinship, it has been argued that under feudalism, ties of vassalage replaced the ties of kinship in Western Europe. As Marc Bloch puts it, 'feudal ties developed when those of kinship proved inadequate' (Bloch 1961: 443). While the transition from lineage society to state forms is said to have occurred in India in the mid-first millennium BC (Thapar 1984), kin ties were not substituted by ties of vassalage. Fox (1971) draws attention to this dimension when he proposes the idea of a 'kin-feudated' state to characterize Rajput polities till the coming of the British.

The importance of the patrilineage as a nodal institution in pre-colonial polities is appropriately situated and analysed in this perspective but the concept of a 'kin-feudated' state also entails an understanding of the political and matrimonial alliances of intermediate rulers, which Fox (1971, 1977) eschews. Unfortunately, the orientation of Africanist studies of kinship has been carried over and recognition of the capacity of marriage alliances for building, cementing or reinforcing relations in the political realm in north India, is missing.

The possibility of regarding the Asiatic and the feudal modes of production as variants of a single tributary mode has also been espoused to characterize pre-capitalist societies where the surplus took the form of tribute (Wolf 1982). While it is not the only way of approaching the analysis of pre-capitalist societies, the tributary state model has its attractions for an anthropologist since it draws attention to what has long been considered an associated feature—namely, the importance attached to gift-giving and tribute, subsuming the idea of bestowing women in tribute.

A third and distinctive anthropological approach seeks to apprehend the nature of kinship and gift-giving on the one hand, and the nature of the state on the other, through the study of indigenous vocabularies and concepts, coupled with the analysis of Hindu texts. In this vein, Dumont's (1957) studies of kinship terminology, gift-giving and cross-cousin marriage in south India have brought out the importance of marriage alliance as a principle of kinship that is on par with descent. But, for north India, he avers that the kinship terminology does not deliver the system of marriage, as it were (Dumont 1966). The analysis of traditional texts probed the ideological structure of Hindu kingship. Thus, the domain of kingship was viewed as an expression of the values that were associated with the caste system (Burghart 1983; Das 1977; Dumont 1962). The fact of the Islamic conquest and its repercussions have still to be investigated.

The political uses of cross-cousin marriage in south India and the exceptional pattern of parallel-cousin marriage prevalent in a royal lineage of Sri Lanka in the past have been documented by Trautmann (1981). However, both Dumont and Trautmann are silent about the marriage practices of the Muslim groups in the subcontinent. Have Muslim ruling lineages, too, realized the potential of marriage among cousins in the political realm? And does *kanyadaan* (gift of a daughter) constitute an 'Indian culture of kinship' (Trautmann 1981: 27), with Muslims, too, sharing in this civilizational conception? While appreciating that the meaning of marriage between cousins or the gift of a daughter varies with the cultural context, we need to investigate the characteristic marriage pattern of Muslim rulers in this regard insofar as cousins were not proscribed as spouses among Muslims.

Finally, an exploration in the realm of kinship and marriage that seeks to relate it to the political order does not imply that the content of kinship and marriage is reducible to the political. The social recognition of biological facts signifies an arena of affective bonds where moral rights and obligations are long-term (Maurice Bloch 1973), if not axiomatic. But since both the nature of kinship and the political order are socially constructed, it is the dovetailing of the two and the possibility of simultaneous movements in the analytically distinguishable realms that may be worth exploring.

This paper attempts to discern a pattern from the practice of rulers over time. It has often been argued, against this view, that cultural norms may or may not be observed in practice, and belong to another plane (Schneider 1968). Yet the muting, rediscovering, compromising and abandoning of cultural norms is of interest in itself and may co-vary with what may be regarded as the norms of the political realm. Rulers, moreover, were married where it was considered appropriate. That these marriages conformed to or flouted cultural norms may be what we, as anthropologists, read into their practice. However, a comparison of what was considered appropriate at different points in time, and discontinuities (if any) relative to their own past, affords an idea of both change and continuity, even on the plane of cultural norms. The anthropological interest of this exercise lies in investigating how Muslim rulers utilized the principles of both descent and alliance for ordering their politico-economic concerns. The paper is divided into four parts: Part I briefly discusses the ethnographic and political context of the princely state of Malerkotla in the period under study. Part II relates the mobilization of group identities to the organization of the polity, and investigates the practices of inheritance and succession to chiefship. Part III discusses the alliance practices of the chiefs of Malerkotla for the periods preceding and following the consolidation of British rule, while the last section evaluates the vitality of kinship and marriage ties for apprehending the character of the pre-colonial polity.

I. THE JAGIR/RIYASAT OF MALERKOTLA

The former princely state of Malerkotla in East Punjab affords ample opportunity to delve into the relations between kinship and the polity, stretching back as it does to over five centuries of uninterrupted rule of the descendants of the fifteenth century founder—the Afghan, Sheikh Sadruddin. The circumstances that made this continuity possible were either preserved in legend or recorded in print at later junctures. Unpublished chronicles in the possession of the former rulers, while not strictly accurate (since facts are not cross-referenced to their sources), provide rich material for culling the general principles that expressed the political order in north India.

An unpublished manuscript titled 'History of the Malerkotla state' was made available to me by the last Nawab of Malerkotla, Nawab Iftikhar Ali Khan. The manuscript has sixteen chapters describing what are considered to be the significant events in the reign of each chief. The information includes aspects of relations with the imperial rulers, neighbouring princely states and collaterals within the patrilineage. Accounts of ceremonial practices, disputes over succession and inheritance and some details about the marriages contracted by the Malerkotla chiefs are incorporated in this work. The information was checked, to the extent possible, by the information obtained from published documents and, for the later years, with the oral and written evidence of older relatives of the ruling family and the people who had been in their employ.

The sequence of events

The legendary beginnings of the *jagir* of Malerkotla are recounted in the encounter between Sheikh Sadruddin, a Sufi sage (*pir*), and Bahlol Lodi who was marching toward Delhi to fight for the emperor's throne. Sadruddin prayed for him and Bahlol Lodi went on to conquer Delhi and the imperial throne. Subsequently, Bahlol Lodi offered Sadruddin the hand of his daughter. While titled a Sheikh because of his piety, Sheikh Sadruddin, like Bahlol Lodi, was an Afghan. As such, the marriage of Sadruddin to the Lodi princess was within the same *kaum* (caste). Sadruddin on his marriage was assigned the revenue of twelve large villages and fifty-six small villages. These villages formed the nucleus for the subsequent *jagir* (estate) and *riyasat* (state) of Malerkotla.

The Lodi Afghans lost out to the Mughals in 1525. The descendants of Sadruddin had to recognize the sovereignty of the latter. Since the Mughals, though proximate on the social scale as immigrant Muslims, were a separate *kaum*, entitlement to the land revenue of this *jagir* could no longer be taken for granted. However, the Afghans continued to be the revenue intermediaries and as Muslims buttressed the interests of the ruling Mughals. The *jagir* of Malerkotla was not resumed as *khalsa* (crown) lands.

Right through the Mughal reign, the Afghans at Malerkotla had to lie low—the construction of forts and any manifestation of military might was frowned upon by the empire. The elevation of the Afghans from *jagirdars* to Nawabs did not take place until the reign of Aurangzeb. During Aurangzeb's rule, Bayzid Khan earned the title of a Nawab by aligning his forces with Aurangzeb when the latter staked his claim to the Mughal throne.

However, in the flux that followed Aurangzeb's death, the chiefs of Malerkotla had to work out an alternative to the Mughal support. Subsequently, a second opportunity for using the Afghan connection presented itself to the chiefs of Malerkotla in the person of Ahmad Shah Abdali, who succeeded Nadir Shah as the ruler of Afghanistan. Abdali's might was solicited in resisting Sikh incursions into Punjab. When the imperial grip of the Mughals had loosened, the chiefs at Malerkotla claimed a *riyasat* status, including the right to coinage. Although the *riyasat* of Malerkotla was later independent of the

TABLE 1: CHARACTERISTICS OF JAGIRS AND RIYASATS

Jagir	Riyasat
1. The holders of *jagirs* were entitled to the revenue or to a fraction of it by virtue of an accord with the imperial centre.	1. The *riyasat's* rights to revenue were absolute and independent of a relation with the imperial state.
2. The chief of the *jagirdars* was the senior spokesman on behalf of the patrilineage vis-à-vis imperial rulers.	2. The chief of the *riyasat* as a ruler could exercise fiscal, criminal and civil powers over the lands of his brothers.
3. A *jagir* was viewed as equal, partible inheritance between sons.	3. A *riyasat* stressed the rule of primogeniture and demarcated a much larger share of the land for the eldest son.
4. *Jagirdars* could not strike coins in their own name.	4. The rulers of a *riyasat* had the right to coinage.
5. *Jagirdars* offered *nazars* (tribute) to the imperial rulers.	5. The ruler of a *riyasat*, ideally, did not offer *nazar* to another ruler.
6. *Jagirdars* did not assume honorific titles without the consent of the emperor.	6. As the ruler of a *riyasat*, a fancy title was quite in order.

Mughals it was still contingent on the support of the Afghan, Ahmad Shah Abdali.

In 1810, the British Government prevented the Sikh ruler, Ranjit Singh, from extending his sway over Malerkotla and the latter was declared to be a British protectorate. A period of relative political stability for the *riyasat* of Malerkotla followed.

The political order

A brief portrayal of the state of Malerkotla in terms of the inhabitants' categories is presented here. It affords a representation of the polity as lived, as against a representation of the polity as theorized.

The categories *jagir*, *riyasat* and *Delhi ki Darbar* (the court at Delhi) were employed by the inhabitants at Malerkotla to describe their political context. The holders of *jagirs*—the *jagirdars*—were entitled to the land revenue or to a fraction of it by virtue of an accord with the imperial rulers. As such *jagirs* contrasted with *khalsa* (crown) lands that were administered directly by the imperial rulers through their own appointees who were responsible for collecting the revenue as well.

Secondly, a *jagir* contrasted with a *riyasat* or territory over which the chief and his patrilineage had a sovereign and absolute right to revenue. The *jagir* and *riyasat,* together, were distinguished from the territory governed by the Badshah or Maharaja (i.e., a greater king) whose empire was denoted in popular parlance as the *Delhi ki Darbar.* This classification is sought to be captured in English usages that translate *riyasat* as a little kingdom or a princely state and portray the Mughal Badshahs, for instance, as emperors. However, while a *jagir* was akin to an estate, it was infrequently characterized as such, perhaps because of the latter's association with feudalism as it developed in Western Europe. The characteristics of the two ideal types of *jagir* and *riyasat* as they emerge from a perusal of the chronicles at Malerkotla are delineated in Table 1.

The *jagir/ riyasat* of Malerkotla was based upon the appropriation of a part of the agricultural surplus by members of the ruling patrilineage, primarily in the form of a share of the harvest. Struggles over the apportionment of this land revenue between the intermediate ruling class and the imperial rulers directed the division into *khalsa* areas, *jagirs* and *riyasats.* The power of the imperial state to claim a sizeable surplus in the form of revenue or the lack of it emerged as the determining force in the transformation from *jagirs* to *riyasats* or *khalsa* areas. The kinship and alliance practices of intermediate chiefs invited exploration as both expressions of rule and as stratagems that sought to deal with particular historical conjunctures.

II. KINSHIP OF THE RULING AFGHANS

Identity formation

In the context of the ruling Afghans, the study of kin terms and categories has to look beyond the terminological system to the role that the cultural definition of persons and groups has entailed in the reproduction of that society. The reproduction of the ruling class can be viewed as a 'political endeavour' (Meillassoux 1978: 63). The relation of the person to the group is, simultaneously, that of the definer and the defined (cf. Bourdieu 1977: 38). Often, the group identities activated by the chiefs at Malerkotla were aimed at ensuring the furtherance of their political interests, both within the patrilineage and in relation to the imperial context of power and authority.

The categories for a collectivity, *khandaan, got, kaum, biradiri, jaat,* are taken as the civilizational givens here. Their specificity, however, derives from a particular context, as differences in their usage even within Punjab itself bear out (cf. Ibbetson 1883). The rulers of the *jagir/riyasat* of Malerkotla variously defined their identity as (*i*) Muslim; (*ii*) Afghan (*jaat/kaum*); (*iii*) members of a single clan (*got*), i.e., as Sherwani; (*iv*) as members of a single patrilineage (*biradiri*), i.e., the descendants of the founder of the *jagir*, Sheikh Sadruddin; and (*v*) as members of a sub-lineage (*khandaan*).

Religious affiliation: As Muslims, the chiefs of Malerkotla shared their faith with the imperial Mughal conquerors. While Hindu Rajputs sought to establish their fortunes in the inaccessible terrains (removed from the empire's fertile central plains), the Muslim *jagirdars* of Malerkotla were not displaced from their territory with the onset of Mughal rule. The relations forged between Malerkotla's ruling patrilineage and the imperial Mughal power were cemented by their mutual identification as Muslims of immigrant origin.

Jaat/kaum-Afghan: If the advent of Muslim rule left its mark upon Hindu society the Muslim chiefs of immigrant origin, too, had to come to terms with a pre-existing social order. The classifications of Muslims based on their places of origin and kinship with the line of the Prophet (for example, the Sayyids) were probably strengthened by the encounter with Hindu society. These identities were described as *jaats* in common parlance and as *kaums* by the Muslims literati at Malerkotla. The Sayyids, especially, were regarded as *khalis* (pure) and showed a preference for marriage within the *khandaan* as became the descendants of the Prophet.

The rulers of Malerkotla were known as Afghans, or colloquially, Pathans, because their ancestors had hailed from Afghanistan. Territory of origin had distinguished the Afghans from other Muslims of 'foreign' origin such as the Mughals, Iranis, Turanis and Arabs. As elsewhere in India, the descendants of Muslim immigrants had been accorded a higher status than the more recent converts to Islam (cf. Imtiaz Ahmad 1973). The 'Afghan' identity, moreover, had enabled the mobilization of ties with the imperial Lodi Afghans and other Afghans living outside Malerkotla.

Got-Sherwani: The *jagirdars* of Malerkotla were known as Afghan Sherwanis ever since the *jagir* came into being. The appellation 'Sherwani' was explained by reference to two factors—immigrant origin, and a relation with a well-known ruling dynasty.

On the one hand, it was believed that the place of origin underlay the name 'Sherwani', the term being derived from the town of Sherwan in north Persia where Sheikh Sadruddin's forefathers had lived before migrating to Afghanistan (M.I. Hussain 1922). On the other hand, it was reported that Sheikh Hussain had three sons—Ghilzi, Lodi and Sherwani. While the former two had founded the Ghilzi and Lodi dynasties (Government of Punjab 1904), the descendants of the third were known as Sherwanis.

Over time the two elements of the Afghan—Sherwani identity came to be conceptualized through the indigenous terms, *jaat* and *got.* The former term referred to Afghan, the more inclusive category, and the latter to Sherwani, the less inclusive category. This manner of referring to them was not limited to non-Afghan Sherwani inhabitants but was employed by the Afghans to designate their own identity. Yusufzai, Lodi and Lohani were perceived as other Afghan *gots.* The latter *gots* were remembered as the original divisions of the Afghans and employed for denoting their descendants in India.

A *got,* thus, did not correspond to the Brahminical *gotra* that included several clans affiliated to a *rishi.* It described an identity that assumed descent from a common male ancestor among the Afghan Sherwanis, in consonance with the practice of the other East Punjab inhabitants (cf. Hershman 1981).

Members of different *gots* came together to form a *biradiri* (literally, a brotherhood) that was often the endogamous unit in this region. The Afghan Sherwanis, however, confined its usage to agnates alone. Members of the *biradiri* were expected to join hands with the chief against outside aggressors, even if they had otherwise fought over the apportionment of the *jagir.* The latter claims could have been exercised only if there was an Afghan Sherwani *jagir/ riyasat* in the first place.

Khandaan: The *khandaans* constituting the patrilineage of Afghan Sherwanis either traced descent from a common chief or backtracked on a sliding generational scale that varied with the issue—to draw attention to social distance or to telescope it; to distinguish the rights in land of collaterals or to focus on common descent. *Khandaans* competed with each other for the chiefship and in the apportionment of rights to the produce of the land.

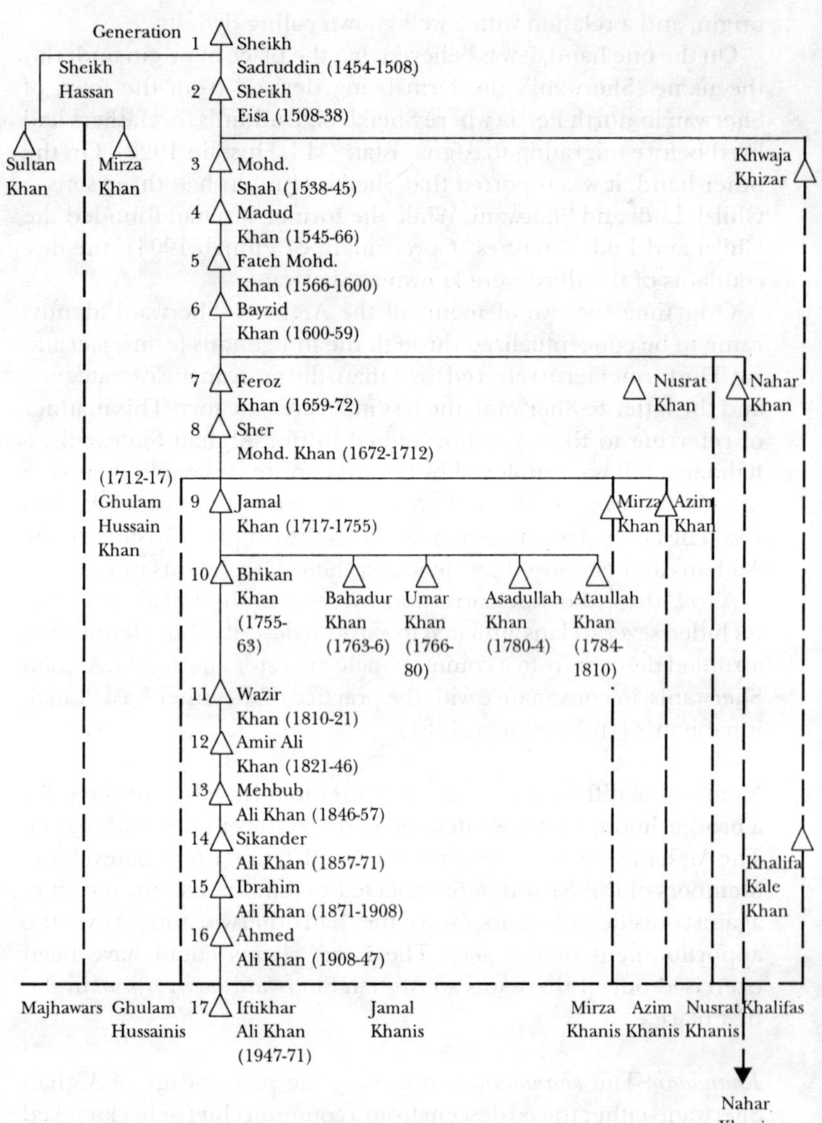

Note: Years of rule are indicated in brackets.

Sources:
(i) Unpublished 'History of the Malerkotla state'.
(ii) M.I. Hussain (1922).
(iii) *Gazetteer of the Malerkotla state* (1904)

FIGURE 1: AFGHAN SHERWANIS: *KHANDAANS* AND PATRILINEAGE

Proximity to the Nawab's *khandaan* (the Jamal Khanis—Figure 1) was a determinant of status within the patrilineage. Marriages contracted with the chiefs' daughters, especially, were considered to have been prestigious by the collaterals belonging to other *khandaans*. This was true even though the status of the chief within the Jamal Khanis was *primus inter pares*. The first Settlement Officer of Malerkotla, F.A. Robertson, was struck by the fact that the other Jamal Khanis claimed 'all the powers of the chief of the family . . .' (Robertson 1889: 1). The sharing of authority with agnates within the *khandaan* had facilitated their military support since their stakes in the continuance of the *jagir/riyasat*, then, were nearly as high as the ruler's.

The universe of linguistic categories was shared by Malerkotla's inhabitants. The use of the categories for expressing identities, however, varied as a consequence of the divergent situations that had to be represented. The formation of ancestor-focused groups was characteristic of members of the ruling patrilineage. *Khandaans* among the Afghan Sherwanis were objectified, named units—Ghulam Hussaini, Azim Khani, etc. By contrast, members of artisan and service castes when asked about their *khandaans* simply said: 'We are the grandsons of X.' The *khandaan*, which signified both status and property here, was a category that they rarely used to designate their own identity.

Who belonged to the *biradiri* for the rulers was a matter of excluding agnates who traced their descent from a remote ancestor while the latter, in turn, persisted in treasuring the fact of common descent. The Afghan Sherwanis had stressed what Alavi represents as the 'vertical axis' of the *biradiri*—that is, the principle of descent (Alavi 1972: 2). The restricted usage of the term *biradiri* was observable among Rajput chiefs as well and it emphasized exclusiveness. Among non-Afghan inhabitants at Malerkotla the horizontal dimension of the *biradiri* was stressed. Here the *biradiri* included agnatic, uterine and affinal kin and often denoted the endogamous group (Alavi 1972; Eglar 1960).

The coalescing of persons along specific identities and the differential use of categories was contingent upon the functions conferred on them. The importance of the categories lay in their capacity to generate groups on the basis of underlying beliefs. The pattern of division into *khandaans* and inheritance as it had obtained within the *biradiri* of Afghan Sherwanis over fifteen generations is presented next.

DIVISION AND INHERITANCE

In terms of ideal-typical features, a *jagir* can be conceived as partible inheritance between sons while a *riyasat* has the formal characteristic of impartibility. The dialectics between the claims of brothers as co-heirs and the chief's appropriation of a larger share of the land made for considerable warring and indeterminacy in the eventual apportionment of chiefs and their brothers (cf. Trautmann 1981: 431).

Generations 1 to 3 (*1454-1545*). The first division within the Afghan Sherwanis of Malerkotla arose in Generation 2 (Figure 1). Sheikh Hassan, the eldest son of the founder, was disinherited because he had not been a party to the rescue mission that freed his widowed sister from the clutches of her in-laws. He was stripped of his right since he had 'failed in this moral duty' (unpublished 'History of the Malerkotla state'). A second version of the story contended that Sheikh Hassan was not worldly-wise and so his *jagir* was easily appropriated by his younger brother, Sheikh Eisa.

Sheikh Hassan's descendants, subsequently, became the *majhawars* (guardians) of Sheikh Sadruddin's tomb. To this day, the Majhawars have a share in the offerings that are made at the founder's shrine. However, the later Nawabs of Malerkotla and their collaterals denied that the Majhawars belonged to the *biradiri* and suggested that they were the descendants of the founder's retainers.

Sheikh Hassan's sons, Sultan Khan and Mirza Khan, attempted to avenge the disinheritance of their father by embarrassing the chief, Khan Mohd. Shah (Generation 3). They assassinated the Mughal officer deputed to look after the affairs of Malerkotla. The *jagir* was subsequently resumed by the Mughals and Khan Mohd. Shah was able to have it restored only through a timely offer of *nazar* (gifts; tribute to a political superior) that was made possible by the assistance of his maternal grandfather. Since Sultan Khan and Mirza Khan had not contributed to the retrieval of the *jagir*, they lost all subsequent claims to its lands.

Generations 4 to 6 (*1545-1659*). Madud Khan (Generation 4) granted one-third of the *jagir's* lands to his brothers. This generosity is bemoaned in the *riyasat's* historical accounts since his brothers also sought to be recognized as chiefs of their *jagirs* by appealing to the Governor of Sirhind, although their endeavours were of no avail.

About Generation 5 it is reported that Fateh Mohd. had not bequeathed his brother a co-heir's share. We are told that the latter's son killed the following Nawab's Bahlil Khan, in a dispute over property (Generation 6).

Generations 7 to 9 (1659-1755). Nawab Feroz Khan (Generation 7) had granted the right over a few villages to his brother 'as a gesture of brotherly affection and goodwill' (unpublished, 'History of the Malerkotla state'). The imperial revenues accruing on their lands, however, had been routed through the Nawab. Their descendants still inhabit Malerkotla and are known as the Nahar Khanis and Nusrat Khanis. Nawab Sher Mohd's brother, Khizar Khan (Generation 8), died heirless on the battlefield.

Nawab Ghulam Hussain Khan (Generation 9) was made to surrender the *gaddi* (chiefship) by his younger brother—Jamal Khan. The former Nawab retired from worldly affairs and subsequently lived on the revenue of five villages. His abdication and Nawab Jamal Khan's flouting of primogeniture was, once again, legitimized in the language of kinship. Nawab Ghulam Hussain Khan had sullied the honour (*izzat*) of the Afghan Sherwanis by giving his daughter in marriage and as tribute to the chief of the warring army when faced with a siege of the *riyasat.* His descendants are still known as the Ghulam Hussainis.

The next Nawab, Jamal Khan, had sought acceptance of his rule on the grounds that his brother had been unable to safeguard the honour of the *biradiri* even though he had preserved the state.

Generations 10 to 13 (1755-1857). The co-sharing of the *riyasat* subsequently vested in the five sons of Jamal Khan. Jamal Khan's younger brothers, Azim Khan and Mirza Khan, however, had been allowed to retain their *jagirs* but the right to the Malerkotla *gaddi* was henceforth confined to the descendants Jamal Khan who came to be known as the Jamal Khanis and Khawanin (senior *jagirdars*).

The Nawab was still only the first among equals (i.e. the Jamal Khanis) and though he succeeded to the title of the chief, the other prerogatives of rulers were shared with his collaterals. The principle of co-sharing was described thus:

> The collaterals have by the existing rule been co-sharers of the State with the Nawab and if a Nawab or collateral died heirless his share (in the case of the Nawab his private share) is divided among the co-sharers according to their shares. (Lall 1892-37)

Generations 14 to 15 (*1857-1908*). Nawab Sikander Ali Khan (Generation 14) had no children and his lands were divided on the above basis between the descendants of Jamal Khan. The *riyasat* was not resumed by the British, however, and the ruler was allowed to adopt Ibrahim Ali Khan and Inayat Ali Khan who were also Jamal Khanis. Later, the British authorities also declared that heirless lands would escheat to the ruler alone. The Khawanin appealed against the encroachment of their traditional rights in 1896 but their case was rejected by the British Government. The verdict of 1899 reduced the Khawanin to being 'mere jagirdars under the suzerainty of the Nawab' (Government of Punjab 1904: 7).

Evidently, the disposal of rights in land within the ruling *khandaan* at Malerkotla ran along a continuum from being regarded as partible and equal inheritance between the chief's brothers, at one extreme to its exclusive, unitary claim by the chief alone, at the other. The study of inheritance practices brought out the play of strategic contest rather than of adherence to an absolute principle (cf. Goody 1966), and often led to the bloodshed of collaterals.

The internal constitution of the ruling patrilineage revealed a pattern of division, occasioned by crises, rather than a precise mapping of genealogical segmentation. Rights to the inheritance of land revenue were set aside if the obligations of honour were sullied or if the collaterals had not contributed to the regaining of lost rights.

Daughters of chiefs were apportioned with land grants upon marriage by their fathers that were determined customarily rather than with reference to Islamic injunctions. The Afghan Sherwanis had practised the customary exclusion of women from the inheritance of patrimony.

Primogenitural and fraternal succession to chiefship

The Quran does not prescribe rules for succession to chiefship. The pattern of succession to the chiefship as it obtained in the Malerkotla state is outlined below.

The rule of primogeniture had not operated in a mechanical fashion. It was first suspended in Generation 2 (Figure 2), i.e. before the Mughals had consolidated their hold over Delhi (Table 2). Thereafter, succession by primogeniture obtained without a break from Generations 3 to 9, the period marked by a mighty Mughal centre. Through the first two centuries of Mughal rule, internecine struggles within the patrilineage at Malerkotla had been effectively controlled by the Chakladars (Governors) of Sirhind who were appointees of the Mughals. The imperial interest rested in the ordered collection of revenue from this *jagir.*

The disarray that spread in the Mughal empire after Aurangzeb's death precipitated fraternal succession to the *gaddi* of Malerkotla. Nawab Ghulam Hussain was overthrown by his younger brother, Jamal Khan. The latter proved to be an extraordinary military leader and could prevent his younger brothers from succeeding to the *gaddi.* After his death, however, fraternal succession had, again, asserted itself and the *riyasat* was ruled, in turn, by his five sons.

Succession by primogeniture was restored when the imperial state established under the British sought to protect the interests of the rulers of the native states. This occurred in the context of their own larger interests of rule over the subcontinent after the 'Mutiny' of 1857.

Fraternal succession to the *gaddi* tended to happen when the imperial power waned and Malerkotla veered towards being a *riyasat* (state). At such junctures *jagirdars* who considered the chief to be the first among equals aspired to the rulership of the *riyasat* on the same basis. Whenever primogenitural succession was overruled, it was legitimized in terms that were acceptable to the populace, such as an affront to the honour of past rulers. However, the dominant presence of an imperial power seemed to swing the balance in favour of the rule of primogeniture at Malerkotla. It is likely that the imperial interests had coincided with those of the Malerkotla chiefs.

The evidence marshalled here suggests the inadequacy of understanding succession to chiefship by recourse to Quranic law or the rules of kinship without considering the political context of the period. Goody (1966) recognizes the constraints of comparing systems of succession without considering the political situation but settles 'at a more limited level' (ibid.: 47).

Both fraternal succession and succession by the eldest son were, in fact, prevalent among Muslim rulers in India. Akbar remarks that in Mughal India 'the fittest rather than the eldest son usually succeeded to his father's throne' (Akbar 1948: 138). The tension between primogenitural and fraternal succession to chiefship appeared to be characteristic of a political order that was based on hereditary rule.

The strain arose because, from one point of view, brothers regarded

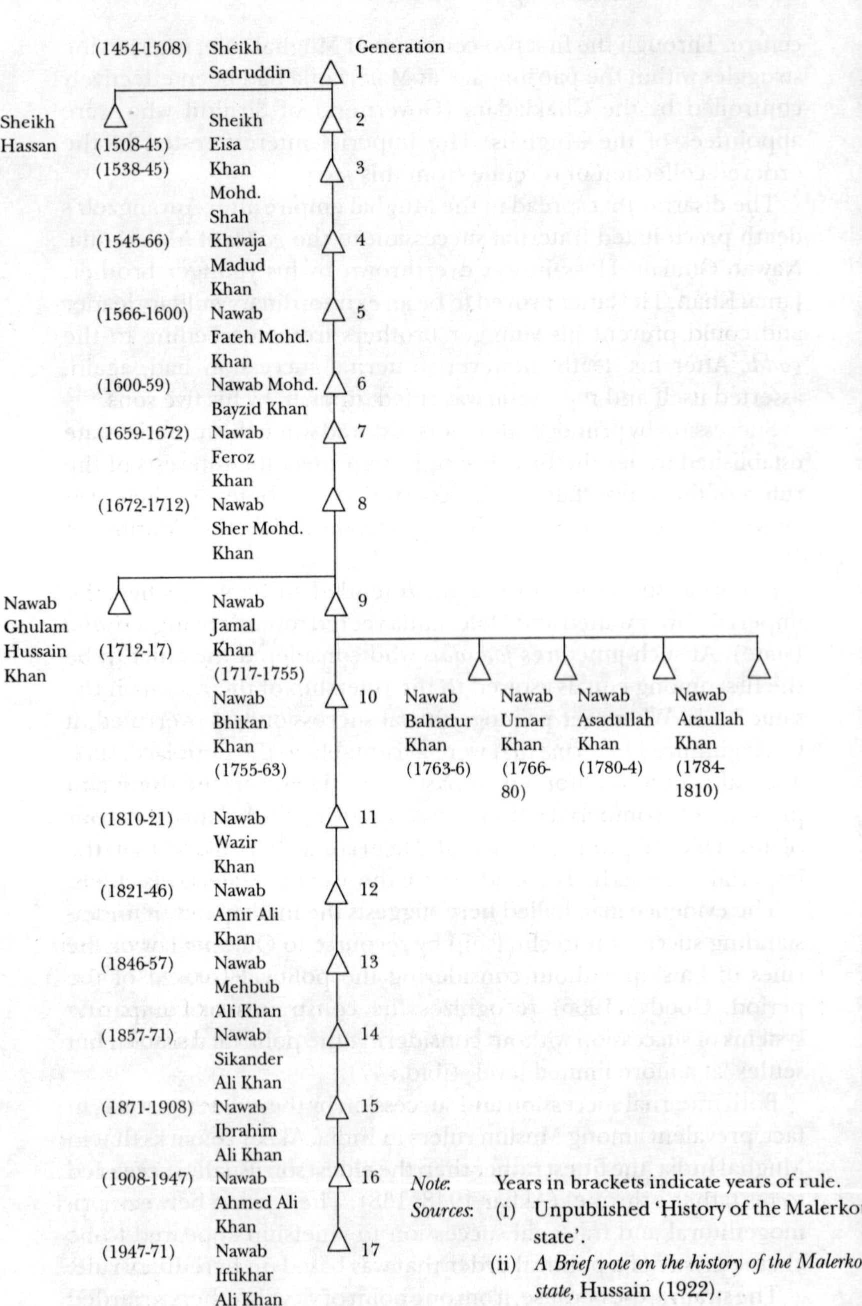
Generation
(1454-1508) Sheikh Sadruddin 1
Sheikh Hassan
Sheikh Eisa (1508-45) 2
(1538-45) Khan Mohd. Shah 3
(1545-66) Khwaja Madud Khan 4
(1566-1600) Nawab Fateh Mohd. Khan 5
(1600-59) Nawab Mohd. Bayzid Khan 6
(1659-1672) Nawab Feroz Khan 7
(1672-1712) Nawab Sher Mohd. Khan 8
Nawab Ghulam Hussain Khan (1712-17)
Nawab Jamal Khan (1717-1755) 9
Nawab Bhikan Khan (1755-63) 10
Nawab Bahadur Khan (1763-6)
Nawab Umar Khan (1766-80)
Nawab Asadullah Khan (1780-4)
Nawab Ataullah Khan (1784-1810)
(1810-21) Nawab Wazir Khan 11
(1821-46) Nawab Amir Ali Khan 12
(1846-57) Nawab Mehbub Ali Khan 13
(1857-71) Nawab Sikander Ali Khan 14
(1871-1908) Nawab Ibrahim Ali Khan 15
(1908-1947) Nawab Ahmed Ali Khan 16
(1947-71) Nawab Iftikhar Ali Khan 17
Note: Years in brackets indicate years of rule.
Sources: (i) Unpublished 'History of the Malerkotla state'.
(ii) A Brief note on the history of the Malerkotla state, Hussain (1922).

FIGURE 2: SUCCESSION TO CHIEFSHIP AT MALERKOTLA

TABLE 2: CHIEFS AT MALERKOTLA AND CORRESPONDING EMPERORS/ GOVERNMENTS AT DELHI (1454-1971)

Chief of Ruling Lineage at Malerkotla	Year of Rule	Corresponding Ruler at Imperial Centre	Years of Rule
1. Sheikh Sadruddin	1454-1508	Bahlol Lodi	1451-89
		Sikander Lodi	1489-1517
2. Sheikh Eisa	1508-38	Sikander Lodi	1489-1517
		Ibrahim Lodi	1517-26
		Babur	1526-30
		Humayun	1530-39
3. Khan Mohd. Shah	1538-45	Humayun	1530-39
		Sher Shah	1539-45
4. Khwaja Madud Khan	1545-66	Salim Shah	1545-55
		Humayun	1555-56
		Akbar	1556-1605
5. Fateh Mohd. Khan	1566-1600	Akbar	1556-1605
6. Nawab Mohd. Bayzid Khan	1600-59	Akbar	1556-1605
		Akbar	1556-1605
		Jahangir	1605-27
		Shahjahan	1627-57
		Aurangzeb	1658-1707
7. Nawab Feroz Khan	1659-72	Aurangzeb	1658-1707
8. Nawab Sher Mohd. Khan	1672-1712	Bahadur Shah	1707-12
9. Nawab Ghulam Hussain Khan	1712-17	Jalandar Shah	1712-13
		Farrukh Siyar	1713-19
10. Nawab Jamal Khan	1717-55	Farrukh Siyar	1713-19
		Muhammad Shah	1719-48
		Alamgir II	1754-59
11. Nawab Bhikan Khan	1755-63	Alamgir II	1754-59
12. Nawab Bahadur Khan	1763-66	Shah Alam II	1762-1806
13. Nawab Umar Khan	1766-80	Shah Alam II	1762-1806
14. Nawab Asadullah Khan	1780-84	Shah Alam II	1762-1806
15. Nawab Ataullah Khan	1784-1810	Shah Alam II	1762-1806
		British Govt.[1]	
16. Nawab Wazir Khan	1810-21	British Govt.	1810-21
17. Nawab Amir Ali Khan	1821-46	British Govt.	1821-46
18. Nawab Mehbub Ali Khan	1846-57	British Govt.	1846-57
19. Nawab Sikander Ali Khan	1857-71	British Govt.	1857-71
20. Nawab Ibrahim Ali Khan	1871-1908	British Govt.	1871-1908
21. Nawab Ahmed Ali Khan	1908-47	British Govt.	1908-47
22. Nawab Iftikhar Ali Khan	1947-71[2]	Govt. of India[3]	1947-71

Notes: [1]In 1809, Malerkotla became a British 'protectorate'.

[2]In 1947, the year of India's Independence, the state of Malerkotla merged with the Union of India.

[3]The privy purses and titles of the former rulers of princely states were revoked in 1971.

Source: Majumdar et al. (1983); the unpublished 'History of the Malerkotla state'.

themselves as equals (Goody 1966; Trautmann 1981: 431); from the other, the eldest son was the chief. But given the political compulsions, he could only be the first among equals. The play between fraternal and primogenitural succession and the partibility or impartibility of the *jagir/riyasat* can be regarded as 'effects produced by the political structure' (Terray 1977: 299).

Kinship of the ruling patrilineages

The pattern of internal differentiation, division, inheritance and succession to chiefship within the patrilineage of Afghan Sherwanis at Malerkotla paralleled the pattern of the princely Rajput lineages in north India. The correspondence of lineage dynamics in relation to the political functions allows for a comparison of the kinship of Afghan and Rajput chiefs. The comparison with Sikh ruling lineages in Punjab is eschewed on account of their relatively shallow depth.

Legends and genealogies, sometimes fictive, connected the history of the ruling patrilineage with mighty heroes and conquerors in both Rajput and Afghan states and were aimed at legitimizing their rule (Jain 1975; Thapar 1984). Rajput patrilineages, too, had reckoned descent from the founder of a *jagir/ riyasat*. The fragmentation into *khandaans* was often occasioned by disputes arising from the division of the *jagir* between brothers (ibid.).

Fusion within the patrilineage was rallied on the basis of a common *got*—Sherwani at Malerkotla; Rathore, Sisodia, Kachchawa and others in the Rajput princely states (Tod 1832). Male agnates of the chief formed a minimal lineage at both Malerkotla and in the princely states of Rajputana. The right of succession to the chiefship lay with the minimal lineage as a corporate group. Collaterals, among both Rajputs and Afghans, were co-sharers of the *jagir/ riyasat*, privileged with complete fiscal, criminal and administrative powers over their domains (ibid.). The chiefs were primarily dependent upon them for military troops.

The presumptive right to the *gaddi* and to the *jagir/ riyasat* had to be periodically restricted to a smaller group of eligibles within the lineage. The satisfactory defence of the *jagir/ riyasat* by the chief and his collaterals against an enemy had often led to the disenfranchisement of the descendants of former chiefs in both the Rajput princely states and at Malerkotla (Tod 1832).

The conflict between the equal division of the *jagir/ riyasat* among the sons of chiefs and the tendency towards impartibility of the realm characterized the history of Rajput princely states as well. Lyall remarks that there was 'a constant struggle between the ordinary rule of Hindu succession to property which divides off the land among the sons at each succession and the rule of political expediency which inclines towards primogeniture' (Lyall 1884: 217).

The rule of primogeniture was often set aside in Rajput kingdoms as well. Affronts to the honour of the ruling patrilineage or defeat in a battle had sometimes concluded in the divestiture of the chief and his descendants in favour of the younger brother. The practice of Rajput patrilineages, too, had precluded an understanding of succession to the *gaddi* in terms of an inviolable 'jural or ideological principle'. (Fox 1971: 81)

Pre-colonial ruling lineages in the colonial period

The British rulers, exceptionally, viewed north Indian polities as autonomous states even though the autonomy of *jagirs* and *riyasats* in north India seemed to be the consequence of a flagging imperial Mughal power. It was apparent that the native states had to be protected in the interests of British rule over the subcontinent. Apart from providing military contingents and reducing administrative costs for the British rulers, the chiefs of princely states were hailed as 'natural leaders' of India after the 'Mutiny' of 1857. These chiefs were useful allies in imparting legitimacy to the alien conquerors (Ramusack 1975).

British protection for the state of Malerkotla in 1810 had gradually altered the basis of the pre-colonial polity. A princely state, it was decreed, should have a single ruler in the interests of satisfactory government. The chief's status as *primus inter pares* was viewed as a 'pernicious custom' (Government of Punjab 1904) that led to the diminution of the ruler's lands and dismissed as not conducive to the efficient functioning of the princely state.

Collaterals, who had been co-sharers of the state, were transformed into *jagirdars* under the Nawab without absolute powers even in their own *jagirs*, marking a departure from the former practice. Heirless holdings which earlier had lapsed to the chief and his male agnates, in the proportion of their shares in the total *jagir*, later escheated to the Nawab alone as the representative of the princedom.

Since the military support of collaterals was not instrumental in perpetuating the chiefship at Malerkotla under the British empire, the Nawab too was emboldened to curtail their powers. The Khawanin (senior *jagirdars*) had remonstrated against the encroachment of their privileges. A similar trend, in fact, was discernible in Rajput princely states. Senior *jagirdars* of Marwar and Bundelkhand, too, had contended that the princely state was their patrimony as much as the chief's (Jain 1975; Tod 1832). Collaterals of both the Alwar and the Malerkotla rulers had registered their protest against the new order of things by refraining from the presentation of *nazars* (tribute) at their investitures (Haynes 1978).

The collapse of the Mughal power had exacerbated conflicts over succession to chiefship in Malerkotla, as in the Rajput princely states. British supremacy tended to reinforce the rule of primogeniture but the *riyasats* were not transformed simultaneously into *jagirs* characterized by partible inheritance, in contradistinction to the tendency under Mughal rule. The ruling patrilineage was dominated by the chief, who later assumed a singular importance.

The political integration in north India during the Mughal period had been nurtured across the ties of descent, caste and religion. The Rajput chiefs had endeavoured to legitimize their alliance with the Mughals by casting them in the role of Kshatriyas (Ziegler 1978). Muslim chiefs, too, had drowned their differences as Iranis, Afghans, etc., and made common cause with the Mughals. Compromises that the chiefs of Rajputs and Afghans had made in the pursuit of power under the Mughals were rendered redundant with the British rulers.

The colonial rulers did not wage a religious war. An imperial state, overtly indifferent to community and religion in promoting its interests, had created the conditions for fostering the distinctiveness of cultural identities that had formerly been tempered by their struggles to retain political control. Ahmad (1991) has argued that cultural assimilation under the British empire ceased to provide 'avenues for mobility' to the former Muslim chiefs, although formerly tendencies of both distinctiveness and fusion were discernible.

The changes context of the princely lineages of Muslim and Hindus in north India led to the unmitigated pursuit of the purity of their descent groups. Rajput rulers averred that they would not marry their daughters to Muslim rulers in future (Plunkett 1973). Afghan chiefs increasingly asserted their Afghan identity by not marrying Rajputs. Irani chiefs, too, had redefined their endogamous unit to exclude the Mughals (Fisher 1983). This idiom of pure and impure allowed the expression of distinctive group identities.

III. AFGHAN ALLIANCES

Preamble

In this section, the term 'alliance' does not refer to what has come to be known as 'alliance theory' in kinship studies. The terminological distinction between kin and affines, correlated with parallel- and cross-cousins, and a continuing relationship of alliance that characterizes this conception is not applicable to the Muslim inhabitants in the northern parts of the subcontinent. Yet, a wider notion of alliance, subsuming both alliances in the political and matrimonial realms, felicitously expresses the marriage practices of Afghans in the pre-colonial era. Trautmann (1981: 358) comments on this dual connotation of the term 'alliance' in French usage.

From the perspective of the Afghans at Malerkotla, the hypergamous conception of marriage relationships synchronized easily with differences in power and status that characterized the polity. Even isogamous marriages in the political realm, with ruling lineages of more or less equivalent standing, were read as rendering explicit what Cohen (1969) terms 'the politics of positions'.

The giving of daughters/sisters always expressed an oriented relationship of tribute to a superior (cf. Kolenda 1984). This contrasted, however, with the Kachins among whom wife-receivers ranked lower than wife-givers and bride-wealth flowed in a direction opposite to that of the movement of women (Leach 1954).

It is possible to approach the subject of Afghan marriage by locating it in the context of Muslim kinship or Afghan kinship and then seeing how far the practice of rulers deviated from the practices of other Afghan *jagirdars*. In this connection, we may note that the marriage of cousins is not prohibited under Islam. Since who should be married is not prescribed either, the expression of cultural preferences is allowed full play.

But the Afghans also share a civilizational conception of marriage that cuts across religious divides. The direct exchange of son-daughter sets in marriage within the *khandaan* or outside was disallowed at Malerkotla in consonance with the practice of distinguishing wife-takers from wife-givers among both the Muslim and Hindu elites. However, instances of direct exchanges of women in marriage among Muslim groups in Afghanistan (Uberoi 1976) and Kabylia (Bourdieu 1977) are known. Or again, daughters were not given in marriage to *jaats/kaums* that were ranked lower in the social hierarchy.

Marriages among the Afghans were practised within the *khandaan*, within the *biradiri*, and with other Afghans, as well as with Rajputs outside Malerkotla. Although the marriages of cousins occurred, this had not featured as the predominant practice of the rulers and *jagirdars* at Malerkotla in the pre-colonial period.

The ruler's *khandaan*, as a corporate ruling entity, could conceive of affinity and alliance too, in corporate terms as the relationship of a group of wife-givers to a distinct group of wife-receivers who were non-residents. Agnatic ties were thus strengthened. Alternatively, the chiefs reached out to new affines. Marriage with the father's brother's daughter (FBD), especially, did not allow for the generation of extra-territorial alliances that were critical for the perpetuation of rule, but worked, at best, as a secondary strategy for both the rulers and the *jagirdars*.

Lastly, while it is possible to recapitulate information on the marriages of Afghan chiefs and their collaterals (the latter through incidental evidence), the comparison with lesser *jagirdars* at Malerkotla cannot be controlled for periods corresponding to those for which data can be obtained for the chiefs. However, I found it useful to compare and contrast the marriage practices of Afghan chiefs with their own past, rather than through the singular frame of a caste, linguistic group or religion.

While *jagirdari* rights had been patrilineally transmitted, the principles of affinity and matrifiliation were often employed by the Afghan chiefs to safeguard their interests in the *jagir/ riyasat.* Marriages contracted by the chiefs of the Afghan Sherwani patrilineage at Malerkotla were recorded by the chroniclers as a part of their narrative. The information pertaining to the years 1755-1846 in the unpublished 'History of the Malerkotla state' is scanty; but, surprisingly, the period 1454 to 1754 has a wealth of information about the wives of former chiefs.

The marriages of the chiefs have been divided into the pre-1858 and the post-1858 periods here. The period from the 1820s to the 1850s was marked by the assertion of colonial rule in Punjab, as in the rest of north India but the British Government refrained from annexing princely states in India after the revolt of 1857. The chiefs of princely states were later viewed as allies by the British imperial power. Under the changed circumstances, the former politico-marital alliances contracted by the Malerkotla chiefs were no longer vital for sustaining the *riyasat.* The period following 1857 marked a turning-point in the marriages of the Malerkotla chiefs to the daughters of Rajput *jagirdars*.

The marriage record from 1850 onwards indicates that in the later period a girl from the *khandaan* became the preferred spouse for the rulers of Malerkotla. This time-span can be taken as marking the heightened importance of the purity of the chiefs' *khandaan* on the one hand, and of asserting their identity as Afghans and Muslims on the other. Other writers on Punjab, too, draw attention to a greater communal awareness following the collapse of Mughal rule and subsequent domination by the British (S.N. Ahmad 1991; Metcalfe 1982; Talbott 1988).

Afghan alliances: pre-1858

Importance of affinal/maternal relatives. Accounts of the *riyasat's* history refer in a matter-of-fact way to the importance of the support that could be provided by maternal or affinal relatives outside the state. Specific instances are cited here:

(*i*) Khan Mohd. Khan (Generation 3) was enabled to resume his custody over the *jagir* of Malerkotla through the assistance of his maternal grandfather, Lobe Khan at Sonepat. The rights of his collaterals were subsequently disenfranchised.

(*ii*) Nawab Fateh Mohd. Khan (Generation 5) was married to an Afghan girl from a Rupar family whose members had held positions of consequence in the Mughal regime. His son, Nawab Bayzid Khan (Generation 6), had hoped to obtain permission for building a fort and residential houses for the Afghan Sherwanis at Malerkotla from the Emperor Shah Jahan at Delhi by virtue of his maternal connections.

(*iii*) Nawab Asadullah Khan (Generation 10), while considering the daughter of the Rajput chief of Bhattian for his son, had been impressed by the prospect of a political alliance. We are told that he was motivated by the desire to 'enlist the sympathy of a powerful chief against a common danger. The chief was probably himself anxious to establish matrimonial relations with the family of the Nawab as he was also in constant danger of raids by the Sikhs of the Patiala State and he thought that this alliance would help in arresting their depredations in future' (unpublished 'History of the Malerkotla state').

Affinal/maternal location. The records of the Malerkotla state show, secondly, that the chiefs of the Afghan Sherwanis had frequently been married to girls belonging to areas outside its territorial limits (Table 3). Affinal connections were traced to the following locations: Delhi, Sonepat, Bazidpur, Kapurthala, Morinda, Rupar, Bahamanian, Jhal and Bhattian. Apart from Delhi, the places cited were within a distance of 200 kilometres from Malerkotla.

The affines of Malerkotla chiefs had been reckoned as political allies. Marital ties in later generations had often followed those that were established by the early Malerkotla rulers:

(*i*) Sheikh Eisa (Generation 2) was married to a girl from a Rajput family at Kapurthala. And again, Nawab Bayzid Khan (Generation 5) was married to a daughter of the same lineage.

(*ii*) The Afghan Sherwanis were linked to the Rajput *jagirdars* of Jhal by Fateh Mohd. Khan's (Generation 5) marriage, in the first instance. These alliances, the chroniclers aver, were periodically reaffirmed by matrimonial ties with later Afghan chiefs or their collaterals. For instance, Dilawar Ali Khan (Generation 12) had been married to a descendant of the same Rajput *jagirdars* at Jhal.

Affinal and maternal relatives outside the *jagir* buttressed the chief's position vis-à-vis collaterals (Generation 3). On having once married a daughter to the chief at Malerkotla, marriages of other daughters of the wife-giving lineage to the chief's collaterals and descendants sometimes followed (Generations 5 and 12). Relations with members of these lineages (as wife-givers to the Malerkotla wife-receivers) continued over time and bound agnates with the ties of descent and affinity. Patrilocal residence entailed that wives of the Afghan *jagirdars* shifted their residence to Malerkotla upon marriage. In the event of an external attack there was the likelihood that the Afghans and their wives would have been cooped within the precincts of their *jagirs.* The armed support of affinal/maternal relatives who lived outside Malerkotla but within its military reach was considered invaluable during such critical periods (Generation 9) and favoured the nurturing of territorial exogamy.

Marriages with Afghans and Rajputs. Apart from the strategic location of affines, what emerges from the indigenous accounts is that the chiefs had, significantly, married both Afghans and Rajputs in the past. The first wives of three Malerkotla chiefs in the period 1545 to

TABLE 3: AFFINES OF MALERKOTLA CHIEFS (1454-1971)

Name of Chief	Year of Reign	Affinal Location	Kaum/Jaat of Affines
Sheikh Sadruddin	(1454-1508)	(i) Delhi	(i) Afghan
		(ii) Kapurthala	(ii) Rajput
Sheikh Eisa	(1508-38)	(i) Sonepat	(i) Afghan
Khan Mohd. Shah	(1538-45)	(i) Morinda	(i) Rajput
Khwaja Madud Khan	(1545-66)	(i) Bazidpur	(i) Rajput
Fateh Mohd. Khan	(1566-1600)	(i) Rupar	(i) Afghan
		(ii) Jhal	(ii) Rajput
Bayzid Khan	(1600-59)	(i) Bahmanian	(i) Rajput
		(ii) Kapurthala	(ii) Rajput
Feroz Khan	(1659-72)	-	-
Sher Mohd. Khan	(1672-1712)	-	-
Ghulam Hussain Khan	(1712-17)	-	-
Jamal Khan	(1717-55)	(i) -	(i) Afghan
		(ii) -	(ii) Rajput
Bhikan Khan	(1755-63)	-	-
Bahadur Khan	(1763-66)	-	-
Umar Khan	(1766-80)	-	-
Asadullah Khan[1]	(1780-84)	-	-
Ataullah Khan[2]	(1784-1810)	-	-
Wazir Khan	(1810-21)	-	-
Amir Ali Khan	(1821-46)	-	-
Mehbub Ali Khan	(1846-57)	-	(i) -
		-	(ii) Rajput
Sikander Ali Khan	(1857-71)	(i) Malerkotla	(i) Afghan
		(ii) Malerkotla	(ii) Afghan
Ibrahim Ali Khan	(1871-1908)	(i) Malerkotla	(i) Afghan
Ahmed Ali Khan	(1908-47)	(i) Malerkotla	(i) Afghan
		(ii) Tonk	(ii) Afghan
		(iii) Malerkotla	(iii) Afghan
		(iv) Malerkotla	(iv) Afghan
		(v) Malerkotla	(v) Afghan
Iftikhar Ali Khan	(1947-71)	(i) Malerkotla	(i) Afghan
		(ii) Tonk	(ii) Afghan
		(iii) Kurwai	(iii) Afghan
		(iv) Tonk	(iv) Afghan
		(v) Malerkotla	(v) Afghan

Notes: [1] His son was married to a Rajput girl from Bhattian.
[2] His son was married to a Rajput girl from Jhal.

Source: Unpublished 'History of the Malerkotla state'.

1659 were Rajputs (Table 3). As the senior wife, and the one most likely to bear heirs for the chief, the fact of her being a Rajput was not viewed as a disqualification at that time in history. The progeny of such marriages were assimilated as Afghans, underscoring patrilineal rather than bilateral transmission of status within the *jaat/kaum.*

The data sources do not say categorically whether the first wives of Afghan chiefs were Muslim Rajputs or Hindu Rajputs. The fact of their having been Rajput seemed to have been of greater consequence for the chroniclers than their religion. However, it may be inferred that they were Muslim Rajputs on two counts:

First, the Afghan Sherwani *jagirdars* were not powerful enough to have made it attractive or incumbent on Hindu Rajputs to give them their daughters in marriage, as was possible for the Mughals. On the other side it has been observed that Muslim Rajputs had not eschewed all their earlier customs after conversion to Islam (Ibbetson 1883). If hypergamous marriages had persisted as the model for Muslim Rajputs, the chiefs of the Afghan Sherwanis would have been eminently suitable as grooms for their daughters. The Afghans, by virtue of their claims to foreign descent, had acquired higher status within the Muslim of the area.[2] The Afghans Sherwanis at Malerkotla emphatically claimed that they were linked to Rajput *jagirdars* as wife-takers to wife-givers.

Second, cross-checking revealed that Muslim Rajput families were indeed *jagirdars* at Morinda, Kapurthala and Jhal at the time the marriages of the Malerkotla chiefs has been contracted with their daughters. This information was culled from old gazetteers covering these locations. However, not all the Rajput families could be traced back to the bases reported in the Malerkotla narrative since the former Rajput *jagirdars* had been displaced by the Jat Sikhs once Sikh power grew in the Punjab.

Politico-marital alliances. Upon the debris of the Mughal empire, the Afghans and Rajputs had together hoped to build a new power that would have replaced the Mughals. Historians point out that Ahmad Shah Abdali's forays in north India revealed a concerted effort towards Afghan rule in the region. Majumdar, Raychaudhuri and Datta put forth the view that these 'were something more than predatory raids. They indicated the revival of the Afghans outside and within India making a fresh bid for supremacy on the ruins of the Mughal Empire' (Majumdar et al. 1983: 577).

The politico-marital alliances of the Afghans and Rajputs would have assumed greater importance once the Sikhs vowed to decimate all the Muslim *jagirs* and *riyasats* in Punjab, even though Malerkotla had been spared devastation during Nawab Sher Mohd.'s reign (1672-1712).[3] The Afghans and Rajputs were special targets of the Sikhs. Rose found that:

> The fact is that within the pale of Sikhism, Rajputs were at a discount. The equality of all men preached by Guru Govind Singh disgusted the haughty Rajputs and they refused to join the standard. They soon paid the penalty of their pride. The Jats who composed the great mass of the Khalsa rose to absolute power and the Rajput who had despised them was the peculiar object of their hatred. The old settlement reports are full of remarks upon the decadence, if not the virtual disappearance of the Rajput gentry in those districts where the Sikh's sway was absolute. (Rose 1919: I, 12)

While the goodwill created by Guru Govind Singh for the Malerkotla chiefs had lasted for a while, the Sikhs later declared that the Malerkotla Afghans were inciting Ahmad Shah Abdali against them. Once the Mughal power had waned, Nawab Jamal Khan had entered into negotiations with the Afghan Ahmad Shah Abdali who had succeeded Nadir Shah as the ruler of Afghanistan. The Afghan Sherwanis of Malerkotla aligned their forces with Abdali who raided Punjab ten times in the years 1747-67. The Muslim Rajputs of the area surrounding Sirhind, too, had supported Ahmad Shah Abdali and Jamal Khan. The latter's son had fought alongside Abdali in the two holocausts dubbed by the Sikhs as the *wadda ghalughara* (the greater holocaust) of 1762 and the *chotta ghalughara* (the lesser holocaust) of 1748.

However, the Afghan-Rajput combine lost out to the Sikhs in the end. The Sikhs had begun to annex the Malerkotla *riyasat's* villages as well. It is stated that during Nawab Sher Mohd. Khan's rule (1672-1712), Malerkotla's territories had extended over thirteen *parganas* (administrative subdivisions). What was left of it in 1809 was what had initially provided the *jagir's* nucleus—that is, the villages given in dowry to Sheikh Sadruddin and the Lodi princess.

The Afghan-Rajput marital and military alliances at Malerkotla were, therefore, not an oddity. We can reasonably assume that the practice of marrying Rajputs persisted until the takeover by the British even though there is a gap in the data concerning the affines of Malerkotla chiefs for the period 1755-1846. This view is supported by the fact that both Nawab Asadullah Khan's (1780-4) son and

Nawab Ataullah Khan's (1784-1810) grandson, Dilawar Ali Khan, were betrothed to Rajput girls. Moreover, the last recorded instance of the Nawab's marriage to a Rajput girl was in fact that of Nawab Mehbub Ali Khan (1846-57).

We see that in the pre-1858 period the Afghan Sherwani chiefs of Malerkotla were both marrying and allying politically with Muslim Rajputs in Punjab. There is no evidence, however, of Afghan marriages with the daughters of other Muslim *jaats/ kaums*, such as the Mughals, Iranis and Arabs, on the one had, and lower caste converts to Islam, on the other.

Marriage alliances confirmed political alliances in north India, as in the imperial state itself. The Mughals had married the daughters of Turanis and Iranis but there are no reported instances of the Mughals allying matrimonially with any lineage of the Afghans (A. Hussain 1972). The Afghans, although Muslims, were considered to be a distinct *jaat/ kaum* that had historically competed with the Mughals for political supremacy in the subcontinent. Marital alliances with the Mughals, Turanis and Iranis appear to have been closed to the Afghans. The latter, however, had allied with Muslim Rajputs in the furtherance of their political interests.

The Afghans claimed that they had received girls from Muslim Rajputs but had not given them their daughters. The daughters of Afghans had been married, as far as possible, only to other Afghans. While some reports suggest that Sheikh Sadruddin's daughter, Bibi Mangi, was married into a family of Muslim Rajputs at Tohana, the chiefs of Malerkotla disputed the evidence contending that Tohana had been in the control of the Afghans (unpublished 'History of the Malerkotla state').

Strikingly, the conception of wife-givers being inferior to wife-receivers was deployed in the expression of the political hierarchy by chiefs both at Malerkotla and Awadh (Fisher 1983). By contrast with the marriage customs of Muslim, Sikh and Hindu cultivators at Malerkotla, who had frequently engaged in direct or three-way exchanges, the Afghan Sherwanis did not favour the exchange of brother-sister sets in marriage. This pattern was in consonance with the unidirectionality of bride-giving among the Hindu elite. Again, daughters of Afghan chiefs were given a dowry upon marriage, sometimes including rights to the revenue of a tract of land. The *mehr* (a sum of cash or other property pledged to the bride by the groom on the wedding day), in contrast with dowry, had not featured in the accounts of Malerkotla's history.

Since Afghan Sherwani marriages were often repeated unidirectionally, the chiefs and their collaterals/descendants at Malerkotla were related to Afghan and Rajput lineages over generations by an extended affinity. Muslim Rajputs had also gradually allowed the marriage of cousins that was permissible under Islam.

The offspring of Afghan-Rajput marriages at Malerkotla had not generated a new caste. The transmission of descent status here was patrilineal rather than bilateral, within limits imposed and accepted by the Afghans themselves.[4] The Mughal emperors, too, had married Rajput princesses but the children resulting from such marriages had been considered to be Mughals. Again, Plunkett remarks that among Rajput rulers 'there is no evidence of formal differentiation among sons of different mothers according to the mother's status as suggested by Dumont (1970: 114)' (Plunkett 1973: 66). At Malerkotla, the determination of descent had indicated an interplay of the organizing principles of caste and clan.

The implications of matrimonial alliances across *jaats/kaums* is a subject that requires further investigation. This is so, especially, for Punjab where marriages across castes were prevalent till recent times. For instance, Bhatnagar observes that in Punjab both customary law and the formal law courts at the turn of the century had recognized marriages between members of different castes to be 'as good and valid' as within the caste (Bhatnagar 1925: 109). The children of *jaats* of proximate statuses were assimilated to the *jaats* of their fathers.

Afghan alliances: post-1858. Warring in the *riyasat* of Malerkotla ceased only after the British authorities had declared it to be a protectorate in 1810. The political aspect of Afghan alliances with Rajput chiefs had obsolesced with the assured British safekeeping of the *riyasat.*

The treaty with the British had affected the balance of power between the chief and his collaterals (Section II). The transformed power relations with the collaterals had enhanced the importance of the chief's line within the Jamal Khanis. Since the Nawab of Malerkotla was no longer constrained to marry out of Malerkotla in the defence of his interests, he had become a much-coveted groom within the

Nawab Sikander Ali Khan (r. 1857-71)	▲	= ○	(FFFFBSD)
Nawab Ibrahim Ali Khan (r. 1871-1908)	▲	= ○	(FFFFFBSSD)
Nawab Ahmed Ali Khan (r. 1908-47)	▲	= ○	(FBD)
Nawab Iftikhar Ali Khan (r. 1947-71)	▲	= ○	(FBDD)

Note: r: years of reign.

FIGURE 3: THE FIRST WIVES OF FOUR MALERKOTLA NAWABS (1857-1971)

khandaan. We find that the first wives of the chiefs who had followed Nawab Mehbub Ali Khan (1846-57) at Malerkotla were women of the Jamal Khani *khandaan*. This practice was a striking contrast to the earlier marriages contracted by the Afghan Sherwani chiefs.

An account of the marriage within the Jamal Khanis follows, particularly in relation to the line of the Nawab. From Nawab Sikander Ali Khan onwards, the Nawabs of Malerkotla had first married a FBD or the nearest genealogical equivalent to a patrilateral woman even if she belonged to an ascendant generation (Fig. 6).

While details of the machinations behind the first and subsequent marriages of the Nawabs were not accessible in all instances, such data as has been gathered about the marriages of these four Nawabs is presented below:

(*i*) Nawab Sikander Ali Khan (r. 1857-71) was married within the Jamal Khanis to the grand-daughter of Nawab Ataullah Khan (marked 1 in Fig. 4). Her father's brother, Rehmat Ali Khan, was his father's rival for the *gaddi* of Malerkotla when the British authorities had reinstated the rule of primogeniture (Government of Punjab 1904). The fact that Nawab Sikander Ali Khan and the Ataullah Khanis were at loggerheads with each other (while the latter persisted in pushing their claims to rulership) did not preclude Nawab Sikander Ali Khan's first marriage with Ataullah Khan's grand-daughter.

(*ii*) Nawab Sikander Ali Khan's children had died in their infancy. There was a dispute over who should succeed him—the next in order of seniority from the chief's line (i.e., Ghulam Mohd. Khan and his sons-a fraternal succession) or any one of the Jamal Khanis (Fig. 4).

The right of choosing a successor in the absence of natural sons, in accordance with 'Mahomedan law', was granted to the Punjab chiefs by the British authorities in 1860. But what was 'Mahomedan law'? The British authorities had interpreted it to mean that the person closer in degree would be preferred as a successor to the more remote. But how was the choice to be exercised between equidistant possibilities?

Nawab Sikander Ali Khan had preferred to adopt Rehmat Ali's grandsons as successors who, like his first wife, were Ataullah Khanis, rather than one of the sons of Ghulam Mohd. Khan. With the adoption of Ibrahim Ali Khan and Inayat Ali Khan, the *khandaan* of the Ataullah Khanis had merged with the Nawab's *khandaan.* The division within the Jamal Khanis was now between the ruler's *khandaan* and the Bahadur Khanis alone. The *khandaans* of Fateh Khan, Nawab Asadullah Khan, and Nawab Umar Khan had already died out (Fig. 4).

Nawab Ibrahim Ali Khan (r. 1871-1908), the adopted successor to Nawab Sikander Ali Khan, was married to Ghulam Mohd. Khan's daughter, i.e. the nearest patrilateral choice (marked 2 in Fig. 4). The hostility between Nawab Sikander Ali Khan and Ghulam Mohd. Khan over the succession to the Malerkotla *gaddi* and the succession of Ibrahim Ali Khan had not prevented the first marriage of Nawab Ibrahim Ali Khan with Ghulam Mohd. Khan's daughter.

(*iii*) Nawab Ahmed Ali Khan (r. 1908-47) was married to his FBD, i.e. Inayat Ali Khan's daughter (marked 3 in Fig. 4). She was the preferred relative, and especially so since she did not have brothers.

Nawab Ahmed Ali Khan was married for the second time to the daughter of the Afghan Nawab of Tonk. Since she was also FZD to the Nawab of Rampur, the match was considered to have been prestigious. His third marriage was to his MBD, i.e. to Ahsan Ali Khan's daughter who was also a Jamal Khani (marked 3a in Fig. 4). His fourth and fifth marriages were to Afghan Sherwani girls from Malerkotla.

(*iv*) Nawab Iftikhar Ali Khan (r. 1947-71) was first married to his FFBDD (marked 4 in Fig. 4), since his genealogical FBD was an infant at that time. His second marriage was to the Nawab of Tonk's brother's daughter. The Nawab was constrained to marry a girl from his father's side in the first instance, even though he was the son of Nawab Ahmed Ali Khan's second wife who had belonged to the ruling house of Tonk. Nawab Ahmed Ali Khan had not had children by his first wife and FBD.

Nawab Iftikhar Ali Khan's third wife was his FZD, who was also the daughter of the Nawab of Kurwai. His fourth marriage was to his

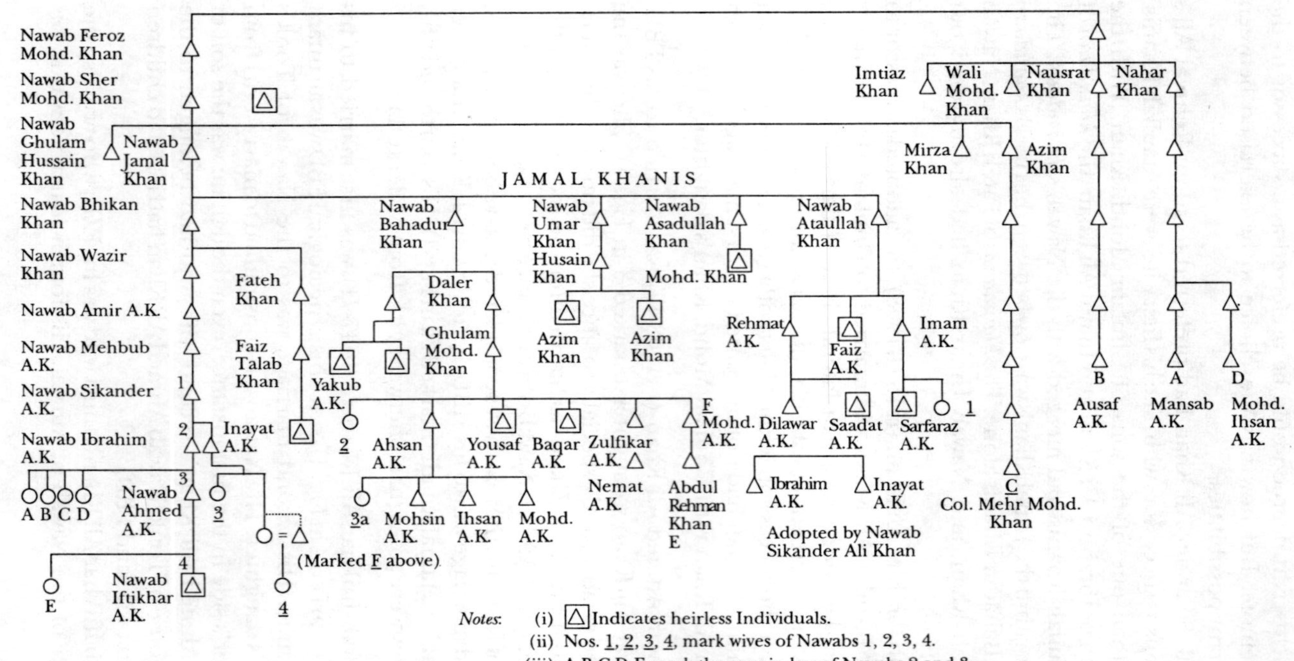

Notes: (i) △ Indicates heirless Individuals.
(ii) Nos. 1, 2, 3, 4, mark wives of Nawabs 1, 2, 3, 4.
(iii) A B C D E mark the sons-in-law of Nawabs 2 and 3.

Source: Constructed from genealogies.

FIGURE 4: MARRIAGES AMONG THE JAMAL KHANIS AND PROXIMATE *KHANDAANS*

MBD from Tonk, since his second wife had died. For the fifth time he had married an Afghan Sherwani girl from Malerkotla.

Marriage within the *khandaan* has been viewed as a mechanism that makes for the exclusiveness of groups (Das 1973). The first marriages of the Nawabs cited above had reflected the desire to provide heirs for the Malerkotla *gaddi* from among the Jamal Khanis only. Moreover, as soon as Nawab Ibrahim Ali Khan and his brother, Inayat Ali Khan, were in a position to make for a more exclusive *khandaan*, they attempted to do so. The marriage of Nawab Ahmed Ali Khan and Nawab Iftikhar Ali Khan to Inayat Ali Khan's daughter and grand-daughter, respectively, bore testimony to this effort (Fig. 4). The first marriages of the Nawabs to patrilateral women were also a means of checking the rivalry between proximate *khandaans*. Contracted after the Nawabs had assumed primacy over their collaterals under British law, marriages to patrilateral women could also be viewed as attempts to reconcile with lineage mates and neutralize the opposition of agnates ([*i*] and [*ii*] above).

The children of a sister, wife's brothers and especially wife's sisters took second place to the closest patrilateral choice insofar as the first marriage of the Nawab was concerned. The desire for the exclusiveness of the descent line had led to the preference for 'the most masculine of women' (Bourdieu 1977: 44). The age of the girls was a consideration between proximate patrilateral choices, but the generation of the spouse-to-be within classificatory relatives was not viewed as a hurdle. While a first marriage with a FZD or a MBD did not facilitate the making of an exclusive *khandaan* at Malerkotla, such marriages had often built up repetitive alliances between ruling houses. This happened, for instance, through the marriage of Nawab Iftikhar Ali Khan to his FZD who was, at the same time, the daughter of the Nawab of Kurwai.

By marrying more than once, it was possible for the Malerkotla chiefs to reconcile through their subsequent marriages the conflicting demands of matrifiliation and affinity in the face of patrilineally organized *khandaans*. Nawab Iftikhar Ali Khan was twice married to girls from his mother's natal family, the ruling house at Tonk. But matrifiliation made demands even when the wife belonged to the same *khandaan* as the ruler. Nawab Ahmed Ali Khan's third marriage, for example, was to his genealogical MBD. That she was also a Jamal Khani was, in this case, a fact of lesser import. The last four Nawabs of Malerkotla did not exceed the permitted number of wives under

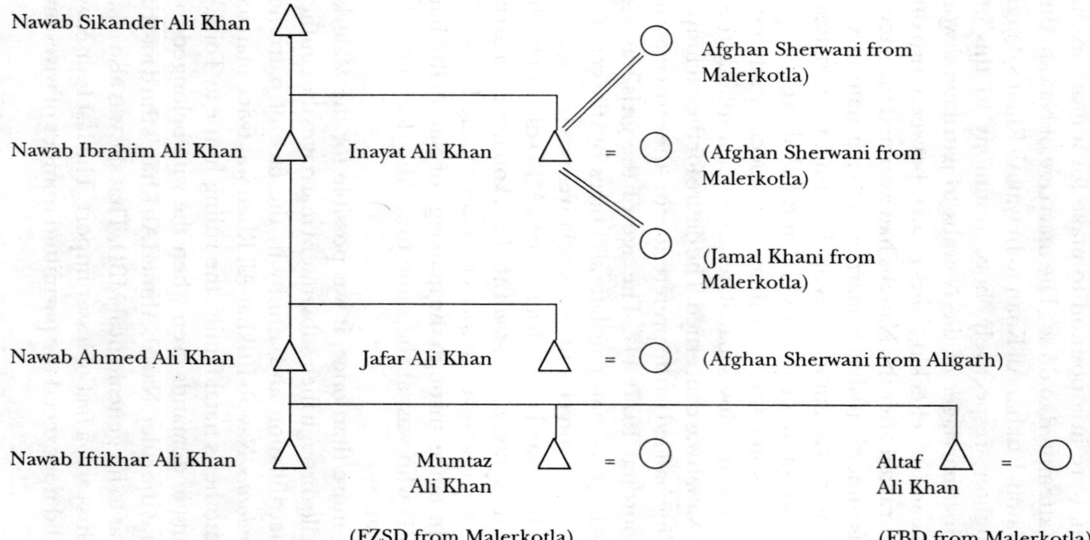

Source: Unpublished 'History of the Malerkotla state'; inhabitants of Malerkotla.

FIGURE 5: MARRIAGES OF YOUNGER SONS OF CHIEFS (1857-1971)

Islam—that is four. Their fifth marriages were contracted only after one of the earlier wives had died.

Younger sons/brothers of chiefs

By contrast with the Nawabs themselves, the younger sons of the chiefs were not faced with pressing marriages to patrilateral women in the absence of FBDs. Information on the marriages of younger sons was obtained for three generations (Fig. 5).

Sahibzada Inayat Ali Khan had married thrice (Fig. 5). His first two wives were the daughters of *jagirdars* at Malerkotla while his third wife was a Jamal Khani (the daughter of Ghulam Mohd. Khan). Sahibzada Jafar Ali Khan, brother of Nawab Ahmed Ali Khan, had married just once. His wife belonged to the Afghan Sherwanis of Aligarh (Uttar Pradesh), a family with whom the Afghan Sherwanis of Malerkotla had not been matrimonially allied in the past.

Sahibzada Mumtaz Ali Khan was married to his genealogical FZSD who was also a Jamal Khani. His younger brother, Sahibzada Altaf Ali Khan, was wedded to his genealogical FBD. It is reported that Nawab Ahmed Ali Khan had to plead with his brother's wife in order to secure this match since his brother had died before the betrothal took place. He, however, had considered it a matter of great pride to have succeeded in marrying his son to his brother's daughter.

As younger brothers, both Inayat Ali Khan and Jafar Ali Khan had first married outside the Jamal Khanis. Jafar Ali Khan was wedded to a girl who was an Afghan Sherwani from another part of the country.

It seems that while the Nawabs sought to make the chief's line exclusive by marriage with patrilateral women, other *khandaans* of the patrilineage had endeavoured to gain proximity to it by vying for the younger brother's hand in marriage for their daughters—a 'marrying up' or hypergamous tendency in relation to the ruler's *khandaan*. Their efforts had succeeded in the absence of closer agnatic women. Otherwise, as in the case of Mumtaz Ali Khan cited earlier, marriages to genealogically proximate patrilateral women were preferred.

Royal daughters/sisters

The ceremonious marriage of the Nawab's daughter to another Nawab of Afghan origin brought glory to the ruling *khandaan*. If eligible chiefs were lacking, the Nawabs had exercised the option of marrying them within the Afghan Sherwanis at Malerkotla itself. The marriages of the daughters of Nawab Ibrahim Ali Khan and Nawab Ahmed Ali Khan are shown in Figure 6.

Nawab Ibrahim Ali Khan had six daughters. Two of his daughters were married to the Nawabs of Khunjpura and Kurwai, respectively. The other four daughters were married to Nahar Khani, Azim Khani and Nusrat Khani *jagirdars* (Fig. 4). Ala Dia Khan, who was a Nahar Khani, had been mentioned in the Settlement Report (1892) of the state as the principal non-Jamal Khani *jagirdar.* His son, Ihsan Ali Khan and nephew, Mansab Ali Khan, were married to two of Nawab Ibrahim Ali Khan's daughters. Both Ausaf Ali Khan and Col. Mehr Mohd. Khan, too, were highly eligible grooms as the only scions of the Azim Khanis and Nusrat Khanis, respectively. All four *jagirdars* were apparently pleased to have the Nawab's daughters as their first wives. The ruling *khandaan,* too, by marrying its daughters to the most eligible *jagirdars,* reclaimed the men who mattered outside the *khandaan* within its fold.

Nawab Ahmed Ali Khan had three daughters. Two of his daughters were married to the Nawabs of Baoni and Khunjpura. The latter Nawab was also the bride's FZS. The third daughter was married to a Jamal Khani—Abdul Rehman Khan—who was also her FMBS (Fig. 4).

The post-1858 marriages of the Nawab's daughters and sons with Afghan chiefs (such as Tonk, Khunjpura and Kurwai) were primarily expressive of solidarity with the Afghan rulers across the country. Contracted under the protective umbrella of the British, they were not akin to the former political alliances arranged between the ruling *khandaan* of Malerkotla and Afghan and Rajput *jagirdars* outside the state but within a distance that could make for military support.

Sons and daughters of chiefs had accomplished different purposes by their marriages. Sons perpetuated the existence of the *khandaan* and the eldest sons, especially, worked towards its exclusiveness by marriage with the nearest patrilateral choice. Daughters enabled prestigious alliances with other ruling families. Rudolph and Rudolph draw attention to the fact that the marriages of daughters in Rajput princley states, too, were 'markers in the pursuit of consolidation of social mobility' (1984: 229). Or alternatively, the marriages of royal daughters, as at Malerkotla, had drawn distant *khandaans* back into a relationship with the chief's line.

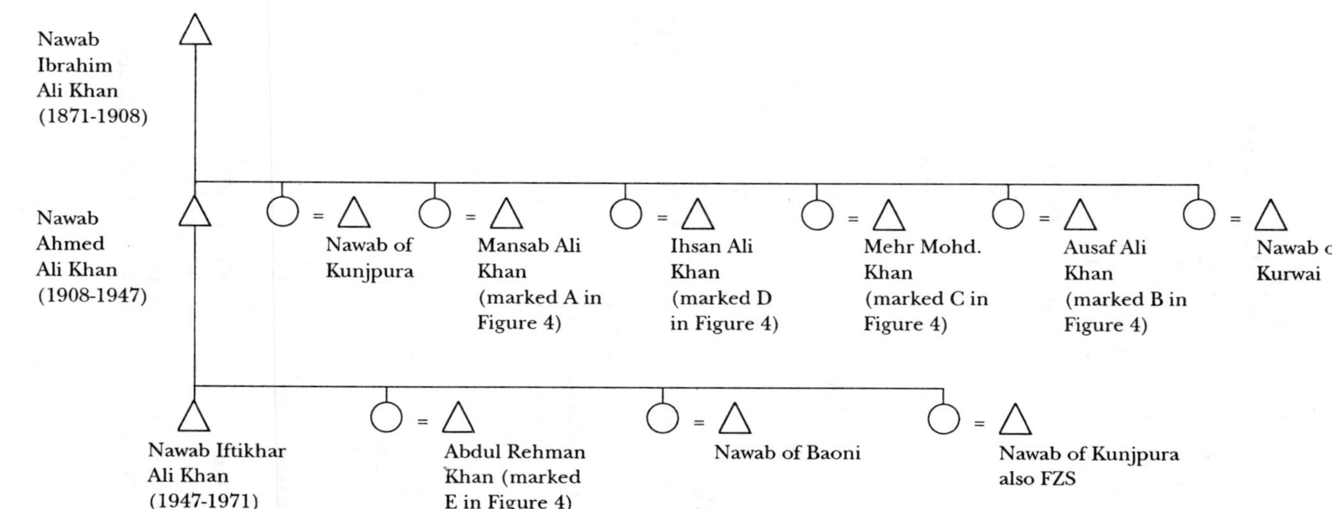

Source: Unpublished 'History of the Malerkotla state'; inhabitants of Malerkotla

FIGURE 6: MARRIAGES OF THE DAUGHTERS OF MALERKOTLA NAWABS (1871-1971)

Comparative Evidence

Under the imperial Mughal regime, *jagirdars* and chiefs and chiefs and emperors were matrimonially linked through the idiom of tribute, wife-givers being inferior to wife-receivers. The Mughals, at the pinnacle of the political hierarchy, were wife-givers to none. After Akbar, the daughters of Mughal emperors had been married within the *khandaan* (A. Hussain 1972). The desirability of politico-marital alliances for the Muslim princely states of Punjab, however, had constrained the possibility of their rulers being exclusively wife-receivers.

Marriage alliances which had sealed and reinforced political alliances for the Malerkotla chiefs, however, had lost their *raison d'être* after 1858. Fisher's account of the marriages of Avadh rulers, too, shows that they revised their marriage strategies once the East India Company had extended its support to them. Formerly, members of the ruling lineage of Awadh had contracted marriages with the Mughals in the pursuit of political ends. Backed by the East India Company, after the downfall of the Mughals, the Awadh ruler had succeeded in reversing the direction of wife-giving. The Awadh Nawab, Ghazi-al-Din Haydar managed to arrange the marriage of his son and heir-apparent to the daughter of the Mughal emperor's brother, Sulayman Shukuh. Through this marriage, he endeavoured to establish the inferiority of the Mughals to the Irani Nawabs of Awadh. Having settled the issue of political rank, as far as the Irani lineage was concerned, the Awadh rulers had subsequently withdrawn from overtly political marriages, concentrated upon Shi'i ideology and confined their marriages to the *khandaan* and a few other Shi'ites.

The decline of Muslim power had led Muslim chiefs to explore other avenues for asserting their superiority in the post-1858 period. Marriage with the FBD, which had earlier been peripheral to the matrimonial strategies of Muslim chiefs in north India, emerged as the most desirable form of marriage. Apart from being the preferred practice in the Middle East where Islam had originated and among the Sayyids, the chief's marriage with the FBD encouraged the fostering of an exclusive and 'pure' descent group as behoved the ruling lineage of an autonomous state. And again, the patrilocal residence of daughters married to other Afghan rulers worked towards both the alliance of distant groups and the generation of an exclusive and 'pure' identity of Afghan rulers across a considerable territorial spread—a translocal Afghan rulers' *khandaan*.

What does kinship theory tell us about the marriages of princesses in the top rungs of feudal regimes? Lévi-Strauss (1969: 479) puts forth the argument that hypergamy could lead to endogamy or to a 'complete paralysis of the body social' unless the eligibility of the groom was enlarged to incorporate personal merit. It is Dumont's (1970: 160) contention as well that the process of hypergamy in north India should have created a problem of grooms for royal daughters. Facts on the ground, however, showed that female infanticide was not prevalent at the apex of the Rajputs' political hierarchy. What obtained was the exchange of daughters/sisters between ruling houses without infringing the taboo on cousin marriage. The tendency toward hypogamy, moreover, was checked by the polygynous alliances contracted by the rulers. Princesses could be wedded to already married kings. Multiple marriages made it possible for Ruler X, for instance, to marry his daughter by Wife A to a house from which he had received Wife B. Plunkett contends that at the peak of the Rajput hierarchy the chain of hypergamy 'appears to loop back on itself rather than terminating sharply' (1973: 80).

At the origin of the Malerkotla state lay the extraordinary marriage of the Lodi king's daughter to a propertyless Sufi sage. However, among the Muslims by and large, the marriage of royal daughters was more easily resolved. At both the highest and the intermediate levels of the Muslim politico-marital hierarchy, the provision of grooms for princesses was enabled by turning inwards to the *khandaan*. Bridegrooms could be drawn from proximate *khandaans* as well by stressing the commonality of descent from a remoter ancestor. However, the vertical extension of the *khandaan* was a face-saving device for the ruler even though it integrated the collaterals who mattered outside the *khandaan* with the main line.

The top of the feudal hierarchy typified a contraction of the marriage circle evident both in the exchange of women as brides among Rajput chiefs and in the marriages of daughters within the *khandaan* among the Mughal rulers—a 'class endogamy', itself engendered by hypergamy (cf. Lévi-Strauss 1969: 475). The pattern of marriage preferences at the intermediate levels of the political system, such as those of the Afghan Sherwani chiefs, however, revealed the coexistence of strategies that worked towards the alliance of groups and strategies that made for their exclusiveness (cf. Das 1973) precluding, perhaps, a theoretical separation.

IV. CONCLUSION

Patterns in Indian kinship and marriage have, by and large, been sought in the discrete religions, castes and linguistic terminologies of its people. However, the framing of Indian kinship mores in terms of caste and religion violates an understanding of the distinctive polity that emerged in north India during the five centuries of Mughal rule. Nor is the striking variation of kinship and marriage practices within the same linguistic group—as between rulers and peasants, for instance, or at different points in time—captured by regarding the limits of languages as the limits of culture.

The kin and marriage practices of the rulers at Malerkotla defy an understanding in terms of exclusive religious, linguistic or ethnic filiations. The pattern of kinship seems to have corresponded closely to the pattern of other intermediate ruling classes, such as the Rajputs, insofar as it relates to lineage organization especially, rather than simply being common to a linguistic group or different across religious divides.

In this paper I have argued for using historical materials to enlighten us about kinship practices in the context of Muslim rule and the pre-colonial political order. The attempt is to discern a pattern from practice and the lived experience of Islam as against a textual view. The limitations of this approach are evident too: practice or observed behaviour cannot deliver an ideal pattern or even a statistical tendency. Yet, I think, the kinship pattern does shed some light on the pre-colonial polity and vice versa.

To what extent had Muslim chiefs participated in the conceptions of north Indian kinship? The importance attached to unidirectional marriage relationships as well as the proscription on exchanging son-daughter sets in marriage within the *khandaan* were striking aspects of Afghan practice at Malerkotla. Wife-takers were distinguished from wife-receivers and the two stood in a hierarchical relationship to each other. This pattern of relationships was isomorphic with relationship in the political realm—political superiors were, conceptually, wife-receivers while inferiors were envisaged as wife-givers. At the level of extant political relationships, this conception was pressed into operation only when a marriage occurred or a woman was bestowed in tribute between groups characterized by relations of superordination and subordination.

The notion of tribute economically expresses ideas that were central to the pre-colonial polity in domains that we may splice as kinship, ritual, political or economic. The importance of ritual, kinship and gift-giving for a south Indian state has been brought out by Dirks (1987). However, while the sacral dimension of gift-giving and *kanyadaan* in north India continues to be the subject of discussion (Parry 1986), the vitality of matrimonial exchanges and tribute for north Indian polities has not been probed. Anthropologists have shied away from investigating the ideological rendition of rulership, and the networks of alliance and tribute that accompanied Mughal rule. For this period, which is widely recognized for its civilizational significance, the understanding of the ruling class and the nature of the political order entails the simultaneous study of kinship and marriage.

A tributary mode of production has been defined as a system in which the ruling class appropriates an agrarian surplus in the form of tribute from a subject peasantry. The collision of the tributary mode and what has been termed as the 'colonial' mode of production by analysts of the Indian economy had implications for kinship and the political order that have, by and large, not been considered. Perhaps such analysis, too, can incorporate changes in the domain of kinship and marriage alliance as an expression of changes occurring in the mode of production. Agnatic ties alone were insufficient for affording political protection and ensuring the perpetuity of rule by pre-colonial chiefs. These ties were coupled with marital and political alliances but kinship bonds were not substituted by the solely political ties of vassal and lord, as in Western Europe.

Whether kin-feudated or tributary, pre-colonial polities and patterns of marriage, inheritance, succession to chiefship and identity formation that corresponded with the former political order were transformed in the wake of colonial rule. The reign of non-resident emperors by proxies had begun and the former strategies of kinship and marriage alliance were no longer integral to the process of empire-building in the subcontinent.

NOTES

* *Acknowledgements*: I am grateful to Prof. Veena Das and Dr. Patricia Uberoi for their helpful comments on an earlier draft of this paper.

1. *Khandaan*: a group of kinsmen tracing descent from an identifiable ancestor; *got*: a group of men identified by a common name who assume descent from a common ancestor; *kaum*: a group identified by ethnic origin, occupation or religion or, as nowadays, by nationality; *biradiri*: a group composed of patrilineally related men, also used to express the endogamous unit or a sub-caste; *jaat*: a collectivity characterized as a natural species, generally identified as caste, but can also denote the clan. The meaning of these categories is unambiguous only within a context, as emphasized by Alavi (1972), Das (1976) and Hershman (1981).
2. Dumont remarks that Muslim Rajputs desired to be assimilated as Afghans: 'Mughals and Pathans (60,000 and 9,60,000) correspond rather to Hindu Kshatriyas, and at the very time of the census the number of Pathans was swelling by many converted Rajputs declaring themselves as such' (Dumont 1970: 253). The reference is to the Census of India conducted in 1911.
3. During Sher Mohd's reign the *riyasat's* chronicles report: 'The small Muslim states of Punjab were scenes of great horror and bloodshed and Sikh atrocities beyond description. On several occasions during these disturbances the Sikhs tried to persuade their leader to attack Malerkotla but he had always pacified them by saying that as Nawab Sher Mohd. Khan was dear to Guru Gobind Singh he would never think of attacking the ruler of Malerkotla.'
4. I have not been able to comment on concubinage and the limited rights of children born of such liaisons in this paper.

REFERENCES

Ahmad, Aziz. 1967. *Islamic Modernism in India and Pakistan, 1857-1964.* London: Oxford University Press.

Ahmad, Imtiaz, ed. 1973. *Caste and Social Stratification among Muslims in India.* New Delhi: Manohar.

Ahmad, Syed Nesar. 1991. *Origins of Muslim Consciousness in India.* U.S.A.: Greenwood Press.

Akbar, Muhammad. 1948. *The Punjab under the Mughals.* Lahore: Ripon Printing Press.

Alavi, H.A. 1972. 'Kinship in West Punjab Villages'. *Contributions to Indian Sociology* (n.s.) 6: 1-27.

Bhatnagar, Mohan Lal. 1925. *The Punjab Land Revenue Act, 1887.* Ferozepore. Anonymous.

Bloch, Marc. 1961. *Feudal Society*. London: Routledge and Kegan Paul.

Bloch, Maurice. 1973. 'The long term and the short term: The economic and political significance of kinship'. In J. Goody, ed., *The Character of Kinship*, pp. 75-87. Cambridge: Cambridge University Press.

Bourdieu, Pierre. 1977. *Outline of a Theory of Practice*. Cambridge: Cambridge University Press.

Burghart, Richard D. 1983. 'For a sociology of India: An intracultural approach to the study of Hindu society'. *Contributions to Indian Sociology* (n.s.) 17: 275-99.

Cohen, Abner. 1969. 'Political anthropology: The analysis of the symbolism of power relations'. *Man* (n.s.) 4: 217-35.

Cohn, Bernard S. 1962. 'Political systems in eighteenth century India: The Benares region'. *Journal of the American Oriental Society* 83: 312-20.

Das, Veena. 1973. 'The structure of marriage preferences: An account from Pakistani fiction'. *Man* (n.s.) 9: 312-45.

———. 1976. 'Masks and faces: An essay on Punjabi Kinship'. *Contributions to Indian Sociology* (n.s.) 10: 1-30.

———. 1977. *Structure and Cognition*. Delhi: Oxford University Press.

Dirks, Nicholas B. 1987. *The Hollow Crown: Ethnohistory of an Indian Kingdom*. Cambridge: Cambridge University Press.

Dumont, Louis. 1957. *Hierarchy and Marriage Alliance in South Indian Kinship*. Occasional paper no. 12 of the Royal Anthropological Institute of Great Britain. London: Royal Anthropological Institute.

———. 1962. 'The conception of kingship in ancient India'. *Contributions to Indian Sociology* 6: 48-77.

———. 1966. 'Marriage in India: The present state of the question'. Part III. *Contributions to Indian Sociology* 9: 90-114.

———. 1970. *Homo Hierarchicus: The Caste System and its Implications*. London: Weidenfeld and Nicholson.

Eglar, Zekiye. 1960. *A Punjabi Village in Pakistan*. New York: Columbia University Press.

Fisher, Michael H. 1983. 'Political marriage alliances at the Shi'i court of Avadh'. *Comparative Studies in Society and History* 4: 593-616.

Fortes, M. and E.E. Evans-Pritchard. 1941. *African Political Systems*. Oxford: Oxford University Press.

Fox, Richard G. 1971. *Kin, Clan, Raja and Rule. State-hinterland relations in pre-industrial India*. Bombay: Oxford University Press.

———. 1977. Introduction. In R.G. Fox, ed. *Realm and Region in Traditional India*, pp. ix-xxv. Delhi: Vikas.

Frykenberg, Robert Eric. 1963. 'Traditional sources of power in south India: An historical analysis of local influences'. *Indian Economic and Social History Review* 1: 122-42.

Goody, Jack. 1966. *Succession to High Office*. Cambridge: Cambridge University Press.

Government of Punjab. 1904. *Punjab State Gazetteers*, vol. XV A. Delhi: Government Printing.

Haynes, Edward S. 1978. 'Bureaucracy versus traditional rulership: Raja, jagirdars and new administrators, 1892-1910'. In R. Jeffrey, ed., *People, Princes and Paramount Power*, pp. 32-64. Delhi: Oxford University Press.

Hershman, Paul. 1981. *Punjabi Kinship and Marriage*. Delhi: Hindustan Publishing Corporation.

Hussain, Afzal. 1972. 'Marriages among Mughal nobles as an index of status and aristocratic integration'. *Proceedings of the Indian History Congress*, pp. 304-12.

Hussain, Mirja Ijaz. 1922. *A brief note on the history of the Malerkotla state*. Lahore: Civil and Military Gazette Press.

Ibbetson, D.C.J. 1883. *Report on the Census of the Punjab taken on 17th February 1881*. Calcutta: Government Printing.

Jain, R.K. 1975. 'Bundela genealogy and legends: The past of an indigenous ruling group of central India'. In J.H.M. Beattie and J. Lienhardt, eds., *Studies in Social Anthropology: Essays in Memory of E.E. Evans-Pritchard*, pp. 238-72. Oxford: Oxford University Press.

Kolenda, Pauline. 1984. 'Women as tribute; Woman as flower'. *American Ethnologist* 11: 98-117.

Lall, I.C. 1892. *Report on the Settlement of Malerkotla, Kalsia and Pataudi States, 1888-92*. Delhi: IMH Press.

Leach, E.R. 1954. *Political Systems of Highland Burma*. Cambridge, Mass: Harvard University Press.

Lévi-Strauss, Claude. 1969. *The Elementary Structures of Kinship* (trans. J. Bell, J. Von Sturmer and R. Needham). London: Eyre and Spottiswoode.

Lyall, Alfred. 1884. *Asiatic Researches, Religious and Social*. London: John Murray.

Majumdar, R.C., H.C. Raychaudhuri and K. Datta. 1983. *An Advanced History of India*. Delhi: Macmillan.

Meillassoux, Claude. 1978. 'The economy in agricultural self-sustaining societies: A pre-liminary analysis'. In David Seddon, ed., *Relations of Production*, pp. 127-58. London: Frank Cass.

Metcalfe, Barbara Daly. 1982. *Islamic Revival in British India: Deoband, 1860-1900*. Princeton: Princeton University Press.

Parry, Jonathan P. 1986. 'The gift, the Indian gift and the "Indian gift"'. *Man* (n.s.) 21: 453-73.

Plunkett, Frances Taft. 1973. 'Royal marriages in Rajasthan'. *Contributions to Indian Sociology* (n.s.) 7: 64-80.

Ramusack, Barbara. 1975. 'The princely states of Punjab'. In W.E. Gustafson and K.W. Jones, eds., *Sources on Punjab History*, pp. 374-449. New Delhi: Manohar.

Robertson, F.A. 1889. *Report on the Result of Enquiries into the Rights and Status of Cultivators in the Malerkotla State*. Lahore: Punjab Government Press.

Rose, H.A. 1919. *A Glossary of the Castes and Tribes of the Punjab and North-West Frontier Province.* Lahore: Punjab Government Press.

Rudolph, Susanne, H. and L. Rudolph. 1984. *Essays on Rajputana.* Delhi: Concept.

Schneider, David M. 1968. *American Kinship: A Cultural Account.* Englewood Cliffs: Prentice-Hall.

Shah, A.M. 1964. 'Political system in eighteenth century Gujarat'. *Enquiry* 1: 83-95.

Southall, Aidan W. 1956. *Alur Society: A Study in Processes and Types of Domination.* Cambridge: Cambridge University Press.

———. 1965. 'A critique of the typology of states and political systems'. In Michael Banton, ed., *Political Systems and the Distribution of Power,* pp. 113-40. New York: Frederick A. Praeger.

Stein, Burton. 1977. 'The segmentary state in south Indian history'. In R.G. Fox, ed., *Realm and Region in Traditional India,* pp. 3-51. Delhi: Vikas.

———. 1980. *Peasant State and Society in Medieval South India.* Delhi: Oxford University Press.

Talbott, Ian. 1988. *Punjab and the Raj.* New Delhi: Manohar.

Terray, E. 1977. 'Event, structure and history: The formation of the Abron kingdom of Gyaman (1700-1800)'. In J.F. Friedman and M.T. Rowlands, eds., *The Evolution of Social Systems,* pp. 279-301. Gloucester: Duckworth.

Thapar, Romila. 1984. *From Lineage to State.* Bombay: Oxford University Press.

Tod, James. 1832. *Annals and Antiquities of Rajasthan,* vols. I and II. Delhi: M.N. Publishers (rpt. 1983).

Trautmann, Thomas R. 1981. *Dravidian Kinship.* Cambridge: Cambridge University Press.

Uberoi, J.P.S. 1976. 'Men, women and property in northern Afghanistan'. In S.T. Lokhandwala, ed., *India and Contemporary Islam,* pp. 398-416. Simla: IIAS.

Wolf, E.R. 1982. *Europe and the Peoples without History.* Berkeley: University of California Press.

Ziegler, Norman P. 1978. 'Some notes on Rajput loyalties during the Mughal period'. In J.F. Richards, ed., *Kingship and Authority in South Asia,* pp. 215-51. Madison: University of Wisconsin Press.

Circumcision, Body and Community

DEEPAK MEHTA
(1996)

This paper explores the significance of circumcision among the Ansaris.[1] The analysis is divided into two parts. The first details the ritual of circumcision and the second the everyday talk surrounding the fact of being circumcised. In the process of explaining the two sections, the paper marks out the discursive terrain of two terms, *khatna* and *musalmani*, used respectively to describe the ritual and the everyday discourse. Common to both sections is my concern to understand how particular Muslim groups claim membership to Islam.

In the context of the circumcision ritual, we find that it is not read from within the domain of Islam. When recognised, as among various tribal societies of tropical Africa (Lewis 1966; Trimingham 1964), it is explained as a puberty ritual. In other cases it is not seen as a rite of initiation (Watt 1965). The second position need not concern us. As a ritual of entry, Bourdieu (1977: 225, n. 56), for example, says that circumcision is a purifying cut protecting the male from the dangers of sexual union. Simultaneously, as part of structure of practices, the ritual shows how individuals are socialized into groups. This paper follows this line of arguments, but also suggests that through the ritual and the everyday discourse a claim is being made to an Islamic heritage.

At the heart of the analysis in this paper, then, is a larger question: what is the relationship of local Muslim groups, such as the Ansaris, to Islam? There could be, at least, two ways of answering this question. Given that the Ansaris are low-caste Muslims,[2] generally illiterate in sacred affairs, we could argue that they typify a 'folk' imagination of Islam. This imagination is necessarily limited to a local context. Consequently, the meanings generated regarding it are also enclosed within the world of Ansaris. Alternately, in their mode of worship we could isolate general characteristics, such as the repetition of sacred formulae and the liturgy, by which they share the same properties as other Muslim groups. In this case, such characteristics point to an orthodox imagination of Islam and are not concerned with the cultural location of the Ansaris. An orthodox point of view assumes that for Muslims Islam is the universal form of human experience, incontestable and invariable. On the other hand, a folk theology of Islam shows, at least partially, how people live their everyday lives and the relationship of their lives to the sacred.

El-Zein (1977) argues for an anthropology of Islam by negotiating the two positions. In the distinction between 'folk and elite Islam, anthropology studies the former, yet its principles of analysis resemble the latter' (ibid.: 246). But, he says, the orthodox and folk theologies of Islam are complementary since each defines and occasions the latter. If orthodox Islam relies on sacred formulae and an inviolable tradition and finds truth first in the Quran, the folk theologies of Islam locate meaning in nature and then place the Quran within that general order (ibid.: 248). An orthodox position shows that the Quran produces a context, while a folk perspective embeds the Quran within a natural order.

In either case, interpretation assumes the universality of Islam. This position, El-Zein argues, is shared by an anthropology of Islam. As a counterpoint, if one assumes that Islam is not characterized by fixed meanings, it becomes possible to collapse the distinction between the orthodox and the folk. This is because Islam is found in the content of what is being studied, one that highlights 'structural relations' in a way that Islam is a product of such relations. If cultures are diverse it is impossible to speak, at least anthropologically, of a universal meaning of Islam. Indeed, the 'logic of Islam' (1977: 252) is immanent in the content of what is being studied. Anthropologically, then, Islam does not exist as a fixed and autonomous form.

I take the above position as a point of departure in the present paper. Focusing both on the content of the ritual and everyday conversations, I argue that the novice's introduction to Islam cannot be separated from his structural position in his domestic group and the Ansari social structure. I do not treat circumcision as part of puberty rituals or situate it within a rite of passage framework if only because the age at which boys are circumcised varies from between 2 to 6 years.[3] I will show that the ritual, in constituting the body of the male, allows it to simultaneously enter into the life-cycle of the domestic group and the community of Islam. This simultaneity is found when we focus on the gestural and graphic engraving of the ritual on the body.

There are three modes in which the gestural and graphic unfold. I understand this operation through the term 'biunity'.[4] Biunity is the signature, par excellence, of the ritual. In conferring an identity on the novice, this signature inscribes it on his body. It shows the combination of male and female characteristics. The medium is primarily gestural. Second, this signature shows how the body as an object is posited. This positing is found in the regimen of three types of signs impressed on the novice. The medium is both verbal and gestural. Finally, the signature implies the agency of the other. The other is the mark of the domestic group, but also the word of God embossed on the novice's body. The medium is primarily verbal.

The discourse on circumcision, however, is not limited by its ritual context, but is part of the everyday vocabulary of the men of the community. This vocabulary does not refer to the body of the circumcised but attempts to orally constitute the boundaries of 'being Muslim'. This constitution is achieved by separating Muslims from non-Muslims. In locating circumcision both within its ritual matrix and as it is constituted orally in everyday life, this paper suggests that the relation between the everyday and the extraordinary can be mapped along a continuum. Through the agency of the wound the ritual inscribes the divisions of the social structure on the novice's body, while in the everyday conversations the discourse on the wound is a mode by which the boundaries of the Muslim community are established. In the process the focal point of everyday conversations is no longer the body of the person undergoing circumcision, but the body of the male Ansari community taken as a unity. This paper attempts to read the ritual and show the transitions and connections from and with it in the everyday life of the community.

I. THE RITE TO BE MALE

In the context of my fieldwork references to circumcision, initially elliptical, later ironic, were neither directly solicited nor framed within an ethnographic setting. I was witness to one circumcision ceremony, that too inadvertently. Sometime in August 1985, I was staying in the house of Sadiq Ali when he decided to have his young son circumcised.[5] My presence in the house led to an ambiguous situation. Sadiq Ali was not sure whether I, a non-Muslim, was allowed to remain in the house during the ceremony. After consulting with the elders he asked me to stay. I started taking notes on circumcision a month later after a Hindu *patwari* (village administrative officer) informed me that because of my association with Muslim, commensal and residential, I was an 'uncircumcised mullah'. I will reproduce the conversation since it is instructive. It points both to the body as a referential object and the verbal discourse surrounding circumcision.

Most evenings a few of us would sit around a local tea-stall talking of the day's activities. Towards the end of September 1985 there was a marked difference in the content of our conversations. Some of my friends were greatly agitated over the emerging controversy in Ayodhaya,[6] barely 30 km east of the villages of this fieldwork. The conversations reflected the fear of violence touching the area. During one of these sessions I was introduced to the *patwari*.

P: Your name? (*Apka nam?*)
DM: Deepak.
P: Deepak what? (Deepak *kya?*)
DM: Deepak Mehta.
P: Are you a Srivastava? (Srivastava *ho?*)
DM: No, I am a Punjabi Khatri. (*Nahin, men Punjabi Khatri hun.*)
P: That's the same thing. Where do you stay? (*Ek hi bat. Kahan rahat ho?*)
DM: Sometime Mawai, sometime Gulharia. (*Kabhi Mawai, Kabhi Gulharia.*)
P: Oh! Do you stay in a Pasi household? (*Achcha! Pasi ke ghar men rahat ho?*)
DM: No. I stay with a Khan Saheb's family. (*Nahin. Khan Saheb ke sath.*)
P: Is that so? Then you must be eating their food? (*Samjha! To unka khana bhi khate ho?*)
DM: Yes. (*Ji.*)
P: This is the first time I have come across an uncircumcised mullah. (*Pehli bar humko mullah mila jisne musalmani nahin karvai ho.*)

The *patwari* met me a few days later. I was advised not to talk to him. 'Good day, wise man. Have you been circumcised?' (*Salam alai kum miyan. Musalmani karva li?*) [On receiving no response] 'What happened? You can't read the *namaz* without being circumcised?' (*Kya hua? Musalmani ke begair namaz nahin pad sakat?*)

I did not know that *musalmani* referred to circumcision. When I asked my friends the meaning of the term, I was told that that was how one became Muslim? Intrigued and rather naively I asked how indeed did one became Muslim? In exasperation, one of my friends visually mimed the operation. *Musalmani* is the most oft-used term denoting circumcision in the field. Other terms, both Persian and Arabic, are restricted to describe the ritual. The classical term *khitan* is not used, but *khatna* (to cut) is. *Khatna* is employed in the company of *tuhr* (to clean). In turn, *tuhr* is associated with other terms, most notably *ghusl* (to bathe), *hajamat* (hair cut) and *istibra* (the removal of the last drop of urine). In this sense, circumcision is a way of experiencing one's body, of apprehending it, of assuming it positively and fully. It is linked to the paring of nails, the removal of hair and the invigoration of the body through oil massages.

The two terms (*musalmani* and *khatna*) denoting circumcision, each constituting a different terrain of action, are used on specific occasions. *Musalmani* discursively establishes being Muslim, pointing in this specific case to the difference between Hindus and Muslims. The second section of the paper develops this discourse. *Khatna* describes the ritual. Before I discuss the ritual I will introduce the main argument of the first half of the paper.

The ritual is characterized by two types of acts: the gestural and the graphic. In describing the enactment of the ritual the paper focuses on the inscription of a mark on the body. Here, what is marked on the body is already part of the body's production since it is included in the body. The body in this sense is referential: an object is carved out by means of a gesture. Together with the gesture, a second movement is discernible in the ritual. This refers to the blowing of the word in the initiate's right ear. Here the mark on the body emerges from an external environment. If the body acquires through gestures an authorized mode of behaviour, with the word it is attached to the community of Islam. Both the word and the gesture are co-present on the surface of the body. Implicit in this ritual, then, is a triadic division of the male body into a depth, a surface and a celestial height.

The setting

The Ansaris circumcise their male offspring in the *zanana* of their household.[7] The courtyard of the *zanana* and the quilt room are especially prepared for the ceremony. The western wall of the courtyard is cleared of impedimenta and made to resemble the blank western wall of the mosque. All ritual connected with circumcision is directed towards the wall. In contrast, the quilt room[8] is decorated with the choicest marriage quilts, the nuptial bed is made and a little flour sprinkled on the bed. An earthen pot, placed in one of the corners of the room, will be broken after the operation.

The day of circumcision is often referred to as *barat*, the day when marriage is consummated. It may be argued that the two ceremonies, of marriage and circumcision, are similarly structured. The practices of sprinkling the nuptial bed with flour, of the ritual bath under the aegis of the mother and the barber, have much in common in either case. It is as if circumcision were a mimicry of marriage, and the removal of the foreskin an anticipation of that of the hymen, or that circumcision is a preparation for deflowering (Bouhdiba 1985: 182). Whether circumcision mimics marriage or is equivalent to the rupture of the hymen are not issues I will examine. Instead, I will show that the ritual enables men to enter into the world of women. Far from separating the sexes, the ritual premises a unity between them. The site of enacting this unity is the body of the novice.

The dramatis personae of the ritual

Broadly, four types of people are involved in the ceremony: the novice, his mother, the female barber and those who witness the ceremony. The last includes the father of the novice, his mother's brother and all his father's circumcised agnates. This comprises the circumcised members of the novice's generation. The mother and the female barber work on the body of the novice while the witnesses authenticate this work by providing verbal legitimacy to the act. They are the only ones who talk of circumcision in the public domain.[9]

The mother

A day before his circumcision, the novice child is under the exclusive custody of his mother.[10] She ensures his hair is cut, his nails pared. Later he is massaged with mustard oil. Of these, the paring of nails is the most significant. It is believed that the novice is susceptible to involuntary corruption just before circumcision. Dirty fingernails aid in this corruption because the devil takes up his dwelling in the dirt lying between the nail and the flesh. Ideally, nails are pared on a Thursday or Friday preceding circumcision as this assures wealth to the circumcised. The parings are buried so that sorcerers are unable to play with them. I was given a second explanation for the burial: they are part of the human body and have to be buried like the body itself. The mother performs the burial in secrecy. After the oil massage and the paring of nails, the mother bathes her child in flowing water. Subsequently she introduces the child to her guests.

In the present instance, after Shabnam (Sadiq Ali's wife) had bathed her child, he was made to eat cooling foods. Immediately after the midday meal Sadiq Ali's agnates, his elder brother and his wife's brother gathered in Sadiq Ali's dwelling. They were accommodated in the courtyard of the *zanana*. In their presence Shabnam introduced her son. Pointing to him she spoke as if he were a stranger. She used the formal third person honorific *ap* and not *yeh*: '*Ap hain Shujat Ahmad. Apki umar teen sal hai. Kal ap Hindu se Musalman honge*' (Here is Shujat Ahmad. He is 3 years old. Tomorrow he will become Musalman from Hindu). The people gathered responded '*Bismillah-al-Rahim*'. After this simple introduction, the boy was asked to sit at the head of the cot on which his father was sitting.

The most important part of the day preceding the ritual is the preparation of the novice. Some Ansaris say the novice is given his first bath on this day and that this is his *ghusl*. Henceforth, he should repeat this process of ablution every Friday: oil massage, paring of nails and bath in flowing water. The removal of pollution is not so much an attempt to exorcise the person of sin as it is to practise an 'ethics of the sphincters' (Ferenczi, quoted in Bouhdiba 1985: 48). Such purificatory techniques then extend to cover a wide range of functions: eating, drinking, defecation, sexual intercourse, etc. The purified body will be discussed later. Through the agency of the mother the first *ghusl* initiates the process of inscribing a subjectivity on the novice's body. Every subsequent *ghusl* enacts this inscription.

On the day of the ritual the mother, after bathing her child, dresses him in the headdress of a groom and leads him to the compound of the *zanana*. The novice is handed over to his MB. In direct contrast to the preceding day, the MB introduces the guests to the child by their genealogically appropriate term. After the introduction, the child is handed over either to his father or the eldest male of the agnatic line. This man, in turn, places him in the custody of the female barber. Meanwhile, the mother places a red piece of cloth near the western wall and holds up a green cloth to the gaze of the assembled. For the duration of the operation the novice is seated on the red cloth. The green cloth is used to wrap mother and child after the operation.

After the prepuce is removed the child is held up by his mother so that blood from the wound runs down her chest. In this way it is believed blood and milk co-mingle in producing a healthy male. Blood and milk are considered vital ingredients of the body and it is important that a proper balance be struck between the two. Balance is achieved only after the mother relinquishes her existing bond with her child. This interpretation is suggested from my conversations with two women, Shabnam and Miriam. Shabnam, in her mid-thirties in August 1985, had participated in her first son's ceremony. Miriam, in her early seventies and the wife of a Muhammad Umar, is considered by community members to be an authority on traditional matters. Muhammad Umar, himself, is a master weaver.

While describing her son's ceremony, Shabnam pointed to the alienation of her son from herself. She began by saying, 'When I was small my father always said to me, "Don't sit next to your classificatory brothers otherwise you will become like them. Play with other girls. In this lies your honour." When Shujat [referring to her son by his formal name] became Muslim, I had to forget he was my Munna [an affectionate diminutive term], because this is what my father meant. I must pass on this *amanat* (thing held in trust, in this case her son) to his father. Soon enough I will not be able to play with him, to hold him, to caress him for he will have become male (*mard*).' I asked, 'What does becoming a male mean?' I was given what appears to me a formal answer. 'It means having enough blood to produce an offspring, observing *namaz*, fasting, pilgrimage to Mecca and alms-giving.'

Shabnam's reiteration of the pillars of Islam was balanced by Miriam's comments. Circumcision is the recognition of the co-presence of male and female in everyone. This recognition is implied in the combination of blood and milk. Every human is composed of two elements—blood inherited from the father and milk from the mother. In holding up the circumcised boy to her breast the mother gives to her child the gift of milk, one that balances the blood of the father. Blood, she says, is red because it implies fire under which everything is either incorporated or ravaged. It stands alone. She compared the singularity of blood to the letter *alif*, the first letter of the Arabic alphabet. Both imply a movement of people towards the sky.

However, for Miriam, blood emerges from the earth and is nurturing. The prime example of nurture is the milk of the mother. This milk balances and often counters the excessive strength and anger given in blood. By a balance she means that if there is an excess of blood in the persons s/he is disposed towards anger. If milk is dominant the person is inclined towards corpulence (*mutapa*) and sadness or hardship (*dukh*). I asked her whether this balance operated in men and women in the same way. In her opinion, women are born with blood and milk, whereas men are gifted the latter. This gift enables them to enter into the world of women. Hence, circumcision is for those who will become men. Furthermore, circumcision is the necessary prelude to marriage for in its absence the product of the union between man and woman is either sterile or consumed by violent passions. The gift of milk is the last gift of the mother to her child. From the point of view of the child the ceremony, carried out in blood and pain, is rivalled by the nostalgia the mother feels when she contemplates her relationship with her mature son: '*khatna ke sath apne walid ka beta ban jata hai*' (with circumcision he becomes his father's son).

This double movement, of affirmation and denial, is the paradigmatic expression of the ritual and its organizing principle. On the one hand, the mother's preparation of the child maintains the security of the enactment and the object of this enactment (the novice's body). Each tirelessly produces in its subjects the conditions of its possibility: the past appears through the act of production. On the other hand, the reappearance of this past is premised on the mother almost wilfully forgetting that she shared a relationship with her child before he was circumcised.

The barber

As ritual specialist the barber transgresses various boundaries, most often those codifying sexuality. In the present ceremony she maintained a constant monologue on the sexuality of the Ansaris of Mawai. In her opinion, they did not know how to be men because they were inadequately circumcised. It was, she said, left to Sadiq Ali's son to rectify this woeful imbalance. Often she would single out one or other male member present and talk of his ceremony, his sexual prowess or lack of it. Her monologue stopped when the wailing child was handed over to her. She examined his penis and commented on its power to impregnate all womankind. To the delight of the witnesses she mentioned that even she, an old crone and thoroughly experienced in matters sexual, looked with envy at the potential sexual prowess of the boy. Then holding the prepuce she snipped off the outer end in one smooth motion. The child had lapsed into whimpers. During the operation not a drop of blood fell on the ground. Subsequently, Sadiq Ali's FB whispered the *azan* and the child's name in his right ear. Immediately after, the men offered prayers facing the western wall.

The barber's transgression of social codes during the ceremony succeeds because, through her dramatic banter, she points towards another code different from male Ansari notions of sexuality. The latter not only prohibit women from discussing sexual matters but also believe women are incapable of exercising judgement in sexual affairs. This code is sustained by a radical separation of the sexes; indeed this very separation is its prerequisite. In making her statement about the boy's sexuality, the barber refers to a domain of feelings that are not merely corporeal and aspiring to pleasure, but also point towards the investiture of a masculinity on the child. She categorically told me the penis was the boy and without it he was nothing.

I talked to the barber more than a month after the ceremony. I began by speaking of the ritual through circumlocutions. I recounted my conversation with the *patwari*, of the term *musalmani* and of her role during the ritual. Referring to the *patwari* she abused him for giving a bad name to a sacred act and said this was the viewpoint of the castrated (*khasi*), not the circumcised. Distinguishing between the two she said the former was achieved by the removal of one or both testicles, whereas *khatna* ensured the sympathy between the male and the female. She designated this sympathy by the term *hamdami* (of one breath), for only this sharing of breath makes possible the male vision (*shuhud*) of the female and the female vision of the male. The conjunction between the male and the female has two aspects: in the male it is the *shauq* (passion or desire) for the female, and in the female, the realization of this *shauq*. *Shauq*, the barber adds, does not refer to two heterogeneous beings, but one person, either male or female, encountering him/herself as the other, at once a biunity, something that people tend to forget. In this interdependence each finds recognition from the other.

Biunity, in the sense elaborated above, is a given but one that must be uncovered by circumcision. Her role is to truthfully reproduce this framed world. She says the operation recognizes the biunity between male and female. The operating instrument, a small and sharp blade called *naharni*, is used. The same blade is also employed to remove the hair of the bride a few days before her marriage. The barber says the *naharni* is deliberately used to remove excess bodily material on both the bride and the novice male child because both will experience a second birth. The *naharni* then is the instrument of *hamdami*. A sure sign of this blowing together is seen in the operation. If the act is swift and smooth the circumcised will be potent. If, however, the prepuce cannot be removed in one flowing motion, he will find it difficult to marry and raise children. If circumcision cannot be performed on the prescribed day the child will become a saint (*pir*).

In the above account, as distinct from that of the mother, the barber is outside the act. Her account is based on a framed portion of a prior world that she undertakes to represent accurately. For the mother there is nothing to retrieve, save the act by which her child becomes alien to her. Simultaneously she acquires agency over her child since she initiates the system of signs given in the act of circumcision. The barber, on the other hand, is engaged in the theme of portraiture. Her portrait is organized around the removal of the foreskin, an act of violence by which the body is precipitated into an alterity. This alterity plots the progression of the boy's career in the domestic group: the labouring body, the impregnating body, the authorizing body. Also, with mutilation the biographical time of the body is encoded so that to enter into the life of the domestic group is to enter the community of Islam. Through such violence the body becomes a metonym of the social space of the domestic group and is simultaneously constituted as an imaginary space for the reception of Islam. Both mother and barber constitute the body of the novice, the barber by recourse to a prior world and the mother by establishing agency over him.

The novice

From the account described so far, the child acquires a gender and subjectivity only after the ritual. I will describe the inscription of this subjectivity by focusing on the way his body is constituted.

There could be multiple interpretations of the details through which the novice's body is marked. We could, for example, show the profound relationship of the ritual to marriage, or from a different perspective, focus on the problematic reconstruction of 'facts' since this paper is dependent almost solely on representative testimony. The interpretation I follow here, however, is suggested in the accounts of both Miriam and the barber. I will argue that the boy's body is fashioned as a biunity. As I understand it, biunity has three dimensions. First, it confers a gender on the child, one found in the combination of blood and milk and male and female. This gendered identity is available in the accounts of the mother and the barber. Second, biunity establishes a relation of substitution between the physical object of the body and the regime of signs that play on it.[11] Finally, biunity forms a relationship of identity between the spiritual and the corporeal.

With the three dimensions the novice's body is simultaneously a system of signs and the object that is marked, worked upon and quite literally produced through the ritual. The regime of signs is understood through three terms: *ghusl* (ritual bath), *istibra* (cleaning the last drop of urine, preferably on a stone) and *kalimah* (the word, to be understood as one through which the novice is impregnated with Islam). Together these three terms constitute the state of being pure (*tuhr*) and in this way point to the conception of masculinity. As an object the body provides the depth on which the state of being pure is enacted. It is almost as if the body has no surface, no inside or outside, no container or contained. In other words it does not have a precise limit. Furthermore, as an object the body is fragmented and dissociated. In mapping the three terms onto the physical object the body acquires visible social organs and an authorized code of con-duct. I will focus on the three terms.

Ghusl

As the major purifying ritual of the body, the importance of *ghusl* cannot be overstressed. Miriam was clear on what *ghusl* attempts to remove. Its main object is to eliminate dirt. The prime source of dirt is the human body, a dirt that is dangerous since it impinges on the tidy insularity of the body. Dirt is composed of secretion and contact is contaminating. Thus, a special regime of hygiene is associated with the secreting areas of body, in particular the armpits and the genital zones. In adults the hair from these areas is assiduously removed. The second fear, after contamination, is of decay—a rotting in the depths of the body—which must be brought to the surface to be excised. All bodily refuse is a sign of decay: urine and faeces for all humans. In addition, for men, pared nails and hair that is cut are signs of decay. In men indications of rot manifest when they are unable to procreate, while in women degeneration reveals itself in the inability to menstruate regularly (pregnant women are of course exempt).

The ritual is the first attempt to rid the body of dirt and decay. The paring of nails, the first hair cut, the oil massage and the subsequent vigorous bath are to be understood in this light. The massage brings to the surface the decay in the depth of the body, while during the bath particular attention is given to cleaning the anus and genitals. Henceforth, the male child removes all excrement by means of water.

Istibra

One of the meanings circumcision lends itself to is the removal of impurity associated with urine. The removal of the prepuce prevents the residue of urine and sperm from accumulating inside the body. Immediately after the operation it is thought to be a good omen if the boy urinates (which I am told happens invariably), for it indicates good health. On all subsequent occasions the boy rids himself of the last drop of urine by an elaborate technical procedure. It is inadvisable to urinate standing. One must urinate with the buttocks resting on the ankles. After urination the penis taken by the left hand is rubbed several times against a stone. *Istibra* is continued until nothing remains in the urinary tract. The removal of the prepuce, however, is not merely an attempt to remove the body of impurities but also the first step towards conjugal union. This is suggested since *istibra* is recommended for the recently married male. Here *istibra* is thought to be an important way by which the male cleans himself after sexual contact.

Lawful conjugal association between man and woman presupposes the circumcised male. If we focus on the bride on her nuptial night, it is possible to infer that her deflowering, carried out almost publicly in the *zanana*, is equivalent to circumcision. The bride, escorted by the groom's father's sister, is led to the nuptial bed and formally introduced to the groom. She is made to sit on the bed while the women of the *zanana* throw flour on her and sing songs. The groom is asked to come sit by his bride while the women congregate outside the nuptial room. Sometime during the night the nuptial sheet is put up for display, showing that the bride was a virgin, or else she is forever branded as someone who cannot be married. In this sense, both circumcision and the deflowering of the virgin are marked by a cruel wound, a forced narcissistic experience of oneself (Bouhdiba 1985: 187).

Here circumcision is an initiation into legitimate sexual desire, but one fraught with negative consequences. This is evident since all the areas of the body producing secretion from them is a sign that life is anxiety and danger. The ritual in effect teaches how that danger can be resolved. Bouhdiba says that circumcision is 'a vaccination against the dangers of sexuality' (1985: 185). Circumcision and the deflowering of the virgin, then, occur within a frame where festivities, blood, pain and exhibitionism accompany the traumata wittingly inflicted by the group to maintain its cohesion. The problem with this analysis is that it posits a perfect symmetry between deflowering and circumcision. This relationship becomes possible after Bouhdiba excises religious legitimacy from the ritual of circumcision and instead considers it only insofar as it reflects on sexuality. This is not to deny that circumcision is of importance for a correct sexuality, but to suggest, at least in the context of this fieldwork, an asymmetry by which circumcision is productive of both correct male sexuality and the imagination of oneself as a member of the Islamic community. In the case of defilement, the only religious legitimacy is provided by the circumcised male.

Kalimah

With *ghusl* and *istibra* the body acquires a socially recognized materiality. This recognition is incomplete if the body does not acquire sound. The blowing of the *azan* in the boy's right ear is succeeded by saying his formal name. Blowing points in two directions: in the first the boy is initiated into the enunciation of the *azan*; in the second his name is linked to the verbal intonation present in the liturgy. By juxtaposing the name with the liturgy a sympathy is created between the two, at once corporeal and spiritual. Simultaneously, blowing gives depth to the body.

It is important to remember that the novice is not the product of the union between a sacred primordial nature and a corporeal nature. If this were the case the boy would be a hypostatized being. The union between the *azan* and the human form is one where the latter ingests God. The name makes visible such ingestion. This interpretation is suggested from my conversation with Sadiq Ali on the use of the formal name during the ceremony. For him this use points to a condition in which the novice boy recognizes the omniscient suzerainty of Allah. The name is crucial in such recognition for Allah has given a name to everything and everybody in this world. I asked him, 'Why do you call him Shujat and not, for example, by your name?' 'My name Sadiq points to the way in which this being [pointing of himself] manifests (*zahir*) the lord (*rabb*) in its own peculiar way. It would be sacrilege (*haram*) for me to call him by my name for otherwise he [his son] will be unable to manifest the lord in his way.'

The above argument, as I understand it, has two aspects. First, each name manifests the lord since He has named everything in the universe. Second, each human being, insofar as he carries a name designated by Allah, is a particular aspect of that manifestation. The sympathy occurring between the two is dialogic since each name is an exemplary indication of the conjunction between the spiritual and the corporeal. Evident in Sadiq Ali's insight is that the acquisition of sound by the body occurs through the convocation with another voice. In this way, the body acquiring sound learns to be obedient: to listen to the voice is to obey. Henceforth, it is natural for the boy to obey his father.

The problem, however, remains: why is the formal name uttered during the ritual? The gestural and verbal inscription on the body are two series regulated by the body. Through the first, the body is marked so that it enters into the productive and reproductive life of the domestic group. The evidence is the wound as an eternal truth. The second series reverses the sequential temporal ordering of the body so that through enunciation it enters into the community of Islam. The evidence is the *azan* written on the body. The *azan* facilitates the transition from one series to another since the communication between the verbal and the gestural is possible only after the *azan* is uttered. The name in this scheme guarantees the conjunction, albeit a particular one, between the corporeal and the spiritual.

The body of the novice thus described is understood through two sets of polarities: the gestural and the graphic and the corporeal and the spiritual. The former shows how certain events are marked on the boy's body, while the second set shows how the body is related to its internal and external environment. Further, the first set refers to a series of events and the latter to a series of attributes. The two divide the body into a surface and a depth, and in the process show how the body as an object is linked to the regime of signs impressed on it.

The surface and the depth

The novice boy, in terms of a geography of his body, is situated in three realms: a depth, a celestial height and the surface of the body. The depth, in the sense of emissions that are polluting and dangerous, must forever be controlled. In the heights he finds the word of God writ large. He must always ascend or descend to the surface and in this way claim the new status thrust on him. The body cannot be located in the celestial domain because then it would either lose its corporeality and ability to procreate, or, in the words of Miriam, have the characteristics of an ungrounded *alif*.

What, then, is the surface of the body? As I understand it, the surface is frontier available in a series of signs laying down an acceptable and accepted mode of behaviour. These signs, embossed on the body both through word and gesture, enter into a surface organization which assures the resonance of the series of events and of the attributes. The surface of signs does not yet, however, imply a unity of direction or community of organs. As a series of events it is primarily the sexuality of the male that is constituted at the surface of the body. The barber's comment that the boy is the penis and without it he is nothing is an example. But more important, the penis must be made visible and in this way forced into a hygienic sexuality. The ritual distinguishes between the depths of the body, always corrupting and therefore to be guarded against, and the zones of the surface, erogenous but always to be legitimated. All the events of the ritual are, in this sense, coordinated in the genital zone. Here, the phallus does not so much play the role of an organ as of an image that shows the healthy male, thereby pointing to its synecdochal character.

Yet it is recognized that a body will emit both fluid elements (urine, faeces, phlegm, semen) and hard substances (nails, teeth). Elements and substances either emanate from the depth or detach from the surface. Sounds, smells, tastes and temperatures refer to emissions from the depth whereas visual determinations refer to the surface. The relation between the depth and the surface is one where emissions, arising from the depth, pass through the surface, and as they detach from the body are replaced by a formerly concealed stratum. Such emissions are understood as being located on and in the physical object of the body since they are recognized and controlled by another.

The other is neither an object of gaze nor a subject. It is an a priori structure of the possible designating the genealogical positions and conjugal relationships potentially available to the boy undergoing circumcision. Thus, the other is a distillation of time by which the rhythms of the body are broken up into units.

There is a second way in which the other is conceived. Through the recitation of the *azan* and the whispering of the name, a theophanic other is sought to be created. The source of this home is an external environment since it emerges from a celestial height. Creation itself has two sides. First, its seat of residence (the depth of the body) manifests divinity by which the body becomes transparent. Second, the recitation of the *azan* is embedded in a corporeality and because of this linked to a particular apprehension of divinity. Each recitation of prayer in the ritual, in the sense noted above, becomes a recurrence of creation. The breath of prayer in the right ear of the circumcised introduces the idea of the guide who stands before the faithful. The other in this sense is the aid. The second part of the recitation—the whispering of the name in the right ear—is based on the attitude of the body prescribed in the course of ritual prayer: erect stance (*qiyam*), inclination (*ruku*) and prostration (*sujud*). The name of man and the prayer of God are thus co-present. Muhammad Umar, mentions that each living being manifests one or all the three postures given in prayer: the upright stance of the faithful corresponding to Miriam's *alif* or the celestial height; the movement of animals similar to the surface of bodies; and the descending movement of plants corresponding to the depth of the body. *Khatna*, he says, recognizes the three dimensions of prayer since it has the three postures of the body built into it: erect stance of the mother and child as they are draped over by the green cloth; the descending movement of the child's blood after his prepuce is removed; the burial of the prepuce under the nuptial bed. Each of these three postures is informed by the *azan*. Circumcision refers to the body in these three dimensions.

What is the body composed of after the ritual has been enacted? With its depth it is constitutive of emissions that are to be purified and controlled. In terms of a celestial height, the body is suffused with the word of God. And through the regime of signs playing on its surface the body recognizes the presence of the other. This surface, in the words of the barber, is the communion of the body with its other, evidenced in the first instance through vision (*shuhud*).

II. THE EVERYDAY DISCOURSE ON CIRCUMCISION

As we explore the terrain of the ritual, we find that the procedures characterizing the operation also organize the construction of the ritual. Meaning is structured around the processes of inscribing the ritual wound on the body. Thus an object marks the discourse on the ritual. Contrarily, in this section an object does not fashion the discourse in everyday life. The discourse on circumcision substitutes signs of the real for the real itself: the body becomes invisible in everyday conversations. Instead, *musalmani* shows the simulated generation of differences between the circumcised and the non-circumcised. Such differences cement a sense of community and posit pain as defining one's station in life. The ritual wound indicates forbearance. The referent, in the sense of the ritual wound, becomes an ornamental inscription on the sign. This section is concerned with the way the body is absented in everyday discourse and the substitution of *khatna* by the signs of *musalmani.*

This is not to suggest an irreconcilable difference between *khatna* and *musalmani.* An authority links the two and allows for an interchange. This authority, drawn from individual and collective memory, enables a reversal and a transition into a community. This community is delineated by recalling the ritual as it has been effected on someone else. Furthermore, this recall is founded not so much on an orthodoxy (of texts, ritual practices and formal exegesis) as on the capacity of *musalmani* to enter into a duplicative relationship with other terms, such as *iman* (belief) and *azan.* In showing the connection between *khatna* and *musalmani,* I do not postulate two opposed terms whose antinomies are transcended by a third. I assume circumcision is subject to multiple meanings.

Everyday speech and the disappearance of the body

As we chart the verbal representations of *musalmani,* we hear a fragmented discourse articulated on the heterogeneous practices of the community. These practices are located within the domain of the everyday.[12] They range from the act of weaving to social intercourse around a tea-stall. The verbal representations of women are absent. The body is absented in two ways. The ritual wound is imbued with an incorporeal value while the body is often seen as an appendage of the community.

Musalmani, when it refers to the genital zone, situates the latter within a speech domain where the emphasis is not so much on the physical condition of the body as on its incorporeal value. The incorporeality of the body issues from the following conversation immediately after the *patwari,* mentioned in the beginning of the paper, had made his comments and left us. The *patwari* asked his questions in a gathering among which I knew four others: Azeer, Kalimullah, Itrat and Rafiq. The first three, roughly of the same age, were friends of mine. Azeer was my companion on my initial reconnaissance field trips, and in 1985 the only unmarried one among the three. Rafiq is older. He was an outsider in this conversation. After the *patwari* left us I asked Azeer the meaning of the term *musalmani.*

A: With *musalmani* we become Muslim. (*Musalmani se hum musalman bante hain.*)

DM: But what is the meaning of *musalmani*? (*Par musalmani ka matlab kya hai*?)

To the amusement of the others Kalim visually mimed the operation of *khatna* from the perspective of the barber and then asked mockingly,

K: Do you want to become Muslim? (*Tumhe musalman banna hai*?)

Ignoring the rhetorical question I asked,

DM: What were you before *musalmani*? (*Musalmani ke pehle kya the tum*?)

K: The property of my mother. (*Ma ki amanat.*)

Itrat and Rafiq nodded assent. Azeer, turning to me, asked,

A: Do you know that masculinity is? (*Mardangi malum hai kya hovat*?)

I did not reply. Then Itrat gently pushing and in an ironic tone opined,

I: What does he know? In the city everyone is adept at masturbation. With *musalmani* the body acquires strength and we do not have any desire to masturbate. *Musalmani* and belief are twins. (*Isko kya malum? Shahr men sab apna hi pani nikalat. Musalmani ke sath jism men dum paida hovat aur pani chorne ka koi shauq nahin rahta. Musalmani aur iman jodi hain.*)

DM: How does the body acquire strength? (*Jism men dum kaise banta hai?*)

I: Strength? I've already told you. We don't masturbate. (*Dum? Kahe to diya. Him pani nahin nikalat.*)

DM: So? If you don't masturbate you become strong? I'm asking what is the connection between strength and non-masturbation? (*To? Agar ap pani nahin chorain jism men dum ata hai? Men puch raha hun dum aur pani ne chorne men kya taluk?*)

R: The meaning is clear. It is a miracle of nature that whenever a Muslim thinks of *musalmani* his heart overflows with spiritual words. With them the body acquires strength. (*Matlab saf hai. Qudrat ka kamal hai ki jab bhi koi Musalman musalmani ke bare men soche to uske dil men ruhani baten ubharne lagte hain. In se jism men dum ata hai.*)

K: Go on, you fraud! (*Chal pakhandbaj*!)

R: Are you showing your hand? This hero is going to begin his performance. (*Hath dikhariya hai? Yeh lumbardar apni nautanki karega.*)[13]

The conversation then examined the difference between the circumcised and the non-circumcised. I will consider this issue later.

An obvious aspect of the conversation is the correspondence established between body and speech. First we find a similarity between seeing and speaking. Kalim, in miming the operation of *khatna*, presents his body to the gaze of the other, a gaze where the body making a gesture prompts an understanding contrary to what it indicates. The gesture evokes the sexual organ and ironically reflects on the preceding question: 'But what is the meaning of the term *musalmani*?' In this sense the gaze divides the meaning of circumcision. While an explanation of *musalmani* is the operation of speech, pantomime is that of body. This speech, in Rafiq's view, has a spiritual essence since in his mode of reasoning it is animated with '*ruh*'.

However, it is not enough to say that the body is mimicry and speech is spiritual for in the conversation one does not know whether pantomime reasons or reason mimics. There is a complex relation between gaze and speech, for the latter takes on the mode of the former, while the body is effaced under the surface of verbal signs. If sight is ironic, so too is speech. Just as Kalim's gestures are interpreted contrary to their indication, so also his question to me ('Do you want to become Muslim?') and Itrat's observations on city folk are ironic reflections.

Such speech reflects on the body in a particular way (Itrat's observations of the body as strength, as belief, as the retention of semen, Azeer's opinion of masculinity and Rafiq's view of the body as spiritual). This speech stands for the body of the circumcised or, more appropriately, substitutes the physical sign on the body by verbal signs. This replacement is one of substitution: the speech of *musalmani* takes over and selectively arranges those meanings of *khatna* that evoke the tradition of Islam. In the process this speech suppresses the entire range of meanings available in *khatna.* This substitution is developed in the following conversation with Rafiq.[14]

Rafiq began by saying the *patwari* was a dangerous man although what he had said of *musalmani* was true: you cannot utter the *namaz* without *khatna.* More important, *khatna* not only makes the *namaz* available for the person in question but also enables this person to carry out his *duasalam.* For Rafiq *khatna* is the precondition of *musalmani.* But *musalmani* and *khatna* are not the same things. Whereas *khatna* cleanses the body of impurities, *musalmani* teaches the person how to approach the Quran and live a pious life. An obvious connection exists between the purification of the body and the conditions necessary for approaching the teachings of the Quran: the latter prescribe an elaborate procedure of purifying the body. However, for Rafiq, *khatna* is sanctioned after the Quran has constituted the world in which a Muslim lives. I asked Rafiq the meaning of '*ruh*' in *musalmani.* In its widest sense *musalmani* is the recitation of the Quran. Following this it refers to the five pillars. *Khatna* is linked to the second pillar (prayer) since the latter requires ablution. But *khatna* is more than the purification of the body. It is, Rafiq says, a mark of remembrance that one has heard the Quran and voluntarily recited *it (khatna se Quran ka zikr karte hain)*.

In Rafiq's account of *khatna* and *musalmani* two moments are discernible. First, *khatna* is linked to prayer. Second, both *khatna* and *musalmani* are subsumed under the power of the recited word. The conjunction of *khatna* with prayer, while utilizing the liturgy of official prayer, is not merely a public collective act, but also a divine practised by the fact of being circumcised. The conjunction represents the process of individuation, enabling the person to internalize the liturgy.

The inscription of the liturgy on the circumcised keeps the person's body within the limits set by the norms of various hygienic practices and legitimate conjugal relationships. Rafiq's account tells a more fundamental truth. It makes the body describe the order of *musalmani,* since *khatna* is the precondition of *musalmani. Khatna* in his estimation produces the practitioners of the norm of *musalmani.* In its most specific occurrence this norm is the inscription of the liturgy on the body, and in its most general manifestation it is the recitation of the Quran.

To the extent that this norm, inscribed on bodies and recounted by them, is repeated in every act of *khatna,* we find the emergence of a discourse centred on a tradition. From the point of view of *musalmani* this tradition makes of the body a text that emits signs and functions as a censor which channels and codes bodies. This censoring of the body emerges from the conversation I had with Muhammad Umar after the ceremony of Sadiq Ali's son.

A few days after the ceremony I had shifted to the house of Muhammad Umar who had consented to teach me how to operate the loom. I was a rather poor learner, easily bored by the interminable clapping of shuttles. During one of these sessions Umar remarked that my hand was unsteady because I did not know the discipline of *musalmani.* First, according to him, the craft of weaving demands the perfectly still body of the weaver. Second, this stillness must be interrupted by regular and abrupt movements of the hands and feet. Such movements are possible if all the motions of weaving originate from the centre of the body—the loins. For this reason, the loins must be particularly resilient and sturdy in maintaining the still and staccato body. The resilience of the loins is given, first, through the act of *khatna,* an act by which one learns the value of pain. The full understanding of pain, Muhammad Umar says, comes from a knowledge of the lives of the *peghambars* of Islam, all of whom endured Herculean hardship (the Prophet, Ali, Husain, Ayub Ansari and Sis Ali Salaam). To be knowledgeable of their lives is to bear witness. Weavers who are unsteady of hand and slow on their feet are inadequately schooled in the knowledge of pain. Conversely, the strength to bear such pain makes the weaver 'strong of speech' and a 'wise weaver'. *Musalmani,* he says, is the recognition by the boy of the pain he feels while being circumcised. This recognition he then links to weaving: to be a Muslim is not merely a question of enduring the pain of the operation, but also one by which the values of resilience, strong speech and wisdom are constituted.

Muhammad Umar isolates the gesture (the movement of the hands and feet in weaving) to organize his discursive space on *musalmani.* This gesture maps this space so that its occupants become available for observation and information: whether they are adequate Muslims and weavers. The gesture becomes visible when it shows the inadequacy of the functioning of the working body. A good gesture does not refer to the body but to the positive discourse of *musalmani,* which talks of pain, wisdom and speech. Thus, a non-discursive gesture is articulated in the language of *musalmani.* This gesture is a metonymic figure of *musalmani,* but also a figure where the bodies of its practitioners are made to speak the truth of *musalmani.* His statement derives its credibility from what it believes is the sign of pain and its union with weaving.

The community

In the above conversations *musalmani* is expressed and interpreted in various ways. The speakers see it as a statement of belief, the excess of *khatna,* pain and hardship. I have suggested that it may be seen as substitutive of the ritual, as the truth and censor of the circumcised body. In this sense *musalmani* produces multiple meanings. In one respect, however, all those I talked to were united in their opinion on the connotation of the term. Each maintained that *musalmani* represented a fundamental difference between Hindus and Muslims.

The dialogue mentioned in the beginning of this section (between Rafiq, Kalim, Itrat, Azeer and me) finally considered the difference between the circumcised and the non-circumcised. This occurred after Rafiq had left us. Kalim was scolded by Itrat for showing disrespect to Rafiq. Kalim launched into a colourful characterization of Rafiq and then commented:

K: What is the connection between *musalmani* and *ruh*? *Musalmani* and pain are twins. (*Musalmani aur ruh men kya taluk? Musalmani aur dard jodi hain.*)

I: You speak like a non-believer! There is some depth in Rafiq's statement. (*Jahil jaise bolat ho! Rafiq ki bat men kuch gherai hai.*)

K: (sarcastically): Then make me understand. (*To humko bhi samjha do.*)

I: Rafiq said that with *musalmani* the body learns to recognize pain. The distinctiveness of this recognition is that with it our belief increases. (*Rafiq ne kaha ki musalmani ke sath jism dard pehchanne lagat. Is pehchan ki khoobiyat asi hai ki hamara iman badta hai.*)

K: Tell me, do you remember the pain you felt? (*Batao, tumko dard ki yad hai?*)

I: Not at all. But this is what Rafiq meant. We don't remember our pain because it is part of our belief. That is why *musalmani* and pain are twins. (*Bilkul nahin. Par Rafiq ka yahi matlab tha. Him dard ka zikr nahin karte kyonke yeh dukh hamara iman hai. Is liye musalmani aur iman jodi hain.*)

A: Through belief we are separate from Hindus. (*Iman se hum Hinduon se ilaida hain.*)

I: Yes. But the meaning of the twinning [between *musalmani* and belief] is also that their [the Hindus'] pain is not productive of spirituality. The Hindu cannot tolerate his own pain. It is true that he can have himself cut in the hospital. But where is the spirit in that operation? (*Ji. Par jodi ka matlab yeh bhi hai ki unke dard se ruh nahin nikalta. Hindu apna dard nahin seh sakat. Yeh such hai ki woh apne ap ko hospital men katwa sakta hai. Par us operation men ruh kahan?*)

Later Rafiq made the same point. When I asked him whether *musalmani* distinguished Hindus from Muslims he said:

> It is true that the other word for *musalmani* is belief that is distinctive to Muslims. This is how we are different from Hindus because for us to be Muslim is to be pure and to have recited the Quran. The Quran is recited with knowledge only after we have removed all that causes impurity in our bodies. The Hindus lack this purity because they are afraid of shedding their blood.

Explaining the difference between Hindus and Muslims, Umar distinguished between the weavers of the two communities.

The Hindu weavers here, known as the Kohris, migrated to the city long ago. Sometimes I wish they had stayed because then the *nurbaf*[15] would have been able to show to them how the weft is made. We are able to weave the weft perfectly straight and without a single knot or break for up to six yards. How is this possible? *Musalmani* is our secret prayer. Through it we learn to educate our hands and feet, but also to maintain the steadfastness of our gaze.

I asked at what the gaze was directed. 'This vision is of the witness who has learnt to recognize pain, to pray with this recognition. *Musalmani* is the prayer of this pain'.

In each of the conversations *musalmani* is suffixed by a metonymic and metaphoric progression of meaning. First, *musalmani* is linked to the recognition of pain which, in turn, is associated with spirituality and subsequently becomes part of the belief of the group. Finally this series of meanings empowers the body of the Musalman, distinguished from the Hindu whose pain is not spiritually elevating. In the second conversation Rafiq connects *musalmani* to the removal of bodily impurity, links the pure body to the recitation of the Quran and concludes that this progression is the belief of the Musalman. The Hindu, in contrast, lacks bodily purity because he fears shedding his blood. In the last conversation, Umar considers the Musalman and the *nurbaf* to be synonyms. The *nurbaf* is an accomplished weaver because he is witness to pain. Consisting of both gesture and sight, this achievement is recognized in prayer. The *nurbaf* is contrasted with the Hindu Kohri who is a poor weaver because he is inadequately experienced in pain. In each of the conversations the body becomes a metonym of *musalmani*. However, the full meaning of the term is achieved only when *musalmani* is linked to general metaphors by which the community is defined.

Common to the three conversations is the ability of each speaker to talk on behalf of the community: each uses the plural in talking of *musalmani*. The community is framed in two ways. First, such speech replaces the signs on the body by attaching to *musalmani* meanings that are external to those found in the ritual. *Musalmani* is an index of such externality and a way of separation from Hindus.

Second, in the estimation of the speakers the community is represented both as a separation from Hindus and by the arrogation of a positive meaning. This is seen in the linking of *musalmani* to terms such as belief, strength, and removal of bodily impurity. Here, *musalmani* always exists as a double meaning: the utterance containing or related to *musalmani* signifies like any other, but also intervenes as an element of metasignification by which the entire utterance acquires a theme. As a symbol *musalmani* harbours a double meaning. The obvious meaning both covers and uncovers a figurative one. It is single signifier with multiple signifieds. Unlike a symbol, however, *musalmani institutes* a relation between itself and various metaphors. Through this relationship the body is described (and eventually annexed). In other words, *musalmani* establishes a duplicative relation between itself and other terms such as *iman, ruh* and *dard.* This is tantamount to saying that the relationship between *musalmani* and, for example, *iman,* depends upon the decoder's ability to make the substitutions necessary to pass from one register to another. Yet, the understanding of *musalmani* is not solipsistic, if only because the task of establishing equivalences is already encoded in *musalmani. Musalmani,* Muslim, *iman, ruh, dard* and *nurbaf* all enter into a duplicative relationship. Whatever the relation between *musalmani* and other terms, all the speakers enclose *musalmani* by the term 'Hindu'.

If *musalmani* enters into a duplicative relationship with terms such as *iman, ruh* and *namaz,* it is important to remember that the speakers mention pain (*dard, dukh*) as its experiential core. The speakers reflect on this term but in such a way that pain is not linked to the physical impairment of the body. The experience of such pain is spatial not because it is restricted to any one body, but because the body of the community, taken as one whole, is a body formed in pain. In the case of Umar the pain borne out of witnessing the hardship of the icons of Islam becomes the object of prayer, while for Itrat, in his interpretation of Rafiq's view, pain is belief. Pain, in this sense, is incorporated into the definition of the community, neither disrupting the intentions of its members, nor alienating them from the group.

From the account of the conversations it is possible to make a further inference: the community becomes a presence when the characteristics used to describe it are those by which the body is so delineated. The speakers believe *musalmani* justifies the pain one feels during the ritual. There is one important way in which this presence is affected. When I asked each speaker whether he remembered his ceremony I was categorically told no one remembers his ceremony, but that every male at some point in his life is expected to be present at someone else's. Umar maintains it is only by participating in another's ceremony that one understands the significance of *khatna* for oneself and its link with *musalmani. Khatna,* for him, replicates the physical hardship endured by the icons of Islam while *musalmani* is the prayer of this pain. Rafiq describes the significance of *khatna* as one where the person, who is witness to the ceremony, can see how he is part of the community of Islam. In this respect such participation in the *ummah* arises only after the ritual has been presented to the witness. The significance of this presentation, Rafiq holds, is found in the meaning of *musalmani.* In its widest sense this meaning is derived from the recitation of the Quran; in its most particular manifestation it refers to the purity of the body signalled by *khatna.* Itrat holds that the ritual is the first test of hardship for the boy undergoing it. The boy's recognition of this hardship can, however, only be undertaken on his behalf by his male agnates. In turn the boy will understand the meaning of this recognition in his capacity as a witness.

In this respect the speakers base their sense of community on the claim to being members in the community of Islam. In so doing they establish links to that tradition. Their interpretation conceals the work of the ritual that is not connected with pain and belief. An interpretation that reflects on the union of milk and blood, the combination of male and female and that of *hamdami,* is ignored. It is almost as if that version of the ritual is valorised which, in invoking a tradition, constitutes the body as a zone of hygienic practices, but as practices that commemorate the community. Both Miriam and Shabnam take recourse to an argument that is legitimated by reference to an inherited tradition and the regeneration of the group. The barber, too, bases her argument on the reproduction of a framed world where the novice eventually recognizes the presence of the other inside his body. The speakers establish the validity of their case by invoking Islam in one way or another. In this invocation the material properties of the sign, as inscribed on the body of the novice, are effaced. Instead another discourse, one that talks of belief and pain, replaces the materiality of the embodied sign.

The replacement of the embodied sign by the discourse of *musalmani* is evident in the constitution of a collective memory. None of the speakers remembers his ceremony, and Rafiq says that it is more significant for the witnesses. In this sense the recall of *khatna* is based not on its individual inscription on the speaker, but on its distribution among every male member of the community. In describing the common thread that binds one circumcised body to another, the speakers attach a retrospective ordering to the ritual. This ordering, evidenced in the discourse of *musalmani,* transforms individual bodies into a communal body.

Two main operations characterize this memory. The first removes something excessive or adds to the discourse. Second, the credibility of this discourse consists in making each body describe its (the discourse's) code. The act of extracting or adding situates the members of the community within the limits established by the twinning of *musalmani* with another term. In this respect, through the disciplinary instrument of the ritual wound, the discourse of *musalmani* is the way by which a social law maintains its hold on bodies and its members. Because this law is incarnated in a physical practice, it makes adherents believe that it speaks in the name of the community of Islam.

The credibility of the discourse of *musalmani* operates through the instrument of the ritual wound since the latter allows for linking *musalmani* with pain and prayer. Here, the wound is an instrument because it allows living beings to become sings that must recur from one body to another. By situating the wound within its fold, the discourse of *musalmani* incorporates the ritual of *khatna,* not as a repetition of the ritual in its filigreed detail, but as a community reminding itself of its identity as represented and told by conjoining *musalmani* with pain and belief. *Musalmani* commemorates the past as a collective autobiography—a master narrative, more than a story told. It is a cult enacted in its telling.

III. CONCLUSION

Bloch (1986) provides a diachronic reading of the circumcision ritual with the intention of showing the principles of change both in the form of the ritual and its constitution as a symbolic system. He says the ritual is historically ordered since it is affected by events external to its framework. However, the '[t]wo images of the world, the ritual and the everyday, cannot in ordinary, non-revolutionary circumstances, compete with each other' (ibid.: 188) because of the peculiar nature of rituals. The ritual is related to the non-ritual not so much competitively, as in enacting what the latter cannot. The ritual establishes a generalized authority. Allied with this authority is a strong emotional appeal. Together, the ritual's authority and effect explain its individual and collective relevance.

The conclusions of this paper are the opposite of what Bloch shows, especially regarding the relation between the ritual and the everyday conversations that reflect on it. The relation between the ritual and the everyday is one where the latter selectively incorporates those elements privileging a sense of the community of Islam. Though this community is not identical with that posited in the ritual—the conjunction of the name with the *azan*—it establishes a continuity with the ritual insofar as the wound becomes, in everyday conversations, an index of pain and belief. In so doing, such conversations attach a significance to the wound in a way that it is external to the frame of the ritual. This significance marks a separation from the term 'Hindu'. In the ritual this term conveys a state of being undifferentiated which the ritual then disaggregates. The conversations, on the other hand, value the term so that it offers a counterpoint to what the Muslim is not.

The appropriation of the ritual wound by the conversations raises a second point. It is possible to argue that the ritual, more than the everyday, has a plasticity built into it and is subject to plural interpretations: the accounts of the mother and the barber and the valorising of the body. This is not to deny that the ritual has a transcendental authority, both collective and individual, built into it—the conjunction of the *azan* with the name that is mapped on to the body of the novice. But it is not as if such transcendence is absent in everyday conversations. The sense of community posited by the speakers is based on an apprehension of the *ummah*, but a community that is established eventually through an act of memory. In contrast, the ritual inscribes the community on the body of the novice.

In the case of this study, then, the basis of separating the ritual from the everyday is not the absence or presence of transcendental authority, but the presencing or absenting of the body. In the ritual the body is the object that is worked upon, while in the conversations it is pushed into the background. The ritual, we have seen, not only valorises the body as the site where the social structure and the community of Islam are enacted but also brings the body in existence in the elements of language. In this sense the circumcision of every male child is the reproduction of the community.

This reproduction, it must be acknowledged, is initiated through the agency of the ritual wound. With the ritual, the body becomes the object of reference and with the everyday conversations the referentiality of the body is substituted by an imagination that constitutes the boundaries of being Muslim. The link between the two (*khatna* and *musalmani*) is provided by the significance attached to the ritual wound. Scarry (1985: 161-326) shows how physical pain is insinuated in the making of the world. In this making, wounding establishes an identifiable relation between the human body and an imagined object.[16]

Following from Scarry's argument we might say that the body as a created object occupies two dimensions: the corporeal and the imagined. The body is corporeal insofar as it 'has all the sturdiness and vibrancy of presence of the natural world' (1985: 280). The body is also imagination because in the moment of its making it is embossed with a future. Much of this paper has followed Scarry's argument in the second half of her book. However, rather than argue for a referential relationship between pain and making, I have suggested that the link between pain and wounding institutes the imagination of *musalmani*. With the ritual we find an imagination that is projected on the physical surface of the body. Here, the act of wounding is willed and legitimated since it restores the body to the community. In this legitimation the self-referentiality of the physical body (found, for example, in its emissions) is socially censored. Simultaneously, the wound also constitutes the metaphysical body, but here the act of wounding is produced in accordance with an already ordained world (found in the conjunction between the name and the *azan*).

In incorporating the wound, the everyday conversations do not recreate the ritual body. In fact, they deny it its complete referentiality (the union of male and female). In linking *musalmani* with pain and prayer, the speakers constitute the future and past as unlimited since the community is not invested with the telos. For the speakers the community must exist for all time and every wound must recreate that existence. Each speaker, it is true, bears the wound within his own body, but the power of the wound and its linking with pain is such that the body is invited into it. In this sense the wound exists before the speaker. He is born to embody it. For this reason, both the ritual and the conversations show how the whole body exchanges its organic will for a social and spiritual one.

NOTES

* *Acknowledgements*: In the writing of this paper Jit Uberoi and Veena Das have exercised a formative influence. I thank Roma Chatterji and Radhika Chopra for their criticisms and Jaya Chatterji for her editorial help.

1. Fieldwork, on which this paper is based, was conducted in two villages of Barabanki district, Uttar Pradesh (1985-6) among a community of weavers, popularly known as Julaha. These weavers call themselves Ansaris. For a discussion of the ramification of the term Julaha, see Pandey (1990) and Crooke (1974). Ansari (1960) discusses the social structure and caste ranking of the Ansaris. I have discussed elsewhere the conception of weaving and its relationship to the Ansari social structure (see Mehta 1992).
2. As far as the circumcision ritual is concerned, I cannot generalize for all Muslim communities in India. We could expect a considerable variation in the content of the ritual across high and low castes. For one, the ritual specialist is different—among high castes it is the male barber. Second, upper-caste Muslims in Uttar Pradesh do not use the term *khatna* to describe the ritual, but prefer *sunna* or *sunnat.*
3. The Ansaris, like most other Muslim groups in India, do not practise female circumcision.
4. I use the term biunity deliberately for my concern is to show how the male body, in its unity, is composed simultaneously of male and female elements. In this context, co-presence or conjunction would always imply two bodies.
5. The male head of the dwelling, in consultation with the elders of his agnatic line, decides on the date of his child's circumcision. Sadiq Ali says children are not circumcised during the 'dark' months of Muharram, Sabrat and Roza since this is a period of solemnity. During Muharram, he adds, some Ansaris are in mourning, in Sabrat old members of the community pray for deliverance, while during Roza the entire community fasts. Circumcision is usually done in the months of Id, the beginning of the new year, or in Chahullam, the most important Ansari festival.
6. In 1985, the year of this fieldwork, the controversy in Ayodhaya had only just begun. The gates of the Babri Masjid, it was rumoured in the field, had been thrown open to the Hindu worshippers of Ram. There were extended debates on the implications of this move, widely believed to have been orchestrated by the central government in Delhi. My friends in the field argued, in hindsight presciently, that this move would change forever the landscape of Hindu-Muslim relations.
7. The house is the centre around which both weaving and the ritual are enacted. Broadly, the house is divided into a male (*mardana*) and female (*zanana*) section. The male part consists of an uncovered courtyard and the work shed, where the loom is housed, while the female part comprises the room of the nuptial night, a covered courtyard and the kitchen.
8. The quilt room (*dul'ai kamra*), located in the *zanana*, is the place where quilts are made and where a part of the weaving process is executed. The woman head of the household oversees both these activities and exercises

control over them. For the purposes of the ritual the quilt room offers a contrast to the courtyard of the *zanana*.

9. None of the Ansari men I talked to remembered their own ceremony, but they were eloquent in describing someone else's. In this sense descriptions never refer to the speaker. They show how a collective memory is, through the ritual, inscribed on the paper.
10. Among Ansaris this day is marked by its relative lack of ostentation and display. Wensinck (1986) reports that in Mecca, on the day preceding circumcision, the boy, clad in costly garments, is paraded through the streets on horseback and is accompanied by footmen and his father's elderly black handmaid. The second part of the procession is composed of the boy's poor comrades. The procession traverses the main streets. Similarly, in Egypt the boy is paraded through the streets. Dressed as a girl, he has his face covered by a kerchief. As in Mecca, he is preceded by musicians. In contrast, circumcision among the Ansaris of Barabanki is confined exclusively to the household.
11. These signs indicate, manifest and signify. As indexicals they function by associating particular words with particular objects or images. In themselves these terms are empty of content, but are filled in through a relationship of externality and referentiality. There is a strict relationship of referentiality between *istibra* and the penis, between *ghusl* and the purified body, and indeed between the name and the person. Further, the terms are indexical in a special sense: They forms material singularities by indicating how each male body is to conduct itself. However, *ghusl*, *istibra* and the name are more than indicators. Through them the novice reflects a socially recognized masculinity and constitutes for himself the domain of the personal. The third dimension of his regime of signs—signification—relates each of the terms to general or universal concepts. Here, signification implies promises and commitments to both the domestic group and the community of Islam.
12. I take the concept of the everyday from Heller (1984). Rather than argue for a separation between the everyday and the ritual, I will show that the former selectively incorporates the ritual.
13. Rafiq is making a sarcastic comment. Nautankis are, in the field, popular theatrical performances influenced almost entirely by Hindi films. Rafiq is obviously commenting on Kalim's penchant for mockery.
14. Rafiq, one of the members present at the circumcision, is Sadiq Ali's father's brother's daughter's husband. Affinally, he is Sadiq Ali's wife's sister's husband's brother. For the purpose of the ceremony he traced his relationship with Sadiq Ali through consanguinity.
15. The traditional term for the weavers was *nurbaf* (weavers of light). Whenever they describe their stories of origin they always represent themselves as 'weavers of white light'.

16. There are three stages by which the body is so delineated. In the first stage the human body and God's voice occur on separate registers, but the events occurring on one register confirm those occurring on the esecond. Stage two shows how, with the conflation of wounding and creating, the body is engulfed with the voice and vice versa. In the last stage creation and wounding are, as categories of action, separated so that the sentient body is substantiated by material and verbal artifacts (Scarry 1985: 184).

REFERENCES

Ansari, G. 1960. *Muslim Caste in Uttar Pradesh.* Lucknow: Lucknow University Press.

Bloch, M. 1986. *From Blessing to Violence: History and Ideology in the Circumcision Ritual of the Merina of Madagascar.* Cambridge: Cambridge University Press.

Bouhdiba, A. 1985. *Sexuality in Islam* (trans. A. Sheridan). London: Routledge and Kegan Paul.

Bourdieu, P. 1977. *Outline of a Theory of Practice* (trans. R. Nice). Cambridge: Cambridge University Press.

Crooke, W. 1977. *The Tribes and Castes of North India,* Vol. III. Delhi: Cosmo.

El-Zein, A. 1977. 'Beyond ideology and theology: The search for an anthropology of Islam'. *Annual Review of Anthropology* 6: 227-54.

Heller, A. 1984. *Everyday Life* (trans. G. Campbell). London: Routledge and Kegan Paul.

Lewis, I.M., ed. 1966. *Islam in Tropical Africa.* Oxford: Oxford University Press.

Mehta, D. 1992. 'The semiotics of weaving: A case study'. *Contributions to Indian Sociology* (n.s.) 26, 1: 77-113.

Pandey, G. 1990. *The Construction of Communalism in Colonial North India.* Delhi: Oxford University Press.

Scarry, E. 1985. *The Body in Pain: The Making and Unmaking of the World.* New York: Oxford University Press.

Trimingham, J. 1964. *Islam in East Africa.* Oxford: Clarendon Press.

Watt, M. 1965. 'Conditions of membership of the Islamic community'. In C.J. Bleeker, ed., *Initiation,* pp. 195-201. Leiden: E.J. Brill.

Wensinck, A. 1986. 'Khitan'. In *The Encyclopaedia of Islam,* vol. V (new edition), pp. 20-2. Leiden: E.J. Brill.

Caste in Islam and the Problem of Deviant Systems: A Critique of Recent Theory

CHARLES LINDHOLM

(1986)

Recent discussions on the role of Islam in India have given rise to a stimulating theoretical controversy. Among the debaters it has been recognized by all that there are many versions of Islamic practice and belief; the controversy is how to define these forms within an Indian context. At the centre of the debate are three volumes edited by Ahmad (1976, 1978, 1981). In these books he makes the general claim that Islamic beliefs and practices in India have accommodated themselves to fit within the larger Hindu community, so that really there are two Islam, 'one ultimate and formal, derived from the Islamic texts; the other proximate and local, validated by custom' (1981: 15). This dualist image is reiterated by Madan, who says Muslims (and Hindus) have 'two sets of representations, one stemming from ideological considerations and the other from the compulsions of living' (1981: 58). Local practice among Muslims is therefore an adaptive response to the constraints of the Indian environment. But along with this functionalist adaptive argument there is an assertion that belief systems, particularly Islamic belief systems, exist as 'ultimate and formal' essences.

Other writers, such as Carroll (1983) and Robinson (1983) make their essentialist statements more obviously. Carroll writes that Ahmad ignores Islamic law. It is clear that Carroll considers the normative commands of Islamic law to be crucial in articulating differences between Hindu and Muslim. Robinson takes this position further, arguing that there is an inexorable worldwide trend toward orthodoxy among Indian Muslims; a 'continual, if sometimes slow and barely perceptible, movement between visions of perfect Muslim life and those which ordinary Muslims lead' (1983: 201). This historical teleology assumes, of course, that there is a 'perfect' Muslim life one can approach. Normative visions of Islam are also characteristic (with some exceptions and qualifications) of Metcalf's edited volume (1984) on the place of *adab* in South Asian Islam.

The essentialist position is strongly opposed by Das, who takes a 'Geertzian' tack, proposing a more 'reflective' mode of analysis that gives credit to creative interpretation and denies the attribution of any 'essence' to Islam. According to Das, Islam is instead continually reworked through a 'folk theology' of discourse about scripture and practice. This approach tends to focus on usage, particularly on the manner in which scripture is understood and enacted at the village level. The aim is to construct the 'native's point of view' through the way in which meaning is given to a text. For Das, then, the important problem is not to discern ultimate values, but rather to understand the dialectic between norms and action in achieving consensus. Her focus is upon 'the active role of the community of believers in sustaining the ideals of Islam' (1984: 297).

The normative and interpretive schools are in many respects quite at odds. But I wish to argue here that both share fundamental underlying premises rooted in a mutual concern with the centrality of meaning in social life. Interpretation is the anthropologist's attempt to convey the native's efforts to construct a coherent model of the world and of action in it. This effort, however, is constrained by and directed to an ultimate text containing the 'norms' or 'values' that are being reworked. The emphasis on the word and its interpretation can thereby be seen as a more sophisticated and open-ended local level version of the essentialist case for ideal values. The essentialist claims these values are given, while for the interpretive school meaning is constructed by discourse within the community. This distinction is important, since the constructionist argument permits (at least in theory) the possibility of communication across cultures and of internal conflict over the 'proper' interpretation. None the less both approaches imply that the object of their study is irreducible and unique. Both also consider texts and the elucidation of texts to be crucial. In a sense, they are different subsets of what might be called a 'systems of meaning' or 'symbolic' theory.

These approaches, with their concern for meaning, stand opposed to another major strand of theory, now rather discredited, but hard to ignore. This is the comparative orientation, usually utilizing the arguments of structural-functionalism of diffusionism. This school sees interpretation and normative values as secondary phenomena lying above more fundamental social processes. Furthermore, it denies the absolute uniqueness of culture, favouring either the analysis of basic structural forms, or of functional adaptation of traits.

In the following essay, I will argue that both the comparative and the symbolic schools may be adequate in ordinary circumstances; but are inadequate when different 'world-views' come into contact, as occurs when Hindu and Muslim meet. It is then that the 'givens' of a particular social order become matters of self-consciousness, and the underlying premises of social life are opened to inquiry. This opening throws into question people's own self-definition, and also permits the consideration of theory in a new light.

Nowhere is the potential for a theoretical critique more evident than in the question of the place of Muslims in a caste system. Caste is a cultural meeting point that is exceptionally rich, since it is in caste ideology that Hindu and Muslim are most at odds: the former ratifying hierarchy, the latter proclaiming equality. Furthermore, the concept of caste has itself attracted considerable sophisticated theoretical interest which can be both used and re-evaluated in the light of the excellent material collected by Ahmad and his colleagues. In this essay, then I intend to look at the premises that lie beneath the theories of caste among Muslims in order to show the internal difficulties of assuming either a symbolic interpretive/normative stance or a comparative structural diffusionist view. I will conclude with a tentative proposal of a conflict model that may be more appropriate to the situation.[1]

Debate on the nature of caste has been long, complex and sometimes acrimonious: but with all the sound and fury, no consensus has been reached. Basically, the various positions boil down to the two mutually exclusive arguments outlined above. This first is structural-functional and views caste as a category or type, comparable in many respects to similar type-systems elsewhere. According to Berreman, a proponent of this approach, 'a caste system resembles a plural society whose discrete sections are all ranked vertically' (1967: 55). Caste can therefore, in Berreman's view, be useful compared to other rank societies, such as the American ranking of blacks and whites. A related argument is not as concerned with structural similarities but looks instead at the mixture of traits found within a particular society. This diffusionist approach uses comparison primarily to link trait complexes with one another.

The second school understands caste as a total symbolic world, unique and not comparable with other systems. Most of these theorists would agree with Bougle, who wrote that 'the spirit of caste unites these three tendencies: repulsion, hierarchy and hereditary specialization' (1971: 9). Dumont, the best known of this group, stresses the attributes of hierarchy and repulsion. He pays special attention to the rigidity of caste positions at each end of the hierarchical scale and to a supposed radical opposition in Hindu thought between categories of power and categories of status (Dumont 1970). Leach, on the other hand, gives first place to hereditary specialization, and the diagnostic of the system, of him, is that 'every caste, not merely the upper elite, has its special 'privileges' (1960: 7).

A somewhat different approach is taken by Marriott and Inden. Instead of focusing on patterns of opposition and inclusion in the fashion of Dumont and Leach, they postulate an indigenous monism, grounded in the assumption that 'all living beings are differentiated into genera, or classes, each of which is thought to possess a defining substance' (1974: 983). These substances, according to the theory, are formed by various transactions, particularly transactions involving food. Although the authors allow that 'rudimentary caste systems have appeared elsewhere' than India (ibid.: 991), it is evident that the symbolic universe of differentiated transactional substances is most fully elaborated in the subcontinent. Thus, they share with Dumont, Leach and others of the symbolic school an emphasis on the coherence and singularity of the Hindu caste system.

How, then, do Ahmad and his contributors handle caste? A basic concern of most of the essays, and of the editor, is the delineation of the effect of caste ideology upon the Muslim community. Caste, in this instance, is viewed in a fashion that much resembles Bougle's definition. The Muslim groups involved are endogamous, hierarchical, and occupationally specialised, with an ideology that restricts relations between the ranked units: they are therefore considered to be within the framework of caste.

From these premises it would seem that no comparison with Muslim peoples outside of South Asia is possible, since Islam is an ideology of radical equality, totally opposed to an assertion of intrinsic hierarchies among believers. The discriminatory barriers between Muslims in India thus must be a result of the influence of caste. As Dumont writes, Indian Muslims 'are contaminated by the caste spirit, although they have not absolutely succumbed to it' (1970: 207).

Ahmad and his contributors do not take quite so simple a position. For instance, Ahmad writes that despite doctrinaire pronouncements of equality, Islamic history shows much evidence of ranking. Even during the era of Muhammad himself, the Quraish tribe claimed first place among all Arabs, while contemporary Arabs divide themselves between the pure Asilin and the inferior people of mixed blood. During the Umayyad dynasty non-Arab subjects were held to be markedly inferior to their conquerors; an inferiority that did not cease with conversion to Islam. In fact, marriage between the two categories was 'regarded as an appalling misalliance' (Lewis 1966: 70). The resentment felt by conquered peoples at this injustice is often cited as one of the root causes of the Abbasid revolt and the rise of Shiism.

Despite the historical gap between the Muslim ideology of equality and the reality of hierarchy, Ahmad still writes that 'Muslim social stratification does not approximate even remotely to the Indian model' and he concludes that 'caste among the Muslims in India owes itself directly to Hindu influences, but it has been reinforced by the justification offered for the idea of birth and descent as criteria of status in Islamic law' (1978: 15). Therefore, 'It is clear that caste exists as a basis of social relations among (Indian Muslims), but its form has been greatly weakened and modified and it differs from the Hindu caste model in certain details' (ibid.: 12). With some equivocation, Ahmad considers caste to be a unique and all-encompassing social phenomenon, an 'essence', and thus remains within the symbolic camp on this point.

Here I would like to take another look at the comparative arguments from which Ahmad turned aside. In fact, is the South Asian world so very different from the world of the Middle East? The argument that the differences obscure underlying similarities has been made most cogently by Barth, who claims that the Swat Pathans, Sunni Muslim people living in the mountains of northern Pakistan, have a type of caste system: but this system is not derived from Indian influence. Rather, he says that Pathan caste is typically Middle Eastern. Barth believes that the Middle Eastern world, like the world of India, is characterized by endogamous, occupationally specialized groups, ideologically separated and ranked in a rough hierarchy. The concept of pollution, so typical of India, is absent, but its place is taken structurally by the notion of shame. Barth also makes an analogy between Pathan holy men, who are venerated even though ideally they must shun political power, and the apolitical Brahmin. Furthermore, at the low end of the social scale, the despised Pathan leather-worker, barber, dancer and sweeper are as much locked in their roles as the Hindu Untouchable is in his. As in India, the Pathan sweeper is even forbidden commensality. For Barth each position in the Pathan hierarchy, like each position in the Hindu caste system, is a summation of statuses, ratified by restrictions on commensality and other forms of social intercourse. Caste is, therefore, considered to be one variant on a more general formal pattern (Barth 1960).

Barth's argument should be considered in the context of Middle Eastern ethnography. For instance, the Marri Baluch are called a caste society by their ethnographer (Pehrson 1966). As among the Pathans, the Baluch clearly mark off the lower orders of serfs, gypsies, smiths and musicians, while the group leader is regarded with religious awe as a being apart and holy. In Persia, the agricultural peoples of Kirman are divided into named endogamous groups within the framework of what looks very much like the Hindu varna system of priest/warrior/clerk/farmer. Once again, there is a set of polluted castes (English 1966). A similar situation is found in South Yemen, where Brahmin-like holy men outrank and mediate among hierarchic endogamous groups, bounded at the lowest level by a set of despised 'Untouchables' with whom commensality is not permitted. The ethnographer (Bujra 1971), has no qualms about calling this a caste society. Other societies with similar patterns, selected more or less at random, include the Kabyle (Berque 1955), the Rif Berbers (Coon 1953), the Tuareg (Briggs 1960) and the Daghara Arabs of Iraq (Fernea 1970). Gaborieau, who uses legal codes in his discussion of Islamic social organization, is thus in error when he asserts that Muslims have no collective impurity or refusal of commensality (1978a). As Carroll notes (1983), practice and law often do not coincide, even in the Muslim heartland. Discrimination against 'inferior' groups, though ostensibly prohibited by Koranic law, is a practical fact in very many Muslim societies.

The resemblances between the two systems go even deeper. Coon proposes a model for Middle Eastern society, which he calls the 'mosaic' system. It has nothing to do with Moses, but instead closely resembles the standard definition of caste accepted by those of the symbolic school. According to Coon, each ethnic group in the Middle East has its own insignia and imputed characteristics. A premium is placed on difference and specialization (one group has even evolved into professional archaeological excavators), and it is easy to tell by looking at a man's clothing and head-dress his status, race and occupation, since all are united. The old cities of the Middle East also present a familiar picture to the Indianist: small wards of interrelated occupational specialists, hierarchically ranked and endogamous. The words Coon uses to describe this world are equally appropriate for India. 'The mosaic system is best suited for a civilization in which trades require a maximum of skill, taught from father to son, and a minimum of organizational complexity': it is a system that 'treats the various segments of the landscape as part of a coordinated whole, rather than as separate economic realms (Coon 1953: 153, 171).

Coon himself does not compare his mosaic model with caste, since it is possible both to change occupations and to marry outside one's own group in the Middle East. But many South Asianists have shown that the rigidity of caste has been greatly overstated (cf. Harper 1959), and that the system was probably even more flexible prior to its codification by British census takers. Furthermore, in both worlds exogamy, when it does occur, tends to be a phenomenon limited to the elite, or to urbanites; it is also generally hypergamous and validates rank. For instance, among the Pathans the holy lineages take wives from the warrior clans without reciprocity, thereby validating their ideological superiority, while Indian upper castes may follow the same pattern.

In none of the Middle Eastern societies is the notion of pollution as highly developed as it is in India. None the less, there are some similarities. The lowest social groups in the Middle East cannot give food to those higher, though food can be received by them; a situation analogous to that of the Indian Untouchable. As in India, eating together and sharing food expresses social solidarity and equality. In both cultures giving food or gifts to religious mendicants is an act of piety for which blessings are returned. Like the Hindu Brahmin, the Muslim Saint converts worldly gifts into divine grace. Finally, it is shameful for a Muslim to receive without giving in return, while giving without reciprocity is considered the height of honour (Lindholm 1982). Moral rank, as well as political rank, is thereby manifested in similar sorts of exchanges both in India and in the Middle East, though the idiom utilized is different.

It seems then, that following Barth's lead and looking for structural equivalents to caste in the Middle East throws some of the assumptions about the uniqueness of caste into question. Leach's definition of caste as 'a system of labour division from which the element of competition among the workers has largely been excluded' (1960: 5) is applicable to the Middle East. The inclusive hierarchy with rigid lines drawn at the top and at the bottom, as described by Dumont, is also a Middle Eastern feature, and so is the revered figure of the charismatic world renouncer who stands above the ranks and unites them by his holiness. As in India, transactions of food and other 'substance codes' reveal rank and differentiation: there is even a way of morally ranking the various units. It is quite possible, therefore, to be devil's advocate and argue that the similarities between South Asian Muslims and Hindus are not a result of assimilation, but rather of structural correspondence. The aspects of South Asian Muslim life which Ahmad and his colleagues see as deriving from Hindu influence, may instead be seen as reflections of characteristic features of the Middle East!

A diffusionist argument is also possible. At the simplest level, it could be said that the invidious distinction made by many Indian Muslims between the Ashraf, who claim foreign descent, and the Ajlaf, who are converts from Hinduism, is extrinsic to the Indian world, resembling instead the status barriers erected between early Arab conquerors and their subjects. This hierarchy of rank may be a 'trait' adapted to India, but derived from the Middle East by cultural diffusion.

A similar diffusionist case has been made against Ahmad by both Das (1984) and Robinson (1983), who cite the use of holy amulets and the prevalence of 'saint' worship in the Middle Eastern core communities as a counter argument to Ahmad's claim of Islamic assimilation into India. But for a really thorough diffusionist approach one must run instead to Gaborieau, who has written a series of articles and books dealing mainly with the place of Muslim bangle-makers in Nepal (1977). He calls this group 'a hybrid type' (1978b: 170), combining Hindu and Muslim elements. None the less, Gaborieau considers the bangle-makers to be part of a caste system. Like Ahmad, he uses Bougle's model, and sees the bangle-makers as an endogamous specialist group located within an overarching hierarchy who follow, though in an attenuated form, many Hindu practices. According to Gaborieau, the bangle-makers even '*acceptent au moins les principes concernant la pollution, base du systéme des castes*' (1966: 89). Therefore they must be categorized as a caste group, though of a mixed variety, tainted by Muslim influence.

But Gaborieau also shows clearly that the bangle-makers are different from Hindus in many respects: their social structure is unlike that of the Hindus in that they have more fragmented lineages of shallower depth (1978a, 1978b): they are also much less concerned with pollution and stand in an ambiguous position in the Nepalese caste structure (1972). Even more important, Hindus link political and ritual authority, while Muslims 'avoid anything which may appear as sacralization of the social order from congregational worship' (1979: 191). According to Gaborieau, this attitude derived from differences in concepts of religion, effectively prevents the full integration of Muslims into Hindu polity, since there is a fundamental refusal among Muslims to accept the Hindu deification of authority. Muslim notions of religious hierarchy and of the place of religious specialists also are at odds with the Hindu model; in particular there is no figure analogous to the Brahmin, since the 'Muslim can always purify himself (ibid.: 190). Thus the Brahmin has disappeared' (ibid.: 194). Given these many divergences, is Gaborieau's assertion of caste among the bangle-makers logically permissible within the premises of the symbolic framework?

I would say that it is not. The diffusionist acceptance of cultural mixtures, as well as the structural-functional claim for underlying formal patterns, denies a central postulate of the symbolist position. This is the postulate of the uniqueness and ideological coherence of the system; a coherence derived from sacred texts and doctrine accepted (and interpreted) by every member of the society. The Hindu world-view, with its sacralization of hierarchy and dominance, is not found in the cases cited by Barth or Gaborieau. Pathan leaders, as Dumont accurately notes, have no recourse to religious hierarchy to justify their rule as the Kshatriya warriors must in India. Therefore, Dumont says that Barth's Pathan caste is not caste at all; rather 'the Hindu system is here beheaded, subordinated to a different system' (1970: 329). He would undoubtedly make the same argument in the case of the 'truncated' structure of the Nepalese bangle-makers.

If it is accepted that the 'systems of meaning' approach for castes rests on the assertion of an internalized, inclusive coherent world-view (which, for the interpretive school, is reworked at the local level through discourse on the sacred texts) then we must reconsider the portrait drawn of Muslims in India by Ahmad and his co-workers. Although his general conclusion is that caste is a fundamentally

Indian institution which has profoundly influenced local Muslims, Ahmad simultaneously says that 'all the contributors to this volume are agreed that the Hindu ideological justification of the caste system does not exist in the case of Muslims' (1978: 11).

If the symbolist view of caste is that it is 'in the mind' then Indian Muslims cannot accurately be said to partake of the caste system, since they disavow the basic premises for stratification and affirm instead the basic equality of all believers. As Madan writes, the existence of caste depends in part upon whose point of view is taken: the Hindu's, the Muslim's, or the observer's (1981: 61). But, in fact, caste and ranking are not easily clarified even by taking 'the native's point of view', since there are contradictions within each position. For instance, Bhattacharya notes that ambiguities among Muslims between ideals of equality and actualities of ranking pose a 'mental dilemma' for his Bengali informants. Their solution is to rationalize realities of hierarchy by claiming that the low-ranked Muslim groups are dirty and sexually immoral (1978: 294-6). For Bhattacharya, this justification shows the influence of Hinduism on Muslims. Such explanations of inferiority, however, are not utilized in the caste ideology. The Hindu may believe that lower ranked groups are dirty and immoral, yet this belief is not cited as the *reason for* the inferiority of the low; it is instead a *consequence* of fundamental differences assumed to be pre-existent. Obviously, the contradiction between ideal and act is not solved by simply claiming that Muslims behave 'as if' they believed in caste, since it is the very congruence between belief and action that is in question.[2]

A more sophisticated treatment of Muslims 'mental dilemma' within the caste system has been offered by Marriott and Inden, who try to reconcile differences as patterned transformations within the basic caste model of transaction. Variation is explicable 'as replication or deletion, as permutation and combination, as negative and reciprocal transformations of coded substance. . .' (Marriott and Inden 1977: 236).

Within this inclusive model 'the structure that appear to "deviate" are in fact homologous and connected, capable of additive treatment since they are generated from the same monistic premises by the same transactional logics' (Marriott 1976: 133). The problem, however, with such a holistic system is that all deviance is assumed to derive from the postulated principles by a series of transformations. the task of the analyst is to show how this occurs. But the model is stretched beyond recognition when deviation is too great, as it is among Indian Muslims. Marriott himself reports that 'only in Muslim parts of South Asia do greater departures appear sometimes to occur from this general transactional structure. . . . Only pious giving matters and . . . the natures of the recievers are not altered by what they receive' (ibid.: 131). In the light of the ethnographic data, it is evident that the assertion of 'monistic premises' among Indian Muslims does not hold, and that the model of transactional structuring also does not extend quite as far as its authors have aspired.

If the symbolic approach is not satisfactory in handling Muslim society, what other possibilities remain? In the pages above several other, more comparative, approaches have been outlined. A structural-functional argument, such as Barth's would attempt a general theory of social organization, not necessarily incompatible with diffusionism, and would claim that Indian Muslims have their own form of status summation (to use Barth's terminology), which resembles, but is not exactly equivalent to, the caste system; both forms being seen as subtypes of social stratification.

Another alternative would be to avoid such grand theory and simply make the diffusionist claim that the caste-like quality of Muslim groups in India is either a retention of a typically Middle Eastern heritage of ranking and social differentiation, or, less radically, that what exists is a combination of Middle Eastern and South Asian features. This is, essentially, the path taken by Gaborieau.

Unfortunately, these options are not especially satisfactory in terms of social theory. Their difficulties are well known. Diffusionism, though giving proper credit to complexity, tends to degenerate into a 'shreds and patches' vision of culture, with various abstract traits laid randomly side by side. The structural approach, on the other hand, runs the risk of isolating details for comparative purposes, thus falsifying cultural integrity and distorting context; it also tends toward sterile exercises in categorization and typologizing. Traits are abstracted, and every society becomes an analytical subtype in what Leach has satirised as a butterfly collection of social structures.

But if structural-functionalism errs in the direction of comparing what is not comparable and of distorting social reality for the sake of typologies, and if diffusionism ends in mere lists of traits, then the symbolic school errs in quite another direction. By stressing the unity and uniqueness of each culture this school tends to subsume all divergence and deviance into a supposed integrated whole. The 'essentialists' stop here, but he interpretive constructionist school has greater flexibility, since it looks at local level discourse over principles. The attention to what is actually said is, of course, extremely important, as is the concern with the dialectic between textual norms and action. But too great an emphasis on meaning and interpretation of 'the word' tends toward a constrictive analysis that cannot move beyond its subject, nor even beyond the words the individuals use to define themselves. Conflict revolved around interpretation of internalized values that characterize the society at large, while comparison becomes impossible, since each system has its own irreducible originality. Where structural diffusionist theory breaks societies down into components and displays on endless array of types, symbolic theory erects barriers and proclaims the inviolability of each specimen.

In reality, the practitioners of both schools are more alert to nuance, and far more willing to permit other factors into their analysis than I have allowed here.[3] My portrayal of the theoretical difficulties of both approaches in exaggerated chiaroscuro is, however, for a purpose. I have focused on the symbolic viewpoint since it is, at present, dominant, and since the problems of structural-functionalism and diffusionism are better known. It is, I think, quite evident that none of these theories can deal adequately with the particular question considered here; that of the position of Indian Muslims within the caste society.

There is, however, another way to analyse the situation of an oppositional subculture. This approach is prefigured, to an extent, in several articles. For instance, in his study of Muslim Tamils, Mines does not attempt to show how these people have adapted to the value system of the dominant Hindus. Instead, he focuses on the divergences between Muslims and Hindus. Muslims in Tamilnadu, Mines says, are egalitarian, hardworking, independent and upwardly mobile; all attributes which contrast with their Hindu neighbours (1978: 160). Several factors are certainly at work here—one is probably the absence of the Ashraf/Ajlaf distinction in Tamilnadu. But the essential point which I wish to bring out concerns the identity and social position of the Muslim converts. Ahmad notes in his introduction that most converts of Islam in India were from the lower and middle castes, But Mines is more specific. He suggests that Islam, with its message of equality and individualism, had what Weber would call an elective affinity for the trading classes and specialists who wished to free themselves from restrictive *jajmani* ties of caste obligation. An analogous case has been made by Pocock for Islamic converts in Gujarat (1962), and the connection between Islam and mercantilism is evident not only in the Middle East, but in South-East Asia as well. Implicit in Mines' article is an assumption that different value systems will be utilized by opposing interest groups. Even more essential, from my perspective, is an emphasis on the conflict of ideologies.[4]

Other authors may take a similar perspective. Although Gaborieau's major theoretical orientation is diffusionist, his complex view of trait combinations permits him to note that opinions about the place of Muslims shift according to the criteria emphasized: if religion is the focus, they will be seen as low and integrated (1972). Integration into the caste structure will also be effected by a number of other factors: the size of the Muslim group, their political power, their internal differentiation, their exposure to Muslim propaganda, etc. But the crucial point is that '*le modèle d'un groupe de Musulmans considéré comme caste dans une société de castes doit donc etre limitê aux cas de minorités dont la position économique est bassé*' (1966: 91). An analogous argument is made in passing by Madan, who writes that the cooperation between Hindu and Muslim in Kashmir is 'dependent both on ideological compromise and upon politico-economic power' (1981: 59).

These various approaches suggest that it is the interplay of the economy, social position, and ideology that is of central importance in understanding the place of Islam in South Asia. It is the study of this interplay that will give insights into the confrontation of cultures.

This indicates that an appropriate way to look at cultures, particularly at complex cultures with internal minorities, is not to give primary attention to question of how much influence the encompassing system has had on the encompassed; nor on how the natives interpret their texts; nor on showing how traits diffuse into hybrids; nor on making the relationships between the minority and the majority fit within a typology. These approaches are all very useful, especially in defining the parameters of the systems under consideration, but their weaknesses become evident when confronted with deviant cases. The fundamental difficulty is that these theoretical stances reify social orders or beliefs into *things*, i.e., objects with properties that are either divisible or united, according to one's approach. The analyst's job, given this fundamental reifying premise, is to search for relations within or between social systems, as his predilection demands. Either the system makes 'sense' in and of itself, or it makes 'sense' as it fits into categories of similar systems.

Instead, I would argue for an approach that focuses on relationships, *first,* especially relationships of antagonism and contradiction, and which sees order and belief growing from these oppositional relations. This mode of analysis assumes that cultures and values are chosen and defined in relation to what is ignored, denied or negated. Consequently, the analysis of opposition, exclusion, and the struggle for identity within a framework of often opposing interests is a necessity for social theory, particularly theory of change. What people believe and what people do grows from experience and antagonism both within and without the community. The articulation of interests is no doubt structured by the vocabulary available, but in hearing the words we must not forget the realities that lie beneath them. With this perspective in mind, the importance of the study of subcultures is crucial, both for the definition of the larger culture and the smaller. Therefore, the interesting questions raised by Ahmad's collections and by the controversy they have engendered are not only how and why Indian Muslims have been assimilated, but also how and why they have resisted assimilation; not only how religion is discussed and interpreted, but by whom, and for what purpose.

NOTES

1. The first version of this paper was presented to the Association for Asian studies in 1981, and a later version was published in the *European Journal of Sociology.* This version has been considerably expanded and revised to deal with new material.
2. It is here, by the way, that the interpretive approach and the essentialist approach are weakest, since both assume that a stated shared belief and motivation to action are united, with belief as the causal factor. Belief, however, is often after the fact; a rationale that aims to justify or make sense of action within a cultural framework. The action itself may have quite another significance than local interpretation allows it, as Durkheim pointed out long ago in his analysis of religious cosmologies and myths. This problem is not evident in the functionalist approach, which assumes that 'meaning' is secondary to more vital necessities of structure.
3. For example, Das draws attention to consider 'social conditions which bring about these variations in emphasis' in folk beliefs (1984: 296).

4. In a later paper, Mines seems to retreat from this position, arguing that 'internal needs to acquire status and a sense of social position' are the cause for Islamicisation (1981: 67). Rivalry with Hindus is seen as irrelevant. But Mines retains his dichotomy between Hindu and Muslim value orientations; a dichotomy that favours Muslim business success. The Islamic values of Urban Muslims can then still be considered to be related to their economic interests, though competition for status among Muslims is also important.

REFERENCES

Ahmad, I. ed. 1976. *Family, Kinship and Marriage among Muslim in India.* New Delhi: Manohar.

———. 1978. *Caste and Stratification among Muslims in India.* New Delhi: Manohar.

———. 1981. *Ritual and Religion among Muslims in India.* New Delhi: Manohar.

Barth, F. 1960. 'The system of social stratification in Swat, North Pakistan'. In E. Leach, ed., *Aspects of Caste in South India, Ceylon, and North-West Pakistan.* Cambridge: Cambridge University Press.

Berque, J. 1955. *Structures sociales de haut atlas.* Paris: Universitaires de France.

Berreman, J. 1967. 'Caste as a structural principle'. In A. deReuc and J. Knight, eds., *Caste and Race: Comparative Approaches.* London: Churchill.

Bhattacharya, R. 1978. 'The concept and ideology of caste among the Muslims of rural West Bengal'. In I. Ahmad, ed., op. cit.

Bougle, C. 1971. *Essays on the Caste System.* Cambridge: Cambridge University Press.

Briggs, L. 1960. *Tribes of the Sahara.* Boston: Harvard University Press.

Bujra, A. 1971. The Politics of Stratification. Oxford: Oxford University Press.

Carroll, L. 1983. 'The Muslim family in India: Law, custom and empirical research'. *Contributions to Indian Sociology* (n.s.) 17: 205-22.

Coon, C. 1953. *Caravan: The Story of the Middle East.* New York: Holt.

Das, V. 1984. 'For a folk-theology and theoretical anthropology of Islam'. *Contributions to Indian Sociology* (n.s.) 18: 293-300.

Dumont, L. 1970. *Homo Hierarchicus: An Essay on the Caste System.* Chicago: University of Chicago Press.

English, P. 1966. *City and Village in Iran.* Madison: University of Wisconsin Press.

Fernea, R. 1970. *Shaiykh and Effendi.* Boston: Harvard University Press.

Gaborieau, M. 1966. 'Les Curaute de Moyen Nepal: place d' un groupe de Musulmans dans une societe de castes'. *L'Homme* 6: 81-91.

———. 1972. 'Muslims in the Hindu kingdom of Nepal'. *Contributions to Indian Sociology* (n.s.) 6: 84-105.

———. 1977. *Minorities, Musulmanes dans le royayme Hindu du Nepal.* Nanterre: Laboratorie d'ethnologie.

———. 1978a. 'Aspects of the lineage among the Muslim bangle-makers of Nepal'. *Contributions to Indian Sociology* (n.s.) 12: 155-72.

———. 1978b. 'Le partage du pouvoir être les lineages dans un localité du Népal central'. *L'Homme* 18: 37-65.

———. 1979. 'Traditional patterns of dominance among South Asian Muslims'. In *Colloques Internationaux du Centre National de la Recherche Scientifique, 582, Asie du Sud: traditions et changements.*

Harper, E. 1959. 'Two systems of economic exchange in village India'. *American Anthropologist* 61: 760-80.

Leach, E. 1960. 'What should we mean by caste?' In E. Leach, ed., op. cit.

Lewis, B. 1966. *The Arabs in History.* New York: Harper and Row.

Lindholm, C. 1982. *Generosity and Jealousy: The Swat Pukhtun of Northern Pakistan.* New York: Columbia University Press.

Madan. T.N. 1981. 'Religious ideology and social structure: The Muslims and Hindus of Kashmir'. In I. Ahmad, op. cit.

Marriott, M. 1976. 'Hindu transactions: Diversity without dualism'. In B. Kapferer, ed., *Transaction and meaning.* Philadelphia: Institute for the Study of Human Issues.

Marriott, M. and R. Inden. 1974. 'Caste systems'. *Encyclopedia Britannica, Macropaedia* 3, 982-91.

———. 1977. 'Toward an ethnosociology of South Asian caste systems'. In K. David, ed., *The New Wind: Changing Identities in South Asia.* The Hague: Mouton.

Metcalf, B. 1984. *Moral Conduct and Authority: The Place of Adab in South Asian Islam.* Berkeley: University of California Press.

Mines, M. 1978. 'Social stratification among Muslim Tamils in Tamilnadu, South India'. In I. Ahmad, ed., op.cit.

———. 1981. 'Islamicization and Muslim ethnicity in South India'. In I. Ahmad, ed., op.cit.

Pehrson, R. 1966. *The Social Organization of the Marri Baluch.* New York: Wenner-Gren.

Pocock, D. 1962. 'Notes on jajmani relationships'. *Contributions to Indian Sociology* 6: 78-95.

Robinson, F. 1983. 'Islam and Muslim society in South Asia', *Contributions to Indian Sociology* (*n.s.*) 17: 185-203.

Arabs, Moors, and Muslims: Sri Lankan Muslim Ethnicity in Regional Perspective

DENNIS B. McGILVRAY
(1998)

Nearly 8 per cent of Sri Lanka's people are Muslims, as compared with 18 per cent who are Tamils, but these simple-sounding minority labels actually conceal more than they reveal of the island's ethnic complexity. For the past 100 years the urban leaders and political spokesmen of the Muslim community have strongly denied any suggestion that they could be seen as 'Tamil Muslims' or 'Muslim Tamils', even though they speak Tamil at home, share many Tamil kinship and domestic practices, and have even composed Muslim commentaries and devotional works in Tamil, some of them written in Arabic-Tamil script (Uwise 1986, 1990). The bewildering list of terms for the Sri Lankan Muslims is symptomatic of the identity issues which they have faced over the centuries in differing colonial European, Tamil, and Sinhalese contexts.

From the beginning of the colonial period in the early sixteenth century, members of the predominant Tamil-speaking Muslim community in Sri Lanka were designated by the term 'Moor' (*Mouro*, 'Moroccan') which the Portuguese applied to Muslims throughout their African and Asian empire, as well as by such familiar European terms as 'Mohammedan' or 'Mussalman'. In the early 1970s, when I began my fieldwork among the Moors of eastern Sri Lanka, I found that 'Muslim' was the most common term they used when speaking in their own native Tamil, although strictly speaking, the religious term 'Muslim' should encompass the ethnically-distinct Malays and the small Gujarati trading groups as well.[1] The term *Cōṉakar* (Sonagar, Jonagar), an older Tamil and Malayalam word which originally denoted West Asians, especially Arabs or Greeks, seems to be falling out of fashion, although 'Lanka Yonaka' was still used as an ethnonym for the Sri Lankan Moors in the 1971 Census.[2] In common English parlance, both 'Moor' and 'Muslim' are used interchangeably today

TABLE 1. SRI LANKAN POPULATION BY ETHNICITY AND RELIGION

Population of Sri Lanka (1997 estimated)		18.7 million
Sinhalese	74 %	13.8 million
Sri Lankan Tamils	12.7 %	2.4 million
Indian Tamils	5.5 %	1.0 million
Moors	7 %	1.3 million
Others (Malays, Burghers, Veddahs, etc.)	1 %	.2 million
Buddhists	69 %	12.9 million
Hindus	15 %	2.8 million
Muslims (including Moors and Malays)	8 %	1.5 million
Christians	8 %	1.5 million

Sources: *CIA World Factbook 1997* and Embassy of Sri Lanka website (http://www.slembassy.org). The most recent Sri Lankan census was conducted in 1981.

to refer to indigenous Tamil speaking Muslim Sri Lankans, 93 per cent of all followers of Islam in the island, most of whom are orthodox (Sunni) members of the Shāfi'ī school of Muslim jurisprudence.[3]

The fact that Sri Lankan Muslims would prefer an ethnic label which is European or Islamic, rather than Dravidian in origin, points to one of the major cleavages within Sri Lanka's Tamil-speaking minority. Recently, a few historians and spokesmen for the Muslim community have even asserted that 'Muslims have no commitment to any particular language', citing the willingness of Moors living in Sinhala-majority districts to enroll their children in Sinhala-medium schools (Shukri 1986b: 70; see also K.M. de Silva 1988: 202). One author contends that the Muslims are becoming 'a linguistically divided community' because young Muslims in Sinhalese districts are learning Sinhalese instead of Tamil (Ali 1986-7: 167). Whether this process will soon result in the loss of Tamil, and the widespread substitution of Sinhala, as the language of the Moorish home seems to me dubious, not least because of the chronic shortage of Muslim teachers qualified in Sinhala (Mohan 1987: 107, Uwise 1986).[4]

The ethnic identity and political stance of the Sri Lankan Muslim community, like that of many culturally-defined groups contesting for a secure place in the world today, has undergone change over the past century in response to colonial and post-colonial pressures and from the internal dynamics of the Muslim community itself. The Moors played a pivotal role in post-Independence Sri Lankan politics, but this became especially true after 1983, when the armed conflict over Tamil Eelam suddenly placed many of them in an extremely tight position, caught between the Sri Lankan security forces and the Tamil rebels of the LTTE.[5] In order to reveal the roots of the dilemma which the Sri Lankan Muslims currently face, I will first trace the historical development of the Moorish ethnic identity in Sri Lanka in comparison with two south Indian Muslim groups to whom the Moors are closely related, the Māppiḷas of Kerala and the Marakkāyars of Tamil Nadu. Then, with this historical background in mind, I will ethnographically explore the tense relations between Tamils and Muslims living in Sri Lanka's eastern region where the future outcome—either ethnic accommodation or ethnic division—still hangs in the balance.

DIVERGENT DEVELOPMENT OF MUSLIM ETHNICITY IN KERALA, TAMIL NADU, AND SRI LANKA

Both in Sri Lanka and in Tamil Nadu, Christians whose native tongue is Tamil generally think of themselves as Tamil Christians, but among Sri Lankan Muslims such a parallel does not hold. In their aversion to identifying themselves as Tamils who happen to follow the Muslim faith,[6] the Moors of Sri Lanka stand in striking contrast to the Marakkāyar Muslims of Tamil Nadu, who, apart from their Islamic theology, have regarded themselves as fully contributing members of the Tamil literary and cultural tradition. If we include one more Muslim group, the historically militant and rebellious Māppiḷas of Kerala, we have the opportunity to conduct an interesting three-way comparison of Muslim ethnicity in south India and Sri Lanka (Map 1). All three Muslim communities preserve elements of matrilineal and/or matrilocal social structure which suggest close connections (involving both intermarriage and conversion) with the matrilineal Hindu castes of the Malabar Coast, and possibly also with the matrilineal Hindu Maravars of Ramnad. Malayalam, the language of Kerala today, was 'effectively a dialect of Tamil until the fourteenth century'—seven hundred years *after* the advent of Islam and the expansion of Arab trade in the Indian Ocean (Shackle 1989: 405). Communication and social interaction between Muslims of Calicut, Kayalpattinam, and Colombo was once a great deal freer than it is today, part of a more widespread 'traffic in commodities, bodies, and myths' from south India into Sri Lanka over the last 700 years (Roberts 1980).

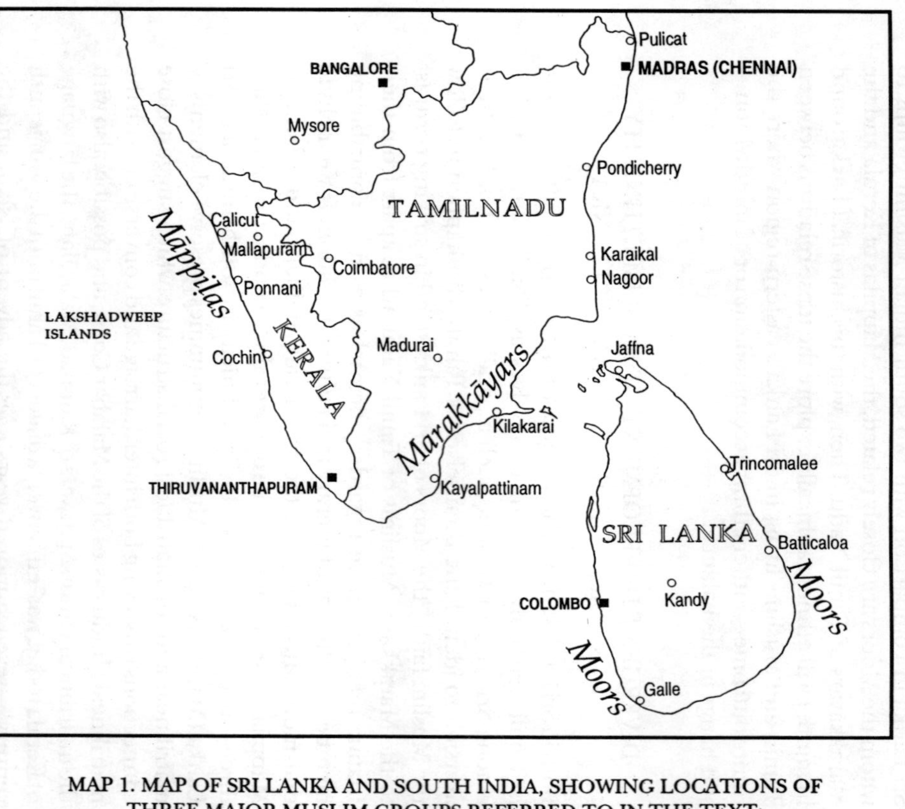

MAP 1. MAP OF SRI LANKA AND SOUTH INDIA, SHOWING LOCATIONS OF THREE MAJOR MUSLIM GROUPS REFERRED TO IN THE TEXT: MAPPIḶAS, MARAKKĀYARS, AND MOORS

As a world systems or macro-economic history approach might predict (Wallerstein 1976, Wolf 1982, Bose 1990), there is a striking similarity in the historical circumstances under which these three Muslim communities came into existence. They were all largely founded by Arab and Persian traders who supplied the Mediterranean market for spices and Indian textiles. From the late fifteenth century onward, all three Muslim communities experienced similar conquest and repression by the colonial Portuguese, Dutch, and British empires, which were then expanding from the European core to exploit the resources of the African and Asian periphery. Yet despite these initial similarities, a comparison of Muslims in Kerala, Tamil Nadu, and Sri Lanka reveals some striking divergences in the way modern Muslim ethnic identities developed in these three geographically adjacent regions.[7]

The Māppiḷas of Kerala

The Muslims of Kerala, known as Māppiḷas (Mappilla, Moplah)[8] were originally the mixed descendants and religious converts of Arab Muslim spice traders who had been actively patronized by the Hindu rulers of the Malabar coast, especially the Zamorins of Calicut. They constitute 23 per cent of the population of the state (Hasan 1997: 2-3), making them a much more substantial political bloc than Muslims in Sri Lanka or Tamil Nadu. Today the Māppiḷas are not only traders and coastal fishermen, but they also form a large segment (25-60 per cent) of the impoverished rural agrarian tenant class in some of the inland districts of northern Kerala, especially in the south Malabar region (Miller 1976, Gabriel 1996). As with local Hindu castes, some Māppiḷas are matrilineal and some patrilineal in tracing their lineage ancestry, but the pattern of residence after marriage for all Māppiḷas is matrilocal. There are also several clearly ranked, endogamous, caste-like subsections within the Māppiḷa community, a pattern also found in the Lakshadweep Islands 200 km west of the Kerala coast (D'Souza 1959, 1973; Ibrahim Kunju 1989: 178-80; Gabriel 1989; Kutty 1972).

Of all the coastal Muslim groups in south India and Sri Lanka, the Māppiḷas were by far the most militant and rebellious during the British colonial period, sustaining a tradition of Islamic martyrdom through violent, suicidal outbreaks (*jihād*) against colonial authorities and dominant high-caste Hindu landlords, the last of which, in 1922, vainly sought to establish an Islamic theocratic sultanate in south Malabar. A few charismatic Sufi holy men actively encouraged these suicidal attacks against the infidel authorities, and annual *nércca* mosque festivals today still commemorate slain Māppiḷa martyrs (Dale and Menon 1978). After a vain effort to forge a separate state of 'Mappilastan' at the time of Indian Independence, the Māppiḷas effectively focused their political power through the Muslim League and offered grass-roots support for Kerala's successful land reform movement (Herring 1991, Gabriel 1996). Since then, Māppiḷa political tactics have been brilliantly pragmatic, switching coalition partnerships between Congress and Communist parties at various times (Wright 1966, Miller 1976: 158-72). A major achievement of the modern era was the creation of Mallapuram District in 1969, the first Māppiḷa-majority electorate in Kerala (Dale 1980: 225-6).

The Marakkāyars and Labbais of Tamil Nadu

Unlike Kerala, where many coastal Māppiḷas spread directly inland and created a large population of tenant farmers, the Muslim community of Tamil Nadu has two points of origin, and two major internal subdivisions corresponding to the Shāfi'ī versus Hanafī legal schools (Fanselow 1989). The prosperous Muslims of Kayalpattinam, Kilakarai, Karaikal and other early Indo-Arab port settlements along the coast of Tamil Nadu call themselves *Marakkāyars* (var. Maraikkāyar, Maraikkār) probably from the Tamil word *marakkalam*, boat or 'wooden vessel'),[9] insist upon endogamous marriages, and claim the highest status among all Tamil Muslims (More 1991). The numerically larger population of Tamil-speaking Muslim artisans, weavers, tanners, and merchants of the inland districts of Tamil Nadu have been loosely termed Labbais, to which must be added a smattering of 'martial' lines such as Navāyats, Rāvuttars, and Pathāns (Mines 1973, Bayly 1989: 71-103, Fanselow 1989).[10] Overall, Muslims represent 5.5 per cent of Tamil Nadu's population (Hasan 1997: 2-3). While the Labbais constitute the bulk of Tamil Muslims today, it has been the elite Marakkāyar traders who seem to have had the earliest historical connection with the Moors of Sri Lanka.

The Marakkāyars of Kayalpattinam have some shallow matrilineages but no formally organized matrilineal clans as in Kerala or eastern Sri Lanka. Post-marital residence is matrilocal for at least a year or so after the wedding, with the married couple eventually living either with the bride's parents in her natal home or in a newly built dowry house in the same *mohulla,* or corporate neighbourhood. Either way, every daughter receives a house at marriage, in addition to jewelry and other movable goods (personal fieldwork in 1983; 'Kayalar' in Thurston and Rangachari 1909, v.3: 267; More 1991; Bayly 1986: 42). Unlike the Labbais who generally follow Hanafī law, members of the Marakkāyar commercial and gem-trading elite, like the Māppiḷas of Kerala and the Sri Lankan Moors, all belong to the Shāfi'ī legal school. Like the Māppiḷas, too, the Marakkāyars have a long history of seafaring, but instead of a warrior tradition they cultivated a reputation for religious, philanthropic, and literary pursuits. Marakkāyar towns are noted for their profusion of mosques and tombs of Sufi scholar-mystics, some of which were also patronized by Tamil Hindu kings, as well as being famed for their wealth and smuggling activities (Bayly 1986, Fanselow 1989: 276).

Marakkāyars take pride in having authored many commentaries and religious works in Arabic-Tamil, including the *Cīrāpppurāṇam,* an epic poem on the life of the Prophet modelled on the Tamil version of the Hindu *Ramayana* (Casie Chitty 1853-55; Mauroof 1972: 67-8; Shulman 1984; Mahroof 1986a: 87; Uwise 1990, Richman 1993, Rao, Shulman, and Subrahmanyam 1992: 264-304). The most renowned regional pilgrimage centre for Muslims in Tamil Nadu and Sri Lanka, the *dargāh* (tomb-shrine) of the Sufi mystic Abdul Q̣ādir Shāhul Hamīd at Nagoor, is a Marakkāyar foundation (Bayly 1986, 1989: Chs. 2-3). Although some urban 'Islamisation' is now occurring, over the centuries most Muslims in Tamil Nadu have identified strongly with, and have been recognized as contributing to, the Tamil literary and cultural tradition (Cutler 1983: 280, 286; Uwise 1990, MacPherson 1969; Mines 1983: 112; More 1993a, 1997). Their politics, quite unlike that of the Māppiḷas in Ḳerala, has not been conspicuously communal or confrontational. They have often supported the Dravidian nationalist parties (DMK, ADMK) or the Congress and have not shown great loyalty to the Muslim League (Wright 1966, McPherson 1969, Mines 1981: 72-4). A recent outbreak of Hindu and Muslim fundamentalist violence in 1997-8 in Coimbatore may signal a breakdown in the Dravidian solidarity of the Muslims of Tamil Nadu (Gopalan 1998), but it is worth noting that Hindu-Muslim violence has so far not spread from the inland centres of the Labbai and Deccani population to the coastal towns of the Marakkāyars.[11]

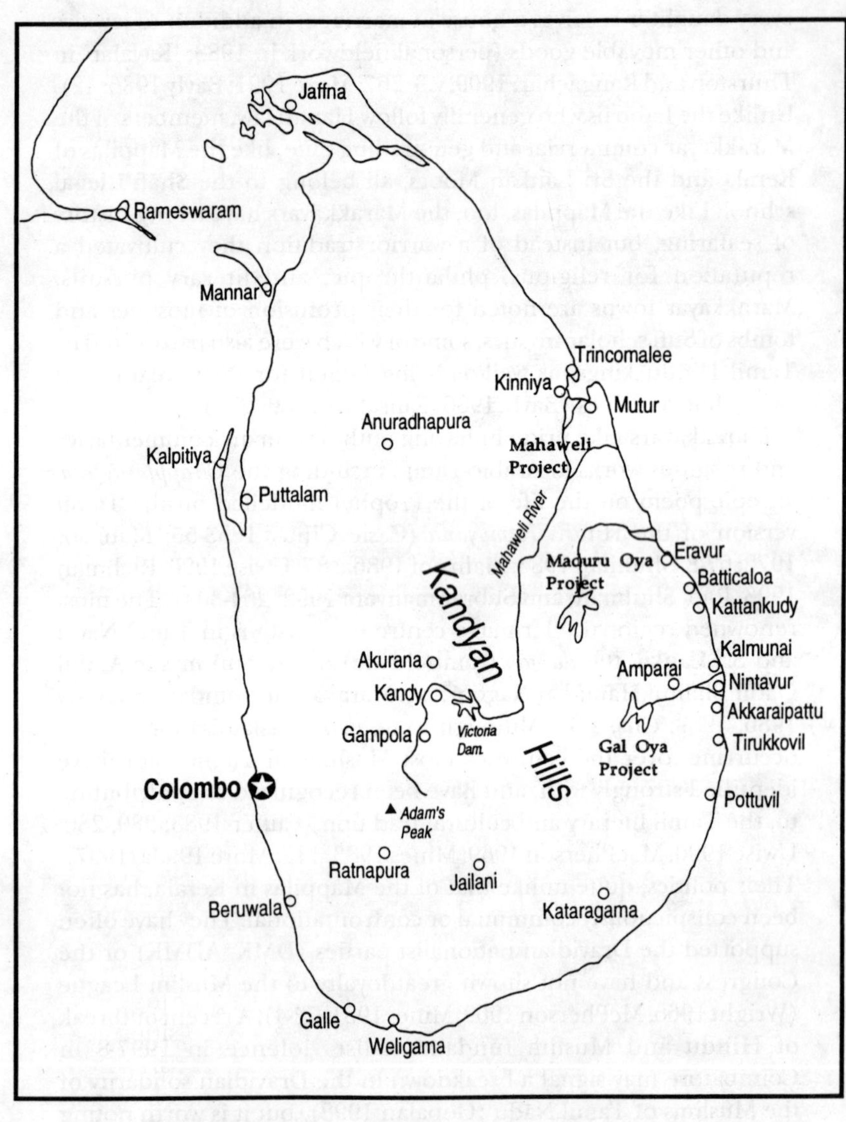

MAP 2. MAP OF SRI LANKA, SHOWING LOCATIONS OF SOME OF THE MAJOR MOORISH (MUSLIM) SETTLEMENTS REFERRED TO IN THE TEXT

The Moors of Sri Lanka[12]

There are many cultural similarities between the Māppiḷas of Kerala, the Marakkāyars of Tamil Nadu, and the Moors of Sri Lanka which point to common origins. All three groups are Sunni Muslims of the Shāfi'ī legal school, a shared legacy of their earliest south Arabian forefathers (Fanselow 1989). All three groups began as Indian Ocean trading communities patronized by local Hindu and Buddhist kings, and commerce remains one of their chief occupations today. The influence of Sufi saints and scholars has been quite strong, first linking the Malabar and Coromandel coasts, then spreading to Sri Lanka (Ibrahim Kunju 1995, Mauroof 1972, Ali 1980, Ch.4, Shukri 1986c, Bayly 1989). In fact, two of the most widespread devotional cults of Sufi saints among Sri Lankan Muslims have clear connections both with Kerala and with Tamil Nadu. The first is that of Shaykh Muhiyadeen Abdul Qādir Jīlānī (d. AD 1166), popularly known in Tamil as Mohideen *Āṇṭavar* ('Lord Mohideen'), Persian-born founder of the Qādiriyya Order whose popularity extends throughout the South Asian Muslim world (Sanyal 1994: 48). He is the subject of the earliest (AD 1607) and most highly regarded Muslim *malappatt* or saintly praise-poem in the Arabic-Malayalam literature of Kerala (Ibrahim Kunju 1989: 198-200), and his *dargāh* shrines are the most widespread in Tamil Nadu (Mines 1981: 69). He is believed to have visited the popular cave-mosque of Daftar Jailani at Kuragala near Balangoda, Sri Lanka, while on a pilgrimage to Adam's Peak (Aboosally 1975).

A second devotional cult popular with Sri Lankan Moors is that of sixteenth century saint Shāhul Hamīd, sometimes referred to in Sri Lanka as Mīrān Sāhib, whose impressively-endowed tomb-shrine on the Coromandel coast at Nagoor attracts Muslim pilgrims from both south India and Sri Lanka to witness the death anniversary festival (*kantūri*) at which the saint's tomb is ritually anointed with cooling sandalwood paste from a special container (*cantanakkūṭu*) which is brought in a grand procession (Nambiar & Narayana Kurup 1968; Bayly 1986). The Nagoor saint is believed to have traced the footsteps of Abdul Qādir Jīlānī to Bagdad and to Balangoda, visiting the Maldive Islands and South-East Asia as well (Shaik Hasan Sahib 1980). Several physically empty but spiritually filled 'branch office' tomb-shrines in Sri Lanka and Singapore celebrate Shāhul Hamīd's death anniversary with flag-raising and *kantūri* celebrations timed to coincide with those at Nagoor (Shams-ud-di'n 1881, McGilvray 1988b). The saint is renowned for his magical power to plug leaks in sinking ships at sea, precisely the sort of boon which would prove useful to his major patrons and devotees, the Marakkāyar sea-traders of Kayalpattinam and Colombo (Sharif 1921: 199, Van Sanden 1926: 31).

All three groups under discussion—Māppiḷas, Marakkāyars, and Moors—as well, in fact, as the coastal Navāyat Muslims of Bhatkal in North Kanara (D'Souza 1955), follow, or at least prefer, some form of matrilocal marriage and household pattern, and many of them also recognize some type of matrilineal descent. The nature of the Sri Lankan Moorish matrilineal system is best documented for the east coast Moors of the Batticaloa and Amparai Districts, where a system of exogamous ranked matriclans, matrilocal residence, and *de facto* pre-mortem matrilineal transmission of houses and lands to daughters through dowry is followed by the Tamil Hindus as well (Yalman 1967; McGilvray 1989). Published research on Moorish kinship in central and western Sri Lanka is still meagre, but matrilocal residence has been reported in a Moorish village in Wellassa (Yalman 1967, Ch. 13; de Munck 1993, 1996), among the upper class Moors of late nineteenth century Galle (Bawa 1888), as well as in 8 out of 12 Moorish households in modern Colombo studied linguistically by Raheem (1975: 59).[13] On trips to Colombo and Galle in 1993 I found matrilocal residence in almost all of the middle-class Moorish families I visited. Some Moors were also well aware that other Muslims, such as the Gujarati-speaking Bohras, follow a contrary patrilocal rule.

The title of *Marakkār* or *Marakkāyar* is found among Muslim maritime trading groups from the Navāyats of the Kanara coast (D'Souza 1955: 43ff.) to the Moors of Sri Lanka. It was borne by the daring Muslim Kunjali admirals of the Zamorin's fleet as well as by more humble Hindu Mukkuvar boatmen of Kerala (Narayan 1995: 94, Thurston and Rangachari 1909 v. 5: 112, Gabriel 1996: 121 ff.). In Sri Lanka, the term is often rendered as *Maraikkār* (Marikar, Marcar, etc.); it appears both in leading Moorish family names as well as in the customary title of the office of mosque trustee, a leader of the local Moorish community (Mahroof 1986a, McGilvray 1974, Ali 1981a). Commercial, cultural, and even migrational links between the Marakkāyar towns of southern Tamil Nadu and Sri Lankan Moorish settlements are attested in the historical traditions of Beruwela, Kalpitiya, Jaffna, and other coastal settlements where some Muslims have lived for centuries (Casie Chitty 1834: 254ff.; Denham 1912: 234, Ali 1981a). Such connections may continue even today: during my early fieldwork in Akkaraipattu (Amparai district) in 1969-71 my Moorish landlord mentioned that he had spent several years as a youth apprenticed to a Marakkāyar merchant in Kayalpattinam, a fact I personally verified on a visit to south India in 1983. Evidence of long-term migration and presumed intermarriage between the Marakkāyars (and Kāyalārs) of Tamil Nadu, the Māppiḷas of Kerala, and the Moors of Sri Lanka is also found in the fact that all three groups share a set of distinctive Tamil kinship terms for parents and elder siblings which are not found among the Labbais or other Tamil-speaking Muslim groups in Tamil Nadu (Mines 1972: 26-7).[14]

The traditional institution of Moorish community decision-making on the west coast of Sri Lanka was a sort of village or neighbourhood assembly (*ūr kūṭṭam*) under the leadership of the chief mosque trustee, who bore the title of *Maraikkār, Matticam*, or *Nāṭṭāṇmaikkārar* (Mahroof 1986a).[15] Such a pattern of local assemblies was also characteristic of medieval Kerala, where they formed a hierarchy of increasing political authority from the village (*tārā kūṭṭam*), to the district (*nāṭṭu kūṭṭam*), to even broader territorial units (Padmanabha Menon 1924: 250-69). Even today, the oral tradition of district assemblies (*nāṭṭu kūṭṭam*) is still recalled by the matrilineal Tamils of the eastern coast of Sri Lanka, part of a pre-colonial political legacy which they apparently share with the west coast Moors. The likelihood that a prior 'Kerala connection' accounts for many of these matrilineal and maritime Muslim traits among both the Marakkāyars of Tamil Nadu and the Moors of Sri Lanka—as well as among the matrilineal Hindu Tamils of the east coast, and even the 'Malabar inhabitants' of Jaffna—seems quite strong (Raghavan 1971: 199-217).[16]

However, there are other respects in which the Moors of Sri Lanka are historically and sociologically distinct from their closest Muslim neighbours in India. In terms of ascriptive status, the Sri Lankan Muslim community as whole is more egalitarian and homogenous than its south Indian counterparts. Although the wealth and class structure descends steeply from elite gem-trading millionaires, to urban entrepreneurs, to rural farmers and boutique keepers (Mauroof 1972), there do not appear to be the sorts of hereditary, endogamous, caste-like divisions among the Sri Lankan Moors which have been documented among the Māppiḷas and between the

Marakkāyars and Labbais in South India.[17] Also, as Fanselow (1989) has pointed out, the Māppiḷas, Marakkāyars, and Deccani Muslims of south India either supplied local Hindu kings with strategic military technologies (naval squadrons, cavalry horses) or were themselves part of the Urdu-speaking political elite under the Nawābs of Arcot.[18] The Moors never played such a strategic military or political role in the history of Sri Lanka (Ali 1981a, Dewaraja 1986, C.R. De Silva 1968), and as a result they did not become identified with the state nor did they develop their own political or military ideology of sovereignty.

One must consider, too, the distinctive features of Sri Lankan Moorish geography and demography. In the districts of northern Malabar, the Māppiḷas form a single Muslim population stretching from the urban coastal cities well into the agricultural hinterlands, whereas in Tamil Nadu the coastal urban Marakkāyar trading elite has erected endogamous barriers separating them from the inland Labbai population. Neither of these Tamil Nadu Muslim groups incorporates a large rural peasantry. Among the Sri Lankan Muslims, in contrast, there is both an urban Muslim elite and a rural Muslim agrarian population, but each is found on opposite sides of the island, separated by the Kandyan Hills (see Map 2). The numerous Moorish farmers on the northern and eastern coast are not only distanced geographically, but separated socio-economically and culturally as well, from the more affluent and cosmopolitan centres of Muslim trade and political influence in the central and western parts of the island. The west coast and up-country Muslims are a widely dispersed minority except in certain well-known enclaves (Beruwela, Akurana, Puttalam/Kalpitiya, Mannar, some neighbourhoods of Colombo and Galle, for example).[19] The east coast Moorish paddy farming towns, on the other hand, which are more substantial and concentrated—but also more agrarian-based and integrated into a distinctive regional subculture—represent nearly one-thirds of all Sri Lankan Muslims. At Mutur and Kinniya south of Trincomalee and in some of the major towns and paddy-growing areas of Batticaloa and Amparai Districts (e.g. Eravur, Kattankudy, Kalmunai, Sammanturai, Nindavur, Akkaraipattu, Pottuvil), half to three-quarters of the population are Moors, making this eastern region the only demographically feasible site in the entire island for a Muslim-dominated electorate (Kurukulasuriya, et al. 1988: 94-102).

MOORISH POLITICAL ETHNICITY IN THE 20TH CENTURY

In the modern era, the Muslims of Kerala and Tamil Nadu— despite their cultural diversity and internal social divisions—have felt reasonably secure about 'who' they are. In contrast, the leading spokesmen for the Moors of Sri Lanka from the late nineteenth century onwards seem to have been perennially vexed by questions of their biological and cultural origins and the most advantageous formulation of their ethnic identity within an increasingly communalized political arena. Cut off from major south Indian Muslim centres of learning to some extent during 300 years of Portuguese and Dutch colonial repression, the Moors were grateful to be emancipated from feudal obligations in the Sinhalese areas of the island in reward for their loyalty to the British crown during the Kandyan Rebellion of 1817-18. In the first half of the nineteenth century they took advantage of gradually liberalized British policies permitting freedom of commerce, urban property rights, purchase of Crown land, and the appointment of local Moorish Headmen. However, the degree to which the Sri Lankan Moors in the late eighteenth and early nineteenth centuries constituted a self-conscious and internally organized minority community is difficult to judge. It is only clear that the Moors formed a visible and distinct census category for British colonial administrators and the compilers of local gazetteers such as Simon Casie Chitty (1834).

Ironically, according to Ameer Ali, whose unpublished Ph.D. thesis offers the most insightful and detailed interpretation of the Muslims in nineteenth and early twentieth century Ceylon, the indigenous Moors seized upon these new colonial opportunities to become even more aloof and inward-looking as a community.[20] He observes that they remained absorbed in their customary modes of livelihood and mosque-based institutions, influenced by Sufi disciples and ritualistic ālims and pious Indian Muslim trader/missionaries from Kayalpattinam and Kilakarai, and strongly averse to mass-literacy, the printing press, and English-medium education, which was then available only through Christian mission schools (Ali 1980, Shukri 1986c: 348ff.). The British-imposed exile to Sri Lanka in 1883 of a charismatic Egyptian revolutionary, Arabi Pasha, finally served to catalyze an Islamic revival and a movement to establish Muslim schools offering a secular western curriculum (Mahroof 1986b, 1986c), but this still placed them far behind the Sinhalese, and even farther behind the Tamils, who had begun to enroll in Christian mission schools in Jaffna 60 years earlier. In any case, the Muslim educational movement was religiously exclusionary and aimed solely at the west coast urban elite; not a single Muslim school was founded for the children of the Moorish farmers of the east coast (Samaraweera 1978: 471).[21]

The mid-to-late-nineteenth century Tamil Hindu and Sinhala Buddhist cultural revivals spurred by Arumuga Navalar, Anagarika Dharmapala, and the European Theosophists were well under way before the Muslims had even begun to organize. By the end of the century, however, the west coast urban Muslim elite had commenced to promote their unique identity as 'Ceylon Moors' in response to several factors. In the first place, being 'Ceylon Moors' established their legitimate claim for seats in the formal system of communal representation which the British instituted and maintained for 100 years (Nissan and Stirrat 1990: 28-9). Muslim representatives (some elected, some appointed) had begun to serve on local Municipal Councils as early as 1866 (Asad 1993: 82), but until 1889 the Moors had been tacitly represented on the all-island Legislative Council by a government-appointed Tamil member, the last of whom was (later Sir) Ponnambalam Ramanathan, a highly influential figure among both Sinhala and Tamil nationalists. By the 1880s, however, the Moors as well as the Sinhala Buddhists had begun to press for separate representation so as to forestall the appointment of better educated or more influential Hindus and Christians to represent them (Wagner 1990: 67).

The underlying colonial discourse in the nineteenth century assumed 'race' as the criterion for political representation (Rogers 1995). In a strategically calculated speech to the Legislative Council in 1885, Ramanathan marshalled linguistic and ethnographic evidence to argue that, apart from religion, the Moors and Tamils shared a great many cultural and linguistic traits resulting from conversion and intermarriage over the centuries. When he published it three years later as an academic essay on 'The Ethnology of the 'Moors' of Ceylon' in the *Journal of the Royal Asiatic Society, Ceylon Branch,* Ramanathan's views might have appeared to gain the imprimatur of the British colonial establishment (Ramanathan 1888). His well-argued but politically motivated conclusion, that the Moors were simply Muslim members of the Tamil 'race,' was immediately perceived by Moorish leaders as 'planned sabotage' of their hopes for the appointment of a separate Muslim Member of the Legislative Council and as an academic excuse for the continued domination of the Moors by the Tamil leadership (Ali 1980: 102n). Ironically enough, Ramanathan was promulgating a more inclusive definition of 'Tamilness' than many high-caste Hindus of Jaffna and Batticaloa would have liked, given their aristocratic reluctance to recognize members of the lowest castes as 'Tamils'.[22]

Ramanathan's strategy abruptly failed when the British Governor appointed a Moor to the Council a year later. However his essay seemed to embody the patronizing Tamil outlook found in many rural areas of the island, where even today high caste Hindus look down upon the Moors as their inferior and uneducated neighbours. In the narrow rhetorical space of colonial politics, the logic of Ramanathan's aggrandizing ethnological thesis forced the Moors to further repudiate their Tamil-ness and to claim they were 'an entirely different race of Arab origin'. Indeed, from that point onward, the Ceylon Muslim leadership embraced the label of 'Ceylon Moor' with great tenacity (Ali 1980: 102). Twenty years later, in 1907, the Moorish editor I.L.M. Abdul Azeez finally published a lengthy rebuttal acknowledging that the Moors' Dravidian traits had resulted from conversion and intermarriage with Tamil women, but insisting that the very earliest forefathers of the Ceylon Moorish 'race'—who may have numbered 'not much more than 100'—had certainly not come from Kayalpattinam in south India and were 'purely Arabs in blood' (Azeez 1907: 22, 46).

Qadri Ismail has provided an insightful deconstruction of Azeez's strategically composed text, with its portrayal of the Moors as peaceful Arab traders (not warlike Tamil invaders) of high religious rank (members of the Prophet's own Hashemite tribe) who thought of themselves virtually as natives (because Adam had fallen from Paradise to earth in Ceylon),[23] tracing exclusively patrilineal descent from Arab males (thereby ignoring all affinal and maternal connections with their Tamil wives and mothers), and conversing in Tamil only as a 'borrowed' language of mercantile convenience (Ismail 1995: 69-70). To keep the story simple, no mention was made of the Persian traders and pilgrims in Sri Lanka reported by Ibn Batuta in the fourteenth century, much less the vestigial evidence of nineteenth century Persian influence or Shi'ite Muharram festivals in Puttalam (Ali 1981a: 74-6, Macready 1888-9). The essential subtext of Azeez's historical treatise was that the Ceylon Moors would refuse to be patronized or subsumed as 'Muslim Tamils' in the twentieth century. Thus, a hypostatized Arab 'racial' pedigree was promoted to separate the Moorish from the Sinhala and Tamil 'races'.[24] The claim of a shared Tamil ethnic identity for both Tamils and Muslims has continued to be rejected by Moorish leaders throughout the twentieth century, notes K.M. de Silva, 'because of its implications of a subordinate role for them vis-à-vis the Tamils, and the assumption of a Tamil tutelage over them' (1994: 43). As we shall see, Muslim/Tamil acrimony over Ramanathan's 'ethnological' thesis has been festering for over a century now, coming visibly to the surface several times in the post-Independence era.

In their determination to foster a unique Ceylonese-Arab identity, however, the Moorish leadership ignored a growing public resentment of their 'extra-territorial allegiance'. As Ameer Ali has noted, the Ceylon Moorish elite at the turn of the century—miming the theatrical loyalism of that exiled dissident, Arabi Pasha, who was yearning to return to Egypt (Asad 1993: 42-3)—was so conspicuously devoted to the British monarch, so flattered by the attentions of the Ottoman Caliph, and so proud of their financial donations to build the Hejaz Railway from Damascus to Medina, that their credibility with Ceylonese nationalist leaders was deeply compromised. Even the celebrated 'fight for the fez', in which a prominent Moorish lawyer secured before the Privy Council his right to plead in court wearing a Turkish fez instead of a barrister's horsehair wig, was defined as an exclusively Muslim issue, not as a Ceylonese nationalist cause around which Sinhalese and Tamils could also rally (Ali 1980: Ch.7).

Like the Ceylon Moors, both the Marakkāyar Muslims of Tamil Nadu and the highest-status Māppiḷas of Kerala boasted of their primordial Indo-Arab ancestry, but the Moors were reluctant to amalgamate with such a south Indian 'race', fearing it could undermine their rights as fully enfranchised natives of Ceylon. Reinforcing this aversion was the Moors' resentment of the immigrant south Indian Muslims (the so-called 'Coast Moors') who had effectively displaced the Ceylon Muslim traders from the export/import sector, and from other local markets as well, during the expansion of the plantation economy in the second half of the nineteenth century. The Ceylon Moors showed marked ambivalence toward the Coast Moors, looking to these successful Indian Muslim 'brothers' for a model of wealth and piety, sometimes even defending them in the

Colombo press,[25] but resenting at the same time their exclusionary trading practices, their ascetic overhead expenditures, and their sharp business dealings (Ali 1980: chs. 6-7, 1981b: 14). Echoes of this rivalry can be found in references to jealous quarrels over the congregational rights of the Coast Moors and the Malays in Colombo mosques in the early twentieth century.[26]

At the beginning of the twentieth century other Ceylon ethnic groups were likewise crafting their identities in terms of 'race' and patrilineal 'blood', two familiar European colonial discourses of the period. I.L.M. Azeez himself pointed to the Parsees of Bombay as an economically and politically successful ethnic-cum-racial minority to emulate (Azeez 1907: 15). In the final analysis, the Ceylon Moors pursued a strategy very similar to that of the Burghers (Eurasians) of Ceylon, who emphasized distant patrilineal Dutch 'racial' pedigrees while downplaying their much stronger maternal Luso-Ceylonese ancestry, extolled a moribund linguistic patrimony (Dutch) while speaking and singing a much livelier vernacular (Portuguese Creole) at home, and all the while lobbied for favourable political treatment through an ethnic association which published historical footnotes and northern European family trees. Eventually the Moors Islamic Cultural Home, founded in 1944 by Senator A.R.A. Razik (later Sir Razik Fareed), began to publish the same sorts of historical articles and genealogical pedigrees for the Moorish community as the Dutch Burgher Union had been publishing for the Burghers since 1908 (McGilvray 1982a; Roberts et al. 1989; Jackson 1990; Moors' Islamic Cultural Home 1965, 1970, 1978, 1983, 1994; Marikar, Lafir, and Macan Markar, eds. 1976).

In the twentieth century, however, the social construction of the 'Ceylon Moor' identity has not gone unchallenged, nor has it remained stable (Ismail 1995). Despite the Moors' obviously complex and plural origins, a simplistic dichotomous racial debate over 'Arab' versus 'Tamil' was sustained for many years, with more or less the same political subtext of ethnic estrangement and rivalry. However, by mid-century a long-standing quarrel had intensified within the community itself as to whether 'Moor or 'Muslim' was preferable as a group designation, nativistic 'Moor' partisans incorrectly asserting that the Portuguese applied this term only to racially pure Arabs (Azeez 1907: 4; Mohan 1987: 27-31, 117; Yule and Burnell 1903: 502), and 'Muslim' adherents emphasizing a broader pan-Islamic religious identity which would ignore race and language, and incidentally make room for the Malays and Coast Moors. This discursive debate was reflected in the names of rival 'Moor' versus 'Muslim' political and cultural associations which from the turn of the century served as political fronts for two rival west coast gem-trading dynasties, both of recent Kerala origin, that of M. Macan Markar (Ceylon Moors' Association) and that of Abdul Caffoor (Ceylon Muslim League).[27] Leaders of these two wealthy families also vied jealously for British knighthoods, litigated over control of the Colombo Maradana mosque, and cultivated rival Sufi brotherhoods, with Macan Markar heading the Sri Lankan Shazuliya order and Abdul Caffoor leading the Qādiriyya order (Wagner 1990: 84-117, and personal communication; de Jong 1986; Samaraweera 1979: 252; Mauroof personal communication).[28] At one point in 1945 the leaders of the Muslim League threatened to pronounce a *fatwa* expelling anyone who called himself a 'Moor' from the Muslim faith, a political ploy clearly intended to discredit the rival Moors' Association under the leadership of Razik Fareed (Wagner 1990: 143). Perhaps one of Fareed's most clever strokes is seen in the omnibus name he chose for the Moors' Islamic Cultural Home, a title which proclaims at once a domesticated, racial, religious, and ethnic identity for the Moors.[29]

In the period between World War I and Sri Lankan Independence in 1948 the Moors fluctuated in their political stance, a consequence of the most terrifying episode of their pre-Independence history, the 1915 Sinhala-Muslim Riots.[30] The multiple causes of this island-wide outbreak of Sinhalese violence against Muslim shopkeepers and workers are still hotly debated. Whether conditioned by Sinhala Buddhist revivalism and anti-British sentiment (Roberts 1994a), or fuelled by resentment against Muslim business practices and triggered by confrontational Islamic zealotry on the part of Coast Moors from Kayalpattinam (Ali 1980, 1981b), the rioting was staunchly repressed by the British, giving Moors good reason to be grateful for British protection and muting their support for the anti-British Khilāfat movement to restore the Sultan of Turkey as the Caliph, or leader, of all the world's Muslims. Indeed, given the Moorish leadership's fawning display of loyalty to the British Raj—a pattern seen in other Sri Lankan communities as well—it is difficult to imagine that the most violent and bloody of the anti-British, anti-Hindu 'Māppiḷa rebellions' was occurring only 400 miles away in Kerala at roughly the same period (1922). The 1915 violence also embittered the Moors against the Tamil elite, still led by Ponnambalam Ramanathan, who sought to retain his prominence in the Ceylonese nationalist movement by rising to defend the Sinhalese rioters against harsh British justice. In Muslim eyes, Ramanathan's stance revealed the hypocrisy of 'Tamil-speaking' solidarity, and this event was later recalled bitterly by Moorish politicians at crucial moments in the 1950s and 1960s (Hassan 1968:101, Sivathamby 1987: 204).

In the 1920s and 30s the Moors—divided between the two rival dynastic political organizations, the All-Ceylon Muslim League and the All-Ceylon Moors' Association, and unable to rally behind the leadership of both a Malay (T.B. Jayah) and a Moor (Razik Fareed)—initially followed the Ceylon Tamil leadership in vainly seeking guaranteed '50-50' minority representation under new constitutional reforms (Russell 1982: Ch.12). However, after the disastrous defeat of all their candidates in the 1936 election, which they correctly interpreted as an omen of Sinhalese majoritarian domination on the horizon, the Moorish leadership strategically transferred their support to the Sinhalese-majority parties, explicitly denying any necessary link between Moorish ethnicity and the Tamil language.[31] This accommodating gesture guaranteed both senior Muslim leaders (T.B. Jayah and Razik Fareed) their charter memberships in the leading Sinhala-dominated party at the time of Independence in 1948, the United National Party (K.M. de Silva 1986a, 1986b).[32] Just as most leading Sri Lankan Tamil MPs in the newly established parliament, hoping to salvage some goodwill from the Sinhalese majority in parliament, eventually broke ranks and voted with the UNP MPs to disenfranchise the 7,80,000 Indian Estate Tamils working on up-country tea plantations, so the Muslim MPs voted to disenfranchise the 35,000 Indian Muslims still doing business in Sri Lanka. Both measures testified to the success of D.S. Senanayake in fostering divisions between the Tamil-speaking communities of the island and thus increasing Sinhala electoral dominance in the post-Independence era (Ali 1986-7: 155-6; Ismail 1995: 71-2, 84-5; and especially Shastri in press).

Apart from an ephemeral east coast Tamil-Moor Federal Party alliance in the 1956 elections, the Moors from Independence up to the mid-1980s consistently opted for a strategy of coalition politics within the two major Sinhalese nationalist parties, the UNP and the SLFP, in the course of which certain Moorish politicians earned a legendary reputation for switching tickets and crossing the floor to join whichever party had come to power (Phadnis 1979; Mohan 1987: 47). Sir Razik Fareed, who emerged as the leading Moorish spokesman in the early decades of Independence, conspicuously endorsed the Sinhala Only national language policy in 1956 and railed against what he called 'political genocide' of the Moors under the 'the Tamil yoke'. His speeches accused the Tamils of discrimination against the Moors in education and in local administrative appointments, as well as apathy and indifference wherever Moorish voters were politically underrepresented. During the Official Language debate in 1956, a Tamil MP sarcastically accused him of being a Sinhala defector. Fareed rhetorically turned the tables by asserting that he and the Moorish community could never be considered 'Tamil converts'. A heated replay of the old Ramanathan-Azeez 'ethnological' argument of 1888-1907 immediately ensued on the floor of Parliament (Hassan 1968: 96-106).

As Kingsley de Silva forthrightly notes, 'Tamil-Muslim rivalry in Sri Lanka is a political reality, and the Muslims themselves have responded with alacrity to Sinhalese overtures to back them against the Tamils' (K.M. de Silva 1986a: 449). In this sense, Moorish politics in independent Sri Lanka coupled the mainstream majority party strategy of the Tamil Nadu Muslims with the shrewd communal opportunism of the Kerala Māppiṟas, but all under the rubric of a carefully constructed 'non-Tamil' Moorish ethnicity which was orchestrated from Colombo. De Silva and others have approvingly viewed the Muslims' cultural assimilation into Sinhalese society, and their pragmatic accommodationist politics, as the mark of a 'good' minority, implicitly contrasting them with the troublesome and uncooperative Tamils (K.M. de Silva 1986a, 1988; Dewaraja 1994, 1995). A tangible reward for this pliant behaviour, and a token of the government's desire to maintain strong economic ties with the Muslim countries of the Middle East (Ali 1984), was the establishment of a separate system of government schools for Muslim students in the 1970s and the training of a corps of Muslim teachers to staff them. Apart from standard academic subjects, the curriculum in the Muslim schools includes Islam and optional Arabic language, and in recent years a distinctive Muslim school uniform has been introduced. This has improved Muslim educational success (Ali 1986-7, 1992a), but has arguably worsened ethnic tensions by restricting direct face-to-face contact between students and faculty from different ethnic communities. It also represents a unique political concession to the Muslim community which 'vitiates the principle of non-sectarian state education which has been the declared policy of all governments since 1960' (K.M. de Silva 1997:33).

As Christian Wagner has documented in detail, this effort to extract rewards from the Sinhala-majority parties for a geographically divided and class-stratified Muslim minority depended upon rural east coast Moorish farmers and fishermen electing back-bench Moorish MPs, while a few rich, well-connected west coast Moorish politicians—whose private interests did not often coincide with those of the rural east coast Moors—received influential cabinet appointments. This continued even while Muslim shops, shrines, and paddy fields were periodically threatened by local Sinhalese mobs (M.I.M. Mohideen 1986: 42-4; Wagner 1990: 136-184; 1991; Roberts 1994b: 283).[33] As an educated Muslim middle class began to emerge in the 1970s and 1980s, its demands for practical socio-economic concessions (university admissions and job quotas, for example) were placated with a broad array of Islamic religious and cultural self-esteem programmes, some of them funded by rival Sunni and Shia regimes in the Middle East, which cost the government nothing (O'Sullivan 1997).

This imperfect arrangement, which privileged the western Moorish elite politically just as it disempowered the eastern Moorish peasantry socio-economically, might have continued indefinitely, if not for the fact that after 1983 the government could no longer guarantee the lives and property of Moors in the east coast Tamil guerrilla combat zone. In the mid-1980s, when President Jayawardene's UNP government employed Israeli military advisors and proposed submerging the key Moorish parliamentary constituencies of Amparai district within an enlarged Sinhalese-dominated Province of Uva, the Moors, led by east coast sentiment, finally broke with the UNP and SLFP, organizing the first distinct Muslim political parties in independent Sri Lanka. These included the East Sri Lanka Muslim Front (ESLMF), which later became the Muslim United Liberation Front (MULF), and the Sri Lanka Muslim Congress (SLMC). When in 1989 the SLMC won four parliamentary seats, the political initiative within the Moorish community had been seized for the first time by leaders self-consciously representing the Eastern Province (Wagner 1990, 1991; Ali 1992b; Hennayake n.d.). More recently, however, the success of UNP Muslim candidates from central and western districts in the 1994 elections may signal a growing political cleavage between the assertive policies of the SLMC defending the territorial interests of agricultural Muslims concentrated in the north-east region and the non-confrontational desires of a prosperous and vulnerable Muslim middle class living interspersed with Sinhalese in the island's Wet Zone (O'Sullivan 1997).

A CRUCIAL TEST: MOORS AND TAMILS IN THE EASTERN REGION

Today, in response to the cues of their political leaders and in reaction against the neglect and disrespect they have suffered from the Tamils, the Moors of Sri Lanka have acquired a clearer image of themselves as a distinct ethnic and religious group. Since the outbreak of the Eelam conflict in the early 1980s, communal interests represented by the Sinhalese majority parties have sought to deepen this schism by deliberately provoking and exacerbating local violence between the Moors and Tamils in order to prevent the formation of a unified Tamil-speaking front comprising both groups (Ali 1986-7: 164; UTHR Report 7, 1991; personal fieldwork data 1993 and 1995). From 1990 onward, the LTTE guerrillas themselves have committed massacres of Muslims at prayer as well as the forced expulsion of the entire Muslim population from Jaffna and the north of the island (Sivaram 1992, Hasbullah 1996). All of this has drawn attention away from the historically-rooted commonalities of language, social organization, and cultural practices which the eastern Moors and Tamils continue to share at the village level. It is especially in the Trincomalee, Batticaloa, and Amparai districts of the east coast that large numbers of Muslims and Tamils live as paddy-farming neighbours, competing strongly for the same economic and political resources, testing the limits of their shared cultural heritage. It is here that one of the pivotal issues of the Tamil separatist movement must be decided: will the east coast Moors eventually agree to join the Tamil-led movement for a Tamil-speaking homeland, perhaps with a constitutional provision for Muslim-majority subregions to safeguard their minority rights? Or will they prefer to remain an even smaller and more submerged minority within the Sinhalese-dominated districts?

Based upon my fieldwork (1969-71, 1975, 1978, 1993, 1995) among Tamils and Moors in Akkaraipattu, a large Muslim and

Hindu farming town east of Amparai (pop. 37,000 in 1981), as well as shorter fieldwork in other parts of Batticaloa and Amparai districts, I can sketch some of the cultural background to Tamil-Muslim relations in this suddenly strategic region of the island. Although written in the 'ethnographic present', the description I offer is largely based upon fieldwork I carried out in the 1970s. On two short research trips to the region in 1993 and 1995, I was able to verify that, despite more than a decade of war and strife, the major patterns of Tamil and Moorish matrilineal social organization and popular religiosity are still honoured wherever possible. However, economic hardships, deaths, disappearances, militant recruitments, and diasporic emigrations abroad have all significantly disrupted normal marriage patterns and public acts of worship. More detailed fieldwork will be necessary to determine what long-term social and cultural changes may emerge as a result of the Eelam Wars. In any case, my baseline ethnographic data from the 1970s can help us to understand the tense but relatively stable pattern of Tamil-Moor relations that existed prior to the radical and bitter communal polarization of the late 1980s.

History, economy, and settlement of the eastern Moors

Apart from King Senerat's poorly documented 1626 resettlement of Portuguese-exiled Moors from Kandy to Batticaloa, there are no firm dates for the earliest Moorish communities on the east coast—although the preponderance of Muslims in medieval coastal trade leads me to assume they long predate the Portuguese arrival—and very little Sri Lankan scholarship on the subject.[34] I heard about direct Arab origins here mainly from miraculous tales of Muslim holy men who 'floated ashore on a plank (*palakai*)' directly from the Middle East. There is also a widespread folk tradition, known to both Tamils and Moors, which recounts a caste war between the Tamil Mukkuvars and their rivals, the Timilars, for regional dominance, in which the Mukkuvars are said to have enlisted the aid of the local Muslims. As their reward for victory, it is said, the Muslims shrewdly chose Tamil wives, knowing that under the local system of matrilineal inheritance, their spouses would bring land with them as well (Kadramer 1934).

Although its historicity is problematic, this popular legend does tacitly acknowledge that, in the past, there had been a good deal of intermarriage between local Tamils (especially the dominant caste Mukkuvars) and Muslims. Certainly the fact that the marriage and descent systems of the Tamils and Moors today are identically matrilocal and matrilineal—even to the point of some identical matriclan (*kuṭi*) names—lends popularly-agreed support to this view (Saleem 1990: 29). There is also the possibility that some Hindu Tamils converted to Islam, especially the more impoverished and oppressed members of the Mukkuvar community. Although I have no historical proof of this, a tendency toward Muslim and Catholic conversion has been noted among the Mukkuvar fishing caste in Kerala and Tamil Nadu (Ram 1991; More 1993b:78). Under the pre-colonial Mukkuvar chiefdoms of the Batticaloa region, the Moors appear to have occupied a subordinate, or at least somewhat circumscribed, social position. Although mercantile trade, bullock transport, handloom weaving, carpentry, and coastal fishing appear to have been successful Moorish specialties from an early date, their overall rank and influence within the Tamil-dominated social system was below that of the high caste Vēḷāḷar and Mukkuvar landowners (*pōṭiyārs*). Vestiges of the hereditary incorporation of Moors into the hierarchical caste and matriclan-based rituals of major Hindu temples continued well into the twentieth century in some areas (e.g. Kokkatticcolai, Tirukkovil), before the awakening of Moorish religious and ethnic consciousness led to a renunciation of these duties. From the high caste Tamil Hindu point of view, of course, such Moorish 'shares' (*paṅku*) in temple ritual should be seen as a privilege and honour rather than as a burdensome or degrading service obligation.

Along the east coast, the present-day pattern is one of alternating Tamil and Moorish towns and villages, as well as some internally divided Tamil/Moorish settlements, with the bulk of the population living within a mile or two of the beach. The mainstay of the economy is irrigated rice cultivation, with many Tamil and Moorish farmers commuting daily to their fields from homes in the coastal towns. The east coast Tamils and Moors cultivate adjacent tracts of paddy land, but their houses are located in ethnically segregated residential neighbourhoods. Tamils and Moors may sometimes live on opposite sides of the street, but their houses are almost never interspersed one beside the other. This ethnic partitioning generally coincides with electoral wards or local Headmen's Divisions, sometimes separated by no more than a narrow sandy lane. Among the Tamils, a pattern of Hindu caste segregation is found as well, with certain streets, wards, and even separate outlying hamlets, reserved for specific hereditary professions such as the Untouchable Paraiyar Drummers (McGilvray 1983). However, apart from a small, endogamous, low-status group of hereditary Muslim barber-circumcisers (*Ostā,* from Arabic *ustād,* master), the Moors have not created a parallel caste hierarchy of their own. The only religious elites are some *Maulānā* families (Sayyids, patrilineal descendants of the Prophet) and some local *Bāwās,* who are members of ecstatic Sufi orders (McGilvray 1988b; Aniff 1990, Mahroof 1991). Fieldwork in 1993 and 1995 revealed that Sufism itself is growing in popularity among middle-class Moors, with itinerant Sheikhs from Kerala and the Lakshadweep Islands teaching the distinctive *dhikr* of the Rifā'ī order, among others, to Muslims in Kattankudy, Kalmunai, Akkaraipattu and elsewhere in the island (McGilvray, 1997a).

To the west, once largely a Dry Zone jungle thinly inhabited by Veddah hunters and poor Sinhalese chena cultivators (Pieris 1965), there are now well over 150,000 Sinhalese peasants who have been resettled onto lands adjacent to the ancient Digavapi Buddhist stupa watered by the Gal Oya project, Sri Lanka's first post-Independence peasant colonization scheme. Here, as in all the ethnic frontier districts farther north, the government's use of internationally-funded irrigation projects (see Map 2) to resettle major Sinhalese populations in immediate proximity to well-established Tamil-speaking districts has been 'successful' but highly incendiary from the standpoint of both Tamils and Moors (Manogaran 1987; M.I.M. Mohideen 1986, Peebles 1990; Shastri 1990; UTHR Report 3, 1990). Profound demographic shifts have occurred in parts of Amparai and Trincomalee districts, where the Tamils and the Moors have lost their majority status to the Sinhalese (Kearney 1987). This also means the Tamil-majority districts on the east coast are no longer geographically contiguous, so some kind of Tamil-Moor political accommodation will be necessary if a territorially unified Tamil Eelam or north-eastern provincial homeland is to be created.

Tamils and Moors: similarities and differences

Residential neighbourhoods of Tamils and Moors often look quite similar to the eye. They are laid out along a gridwork of sandy lanes, each household lot guarded by perimeter walls or formidable barbed-wire fences and lushly planted with hibiscus, coconut, arecanut, and mango trees. Ordinary Tamil houses tend to follow a traditional floor-plan oriented toward a carefully raked sandy yard to the east and incorporating a windowless interior Hindu shrine-room at the middle of the western wall. Moorish houses show more variation from this basic floorplan. For example, Moorish families usually allocate the windowless centre room to the husband and wife as their bedroom, and they generally make some provision for female seclusion, such as a high masonry wall extending from the house into the front garden and interior walls or curtains to block the view of male visitors. For more details and floorplan drawings see McGilvray 1989: 195-8. Newer Moorish houses also display more external ornamentation and use of colour than Tamil homes. This tendency is even more strongly marked in the way Moors decorate their bullock carts and fishing boats with colourfully painted floral designs and protective '786' numerology.[35] For reasons no one could explain, Tamil carts and boats are devoid of ornamentation of any kind.

As with the popularly alleged 'racial' differences between Sinhalese and Tamils, outward physical differences between Tamils and Moors are often difficult for an outside observer to detect. Local people would occasionally point out Moors with lighter skin and aquiline features as evidence of their Arab ancestry. However, the most reliable marks of Tamil *versus* Moorish identity 'on the street' are the cultural ones: dress, occupation, and to some degree vocabulary and dialect.[36] Although western-style shirts are nearly universal, Moorish men tend more often to wear as a lower garment a tubular stitched cotton sarong (*cāram)*, typically in a plaid or check pattern, sometimes with a wide black belt, while Tamil men more often wear a plain white unstitched cotton *vēṭṭi* and never a belt. Both Tamil and Moorish women wear a sari and blouse, but Islamic modesty requires Moorish women to cover the head and part of the face with the end of their saris in public, a practice locally known as *mukkāṭu.* Hindu Saivite face and body markings (sacred ash, sandalwood paste, vermilion powder, male earrings) are unmistakably Tamil. Simple white kerchiefs, embroidered skullcaps, or the rare fez may be worn by Moorish men, especially as the hours of prayer approach. However, ambiguity and disguise are always possible: during anti-Tamil riots in Sinhalese areas, Moorish men have sometimes escaped mistaken slaughter only by displaying anatomical proof of circumcision.

Within their ethnically homogeneous wards and neighbourhoods, the Tamils and the Moors maintain places of worship, which are usually managed on a matrilineal basis. Both temples and mosques are governed by boards of male trustees (called *vaṇṇakkars* by the Tamils and *maraikkārs* by the Moors), each trustee representing one of the major matrilineal clans (*kuṭi*) found among the local temple or mosque congregation, and each seeking to preserve the honour and status of his matriclan at annual rituals, whether Hindu temple festivals or Muslim *kantūri* feasts. In the course of fieldwork, I was struck by the difference in religious styles between the Tamils and the Moors. Most of the Tamils I knew enjoyed ritual, and they often encouraged me to enter temples and attend pujas without any doctrinal commitment, whereas the Moors were sometimes more protective of their sacred spaces and more eager to engage in theological debates concerning my personal religious beliefs. As a first approximation, the distinction between Hindu 'orthopraxy' and Muslim 'orthodoxy' does seem to work pretty well, although the east coast Tamil Hindus tend to be less Sanskritic in their rituals than one would find in the agamic temples of Jaffna (McGilvray 1988a). In the sphere of public worship, there is now very little crossover or joint participation by Hindus and Muslims. The only exceptions I noted were some Tamil Hindus who made vows and offerings at the tombs of Muslim saints (*auliyā*) located in mosques (*paḷḷi*) and small chapels (*taikkiyā*).

Moors and Tamils share very similar cultural understandings of sexuality and the body, of heating and cooling foods and substances, and of folk medicine derived from the Siddha and Ayurvedic traditions (McGilvray 1998). Local specialists in both communities are called 'curers' (*parikāri*; colloq. *paricāri*); no one in Akkaraipattu uses the title of *hakīm* or identifies with the Arabic Ūnāni medical system. At the level of ghosts and malevolent spirits (*pēy, picāsu,* Muslim *jinn*), the Tamils and the Moors have a similar construction of the supernatural. There are both Tamil and Muslim *mantiravātis* (experts in the use of mantras to control demonic forces), and there is a propitiatory cult of local female spirits (*tāymār,* 'the mothers') conducted by Moorish women. Until venturing outside of one's own ethnic neighbourhood became a dangerous undertaking as the Eelam 'problems' progressively worsened, some Moors would consult Tamil astrologers concerning marriage, career, and other personal problems. Similar guidance remains available from Moorish numerologists and ink-readers.

Young Muslim children of both sexes continue to attend traditional neighbourhood Koranic 'recitation schools' (*ōtuppaḷḷikkūṭam*) to memorize Arabic scripture, but the agents of modern pan-Islamism are nowadays more visible, particularly young ālims and maulavis, college and seminary-trained teachers of Islam in the Muslim government schools. Their efforts to suppress local traditions and practices as 'non-Islamic' have met with mixed success, and it is sometimes difficult to differentiate the pro-Islamic from the anti-Tamil motives which may lie behind such actions. For example, many Moorish women continue to publicly attend a regional festival celebrating the south Indian saint Shāhul Hamīd of Nagoor at the 'Beach Mosque' (*kaṭaṟkaraip paḷḷi*) near Kalmunai, despite efforts to impose purdah restrictions. For practical reasons, poorer Moorish women still work as members of female weeding and threshing teams in the fields, bringing home cash or a share of the paddy harvest for their families. At the same time, Moors in many areas have stopped employing Hindu caste musicians at local ceremonies and circumcisions because this Islamic 'purification' also enables an anti-Tamil economic boycott. During my visits to Akkaraipattu in 1993 and 1995, many Moors still employed Tamil Washermen for domestic laundry services, and Tamil Blacksmiths still forged agricultural tools and bullock cart wheels for Moorish farmers, despite the heightened ethnic tensions of Eelam War III.

Despite the lifeways they have in common, there are barriers to direct social interaction between the Tamils and the Moors, such as the bifurcated school system. There seem to be virtually no Tamil-Moorish intermarriages today, although they must have occurred widely in the distant past. Similarly, contemporary Tamil converts to Islam are rare; I came across only one or two in my entire fieldwork, always by Tamil women who married Moorish men. I observed very few Tamil-Moor inter-household visitations, gift-giving relationships, or food exchanges except those associated with landlord/tenant obligations or with hereditary low caste Tamil service to Moorish land owners. Women are generally shielded from contact with the opposite community more than men, and Moorish women are shielded most of all.

The remaining opportunities for direct Tamil-Moor social interaction are largely vocational and economic. In the 1970s, before the escalation of the Eelam conflict, Tamils and Moors might cultivate paddy on adjacent tracts of land, in which case they would also participate together on irrigation committees. Tamil and Moorish landowners would also recruit tenant cultivators and field labourers from the opposite community. As a result of violence starting in the 1980s, paddy cultivation and land tenure patterns have been severely disrupted, and farmers in some areas have lost control of their fields to members of other ethnic communities, or to the LTTE itself. I do not know whether joint Tamil-Muslim irrigation committees continue to function today, but many Tamil labourers are still reported to be employed by Muslim landowners in Akkaraipattu (UTHR Bulletin 11, 1996). In the 1970s, shoppers could choose to patronize Tamil or Moorish or Low Country Sinhalese merchants in Akkaraipattu, depending upon a complex set of considerations (price, selection, convenience, credit, and personal trust). However, ethnic resentment and suspicion was often noted, particularly among the Tamils, because the majority of retail establishments in a town such as Akkaraipattu were owned by Moors or Sinhalese or 'Jaffnese' Tamils. Public markets and shops are culturally defined as a male domain into which respectable women should not venture without a chaperone. Tamil women may shop together or with a male relative, but Moorish women must dispatch men or boys to fetch merchandise samples to view at home. Nowadays the purchasing power of Tamils in a town such as Akkaraipattu has been drastically reduced by the Eelam conflict, while the Muslims are visibly more prosperous (UTHR Bulletin 11, 1996).

At the level of popular culture and day-to-day problem-solving, the Tamils and Moors still have a great deal in common, although they rarely stop to reflect upon it. In addition to a common language, their farming practices, matrilocal marriage and household patterns, matrilineal kinship rules, rites of passage, dietary and medical lore, and magical beliefs are identical or closely related in many cases (McGilvray 1982c, 1989). These are the sorts of everyday patterns which, from an anthropological perspective, give the whole Batticaloa region its distinctive cultural identity in contrast to Jaffna or Tamil Nadu, and frankly my own bias would be to read these data optimistically as evidence of consensus rather than conflict. Unfortunately, as the examples of Lebanon, Bosnia, and Northern Ireland prove, in a politically-charged situation these elements of shared regional culture are not necessarily enough to forestall bitter political schism legitimated by history and other markers of cultural difference.

Ethnic stereotypes and self-perceptions

The high-caste Tamils with whom I became acquainted expressed at least a vague awareness of being heirs to a Tamil cultural tradition, a Dravidian civilization with plausible claims to linguistic roots going back to the pre-Vedic Indus Valley culture—and therefore much older than either Buddhism or Islam (Fairservis & Southworth 1989). Yet, although the linguistic and cultural chauvinism which has characterized Tamil politics in the twentieth century has clearly been felt on the east coast, there is also a tinge of ambivalence about the arrogance and presumed cultural authority of the Jaffna Tamils who have led this movement. My Tamil friends were not outspoken on these issues, but they prided themselves on adhering to a coherent and time-tested set of rules for living, including standards for Tamil food and attire, Tamil family patterns, Tamil religiosity, Tamil language and manners. They did not expect me, as a *veḷḷaikkāran* (whiteman), to follow the same regimen, but they were appalled when I seemed to have no systematic rules of my own. My blatant dietary promiscuity and my groggy morning regimen seemed particularly lax to them, and the American kinship system struck both the Tamils and Moors as appallingly flaccid. When the postman brought a wedding invitation from my mother's brother's daughter in California, I was admonished for not having closely scrutinized her fiancé, obviously a rival for my cross-cousin's hand.

Many of the very same elements are found in Moorish self-perceptions, especially the concern to evince a well-ordered cultural system for living. However, the Moors have the option of drawing upon both the Islamic and the Tamil traditions, and sometimes there can be debate over which one to emphasize. From the religious point of view, the Moors enjoy a robust, unequivocal self-definition as orthodox Muslims; indeed some of my friends urgently referred me to locally respected treatises on *sunnā* and *hadīth*, especially the nineteenth century Arabic-Tamil work of 'Māppiḷḷai Ālim' (Ahmad Lebbai 1873/1963). Among some of the young educated Moorish men who became my close friends during fieldwork in the 1970s there was some concern about their own 'hybrid' cultural traits, which they sometimes humorously caricatured as consisting of an Arabic religion, together with a south Indian language, and a mixed programme of clothing and cuisine. Shouldn't the Moors have their own unique 'national dress', some of them asked, instead of just borrowing a Sinhala-Malay sarong and a Tamil sari? A further complication in the 1970s was the official adoption of a Pakistani school uniform, the 'Punjabi costume' of *salwar kameez*, for Moorish high school girls, more recently augmented with an Iraqi-inspired white hooded head-covering (referred to as *partā*, purdah). With grudging admiration, a Moorish friend of mine remarked that, regardless of where in the world she might live, a Tamil woman would unhesitatingly prefer to wear a traditional Kanchipuram sari and tie the customary jasmine blossoms in her hair. Lacking such a strong cultural identity, a Muslim woman, he felt, would be more inclined to adopt local, or more western, dress.

In agriculture and business, however, the Moorish identity is strong and unequivocal: they see themselves as—and are acknowledged by the Tamils to be—shrewd, hard-working, and successful. In the 1970s, east coast Moors readily admitted to me that their MPs would 'reverse hats' (*toppi tiruppuvān*), i.e., switch party affiliations, to ally themselves with the party in power, a manoeuvre perfected by the late Gate Mudaliyar M.S. Karaiyapper of Kalmunai, his son-in-law M.M. Mustapha, and his nephew M.C. Ahmed (Phadnis 1979: 45-6; Mohan 1987: 47; Wagner 1990: 157). It should be noted, however, that several east coast Tamil MPs also learned to emulate this tactic quite well (UTHR Report 7, 1991: 45-6).

There are many different perceptions and opinions of Tamil/Moor cultural difference, but some basic themes emerged in offhand remarks I heard from members of each group. Tamils generally concede that the Moors are extremely energetic and hardworking, a fact visibly reflected in their improved houses and growing material wealth. In fact, the increasing prosperity of the Moors is of acute concern to many high caste Tamils, because it challenges their traditionally dominant position in society. Not only are the Moors getting richer, they are also accused of having too many children. It is true that the Moors have maintained the highest birth-rate of any ethnic community in the country over the past 50 years (Kurukulasuriya, et al. 1988: 191), a trend which is also true among Muslims in India. With demographic and electoral trends in mind, many Tamils and Moors—and nowadays some Sinhalese as well (Schrijvers 1998: 12)—view such persistent fecundity as a political act.

I also encountered a more covert level of ethnic stereotyping which was constructed from private beliefs and suspicions, a more concealed discourse among younger men with whom I spent time which reflected both their curiosity and anxiety about matters of the body. Whether these ideas have had any real impact at all upon Tamil-Muslim communal politics is impossible for me to say, but at some level they form part of the symbolic web of cultural images which separates the two groups. I found that the more intimate domains of Muslim diet, sexuality, and hygiene, because they are blocked from public view, typically generated the most Tamil gossip. Some Tamils theorize that the Moors' vigour and fertility come from their consumption of beef, in Hindu eyes a polluting and highly 'heating' meat that energizes the body and the libido. Indeed, according to Māppiḷḷai Ālim's influential nineteenth century Arabic-Tamil treatise on Islamic teachings, Muslims are encouraged to consume meat and flesh for this purpose (Ahmad Lebbai 1873/1963: 255-67). One inventive Tamil informant hypothesized that Moorish circumcision dulls male sensitivity, prolongs intercourse, and allows more Moorish women to achieve orgasm, thereby promoting conception (McGilvray 1982b). I once also heard some Tamil youths jokingly refer to the Moors as 'three-quarters' (*mukkāl*), revealing their muddled fantasies of what was actually severed during male circumcision, an operation which in Akkaraipattu is usually conducted around the age of 9 or 10 with considerable domestic celebration and formal hospitality. The Moorish male circumcision ritual itself is colloquially referred to as a 'circumcision wedding' (*cunattu kaliyāṇam*), and it parallels in interesting ways the Tamil and Moorish female puberty ceremony, which is also referred to as a 'wedding,' i.e., an auspicious rite of passage (McGilvray 1982b). The Moorish practice of female circumcision was, however, completely unknown to the Tamils with whom I spoke in Akkaraipattu. This mandatory (*wājib*) operation (Ahmad Lebbai 1873/1963: 479) conducted by the circumciser's wife (*ostā māmi*) within 40 days of birth was described by my male friends—who had to turn to their wives and elder sisters for specific information on the topic—as a symbolic cutting of the skin over the baby's clitoris sufficient to draw a drop of blood, but not as full scale genital excision or clitoridectomy.[37]

There are some other grooming and adornment practices as well which serve to distinguish the Moors from the Tamils. It is considered good (*sunnat*) for Moorish men and women to shave or clip their armpit and pubic hair every forty days in order to ensure that all parts of the body are moistened during bathing to remove ritual pollution (*mulukku*).[38] Some informants also told me there was a *hadīth* against body hair long enough to grasp. I knew a number of older, more traditional Moorish men in the 1970s who had their heads and armpits shaven monthly by a Moorish barber (*ostā*), while there was no corresponding tonsorial practice among the Tamils apart from shaving the head to fulfil personal Hindu vows. While women of both communities wear pierced earrings, and Tamil women wear nose ornaments, it is *harām* (forbidden in Islam) for Moorish women to pierce the septum. Similarly, unlike traditional Hindu Tamils, Moorish men must not pierce their ears or wear earrings (Ahmad Lebbai 1873/1963: 480).

In the sort of intimate observation which only a few of my closest male Moorish and Tamil friends ventured to offer, it was suggested that the substantive focus of everyday pollution anxiety is somewhat different among the Tamils and Moors. While both communities share an aversion to contact with blood, semen, menstrual and childbirth substances, the Tamils have a marked aversion to saliva (*eccil*) which is not reciprocated as strongly among the Moors. Indeed, some ecstatic Sufi rituals conducted by local Bawas involve the transfer of sacred power to implements of self-mortification from the breath and saliva of the presiding *kalifā* (McGilvray 1988b; Bayly 1989: 127-8). The Moors, on the other hand, seem to have stronger taboos on contact with excreta, especially urine and sexual fluids. Moorish men are taught to take special precautions when they squat to urinate so that no urine touches their sarong or other clothing, a form of contamination which would bar them from the mosque and from Muslim prayers. Some male friends of mine said they would use a porous piece of brick to absorb the last drops of urine. Islamic rules also require a full head-bath not only after, but *between*, all acts of sexual intercourse, a fact which can make it something of an embarrassment when the sound of the well-sweep is heard late at night in Moorish neighbourhoods.

The most frequent complaints I heard from Tamils concerning the Moors as a group were that they were politically unreliable, that they were relatively less educated (which was true earlier in the century, but not now), that they lived in unhealthily overcrowded houses and neighbourhoods (for example, in Kattankudy, the most densely-inhabited town in Sri Lanka), that they ate beef (a source of Hindu regret but not anger), and—admittedly a minor point—that they had a fondness for asphyxiating scents and perfumes (*attar*). The latter is obviously a case of selective criticism, for the Tamils burn strongly aromatic camphor and apply sweet-smelling sandalwood paste in all their Hindu rituals. Māppiḷḷai Ālim's treatise on Muslim practices commends the use of perfume before attending Friday prayers (Ahmad Lebbai 1873/1963: 274), and I found that long-lasting, concentrated *attar* scent was also routinely applied to guests and participants at many other Moorish events in order to enhance the sense of ritual occasion.

Moorish stereotypes of the Tamils reflected much less voyeuristic concern with the details of grooming and sexual practices. Instead, Moors complained to me about the monopoly of Tamils in the professions and the civil service, a charge more properly directed against the Jaffna Tamils, who have far outnumbered the local Batticaloa Tamils in these career paths. Moors would acknowledge that, until recent decades, the Tamils had been better educated, both in traditional Tamil culture as well as in the modern professions, but they resented the Tamils' unnecessary arrogance and ingrained attitudes of superiority. Moors attributed much of this to the rigidity of the Hindu caste system and to the inegalitarian hierarchical frame of mind upon which it is based. All Muslims, they assured me, are equal before Allah. Although my fieldwork eventually turned up some very small hereditarily ranked endogamous Moorish sub-groups (*Ostā* barber-circumcisers, *Maulānā* Sayyids), the claim of broad ritual equality among the Moors is indeed valid. In a town like Akkaraipattu, however, wealth differences seem more pronounced among the Muslims than among the Tamils.[39] Tamils are stigmatized in the eyes of the Moors for their propensity to waste time and money drinking alcohol, although some Moors are also known to imbibe surreptitiously on occasion. Finally, although they had little eyewitness knowledge of these matters, the Moors' opinion of Hindu religious practices was uniformly negative. Tamil Saivism was criticized for being polytheistic, idolatrous, and demonic, and for not being a prophetic Religion of the Book. On this issue, the local Muslims and the Christians definitely saw eye to eye.

Communal disturbances in the Batticaloa region

Popular memory recounts the many localized Tamil-Moor riots and disturbances (*kuḷappam,* 'mix-up', *canṭai,* 'fight') which have plagued communal relations on the east coast throughout the twentieth century and probably earlier.[40] Although I directly witnessed no local

Tamil-Moor violence, I did gather oral accounts of such outbreaks. One type of incident was the post-election reprisal, typically an attack upon members of the opposite community for failure to deliver blocs of votes which had been purchased in advance with money or arrack (and sometimes purchased twice, by different candidates!). A second type of conflict would arise from an individual provocation, which was perceived as a generalized insult to the entire Tamil or Moorish community. When, for example, in the late 1960s a drunken Moorish man allegedly snipped off the braided hair of a Tamil woman who had spurned his advances in public, an innocent Moorish bystander soon lost his ear, and there were communal ambushes and roadblocks for a week. A year or so later, Moorish youths organized Akkaraipattu's very first Gandhian-inspired Shramadana community self-help project: a new road allowing Moorish cultivators to circumambulate Tamil villages to evade ambush whenever they travel to their fields during future communal riots.

A third type of violence was related to a growing competition for land, including residential building sites. The historical tendency over the last 150 years has been for successful Moors to expand their agricultural landholdings and businesses, while upwardly mobile Tamils have favoured education and a career in the professions. Recognizing the gradual decline in Tamil-owned paddy fields, the Tamils are now chagrined and resentful. Because of the determination of Moors to reside together in established Muslim enclaves, the pressure on adjoining Tamil neighbourhoods has resulted in both irresistible buy-outs and violent evictions of Tamil residents by their Moorish neighbours. For example, lower caste Tamils have been forcibly driven out of their neighbourhoods in the Kalmunai-Sainthamaruthu area, and Moors have quickly moved in (UTHR Report 7, 1991: 49-55, and my own fieldnotes).

Based upon accounts of Hindu-Muslim rioting in north India, I had initially assumed that Tamil-Moorish conflicts in Sri Lanka would be sparked by religious provocations: Muslim cow slaughter, Hindu processions near mosques, and the like. However, the actual incidents I recorded suggest that 'religious' issues have never been a frequent trigger, not even a major underlying cause, of local Moorish/Tamil violence on the east coast. Even when religious sites have been targeted, such as the destruction of the Bhadrakali Hindu temple in Akkaraipattu by Muslims (with the acquiescence of the Sri

Lankan Army) after the withdrawal of the Indian Peace-Keeping Force in 1989, the underlying motive appears to have been a desire to expand the boundaries of the Moorish residential neighbourhood near which the temple was situated.[41] With the upsurge of warfare between Tamil guerrillas and Sri Lankan armed forces in the region since 1983, Moorish seizure of agricultural lands abandoned by fleeing Tamil refugees and reprisal depredation by Tamils of exposed Moorish fields have further enflamed the inter-ethnic situation (UTHR Report 7, 1991; Report 11, 1993).

Difficult as it is to take a longer view of such events, they must nevertheless be understood as part of the gradual emancipation of the Moorish community from the thralldom of pre-modern Tamil Hindu political domination, caste hierarchies, and feudalistic land tenure systems in this region (McGilvray 1982c, and book manuscript in progress). Nowadays the Moors enjoy a degree of economic prosperity and political independence from the Tamils that would have been impossible to imagine a century earlier. The wealthier, higher-caste Tamils are particularly aware of this trend, which represents the loss—or the increasing irrelevance—of their hereditary status privileges. The Moors are fully aware that many high caste Tamils still look down upon them as their recent inferiors, and this has spurred the younger and more professionally-oriented Moors to strive for modern careers and avenues of self-respect quite independent of the Tamils.

More recently, the deliberate provocation of intercommunal violence by those seeking to block the creation of any east coast Tamil-Moorish political alliance, as well as massacres and reprisals against members of both ethnic communities arising from differences over Tamil Eelam and the future of the north-eastern region, have established a climate of hatred and distrust which may poison Tamil-Moorish inter-communal amity for years to come (UTHR Report 10, 1993). The depth of misunderstanding and miscalculation was illustrated by a speech given in 1990 by Tamil Tiger spokesman Y. Yogi, scolding the Moors for failing to properly identify themselves as Tamils and justifying the mass expulsion of Muslims from Jaffna and Mannar by the LTTE as punishment for their alleged ethnic betrayal. Tragically, this was Ponnambalam Ramanathan's 1888 'ethnological' thesis yet again, but this time enforced with Kalashnikov rifles and a brutal agenda of ethnic cleansing.[42]

OPTIONS FOR THE FUTURE

A low point in Muslim-Tamil relations definitely occurred in 1990, but to leave the story there would be, I think, too pessimistic. Cultural membership is always contextual and historically conditioned, and a great deal of new history is presently being made in Sri Lanka. We have already seen that Muslims in three neighbouring regions of the subcontinent were capable of forging divergent cultural styles, ethnic identities, and political strategies over the past four centuries: violent *jihād* in Kerala, literary and spiritual synthesis in Tamil Nadu, 'non-Tamil' political ethnicity in Sri Lanka. Several modern observers have suggested that for all the demographic, political, and cultural reasons enumerated earlier, the Moors of Sri Lanka are now starting to differentiate themselves into several distinct subregional identities within the island, the most significant of which would distinguish the one-third of all Muslims concentrated in the agricultural north-east from the remaining two-thirds who live widely dispersed in the Sinhalese areas of the south-west (Sivathamby 1987; Ali 1992b; Ismail 1995).

It was the nineteenth and twentieth century British colonial regime which provided tangible political rewards for establishing a 'racial' distinction between Moor and Tamil, thus defining the competitive arenas within which modern communal politics in Sri Lanka would be forged. After Independence came the 'interactive ethnonationalism' of Sinhalese majoritarian politics (Hennayake 1992) and shrewd accommodations by the Muslim elite defending its west-coast urban interests within Sinhala society. During the Eelam Wars of the past two decades, calculated acts of inter-ethnic sabotage by government forces and by Tamil militants have intentionally widened the division between the Moors and the Tamils into a political chasm. Yet, despite unforgivable atrocities on all sides, the general awareness of this sad history is by now so widely shared, and the sheer terror and exhaustion of the Eelam conflict is so desperately felt in the eastern war zone, that the basis for a pragmatic rapprochement between the Tamils and Moors of the Batticaloa region may still be possible (Lawrence 1997, 1998, and in press; McGilvray 1997b; Schrijvers 1998; see Krishna 1994 for a more pessimistic view).

The original Federal Party slogan of S.J.V. Chelvanayagam who sought to unite all of Sri Lanka's 'Tamil-speaking peoples' under one political umbrella was scornfully rejected by earlier Colombo-based Moorish leaders such as Sir Razik Fareed, even though there is a great deal of Tamil poetry, folklore, and religious literature by Sri Lankan Muslims from Batticaloa, Jaffna, Mannar, and elsewhere (Kandiah 1964; Sivathamby 1987; Uwise 1986, 1990; Saleem 1990). In fact, when the Eelam War first broke out in the 1980s, Tamil militant groups, including the LTTE, were able to recruit and train a significant cohort of Muslim fighters from the Eastern and Northern Provinces on the basis of regional loyalty to the idea of a 'Tamil-speaking' homeland. This militant collaboration between Tamil and Muslim youths, with its echo of the historic Moor-Mukkuvar alliance celebrated in Batticaloa legend, was shattered in 1990 when the eastern command of the LTTE, acting on local enmities and resentments, launched a series of attacks and pogroms against Muslims, including the well-publicized Kattankudy Mosque massacre (Sivaram 1991, 1992; McGilvray 1997b). Muslim cadres abruptly fled the LTTE organization, and there seemed no hope for further dialogue.

Despite this profound Tamil betrayal, the pragmatic needs of local Muslim traders and the geographical vulnerability of both Tamils and Moors to mutual retribution soon resulted in a series of private contacts and locally-based understandings between the LTTE and Moorish village leaders and merchants which continue to the present. At the same time, working against the reestablishment of Tamil-Muslim cordiality are the various armed and thuggish 'ex-militant' Tamil groups (e.g. PLOTE, TELO, EPRLF) who implement the Sri Lankan Security Forces' strategy of divide and rule in the Batticaloa region (Krishna 1994: 312). At a broader level, one of the perennial obstacles to a parliamentary accord between the Muslim SLMC and the Tamil TULF parties has been the lack of minority safeguards and explicitly defined territorial rights for the Muslims within a larger federated Tamil region (Sivathamby 1987). Recently, in 1997, there were some signs of movement toward the creation of the first Moorish-majority district in Sri Lanka stretching from Kalmunai to Pottuvil in the south-eastern part of the island, just as the Māppiḷas of Kerala had carved out the newly created Mallapuram District for themselves in 1969.

At this late date, the distinct 'non-Tamil' ethnic ideology of the Moorish establishment and their 50-year record of political collaboration with the main Sinhalese parties, coupled with the uncompromising, short-sighted, and brutal militancy of the Tamil guerrillas, have made a rapprochement based upon a recognition of Tamil and Moorish cultural affinities and common interests on the east coast extremely difficult to achieve. First colonially-engineered competition, then ethnic party politics, and eventually civil war, have pre-empted whatever goodwill might have developed between the two groups under more foresighted leadership. However, because their common geohistorical destiny offers them little choice, the Tamils and Moors in the eastern Batticaloa region may eventually come to a renewed appreciation of their shared cultural roots, as well as an honest appraisal of their past prejudices. The cultural, political, and economic basis for a lasting inter-ethnic community of interest between the Tamils and the Moors is still there, at least in the geographically delimited eastern coastal region, but in the wake of massacres and reprisals, expulsions, displacements, land thefts, and masked betrayals, both deep compassion and true ethnic statesmanship on all sides will be needed to nurture it.

NOTES

1. The Sri Lankan Malays, so termed by the British because of their Indonesian Malay lingua franca, are Sunni Muslims. Their ancestors were exiled Javanese princes as well as a medley of banished criminals and Dutch Company soldiers of diverse Indonesian origin dispatched from Batavia during the eighteenth century (Hussainmiya 1986; Mahroof 1994). There are also some small groups of Bombay and Gujarati traders who have businesses in Colombo: Bohras and Khojas (both Ismailis), and Memons (who are Sunnis). Some schismatic Qādiyāṇis (Ahmadiyyas) are said to be found in the Gampola region, remnants of a group once influential in Colombo as well (Abdul Majeed 1971).
2. Denham (1912: 232n.) observed a half-century ago that *Cōni* ('Sōṇi' or 'Chōni', short for *Cōṉkar*) was commonly used as a term for Muslims in the Batticaloa region, although the nickname has derogatory overtones today. Two other negative slang terms are *Nānāmār* and *Kākkā*, regionally variant Moorish kin terms for 'elder brother', the latter unfortunately also a colloquial homonym for 'crow' in Tamil. Additional Sri Lankan terms for the so-called 'Coast Moors', expatriate Muslim traders from the south Indian coast, include *Marakkala Minissu* (Sinh. 'boat-people'), *Hambaya* or *Hambankāraya* (Sinh.) and *Cammankārar* (Tam.), both either from Malay *sampan* 'skiff' or from Tamil *cāmān* 'goods', and Tambey (Tam. *tampi*, younger brother), a British colonial term for

itinerant trader. See Ameer Ali 1980: 99ff. and 1981a for a general discussion.

3. I use both terms in this essay, with no intended implications about the basis of contemporary group identity.
4. Colombo is the *only* place in the island where I have ever met a Moor who could not speak Tamil. Multilingualism is, however, gaining among middle-class Colombo Muslims, some of whom prefer to send their children to Sinhala or English medium schools to hedge their bets about the future of the country. The sermons in some Colombo mosques are also delivered in Sinhala or English on certain days (Nilam Hamead, personal communication).
5. For an up to date overview of the Sri Lankan ethnic conflict see Nissan 1996. For more background on the failure of democratic institutions see Tambiah 1986.
6. Ismail discerns a 'terror' of being viewed as Tamils in elite Muslim discourses (1995: 66 fn.26).
7. For a closer review of the literature on the early history of the Sri Lankan Moors, and a more detailed discussion of the Māppiḷas and the Marakkāyars, please see the original version of this article which appeared in *Contributions to Indian Sociology* (n.s.) 32, 2 (1998).
8. Miller (1976: 30-2) reviews eight etymologies for the term, settling upon 'bridegroom, or new husband' (Tamil, *māppiḷḷai*) as the most plausible, given the historical pattern of marriage between Arab traders and local Kerala women. The term was once also used for Christian and Jewish settlers in Malabar (Thurston and Rangachari 1909, v. 4: 460).
9. There is an enduring etymological debate about the origin of this word. Proponents of Arab ethnic identity prefer to derive the term from *markāb* (Arabic, boat). Others derive it from *mārkkam* (Tamil and Malayalam, religion). More (1997: 22) reports that Marakkāyars today favour an etymology derived from *marakkalarāyar* ('ruler of the boats'). Besides being a Sinhalese term for Indian 'Coast Moors', the term *Marakkala* is similar to a caste title found among the Moger coastal fishermen in South Kanara. See D'Souza (1955: 41-7) and Ameer Ali 1981a: 68-70) for exhaustive discussions.
10. The Labbai/ Marakkāyar distinction is not uniformly observed within Tamil Nadu, nor is it more than three centuries old. The contrast dissolves among the Muslims of Pulicat north of Madras, where even the exclusive endogamous Arab-descended coastal traders are called 'Labbay' (Pandian 1987: 128-33). Rao, Shulman, and Subrahmanyam (1992: 265) assign the term Labbai to 'coastal fishermen, divers, weavers, artisans and husbandmen' who were not clearly differentiated from the Marakkāyars in the seventeenth century. J.B.P. More (1997: 21-5) notes that in the fifteenth and sixteenth centuries most Tamil Muslims were referred to as 'Turks' (*tulukkar*), a term which I also occasionally heard in Sri Lanka in the 1970s.

11. My sources are the south Indian newsmagazines *The Week* (1 March 1998) and *Frontline* (20 March 1998).
12. A series of photographs illustrating aspects of modern Sri Lankan Muslim culture may be found in the original version of this article which appeared in *Contributions to Indian Sociology* (n.s.) 32, 2 (1998).
13. Formal matrilineal descent units (matrilineages, matriclans) have not been documented among Moors outside of the east coast. One author briefly alludes to patrilineal kinship among the Moors of Kalutara and Mannar (M.Z. Mohideen 1965: 25).
14. Father, *vāppā*; mother, *ummā;* elder brother, *kākkā*; elder sister, *rāttā* or *tāttā*. For the Māppiḷa kin-terms see Gough 1961: 439-42 and Puthenkalam 1977: 228-32. In the absence of a full list of Marakkāyar kin-terms, I do not know what other kin-terms they may share with the Moors of Sri Lanka. Muslims in Colombo and south-western Sri Lanka recognize as a substitute for *kākkā* (elder brother) the term *nānā,* which is also a Singaporean term for the wealthier Tamil Muslims who come from coastal *Marakkāyar* towns such as Karaikal and Nagapattinam (Mani 1992: 341).
15. Mattisam is derived from the Tamil word *mattiyam* or *mattiyastam,* adjudication or mediation. *Nāṭṭāṇmaikkārar* is a term for certain regional caste headmen in Tamil Nadu.
16. According to a Māppiḷa tradition, the Marakkāyars themselves were originally a merchant group in Cochin (Nambiar 1963: 59). Some Sinhalese cultural patterns, too, are historically of Kerala origin (Roberts 1980; Obeyesekere 1984: 425-52).
17. Mines (1973) reports relatively open and egalitarian relations between different Labbai subdivisions in a suburb of Madras, and other writers have pointed to important ways in which Muslim social divisions are *unlike* Hindu castes (Mauroof 1986; Mujahid 1989). Still, the evidence of endogamous status barriers between Marakkāyars and other Tamil Muslim groups remains quite strong (More 1991; Bayly 1989; Pandian 1987: Chs. 6-8; my own fieldwork in Kayalpattinam 1983). Both the Māppiḷas and the Sri Lankan Moors have traditionally assigned the task of circumcision to a hereditary low-status group of Muslim barbers called *Ossan* in northern Kerala, *Ostā* in Travancore and in Sri Lanka (McGilvray 1974: 306-12). The existence of smaller endogamous marriage circles—possibly even the perpetuation of Marakkāyar pedigrees from Kayalpattinam—among the wealthy Muslim gem-trading families of Colombo, Beruwela, and Galle has been asserted by Mauroof (1972: 69-80), but without supporting data.
18. For a brief period in the mid-eighteenth century a coastal Navāyat dynasty held the Nawābship (Fanselow 1989: 273).
19. The largest single urban concentration of Sri Lankan Muslims (18 per cent of the total Muslim population) is within the municipal district of Colombo (Phadnis 1979: 29-32).

20. Another author, M.M.M. Mahroof, has called it the 'Kasbah mentality' (1990: 91).
21. A similar picture emerges with respect to the older, more traditional madrasas or Arabic Muslim seminaries, which were primarily founded in the southernmost Galle-Weligama region (Asad 1994).
22. I found in the 1970s that high-ranking Vēḷāḷars and Mukkuvars in the Batticaloa region still generally referred to members of low castes such as Washermen (*Vaṇṇāṉ*) and Drummers (*Paṟaiyaṉ*) by their specific caste names, reserving the collective term 'Tamil' (*Tamiḷaṉ*) solely for the highest castes. I am grateful to John Rogers for reminding me this was true in Jaffna as well.
23. Although it is not widely recounted in Sri Lanka, there is an extra-Quranic tradition that Adam, having rejoined his wife Eve at Arafat near Mecca, returned with her to Sri Lanka where they gave birth to the human race (Wadood 1976). Any acknowledgement of the many alternative legends which place Adam's fall in India (al-Ṭabarī 1989) would have been awkward from Azeez's point of view.
24. For critical examination of the Sinhalese and Tamil 'racial' constructions, see Gunawardena 1990, Rogers 1995, and Hellman-Rajanayagam 1995.
25. Indeed, only three years prior to publishing his racially exclusivist rebuttal of Ramanathan, I.L.M. Abdul Azeez had defended the Coast Moors in his Tamil newspaper, the *Muslim Guardian*, arguing that, in addition to their shared bonds as loyal British subjects, 'the Northern Coast [Indian] Moors and the Ceylon Moors are related in terms of their religion and to an extent in terms of their race'. His Tamil word for race was *cāti*, which could also mean caṣte. 'Northern Coast Moor' is my translation of the phrase *vaṭakarai cōṉakar* (cf. Ameer Ali 1981: 14, 20n).
26. *Ceylon Legislative Council Debates.* 21 August 1924, pp. 277-301. 'History of the Maradana Mosquē', (anonymous), 38 pp. typescript. Catalogue #297.3595493/1187 in the library of the Moors Islamic Cultural Home, Bristol Street, Colombo. For the Malays see also Asad 1993: 80, 90; Ossman 1990.
27. Michael Roberts asserts that 'the Macan Markars and the Abdul Cafoors' migrated to Sri Lanka in the eighteenth or nineteenth centuries from Kerala (1980: 38, 46n).
28. The possibility of something like a dynastic moiety system within the west coast Muslim elite remains strong, as evidenced by the nearly simultaneous publication of two independently sponsored scholarly collections of essays on the history and culture of the Sri Lankan Muslims. One of these volumes enjoys the patronage of a third and newer Moorish gem-trading dynasty, that of Naleem Hadjiar (Mahroof et al. 1986; Shukri, ed. 1986a; Mauroof 1972: 69).

29. Fareed's Tamil name for the MICH is *Cōṉaka Islāmiya Kalācāra Nilaiyam.*
30. Six papers in the Ceylon Studies Seminar 1969/70 Series are devoted to this event, four of them also published in the *Journal of Asian Studies* 29, no. 2 (1970). See also Ameer Ali 1981b, Roberts 1994a.
31. Note, however, that as late as 1930 there was a daily Colombo newspaper for Muslims, *Tina Tapāl* (Daily Post), published in Tamil (Mahroof 1990: 94).
32. At the very same time, an Indian Muslim radical who had agitated for an independent 'Mappilastan' in Kerala was proposing to create 'Nasaristan' for the Moors in eastern Sri Lanka and 'Safiistan' for west coast Moors. Because of their strategic decision to work within the Sinhalese nationalist parties, the Moorish leadership paid no attention to his efforts (Rahmat Ali 1943; Gabriel 1996: 294 ff.).
33. In recent decades the Muslim cave-shrine at Daftar Jailani has been the scene of volatile confrontations between Muslim devotees and Sinhalese monks and politicians who wish to reclaim it as an ancient Buddhist site (Hon. M.L.M Aboosally, M.P., Chief Trustee of the shrine, personal communication 27 August 1993).
34. An exception is the recent local history of Akkaraipattu by Saleem 1990. See also Kandiah 1964.
35. The number 786, frequently painted on sea-going fishing craft, is numerological short-hand for the Islamic invocation *Bismillāhi 'l-Rahmān 'l-Rahīm* ('In the Name of God, the Beneficent, the Merciful').
36. The Tamil spoken by the Moors of the Batticaloa region contains a number of Islamic and Arabic-derived words as well as alternative Tamil expressions and kin-terms which are distinctive to Muslim usage. Their pronunciation, however, is broadly similar to the Tamils of the eastern region, as compared, for example, with the notably different Muslim Tamil speech patterns around Galle and the southern coast.
37. The *Fat-Hud-Dayyān* instructs: 'What is necessary to be done in the case of a male is to have the entire foreskin cut off. What is necessary to be done in the case of a female is to cut off a small bit of the flesh of the cock's-comb-like clitoris that lies above the urinary duct. It is *sunnat* to have the circumcision of a male known, and the circumcision of a female kept secret' (Ahmad Lebbai 1873/1963: 479). A recent wire service story (IPS, 19 August 1997) claims that radical female genital mutilation (clitoridectomy) is practiced on forty-day old Muslim girls by *ostā māmis* in the Colombo neighbourhoods of Dematagoda, Maskade, and Maradana, but my information from Colombo Muslim sources does not corroborate this report.
38. *Muḷukku* (a Tamil word which also means 'immersion') is the Moorish equivalent of *tuṭakku,* the common Tamil term for ritual pollution in the Batticaloa region. Arabic Islamic terms such as *najīs* (filth), *janāba*

(sexual pollution), and *nifās* (childbirth pollution) are available (Ahmad Lebbai 1873/1963) but are rarely used.

39. Neighbouring Muslim towns such as Nintavur and Sammanturai are said to have even greater concentrations of landed wealth in the hands of Moorish *pōṭiyārs.*
40. Interestingly enough, E.B. Denham, the Government Agent in Batticaloa, reported 'no trouble of any kind in this Province' at the time of the 1915 Sinhala-Muslim riots (Denham 1915: E5).
41. Fieldwork in Akkaraipattu in 1993 revealed the temple I had studied intensively in the 1970s is now totally demolished. Cattle bones have been tossed into the temple well to pollute the site and to discourage the Tamils from rebuilding the temple at the same location. A land sale was one of the few options available to the temple trustees (McGilvray 1997b).
42 'Muslims claim that they are neither Sinhalese nor Tamils, but are Arabs. They use this in pursuit of their selfish aims. . . . They are Tamils. They study in Tamil at Tamil schools. Their culture is not Arab. . . . we did not rape them or loot their property. We only sent them out. . . . We made several promises to the Muslims. . . . On the contrary, they joined forces with the Sinhalese army and the Sri Lankan state and set about destroying us. . . . The Muslims must accept that they are Tamils. They must understand that they are descendants of Arabs who married Tamil women' (UTHR Report 7, 1991: 42-3). For a discussion of LTTE expulsion of Muslims from the Northern Province, see Hennayake 1993 and Hasbullah 1996. For an ominous reiteration of this ultimatum to the Moors see Mohamed 1996.

REFERENCES

Abdul Majeed, O. 1971. *The learned Ceylon Muslims' opinion on Ahmadiyya movement* (Pamphlet). Colombo: Ceylon Ahmadiyya Muslim Association.

Aboosally, M.L.M. 1975. 'Did Shayk Abdul Kader Jilani visit Adam's Peak in Sri Lanka?' *The Muslim Digest* (South Africa) September-October 1975: 167-70.

Ahmad Lebbai, Seyyid Muhammad Ibn. 1963. *Fat-Hud-Dayyān: Fi Fiqhi Khairil Adyan.* (A compendium on Muslim theology and jurisprudence). Saifuddin J. Aniff-Doray, trans. Colombo: Fat-Hud-Dayyan Publication Committee. First published in Arabic-Tamil in 1873.

al-Ṭabarī, Abū Ja'far Muhammad b. Jarīr. 1989. *The history of al-Ṭabarī,* vol. 1: *General introduction and from the Creation to the Flood.* Franz Rosenthal, trans. Albany: State University of New York Press.

Ali, A.C.L. Ameer 1980. Some aspects of religio-economic precepts and practices in Islam: A case study of the Muslim community in Ceylon during the period *c.* 1800-1915. Unpublished Ph.D. thesis. Perth: University of Western Australia.

———. 1981a. 'The genesis of the Muslim community in Ceylon (Sri Lanka): A historical summary'. *Asian Studies* 19: 65-82.

———. 1981b. 'The 1815 racial riots in Ceylon (Sri Lanka): A reappraisal of its causes.' *South Asia* 4: 1-20.

———. 1984. 'Muslims and Sri Lanka's ethnic troubles'. *Muslim World League Journal.* Aug-Sept. 1984: 55-8.

———. 1986-7. 'Politics of survival: Past strategies and present predicament of the Muslim community in Sri Lanka'. *Journal Institute of Muslim Minority Affairs* 7-8: 147-70.

———. 1992a. 'The quest for cultural identity and material advancement: Parallels and contrasts in Muslim minority experience in secular India and Buddhist Sri Lanka'. *Journal Institute of Muslim Minority Affairs* 13 (1): 33-58.

———. 1992b. 'Sri Lanka's ethnic war: The Muslim dimension'. *Pravāda* 1(11): 5-7. (Reprinted in *Tamil Times,* 15 November 1992, pp. 13-14, 16).

Aniff, Fareed. 1990. 'They drive spikes into their heads'. *Weekend* magazine, 6 April 1990. Colombo.

Asad, M.N.M. 1993. *The Muslims of Sri Lanka under British Rule.* New Delhi: Navrang.

———. 1994. 'Muslim education in Sri Lanka: The British colonial period'. *Journal Institute of Muslim Minority Affairs* 14(1&2): 35-45.

Azeez, I.L.M. Abdul. 1907. A criticism of Mr. Ramanathan's 'Ethnology of the "Moors" of Ceylon'. Colombo: Moors' Union. (Reprinted 1957, Colombo: Moors' Islamic Cultural Home.)

Bawa, Ahamadu. 1888. The marriage customs of the Moors of Ceylon. *Journal of the Royal Asiatic Society, Ceylon Branch* 10(36): 219-33.

Bayly, Susan. 1986. 'Islam in southern India: "purist" or "syncretic"?' In C.A. Bayly and D.H.A. Kolff, eds., *Two Colonial Empires: Comparative Essays on the History of India and Indonesia in the Nineteenth Century,* pp. 35-73. Dordrecht: Martinus Nijhoff.

———. 1989. *Saints, goddesses, and kings: Muslims and Christians in south Indian society, 1700-1900.* Cambridge: Cambridge University Press.

Bose, Sugata, ed. 1990. *South Asia and World Capitalism.* New Delhi: Oxford University Press.

Casie Chitty, Simon. 1834. *The Ceylon Gazetteer.* Ceylon: Cotta Church Mission Press. (Reprinted 1989. New Delhi: Navrang.)

———. 1853-5. 'An analysis of the great historical poem of the Moors, entitled "Seerah".' *Journal of the Royal Asiatic Society, Ceylon Branch* 2: 90-102.

Cutler, Norman. 1983. 'The fish-eyed goddess meets the movie star: an eyewitness account of the Fifth International Tamil Conference'. *Pacific Affairs* 56: 270-87.

D'Souza, Victor S. 1955. *The Navayats of Kanara: a study in culture contact.* K.R.I. monographs series 3. Dharwar: Kannada Research Institute.

———. 1959. 'Social organization and marriage customs of the Moplahs on the south-west coast of India'. *Anthropos* 54: 487-516.

———. 1973. 'Status groups among the Moplahs on the south-west coast of India'. In Imtiaz Ahmad, ed., *Caste and Social Stratification among the Muslims*, pp. 45-60. New Delhi: Manohar.

Dale, Stephen Frederic. 1980. *The Māppiḷas of Malabar, 1498-1922: Islamic society on the South Asian frontier.* Oxford: Clarendon Press.

Dale, Stephen Frederic and M. Gangadhara Menon. 1978. 'Nérccas: saint-martyr worship among the Muslims of Kerala'. *Bulletin of the School of Oriental and African Studies* 41: 523-38. (Reprinted in Asghar Ali Engineer, ed., 1995. *Kerala Muslims: a historical perspective*, pp. 174-99. Delhi: Ajanta Publications.)

de Jong, Fred. 1986. 'Note sur les confréries soufies à Sri Lanka'. In André Popovic and Gilles Veinstein, eds., *Les ordres mystiques dan l'Islam: cheminements et situation actuelle*, pp. 135-7. Recherches d'histoire et de sciences sociales 13. Paris: Editions de l'Ecole des Hautes Etudes en Sciences Sociales.

de Munck, Victor C. 1993. *Seasonal cycles: a study of social change and continuity in a Sri Lankan village.* New Delhi and Madras: Asian Educational Services.

———. 1996. 'Love and marriage in a Sri Lankan Muslim community: toward a reevaluation of Dravidian marriage practices'. *American Ethnologist* 23(4): 698-716.

Denham, E.B. 1912. *Ceylon at the Census of 1911.* Colombo: H.C. Cottle, Government Printer.

———. 1915. Report of Mr. E.B. Denham, Government Agent. Administration Reports, 1915. Part 1. Civil-Provincial Administration. Eastern Province, Ceylon.

de Silva, C.R. 1968. 'Portuguese policy towards the Muslims in Ceylon, 1505-1626'. *Proceedings of the First International Conference Seminar of Tamil Studies, Kuala Lumpur 1966*, pp. 113-19. Kuala Lumpur: International Association for Tamil Research.

de Silva, Kingsley M. 1986a. 'The Muslim minority in a democratic polity—the case of Sri Lanka: reflections on a theme'. In M.A.M. Shukri, ed., pp. 443-52.

———. 1986b. 'Muslim leaders and the nationalist movement'. In M.A.M. Shukri, ed., pp. 453-72.

———. 1988. 'Sri Lanka's Muslim minority'. In K.M. de Silva, Pensri Duke, Ellen S. Goldberg and Nathan Katz, eds., *Ethnic conflict in Buddhist societies: Sri Lanka, Thailand and Burma*, pp. 202-14. Boulder: Westview.

———. 1994. *The 'traditional homelands' of the Tamils, separatist ideology in Sri*

Lanka: a historical appraisal. Revised 2nd edn. Kandy, Sri Lanka: International Centre for Ethnic Studies.

———. 1997. 'Multi-culturalism in Sri Lanka: historical legacy and contemporary political reality'. *Ethnic Studies Report* 15 (1): 1-44.

Dewaraja, Lorna. 1986. 'The Muslims in the Kandyan kingdom (*c.*1600-1815): a study of ethnic integration'. In M.A.M. Shukri, ed., pp. 211-34.

———. 1994. *The Muslims of Sri Lanka: One thousand years of ethnic harmony, 900-1915.* Colombo: The Lanka Islamic Foundation.

———. 1995. 'The indigenisation of the Muslims of Sri Lanka'. In G.P.S.H. de Silva and C.G. Uragoda, eds., *Sesquicentennial commemorative volume of the Royal Asiatic Society of Sri Lanka, 1845-1995,* pp. 427-39.

Fairservis, Walter A. and Franklin C. Southworth. 1989. 'Linguistic archaeology and the Indus valley culture'. In Jonathan M. Kenoyer, ed., *Old problems and new perspectives in the archaeology of South Asia.* Wisconsin archaeological reports 2: 133-41. Madison: University of Wisconsin.

Fanselow, Frank S. 1989. 'Muslim society in Tamil Nadu (India): An historical perspective'. *Journal Institute of Muslim Minority Affairs* 10(1): 264-89.

Gabriel, Theodore P.C. 1989. *Lakshadweep: history, religion and society.* New Delhi: Books & Books.

———. 1996. *Hindu-Muslim relations in North Malabar, 1498-1947.* Lewiston, NY: Edwin Mellen Press.

Gopalan, T.N. 1998. 'Muslims, friendless in Tamil Nadu?' *Tamil Times* 17(4): 27-9.

Gough, Kathleen. 1961. 'Mappilla: North Kerala'. In David Schneider & Kathleen Gough, eds., *Matrilineal Kinship.*, pp. 415-42. Berkeley: University of California Press.

Gunawardana, R.A.L.H. 1990. 'The people of the lion: the Sinhala identity and ideology in history and historiography'. In Jonathan Spencer, ed., *Sri Lanka: history and the roots of conflict,* pp. 45-86. London and New York: Routledge.

Hasan, Mushirul. 1997. 'Legacy of a divided nation: India's Muslims since Independence'. Boulder: Westview Press.

Hasbullah, S.H. 1996. *Refugees are people.* Proceedings of the Workshop on the Resettlement Programme for the Forcibly Evicted Muslims of the Northern Province, Sri Lanka. Puttalam, 13-14 January 1996. Colombo: Northern Muslims' Rights Organization. 15A Rohini Road, Colombo 6.

Hassan, M.C.A. 1968. *Sir Razik Fareed.* Colombo: Sir Razik Fareed Foundation.

Hellman-Rajanayagam, Dagmar. 1995. 'Is there a Tamil race?' In Peter Robb, ed., *The concept of race in South Asia,* pp. 109-45. Delhi: Oxford University Press.

Hennayake, Shantha K. 1992. 'Interactive ethnonationalism: An alternative explanation of minority ethnonationalism'. *Political Geography* 11(6): 526-49.

———. 1993. 'Sri Lanka in 1992: Opportunity missed in the ethno-nationalist crisis'. *Asian Survey* 33(2): 157-64.

———. n.d. 'The Muslim community in the ethnonationalist crisis of Sri Lanka'. Sri Lanka: Peradeniya University, ms.

Herring, Ronald J. 1991. 'From structural conflict to agrarian stalemate: agrarian reforms in South India'. *Journal of Asian and African Studies* 26(3-4): 169-88.

Hussainmiya, B.A. 1986. 'Princes and soldiers: the antecedents of the Sri Lankan Malays'. In M.A.M. Shukri, ed., pp. 279-309.

Ibrahim Kunju, A.P. 1989. *Mappila Muslims of Kerala: their history and culture.* Trivandrum: Sandhya Publications.

———. 1995. 'Origin and spread of Islam in Kerala'. In Ali Asghar Engineer, ed., *Kerala Muslims: a historical perspective,* pp. 17-34. Delhi: Ajanta.

Ismail, Qadri. 1995. 'Unmooring identity: the antinomies of elite Muslim self-representation in modern Sri Lanka'. In Pradeep Jeganathan and Qadri Ismail, eds.. *Unmaking the nation: the politics of identity and history in modern Sri Lanka,* pp. 55-105. Colombo: Social Scientists' Association.

Jackson, K. David. 1990. *Sing without shame: oral traditions in Indo-Portuguese creole verse.* Amsterdam, Philadelphia & Macau: John Benjamins Publishing & Instituto Cultural de Macau.

Kadramer, D.W.N. 1934. *Landmarks of ancient Batticaloa and other contributions to the Ceylon press.* Batticaloa, Sri Lanka: Catholic Orphanage Press.

Kandiah, V.C. 1964. *Maṭṭakkaḷappuṭ tamiḷakam* (Batticaloa Tamil Homeland). Jaffna: Iḷākécari Ponnaiyā Ninaivu Veḷiyīṭṭu Maṉīṟam.

Kearney, Robert N. 1987. 'Territorial elements of Tamil separatism in Sri Lanka'. *Pacific Affairs* 60(4): 561-577.

Krishna, Sankaran. 1994. 'Notes on a trip to the Eastern Province, June 25 to June 29, 1994'. *Serendipity* 7: 301-3. Sri Lanka Academic Interests Group.

Kurukulasuriya, G.I.O.M., Abdul Gafoor and M.A.M. Hussein. 1988. *The Muslim community of Sri Lanka.* (Reprint of a study prepared for the Dr. Shaikh Shams Al-Fassi Foundation of Sri Lanka in 1984-5). Colombo: Marga Institute.

Kutty, A.R. 1972. *Marriage and Kinship in an Island Society.* Delhi: National.

Lawrence, Patricia. 1997. 'The changing amman: notes on the injury of war in eastern Sri Lanka'. *South Asia* 20: 215-36.

———. 1998. 'Grief on the body: the work of oracles in eastern Sri Lanka'. In Michael Roberts, ed., *Collective Identities Revisited,* vol. 2: 271-94. Delhi: Navrang.

———. in press. 'Violence, suffering, amman: the work of oracles in Sri Lanka's eastern war zone'. In Veena Das, Arthur Kleinman, Mamphela Ramphele, and Pamela Reynolds, eds., *Violence, political agency, and the self.* Berkeley and London: University of California Press.

MacPherson, Kenneth. 1969. 'The social background and politics of the Muslims of Tamil Nad, 1901-1937'. *Indian Economic and Social History Review* 6: 381-402.

Macready, W.C. 1888-9. 'The jungles of Rajavanni Pattu and the ceremony of passing through the fire'. *The Orientalist* 3: 188-93.

Mahroof, M.M.M. 1986a. 'Muslim social organisation'. In M.M.M. Mahroof, et al., pp. 125-44.

———. 1986b. 'British rule and the Muslims (1800-1900)'. In M.M.M. Mahroof, et al., pp. 61-95.

———. 1986c. 'Muslim education'. In M.M.M. Mahroof, et al., pp. 166-82.

———. 1990. 'Muslims in Sri Lanka: the long road to accommodation'. *Journal Institute of Muslim Minority Affairs* 11 (1): 88-99.

———. 1991. 'Mendicants and troubadours: toward a historical taxonomy of the faqirs of Sri Lanka'. *Islamic Studies* 30: 501-16.

———. 1994. 'Community of Sri Lankan Malays: notes toward a socio-historical analysis'. *Journal Institute of Muslim Minority Affairs* 14 (1&2): 143-55.

Mahroof, M.M.M., Marina Azeez, M.M. Uwise, H.M.Z. Farouque and M.J.A. Rahim. 1986. *An ethnological survey of the Muslims of Sri Lanka from earliest times to Independence.* Colombo: Sir Razik Fareed Foundation.

Mani, A. 1992. 'Aspects of identity and change among Tamil Muslims in Singapore'. *Journal Institute of Muslim Minority Affairs* 13 (2): 337-57.

Manogaran, Chelvadurai. 1987. *Ethnic conflict and reconciliation in Sri Lanka.* Honolulu: University of Hawaii Press.

Marikar, A..I.L., A.L.M. Lafir and A.H. Macan Markar, eds. 1976. *Glimpses of the past of the Moors of Sri Lanka.* Colombo: Moors' Islamic Cultural Home.

Mauroof, Mohamed. 1972. 'Aspects of religion, economy, and society among the Muslims of Ceylon'. *Contributions to Indian Sociology* 6: 66-83. (Reprinted in T.N. Madan, ed., 1976. *Muslim communities of South Asia: culture and society,* pp. 66-83. New Delhi: Vikas.)

———. 1986. 'A sociology of Muslims in southern India and Sri Lanka'. In M.A.M. Shukri, ed., pp. 319-36.

McGilvray, Dennis B. 1974. 'Tamils and Moors: Caste and matriclan structure in eastern Sri Lanka'. Unpublished Ph.D. thesis. University of Chicago.

———. 1982a. 'Dutch Burghers and Portuguese mechanics: Eurasian ethnicity in Sri Lanka'. *Comparative Studies in Society and History* 24(1): 235-63.

———. 1982b. 'Sexual power and fertility in Sri Lanka: Batticaloa Tamils and Moors'. In Carol P. MacCormack, ed., *Ethnography of fertility and birth,* pp. 25-73. London: Academic Press. (Second edition 1994. Prospect Heights: Waveland Press, pp. 15-63.)

———. 1982c. 'Mukkuvar vannimai: Tamil caste and matriclan structure in Batticaloa, Sri Lanka'. In D.B. McGilvray, ed., *Caste ideology and interaction,* pp. 34-97. Cambridge papers in *Social Anthropology* 9. Cambridge University Press.

———. 1983. 'Paraiyar drummers of Sri Lanka: consensus and constraint in an untouchable caste'. *American Ethnologist* 10: 97-115.

———. 1988a. 'The 1987 Stirling Award essay: sex, repression, and Sanskritization in Sri Lanka?' *Ethos* 16(2): 99-127.

———. 1988b. 'Village Sufism in Sri Lanka: an ethnographic report'. *La transmission du savoir dans le monde musulman peripherique,* pp. 1-12. Lettre d'information 8. Programme de recherches interdisciplinaires sur le monde musulman peripherique. Paris: Ecole des Hautes Etudes en Sciences Sociales.

———. 1989. 'Households in Akkaraipattu: dowry and domestic organization among the matrilineal Tamils and Moors of Sri Lanka'. In John N. Gray and David J. Mearns, eds., *Society from the inside out: Anthropological perspectives on the South Asian household,* pp. 192-235. New Delhi, Newbury Park, & London: Sage.

———. 1997a. 'Sufi circuits in/to Sri Lanka. Paper presented at the 26th Annual Conference on South Asia'. University of Wisconsin-Madison. 16-19 October 1997.

———. 1997b. 'Tamils and Muslims in the shadow of war: schism or continuity?' *South Asia* 20: 239-53.

———. 1998. *Symbolic heat: gender, health, and worship among the Tamils of South India and Sri Lanka.* Ahmedabad: Mapin.

Miller, Roland E. 1976. *Mappila Muslims of Kerala: a study in Islamic trends.* Madras: Orient Longman.

Mines, Mattison. 1972. *Muslim merchants: the economic behaviour of an Indian Muslim community.* New Delhi: Shri Ram Centre for Industrial Relations and Human Resources.

———. 1973. 'Social stratification among Muslim Tamils in Tamil Nadu, South India'. In Imtiaz Ahmed, ed., *Caste and Social Stratification among the Muslims,* pp. 61-71. New Delhi: Manohar.

———. 1981. 'Islamization and Muslim ethnicity in South India'. In Imtiaz Ahmad, ed., *Ritual and Religion among Muslims in India,* pp. 65-90. New Delhi: Manohar.

———. 1983. 'Kin centres and ethnicity among Muslim Tamilians'. In Imtiaz Ahmad, ed., *Modernization and Social Change among Muslims in India,* pp. 99-118. New Delhi: Manohar.

Mohamed, Peer. 1996. 'Tamil Muslims and Tamil Eelam'. *Proceedings of the international conference on the conflict in Sri Lanka: peace with justice.*

27-8 June 1996. Canberra, Australia. http://www.tamilnet.com/conference_papers/pwj/

Mohan, R. Vasundhara. 1987. *Identity crisis of Sri Lankan Muslims.* Delhi: Mittal.

Mohideen, M.I.M. 1986. *Sri Lanka Muslims and ethnic grievances.* Colombo: M.I.M. Mohideen.

Mohideen, M.Z. 1965. 'The "kudi" maraikayars of Batticaloa south'. *Moors' Islamic Cultural Home: the first twenty-one years.* Colombo, pp. 25-7.

Moors' Islamic Cultural Home, 1965, *Moors' Islamic Cultural Home: the first twenty-one years.* Colombo, Sri Lanka.

———. 1970. *Moors' Islamic Cultural Home: silver jubilee sourvenir 1944-1969.* Colombo, Sri Lanka.

———. 1978. *Moors' Islamic Cultural Home: souvenir III 1970-76.* Colombo, Sri Lanka.

———. 1983. *Moors' Islamic Cultural Home: souvenir IV 1977-1982.* Colombo, Sri Lanka.

———. 1994. *Moors' Islamic Cultural Home: golden jubilee souvenir 1944-1994.* Colombo, Sri Lanka.

More, J.B.P. 1991. 'The Marakkayar Muslims of Karikal, South India'. *Journal of Islamic Studies* 2: 25-44.

———. 1993a. 'Tamil Muslims and non-Brahmin atheists, 1925-1940'. *Contributions to Indian Sociology* 27: 83-104.

———. 1993b. 'Muslim evolution and conversions in Karikal, South India'. *Islam and Christian-Muslim Relations* 4(1): 65-82.

———. 1997. *The political evolution of Muslims in Tamil Nadu and Madras, 1930-1947.* Hyderabad: Orient Longman.

Mujahid, Abdul Malik. 1989. *Conversion to Islam: untouchables' strategy for protest in India.* Chambersburg, PA: Anima Publications.

Nambiar, O.K. 1963. *The Kunjalis, admirals of Calicut.* London: Asia Publishing House.

Nambiar, P.K. and K.C. Narayana Kurup. 1968. 'Festival of Saint Quadar Wali at Nagore'. Census of India 1961, vol. IX: *Madras,* Part VII-B: *Fairs and Festivals,* pp. 59-60 plus 8 pages of photographs.

Narayan, M.T. 1995. 'Kunjalis—the Muslim admirals of Calicut'. In Asghar Ali Engineer, ed., *Kerala Muslims: a historical perspective,* pp. 91-102. Delhi: Ajanta.

Nissen, Elizabeth. 1996. *Sri Lanka: a bitter harvest.* London: Minority Rights Group International.

Nissan, Elizabeth and R.L. Stirrat. 1990. 'The generation of communal identities'. In Jonathan Spencer, ed. *Sri Lanka: history and the roots of conflict,* pp. 19-44. London and New York: Routledge.

Obeyesekere, Gananath. *The cult of the goddess Pattini.* Chicago: University of Chicago Press.

Ossman, M.S. 1990. 'Status of Malays in Sri Lanka past-present'. *Challenge for change: profile of a community,* pp. 32-42. Colombo: Muslim Women's Research and Action Front.

O'Sullivan, Meghan. 1997. 'Conflict as a catalyst: the changing politics of the Sri Lankan Muslims'. *South Asia* 20: 281-308.

Padmanabha Menon, K.P. 1924. *A history of Kerala,* vol. 1. Ernakulam: Cochin Govt. Press.

Pandian, Jacob. 1987. *Caste, nationalism and ethnicity: an interpretation of Tamil cultural history and social order.* Bombay: Popular Prakashan.

Peebles, Patrick. 1990. 'Colonization and ethnic conflict in the Dry Zone of Sri Lanka'. *Journal of Asian Studies* 49(1): 30-55.

Peiris, Ralph. 1965. 'The effects of technological development on the population of the Gal Oya valley, Ceylon'. *Ceylon Journal of Historical and Social Studies* 8(1&2): 163-92.

Phadnis, Urmila. 1979. 'Political profile of the Muslim minority of Sri Lanka'. *International Studies* 18: 27-48.

Puthenkalam, Fr. J. 1977. *Marriage and family in Kerala, with special reference to matrilineal castes.* Calgary: Journal of comparative family studies monograph series.

Raghavan, M.D. 1971. *Tamil culture in Ceylon: a general introduction.* Colombo: Kalai Nilayam.

Raheem, Raihana. 1975. 'A study of the kinship terms of the Moor community in Ceylon'. Unpublished Ph.D. thesis, University of Leeds.

Rahmat Ali, Choudhary. 1943. *The millat and her minorities: foundation of Nasaristan for Muslims of E. Ceylon* (pamphlet). Cambridge: Nasaristan National Movement.

Ram, Kalpana. 1991. *Mukkuvar women: gender, hegemony and capitalist transformation in a south Indian fishing community.* London: Zed Books.

Ramanathan, Ponnambalam. 1888. 'The ethnology of the "'Moors' of Ceylon'". *Journal of the Royal Asiatic Society, Ceylon Branch* 10(36): 234-62.

Rao, Velcheru Narayan, David Shulman and Sanjay Subrahmanyam. 1992. *Symbols of substance: court and state in Nāyaka period Tamil Nadu.* Oxford University Press.

Richman, Paula. 1993. 'Veneration of the Prophet Muhammad in an Islamic *piḷḷaittamiḻ*'. *Journal of the American Oriental Society* 113(1): 57-73.

Roberts, Michael. 1980. 'From southern India to Lanka: The traffic in commodities, bodies, and myths from the thirteenth century onwards'. *South Asia* 3: 36-47.

———. 1994a. 'Mentalities: ideologues, assailants, historians and the pogrom against the Moors in 1915'. In Michael Roberts, *Exploring confrontation: Sri Lanka: politics, culture and history,* pp. 183-212. Chur, Switzerland: Harwood Academic Publishers.

———. 1994b. 'Ethnicity in riposte at a cricket match: the past for the present'. In Michael Roberts, *Exploring confrontation: Sri Lanka: politics, culture and history*, pp. 269-95. Chur, Switzerland: Harwood Academic Publishers.

Roberts, Michael, Ismeth Raheem and Percy Colin-Thome. 1989. *People inbetween,* vol. 1: *the Burghers and the middle class in the transformations within Sri Lanka, 1790s-1960s.* Ratmalana, Sri Lanka: Sarvodaya Book Publishing Services.

Rogers, John D. 1995. 'Racial identities and politics in early modern Sri Lanka'. In Peter Robb, ed., *The Concept of Race in South Asia,* pp. 146-64. Delhi: Oxford University Press.

Russell, Jane. 1982. *Communal Politics under the Donoughmore Constitution, 1931-1947.* Dehiwala, Sri Lanka: Tisara Prakasakayo.

Saleem, A.R.M. 1990. *Akkaraippaṟṟu varalāṟu.* (History of Akkaraipattu). Akkaraipattu, Sri Lanka: Hiraa Publications.

Samaraweera, Vijaya. 1978. 'Some sociological aspects of the Muslim revivalism in Sri Lanka'. *Social Compass* 25: 465-75.

———. 1979. 'The Muslim revivalist movement, 1880-1915'. In Michael Roberts, ed., *Collective identities, nationalisms and protest in modern Sri Lanka,* pp. 243-76. Colombo: Marga Institute.

Sanyal, Usha. 1994. '*Pir, Shaikh,* and Prophet: the personalisation of religious authority in Ahmad Riza Khan's life'. *Contributions to Indian Sociology* 28: 35-66.

Schrijvers, Joke. 1998. 'We were like cocoanut and flour in the pittu': Tamil-Muslim violence, gender and ethnic relations in eastern Sri Lanka'. *Nēthrā* 2(3): 10-39.

Shackle, Christopher. 1989. 'Languages'. In Francis Robinson, ed., *The Cambridge Encyclopedia of India, Pakistan, Bangladesh, Sri Lanka, Nepal, Bhutan and the Maldives,* pp. 402-5. Cambridge: Cambridge University Press.

Shaik Hasan Sahib, S.A. 1980. *The divine light of Nagore.* Nagoor: S.K. Nazeer Ahmad.

Shams-ud-di'n, A.T. 1881. 'Note on the "mira kantiri" festival of the Muhammadans'. *Journal of the Royal Asiatic Society, Ceylon Branch* 7: 125-36.

Sharif, Ja'far. 1921. *Islam in India or the Qanun-i-Islam: the customs of the Musalmans of India, comprising a full and exact account of their various rites and ceremonies from the moment of birth to the hour of death.* William Crooke, ed., G.A. Herklots, trans. Oxford University Press. (Reprinted 1972, New Delhi: Oriental Books Reprint Corp.)

Shastri, Amita. 1990. 'The material basis for separatism: the Tamil Eelam movement in Sri Lanka'. *Journal of Asian Studies* 49(1): 56-77.

———. in press. 'The Estate Tamils, the Ceylon Citizenship Act of 1948, and Sri Lankan politics'. *Contemporary South Asia.*

Shukri, M.A.M., ed. 1986a. *Muslims of Sri Lanka: avenues to antiquity.* Beruwala, Sri Lanka: Jamiah Naleemia Institute.

———. 1986b. 'Introduction'. In M.A.M. Shukri, ed., pp. 1-81.
———. 1986c. 'Muslims of Sri Lanka: a cultural perspective'. In M.A.M. Shukri, ed., pp. 337-62.
Shulman, David. 1984. 'Muslim popular literature in Tamil: the *Tamīmaṇacāri Mālai*'. In Yohanan Friedmann, ed., *Islam in Asia, volume 1, South Asia*, pp. 174-207. Boulder: Westview.
Sivaram, D.P. (Taraki, *pseud.*). 1991. *The eluding peace, an insider's political analysis of the ethnic conflict in Sri Lanka.* Sarcelles, France: ASSEAY (Arts Social Sciences of Eelam Academy, France).
———. 1992. 'LTTE's Eelam project and the Muslim people'. *Tamil Times.* 15 November 1992, pp. 20, 24.
Sivathamby, Karthigesu. 1987. 'The Sri Lankan ethnic crisis and Muslim-Tamil relationships—a socio-political view'. In Charles Abeysekera and Newton Gunasinghe, eds., *Facets of ethnicity in Sri Lanka,* pp. 192-225. Colombo: Social Scientists' Association.
Tambiah, Stanley J. 1986. *Sri Lanka: ethnic fratricide and the dismantling of democracy.* Chicago and London: University of Chicago Press.
Thurston, Edgar and K. Rangachari. 1909. *Castes and tribes of southern India.* 7 vols. Madras: Government Press.
UTHR (University Teachers for Human Rights, Jaffna). 1990. *Report 3: the war and its consequences in the Amparai District.* Issued 16 October 1990. UTHR(J): Thirunelvely, Jaffna, Sri Lanka.
———. 1991. *Report 7: the clash of ideologies and the continuing tragedy in the Batticaloa and Amparai Districts.* Issued 8 May 1991. UTHR(J): Thirunelvely, Jaffna, Sri Lanka.
———. 1993. *Report 10: rays of hope amidst deepening gloom.* Issued 15 January 1993. UTHR(J): Thirunelvely, Jaffna, Sri Lanka.
———. 1993. *Report 11: land, human rights and the eastern predicament.* Issued 15 April 1993. UTHR(J): Thirunelvely, Jaffna, Sri Lanka.
———. 1996. *Information bulletin 11: the quest for economic survival and human dignity: Batticaloa and Amparai Districts, June 1996.* UTHR(J). Internet source: JHOOLE@THUBAN.AC.HMC.EDU.
Uwise, M.M. 1986. 'The language and literature of the Muslims'. In M.M.M. Mahroof, et al., pp. 150-65.
———. 1990. *Muslim contribution to Tamil literature.* Kilakarai, Tamil Nadu: Fifth International Islamic Tamil Literary Conference.
Van Sanden, J.C.. 1926. *Sonahar: a brief history of the Moors of Ceylon.* Colombo: Van Sanden & Wright.
Wadood, A.C.A. 1976. 'Sri Pada—the Muslim view'. In Marikar, Lafir and Macan Markar, eds. pp. 8-9.
Wagner, Christian. 1990. *Die Muslime Sri Lankas: eine volksgruppe in spannungsfeld des ethnischen konflikts zwischen Singhalesen und Tamilen.* Freiburger beiträge zu entwicklung und politik 5. Freiburg: Arnold Bergstraesser Institut.

———. 1991. 'A Muslim minority in a multiethnic state: the case of Sri Lanka'. In Diethelm Weidemann, ed., *Nationalism, ethnicity and political development: South Asian perspectives*, pp. 93-112. New Delhi: Manohar.

Wallerstein, Immanuel. 1976. *The modern world system: capitalist agriculture and the origins of the European world-economy in the sixteenth century.* New York: Academic Press.

Wolf, Eric. 1982. *Europe and the people without history.* Berkeley: University of California Press.

Wright, Theodore P. Jr. 1966. 'The Muslim League in South India since Independence: a study in minority group political strategies'. *American Political Science Review* 60: 579-99.

Yalman, Nur. 1967. *Under the Bo tree: studies in caste, kinship, and marriage in the interior of Ceylon.* Berkeley and London: University of California Press.

Yule, Henry, and A.C. Burnell. 1903. *Hobson-jobson: a glossary of colloquial Anglo-Indian words and phrases.* 2nd edn. William Crooke, ed. London: John Murray.

Sufi, Reformist and National Models of Identity: The History of a Muslim Village Festival in Sri Lanka

VICTOR C. DE MUNCK
(1994)

I. INTRODUCTION[1]

This paper is an analysis of the confluence of local, national, and pan-Islamic processes as manifested in a Sri Lankan Muslim village festival. Annually, the 1,000 villagers of Kutali hold a festival called *Burdha Kandhoori.*[2] The festival is presided over by a *Moulana,* who claims direct descent from the Prophet Muhammad through Fatima.[3] Considered a 'holy man' (or *pir*) by the villagers, he is said to be capable of performing miracles. The express theme of the festival is to address the material and spiritual concerns of the villagers through the supernatural capacities of the Moulana. The festival is, in origin, content and form, a Sufi festival (Gilsenan 1973; van der Veer 1992). Over time, as I will show, the importance of the festival as an Islamic-Muslim boundary ritual distinguish villagers from their Sinhala Buddhist neighbours has diminished.

Bloch (1988), Connerton (1989) and many others view ritual as interactively linked with historical and political processes in the production of ideology and authority structures, rather than as a representation or explanation of social solidarity. This approach induces scholars to think about ritual as contingent and performative, rather than as fixed and reflective. Ritual performances (re) shape as much as reveal 'social memory' and, to the extent they are accepted, provide a 'measure of insurance' against alternative re-shapings of the past (Connerton 1989: 102).

Ritual performances are practices enacted to resist change and legitimate the social order; conversely, they can be recast as practices that induce change and question the social order. The 'productions of ideology and authority structures' are in part shaped by the contingencies that influence recollections. The ideological and authority structures that interact and are singled out for analysis in this paper concern Sri Lankan nationalism, Sufi traditions, and the *Tablighi Jama'at,* a pan-Islamic reformist movement.[4] As a cultural performance, the festival serves as a socio-temporal site for the meeting of contrasting and contesting narratives and modes of interpretation. As will be shown, the festival has been, at different times, a site both for invoking and for resisting change. Ideological and authority structures are recast over time; new modes of experience and knowledge are shaped through the ritual performances.

The villagers of Kutali identify themselves in terms of many different social identities: they are villagers, Sri Lankans, members of the Qadariya Tariqat (a Sufi Brotherhood), Sunni Muslims, and some are '*Tablighis*'.[5] Depending on context, villagers can variously claim membership in all these groups. However, such identity shifting, a part of daily life everywhere, has become increasingly difficult in the light of the inter-ethnic violence in Sri Lanka and the rise of Islamic reform movements. Identities have histories and signify different socio-political formations (White 1992). In Sri Lanka, local, national, and transnational forms of identity emphasize different temporalities, histories and socio-political orientations, making any kind of tripartite integration problematic, if not impossible.

Burdha Kandhoori was begun in 1914 and was part of a national wave of religious and ethnic revivalism. For Kutali Muslims, the festival represented a turn towards Islam and away from Islamic-Buddhist/Hindu syncretism. Today, the Tablighi Jama'at provides a counterpoint to the Moulana Burdha Kandhoori, rejecting the latter as a form of saint worship and, thus, a corruption of Islam. While the content of this religious debate is expressly apolitical it is, nevertheless, partially motivated by and embedded in national and transnational political events and discourses.[6]

II. THE SETTING

Kutali is a village of approximately 1,000 Muslims, located in the south-central plains of Uva Basin. The village is relatively remote, bounded on the east by the Nilgala forest and by secondary forest growth in the other directions. Sinhala Buddhists live in hamlets scattered in the area. Like their neighbours the villagers of Kutali rely mostly on their rice paddy and *chena* (swidden) fields for their subsistence and income.

In 1980, for the first time ever, the *Marikars* (administrators) of the sole functioning village mosque cancelled Burdha Kandhoori. In 1981, upon the insistence of the villagers and faced with the possibility of being replaced themselves, the Marikars agreed to invite the Moulana for the festival. What caused this one year hiatus? The cancellation and resumption of Burdha Kandhoori provides us with an extended 'diagnostic' event through which 'competing cultural claims' are expressed and may be recognized (Moore 1987: 729-30). One such claim is that of Sri Lankan nationalism.

III. THE RHETORIC OF SRI LANKAN NATIONALISM

Benjamin (1973) and Anderson (1983) have argued that twentieth century nationalist ideologies involve the merging of an 'objective modernity' with 'a subjective antiquity' (Anderson 1983: 14). Nationalism, in other words, moulds a romanticised vision of the past with a contemporary image of an idealized future. In Sri Lanka, this potent and paradoxical mixture of reactionary and progressive ideologies has produced a model for nationalism based on a Sinhala Buddhist 'pastoral past' (Spencer 1990: 138-64).[7]

Tambiah (1986), Tenekoon (1988), Brow (1988, 1990), Peebles (1990), Shastri (1990), Spencer (1990) among many others, have described how politicians, Buddhist monks, and local-level Sinhala leaders have 'mythicised' ethnically laden symbols and then use them to promote rituals to nationalism (Peebles 1990: 48). Politicians have rhetorically cast the nation in terms of a tripartite image consisting of a Buddhist temple, rice paddy fields, and irrigation schemes (Spencer 1990; Tenekoon 1988). This culturally reductionist 'official nationalism' necessarily delegitimises alternative Sinhala and ethnic minority national models (Anderson 1983: 50). Obeyesekere's (1979) infamous equations—'Sri Lanka = Sinhala = Buddhism'—distills Sri Lankan nationalism to its essence.

Spencer suggests that cultural homogenization may be a necessary consequence of nationalism as it '. . . involves a process of cultural transformation in which local differences come up against an ideal of national similarity' (1990: 250). The doxa of self-similarity supersedes and subsumes that of heterogeneity (White

1992: 17). In Sri Lanka, the national identity is formulated from just such a homogenized vision of a heroic Sinhalese Buddhist past that subordinates and subsumes all other ethnic histories.

Such assertions compel ethnic minorities to refute the 'official' version of Sri Lankan nationalism and to locate their own communal identities in their own past. Consequently, historical grievances and conflicts are revised and renewed. Each historical 'fact' becomes grist for the mill of ethnic polemics and hatred. In the process of nation building has come its antithesis: nation razing. The ongoing ethnic strife and pogroms against civilians, and Tamil demands for a separate State (*eelam*), are tragic evidence of the exclusionary effects of an ethnocentric nationalist ideology.

IV. THE MUSLIM DILEMMA: CAUGHT IN THE CENTRE OF THE STORM

Few scholars have described the effects of the last twelve years of ethnic Fratricide on the Sri Lankan Muslim community. The Muslim community is often described as having 'managed' to maintain an 'accommodative' stance between Sri Lankan Tamils and Sinhalese (De Silva 1986; Spencer 1990: 95).

At the turn of the twentieth century, Muslims were ethnically categorized as Tamils primarily because their *lingua franca* is Tamil (Mohan 1987; McGilvray 1991). Tamils claimed that Muslims were of Tamil ancestry and, therefore, did not constitute an ethnically distinct group (Ramanathan 1888). To refute the claim that they were 'Tamil converts to Islam' (Mohan 1987: 7-32), Sri Lankan Muslim leaders emphasized their Arabic heritage and allied themselves with Sinhalese rather than Tamil political parties. Sinhalese leaders, in turn, courted Muslims as a counterpoint to Sri Lankan Tamils and, more recently, as political brokers to the Arab world. The 1915 Sinhalese-Muslim riots, which led to the widespread looting and destruction of Muslim shops, are a vivid reminder to Muslims that such an alliance also poses risks. Tamils have also redoubled their efforts to court the Muslim community, either as partners in the formation of Eelam, or as political allies against the Sinhala majority.

Politically and economically, the pragmatic dilemma of Sri Lankan Muslims is that they are positioned between two larger and opposing ethnic groups. As a result, Muslims do attempt to 'manage' their position and are frequently perceived by Tamils and Sinhala as opportunists (Mohan 1987: 32). This 'accommodative' and 'managed' stance was pithily expressed by a villager who noted that: 'In Tamil areas I am pro-Eelam, in Sinhalese areas I am pro-Sri Lanka.'

Leveraged neutrality does not go without a cost; Muslims are, on the whole, dislike by both Tamils and Sinhalese. The twin pull of nation building and deconstruction not only affects the Sri Lankan Muslims' sense of personal security but their claims to a distinct history and culture.

V. CONSTRUCTING COMMUNITY: HETERODOX AND ORTHODOX INTERPRETATIONS OF ISLAM

Muslim associations represent a secular 'assimilative' response to Sri Lankan nation building (Mohan 1987: 32). Historically they have played, and continue to play, a vital role in the development and education of Sri Lankan Muslims. Since the late 1800s, Muslim associations have focused on issues of religious and secular education and have promoted cultural distinctiveness within a national framework. The Moors Islamic Cultural Home and the All Ceylon Moors' Association Muslim are two prominent national associations. The names, themselves, suggest their apolitical and cultural emphasis. These associations provide religious training; organize public forums for discussion on political, social and religious issues; publish books and instructional material on Islam and Muslim history; and grant scholarships.

Beyond self-help programmes, the associations promote 'communal harmony'. The modernist optimism of association members, mostly urban middle class, promulgates an outlook of liberal eclecticism, religious tolerance and a national identity as Sri Lankan Muslims. The vitality of these Muslim associations depends both on an ethnically heterogeneous notion of nationalism and an ideologically tolerant and broad conception of what it means to be a Sri Lankan Muslim.

The secular bent of these associations excludes them from those debates where 'Muslim' is equated with 'Islam' in the way that 'Sinhala' is equated with 'Buddhism' (Obeyesekere 1979; Tambiah 1988). The theme of this internal debate concerns the 'settings' of the ideological and behavioural parameters permissible within the Muslim 'community'.[8] For the Tablighi Jama'at, representing the reformist position, the settings should be in alignment with Islamic orthodoxy and they oppose many of the beliefs and public practices of the Sufi Brotherhoods. I shall begin by presenting the Sufi 'position' in this debate.

The Sufi tradition on the subcontinent encompasses a wide range of beliefs and practices ranging from 'highbrow' mysticism to public rituals of 'playing' with swords (van der Veer 1992: 553). At the turn of this century, Sufism served as the primary vehicle for ethnic and religious revivalism in Sri Lanka. Shukri (1986) and McGilvray (1991) note that Sri Lankan Muslim religious beliefs and practices have been strongly influenced by Sufi scholars and saints of south India. In Sufism, Sri Lankan (and Indian) Muslims found their religious parallels to popular Buddhism and Hindu forms of worship. Saints, pilgrimages to holy places, sheikhs, devotional practices to tap supernatural powers, and petitioning saints for help are but a few aspects of Sufism that have their counterpart in popular Buddhism (see de Munck 1985 and 1992 for a more extended analysis). Parallelisms do not imply that these practices were historically derived from Buddhism or Hinduism. These Sufi practices are also found among Muslims outside the subcontinent (Crapanzano 1973; Gilsenan 1973; Eickelman 1976).

The historical and continuing importance of Sufism in Kutali is underscored by the villagers' identification of themselves with the Qadariya Tariqat, a Sufi Brotherhood. The Qadariya take their name from Abdul Qadir Mohideen al Gilani, a famous twelfth-century Iraqi Sufi saint and scholar. He is said to have visited Sri Lanka and meditated in a cave for eleven years. Thousands of Muslims from around Sri Lanka and India come to visit this isolated and beautiful spot where a number of Sufi hermits live in caves the year around.

The area called Jailany after the birthplace of the Saint, is a major pilgrimage area. Annually, there is a four week festival that is functionally similar to the Kataragama festival described by Obeyesekere (1977, 1978). Like Kataragama, Jailany is situated in a remote and difficult-to-reach location. Penitents and devotees come to renew their devotion and power through fasting, prayer, trance-inducing rituals, and various forms of self-inflicted torture. Also, pilgrims come to socialize, renew acquaintances, arrange marriages, shop, flirt with members of the opposite sex, and generally enjoy themselves. Nightly there is a procession around the shrine (*dargah*) that concludes with a ritual demonstration of the power of faith by a group of *Rifa'i faqirs*. Led by a *Khalifa*, the faqirs receive his blessings, and accompanied by tambourine music, proceed to pierce themselves with swords, various sharp iron pins, and maces. Members of the audience can also, when so moved, request to be pierced. These actions and the recitations of religious songs are intended to reflect the sacred power of the saint and through him, his devotees. It is this sacred status of saints and the supernatural power that can be harnessed through devotion to the saint which lie at the centre of the internal debate over the acceptable parameters of Muslim beliefs and practices.

Kutali villagers regularly offer vows and provide alms in the name of the *Owlie-akkel* (Saint) Mohideen. Annually, his birthday is celebrated with an eleven-day celebration (*maulid*). Villagers regularly tell stories of how they were saved from danger by calling out 'Ya Mohideen'. Religious priests (called *labbais*) conjoin the recitation of *suras* (verses from the Koran) with those recitations that refer to Mohideen to perform healing or protective rituals. Every Thursday evening Sufi adherents recite *dhikr*: a Sufi practice in which the many names of Allah are repeated in order to harmonize one's inner vibrations with God. Further, both mosques in the villages are referred to as either 'the old' or 'the new Mohideen mosque'.

For the villagers, being members of the Qadariya Brotherhood is primarily a nominal and ascriptive, rather than substantive, affiliation. There is no local *pir-murid* (leader-followers) relationship among the Qadariya. The Brotherhood is not textually based and depends for its continuity on the oral transmission of its traditions. Except for recounting some stories regarding the saint's legendary deeds, there is nothing that villagers could cite to distinguish them from other Sufi Brotherhoods. At the core of their Sufi identity is the belief in saints as sacred intercessors for them in this world, and the various ritual practices that follow from this belief. Opposing this social bricolage of Sufi Brotherhoods are Islamic reformist movements that view saint worship as comparable to polytheism (*shirk*) and call for a rejection of such customs. The largest of these reform movements in Sri Lanka is the Tablighi Jama'at.

The Tablighi Jama'at was founded by Maulana Muhammed Ilyas (1885-1944) in 1926 (Durrany 1993: 22; van der Veer 1992: 552). Ilyas had convinced the Muslims of Mewat, near Delhi, to abandon their 'non-Islamic customs' and, thereafter, continued a campaign of Islamic reform. The reformist aims of the Tablighi Jama'at are directed towards Muslims and include: (1) the rejection of Sufi beliefs in saint worship and saintly power (van der Veer ibid.: 552-3); (2) imitation of the devotional practices of the companions (*Sahabah*) of the Prophet Muhammad (Durrany 1993: 22-3); (3) instilling a devout adherence to the five pillars of Islam, particularly *shahada* (the profession of faith) and *salat* (five times daily prayer); and (4) organizing Tablighis (missions) to contact other Muslims and encourage them to attend the mosque. Van der Veer writes about the 'mission' of the Tablighi Jama'at in Surat, a port town in Gujarat, as follows:

> Public confrontations on religious issues are carefully avoided. Nevertheless, some of their propaganda clearly stands against Sufism, and is well understood among both Sufis and non-Sufis. They do not concern themselves with Hindu participation or Hindu influences in Sufi practices. Their main theme is that Sufi conceptions of hereditary saintliness and saintly power are innovations (*bida't*) that have led Muslims astray. (1992: 553)

Two to three times a year a party of five to ten Tablighi members arrive, usually by car, and stay in Kutali for a few days. Periodically, Pakistani, Bengali, or Indian Muslims are part of the Tablighi, giving it an international flavour. Invariably the lay members of these *jamatis* (missions) are urban-educated professionals who have recently retired. The socio-economic status of these lay members alternatively rankled or impressed the villagers. The Tablighis slept at the mosque and during the day went door to door to talk religion with occupants and invite the males to evening sermons. These sermons were well attended and villagers would be exhorted to join the movement and participate in jamatis. Repeated appeals to participate in jamatis usually enticed a few villagers to raise their hands in consent. However, the large majority listened sympathetically but non-committally.

After the Tablighis leave, the villagers frequently gather and tell amusing stories about encounters with the Tablighis. For example, one villager recounted how he had whispered to his child to tell a party of Tablighis at his door that he was not at home, whereupon the child said, 'My father told me to tell you he is not here'. Other stories expressed local irritation at the intrusive presence of the Tablighis and the felt need for villagers to be on their 'good behaviour'. Over the two years and ten months of my stay in Kutali, between five and ten villagers had become members of the movement. Though these numbers are small, they include all four of the village *Maulevis*, men who obtained a religious education in an Islamic school (*madrasa*).

The four Maulevis are young—three are in their early twenties and the fourth is in his early thirties—and they are highly respected for their religiosity. They are locally perceived to represent a new type of village Muslim, one that contrasts both with the older generation of religious leaders and with the irreligious young adults whom the villagers scornfully refer to as (in English) 'new Muslims'. Except for the eldest Maulevi, the others do not participate in Sufi rituals nor do they openly criticize these practices. Though their position is non-confrontational, as in Surat, the villagers know that the Maulevis disapprove of Sufi practices and beliefs. Their absence from events such as Burdha Kandhoori symbolizes their opposition. Significantly, the three younger Maulevis were the only villagers who, for religious reasons, were reluctant to have their pictures taken by me, viewing it as a form of idolatry (*shirk*). Further, all four Maulevis admonished the villagers not to speak negatively about the Tablighi Jama'at.

In contrast with other Muslim associations, the Tablighi Jama'at emphasizes commitment to *dar al Islam*: that is 'the realm of Islam' in which allegiance is to God and not to the State (Ruthven 1984: 355-6, 380). However, the Tablighi Jama'at is an expressly religious, not a political organization. Yet, from the villagers' perceptions, the international composition and organization of the jamatis and its reformist theme serve to underscore a Muslim identity that is pan-Islamic and anchored in the Arabic heritage of Islam. Through identification and affiliation with the Tablighi Jama'at, the villagers become part of a religiously based network that extends across national boundaries. In India and Sri Lanka, where Muslims are a minority, such transnational reformist movements are, I believe, 'imagined' like 'nationalisms'. There is a dual temporal projection: backwards, to a heroic past where Tablighi members are identified with the Prophet's companions, and forward to a new incorruptible transnational culture of Islam. The return to a heroic Arabic-Islamic past which serves as a template for the future mirrors the dual national vision of a heroic Sinhala-Buddhist past.

Both nationalism and reformist movements conjoin, in their current state, to dislocate Sri Lankan Muslims. On the one hand, Muslims are marginalized by the Sinhalized depiction of Sri Lanka nationhood and, on the other, they are enjoined to become members of a reformist movement that rejects their local history and local knowledge. These various cultural claims and constructions of Muslim identity underlie the motivations that led to the cancellation of Burdha Kandhoori, and its resumption the following year.

VI. THE FESTIVAL AND ITS CHARISMATIC LEADER

Burdha Kandhoori is the largest annual festival in Kutali. Not only is it the creation of the grandfather of the present-day Moulana, but he embodies the expressed purposes for the festival; without him there is no Burdha Kandhoori. While other Muslims claim descent from the Prophet, for the villagers of Kutali there is only one Moulana. Their Moulana is, during the year, a shopkeeper in the southern coastal town of Dikwela. He is a rotund and balding man in his fifties; he is soft-spoken and appears gracious and pleasant in demeanour.

A few months before the festival, the mosque administrators (Marikars) send an invitation to the Moulana, who tells them when he expects to arrive. Months before his arrival, the villagers begin their preparations: teams of volunteers clean the roads and whitewash the mosque; the village women weave colourful reed mats; the Marikars invite prominent Sinhalese and Muslims in the area to attend the final feast day and also to request donations; the villagers clean their own houses and donate funds, livestock, and foodstuff. The collective activities are all organized by the mosque Marikars.

On the day of the Moulana's arrival, the village looks its best: house-fronts have been washed, there is no garbage along the streets and the villagers, dressed in their best clothes, gather at the junction in anticipation. The Moulana usually arrives in a hired van (and sometimes by bus) and from the corner junction is paraded, with pomp and circumstance, down the main dirt road, to the mosque. For the next eight days he will reside at the mosque, taking his meals at the homes of the villagers. Typically the male head of the household serves the meal, and the Moulana eats in relative silence. After the meal, the Moulana, offers a prayer for the general prosperity and health of the family. Thereafter, those present tell him of their most pressing problems. The villagers appeal to him to cure them of illness, offer prayers for prosperity, settle disputes, find a mate for an unmarried daughter, counsel the troubled and, primarily, provide religious assurance for the future well-being of the villager and his family. He responds to the problems with earnest decisiveness. For example, at one home a man explained that a boy's family had agreed to a marriage but backed out at the last moment. The Moulana sent for the boy's parents, listened to both sides, and then adjudicated in favour of the girl's family and a marriage date was set. I was present on this occasion and both parties viewed the Moulana's verdicts as vested with sacred authority and not to be questioned.

The 1979 Burdha Kandhoori was, it seemed, a great success. During the eight days the Moulana's chief occupation was that of miracle worker. On the morning of the eighth day there was a great village feast (*kandhoori*) attended by villagers and outsiders—Muslims and non-Muslims. After the feast, the Moulana recited a benediction for the prosperity and security of the village and those in attendance lined up to receive his personal blessings. In the late afternoon a procession of villagers, singing religious songs and dancing, led him back to the main junction, where a hired van was waiting to drive him back to his home.

During the eight days of the festival, miracles were performed, old animosities and disputes resolved, the sick cured, and the cumulative worries of the villagers wiped away. With a renewed sense of collective pride and anticipation, the villagers faced the coming year. Shortly after the Moulana's visit, the villagers began to clear their swidden (chena) fields for cultivation.

Though neither the villagers nor the Moulana described Burdha Kandhoori as an agricultural festival, it occurs during the period between the end and beginning of the agricultural season. In the final benediction, the Moulana prays for rain and agricultural success. But the festival has more general functions than the agricultural prosperity of the villagers. In contrast with Buddhism, it is an expression and manifestation of sacred power anchored in and derived from Islam.

VII. 1980—THE YEAR THE FESTIVAL WAS CANCELLED

In 1980, the Moulana was not invited; for the first time in the collective memory of the villagers, there had been no Burdha Kandhoori. What had gone wrong? There was a great deal of finger-pointing. The Marikars balmed the drought; they explained that the villagers were simply too poor to put on a proper festival. They argued that it was better to postpone the festival than to hold one that would disgrace the village in the eyes of the Moulana and their neighbours. The villagers, however, did not fully accept this argument, instead, they blamed the Marikars, particularly the Trustee (the head Marikar) who, villagers said, he pocketed 7,000 rupees from the mosque treasury.

The villagers discussed the cancellation of the festival in small private groups; no one wanted outsiders to know that the village was split into hostile factions. The public explanation provided to outsiders was the one promoted by the mosque officials—the drought was to blame. The mosque officials remarked, 'We cannot, in good conscience, ask villagers to make such a sacrifice.' The villagers said, 'We have barely enough to feed ourselves let alone 2,000 guests.' Mosque officials and villagers were in accord in presenting this explanation to outsiders, including other Muslims.[9] Within the village boundaries, the villager complained bitterly about the Marikars and, as with discussions about politicians anywhere in the world, the villagers wanted to 'throw the crooks out of office'.

In January 1981, usually the time an invitation is sent to the Moulana, the Trustee proposed that they postpone Burdha Kandhoori by one more year. There had been another drought; yields were likely to be poor. 'How', he asked, 'can we hold a Burdha Kandhoori when our fields lie barren?' This time, however, the villagers were not only angry but afraid; many criticized the Trustee and the Marikars and believed that the cancellation itself had caused the drought. Stories were told of rich men who had come to ruin: they had become arrogant and had neglected their religious obligations. The villagers whispered that the continued drought was a sure sign of the Moulana's, Allah's, and the Prophet's wrath. As one villager remarked, 'Somehow or other we must hold the festival, for without it we are lost.' Rumours circulated that the Marikars feared the Moulana would demand their resignations and that was the reason why they wanted to cancel the festival. As gossip, recriminations, and animosity mounted, the village threatened to schism into two groups: the Marikars and their (few) supporters, and the villagers who called for the resumption of the festival.

The latter were spearheaded by a group of 'young Turks'—males between the ages of 25 and 40 who had become successful businessmen (*mudalali*). They decided to independently sponsor the festival and invite the Moulana. When their intentions became public knowledge, they were hailed as the village heroes. The Marikars were put into an indefensible position for they had claimed that the villagers were too impoverished to fund the festival and, therefore, that they had no choice but to cancel it. Now a groups of villagers had offered to fund and organize the festival.

The Marikars called a meeting with the young Turks and they reached an agreement to co-sponsor the Kandhoori. The compromise benefited the Marikars, who managed to save face and retain official control over the festival. The young Turks also benefited; they were responsible for much of the leg-work and ensuring the success of the festival. Should the upcoming festival be a disaster, the Marikars could always blame it on the young Turks.

VIII. THE 1981 BURDHA KANDHOORI

The 1981 festival was a huge success. The Moulana performed his miracles; Marikars and the young Turks amicably shared the limelight; the Marikars were not asked to resign; old wounds, if not healed, were sutured. An estimated 2,000 outsiders attended the final day of festivities. On this day Muslim, Tamil, Veddah and Sinhalese beggars lined the streets and a merry-go-round and swings were set up on the mosque grounds for the children. The villagers wore new clothes and strolled the muddy eroded main road as if it were a city promenade. For the many women who rarely left the village, this was their single annual opportunity to shop for 'fancy wares' displayed by travelling merchants.[10]

During the feasting, villagers and outsides, rich and poor, Buddhists and Muslims, sat companionably around large deep bowls (*saban*) in which rice, meat and vegetable curries had been ladled. Groups of five, from different denominations and ethnicities, ate with their hands from the same saban. The women ate at the newly built paddy cooperative across from the mosque. These expressions of communal harmony provided a striking contrast to the 'ethnic fratricide' that, too frequently, characterizes communal relations in Sri Lanka.

After the feast, people lined up with bottles of water for the Moulana to bless. The water is saved and used in times of illness. The Moulana concluded with the following benediction:

> Oh Allah, let our sins be forgiven for those who are here and for all villagers. All the people want to pray and I beseech you to help them pray. O Allah, we are poor and uneducated, therefore, send us the means to become rich. Oh Allah, we want to die with lots of merit. Oh Allah, bless our request. Oh Allah, give us plenty of rain and good harvests, give many things to our

village. O Allah, we hope for an abundance of rain and good paddy and chena cultivations. Oh Allah, we hope for better education and more comforts. Oh Allah, please grant our requests.

It is a prayer that mixes the sacred with the profane, but its main theme is instrumental and agricultural. For the villagers, the Moulana is an admixture of religious intermediary and holy man; through him sacred power is tapped for earthly purposes. The resumption of the festival was also a resumption of the villagers' connection with the sacred. To understand the importance of the Moulana as the source of religious power and, thereby, opposed by the Tablighi Jama'at, I return to the historical beginnings of Burdha Kandhoori.

IX. HISTORICAL CONTEXT OF BURDHA KANDHOORI

It was the link between Sufism and ethnic resurgence that spawned Burdha Kandhoori in 1914. Mr. Yassim, a Muslim politician and lay historian, explained that: 'Burdha Kandhoori was intended to revive Muslim faith in their religion . . . and to discourage Muslims from following Hindu customs.'

The Moulana, himself, provides a similar but more detailed explanation:

My grandfather's father started this work in 1914. Earlier there were no Burdha Kandhooris. . . . In those days there was no religion and people had no knowledge of the proper way of reciting prayers so my grandfather would travel to twelve Muslim villages yearly and teach the villagers the proper ways of worshipping. The villages, of which Kutali was one, would put on a feast to honour him. . . .

Being a Moulana is like a caste . . . we are from the blood of the Prophet, no? My daughters must marry other Moulanas, but boys can marry anyone because the blood is passed through the patriline. However, even sons should marry the daughters of Moulana families. All my six sons did so. People respect me because I am of the blood of the Prophet and through me they worship him.

One thing that is significant in his description is the initial motivating reformist charter of the Burdha Kandhoori. It is organized as a Sufi festival in all but name. Even though the Moulana and villagers identify as members of the Qadariya Brotherhood, this identification is muted in the festival. The relation between the Moulana and villagers parallels that of *pir-murid* (leader-disciple) relations in Sufi

Brotherhoods; yet this relationship is circumscribed by, and limited to, Burdha Kandhoori. The festival does not specifically commemorate the saint Abdul Qadir, after whom the Brotherhood is named and whose anniversary (*'urs*) is celebrated another month. Nor does the festival include other aspects typically associated with Sufi festivals such as the presence of *faqirs*, 'playing with swords', Sufi music, or the inducement to trance states.

On the other hand, the Moulana has the attributes of a Sufi pir: he is reckoned to have religious power that stems from his genealogy. The villagers and the Moulana believe, as the Moulana states, that the blood of the Prophet flows in his veins and is therefore present in him. To keep the blood powerful is to keep it pure through practising endogamy (see van der Veer 1992: 559 for a similar account).

Throughout the year the villagers tell stories that recount and reveal the power of the Moulana. One story tells of the time his son had stolen pumpkins from a neighbour's garden. The Moulana asked his son if he had been the thief; the son told him, 'no'. The Moulana, knowing his son was lying, was very angry and commanded his son to 'shut up'. Since that day, the villagers say, his son has been unable to speak. Another man who had become wealthy by village standards had begun to drink. At a Burdha Kandhoori he had been drunk and cursed the Moulana. Thereafter, he began to lose both his wealth and his health. His father and the villagers were convinced that he would die unless he reformed is ways, attended mosque services, and asked forgiveness from Moulana. In 1981, this man begged forgiveness, reformed his ways and, indeed, regained his health.

Despite these stories and the villagers' belief in the Moulana's power, no-one, including the Moulana, referred to him as an *owlie-akkel* (saint). His religious power stems from his genealogical connection and is used for instrumental rather than moral purposes. The Moulana, unlike Sufi pirs generally, is not involved in the day-to-day lives of the villagers. The Moulana had no voice in the discussions over the cancellation of the festival in 1980, nor in its resumption in 1981. His authority is constrained by the contextual and temporal parameters of the festival. Thus, his role as pir depends solely on the consent of the villagers. For the villagers, the Moulana represents and is a conduit to the sacred; but he is not, through his own deeds nor wisdom, himself sacred.

There are only twelve villages in Sri Lanka where the Burdha Kandhoori is held. The Moulana noted that the Burdha Kandhoori had been cancelled in other villages. In one village it had been postponed for three continuous years. The Moulana said that he expected that eventually all the villages would cease to invite him. The success of the 1981 Burdha Kandhoori testified to its importance for the villagers. Why, I asked the Moulana, might Burdha Kandhoori be eliminated in the future? The Moulana said simply, 'More and more villagers are against it.'[11] But to understand this point we need to examine the underlying reasons for this perceived opposition to Burdha Kandhoori. As described above, villagers perceived the festivals' cancellation as embedded in local politics not in wider religious and political issues. But, corruption and drought are not new social and environmental phenomena. The festival was originally motivated by national resurgences of ethnic revivalism; today, new national and international forces are reshaping the meaning of the Burdha Kandhoori. Village narratives, I believe, are motivated and shaped by these more inclusive socio-cultural forces.

X. THE FUTURE OF BURDHA KANDHOORI

In 1914, rural Muslim villages such as Kutali were largely isolated from the nationalist strivings and pan-Islamic activities of the urban Muslims of Sri Lanka and the subcontinent. Local Muslim beliefs and practices had been, and remain, a syncretic mix. Villagers call on Buddhist folk healers (*aeduro*) to diagnose and cure illnesses thought to be caused by demons (*yakko*) or the evil eye (*kan nur*). for children's contagious diseases, villagers congregate in the evening and recite Tamil texts for the Hindu goddess Maria Amman (or Pattini). The belief in supernatural agents as acting on the personal and collective fortunes of villagers and the practice of engaging and influencing these agents through ritual specialists remains intact.

Through the leadership of a pir or *sheikh* and the worship of saints, Sufism has historically provided a distinctive Islamic alternative to these syncretic practices. The complex bricolage of beliefs and practices that one can label 'Sufi' parallel, but do not necessarily incorporate, Hindu-Buddhist practices. In their expression, as is evident by the Moulana's benediction, they commemorate and therefore remain true to the essential tenet of Islam: the omnipotent singularity of Allah. Most villagers recognize that neither the Moulana nor saints are independent creators of power and that this power is ultimately and unambiguously derived from Allah. Sacred power originates only in Allah and nowhere else; the saints and the Moulana are important as intermediaries and not, as in the Buddhist-Hindu pantheons, as distinct supernatural entities. Thus, these Sufi practices are fundamentally different from local Buddhist-Hindu practices and beliefs in that there is no conscious assertion of polytheism in the former.

In its contemporary context, the festival commemorates the relation between the instruments of religious power and the social estate of villagers as peasant farmers. Its performative aspects recall the miraculous deeds of the Prophet, not his ethical actions. The stories told are about the uses and misuses of religious power, not of good versus evil. Religious instruction on the nature of good and evil, heaven and hell, and the proper forms of worship and conduct for Muslims are the province of religious virtuosi and reformers, not the Moulana.

The resilience of the festival lies in the villagers' unwavering belief in the genealogical transmission of religious power. The Moulana's power stems solely from his genealogical link with the Prophet. Rain and religion are annealed through ritual. This axiomatic triad of rain, genealogically transmitted power and ritual use of this power is rejected by the Tablighi Jama'at, who argue that the belief in the ability of ritual practitioners to control natural forces, at best, presumes a religious hierarchy that is contrary to the egalitarian spirit of Islam (van der Veer 1992: 561). This opposition, however non-confrontational, conceptually places the festival in the syncretic and, hence, un-Islamic complex of Buddhist-Hindu religious practices and beliefs. Burdha Kandhoori can now be 'read' as being precisely part of that process of religious assimilation which it was originally designed to oppose.

The villagers' answers to questions as to why the 1980 festival was cancelled are not wholly satisfying. The villagers argue that the festival was cancelled because the Marikars were corrupt; the latter explain that the festival was cancelled as a result of the drought. Both responses ring true but incomplete. Neither of these conditions is unique: it is not uncommon to accuse Marikars of corruption; nor is a drought year, such as 1980 or 1981, exceptional. But the cancellation of the festival certainly was a unique event. Other explanations are necessary. What has happened, I think, is that Burdha Kandhoori as a ritual system is no longer completely 'healthy' and cannot tolerate the hardships that it once could. The muted but known disapproval of the four Maulevis and the Tablighi Jama'at's preachings against Sufi practices lower the villagers' motivations for holding the festival. Disputes, droughts, and corruption have become reasons enough for cancelling the festival.

The clamour for the resumption of the festival the following year is evidence of its continued popularity. Yet its appeal has necessarily been diminished since the Tablighi Jama'at has ascended to the reformist role. The festival's resilience lies in its performative commemoration and assertion of the earthly expressions of Islamic power. In its historical context, the Moulana and Burdha Kandhoori were ritually contrasted with Buddhism and Buddhist influences. In this historically salient contrastive context, the Moulana-Burdha Kandhoori complex was identified with Islam and served to mark ethnic boundaries. Today, however, the culturally relevant contrast is with the Tablighi Jama'at. In this context, the Moulana-Burdha Kandhoori complex represents an impure and syncretic conceptualization of Islam. As the contextual contrast set has changed over time, so has the meaning of the festival. As once it stood for 'genuine' Islam, it now stands, for some, for a 'spurious' Islam.

Van der Veer (1992: 553) and Durrany (1993: 21-2, 146) have remarked that the Tablighi Jama'at is expressly apolitical and non-confrontational. Despite this, van der Veer (1992: 549, 552-3) refers to the Tablighi Jama'at as the 'main Muslim opponent' to Sufism in Surat. Durrany (1993: 147, 151) categorizes the Tablighi Jama'at with Islamic 'fundamentalism' and states that members preach that 'worldly constitutions and the governments are imperfect and subject to change and corruption' and espouse the 'establishment of an Islamic social order'. We can best summarize the Tablighi Jama'at's position as 'non-confrontational opposition'. This position expresses sets of contrasts that have important socio-cultural ramifications for Kutali, Sri Lankan, and South Asian Muslims. In the one contrast, discussed above, the Tablighi Jama'at reformers claim to represent Islam, and Sufism that which is not Islam, and thus its followers are *kafir* (heretical). In yet another set, the Tablighi Jama'at contrasts with 'nation'.

XI. CONCLUSION: TRANSNATIONAL, NATIONAL, AND LOCAL CONFLUENCES AND CONUNDRUMS

Sri Lankan Muslims, whatever their religious persuasion, want to be granted full birthright status as citizens of the nation. But as Spencer (1990: 240-1) and others indicate, Muslims remain excluded from the socio-moral compass of Sinhalese and Tamil nationalisms. Their inclusion in these nationalisms usually invokes cynical references to 'realpolitik'. For the Sinhalese and Tamils, the inclusion of Muslims in their respective nationalist schemes is interpreted, by all concerned, as a zero-sum game manoeuvre to gain an ethnic ally at the expense of the opposition. Similarly, the Muslim community maintains its 'advantage position' within this inter-ethnic '*tertius gaudens*' (literally, 'the one who enjoys' as a consequence of one's position between two antagonists) by resorting to a collective strategy of 'managed' neutrality (De Silva 1986; Simmel 1950: 154-62). These kinds of realpolitik stratagems and counter ploys obviate, or make problematic, avowals that Muslims are full citizens of the nation in the most inclusive sense of 'citizenship'.

A nation is more than an 'imagined community'; it also includes the social 'habit' of tracing the present to a substantive past through historical remindings (Connerton 1989: 23). These habitual remindings of the past become grist for a conceptual mill that grinds out seeds with which to sow unity and/or enmity. Nation is legitimized, in part, through the habitual remindings and tracings of historical commonality, not communal rivalry. The remindings of Sri Lankan histories, as presented by Sri Lankan politicians and in national ceremonies, do not include Muslims (Brow 1988; Tenekoon 1988). Sri Lankan Sinhalese Buddhist unity is recreated, while Tamil Hindus are re-established as the historical foe (Kapferer 1988). For Sri Lankan Muslims their historical tracings are situated both in local and Arabic temporalities.

Because of the acknowledgements of the pragmatic motivations for building alliances, Muslims recognize the importance of establishing a unified community. Only through the perception, if not the reality, of ethnic unity can Muslims maintain their advantaged position. Further, it is also important to remain politically neutral and situationally expedient. These national constraints illuminate the basis for Tablighi Jama'at policies towards Sufi Brotherhoods and the nation.

The immediate goal of the Tablighi Jama'at is to recruit new members through weekly *ijtimas* (public meetings) and by organizing preaching parties that visit Muslim communities. In their dual identities as members of an ethnic minority and as a reformist organization, the goals of the Tablighi Jama'at can best be achieved through adopting a non-confrontational and apolitical stance. The religious appeal of the Tablighi Jama'at lies in its repetitive commemoration of the heroic and pure Islamic social order founded by the Prophet and continued with the four subsequent Caliphas (Durrany 1993: 147). It commemorates in two ways: (1) through the simplicity of the preaching which emphasizes prayer and the shahada ('There is no God but Allah and Muhammad is his Prophet') as practices, and the Sunnah and Quran as the doctrinal bases of Islam; and (2) through the circuits of preaching and the simple habits of the Tablighi Jama'at members, many of whom are wealthy, recalling the simple and pure religious activities of the Prophet and his companions.

Through these practices, the Tablighi Jama'at cognitively, bodily, and visually symbolizes a puritan view of Islam that denies the later temporal accretions of Sufism. The Tablighi Jama'at, through practices and sermons, restages and thereby reminds Muslims of their origins and the purist impulses of Islam. Of course, there were no Muslim saints, nor Sufi practices, at the time of the Prophet. Opposition need not be direct or overt to be understood and effective. I must add that open confrontations have increased, and reformists occasionally organize at major Sufi sites to protest these practices. However, these activities are not condoned by the Tablighi Jama'at.

In India, Ahmed (1988: 228) explains that nationalism '. . . has created ambiguity and tension among Muslims. . .' since the affirmation of a nation entails loyalty to the State, national boundaries, citizenship and adherence to the laws of the nation. These definitions of personhood and law are opposed to the Islamic concepts of the *Ummah* (unity and equality among all Muslims) and *Shari'a,* both of which supersede and stand, ideologically, in opposition to nationalism. Thus, Ahmed (ibid.) states that in countries with Muslim majorities, 'Islam was equated with nationalism'.

This equation is somewhat misleading because it is the nation that is conceptually subsumed by Islam. In principle, Islam is a universalist religion that extends beyond national and cultural borders. All Islamic nations are, in principle, alike in their mode of governing. In countries where Muslims are a minority this equation cannot be obtained, hence the 'ambiguity and tension among Muslims'. The Tablighi Jama'at is a transnational organization with its focus on religion rather than economics or politics. Though apolitical, the movement preaches that governments based on secular principles are 'imperfect'. Further, the movement does restrict participation in political elections and rejects the principle of parliamentary democracy (Durrany 1993: 151). Its apolitical stance signifies the negation of participation in non-Islamic (i.e. Sri Lankan) national politics. Thus, the managed neutrality of Sri Lankan Muslims has both political and religious undertones.

The Moulana and Burdha Kandhoori are, oddly enough, products of a simpler time. But the temporality of Burdha Kandhoori is local and conditional. It recollects a time of miracles, both in stories and practice, and, in so doing, answers the villagers' (and our) eternal wish for control over their bodies and their environment. It is the eternalness of unpredictability, of chance and whimsy, that ultimately provides Burdha Kandhoori with its durability.

Through the transformative processes of modernization by which villagers become part of a wider world, local identities become less relevant. As local history fades and becomes archived by the local historians, common memories must be traced back to more inclusive generalities. The tracings to a common history convey, for Kutali and South Asian Muslims, back to the beginning of Islam in the Arabic plains of Mecca and Medina. The Tablighi Jama'at offers not only commemorations but a means to 'practise' that past and, thus, a means to establish full citizenship in a pan-Islamic identity. Sufism provides miracles and a local sectarian identity. Nationalism, as presently constituted in Sri Lanka, offers nominal rather than substantive inclusion into the national identity.

In the contemporary political contesting for position, and on a landscape racked by eruptions of violence, Muslims, Sinhalese and Tamils look backwards to their own heroic ages. Ironically, these habitual remindings exclude the imagining of a morally inclusive pluralist nation. The ethnically homogenized recreations of the past necessarily perpetuate violence in the present. None of these three identities—the local, national, and transnational—need necessarily exclude the other. Each has its particular niche. The disallowance of the coexistence of multiple narratives and histories perpetuates and recreates animosities.

Within the village of Kutali, multiple narratives are permitted; the animosities are expressed in terms of actions, not ideologies. The past is not problematized, but coded in these local narratives and arguments as the dilemmas of a nation.

NOTES

1. I wish to thank Alan Beals, David B. Kronenfeld, Steven Reyna, Barbara Larson, Nina Glick-Schiller, and the referee for their incisive comments and responses to earlier versions of this paper.
2. Kutali is a pseudonym I have used in other articles.
3. Moulana is a title designating the leader of a religious group. When used self-referentially by the 'Moulana' and by villagers in reference to him, the genealogical connection to the Prophet is the critical attribute of the title. More generally, a direct descendant of the Prophet is referred to as *Sayyid.*
4. This is one of the fastest growing Muslim reform movements on the subcontinent. Only recently has it become the subject of much literature (see Haq 1972; van der Veer 1992; Durrany 1993).
5. The Qadariya or Qadiriya are named after Abdul Qadir Gilani and are also to be associated with the Rifa'i Tariqat in India (van der Veer 1992: 550). Rifa'i *faqirs* are featured at the annual festival at Jailany, Sri Lanka, for Abdul Qadir.
6. Similar debates have been described and identified elsewhere on the subcontinent (see, for example, Robinson 1983; Metcalf 1984; Ewing 1988; Engineer 1991; van der Veer 1992).
7. Of the Sri Lankan population 67 per cent is Sinhala Buddhist and 7 per cent is Muslim (1981 census).
8. The idea of ideological 'parameters' and 'variability' is taken from Gregory Bateson (1958: 292). Parameters refer to the settings that configure a socio-cultural system. The behavioural or ideological variation within those parameters is neither indicative nor a catalyst for social change.
9. These quotes are syntheses of statements made by the villagers. Indeed the villagers are very jealous of the reputation of the village as a whole. During Ramadan, villagers were particularly admonished not to eat, drink or smoke outside the village.
10. Rarely did village women leave the local area. A young woman married to a young Turk told me she fainted the first (and only) time she had

gone to Bibile, the nearest town of approximately 15,000 people.

11. This is not a transliteration of his response, but is accurate in conveying his main point.

REFERENCES

Ahmed, Akbar S. 1988. *Discovering Islam: Making Sense of Muslim History and Society.* New York: Routledge and Kegan Paul.

Anderson, Benedict. 1983. *Imagined Communities.* London: New Left Books.

Bateson, Gregory. 1958. *Naven* (2nd edn.) Stanford: Stanford University Press.

Benjamin, Walter. 1973. *Illuminations.* London: Fontana.

Bloch, Maurice. 1988. *Ritual, History and Power: Selected papers in Anthropology.* Atlantic Highlands (NJ): Athlone Press.

Brow, James. 1988. 'In pursuit of hegemony: Representations of authority and justice in a Sri Lankan village'. *American Ethnologist* 15, 2: 311-27.

———. 1990. 'Notes on community, hegemony, and the uses of the past'. *Anthropological Quarterly* 63, 1: 1-6.

Connerton, Paul. 1989. *How Societies Remember.* Cambridge: Cambridge University Press.

Crapanzano, Vincent. 1973. *The Hamadsha.* Berkeley: University of California Press.

de Munck, Victor. 1985. *Cross Currents of Conflict and Cooperation in a Sri Lankan Muslim Community.* Ann Arbor: University Microfilms.

———. 1992. 'The fallacy of the misplaced self: Gender relations and the construction of multiple selves among Sri Lankan Muslims'. *Ethos* 20, 2: 167-90.

De Silva, K.M. 1986. *Managing Ethnic Tensions in Multiethnic Societies: Sri Lanka 1880-1985.* Lanham: University Press of America.

Durrany, K.S. 1993. *The Impact of Islamic Fundamentalism.* Delhi: Indian Society for Promoting Christian Knowledge (Religion Series 30).

Eickelman, Dale. 1976. *Moroccan Islam,* Austin: University of Texas Press.

Engineer, Asghar Ali. 1991. Sufism and Communal Harmony. Jaipur: Rupa.

Ewing, Katherine P. 1988. Shari'at and Ambiguity in South Asian Islam. Berkeley: University of California Press.

Gilsenan, Michael. 1973. *Recognizing Islam: Religion and Society in the Modern Arab World.* New York: Pantheon Books.

Haq, Anwar. 1972. *The faith movement of Mawlana Muhammad Ilyas.* London: Allen and Unwin.

Kapferer, Bruce. 1988. *Legends of People Myths of State.* Washington D.C.: Smithsonian Institution Press.

Metcalf, Barbara. 1984. *Moral Conduct and Authority.* Berkeley: University of California Press.

McGilvray, Dennis B. 1991. 'Arabs, Moors, and Muslims: The mobilization of Muslim identity in Sri Lanka'. Paper presented at the Third Sri Lanka Conference, Amsterdam, The Netherlands.

Mohan, Vasundhara R. 1987. *Identity Crisis of Sri Lankan Muslims.* Delhi: Mittal.

Moore, Sally Falk. 1987. 'Explaining the present: Theoretical dilemmas in processual ethnography'. *American Ethnologist* 14, 4: 727-50.

Obeyesekere, Gananath. 1977. 'Social change and the deities: The rise of the Kataragama cult in modern Sri Lanka'. *Man* 12: 377-96.

———. 1978. 'The firewalkers of Kataragama: The rise of bhakti religiosity in Buddhist Sri Lanka'. *Journal of Asian Studies* 36: 457-76.

———. 1979. 'The vicissitudes of the Sinhalese-Buddhist identity through time and change.' In Michael Roberts, ed., *Collective Identities Nationalism and Protest in Modern Sri Lanka,* pp. 279-313. Colombo: Marga Institute.

Peebles, Patrick 1990. 'Colonization and ethnic conflict in the dry zone of Sri Lanka'. *Journal of Asian Studies* 49: 30-55.

Ramanathan, P. 1888. 'The ethnology of the Moors of Ceylon'. *Journal of the Royal Asiatic Society* (Ceylon Branch) 10, 36: 234-62.

Robinson, Francis. 1983. 'Islam and Muslim society in South Asia'. *Contributions to Indian Sociology* 17: 185-203.

Ruthven, Malise. 1984. *Islam in the World.* New York: Oxford University Press.

Shastri, Amita. 1990. 'The material basis of separatism: The Tamil Eelam movement in Sri Lanka'. *Journal of Asian Studies* 49: 56-77.

Shukri, M.A.W. 1986. *Muslims of Sri Lanka: Avenues to Antiquity.* Beruwala (Sri Lanka): Jamiah Naleemia Institute.

Simmel, Georg. 1950. *The Sociology of Georg Simmel.* New York: Free Press.

Spencer, Jonathan. 1990. *A Sinhala Village in a Time of Trouble: Politics and Change in Rural Sri Lanka.* Delhi: Oxford University Press.

Tambiah, Stanley J. 1986. *Sri Lanka: Ethnic Fratricide and the Dismantling of Democracy.* London: I.B., Tauris.

———. 1988. 'Ethnic fratricide in Sri Lanka: An update'. In Gudieri, Pellizzi, Tambiah, eds., *Ethnicities and Nations,* pp. 293-319. Austin: University of Texas Press.

Tenekoon, N.S. 1988. 'Rituals of Development: The accelerated Mahavali development program of Sri Lanka'. *American Ethnologist* 15: 294-310.

van der Veer, Peter. 1992. 'Playing or praying: A Sufi Saint's day in Surat'. *Journal of Asian Studies* 51, 3: 545-64.

White, Harrison C. 1992. *Identity and Control: A Structural Theory of Social Action.* Princeton: Princeton University Press.

Contributors

AKBAR S. AHMED, a senior member of the Pakistan Civil Service, is currently Visiting Iqbal Fellow, and Fellow of Selwyn College, University of Cambridge. A prolific author, Dr. Ahmed has a large number of books and research papers to his credit, including *Pukhtun Economy and Society* (Routledge, London, 1980), *Pakistan Society* (Oxford, Karachi, 1986), *Discovering Islam* (Routledge, 1990), *Resistance and Control in Pakistan* (Routledge, 1991) and *Postmodernism and Islam* (Routledge, 1992).

HAMZA ALAVI. On retirement from the Department of Sociology at the University of Manchester Hamza Alavi has served as Professor in the Social Sciences at the University of Denver and, following that, as Visiting Professorial Fellow at the Centre for Social Theory and Comparative History at the University of California, Los Angeles. He now lives in Karachi: P.O. Box 3880, Karachi 75600. He is currently working on a book on 'Pakistan: Power and Ideology' to be published by OUP, Karachi.

PETER J. BERTOCCI is a professor in the Department of Anthropology and Sociology, Oakland University, Rochester, Michigan, USA. He has carried out extensively fieldwork in Bangladesh, and written about different aspects of its social organization.

RITA BARARA teaches at the Department of Sociolgy, University of Delhi. Her areas of research include kinship, ecology and rural development. Currently she is working on a book about village commons.

VICTOR C. DE MUNCK is Assistant Professor of Anthropology at the University of New Hampshire. He received his Ph.D from the University of California, Riverside in 1985. He has published a monograph and 12 articles on Sri Lankan Muslim Culture.

MARC GABORIEAU is Director of Studies at the School for Higher Studies in Social Sciences (EHESS) and Director of Research at the

National Centre for Scientific Research (CNRS), Paris. He is interested in the study of the Muslim Communities of Nepal and India. His publications include *Minoritiés musalmanes dans le royaume hindou du Nepal* (Societe d' ethnologie, Nanterre, 1977), *Le Nepal el ses populations* (PUP, Paris, 1978), *Ni brahmanes ni ancestres* (Societe d' ethnologie, Nanterre, 1993).

KATY GARDNER studied for her Ph.D, which was based on field work in Sylhet, Bangladesh, at the London School of Economics. Since then she has worked for the British Overseas Development Administration, and at the University of Kent. She is currently a lecturer in Anthropology at the University of Sussex. She is author of *Songs at the River's Edge: Stories from a Bangladesh Village* (Virago, 1991)

GOPAL KRISHNA was a foundation Fellow at the Centre for the Study of Developing Societies, New Delhi. A historian by training, he is the author of many research papers and has edited two volumes of *Contributions to South Asian Studies.* After retirement he divides his time between Delhi and Oxford.

CHARLES LINDHOLM is a University Professor and member of the Department of Anthropology at Boston University. His research is on passionate relationships of identification and on complex societies with egalitarian ideologies. His books include *Generosity and Jealousy among the Swat Pukhtun of Northern Pakistan* (Columbia University Press, 1983).

T.N. MADAN is Honorary Professor of Sociology at the Institute of Economic Growth, Delhi. An Honorary Fellow of the Royal Anthropological Institute of Great Britain and Ireland and Doeteur Honoris Causa of the University of Paris X (Nanterre), his most recent publications are, *Pathways: Approaches to the Study of Hindu Society* (Oxford, Delhi, 1994), *Modern Myths, Locked Minds: Secularism and Fundamentalism in India* (Oxford, Delhi, 1997), and, as editor, *Religion in India* (Oxford, Delhi, 1991).

DENNIS B. MCGILVRAY is Associate Professor of anthropology at the University of Colorado at Boulder. His reserach among the Tamils and Muslim of Sri Lanka has been of wide scope and has resulted in many publications. It has focused on among other themes colonial and contemporary politics. His recent photographic book is *Symbolic*

Heat: Gender, Health and Worship among the Tamils of South India and Sri Lanka (Mapin, Ahmedabad, 1998).

DEEPAK MEHTA teaches at the Department of Sociology, University of Delhi. He is the author of *Work, Ritual, Biography: A Muslim Community in North India* (OUP, 1997) and a number of research papers.

J.B.P. MORE was educated in Pondicherry and in Paris. He obtained a Ph.D in History at the Ecole des Hautes Etudes en Sciences Sociales, Paris.

APARNA RAO did her schooling in India before studying Social Anthropology, Sociology, Human Geography, Islamic Studies and French Literature at the Universities of Paris (Sorbonne) and Srasbourg. She has researched mobile populations of peripatetics and pastoralists, in France, Afghanistan and the Western Himalayas (Kashmir), and published extensively on aspects of social organization, economy, gender relations and ethnicity. She has taught Anthropology at Cologne University and is acting Head of Department, Anthropology, University of Heidelberg.

USHA SANYAL earned her Ph.D in History from Columbia University in 1990. She has taught undergraduate courses on South Asia at Western Washington University, Washington State, and on Islam at Rutgers University, New Jersey. Her research interests are in the history of South Asian Islam and in the South Asian Muslim diaspora to the United States. Her book, *In the Path of the Prophet: Maulana Ahmad Riza Khan Barelwi and the Ahl-e Sunnat wa Jama'at Movement, c. 1870-1921,* is being published by Oxford University Press, Delhi.

PNINA WERBNER is Senior Lecturer in Social Anthropology at the University of Keele, UK, and Research Administrator of the International Centre for Contemporary Cultural Research (ICCCR) at Keele and Manchester Universities. Her books include: *The Migration Process: Capital, Gifts and Offerings among British Pakistanis* (Berg, Oxford 1990), *Black and Ethnic Leadership in Britain* (co-edited with Muhammed Anwar) (Routledge, 1991) and *Economy and Culture in Pakistan* (co-edited with Hastings Donnan) (Macmillan, 1991). Her current research is on Sufism as a transnational religious movement.

Index

INSTITUTE OF ECONOMIC GROWTH

CONTRIBUTIONS TO INDIAN SOCIOLOGY

OCCASIONAL STUDIES

1. *Muslim Communities of South Asia: Society and Culture,* edited by T.N. Madan, New Delhi: Vikas, 1976.*

2. *Process and Institution in Urban India: Sociological Studies,* edited by Satish Saberwal. New Delhi: Vikas, 1978. Second impression, 1978.*

3. *Way of Life: Kind, Householder, Renouncer: Essays in Honour of Louis Dumont,* edited by T.N. Madan, New Delhi: Vikas; Paris: Maison des Sciences de l'Homme, 1982. Second impression, New Delhi: Vikas, 1982. Second, enlarged edition, New Delhi: Motilal Banarsidass, 1988.

4. *The Word and the World: Fantasy, Symbol, and Record,* edited by Veena Das. New Delhi: Sage, 1986

5. *India through Hindu Categories,* edited by McKim Marriott. New Delhi: Sage, 1990. Third impression, 1993

6. *Muslim Communities of South Asia: Culture, Soceity and Power,* edited by T.N. Madan. New Delhi: Manohar, 1995

7. *Social Reform, Sexuality and the State,* edited by Patricia Uberoi. New Delhi: Sage, 1996.

8. *Tradition, Pluralism and Identity: Essays in honour of T.N. Madan,* edited by Veena Das, Dipankar Gupta and Patricia Uberoi. New Delhi: Sage, 1999.

9. *The World of Indian Industrial Labour,* edited by Jonathan P. Parry, Jan Breman and Karin Kapadia. New Delhi: Sage, 1999.

* out of print